Medieval Chronicles 5

SHORT SCOTTISH PROSE CHRONICLES

Medieval Chronicles

ISSN: 1462–8724

Founding editors
Professor Dan Embree
† Professor Lister M. Matheson

Editorial Board
Caroline D. Eckhardt
Chris Given-Wilson
Edward Donald Kennedy
Erik Kooper

I
'The Chronicles of Rome'
An Edition of the Middle English 'Chronicle of Popes and Emperors'
and 'The Lollard Chronicle'
Edited by Dan Embree

II
Death and Dissent
Two Fifteenth-Century Chronicles
'The Dethe of the Kynge of Scotis' and '"Warkworth's"' Chronicle'
Edited by Lister M. Matheson

III
An English Chronicle 1377–1461: A New Edition
Edited by William Marx

IV
The Oldest Anglo-Norman Prose *Brut* Chronicle
Edited and translated by Julia Marvin

This series publishes scholarly editions of the chronicles of the Middle Ages, particularly those that have never been edited or that exist only in long out-of-date editions. All languages are covered; non-English chronicles are presented with facing translations, English chronicles with glossaries. All volumes contain full apparatus, with introduction, explanatory notes, textual notes and bibliography.

Proposals or queries should be sent in the first instance to Professor Dan Embree or to the publisher, at the addresses given below.

Professor Dan Embree, 2411 Martin Luther King Jr Way, Berkeley, CA 94704, USA

Boydell & Brewer Ltd, PO Box 9, Woodbridge, Suffolk, IP12 3DF, UK

Short Scottish Prose Chronicles

La Vraie Cronicque d'Escoce
The Scottis Originale
The Chronicle of the Scots
The Ynglis Chronicle
Nomina Omnium Regum Scotorum
The Brevis Chronica
The St Andrews Chronicle

Edited by

DAN EMBREE, EDWARD DONALD KENNEDY
AND KATHLEEN DALY

with Latin translations by

SUSAN EDGINGTON

THE BOYDELL PRESS

First published 2012
The Boydell Press, Woodbridge

ISBN 978–1–84383–745–9

The Boydell Press is an imprint of Boydell & Brewer Ltd
PO Box 9, Woodbridge, Suffolk IP12 3DF, UK
and of Boydell & Brewer Inc.
668 Mount Hope Ave, Rochester, NY 14620–2731, USA
website: www.boydellandbrewer.com

A CIP catalogue record for this book is available
from the British Library

The publisher has no responsibility for the continued existence or accuracy of
URLs for external or third-party internet websites referred to in this book,
and does not guarantee that any content on such websites is,
or will remain, accurate or appropriate.

Papers used by Boydell & Brewer Ltd are natural, recyclable products
made from wood grown in sustainable forests

Printed from camera-ready copy supplied by Professor Dan Embree

Printed and bound in Great Britain by
CPI Group (UK) Ltd, Croydon, CR0 4YY

TABLE OF CONTENTS

LIST OF ILLUSTRATIONS

ACKNOWLEDGMENTS

For permission to publish these chronicles and the facsimile pages that illustrate them, we thank:
- The Bibliothèque royale de Belgique – Koninkijke Bibliotheek van België (MS 9469–70).
- The Keeper of the Records of Scotland, National Archives of Scotland (MS GD 45/31/1–II); the manuscript was purchased with funding from The National Heritage Trust.
- The Keeper of the Manuscripts and Muniments, University of St Andrews Library (MS DA 775.A6W9).
- The Trustees of the National Library of Scotland (MSS 16500 and Advocates 19.2.4).
- The British Library Board (Royal MS 17.D.xx).

For support over the years of research that went into this project, we thank The University of North Carolina at Chapel Hill and its Research Council; and Mississippi State University and its Criss Fund.

The editors wish to thank those colleagues whose help and advice, generously given, have clarified many linguistic, historical, and paleographical matters: Robert Babcock of The University of North Carolina at Chapel Hill, Alan Borthwick of the National Archives of Scotland, Kenneth Dunn and Ulrike Hogg of the National Library of Scotland, Simon Innes of Harvard University, Maura Lafferty of the University of Tennessee Knoxville, Chris Robinson of the Scottish Language Dictionaries, Carin Ruff of Cornell University, and Tess Tavormina of Michigan State University; and those who provided invaluable technical or logistical expertise: Patricia Dominguez and Tommy Nixon of the Davis Library of The University of North Carolina, Susan Hall of the Mitchell Memorial Library of Mississippi State University, and Rachel Hart and Iris Papaemmanouil of the University of St Andrews Library. We owe a special debt to Michael Chesnutt, whose work in bringing the Dalhousie manuscript to light and in interpreting the chronicles it contained contributed materially to the form of this edition; and to Dauvit Broun, whose critique of the treatment of Scottish history in the notes of an early draft has saved us from many errors. We are, of course, responsible for those that remain.

In Memoriam

Lister Matheson

1948–2012

A Scot, a scholar, an editor, a teacher, a
comrade, a teller of tales, a lover of life.

ABBREVIATIONS

BAd   The Brevis Cronica (Advocates MS)

BAs   The Brevis Cronica (Asloan MS)

N   Nomina Omnium Regum Scotorum

OA   The Scottis Originale (Asloan MS)

OD   The Scottis Originale (Dalhousie MS)

OR   The Scottis Originale (Royal MS)

S   The Chronicle of the Scots

StA   The St Andrews Chronicle

Y   The Ynglis Chronicle

VC   La Vraie Cronicque

INTRODUCTION

Edward Donald Kennedy

Kathleen Daly
(*Vraie Cronicque* and its manuscripts)

The seven short chronicles in this book, all dating from the late fifteenth or early sixteenth century, are abbreviations and popularizations of an older Scottish historiographical tradition that were written to respond to contemporary events. The overwhelming political question in Scotland in the sixty years between the end of the Hundred Years' War and the Battle of Flodden was the relation of Scotland to its traditional ally, France, and to its traditional enemy, England. These chronicles are attempts to address this question by extending the historical claims of Scottish nationalism to audiences beyond those familiar with the weighty and scholarly histories of John of Fordun, Walter Bower, John Mair (Major) and Hector Boece. The French *Vraie Cronicque* may have been written, as suggested below, as a briefing note for French representatives about to participate in negotiations with England. The Latin *Nomina Omnium Regum Scotorum* would have been intended for educated readers who lacked the time or the inclination to tackle more than the essentials of Scottish history, and, as its name suggests, would have functioned as a genealogy of the Scottish kings that showed their descent from ancient times.[1] The remaining five, though probably derived from Latin sources, are in the Scots dialect of English.

Four of these seven chronicles were written as propaganda. The *Scottis Originale* (the *Cronycle of Scotland in a Part*), the *Ynglis Chronicle*, and the *Nomina* with its closely associated Scots-English *Brevis Cronica* all assert a history of English treachery opposed by Scottish heroism. They reflect their authors' anxieties about the continuing English threat to Scotland in the late fifteenth and early sixteenth centuries, and they attempt to pass these anxieties on to their readers. At least by implication, they undermine the efforts of some Scottish leaders to improve relations with England. The *Vraie Cronicque*, written with French – not Scottish – interests in mind, also preys on these anxieties. Together with the less politically biased *Chronicle of the*

---

[1] See Edward Donald Kennedy, "The Antiquity of Scottish Civilization: King-Lists and Genealogical Chronicles" in *Broken Lines: Genealogical Literature in Medieval Britain and France*, ed. Raluca L. Radulescu and Edward Donald Kennedy (Turnhout, Belgium: Brepols, 2008), pp. 159–74.

Scots and *St Andrews Chronicle*, they attest to the ancient and distinguished origins of the Scots and the long independence of the Scottish kingdom.

The *Scottis Originale*, the *Brevis Cronica*, the *Ynglis Chronicle*, and the *Chronicle of the Scots* were published in editions of the eighteenth, nineteenth and early twentieth centuries. The first three of these appeared in Craigie's 1923 edition of the miscellany copied by the Edinburgh notary John Asloan in the early sixteenth century, but that edition did not take into account the other manuscripts of the *Scottis Originale* and the *Brevis Cronica*. The *St Andrews Chronicle*, a fragment of an English abstract of part of Hector Boece's Latin *Scotorum Historia* (1526 or 1527), formerly thought to be a copy of the *Brevis Cronica*, is here published for the first time.[2] Robert Anstruther transcribed one manuscript of the *Vraie Cronique* for the Roxburghe Club in 1847,[3] but few copies were printed, and it is inaccessible to most today. Kathleen Daly's edition published here is the first that is based on the four surviving manuscripts, and hers is its first translation into English. The Latin *Nomina Omnium Regum Scotorum*, published in part by David Laing in 1855,[4] is published here in its entirety and translated into English for the first time.

We have omitted two additional short chronicles in the Asloan manuscript since they have been published fairly recently: a transcription of *The Auchinleck Chronicle*, a chronicle of events in the reign of James II, is included as an appendix to Christine McGladdery's 1990 biography of James II;[5] an edition of the other, a brief universal history entitled *The Sex Werkdays and Agis,* was also published in 1990.[6]

The Scots Nation and Nationalism
In his influential book *Imagined Communities*, Benedict Anderson, building upon arguments earlier advanced by Hugh Seton-Watson and others, argues that the idea of "the nation" developed in the early modern period, after the decline

---

[2] It is found in the concluding leaves of one of the manuscripts of Andrew of Wyntoun's *The Original Chronicle of Scotland*, St Andrews University Library, DA 775.A6.W9 (formerly T.T.6.6), fols 449ʳ, 450ʳ–452ʳ.

[3] *La Vraie Cronicque d'Escoce; Pretensions des Anglois à la couronne de France; Diplôme de Jacques VI, roi de la Grande Bretagne*, ed. R[obert] Anstruther, Roxburghe Club (London, 1847).

[4] *The Bannatyne Miscellany*, vol. 3, ed. David Laing, Bannatyne Publications 19 (Edinburgh, 1855; reprint New York: AMS, 1973), pp. 44–60.

[5] McGladdery, *James II* (Edinburgh: John Donald, 1990), pp. 160–73, with discussion pp. 116–24. McGladdery is preparing a revised edition of this book.

[6] *The Sex Werkdays and Agis: An Edition of a Late Medieval Scots Universal History from the Asloan Manuscript*, ed. L. A. J. R. Houwen (Groningen: Egbert Forsten, 1990). For Walter Bower's brief *Liber Extravagans* (Supplementary Book), included with the *Scotichronicon*, see n. 81 below.

of Latin in the West as what Anderson calls a "sacred dead language" and the ascent of the vernaculars and of the printing press. Moreover, Anderson believes that "nationalism," in either the sense of patriotic feeling or advocacy of political independence, developed still later in the eighteenth and nineteenth centuries.[7] A number of Anderson's generalizations about the Middle Ages, however, are questionable. Latin was not a sacred dead language but was, in fact, a learned living language during the Middle Ages and was often used for international communication; it became a dead one with the humanists' emphasis on classical style in the late medieval and early modern periods.[8] The vernaculars, moreover, were in the ascendant long before the early modern period. Although some countries, such as Germany and Italy, would not have a sense of being a nation for years after the Middle Ages had ended, Anderson's thesis is not applicable to countries such as England, France, and Scotland where the concept of "the nation" developed earlier. Even "nationalism," in either of the senses that Anderson mentions (patriotic feeling, advocacy of national independence), is found earlier. Studies such as Gabrielle M. Spiegel's *Romancing the Past*, Bernard Guenée's *States and Rulers in Later Medieval Europe*, and Thorlac Turville-Petre's *England the Nation* discuss the development of the concept of the nation in France and England in the thirteenth, fourteenth, and fifteenth centuries; and Alice Shepherd has argued for a sense of national identity in England as far back as the Anglo-Saxon period.[9] R. James Goldstein, Marjorie Drexler, Alexander Grant, Norbert Kersken, G. W. S. Barrow and Keith Webb, among others, discuss the influence of the wars between England and Scotland in the late thirteenth, fourteenth and fifteenth centuries upon the development of the sense of a nation in Scotland.[10]

---

[7] Anderson, *Imagined Communities: Reflections on the Origin and Spread of Nationalism*, rvsd. edn. (London: Verso, 1991); Hugh Seton-Watson, *Nations and States* (Boulder, CO: Westview Press, 1977), esp. pp. 1–13.

[8] C. S. Lewis writes of the humanists' attempt to restore classical Latin: "[T]he classical spirit ended the history of the Latin tongue. . . . They [the humanists] succeeded in killing the medieval Latin: but not in keeping alive the schoolroom severities of their restored Augustanism. Before they had ceased talking of a rebirth it became evident that they had really built a tomb" (*English Literature in the Sixteenth Century excluding Drama*, Oxford History of English Literature 3 [Oxford: Clarendon Press, 1954], p. 21).

[9] Spiegel, *Romancing the Past: The Rise of Vernacular Prose Historiography in Thirteenth-Century France* (Berkeley: University of California Press, 1993); Guenée, *States and Rulers in Later Medieval Europe*, trans. Juliet Vale (Oxford: Basil Blackwell, 1985); Turville-Petre, *England the Nation: Language, Literature and National Identity 1290–1340* (Oxford: Clarendon Press, 1996); Sheppard, *Families of the King: Writing Identity in the "Anglo-Saxon Chronicle"* (Toronto: University of Toronto Press, 2004), esp. pp. 9–25.

[10] Goldstein, *The Matter of Scotland: Historical Narrative in Medieval Scotland* (Lincoln: University of Nebraska Press, 1993); Drexler, "Fluid Prejudice: Scottish Origin Myths in the Later Middle Ages" in *People, Politics and Community in the Later Middle Ages*, ed. Joel

Scotland's sense of itself as a nation, however, did not develop as did the sense of national identity in some countries. Unlike some nations, it lacked linguistic unity: in the Highlands the majority spoke Gaelic although the Scandinavian language Norn was also spoken in the north and the Northern Isles; in the more racially mixed Lowlands, Anglo-Norman became the language of the court under Malcolm III (traditionally known as Canmore)[11] in the late eleventh century and continued in use until the thirteenth century; English began to be used in the Lowlands during the same period and by the fourteenth century had replaced Anglo-Norman as the dominant language in south and east Scotland. It developed into the dialect that linguists today refer to as "Scots," and its use continued to increase. By about 1500, perhaps only one third of the people had Gaelic as their primary language.[12]

Rosenthal and Colin Richmond (Gloucester: Alan Sutton, 1987), pp. 60–76; Grant, "Aspects of National Consciousness in Medieval Scotland" in *Nations, Nationalism and Patriotism in the European Past*, ed. Claus Bjørn, Alexander Grant and Keith J. Stringer (Copenhagen: Academic Press, 1994), pp. 68–95; Kersken, *Geschichtsschreibung im Europa der "nationes": Nationalgeschichtliche Gesamtdarstellungen im Mittelalter* (Cologne: Böhlau, 1995), pp. 368–98; Barrow, *The Anglo-Norman Era in Scottish History* (Oxford: Clarendon Press, 1980), pp. 147–49; Webb, *The Growth of Nationalism in Scotland* (Glasgow: Molendinar Press, 1977), pp. 14–16. There is further discussion of these matters in the essays in *Concepts of National Identity in the Middle Ages*, ed. Simon Forde, Lesley Johnson, and Alan V. Murray, Leeds Texts and Monographs, n.s. 14 (Leeds: University of Leeds,1995).

[11] Scholars have fairly recently discovered that the name "Canmore," which has been used in the medieval and modern periods to designate Malcolm III (as in the chronicles edited here), was actually a name for his great-grandson Malcolm IV. See A. A. M. Duncan, *The Kingship of the Scots 842–1292: Succession and Independence* (Edinburgh: Edinburgh University Press, 2002), pp. 51–52, 74–75; Richard Oram, *David I: The King Who Made Scotland* (Stroud: Tempus, 2004), p. 17 n. 1. Oram nevertheless refers to him as Canmore in *The Canmores: Kings and Queens of the Scots 1040–1290* (Stroud: Tempus, 2002), p. 11 and in the more recent *The Kings and Queens of Scotland*, ed. Richard Oram, Michael Penman, Christine McGladdery, and Maureen Meikle (Stroud: Tempus, 2004), p. 56.

[12] Initially the dialect of English spoken in Scotland would have been indistinguishable from that of northern England. Modern linguists use the term "Scots" to describe this dialect, even from the earliest times, and that term will be used in subsequent paragraphs of this introduction. In the Middle Ages, however, "Scots" referred to Gaelic until about the fifteenth century (see *Scottish National Dictionary*, s.v. "Scots"; Christine Robinson and Roibeard Ó Maolalaigh, "The Several Tongues of a Single Kingdom: The Languages of Scotland, 1314–1707" in *The Edinburgh History of Scottish Literature*, vol. 1, *From Columba to the Union [until 1707]*, ed. Thomas Owen Clancy et al. [Edinburgh: Edinburgh University Press, 2007], pp. 153–63); and the term probably continued to suggest Gaelic for quite a while after that. William Dunbar, writing in the late fifteenth and early sixteenth centuries, referred to his language as "oure Inglisch," not as Scots (see *Poems*, ed. James Kinsley [Oxford: Clarendon Press, 1958], p. 32). For differences in views, see G. Gregory Smith, *Specimens of Middle Scots* (Edinburgh: William Blackwood, 1903), pp. xi–xvi, who believed, for example, that Barbour's dialect should be described as northern English, and the more recent discussion by Robinson and Ó Maolalaigh who point out differences between Barbour's language and that of northern England ("Several Tongues," pp. 159–60). However, a number of features of Barbour's dialect that Robinson and Ó Maolalaigh discuss can be found in the northern English of Richard Rolle, and what they describe as his use of the "exclusively Scots" *quh-* for *wh-* is not far from the *qw* for

Scotland also lacked racial unity, since the Highlanders were primarily of Gaelic descent and the Lowlanders a mix of Briton, English, French, Norman, Dutch, Flemish, Norse, Gaelic, and, as has recently been argued, from the twelfth century, possibly Jewish.[13] The sense of being a nation did not develop from harmony between the two groups since Lowlanders generally looked upon Highlanders as barbarians, "wild Scots," who were incapable of being civilized; and it did not develop from having a powerful central government that was the source of nationalist sentiments of some countries in later periods.[14]

In Scotland the sense of being a nation developed from other factors. One was territorial: the Romans had conquered the Brythonic Celts in the South and had separated the North from the South with walls built by the Emperor Hadrian and his successor Antonius Pius. The authors of these chronicles see the territory north of these walls as an area that, unlike the territory to the south, had never been conquered (except for possibly the brief period between 360 and 403 when Romans occupied the territory). This is not quite true. Although these chroniclers seem to have been unaware of it, the Romans had also occupied a considerable part of Scotland in the first and second centuries but then withdrew.[15] The land occupied by the Scots also changed over the years, beginning with the settlement of Scots from Ireland in Dál Riata, their taking over lands of the Picts, and eventually their occupying the territory from the Pentland Firth in the north to the

---

wh used by one of the North East Midland scribes of the early fourteenth-century chronicle of the anti-Scottish Robert Mannyng of Brunne. On the latter's dialect, see Mannyng, *The Chronicle*, ed. Idelle Sullens (Binghamton, New York: Binghamton University Press, 1996), pp. 39–51. For features of the dialects of Rolle and Barbour, see Fernand Mossé, *Handbook of Middle English*, trans. James A. Walker (Baltimore: Johns Hopkins University Press, 1952), pp. 377–78, 397–98. On the survival of Gaelic, see Wilson McLeod, *Divided Gaels: Gaelic Cultural Identities in Scotland and Ireland c.1200–c.1650* (Oxford: Oxford University Press, 2004), p. 33. Also see Robinson and Ó Maolalaigh, "Several Tongues," pp. 153–63; Kenneth MacKinnon, "Scottish Gaelic" in *Languages in Britain & Ireland*, ed. Glanville Price (Oxford: Blackwell, 2000), pp. 44–57.

[13] For the latter group, see Elizabeth Caldwell Hirschman and Donald N. Yates, *When Scotland Was Jewish* (Jefferson, NC and London: McFarland, 2007).

[14] Traditionally Scottish government in the Middle Ages has been seen as backward and ineffective, although some scholars have recently questioned this view. The king became stronger under James II in 1455 after the defeat of the Douglases, but weak again during the disastrous reign of James III (1460 to 1488). For a survey of views of the government of Scotland during the later Middle Ages, see Michael Brown, "Stewart Monarchy (1371–1513)" in *Scotland: The Making and Unmaking of the Nation c. 1100–1707*, vol. 1: *The Scottish Nation: Origins to c. 1500*, ed. Bob Harris and A. R. MacDonald (Dundee: University of Dundee Press, 2006), pp. 48–64.

[15] See D. J. Woolliscroft and B. Hoffman, *Rome's First Frontier: The Flavian Occupation of Northern Scotland* (Stroud: Tempus, 2006) and James E. Fraser, *The Roman Conquest of Scotland: The Battle of Mons Graupius AD 84* (Stroud: Tempus, 2005).

Tweed in the south, the area that, by the early thirteenth century, was considered to be Scotland.[16]

Scotland also eventually had a monarchy to which both Highlanders and Lowlanders were generally loyal, even though they might disagree over who that monarch should be. They also believed that Scotland had been a nation for many centuries, that according to chronicles of the late-fourteenth, fifteenth, and sixteenth centuries, it had been independent with its own ruler for almost 2000 years. Finally, Scotland's sense of being a nation developed from the threat to its independence in the late thirteenth and early fourteenth centuries when, during an interregnum in Scotland, England's Edward I tried to get control over it. This threat from England continued into the sixteenth century and gave impetus to the writing of history in Scotland, for although there had been brief annals written in Latin and Gaelic as least as early as the tenth and eleventh centuries,[17] extensive writing of Scottish history, so far as we know, began after the middle of the thirteenth century.[18]

Historical Writing in Scotland

In the 1290s Edward I, trying to gain hegemony over Scotland by taking advantage of the crisis over the succession following the death of Alexander III, ordered his scholars to draw upon Briton and English historical records to show that the kings of Scotland, from the earliest times, owed homage to England. In 1301 the English presented this information to the Pope with the hope of gaining the papacy's support for their desire to control Scotland.[19] The English looked upon themselves as successors to the Britons, whom the Anglo-Saxons had conquered, and they had adopted much of the Briton legendary history as their own. They made extensive use of the pseudo-history in Geoffrey of Monmouth's *Historia Regum Britanniae*, and they accepted the belief, which goes back at least as far as the *Historia Brittonum* (ca. 829/30) but was popularized by Geoffrey and his successors, that the Britons were descended from the Trojans and that

---

[16] Dauvit Broun, *Scottish Independence and the Idea of Britain: From the Picts to Alexander III* (Edinburgh: Edinburgh University Press, 2007), pp. 7–11. Also see *Atlas of Scottish History to 1707*, ed. Peter G. B. McNeill and Hector L. MacQueen (Edinburgh: Scottish Medievalists and Department of Geography, University of Edinburgh, 1996) and Malcolm E. Falkus and John Gillingham, *Historical Atlas of Britain* (New York: Continuum, 1981).

[17] See *Chronicles of the Picts, Chronicles of the Scots and Other Early Memorials of Scottish History*, ed. William F. Skene (Edinburgh, 1867), pp. xviii–xli, 3–116.

[18] Dauvit Broun, "The Birth of Scottish History," *Scottish Historical Review* 76 (1997), 12–15.

[19] For several of the English and Scottish documents, see *Anglo-Scottish Relations 1174–1328: Some Selected Documents*, ed. E. L. G. Stones (London: Nelson, 1965), *passim*.

their founder Brutus was the great-grandson of Aeneas (or grandson, according to one account in the *Historia Brittonum*).[20] According to Geoffrey, the sons of Brutus inherited the three parts of Britain: Locrinus, the eldest, received Loegria (England); Kamber, the second son, Kambria (Wales), and Albanactus, the youngest, Albany (Scotland). Loegria was considered the superior part, and since Albany was inherited by the youngest son, one might infer that it was the least desirable. (The Scots, however, would argue that the three children were peers with none subject to the other.)[21] When Albanactus was killed by the invading Huns, his people fled to Locrinus for protection, thus establishing a precedent for the southern kingdom's rule of the North. The English also did not forget that King Arthur had brought Scotland under his control; and many later Scottish kings, the English claimed, also paid homage to the kings of England.

In making its case for past glory and long independence, Scotland had greater obstacles to overcome than either England or France, since its reputation in Europe did not give it much prestige. Known as a poor country (the home, in fact, of Poverty in the thirteenth-century *Le Roman de la Rose*) and, primarily because of its Highlanders, often a barbarous one, it was defensive. Being a remote northern country did not help, for there had been prejudice since antiquity against the North. Ezekiel had warned of the armies of Gog coming from the North in the final days of the world. Aristotle believed that people from the North were less intelligent than those from the South, that the further people lived from the equator, the more barbarous and miserable they were.[22] To early Christians the North was the region of the heathens, and in religious rituals the priest faced north when reading the gospel in order to confront imaginary pagans. The late-sixteenth-century chronicler and humanist George Buchanan argued in his *De Jure Regni apud Scotos: Dialogus* (1579) against the belief held by many that "in the ice-bound regions of the world men are as far removed from literature, from culture, and from every intellectual pursuit as they are from the sun."[23] Such prejudices,

---

[20] The *Historia Brittonum*, once attributed to Nennius, gives two versions of the ancestry of Britto or Brutus: in one he is the grandson of Aeneas; in the other, the great-grandson as in Geoffrey and most other chronicles. See *British History and The Welsh Annals*, ed. and trans. John Morris (London: Phillimore, 1980), pp. 10, 19 (two different accounts on the latter page).

[21] This was in their response to the Pope ca. 1301 when Edward I had argued to the Pope that England should have hegemony over Scotland. See *Anglo-Scottish Relations*, ed. Stones, p. 113; *Chronicles of the Picts*, ed. Skene, pp. 240–41.

[22] Arthur H. Williamson, "Scots, Indians and Empire: The Scottish Politics of Civilization 1519–1609," *Past & Present* no. 150 (Feb. 1996), 47.

[23] Ibid., 52.

Arthur Williamson observes, seemed particularly applicable to the Scots because of "the predatory inhabitants of the northern mountains, forests and desolate isles."[24] Even the Scots Lowlanders would have been in agreement with this prejudice against the Highlanders.[25]

As Susan Reynolds reminds us, stories concerning the "common origin of a people served to increase or express its sense of solidarity."[26] Just as the English had accepted the Briton legends as a history of the island that they had inherited, some Scots also accepted the Briton legends and attempted to claim some of them as part of their own ancestry: Robert II, for example, proclaimed the Stewart dynasty's Trojan origins, and the Briton origin legends are treated favorably by Barbour and by Andrew of Wyntoun. Some emphasized the Scots' relationship with England through Malcolm III's queen, Margaret, who was descended from the English royal dynasty prior to the Conquest and who, by the mid-thirteenth century, had been canonized. Thus to some Scots, the Briton and English legends were an important part of their own history.[27]

Many Scots, however, saw the need to produce and publicize their own foundation legends, in part to break with an earlier tradition that had regarded the Scots' civilization simply as an offshoot of that of Ireland[28] and in part to respond to the Briton legends taken over by the English. It was also important for the Scots to have legends that would enable them to assert their superiority to, and independence from, both the Britons and the English. Much of the impetus for the development of these origin legends came from the wars of independence against England in the late thirteenth and early fourteenth centuries.[29] Scholars in Scotland searched their historical records for evidence that would show that Scotland had a dynasty and an uninterrupted line of kings that went back to antiquity in contrast to England that had been occupied by Britons, Romans, Anglo-Saxons, Danes, and Normans.[30] Edward I, it was

---

[24] Ibid., p. 47.

[25] The prejudice continued into later periods: James VI (James I of England) would assert in his *Daemonologie* that witchcraft could be found in places like Orkney and Shetland "because where the deuill findes greatest ignorance and barbaritie, there assayles he grosseliest" (Williamson, "Scots, Indians," p. 48).

[26] Reynolds, "Medieval *Origines Gentium* and the Community of the Realm," *History* 68 (1983), 375.

[27] On the points in this paragraph, see Steve Boardman, "Late Medieval Scotland and the Matter of Britain" in *Scottish History: The Power of the Past*, ed. Edward J. Cowan and Richard J. Finlay (Edinburgh: Edinburgh University Press, 2002), pp. 47–72.

[28] On this, see Dauvit Broun, *The Irish Identity of the Kingdom of the Scots in the Twelfth and Thirteenth Centuries* (Woodbridge: Boydell Press, 1999), esp. pp. 195–200.

[29] Broun, *Scottish Independence*, pp. 23, 235–68.

[30] See Drexler, "Fluid Prejudice," pp. 61–62.

argued, destroyed all of the Scottish historical records he could find, but fortunately some survived so that Scottish scholars could offer evidence that their nation had distinguished origins and a long history of independence.[31] According to Dauvit Broun, the earliest extant text that gave Scotland an ancient history was a king-list prepared at the time of John Balliol's inauguration on 30 November 1292: it maintained that the Scottish kingdom was over 1976 years old.[32] During this period, when Edward I was trying to take over Scotland, the argument that Scottish history dated back almost two thousand years was used to bolster the Scottish cause, and evidence concerning its long independence was presented in 1301 in tracts presented to the Pope in opposition to Edward's claims, notably in the *Processus Baldredi contra figmenta Regis Anglie*, attributed to Baldred Bisset.[33] This evidence later was affirmed in the *Declaration of Arbroath*, which the Scottish earls and barons sent to the Pope in 1320.[34]

The Scots' origins were not only different from, but in their eyes superior to, those of any other European country. Most nations of Europe, Bernard Guenée points out, in reminding others of their distinguished origins, turned to legends of Troy or Rome and to stories from the Bible, since the Trojans were sometimes said to be descended from Noah and thus directly from Adam and God.[35] The Celtic Britons, as mentioned above, were ultimately descended from Aeneas, and although claims of Trojan descent are often thought to have been confined to areas occupied by ancient Rome, even some Germanic tribes claimed Trojan ancestry. The Normans, for example, although originally Danes, claimed descent from the Trojans. (Saxons, however, sometimes traced their origins to the troops of Alexander the Great.)[36]

---

[31] Ibid., p. 62; Bower, in his introduction to the *Book of Cowper*, maintains that Edward I destroyed historical records (Bower, *Scotichronicon*, gen. ed. D. E. R. Watt, 9 vols [Aberdeen: Aberdeen University Press, 1987–98)], vol. 9, p. 13).

[32] Broun, "Birth of Scottish History," p. 13.

[33] See "Incipit processus Baldredi contra figmenta Regis Anglie" in Bower, *Scotichronicon*, gen. ed. Watt, XI 57–64 (vol. 6, pp. 168–89); also published in *Chronicles of the Picts*, ed. Skene, pp. 271–84; and in *Liber Pluscardensis*, ed. Felix J. H. Skene, 2 vols (Edinburgh, 1877–1880), vol. 1, pp. 205–18. For discussion of Bisset's pleading and its possible influence on Fordun, see Katherine H. Terrell, "Subversive Histories: Strategies of Identity in Scottish Historiography" in *Cultural Diversity in the British Middle Ages: Archipelago, Island, England*, ed. Jeffrey Jerome Cohen (New York: Palgrave, 2008), pp. 157–61.

[34] A. A. M. Duncan, *The Nation of Scots and the Declaration of Arbroath (1320)* (London: The Historical Association, 1970), pp. 34–37; Edward J. Cowan, *"For Freedom Alone": The Declaration of Arbroath, 1320* (East Linton: Tuckwell Press, 2003), pp. 144–47.

[35] Guenée, *Histoire et culture historique dans l'Occident médiéval* (Paris: Aubier Montaigne, 1980), 58–63; also see Reynolds, "Origines Gentium," pp. 376–77.

[36] Reynolds, "Origines Gentium," pp. 376–77.

The Scots constructed for themselves a legendary past intended to outrank and antedate the origin myths of the Britons and of most other people of Europe: if the Britons were descended from Trojans and Romans, then the Scots would be descended from Greeks and Egyptians; if the Britons dated their origins from the Trojan War at about 1200 BC, then the Scots would date theirs from the Exodus at about 1500 BC, giving themselves a biblical association and descent from a Greek prince, Gathelos, and an Egyptian princess, Scota, daughter of the pharaoh drowned in the Red Sea.[37]

Scotland's sense of its long and distinguished history began to be emphasized in the late thirteenth century, but it became more widely known near the end of the fourteenth when John of Fordun, sometime between 1371 and the mid-1380s, or possibly, as D. E. R. Watt suggests, prior to 1363,[38] wrote his *Chronica Gentis Scotorum*, which covered Scottish history from its legendary beginnings in the days of Moses to the death of King David I in 1153.[39] Fordun's *Chronica* survives in at least eight manuscripts, not counting copies of the text that were altered by Walter Bower when incorporating it into his own *Scotichronicon*.[40] However, the Scottish historical tradition transmitted by Fordun to chroniclers of the late fifteenth and early sixteenth centuries was largely imaginary until he began telling of events relatively late in the medieval period.[41]

The extent to which Fordun is responsible for this narrative is debatable. A traditional view is that he may have had available, for the period before the reign of Kenneth mac Alpin in the mid-ninth century, a bare and discontinuous historical outline, derived principally from Scottish and Pictish king-lists, Irish annals, and perhaps some chronicles no longer extant, stretching back no further than to the end of the fifth century. He would have supplemented this scant record with what he could glean from Roman, Anglo-Saxon, and continental sources and with what he simply invented.

[37] This material has been discussed many times. See, for example, William Matthews, "The Egyptians in Scotland: The Political History of a Myth," *Viator* 1 (1970), 289–306; William Ferguson, *The Identity of the Scottish Nation: An Historic Quest* (Edinburgh: Edinburgh University Press, 1998), pp. 36–55.

[38] See Watt, "Fordun, John," *Oxford Dictionary of National Biography (ODNB)* (2004).

[39] For a good overview of Fordun's work, with excellent references to earlier scholarship, see Kersken, *Geschichtsschreibung*, pp. 375–98.

[40] See Broun, *Irish Identity*, pp. 20–27 for a list of the manuscripts of Fordun's *Chronica*. Six of these were identified and described by William F. Skene in his edition of Fordun, *Chronica Gentis Scotorum*, (Edinburgh, 1871), pp. xv–xviii. There is no recent edition of Fordun. See discussion of Bower's *Scotichronicon* below.

[41] For a recent discussion of Fordun's chronicle, see Terrell, "Subversive Histories."

However, more recently scholars have argued that Fordun's chronicle was possibly based upon some earlier history of Scotland written between 1249 and 1285 that provided the basic narrative for much of his history. It would also have provided material for the early fourteenth-century documents intended to argue Scotland's cause before the Pope, the *Processus* attributed to Baldred Bisset and the *Declaration of Arbroath*.[42] Broun argues that much of the structure of Fordun's *Chronica,* and not just its legendary part, may have been in existence before the beginning of the fourteenth century when the Scots were trying to respond to English claims about their right to control the country.[43] If so, long texts with such breadth have disappeared, and what distinguishes Fordun's chronicle from the surviving works of his predecessors is its scope, its broad focus on all of Scottish history.

Fordun certainly did not invent the Scots' legendary history: references to the Egyptian princess Scota after whom Scotland was supposedly named can be found in documents as early as the ninth century, where, like Geoffrey of Monmouth's legend of Brutus, its origins can be found in the *Historia Brittonum,*[44] and the legend was known in Ireland by the eleventh century in the *Lebor Gabála Érenn* (*Book of the Taking of Ireland*). In some early accounts only Scota is mentioned and not her husband: in Bisset's *Processus,* Scota is said to have sailed to Scotland with a large fleet of ships, "carrying with her the royal seat which this King of England [Edward I] forcibly took away with him from the kingdom of Scotland"; she conquers the Picts and takes over the kingdom.[45] An account in an Anglo-Norman poem dating from the early

---

[42] See Nicola Royan and Dauvit Broun, "Versions of Scottish Nationhood, c. 850–1707" in *The Edinburgh History of Scottish Literature*, pp. 171–72. One possible earlier writer of a general chronicle is the unknown "Veremundus," the reputed source for Hector Boece's lost kings (see below). For a discussion of Veremundus / Richard Vairement, see Nicola R. Royan, "The *Scotorum Historia* of Hector Boece: A Study" (Oxford University D. Phil. Thesis, 1996), pp. 197–215, cited by Broun, "Birth of Scottish History," p. 21; also see Royan, "Boece [Boethius], Hector," *ODNB* and Broun, *Scottish Independence*, pp. 252–63.

[43] Broun, "Birth," pp. 15–16, 21–22.

[44] The name Scota appears in several manuscripts of the *Historia Brittonum*, once attributed to Nennius. There she is the daughter of Pharaoh and her husband is a Scythian of noble birth. See Edward J. Cowan, "Myth and Identity in Early Medieval Scotland," *Scottish Historical Review* 63 (1984),120. Cowan dates the *Historia* at ca. 900 (p. 119) but others date the earliest version ca. 800. See *British History and the Welsh Annals*, ed. and trans. Morris, 2; for the reference to Scota, see p. 21. David Dumville has edited a later version (the "Vatican" recension) that was written 943/44 (*The Historia Brittonum*, ed. Dumville (Cambridge: D. S. Brewer, 1985). Also see Anke Bernau, "Myths of Origin and the Struggle over Nationhood in Medieval and Early Modern England" in *Reading the Medieval in Early Modern England*, ed. Gordon McMullan and David Matthews (Cambridge: Cambridge University Press, 2007), pp. 109–11.

[45] For Bisset's account see Bower, *Scotichronicon,* gen. ed. Watt, XI 62 (vol. 6, pp. 182–84). There is a similar Anglo-Norman report on Bisset's account intended for Edward I; see *Anglo-Scottish Relations,* ed. Stones, p. 113. For recent discussion of Bisset, see R. James

fourteenth century tells of both Scota and her husband arriving in Scotland:

> Gaidelon and Scota brought this stone, when they passed from the land
> of Egypt to Scotland . . . . They named the land Scotland from Scota's
> name. After Scota's death her husband . . . made his dwelling in the
> land of Galloway. From his own name, he gave Galloway its name.[46]

In some early versions, such as the *Historia Brittonum*, her husband was from
Scythia rather than from the more distinguished Greece,[47] and in the twelfth-
century Irish *Chronicum Scotorum* he is a Spaniard who leads an unsuccessful
rebellion in Scythia before fleeing to Egypt.[48] Thus, while Fordun was not the first
to claim that the Scots originated in the days of Moses and that Scotland had
existed for almost two thousand years, his *Chronica* nevertheless popularized
both the legend of Scota and the fiction that Scotland had an ancient civilization.

By the end of the fourteenth century there was a generally accepted chronology of events in Scottish history: the ancestors of the Scots, Gathelos and Scota,
left Egypt in about 1500 BC, and, in most accounts, after settling in Portugal,
their descendants settled first in Ireland and then in Dál Riata in Scotland in
about 443 BC (a date close to the one mentioned in the *Declaration of
Arbroath*).[49] Fergus, son of Ferchard, founded the Dál Riatic line of Scottish
kings in about 330 BC. This kingdom lasted almost seven hundred years until
the Romans conquered it in AD 360. Although Fordun gives the names of only
two kings from this period, Fergus, son of Ferchard, and Fergus, son of Erc, he
says that there were forty-five kings who reigned prior to the Roman conquest
of the Scots. Then after forty-three years, a restoration of Scottish rule took place
under the second Fergus, and from AD 403 the line of Scottish kings continued

Goldstein, "The Scottish Mission to Boniface VIII in 1301: A Reconsideration of the Context
of the *Instructiones* and *Processus*," *Scottish Historical Review* 70 (1991), 1–15; Cowan,
"For Freedom Alone": The Declaration of Arbroath, pp. 44–47 and Matthew Fisher,
"Genealogy Rewritten: Inheriting the Legendary in Insular Historiography" in *Broken Lines*,
ed. Radulescu and Kennedy, pp. 135–36.

[46] For the Anglo-Norman poem and translation, see M. Dominica Legge, "La Piere
d'Escoce," *Scottish Historical Review* 38 (1959), 109–13.

[47] See Cowan, "Myth and Identity," pp. 122–23.

[48] See Edward Donald Kennedy, "Chronicum Scotorum" in *The Encyclopedia of the
Medieval Chronicle*, gen. ed. Graeme Dunphy, 2 vols (Leiden: Brill, 2010), 1:424–25.

[49] According to the *Declaration of Arbroath*, "[O]ur own nation, namely of Scots, . . .
journeyed from Great Scythia by the Tyrrhenian Sea and the Pillars of Hercules, and dwelt
for a long span of time in Spain among the most savage peoples, but nowhere could it be
subjugated by any people, however barbarous. From there it came, twelve hundred years
after the people of Israel crossed the Red Sea and, having first driven out the Britons and
altogether destroyed the Picts, it acquired, with many victories and untold efforts, the places
which it now holds" (Duncan, *Declaration of Arbroath*, p. 34).

to the fourteenth century.[50] Fordun hoped to give the Scots a sense of national identity and, like those who disputed the claims that Edward made to the Pope about England's right to hegemony over Scotland and like the earls and barons who signed the *Declaration of Arbroath*, hoped to show that Scotland, with a past more distinguished than that of the Brythonic Celts or the English, was historically an independent nation over which the English had no claim.

The Scots, of course, have no known Egyptian or Greek ancestry, but are descendants of the Goidelic Celts who migrated westward from central Europe and reached Ireland (Scotia Major, Hibernia), at least by 600 BC and possibly much earlier. By the end of the fifth century AD, some of these Gaels (or Scots) were occupying Argyll and Kyntyre – either because they had recently migrated there from northeast Ireland or because they had long resided there.[51] They were thus the neighbors of the Brythonic Celts (Britons), who had a kingdom centered on the Clyde; of the Picts, the possibly Celtic people whom the Romans had found resident in the northeastern parts of the island of Britain centuries earlier; of the Angles who perhaps by the fifth century were settling on the eastern edge of Britain in Northumbria; and of the Scandinavian raiders and settlers in the far north and the Isles. In the course of the next three-and-a-half centuries, these five peoples jockeyed for position and power in the territory encompassed by modern Scotland — even as the rival cenéla (or kinship groups) of the Scots jockeyed for supremacy within the Scots' southwestern corner. At least by the end of the seventh century, some of the Scots' kingdoms had coalesced into a kingdom called Dál Riata. The uneasy coexistence of the Dál Riata Scots with the Picts – including periods of Pictish domination – ended, by a process not well documented, in their merger in the ninth century into a joint Scottish and Pictish kingdom, whose ruler Kenneth mac Alpin bore the title "King of the Picts." By the early tenth century that kingdom was being called Alba. Although the Picts did not vanish, their language did: its demise came in the reigns of Kenneth's grandsons in the first half of the tenth century.[52]

---

[50] This chronology is based on the summary of events in J. B. Black, "Boece's *Scotorum Historiae*," *University of Aberdeen Quatercentenary of the Death of Hector Boece* (Aberdeen: The University Press, 1937), p. 36.

[51] See Ewen Campbell, "Were the Scots Irish?", *Antiquity* 75 (2001), 285–92.

[52] For kings from Fergus, son of Erc, to Kenneth mac Alpin, see Marjorie Anderson, *Kings and Kingship in Early Scotland*, rvsd. edn. (Edinburgh: Scottish Academic Press, 1980); and from Kenneth to Lulach, see Benjamin T. Hudson, *Kings of Celtic Scotland* (Westport, CT: Greenwood Press, 1994). For what is known of the early centuries of the Dál Riata Scots, see James E. Fraser, *From Caledonia to Pictland: Scotland to 795* (Edinburgh: Edinburgh University Press, 2009). For the transition from Dál Riata to Alba, see Alex Woolf, *From Pictland to Alba, 789–1070* (Edinburgh: Edinburgh University Press, 2007). For early Anglian settlements, also see Frank Stenton, *Anglo-Saxon England*, 2nd edn. (Oxford: Clarendon Press, 1947), pp. 74–77.

Even after the reign of Kenneth, it is anachronistic to speak of a kingdom of Scotland for perhaps another two centuries. The Scots and Picts continued to struggle with the Scandinavians in the north and west and the Angles in the south; there were still Briton kingdoms along the Forth and the Clyde in the tenth century. As the kingdom of Alba extended its power southward, annexing the ports and towns of the Lowlands, it naturally became more cosmopolitan and less Celtic. Nearly four centuries before the chronicles edited here, Malcolm III – called by the *Brevis*-chronicler "the most illustrious King of Scots" – was installed by the English, married to a French-speaking English wife, Margaret, and was presiding in Edinburgh over an increasingly Anglo-Norman-speaking court.[53]

The ethnic and cultural purity claimed by some Scottish chroniclers of the late fifteenth and early sixteenth centuries is thus historically untenable, but was so long implanted as a national historical myth as to pass almost without examination. The Scotland of these patriotic Scots was, as mentioned earlier, home to the remnants of almost every tribe (except for possibly the Romans) who had crossed the North Sea or the Tweed as invaders, courtiers, or refugees during the previous thousand years. But the chroniclers seem not to know that.

Fordun's account of the Scots' legendary past received still further circulation in the fifteenth century: between 1440 and 1447 Walter Bower, Abbot of Inchon, incorporated both the *Chronica* and the *Gesta Annalia*, annals covering the years 1153–1385 often attributed to Fordun,[54] into a much longer chronicle, the *Scotichronicon*, which ended with the murder of James I in 1436/37 and which was intended to further develop the nationalism expressed

---

[53] Malcolm's "English" wife was born in Hungary and spoke French. After the conquest, the influences at the Scottish court would have been Norman. R. L. Graeme Ritchie writes: "It was not with the native English that the King of Scots or his family or his nobles or his envoys had to deal. Southern influences had become Norman influences. Until 1066 the Scottish Kingdom had borrowed little from England. Afterwards it borrowed much. But what it borrowed was French." The "English Margaret," Ritchie observes, "was manifestly a continental." See *The Normans in Scotland* (Edinburgh: Edinburgh University Press, 1954), pp. 68, 70–74. Also see G. W. S. Barrow, *Kingship and Unity: Scotland 1000–1306*, 2nd edn. (Edinburgh: Edinburgh University Press, 2003), pp. 34–37.

[54] In the past scholars assumed that Fordun wrote the *Gesta Annalia*, which consists of brief annals covering the years 1153 to 1363, with a later continuation to 1385, probably compiled by others, and believed that Fordun may have planned to develop the annals he wrote into a chronicle but died before doing so. For this view see D. E. R. Watt, gen. ed., *Scotichronicon*, vol. 9, pp. 226–27. Dauvit Broun, however, does not believe that Fordun wrote the *Annalia*, but that they represent a source that he drew upon. See Broun, "A New Look at the *Gesta Annalia* Attributed to John of Fordun" in *Church, Chronicle and Learning in Medieval and Early Renaissance Scotland*, ed. Barbara E. Crawford (Edinburgh: Mercat Press, 1999), pp. 9–30, as well as Royan and Broun, "Versions," and Broun, *Scottish Independence*, pp. 215–68.

in Fordun's work and further warn against the treachery of the English.[55] As is evident from its recent edition, which includes in its nine volumes eight volumes of Latin text and translation, the *Scotichronicon* is a long, sprawling work, often digressive, and often concerned not with events in Scotland but with those in England and on the Continent. Bower later wrote a revision known as the *Book of Cupar* that he intended as an abridgement, but, as Marjorie Drexler points out, it is not "noticeably shorter than its original."[56] However, a true abridgement, the *Liber Pluscardensis*, once attributed to a Maurice Buchanan but now considered anonymous, was completed in 1461 and survives in six Latin manuscripts and one French.[57] It tended to omit Bower's accounts of European history (except for Franco-Scottish and Franco-English concerns) and to focus more on Scottish history.[58] Sometime around 1480 Patrick Russell, a brother of the Carthusian monastery in Perth, wrote another abridgement that was based upon the *Scotichronicon* and the *Book of Cupar*. John Gibson, a canon of Glasgow, wrote still another in 1501–02; and other abridgments by Richard Striveling, John Law, and the anonymous compiler of the *Extracta e Variis Cronicis Scocie*, as well as three abridgements of the *Book of Cupar*, appeared in the late fifteenth and early sixteenth centuries.[59] There are six manuscripts of the full text of the *Scotichronicon* and four abbreviated ones, and five others that include Fordun's *Chronica* and the *Annalia*.[60] This is a large number for a medieval Scottish work in Latin and indicates that the Scots had great interest in the history of their country.

Some writers attempted to reach a broader audience by writing in the Scots-English dialect. Between 1375 and 1377, at about the time that Fordun was writing, John Barbour produced a historical epic of close to 14,000 lines of Scots four-stress couplets about the heroic adventures of Robert Bruce who fought the English in the late thirteenth and early fourteenth centuries.

---

[55] For a recent study of nationalist sentiment in Bower, see Katherine H. Terrell, "'Lynealy discendit of the devill': Genealogy, Textuality, and Anglophobia in Medieval Scottish Chronicles," *Studies in Philology* 108 (2011), 320–44.

[56] Drexler, "The Extant Abridgements of Walter Bower's *Scotichronicon*," *Scottish Historical Review* 61 (1982), 63.

[57] Sally Mapstone, "The *Scotichronicon*'s First Readers" in *Church, Chronicle and Learning*, pp. 34–35 and 48 n. 23, n. 25. Drexler still attributed it to Buchanan ("Extant Abridgements," 63–64).

[58] Mapstone, "First Readers," p. 39.

[59] Drexler, "Extant Abridgements," pp. 64–66; Mapstone, "First Readers," p. 35. For a modern abridged translation, see Walter Bower, *A History Book for Scots: Selections from the "Scotichronicon,"* ed. D. E. R. Watt (Edinburgh: Mercat Press, 1998).

[60] D. E. R. Watt et al., "The Manuscripts" in Bower, *Scotichronicon*, gen. ed. Watt, vol. 9, pp. 148–202.

Barbour's *The Bruce* was followed in the early fifteenth century by Andrew of Wyntoun's 30,000-line *The Original Chronicle of Scotland*, "original" because it began with the origins of the universe. It covered the history of the world down to 1408 and sought to provide readers with some conception of the importance of Scotland in that universal history. Then between 1476 and 1478, when the unpopular James III was trying to forge an alliance with England, a Scottish author known variously as Blind Harry, Henry the Minstrel, or simply Hary [*sic*], wrote a 12,000-line epic about Wallace, another Scottish hero of the late thirteenth and early fourteenth centuries, to remind the Scots of the treachery of England, the "fals nacioun that we are nychtbouris to."[61]

The tradition of writing long histories in both Latin and Scots continued into the sixteenth century. In 1521 John Mair (Major) published his Latin *Historia Maioris Britanniae* (*History of Greater Britain*, a title that could be translated as *Mair's History of Britain*), in an attempt to eliminate earlier legends about the founding of both Scotland and Britain. His objective was similar to that of the humanist historian Polydore Vergil, whom Henry VII brought to England from Italy and who dismissed as fable the legendary history of Britain that had appeared in English chronicles since Geoffrey of Monmouth.[62] Like Polydore Vergil, Mair, as T. D. Kendrick observes, "sought to smash down the entire top-heavy structure of British and Scottish fabulous history with a few adroit and powerful blows"[63] and to present, in opposition to the pro-French policies of some of those advising the young James V, some basis for better relations between Scotland and England.[64]

Hector Boece's Latin chronicle, *Scotorum Historia* (1526 or 1527; reprinted in 1574 and 1575) is sometimes thought to have been written as a

---

[61] *Hary's Wallace*, ed. Matthew P. McDiarmid, 2 vols, Scottish Text Society, 4th s., 4, 5 (Edinburgh: William Blackwood, 1968–69), IX 115, vol. 1, p. 231. For discussions and bibliography of Fordun, Bower, Barbour, Andrew of Wyntoun, and Hary, see Edward Donald Kennedy, *Chronicles and Other Historical Writing*, vol. 8 of *A Manual of the Writings in Middle English*, gen. ed. Albert E. Hartung (New Haven: Connecticut Academy of Arts and Sciences, 1989), nos. 52, 53, 55, 59, pp. 2679–90, 2692–99, 2891–2913, 2915–2924. Also see Goldstein, *The Matter of Scotland*, and Friedrich Brie, *Die nationale Literatur Schottlands von den Anfängen bis zur Renaissance* (Halle: Niemeyer, 1937).

[62] Polydore Vergil tells how his friend, the Scots poet Gavin Douglas, tried to dissuade him from using Mair's *Historia* and to accept the truth of the story of Gathelos and Scota. Vergil was unwilling to do this. See John MacQueen, "National Spirit and Native Culture" in *Who Are the Scots? and The Scottish Nation*, ed. Gordon Menzies (1971, 1972; reprint, Edinburgh: Edinburgh University Press, 2002), pp. 172–73.

[63] Kendrick, *British Antiquity* (1950; reprint London: Methuen, 1970), p. 78.

[64] See Alexander Broadie, "Mair, John," *ODNB* 2004; R. A. Mason, "Kingship, Nobility, and Anglo-Scottish Union: John Mair's *History of Greater Britain* (1521)" *Innes Review* 41 (1990), 182–222.

reply to Mair's work.[65] Whether or not Boece wrote his work as a response to Mair, it nevertheless reasserted the validity of the medieval accounts of Scottish history and again expressed concerns about attempts to improve relations with England. His chronicle, according to Kendrick, "might at first reading be said to put the clock back about four hundred years."[66] It not only revived interest in the old legends that Mair tried to dismiss and emphasized the classical Greek and Egyptian culture upon which Scottish civilization was supposedly based, but it added detailed information about the forty-five ancient Scottish kings that Fordun had said ruled in the seven hundred years of history between the two Ferguses. Fordun had not given the names of these kings, and no one else seems to have known anything about them. Boece, in 119 pages of his *Historia,* gave what J. B. Black has called "an amazingly full and circumstantial account of the events" of the reigns of these kings. Boece, Black observes, hoping to inspire patriotism, placed the Scottish monarchy on an "apparently unassailable foundation as the most ancient of the civilised world" and presented Scots of that period as "comparatively civilised" with "a political system that would have done credit to any nation many centuries later."[67] Although his book had detractors in England in the sixteenth century,[68] almost no one in Scotland appears to have doubted Boece's account,[69] and it established his reputation as one of the greatest historians of his time.[70] He may, like Geoffrey of Monmouth, have created the previously unknown histories of the early kings himself, or, as is possible in light of his reputation as a scholar, he may not have intended to deceive but may have been drawing upon a now-lost source, identified as the chronicle of Veremundus, which he thought was genuine.[71]

---

[65] See R. A. Mason, "Kingship, Nobility, and Anglo-Scottish Union," p. 184; also for a good study of Mair, see J. H. Burns, *The True Law of Kingship: Concepts of Monarchy in Early-Modern Scotland* (Oxford: Clarendon Press, 1996), esp. p. 77.

[66] Kendrick, *British Antiquity,* p. 65.

[67] Black, "*Scotorum Historiae,*" p. 37.

[68] Kendrick, *British Antiquity,* pp. 65–69.

[69] George Buchanan had reservations about parts of it. See below.

[70] Black, "*Scotorum Historiae,*" p. 37.

[71] Black, "*Scotorum Historiae,*" pp. 48–53. See Royan, "The *Scotorum Historia* of Hector Boece." Also see Royan, "Boece [Boethius], Hector," *ODNB.* For a useful comparison of Mair and Boece, see Burns, *The True Law of Kingship,* pp. 54–92. Kendrick thinks it likely that Boece did not invent the source but "merely embellished and edited a forgery" (*British Antiquity,* p. 66). Dauvit Broun argues that Veremundus could have been a source for both Baldred Bisset's *Processus* and for Boece's *Historia* (*Scottish Independence,* pp. 252–68).

Boece's chronicle was influential. Published when James V was fourteen years old, it was intended to provide political instruction to the young king. It concerns bad kings, who ignored good counsel, and good kings, who followed it. Since it was written in Latin, however, and since James may have been illiterate and unable to read any language, in its original form it would have done the king little good.[72] John Bellenden soon translated the chronicle for him (and supplemented it with material from Bower and Mair), first in a version written between 1531 and 1533 and, after a number of revisions, in a version thought to have been printed sometime between 1536 and 1540.[73] Between 1531 and 1535, at about the same time that Bellenden began translating his prose version, William Stewart prepared another translation for the king, this time in pentameter couplets, a rather unusual medium for a historical work in the sixteenth century, but one that makes sense if it were intended to entertain as well as instruct a possibly illiterate young king.[74] Boece's chronicle was also translated not long after its publication into an anonymous prose account known as the *Mar Lodge Translation*.[75] Although George Buchanan pointed out a number of errors that he thought Boece had made, his *Rerum Scoticarum Historia* (1582) is based to a considerable extent on Boece. John Leslie completed a vernacular continuation of Boece's account (1570), and he later used it when writing a Latin history (1578), which was translated into Scots by James Dalrymple (1596). Robert Lindesay of Pitscottie completed a continuation of Bellenden's Scots version between 1577 and 1579 and

---

[72] It is generally assumed that James V was poorly educated and, since he was said to be unable to even read a letter in English, scholars assume he would not have been able to read Boece's Latin either. David Edward Easson, however, suggests that although English may have been difficult for him, he could nevertheless have been educated in Latin (*Gavin Dunbar, Chancellor of Scotland, Archbishop of Glasgow* [Edinburgh: Oliver and Boyd, 1947], pp. 29–32).

[73] John Bellenden, trans., *The Chronicles of Scotland, Compiled by Hector Boece*, ed. R. W. Chambers, Edith C. Batho, and H. Winifred Husbands, 2 vols, Scottish Text Society, 3rd s., 10, 15 (Edinburgh: William Blackwood, 1938–41). The STS edition is based on an earlier version than that of the sixteenth-century printed edition. See Nicola Royan, "The Relationship between the *Scotorum Historia* of Hector Boece and John Bellenden's *Chronicles of Scotland*" in *The Rose and the Thistle: Essays on the Culture of Late Medieval and Renaissance Scotland*, ed. Sally Mapstone and Juliette Wood (East Linton: Tuckwell, 1998), p. 137; Mapstone, "First Readers," p. 39.

[74] William Stewart, trans., *The Buik of the Croniclis of Scotland; or a Metrical Version of the History of Hector Boece*, ed. William B. Turnbull, Rolls Series 6, 3 vols (London, 1858). On its pedagogical intent, see Thea Summerfield, "Teaching a Young King about History: William Stewart's Metrical *Chronicle* and King James V of Scotland" in *People and Texts: Relationships in Medieval Literature*, ed. Thea Summerfield and Keith Busby (Amsterdam: Rodopi, 2007), pp. 187–98.

[75] *The Mar Lodge Translation of the History of Scotland*, ed. George Watson, Scottish Text Society, 3rd s., 17 (Edinburgh: William Blackwood, 1946). This edition, which was to consist of two volumes, was never completed. Volume 1 ends with the seventh book of the translation of Boece's *Historia*. The manuscript is now New York, Pierpont Morgan Library, MS M.0750.

apparently considered Bellenden's version a standard account of earlier Scottish history. It continued to be influential in the seventeenth century.[76]

Alexander Grant has described the chronicles of Fordun, Wyntoun and Bower as "consolidation[s] of Scottish beliefs about the past."[77] This description would apply to Boece and his translators as well. Their purpose was to give readers a sense of Scotland's distinguished history, its many victories over its enemies, and its independence from earliest times. However, even the abridgments of the *Scotichronicon* were long works. The *Liber Pluscardensis*, for example, runs to about four hundred pages in Felix J. H. Skene's nineteenth-century edition, and Skene omitted the early books that were based on Fordun's *Chronica*. Some of the works were, moreover, in Latin and could have been read by only a limited group. Even those written in Scots like *The Bruce*, *The Wallace* and the translations of Boece's *Historia* might have been too long to have been effective political propaganda, particularly if, like politicians today, an author hoped to reach those without much patience, time, or ability to concentrate, and some must have felt the need to provide what we today would call an "executive summary."

The Short Scottish Chronicles
In the late fifteenth century and in the early years of the sixteenth a series of short chronicles were written in Scots, French, and Latin that were intended to appeal to a wider audience, in part because of what Mapstone describes as Bower's "perceived loquaciousness."[78] The purpose of these short chronicles, like that of the long ones discussed above, was to instill a sense of pride in the Scottish nation; and most, like the longer ones, attempted to alert them to the threat from England. They too are "consolidations of Scottish beliefs about the past": the *Scottis Originale*, the *Ynglis Chronicle*, the *Chronicle of the Scots*, the *Brevis Cronica*, the *St Andrews Chronicle*, and the French *Vraie Cronicque* are short, highly derivative condensations of the more detailed Latin tradition of Scottish history. With the exceptions of the *Chronicle of the Scots* and the *Vraie Cronicque*, they build their versions of medieval events on Scotland's foundation legends and feed the popular appetite for a history that makes the Scots different from, older than, and superior to the

---

[76] George Buchanan, *History of Scotland*, trans. James Aikman, 4 vols (Glasgow, 1827); John Leslie, *History of Scotland*, ed. T. Thomson, Bannatyne Club, 38 (1830) and *Historie of Scotland*, trans. James Dalrymple, ed. E. G. Cody and William Murison, Scottish Text Society 5, 14, 19, 34 (1888–95); and Robert Lindesay (Lindsay), *The Historie and Cronicles of Scotland*, ed. Æ. J. G. Mackay, 3 vols, Scottish Text Society 42, 43, 60 (1899–1911). On the later influence of Boece and Bellenden, see Royan and Broun, "Versions," pp. 178–79.

[77] Grant, "Aspects of National Consciousness in Medieval Scotland," p. 74.

[78] Mapstone, "First Readers," p. 39.

Britons and English. The *Chronicle of the Scots* was different in that it was not written as a piece of propaganda, and the *Vraie Cronique* was written more for a diplomatic audience than for a popular one.

They are in many ways offshoots of the *Declaration of Arbroath*: although the authors of this document tried to win the Pope's sympathy by referring to their country as "poor little Scotland," and although it was written in Latin, the pride in their ancestry (although in this case the origins are in Greater Scythia), their being among the first nations converted to Christianity through the patronage of St Andrew, and the vehemence of their hatred of Edward I and the English anticipate the sentiments of the short chronicles.[79]

Abbreviated chronicles were teaching devices. Like the fourteenth-century English *Short Metrical Chronicle* or John Lydgate's fifteenth-century *Verses on the Kings of England*, or the numerous French, Anglo-Norman, Latin, and English genealogical chronicles that taught through genealogical diagrams accompanied by brief texts,[80] the Scottish ones would have been intended to teach essential facts of their nation's history. They would have been similar in intent to the verse *Liber Extravagans (Supplementary Book)*, an epitome of Scottish and English history that Bower appended to the *Scotichronicon* and that was also a source for some of the information in his longer work.[81] Almost all the paragraphs of three of the chronicles edited here – the *Nomina Omnium Regum Scotorum*, the *Brevis Cronica*, and the *St Andrews Chronicle* – focus on the reign of a king, and so each is essentially a genealogy of the Scottish monarchy. The *Scottis Originale* is an exception in that it does not attempt to tell all of Scottish history; its alternate title – *The Cronycle of Scotland in a Part* – explains that it is just part of Scottish history, and in its vehemence it is even more than the others intended as a piece of propaganda. Similarly the *Ynglis Chronicle* describes itself as "part of þe ynglis cronikle" and is as vitriolic.

Since the strained relationships between England and Scotland from the late thirteenth century led to persistent distrust of the English, it is difficult

---

[79] The Latin text for the *Declaration* is in *Chronicles of the Picts*, ed. Skene, pp. 291–94; translations are in Duncan, *Declaration of Arbroath*, pp. 34–37 and in Cowan, "For Freedom Alone," pp. 144–47.

[80] For the *Short Metrical Chronicle* and the English genealogical chronicles, see Kennedy, *Chronicles and Other Historical Writing*, nos. 6, 42–51, pp. 2622–24, 2674–79, 2807–9, 2888–91; for Lydgate's *Verses on the Kings of England*, see Alain Renoir and C. David Benson's chapter on Lydgate in *A Manual of the Writings in Middle English*, 6 (New Haven: Connecticut Academy of Arts and Sciences, 1980), nos. 100–02, pp. 1864–65, 2125–27, as well as Kennedy, ibid., p. 2599. For Anglo-Norman and French genealogical chronicles, see Olivier de Laborderie, "A New Pattern for English History: The First Genealogical Rolls of the Kings of England" and Marigold Anne Norbye, "Genealogies in Medieval France," both in *Broken Lines*, ed. Radulescu and Kennedy, pp. 45–61, 79–102.

[81] See "*Liber Extravagans* (Supplementary Book)," ed. Dauvit Broun with A. B. Scott in Bower, *Scotichronicon*, gen. ed. Watt, vol. 9, pp. 54–127.

to say that these were written as the result of any particular event, although certainly opposition, from the 1470s on, to attempts of some in Scotland to form an alliance with England could have been an inspiration for most of them. James III, for example, tried in the mid-1470s to arrange matrimonial alliances with the English royal family and, seeing little future in the alliance with France, tried to secure peace with England. His actions were the inspiration for Hary's *The Wallace*.[82] In 1482 James III's brother the Duke of Albany acknowledged Edward IV as his overlord and in return was recognized as King of the Scots; Scotland was spared Edward's imminent invasion by his death in 1483. His brother Richard III, having enough trouble in England, wanted peace with the Scots. Relations with England deteriorated again during the reigns of James IV (1488–1513) and Henry VII of England (1485–1509) until 1502 when James entered into a treaty of perpetual peace with England and the following year married Henry VII's oldest daughter, Margaret. The peace was not perpetual, however, and in 1512 James renewed the alliance with France and, going to war with England, was defeated and killed at Flodden in September 1513. His son James V was a minor until 1528, and his court was torn between those who supported England and those who supported France. This debate was also carried on in the historical literature, with Mair supporting an alliance with England and Boece supporting one with France. When James V began his personal rule, he turned toward France.[83]

Like the longer historical works, most of the short Scottish chronicles were written as propaganda. But with the exception of the *Nomina Omnium Regum Scotorum*, they would likely have been read and understood by more people. The history Fordun synthesized from earlier chronicles and passed on to Bower and Boece was, for the Scottish vernacular chroniclers, apparently too digressive and overly concerned with non-Scottish material. The authors of these short chronicles in Scots at times smoothed out their sources to project a history that is more honorable and less internecine than that reported in the earlier accounts. Drexler's comment about the author of the *Scottis Originale* – "This was an author on the defensive; he systematically rewrote the myth, smoothing over or omitting many episodes which might have been used to raise uncomfortable questions about the Scots' integrity"[84] – is applicable to parts of the *Brevis Cronica* and the *Ynglis Chronicle* as well.

---

[82] McDiarmid, ed., *Hary's Wallace*, vol.1, pp. xiv–xxvi.

[83] William Ferguson, *Scotland's Relations with England: A Survey to 1707* (Edinburgh: John Donald, 1977), pp. 39–41, 54–55.

[84] Drexler, "Fluid Prejudice," p. 69.

A good example of this "smoothing over" is found in the characterization of Gathelos, the legendary Greek prince who gives his name to the Gaels. Fordun presents him as "good looking" but "mentally unstable" (*habens vultu elegantem animo tamen instabilem*). He alienates his father by "many acts of destruction" (*multis cladibus*) and is run out of Greece and escapes to Egypt.[85] This account is preserved by Bower and Boece. As Drexler points out, Fordun's purpose in presenting this negative characterization of Gathelos would probably have been to present him and his Greeks as the "eponymous ancestors of the despicable Gaels" whose "waywardness reflected badly on the whole nation."[86] At one point in his chronicle, Fordun discusses differences between Lowlanders and Highlanders. He describes Lowlanders as being "of domestic and civilized habits, trusty, patient and urbane, decent in their attire, affable, and peaceful, devout in Divine worship, yet always prone to resist a wrong at the hand of their enemies." Although he admits that the Highlanders could be "faithful and obedient to their king and country, and easily made to submit to law, if properly governed," he nevertheless describes them as

> a savage and untamed nation, rude and independent, given to rapine, ease-loving, of a docile and warm disposition, comely in person, but unsightly in dress, hostile to the English people and language, and, owing to diversity of speech, even to their own nation, and exceedingly cruel.[87]

He reinterprets the old origin legend to account for the existence of two peoples within the kingdom, the Highlanders and Lowlanders, who were so different from one another. The Gaelic-speaking and often wild Highlanders would have been closely associated with Gathelos because of the name of their language (as the *Scottis Originale* points out). It could be implied that the Highlanders inherited their unruly nature from him. Though the two races were united through intermarriage, each had its own characteristics and Fordun obviously saw them as two distinct cultures within the nation.[88]

---

[85] Fordun, *Chronica,* I 8, trans. in Fordun, *Chronicle of the Scottish Nation,* pp. 6–7. In Bower, *Scotichronicon,* gen. ed. Watt, I 9 (vol. 1, p. 27).

[86] Drexler, "Fluid Prejudice," p. 69.

[87] Fordun, *Chronicle of the Scottish Nation,* II 9 (vol. 1, p. 38); Bower, *Scotichronicon,* gen. ed. Watt, II 9 (vol. 1, pp. 184–85).

[88] G. W. S. Barrow, *The Anglo-Norman Era in Scottish History,* pp.146–47; Kathleen Daly, "The *Vraie Cronicque dEscoce* and Franco-Scottish Diplomacy: an Historical Work by John Ireland?" *Nottingham Medieval Studies* 35 (1991), 113.

Fordun claims to have derived his characterization of Gathelos from two sources, an anonymous chronicle and a now lost *Legend of St Brendan*,[89] but since there is little extant evidence for this characterization prior to Fordun, he may have created the unruly Gathelos himself.[90] Gathelos is portrayed favorably in a concise late-thirteenth-century Anglo-Norman genealogical chronicle about Scotland that was incorporated into Thomas Gray's fourteenth-century *Scalacronica*. It describes him as chivalrous and the son of a noble knight of Athens.[91] Goldstein believes that "most of the details in Fordun's version [of the story of Gathelos's youth] are his own invention,"[92] and John and Winifred MacQueen point out that Gathelos corresponds to the creator of the Gaelic language Gáedel Glas of the Irish chronicle *Lebor Gabála*,[93] but add "It is curious that his early life [in Fordun] is portrayed in such hostile terms, which have no parallel in the Irish tradition." There might, however, have been a suggestion of his wayward behavior in Irish literature for, as mentioned above, in the *Chronicum Scotorum* the character corresponding to Gathelos has to flee to Egypt after attempting an unsuccessful rebellion in Scythia. Similarly, the MacQueens note that in the *Historia Brittonum* the unnamed Scythian nobleman who marries Scota is expelled from his kingdom, "presumably for some kind of misdeed," and is later driven away by the Egyptians who, after the Hebrews left, feared he might take over the kingdom. Either of these could have given Fordun an initial suggestion

---

[89] Fordun, *Chronicle*, I 8 (vol. 1, p. 7). This is also in Bower, *Scotichronicon*, gen. ed. Watt, I 9 (vol. 1, p. 27).

[90] Sir Thomas Gray also cites the *Legend of St Brendan* as a source for the Gathelos story that he includes in the *Scalacronica*, but he does not give Gathelos the negative characteristics that Fordun does. See his *Scalacronica 1272–1363*, ed. and trans. Andy King, Surtees Society 209 (Woodbridge: Boydell Press, 2005), pp. 18–19.

[91] "[E]n le pays de Attenys en Grece estoit vn noble cheualer, qi out vn fitz, qy auoit a noun Gaidel, qauoit en espouse la feile Pharao le Roy de Egypt, qe out a noune Scota, de qei il auoit bele engendrure. Gaidel estoit cheualerous; se purchasa lez juuenceaux de soun pays se mist en mere en nefe, od sa femme Scota et sez enfauntz, se quist mansioun al auenture en biaunce de le conquer, arryua en Espayne, ou sure vn haut mountain, au couster de la mere Hiberynie, fist edifier vn fort chastel, et le noma Brigans." ([T]here was a noble knight in the country of Athens in Greece, who had a son named Gaidel, who took to wife the daughter of Pharaoh, the King of Egypt, named Scota, by whom he had fair offspring. Gaidel was chivalrous, and having sought out the young men of his region, he set out to sea in a ship, with his wife Scota and their children, and sought a home by chance, in the hope of conquering it. He landed in Spain, where on a high mountain on the coast of the Hibernian sea, he had a strong castle built, and named it Brigantia.) Gray, *Scalacronica*, ed. and trans. King, pp. 18–19. The Anglo-Norman text is also *Chronicles of the Picts*, ed. Skene, pp. 194–95.

[92] Goldstein, *Matter of Scotland*, p. 114.

[93] This form of the name appears in the *Scottis Originale* and a derivative of it, Galiel, in the *Vraie Cronicque*. See discussion of these works below.

for Gathelos's early discreditable behavior that he developed more fully.[94] His innovation, however, was ignored by the vernacular chroniclers.

The *Ynglis Chronicle*, which does not hesitate to emphasize flaws of the ancestors of the kings of the English, "þe mast faltyf pepill of all þe warld," says nothing about Gathelos, referring only to "þe noble Grekis þat we ar cummyn of on þe mannis syd" (Y 11–16). The *Brevis Cronica* identifies him as "King Neolus son of Grece" (BAd 1–2) but does not tell how he came to be in Egypt. The *Scottis Originale* goes further in rehabilitating Gathelos: apparently drawing upon either the *Vraie Cronicque* or a Latin source about the legendary history common to both the *Scottis Originale* and the *Vraie Cronicque*, it explains that he was sent by his father in response to an Egyptian call for help from their Greek allies. And the chronicler makes the contemporary political point explicit by adding, "as now is allyit Fraunce to vs" (OD 5). Similarly, after Gathelos has married the pharaoh's daughter, the eponymous Scota, Fordun and most of his successors are frank about his reasons for leaving Egypt: he is once again run out of the country by Egyptians who fear he will usurp their throne. The *Scottis Originale* says that Gathelos left because of the cruel plagues that afflicted Egypt. The *Brevis Cronica* simply says that he left.

Although the English claimed hegemony over Scotland, a major theme of these chronicles is the uninterrupted independence and freedom of the Scots in contrast to the inhabitants of the southern part of the island. Moreover, since an early conversion to Christianity gave medieval nations prestige, these chronicles emphasize that the Scots had been Christianized before the arrival of Pope Gregory's missionaries to England in 597. The dates that they give vary: the *Chronicle of the Scots*, the least polemic of the chronicles, says the Scots accepted Christianity in 433 (S 23), which is close to the date that some chroniclers give for the translation of some of the bones of St Andrew to Scotland and the founding of St Andrews (but even that is about three hundred years earlier than the actual founding of St Andrews), and it does not try to argue that the Scots were converted before the Britons.[95] Both the *Scottis*

---

[94] John and Winifred MacQueen, eds, *Scotichronicon*, by Bower, gen. ed. Watt, vol. 1 (1993), p. 112. For the reference in the *Historia Brittonum*, see *British History*, ed. and trans. Morris, p. 21. In the brief early fifteenth-century *Tract on the Scots* as well as in a fifteenth-century Latin metrical chronicle, the *Liber Extravagans* (*Supplementary Book*), Scota's husband is from Scythia rather than Greece. See *Chronicles of the Picts*, ed. Skene, pp. lxix, 330–31, 333 and for the *Liber Extravagans*, ed. and trans. Dauvit Broun with A. B. Scott in Bower, *Scotichronicon*, gen. ed. Watt, vol. 9, pp. 66–67.

[95] For the shifting back four hundred years of the arrival of the relics of St Andrew, see Skene, ed., *Chronicles of the Picts*, pp. clxxiv–clxxviii and Edward Donald Kennedy, "John Hardyng and the Holy Grail," *Arthurian Literature* 8 (1989), 193–97, reprinted in *Glastonbury Abbey and the Arthurian Tradition*, ed. James P. Carley (Cambridge: D. S. Brewer, 2001), pp. 256–59.

Originale and the *Brevis Cronica*, however, maintain that the conversion took place about four hundred years before the English, and that "Scotland tuke þe faith of Cryst" in the year 203 and "as ʒitt hes kepit it vndefoulit" (BAs 52–54).[96] They base this date upon the conversion of the English by Augustine and other missionaries that Pope Gregory sent to England in 597, and they choose to ignore the statement in Geoffrey of Monmouth that the Britons had been converted in the second century[97] or even the historical conversion of the Britons in the fourth century when Constantine was emperor of Rome. Like the authors of the *Declaration of Arbroath*, these chroniclers believed that an early conversion to Christianity gave their nation special eminence.[98]

The chroniclers draw sharp distinctions between the Scots of the North and those people of the South, the Celtic Britons and the English. The *Ynglis Chronicle* and the *Scottis Originale*, which use Scottish history to negate English claims, comb their sources for facts that will discredit Briton and English kings, their progeny, and their subjects.

These short chronicles would have been written to supplement the long histories of Scotland in Latin and English written in the fifteenth and sixteenth centuries by Bower, Mair, Boece, and Bellenden, and most would have been intended as polemical works for potentially larger, less educated, often illiterate audiences. The use of history as political propaganda, of course, was not confined to the Scots. Bernard Guenée writes:

> [L]'historien, au Moyen Age, n'eut pas simplement le pouvoir de réinterpréter le passé; il eut celui de le réinventer. . . . Le passé, au Moyen Age, était aussi complaisant qu'il était respecté, aussi malléable qu'il était prestigieux." (The historian in the Middle Ages had not simply the power to reinterpret the past; he had the power to reinvent it. . . . The past in the Middle Ages was as accommodating as it was respected, as malleable as it was prestigious.)[99]

---

[96] See Skene, ed., *Chronicles of the Picts*, p. clxxv (400 years); *Anglo-Scottish Relations*, ed. Stones, p. 114 (500 years).

[97] Geoffrey of Monmouth, *The History of the Kings of Britain*, trans. Lewis Thorpe (Harmondsworth: Penguin, 1966), pp. 124–25, and see Thorpe's time line on p. 287.

[98] Cf. *The Declaration of Arbroath*: "Their [the Scots'] high qualities and merits . . . shine out sufficiently from this: that the king of kings and lord of lords, our lord Jesus Christ, after his passion and resurrection, called them, even though settled in the uttermost ends of the earth, almost the first to his most holy faith. Nor did he wish to confirm them in that faith by anyone but by the first apostle by calling (though second or third in rank) – namely the most gentle Andrew, the blessed Peter's brother, whom he wished to protect them as their patron for ever" (Duncan, *Declaration of Arbroath*, p. 35).

[99] Guenée, *Histoire et culture historique*, pp. 351–52.

These Scots chroniclers usually treat their sources more freely than their counterparts in England, at least when dealing with what we call legendary material; the English vernacular versions of Geoffrey of Monmouth's account, although adding some details and dialogue not in the original Latin texts, and often summarizing what Geoffrey had written, nevertheless remained generally faithful to the main points of Geoffrey's account.[100] It was as if his *Historia* were a canonical text that was to be treated with reverence. The Scots, however, in general felt freer to adapt and modify their exemplars, whether they were writing new Latin adaptations of Bower's *Scotichronicon*, like the abbreviated version in the *Liber Pluscardensis*, or vernacular ones like those edited here. Mapstone observes that readers of the manuscripts of Bower and Fordun apparently saw the material in the *Scotichronicon* as subject to "accretion and recasting." [101] Much of the "recasting" involved producing history that was more focused and more politicized. The propaganda glorified the nation's past, ignored facts that might make questionable the long independence of their country, and distorted earlier accounts by simplifying the characters of the heroes, making the national Scots heroes all good and the English all bad. Of course, earlier Latin historians, like Fordun and Bower, were also writing propaganda, but they were writing for learned groups and generally gave more balanced accounts of both the good and bad on both sides. With the exception of the *Chronicle of the Scots*, the short chronicles written in English represent a more politicized history: they are close in spirit to the anti-English epic *The Wallace*, but they are short and to the point and get their message across as vividly as any modern political pamphlet. The quotation from Mark Twain that Marjorie Drexler cites in her essay on Scottish origin legends – "The very ink with which all history is written is merely fluid prejudice"[102] – is particularly applicable to these works.

These chronicles raise a number of questions about historical interpretation of events. In an essay on different medieval interpretations of the fourteenth-century Peasants' Revolt in England, Derek Pearsall observes that one could argue that since the historical actuality of the revolt has essentially been lost, "the Revolt is significant chiefly as . . . an image of popular insurrection upon which outrage and utopian idealism could alike focus." In

---

[100] For the *Brut* chronicles written in English, see Kennedy, *Chronicles and Other Historical Writing*, nos. 3–17, pp. 2611–47, 2781–2845; for Latin ones that made use of Geoffrey's *Historia*, see Laura Keeler, *Geoffrey of Monmouth and the Late Latin Chroniclers, 1300–1500* (Berkeley: University of California Press, 1946).

[101] Mapstone, "First Readers," pp. 33–34.

[102] Drexler, "Fluid Prejudice," p. 60.

other words, the event becomes "part of English history through the process of interpretation. The importance of history is the way it is read." Pearsall objects to this approach because "it opens history to ideological and propagandist reconstruction," and history becomes indistinguishable from fiction.[103] This is the kind of narrative that these Scottish chroniclers were creating out of the information found in their sources. In the Middle Ages, chroniclers such as Bede and Ranulph Higden tried to get at the truth of events they were presenting by comparing contrasting accounts of them; and, limited as their resources were, they tried to be honest. One finds similar attempts at honesty even in nationalist works like those of Fordun and Bower. However, the authors of most of the short Scottish chronicles were not interested in trying to find objective truth,[104] and it is doubtful that those who listened to or read these chronicles questioned them any more than many people question television commercials today.

The concluding words of Bower's *Scotichronicon* are "Non Scotus est Christe cui liber non placet iste" (Christ! He is not a Scot who is not pleased with this book!).[105] That statement could be added to the vernacular works discussed here: it is safe to say that Scots would have been pleased with them and perhaps so would their allies, the French, but few French would have been able to read works written in Scots. The only large national group outside of Scotland that would have been able to read them would have been the English, who, not being Scots, would not have been pleased by the fluid prejudice that flowed from the pens of their northern neighbors. This would have given satisfaction to the authors of these works.

La Vraie Cronicque d'Escoce
Text and manuscripts
The *Vraie Cronicque* traces the history of Scotland from its origins to the death of the regent Mary of Guelders in December 1463. Four fifteenth-century manuscripts have survived.[106]

– [B] (Brussels, Bibliothèque royale, MS 9469–70) dates from 1467 at the latest, when it was recorded in the inventory of the library of Philip the Good,

---

[103] Pearsall, "Interpretative Models for the Peasants' Revolt" in *Hermeneutics and Medieval Culture*, ed. Patrick J. Gallacher and Helen Damico (Albany: State University of New York Press, 1989), p. 69.

[104] Many argue, of course, that historians cannot be objective. See Hayden White, *The Content of the Form: Narrative Discourse and Historical Representation* (Baltimore: The Johns Hopkins University Press, 1987; reprint 1992), esp. "The Politics of Historical Interpretation: Discipline and De-Sublimation," pp. 58–82.

[105] *Scotichronicon*, gen. ed. Watt, XVI 39 (vol. 8, pp. 340–41).

[106] See manuscript descriptions at the end of the Introduction.

Duke of Burgundy. This manuscript, which was the one published by Robert Anstruther,[107] is the basis for the present edition.

– [A] (Paris, Bibliothèque nationale nouvelle acquisition française MS 20962) belonged to Jacques d'Armagnac, Duke of Nemours.

– [P] (Paris, BNF nouvelle acquisition française 6124), is French, of unknown provenance.

– [G] (Geneva, Bibliothèque publique et universitaire MS français 166), according to a contemporary note in the manuscript, was given to Bérault Stuart, 3rd seigneur d'Aubigny, by John Ireland, better-known as the author of the *Meroure of Wyssdome*.[108]

The first three manuscripts have few significant variants, although none is a direct copy of another. However, two passages emphasizing the historical bases of friendship between the kings of France and Scotland are present only in the Geneva manuscript [G].[109]

The *Vraie*-chronicler's declared aim is to reconcile the conflicting accounts in his chronicle sources and to find what is "most likely and certain" about the history of Scotland (VC 4–15). This is not an innocent quest for truth, however. His range of interest in Scotland is very narrow: he uses a short genealogy of Scottish kings as a vehicle for a politicized history. He focuses on a series of key themes or issues in Scottish history: English claims to overlordship over Scotland; Scottish claims to the English crown and to lands in England; and friendship and alliances between the French and the Scots. The text concludes with some short entries on kings of Scotland from Robert II to the death of James II.

English claims over Scotland

Most of the *Vraie Cronicque*, directly or indirectly, explores the relationship between the kings of Scotland and the kings of England. This becomes apparent in the *Vraie*-chronicler's version of the origin of the Scots. At first reading, much of his account is consistent with the Scottish interpretation of the kingdom's origins. He favors the Irish Scots as the first inhabitants of Scotland, as the descendants of a union between the Egyptian princess Scota

---

[107] Anstruther, *La Vraie Cronicque d'Escoce: Pretensions des Anglois à la Couronne de France; Diplôme de Jacques VI, Roi de la Grande Bretagne*, Roxburghe Club (London, 1847).

[108] J. H. Burns, "Ireland, John (c. 1440–1495)," Philippe Contamine, "Stuart, Bérault (1452/3–1508)," *ODNB*.

[109] See VC 335–45 in the edition and a further revision in VC 399–404. [G] may therefore represent a later and slightly revised version of the text. All the witnesses have their share of mistakes and unique variants. [A] omits the Latin text of the Quitclaim of Canterbury (see VC 260–301). The number of errors and variant readings in [P] set it apart from other witnesses, but as these do not significantly alter the text, not all have been recorded in this edition. However, [P] is still closer to [A] and [B] than to [G].

and the Greek prince Gathelos or Galiel, as he is called here.[110] He asserts that the Irish settled in Scotland before the arrival of any others (that is, the Picts and Britons), that they considered themselves subject to the King of Ireland, that they were led by Rottay, and that the first King of Scotland, Fergus Feradrach, conquered the Picts, who had tried to claim the whole of Scotland.[111] There are a few interesting variations between his account and those of Fordun, Bower, and the short chronicles described below. Agenor and the ancestors of the Picts are given an Egyptian, rather than a Scythian origin, and thus an implicit link with Scota.[112] This may have been an attempt to explain why the descendants of Scota in Ireland were prepared to give the Picts wives and direct them to Scotland (a fact that had puzzled Bower).[113] The author is alert to the problem of explaining how people of different origins and languages could form a political community. In his account, the descendants of Yber-Scota settled, well before the arrival of the Picts, north of the "Scots sea," or Firth of Forth, where their descendants still spoke Gaelic in his own day.

Certain features of his account, however, sit uneasily with a pro-Scottish stance. For example, he accepts that the land "stretching from the duchy of Albany to the river Humber" was the inheritance of Albanact, son of Brutus, where the inhabitants first spoke "British," then, after the Saxon conquest, English. He implies that the Scots as well as the Britons lived both in "part of" the North and in "English" Scotland, whence they were driven out by the Picts, leaving unresolved how the Britons came to live there, and their relationship with the Scots. This potentially weakens a clear case for prior habitation of Scotland by the Scots. He side-steps the issue by emphasizing that the whole territory was united by Kenneth mac Alpin, who expelled the Picts, to form a single "kingdom" of Scotland (VC 131–38). He is therefore far more emphatic than Fordun that the reign of Kenneth mac Alpin molded a people of diverse origins into a kingdom.[114]

The *Vraie Cronicque* targets other key incidents in the dispute over Scottish independence from England: the homage paid by Malcolm IV to Henry II in 1157 and its confirmation by William the Lion at Falaise-Valognes

---

[110] VC 4–59. For the treatment of Gathelos in the *Vraie Cronicque* and the *Scottis Originale*, see the comparison of VC and SO in the section on SO below.

[111] VC 49–88. For the treatment of these events in Scottish sources, see above pp. 12–13.

[112] VC 67–69. The description of Agenor as an Egyptian prince is also found in SO, although there he expels, rather than leads, the Picts (see OD 86–90, OR 83–88, OA 69–74).

[113] Bower, *Scotichronicon*, gen. ed. Watt, I 25 (vol. 1, p. 60).

[114] It is possible that the author also wished to deny the separatist tendencies of the Lordship of the Isles within the Scotland of his own day. Daly, "*Vraie Cronicque*," pp. 112–13.

in 1178 (VC 231–40); the Quitclaim of Canterbury of 1189, when Richard I freed William the Lion of obligations for the kingdom of Scotland (VC 260–301); the Great Cause, when Edward I intervened in the disputed succession to the Scottish throne (VC 346–404); and the Treaty of Northampton, concluded in 1328 between Robert I and Queen Isabella, acting for her young son Edward III (VC 440–50). Once again, the author is far more ambivalent about these key incidents than are his Scottish counterparts. On the one hand, he accepts that Malcolm IV paid homage for the kingdom of Scotland. On the other, he explains that this did not imply Scottish subordination to England as it was an act of friendship rather than a legal duty to an overlord. To reinforce the point, he alleges that the Scots still rejected Malcolm and made William king instead (VC 225–34). He accepts that William in turn was forced to pay homage to Henry II. He then cites a version of the Quitclaim of Canterbury that justifies Scottish independence. However, he also undermines the Quitclaim's value by claiming that the document left the issue of Scottish homage "most unclear" (VC 234–37, 255–301). This indecisiveness is not found in Scottish chroniclers. Even treatment of the crucial issue of the Great Cause is not wholly favorable to the Scots. Whereas the English state that the Scots made submission (at Norham) "acknowledging that the kingdom of Scotland was held from the kingdom of England as their sovereign," the Scots claim "that the submission was made only to their nearest neighbour" (VC 367–73). Once again the author gives a leading role to the Scottish people, who reject Edward I's choice of Balliol, echoing the account in Fordun and Bower that "the sentence was only given in favor of Balliol because he had promised to become the man of the King of England."[115] The task of defending Scotland is left to William Wallace, until his execution by the English. Although the *Vraie*-chronicler's accounts of Balliol's resignation and Bruce's accession are very confused, Bruce is generally depicted in a negative fashion, apparently changing his allegiance only for personal gain. Conflicting English and Scottish interpretations of the Treaty of Northampton are reported without authorial comment (VC 401–18, 446–50). Thus, while broadly sympathetic to the Scots, the *Vraie Cronicque*'s treatment of the issue is ultimately ambivalent and inconclusive.

Scottish claims in England

The *Vraie*-chronicler is equally non-committal when describing Scottish pretensions to the English crown and to lands well south of the border. He alleges that "the kings of Scotland claim to this very day to have a right to the crown of England, and that it should belong to them" through their descent

---

[115] VC 399–404; compare with their role in ousting Malcolm IV in favor of William the Lion (VC 225–34, mentioned above).

from Malcolm III's wife, Saint Margaret, the heiress of the Anglo-Saxon king, Edmund Ironside.[116] The *Vraie Cronicque* is more ambivalent than Scottish sources about the justice of the claim. On the one hand, it notes that "according to the English," Margaret's line returned to the English throne through the marriage of her daughter Matilda to Henry I. On the other hand, it alleges that Malcolm III refused to give up his claims to the English throne and met his death while pursuing his right (VC 196–207, 212–16).

According to the *Vraie Cronicque*, Scottish claims to lands in England also originated from this claim to the English throne, for the children of Malcolm and Margaret received the earldom of Huntingdon, the counties of Northumberland, Cumberland, and the "land" of Tynedale from Henry I in return for giving up their claim to the English throne. However, Malcolm IV subsequently surrendered his northern lands when he granted to Henry II "all the lands on the borders of England and Scotland, from the river Tyne to the river Tweed and from the river [*sic*] Rere Cross and Stainmore to Solway," although according to our text, this grant was not accepted by the Scots (VC 198–204, 228–32). After his defeat by Henry II, William the Lion was forced to surrender the four great fortresses of the eastern march – Stirling, Edinburgh, Berwick, and Roxburgh – to the English king. These places were subsequently returned to the Scots king by the terms of the Quitclaim of Canterbury. It is possible that the *Vraie*-chronicler understood that the treaty also returned Cumberland, Westmorland, and Northumberland, or he may have concluded that the treaty was as unclear on those points as it was on the issue of homage (VC 251–55). By referring to the renewal of the Quitclaim by Henry III and Alexander II, the author implies that later Scottish kings retained their territorial claims, though he does not explicitly state this (VC 315–17). Overall, this is a nuanced picture, presenting information favorable to Scottish claims, but also details that might cast doubt on them.

What significance might the accounts of Scottish royal rights to the English throne and to English lands have had for the chronicler and his audience? The argument that Margaret was the true heiress of the English throne reinforced the status of Scotland as an independent kingdom: it had been used by the Scots at Bamburgh in 1321 to refute English claims to overlordship of Scotland.[117] Malcolm IV's grants to Henry II, confirmed by

---

[116] The *Scottis Originale* also asserts that the reigning King of Scotland is Margaret's heir and that her claim to the English throne was superior to that of William the Conqueror, whose illegitimacy barred him from the succession, although it does not give the details about her Anglo-Saxon predecessors present in Fordun, Bower, and the *Vraie Cronicque*. See OD 172–76, OR 168–75, OA 162–69.

[117] P. Linehan, "A Fourteenth-Century History of Anglo-Scottish Relations in a Spanish Manuscript," *Bulletin of the Institute of Historical Research* 48 (1975), 106–25. The claim was restated by the *Scottis Originale* (OD 173–75, OR 170–74, OA 164–68).

agreements between their successors, were significant to Scottish and English history because they stabilized the border between the kingdoms of England and Scotland, at the Solway Firth to the west and the Tweed to the east.[118] This stability had been undermined during the Scottish Wars of Independence and subsequent campaigns, when northern England and southern Scotland were prime targets for Scottish or English invasions.[119] The *Vraie Cronicque* therefore asserts the integrity of Scotland's boundaries as they existed well before the Great Cause. While there is little evidence that the Scots were actively pursuing pretensions to Cumberland and other lands in England in the 1460s,[120] Scottish claims to Roxburgh and Berwick were still relevant: the Scots had taken Roxburgh as recently as 1460, at the cost of James II's life, while Berwick was ceded in 1461 by Lancastrian claimants to the English throne as the price for Scottish support.[121]

The French and the Scots

The *Vraie*-chronicler's apparent impartiality is abandoned when he discusses the relationship between France and Scotland. Passages in the Geneva manuscript trace the connection between the two kingdoms back to Alexander II and Prince Louis (the future Louis VIII) of France and even suggest the alliance could have originated in the time of Malcolm III.[122] The *Vraie*-chronicler notes that first Balliol, then Bruce, sought French help to defy the English kings, and it is possible that some of his ambivalence arises from the fact that

---

[118] G.W. S. Barrow, "The Anglo-Scottish Border" in Barrow, *The Kingdom of the Scots*, pp. 112–29.

[119] Edward I had taken Berwick, Roxburgh, Stirling and Edinburgh in 1296; Edward Balliol ceded much of southern Scotland to Edward III in 1334; Roxburgh had also been the focus of Scottish campaigns in 1377; in 1417, when Berwick was also attacked; and again in 1436; and both towns had been bargaining chips in Anglo-Scottish negotiations in 1433. Norman Macdougall, *An Antidote to the English: the Auld Alliance 1295–1560* (East Linton: Tuckwell, 2001), pp. 21, 35, 49, 58, 81.

[120] *Pour ce que plusieurs*, written for the same negotiations as the *Vraie Cronicque*, likewise cites Scottish claims to "the county of Huntingdon, Northumberland, Westmorland, Tynedale and other great lordships in England, which the English have taken from them [my translation]," *Debating the Hundred Years War: Pour ce que plusieurs (La Loy Salicque) and A declaration of the trew and dewe title of Henrie VIII*, ed. C. D. Taylor (Cambridge: Cambridge University Press, 2006), p. 112. However, the author of that treatise is not justifying the Scottish claim as such, but using it to show that the English had no right to complain that the King of France had confiscated lands in France claimed by English kings, when the English had taken land from their neighbors.

[121] Macdougall, *Antidote to the English*, pp. 86–87, who notes that these acquisitions removed one of the most obvious incentives for war against the English.

[122] VC 333–42 (present only in the Geneva manuscript). He seems unaware of the tradition that made Achaius, King of the Scots, the ally of the "French" Charlemagne (Daly, "*Vraie Cronicque*," p. 107; on the historical basis for this link, see E. Bonner, "Scotland's 'Auld Alliance,'" *History* 84 [1999], 5–30).

the French signed treaties with each claimant in turn (1295 and 1326). He asserts that some of the French nobles who helped Bruce settled in Scotland, as if affirming that the "auld alliance" was reinforced by blood (VC 411, 433–39). He invents a dramatic scene in which Philip VI of France rejects peace with the English because the King of Scotland would have been excluded, a decision for which the French pay with their blood at the battles of Crécy and Poitiers. He gives a glowing account of the disastrous expedition of the admiral of Vienne to Scotland in 1385 (VC 453–93, 498–502). He recounts how the French gave refuge to David II and offered asylum to the future James I, a plan thwarted by the English (VC 523–27). There is no question here of mutual assistance: the Scots are depicted as debtors, the French as benefactors.

The political context

As we have seen, the *Vraie Cronicque* is much more ambivalent towards the relationship between the Scots and English than are the Scottish chronicles. The use of phrases such as "the English state . . . , the Scots claim" may support the author's stance as a neutral seeker after truth, but they also reinforce a sense of distance between the French and their Scots allies (VC 367–73; see also VC 205–07). In contrast, the text emphasizes the benefits of the "auld alliance" for Scotland rather than France. It seems unlikely, therefore, that it was propaganda intended to convince a French audience of the case for Scottish independence. What, then, was its purpose?

Textual and contextual evidence suggest that the *Vraie Cronicque* was prepared for diplomats as a briefing note that would enable them to defend French, not Scottish, interests and put pressure on the English by reminding them of sensitive issues in Anglo-Scottish history, including the "auld alliance." As the text was completed in 1464, it must originally have been prepared for important Anglo-French negotiations that were scheduled to take place at Saint-Omer the same year. In three manuscripts, the *Vraie Cronicque* accompanies another text that was prepared for the same negotiations and which used history to explain why the English had no claim to the French throne or any lands within France.[123]

By 1464, the French king Louis XI had already demonstrated that he was willing to sacrifice Scotland to his wider interests. On his accession to the throne in 1461, he had failed to renew the Franco-Scottish alliance of 1448. Furthermore, Scotland had not been included in the terms of the truce of Hesdin, which Louis signed with the Yorkist King of England, Edward IV, in October 1463. This was an ominous development, given that Edward IV

---

[123] For this text, *Pour ce que plusieurs* and its context, see Taylor, *Debating the Hundred Years War*, pp. 13–27.

had renewed the traditional English claim for homage from Scotland. By July 1464, it was even rumored at the Scottish court that Edward and Louis planned to attack Scotland together unless James III paid homage to Edward and accepted English sovereignty.

However, to use Scotland against England, Louis had to ensure that the Scots themselves were faithful to the alliance, and this was by no means certain as the Scots had concluded a fifteen-year truce with England on 3 June 1464.[124] Louis was not totally secure in France, either, and he may have been reluctant to alienate the Scots in case they allied with his archenemy, Charles, Count of Charolais and future Duke of Burgundy, and other French princes.[125] This uncertainty may explain why the *Vraie Cronicque*'s interpretation of Scottish history is so nuanced. French diplomats could remind their English counterparts that the Scots had far more reason to trust their traditional allies, the French, than the English, who had betrayed them in the past. On the other hand, should King Louis choose to abandon that alliance, his servants could cite the flaws in the Scottish case for independence from England to justify his actions. In the event, their sophistry was not put to the test, for the peace negotiations, which had originally been scheduled for spring 1464, were postponed to October and then abandoned in favor of specific truces.[126]

The *Vraie Cronicque* is therefore set apart from other short chronicles of Scotland published here not only in its language (French rather than Scots or Latin), but by its methods, objectives and intended audience. The sources of the text are unknown, although there are glaring errors and confusions in the account that form a stark contrast to treatment of the same issues in Scottish chronicles. However, as the *Vraie*-chronicler, like Fordun and Bower, is able to list some of the more obscure possessions of Earl David of Huntingdon, their texts may ultimately have been his source.[127] If the *Vraie Cronicque* was

---

[124] Daly, *"Vraie Cronicque,"* pp. 121–25 and references, for the complex diplomacy of these years in England, Scotland, France and the Low Countries, and more recently, D. Ditchburn, "The Place of Guelders in Scottish Foreign Policy, c. 1449–c. 1542" in *Scotland and the Low Countries: 1124–1994*, ed. G. G. Simpson (East Linton: Tuckwell, 1996), pp. 59–75; Macdougall, *Antidote to the English*, pp. 79–87.

[125] A major noble revolt against Louis, known as the War of the Public Weal and led by the Count of Charolais, erupted in France the following year. See Pierre Roger Gaussin, *Louis XI: un roi entre deux mondes* (Paris: A. Nizet, 1976), p. 106.

[126] J. Calmette and G. Périnelle, *Louis XI et l'Angleterre (1461–1483)* (Paris: A. Picard, 1930), pp. 42–54.

[127] It is uncertain whether Fordun's or Bower's text was circulating in France at this date. The author of the *Liber Pluscardensis*, an abridgment of Bower (see above p. 19), was well informed about Franco-Scottish affairs and must have passed much of his life in France, but he had returned to Scotland before 1464; the availability of the text in France is uncertain before 1519, when it was translated into French with a dedication to John, Duke of Albany, regent of Scotland. See Skene, ed., *Liber Pluscardensis*, vol. 1, p. xv n. 2.

composed directly from such sources, rather than drawing on an intermediate short chronicle such as the *Scottis Originale,* as was previously believed,[128] it marks a radical new departure in French knowledge about Scottish history, in spite of its errors.[129] Faced with the Hesdin–Saint Omer negotiations, it seems likely that Louis XI's officials turned to Scots in France, either in royal service,[130] or at the University of Paris, for their raw materials.[131] An inscription in the Geneva manuscript provides some evidence for this: it states that the anonymous owner was given that copy by Bérault Stuart, 3rd seigneur d'Aubigny, and that it was "made by a great Scottish clerk called Ireland, long nourished in France," an echo of Ireland's assertion in his *Meroure of Wyssdome* that he had been "thirty years nourished in France."[132] Ireland may have given Stuart the *Vraie Cronicque* while both were in Louis XI's service, or during diplomatic negotiations for renewal of the Franco-Scottish alliance in 1483–84, when Ireland had entered the service of James III, and Stuart was serving Louis's successor, Charles VIII. But was he the author? The term "fet," that is "made," is imprecise. It could mean that Ireland merely commissioned a copy of the text, perhaps making the additions found only in the Geneva manuscript, although that in itself would be valuable, as there is little other evidence of his historical interests. On the other hand, it is possible that Ireland played a major role in the original creation of the *Vraie Cronicque,* by devilling for French diplomats and compiling what was known about his country's past. If so, this may have given him an introduction both to French royal service and Franco-Scottish diplomacy: he was in Louis XI's service by

---

[128] For a discussion of the relationship between this Scottish chronicle and the *Vraie Cronicque,* see below, pp. 50–51.

[129] Daly "*Vraie Cronicque,*" pp. 106–108, 126 and note 61; Philippe Contamine, "Froissart and Scotland" in *Scotland and the Low Countries,* ed. Simpson, pp. 43–58.

[130] See, for example, William Monypenny, a veteran negotiator between France and Scotland; he had also been entrusted with a message to Louis XI from James Kennedy, bishop of Saint Andrews, about the dangers of abandoning the Scottish alliance, probably in July 1464. Daly, "*Vraie Cronicque,*" p. 123 and n. 52, and Norman Macdougall, "Monypenny, William," *ODNB.*

[131] The ingenuity of French royal officials in collecting historical materials from scratch was demonstrated in 1462–64 when they used oral testimony as well as chronicles to compile a dossier defending royal rights in Breton bishoprics. See Philippe Contamine, "The Contents of a French Diplomatic Bag in the Fifteenth Century: Louis XI, Regalian Rights and Breton Bishoprics," *Nottingham Medieval Studies* 25 (1981), 52–72.

[132] Sally Mapstone, "A Mirror for a Divine Prince: John Ireland and the Four Daughters of God" in *Bryght Lanternis,* ed. J. D. McClure and M. R. G. Spiller (Aberdeen: Aberdeen University Press, 1989), pp. 308–23. See most recently on Béraud or Bérault Stuart, Philippe Contamine, "Entre France et Écosse: Bérault Stuart, seigneur d'Aubigny (vers 1452–1508): chef de guerre, diplomate, écrivain" in *The Auld Alliance: France and Scotland over 700 Years,* ed. James Laidlaw (Edinburgh: University of Edinburgh Press, 1999), pp. 59–76.

the 1470s, and possibly earlier.[133] In the absence of conclusive evidence, Ireland's role has to remain conjectural. It seems highly likely, however, that one or more of the diplomats involved in the Hesdin–Saint Omer negotiations had a major role in the form and content of the text.[134]

In the past, Scottish interest in Scottish history had been promoted by war and diplomacy. The *Vraie Cronicque* shows that French interest in Scottish history was stimulated by diplomacy, but was also refracted through the prism of French concerns, for the hesitations and equivocations of the author about the relationship between England and Scotland were much more in the interest of the French than the Scots.

The Scottis Originale (*The Cronycle of Scotland in a Part*)

The *Scottis Originale* survives in three versions in three manuscripts: OD in the Dalhousie manuscript (Edinburgh, National Archives of Scotland, Dalhousie Muniments, GD 45/31/1 – II, formerly Brechin Castle, Panmure manuscript); OR in the Royal manuscript (British Library, Royal 17.D.xx), and OA in the Asloan manuscript (National Library of Scotland, MS 16500, formerly Acc 4233). The three versions have all been published separately.[135] The only chronicle written in Scots with more exemplars is Andrew of Wyntoun's *The Original Chronicle of Scotland*, which survives in nine manuscripts. Moreover, Michael Chesnutt observes that the Dalhousie version, judging from wear and tear on the manuscript, was read "much more often" than the other seven items in the manuscript.[136]

Like other short vernacular Scottish chronicles, the *Scottis Originale* is a condensation of Scottish history primarily intended for popular consumption. Its major theme is the uninterrupted independence and freedom of the Scots, and it reads less like history than like political polemic. It is more highly selective than others in that it mentions relatively few kings and presents just part of Scottish history; as its alternate title suggests, it is a "chronicle of Scotland in a part."

---

[133] Arguments for and against Ireland's authorship are discussed more fully in Daly, "*Vraie Cronicque*," pp. 125–29.

[134] A possible candidate may be Guillaume Cousinot. Cousinot had first-hand knowledge of Scotland, having been part of a French embassy to Scotland in 1451. Shortly before the *Vraie Cronicque* was composed, he had visited the court of Henry VI, which had been exiled to Scotland (1463). He has recently been identified as the author of *Pour ce que plusieurs*, the text that accompanies the *Vraie Cronicque* in three manuscripts. See Taylor, ed., "Introduction," *Debating the Hundred Years War*, pp. 7–8.

[135] The editions are listed in the bibliography at the end of this volume.

[136] Chesnutt, "The Dalhousie Manuscript of the *Historia Norvegiae*," *Bibliotheca Arnamagnæana* 38 (1985), 80–81.

The content

A major theme of this work is Scotland's long existence as an independent nation in contrast to the area to its south, which was repeatedly conquered. The Romans conquered the Britons but had to build "twa wallis fra the Est See to the West See" to keep the Scots out (OD 117–18, OR 113–14, OA 103–04). After the departure of the Romans, the Britons were conquered by the Saxons who were later ruled by Danes for thirty years. The chronicler includes a not-historically-verifiable reminder that a "king of Scotland callit Gregore" in the time of Alfred ruled over the English "to the water of Themes, mare than xxx ʒere" (OD 239–40, OR 241–42, OA 236–37). Since the reign of William the Conqueror (or "Bastard," as the author refers to him), Normans have ruled in England. In contrast, we are twice told that Scotland has been independent for 1800 years (OD 188–93, OR 187–92, OA 178–85; and OD 205–07, OR 206–09, OA 198–201). The Scots, moreover, inhabited their land "lang tyme before þat Troy was destroyit and lang or Brute was borne"; Brutus came to the island "lang efter þat" and occupied it "bot to the Scottis See, and nocht be north it" (OD 74–78, OR 72–75, OA 60–62). This is not in agreement with other Scots historians who wrote that the Scots first arrived in Scotland in 443 BC, long after Brutus arrived in the South ca. 1115 BC[137] However, there is some basis for his assertion since Bisset's *Processus* presents the version of the legend in which Scota herself "sailed to Scotland," bringing with her the Stone of Scone, and "conquered and overthrew the Picts and took over that kingdom."[138] In the *Scottis Originale*, however, the Picts arrive after the Scots. Then Fergus Feradach unites the Scots, conquers the Picts and becomes the first King of Scotland (OD 97–103, OR 94–99, OA 82–88). Later, supposedly 700 years before the chronicle was written, Kenneth mac Alpin drives the Picts out of Scotland (OD 167–71, OR 162–67, OA 157–61). The Scots have been independent from their first king Fergus until their present sovereign: "neuer strangeare regnyt on vs na had dominacioun" (OD 111–12, OR 107–08, OA 98–99).

Another important theme is the Scots' distinguished, ancient ancestry that originated in "the tyme of Moyses" (OD 1–2, OR 3–4, OA 3). Their present kings are descended from the ancestors of the Scots, the Greek prince Gayelglas (Gathelos) and his wife, the Egyptian princess Scota, daughter of the pharaoh drowned in the Red Sea. The chronicler omits references to Gayelglas's wayward behavior presented in Fordun and Bower and instead

---

[137] See the chronology for the Britons in Geoffrey of Monmouth, *History of the Kings of Britain*, trans. Thorpe, p. 286.

[138] See the text of the *Processus* in Bower, *Scotichronicon*, gen. ed. Watt, XI 62 (vol. 6, p. 183).

presents Gayelglas as the heroic warrior found in the *Vraie Cronicque* who comes to help the Egyptians by driving the Ethiopians out of the country. In the *Scottis Originale* Gayelglas is rewarded for his valor by Pharaoh's giving him Scota as his wife, and instead of being exiled by the Egyptians, he and his company, made up primarily of "lordis and gentillmen" (OD 58, OR 58, OA 48), leave not because they are forced out but because of concern about plagues that ravage Egypt after Pharaoh's death. According to Fordun and Bower, Gathelos cannot go back to Greece because of the crimes he had committed there, but the *Scottis Originale* says that Gayelglas rules out such a return in accordance with the custom of those days ("as the maner was that tyme" [OD 45, OR 48, OA 39]).

The Scots' lineage is far more distinguished and ancient than that of the Britons who are descended from "the traytouris of Troye" (OD 18, OR 21, OA 19). The Greeks were "the worthiest, it apperis, for thai haue bene twis conquerouris of the warlde," and the Egyptians were the people who "ressauit Crist . . . and nurist him nere vii ʒeris" (OD 25–26, 54–55, OR 28, 54–55, OA 26, 43–44). Gayelglas, Scota and their followers sought new lands, going first to Africa, then to Spain and "Portyngale" (named after "Gayell, oure forefader" (OD 63, OR 63, OA 53), and their descendants settled in Scotland "lang tyme before þat Troy was destroyit and lang or Brute was borne" (OD 75, OR 72–73, OA 60–61).

The foreign king to whom most space is devoted is Arthur, and this chronicle gives the Arthurian story a peculiarly Scottish interpretation that may have originated with the chronicles of Fordun and Bower. None of the earlier Scots chroniclers, however, had been as vitriolic in their presentation of Arthur as the author of the *Scottis Originale*. The hatred of Arthur expressed in the *Scottis Originale* runs counter to the admiration for Arthur expressed by many earlier Scottish writers including Barbour and Wyntoun and counter to the popularity of Arthurian romance in Scotland at this time.[139]

---

[139] On the complexity of attitudes toward King Arthur in Scotland, see Boardman, "Late Medieval Scotland," pp. 50, 53–56; Flora Alexander, "Late Medieval Scottish Attitudes to the Figure of King Arthur: A Reassessment," *Anglia* 93 (1975), 17–34; Nicola Royan, "'Na les vailyeant than ony uthir princes of Britane': Representations of Arthur in Scotland 1480–1540," *Scottish Studies Review* 3.1 (2002), 9–20; Juliette Wood, "Where Does Britain End? The Reception of Geoffrey of Monmouth in Scotland and Wales," and Royan, "The Fine Art of Faint Praise in Older Scots Historiography," both in *The Scots and Medieval Arthurian Legend*, ed. Rhiannon Purdie and Nicola Royan (Cambridge: D. S. Brewer, 2005), pp. 9–23, 43–54. For an earlier view, see Karl Heinz Göller, "King Arthur in the Scottish Chronicles," trans. Edward Donald Kennedy in *King Arthur: A Case Book*, ed. Edward Donald Kennedy (New York: Garland, 1996; reprint New York: Routledge, 2002), pp. 173–84 (originally published as "König Arthur in den schottischen Chroniken," *Anglia* 80 [1962], 390–404). Göller's article emphasizes the negative attitudes toward Arthur in Scotland; Alexander's article was written in response to show that there were also positive portrayals of Arthur in medieval and Renaissance Scottish literature.

Geoffrey of Monmouth had indicated that the Scottish kings owed allegiance to Arthur, and Edward I attempted to draw upon Geoffrey's evidence to further his claims to being overlord of Scotland. These English claims, based upon the chronicles, continued into the reign of Edward III, and they were later revived in 1400 under Henry IV[140] (and still later by Edward IV and Henry VIII). English attempts to gain hegemony over Scotland in the late thirteenth and fourteenth centuries would have given Fordun and Bower impetus to reinterpret the Arthurian material. In their chronicles although Arthur is a great king, he was nevertheless the illegitimate son of Uther and Igerne, and the true heir to the throne was Mordred, who, according to Bower, was the older son of King Lot of Lothian; but Mordred and his brother Gawain were passed over at the time of Uther's death because they were too young to save the country from the invading Saxons. Arthur, who, Fordun admits, had courage and innate goodness, was chosen out of necessity because he was fifteen and thus old enough to take command. The fact that Mordred had not been chosen king, Fordun and Bower suggest, may have caused him to rebel against Arthur many years later.[141]

As Susan Kelly has shown, however, there are differences between the accounts of Arthur in Fordun and in Bower. Bower's changes, Kelly points out, "bridge the enormous gap between the cautiously stated case of Fordun," which she describes as pro-Scottish rather than anti-Arthurian, and the severe denunciation of Arthur in the *Scottis Originale*.[142] Bower had emphasized even more than Fordun the importance of the independence of Scotland and had presented stronger objections to the legitimacy of Arthur's rule, and these became more forceful in the *Scottis Originale*. According to the latter work, Arthur took the realm of Britain from the "rychtwys aire" Mordred. However, the Britons, because Arthur's sister had married a Scotsman, made Arthur king "be the devilry of Merlyn,"[143] and Mordred was passed over because "he was Scottis, & was putt by his rycht." Arthur had no right to the throne because "he was þe son of adultry" (OA) or "a huris sone" (OD, OR). He broke old alliances with the Scots and made war on them. Mordred, "quhen Arthure was

---

[140] E. L. G. Stones, "The Appeal to History in Anglo-Scottish Relations between 1291 and 1401: Part I," *Archives* 9, no. 43 (1970), 11–21, 80–83.

[141] Fordun, *Chronicle of the Scottish Nation*, III 25 (vol. 1, p. 102); Bower, *Scotichronicon*, gen. ed. Watt, III 25 (vol. 2, pp. 66–67).

[142] Susan Kelly, "The Arthurian Material in the *Scotichronicon* of Walter Bower," *Anglia* 97 (1979), 437.

[143] The author is here probably thinking of the sword in the stone episode in either Robert de Boron's *Merlin* or its adaptation into the French prose romances of the Vulgate and Post-Vulgate cycles. Merlin drops out of the story before Arthur is born in Geoffrey of Monmouth's *Historia* and the English chronicles based on his work.

out in his tyrandiis, be all the statis of Britones and Scottis, was . . . crownyt for king of Britones and in his rychtwis querele, he slew this Arthure, and he him" (OD 119–48, OR 109–43, OA 109–39).

This chronicle also scoffs at the authenticity of the Arthurian stories. It assures us "thare is mekle thing said of this Arthur quhilk is nocht suthe, & bot fenȝeit." Thus he dismisses accounts in the English chronicles of Arthur's conquest of France and of Rome: the stories of Arthur's killing Frollo, King of France, and Lucius, Procuratour of Rome, are false because Frollo and Lucius did not exist: "thare was nane sik, as all storyes of Fraunce beris witnes."[144] The *Scottis Originale* further questions the truth of the Arthurian chronicles by asking how likely it is that Arthur conquered thirty realms when he was unable to drive the Saxons from his own kingdom, and the Scottish author implies that the material in the English chronicles had no more truth than the fanciful material of the romances, the stories that "Maister Walter Maple fenȝeit, in his buke of ane callit Lanslot [of] the Lake" (OD 150–55, OR 145–49, OA 141–43). In the Middle Ages Walter Map was erroneously thought to be the author of the French prose romances of the *Vulgate* (*Lancelot-Grail*) *Cycle*, the longest of which was the *Lancelot*.[145]

The only other kings in this chronicle besides the previously mentioned Fergus Feradach, Kenneth mac Alpin, Arthur, Gregor, and William the Conqueror are Edmond Ironside, Malcolm III (here called Canmore), and Henry II. Edmond Ironside had been "vndoutit King of Ingland," and after the death of Edmond, the Scot Malcolm should have ruled since he had married "Edmound Irnesydis sonnis douchter" (OD 174–75, OR 170–74, OA 164–68). The third of these kings, Henry II, had, according to this chronicle, demonic origins. The chronicler includes the story, derived ultimately from

---

[144] The chronicle is, for the most part, correct on this point: The story of Arthur's continental conquests did not appear in most French chronicles, except for a few published in Brittany; being conquered by the British was generally not a part of French historical tradition. See Robert Huntington Fletcher, *The Arthurian Material in the Chronicles, Especially Those of Great Britain and France* (1906), 2nd edn., ed. Roger Sherman Loomis (New York: Burt Franklin, 1966), pp. 209–36. Although there are references in several continental chronicles that Fletcher was not aware of, there are still not many. See Edward Donald Kennedy, "Arthurian Material," *The Encyclopedia of the Medieval Chronicle*, 1:114–18.

[145] He was incorrectly said to be the author in the concluding sentence of the *Quest del Saint Graal* and in the opening sentence of the next and last romance in the series, *La Mort le Roi Artu*. To gauge the impact of this statement comparing the English Arthurian chronicle stories to this French romance, one need only recall that this is the romance that Chaucer mentions in his *Nun's Priest's Tale* when his narrator says that his tale of two chickens is as true as the "book of Launcelot de Lake," which "wommen holde in ful greet reverence" (lines 3212–13 in *The Riverside Chaucer*, 3rd edn., gen. ed. Larry D. Benson [Boston: Houghton Mifflin, 1987], p. 258). The author of the *Scottis Originale* thus relegates the stories in the English Arthurian chronicles to the medieval equivalent of the romances sold in supermarkets today.

the English chronicler Ranulf Higden but here taken more probably from Bower, who attributes the story to Higden, that a distant female ancestor of Henry II flew out a church window and was never seen again. Higden refers to her devilish (*diabolice*) character and reports that Richard the Lionhearted said "hit was no wonder þouȝ þey þat comeþ of suche a kuynde greved everich oþer, as þey þat comeþ of þe devel and schulde goo to þe devil."[146]   The chronicler, in emphasizing this woman's relationship to the Devil, thus shows that Henry II was descended directly from the Devil: "Henry the tyrane . . . was bot the secund fra the Devill", and "all the kingis sensyne ar cummyn of him" (OD 217–19, OR 217–21, OA 212–16). This lineal descent explains the treachery of subsequent English kings.

Relation of the three versions

Because of the differences in the wording of the Asloan and Dalhousie versions, W. E. Craigie, who did not know of the Royal version, assumed that OA and OD were "independent versions from a Latin original."[147] The use of Latin tags (*In primis nota* [OD 1], *Juxta illud* [OD 14, 51, 235], *Versus* [OR15, 51, 237], *Juxta illud metrice dictum* [OA 231]) suggests a Latin source. Michael Chesnutt agrees that they were translated from a Latin source but believes that the differences in the three could be due to their being "(indirect) products of dictation to a team of scribes" and thus "more or less unfaithful witnesses to a common original."[148] Such a method of production makes sense if there was interest in getting a number of copies produced quickly for political propaganda. OD and OR, however, are more closely related to one another than to OA, and it could be argued, as Craigie suggested, that all are independent translations from a lost original. A third and perhaps most likely possibility is that there was a single translation and that the three surviving texts represent independent revisions of it.

One of the ways that the *Scottis Originale* differs from the other short vernacular chronicles is the amount of Latin it contains. The fact that all three agree on leaving certain passages in Latin could point to their being, as Chesnutt suggests, products of dictation from a common English translation that had been made from a Latin original or simply that the three surviving versions represent independent revisions of one written translation. The Latin passages are of

---

[146] Quoted from Trevisa's translation. See *Polychronicon Ranulphi Higden Monachi Cestrensis*, Rolls Ser 41, vol. 8, ed. Joseph Rawson Lumby (London, 1871), pp. 33–35 (bk. 7, ch. 21). This anti-English story is quoted in Bower, *Scotichronicon*, gen. ed. Watt, IX 6 (vol. 5, pp.16–19) and attributed to Higden. Also see Terrell, "'Lynealy discendit of þe devil.'"

[147] Craigie, ed., *Asloan*, vol.1, p. vii.

[148] Chesnutt, "Dalhousie Manuscript," p. 72.

particular types: 1) Latin verses; 2) apparently familiar proverbs (OR 160-61, OA 156; OD 223, OR 225, OA 219–20); and 3) direct quotations from Latin sources such as "Sicut spina rosam sic genuit Judea Mariam" (OD 52, OR 52) or the quotation from Saint Bernard (OD 236–37, OR 238–39, OA 232–33). Only two – OD and OR – contain the Latin "Sicut spina rosam," although it might have been in Asloan's exemplar, and he could have missed it through eyeskip. Alternatively, the quote might have been dropped from his exemplar.

The amount of Latin in the *Scottis Originale* could suggest that it was intended for a learned audience. At least one reference, concerning the date when the first Fergus became king, relies on a reader's ability to understand a Latin phrase that had appeared earlier (see discussion below). Sally Mapstone has pointed out that the inclusion of the *Scottis Originale* in the Dalhousie manuscript "reveals its transmission into the milieu of a distinguished literary patron." It was possibly prepared for Henry Lord Sinclair (d. 1513), patron of the poet Gavin Douglas, or as Chesnutt suggests, compiled from materials inherited by Lord Sinclair.[149] It may therefore have been originally intended for a well-educated group. Mapstone points out that Sinclair was not one of the most important people in James IV's government,[150] but considering the amount of anti-English sentiment at the court of James IV (prior to his marriage to Henry VII's daughter in 1502), it would nevertheless seem appropriate for people who had connections at court.

On the other hand, as Mapstone suggests, its inclusion in Asloan's manuscript indicates "the appeal of this kind of text to a literate laity extending considerably beyond magnate circles."[151] Since most of its main points are presented in Scots, the Latin could be there for decoration, to impress the readers with its author's learning and authority and thus to give more weight to the propaganda being presented (a technique used by Chaucer's Summoner and Pardoner).[152]

The dates of the extant Scots versions

Version OD for many years was thought to have been written in the middle of the fifteenth century: David Laing, the nineteenth-century editor of OD,

---

[149] Mapstone, "First Readers," p. 40; Chesnutt, "Dalhousie Manuscript," p. 88.

[150] Ibid.

[151] Ibid.

[152] The Summoner: "And whan that he wel dronken hadde the wyn, / Thanne wolde he speke no word but Latyn. / A fewe termes hadde he, two or thre, / That he had lerned out of som decree" (*General Prologue* lines 637–40); the Pardoner: "And in Latyn I speke a wordes fewe, / To saffron with my predicacioun [to season my sermon], / And for to stire hem to devocioun" (*Pardoner's Prologue*, lines 344–46). Quotations from *Riverside Chaucer*, gen. ed. Benson, pp. 33, 194.

believed that it was written during the reign of James II and was copied into the Dalhousie manuscript ca. 1460;[153] and others followed suit, dating it *ante* or ca. 1460.[154] The *Scottis Originale*, however, could have been written considerably later than that. Chesnutt believes that OD was written close to 1500. Version OA, which refers to "our souerane lord James þe Fyft þat now is" (OA 96), would have been copied between 1513, when James became king, and ca. 1533, the probable date of the death of John Asloan.[155] Scholars have assumed that he copied the parts of his manuscript over a period of years between 1513 and 1525, and since it was written in fascicles, the parts could have been written in an order different from that in which they appear in the manuscript.[156] OR has been dated 1482–1530, with the date of 1530 suggested by OR's addition to the statement, found in all three versions, that the expulsion of the Picts took place "sewyn hundir ʒeir syne" (OD 169, OR 164, OA 159-60): OR adds, "þat is to say, þe ʒeir of our Lord, aucht hundir xxx and od ʒeiris" (OR 164–65). Thus, according to OR, the expulsion of the Picts occurred sometime in the 830s, and it is now seven hundred years later, in the 1530s ("xxx and od ʒeiris"). All of the extant Scots versions could therefore have been written late in the fifteenth century or in the early sixteenth century. If all three are independent revisions of a translation, the original translation could have been written earlier in the fifteenth century.

The presumed Latin source

As mentioned above, scholars have assumed that the three versions of the *Scottis Originale* were based upon a Latin source. Chesnutt believes that there is little reason for dating the Latin source much earlier than its three Scots translations. Since all three versions state that the Egyptians and Greeks were allied like Scotland and France, he dates the Latin source at ca. 1495, after the

---

[153] Laing, ed., *Bannatyne Miscellany* 3, p. 27.

[154] Ritchie Girvan, ed., *Ratis Raving and Other Early Scots Poems on Morals*, Scottish Text Society, 3rd s., 11 (Edinburgh: Blackwood, 1939), p. liii; Craigie, ed., *Asloan*, p. vii; Flora Alexander, "Late Medieval Scottish Attitudes," p. 21; Daly, *"Vraie Cronicque,"* pp. 108, 110; I. C. Cunningham, "The Asloan Manuscript" in *The Renaissance in Scotland*, ed. A. A. MacDonald, Michael Lynch and Ian B. Cowan (Leiden: E. J. Brill, 1994), p. 110; Catherine Van Buuren, "John Asloan and His Manuscript: An Edinburgh Notary and Scribe in the Days of James III, IV and V (c. 1470–c. 1530)" in *Stewart Style 1513–1542: Essays on the Court of James V*, ed. Janet Hadley Williams (East Linton: Tuckwell, 1996), p. 24.

[155] Asloan's activities are recorded in and around Edinburgh beginning Feb. 1494/95, and scholars once thought that the last reference to him was on 3 March 1529/30. However, in 1985 another document was published on which his name occurs among witnesses to a deed dated 11 December 1532 (*Protocol Book of John Foular, 1528–1534*, ed. John Durkan, Scottish Record Society n. s. 10 [Edinburgh, 1985], 150, cited van Buuren, "John Asloan and His Manuscript," p. 15).

[156] Cunningham, "Asloan Manuscript," p. 133.

renewal in March 1492 of the alliance between Scotland and France.[157]   He believes that it would have been translated into Scots shortly after that, during a period of conflict with the English that lasted until peace was secured in 1502 through the arrangement of the marriage of James IV and Margaret, daughter of Henry VII of England.   He also sees the chronicle as a reaction against the anti-Scottish sentiments in Caxton's *Chronicles of England* (the Prose *Brut*), which was published in 1480 and 1482.

A Latin sentence in both OD and OR, *Sicut spina rosam sic genuit Judea Mariam* (OD 52, OR 52), strengthens the possibility of a date as late as Chesnutt suggests for the Latin source.   This is a chant taken from the middle of a respond *Ad nutum Domini* associated with the nativity of the Virgin and, in Paris and Cambrai, also with the Matins for the feast of the Conception. The respond, in the middle of which the Latin sentence appears, can be found in England as early as the twelfth century in the Use of Salisbury and in the thirteenth century in the antiphonal at Worcester Cathedral as well in Benedictine monasteries in France.[158]   However, buried as it is in the middle of a line in the middle of a respond, this Latin sentence would have been obscure had it not become the title of a mass for the Virgin Mary written by Jacob Obrecht, probably for a church in Antwerp in the 1490s, in all likelihood in 1497 or 1498.[159] Thus the Latin quotation in the *Scottis Originale* could be a reference to Obrecht's work. Moreover, Obrecht's mass was in use in churches in Paris, which is significant since the *Scottis Originale* is related to the French *Vraie Cronicque*.   The Latin source could have been written in Paris by someone familiar with both Obrecht's mass and the *Vraie Cronicque* (or a Latin source upon which *Vraie Cronicque* was based).   On the other hand, if the Latin source of the *Scottis Originale* were written earlier in the fifteenth century, the Latin reference to Obrecht's mass could have been added for the first time to the Scots exemplar upon which the Scots versions represented by OD and OR were based, an exemplar that had been either written in France or written by someone who had recently been to France and had heard Obrecht's mass in Paris.

---

[157] Chesnutt, "Dalhousie Manuscript," pp. 73–75.

[158] See Manfred F. Bukofzer, *Studies in Medieval and Renaissance Music* (New York: Norton, 1950), 309 for references to *Antiphonale Sarisburiense* (Salisbury), *Processionale Monasticum* (Worcester), and *Paléographie musicale* (Benedictine monasteries in France).

[159] See Barton Hudson, "Obrecht's Tribute to Ockeghem," *Tijdschrift van de Vereniging voor Nederlandse Muziekgeschiedenis*, D. 37ste. (1987), pp. 3–13, here p. 9, from http://www.jstor.org, Monday October 16 14.10.41 2006; M. Jennifer Bloxam, "Plainsong and Polyphony for the Blessed Virgin: Notes on Two Masses by Jacob Obrecht," *The Journal of Musicology* 12 (1994), 51–75, esp. 51–64; http://www.jstor.org/ Fri Oct 13 17:13:12 2006.

While Chesnutt's dating for the Latin source at ca. 1495 is possible, there are reasons to believe that it might have been written earlier. The chronicler could have reacted against the anti-Scottish sentiments of the Prose *Brut* long before its publication as Caxton's *Chronicles of England* in 1480 and 1482 since there were many manuscripts of this work in circulation (about 52 of the Anglo-Norman version survive and anywhere from 175–182 of the English, depending on what one counts as a Prose *Brut*).[160] Moreover, although the reference to an alliance between Scotland and France could refer to the renewal of the alliance in 1492, there were many Franco-Scottish alliances.[161] Beginning informally in the late twelfth century and formally in 1295, alliances were renewed in 1326, 1371, 1391, 1428, 1448, 1484, and 1512, as well as 1492.[162] In the periods in between many Scots apparently considered the alliance to be continuously in effect. In 1467 a Scots parliamentary commission wished "to show their loyalty to the French alliance," and in 1471 Edward IV apparently tried to weaken "the Franco-Scottish alliance."[163] Two versions (OD 5, OR 6–7) refer to the alliance in the present tense, but in one (OA 5–6) it could be in the past (even though Asloan was writing after the renewal of the alliance in 1512). An allusion to this long-standing alliance does not necessarily point to a specific date.

Moreover, the chronicle offers evidence of a date earlier than the 1490s and later than 1460. The three translations all include the following information (except for the words *and mare*, which are only in OD and OR):

[160] I list 172 manuscripts in *Chronicles and Other Historical Writing*, pp. 2818–21; Lister Matheson lists 181 in *The Prose "Brut": The Development of a Middle English Chronicle* (Tempe, AZ: Medieval and Renaissance Texts and Studies, 1998), pp. xxiii–xxxi, but both of us include four post-medieval transcripts among them. Matheson classifies several chronicles as Prose *Bruts* that are textually unrelated to most of the others and that I had listed as separate chronicles. After the publication of my list in 1989, one other Prose *Brut*, Brogyntyn MS 8, on deposit at the National Library of Wales, was discovered, and Matheson recognized, as I had not, that the brief history in the Mayor's Calendar, city of Bristol, is an abridgment of the Prose *Brut* and not, as I had thought, of Geoffrey of Monmouth's *Historia Regum Britanniae*. After the publication of Matheson's book, another Prose *Brut* turned up at a Sotheby's sale on 22 June 2004, and is now at Dartmouth College Library. See Elizabeth Bryan, "Prose Brut, English" in *The Encyclopedia of the Medieval Chronicle*, ed. Graeme Dunphy (Leiden: Brill, 2010), 1:1239–40. Thus by my count, the number of surviving manuscripts is 175; by Matheson's, 182.

[161] The paragraphs below are based on Kennedy, "The *Chronicle of Scotland in a Part* and the *Chronicle* of John Hardyng" in *The Medieval Book and a Modern Collector: Essays in Honor of Toshiyuki Takamiya*, ed. Takami Matsuda, Richard A. Linenthal, and John Scahill (Cambridge: D. S. Brewer, 2004), pp. 360–64.

[162] Ranald Nicholson, "Index: Franco-Scottish Alliance" in *Scotland: The Later Middle Ages* (Edinburgh: Oliver & Boyd, 1974), 659; Norman Macdougall, *Antidote to the English,* p. 9 and *passim*.

[163] Nicholson, *Scotland*, pp. 441, 420; W. H. Finlayson, "The Boyds in Bruges," *Scottish Historical Review* 28 (1949), 195.

[T]here is na land, nor зit nacion, þat is nor was fra the begynnyng of the warld, þat standis in fredome sa lang tyme, – that is to say *auchtene hunder зere and mare* vnconquest or subject till ony strange nacioun or king, as we do, bot euer vnder oure awin king, of oure awin blude, *rycht lyne descendand fra oure first King Fergus before said,* till him þat now regnis, quham God sauff. (OD 188–93; cf. OR 187–92 and OA 178–85; emphasis mine)

The phrase "before said" refers to an earlier passage of Latin verse in all versions that mentions Fergus as the first king, who reigned from about 330 BC (*Christum tercentis terdenis prefuit annis* [OD 107, OR 103, OA 93]). Chesnutt observes, "[T]aken at its face value the passage might accordingly be supposed to mean that the author was writing immediately after 1470." Chesnutt's reading, however, may not give enough importance to the phrase *and mare* in OD and OR that extends the date beyond 1470. Chesnutt dismisses the date 1470 as an error because the three texts also refer to the expulsion of the Picts by Kenneth mac Alpin as having taken place seven hundred years ago: "[W]e putt thame vtterly out of the land for euer be oure king Kenneth Makalpyne, the quhilk was done vij^c зere syne" (OD 168–69, OR 163–65, OA 158–60). That would be in 770. Chesnutt writes:

> The traditionally received date of the expulsion of the Picts was ca. 840
> – John of Fordun assigns the event to the period between 839 and 845
> – and it is unlikely, in view of the learning which he displays elsewhere,
> that the author was ignorant of this date.

However, seven hundred years after ca. 840 would date composition about 1540. This is impossible since Asloan died ca. 1533 and, as noted above, the Royal version also appears to have been copied before 1530. Chesnutt argues that the author must therefore have "reckoned his dates to the nearest half century." This would establish "a *terminus a quo* more than six and a half centuries after the expulsion of the Picts, i.e. sometime in the 1490s."[164]

Although this explanation is possible, the chronicler, who was more propagandist than historian and whose accuracy about facts of history is questionable, may have forgotten or ignored the traditional date of ca. 840 or may have used a source with a different date. Although in Fordun the expulsion occurs ca. 839–45, dates vary in other chronicles. As noted above, the Royal chronicler or scribe thought it was ca. 830. In the thirteenth-century *Chronicle of the Picts and Scots* from the priory of St Andrews and in two

---

[164] Chesnutt, "Dalhousie Manuscript," pp. 73–74.

fourteenth-century chronicles apparently based on it, the era of Kenneth mac Alpin is presented as being much earlier. The time from Kenneth to the accession of Alexander in 1251 (actually 1249) is said to be 501 years in two of these chronicles and 567 years in another. Thus Kenneth would have reigned ca. 750 according to two of these chronicles and as early as ca. 684 according to another. These calculations give dates from ninety to more than one hundred years earlier than that found in Fordun and the Royal chronicle, perhaps in order to give the united kingdom of the Scots greater antiquity.[165] If the author of the original version of the *Scottis Originale* considered 750 to be the date for the expulsion, this would suggest a date of composition of 1450, during the reign of James II as scholars once thought. However, 1450 would not correspond to the other date, 1470, suggested by the chronicle.

Another unusual date for the expulsion of the Picts that may be relevant appears in Cambridge, Corpus Christi MS 171 of the *Scotichronicon*, the manuscript belonging to Inchcolm Abbey where Bower was abbot and which was emended "under Bower's own supervision before his death in 1449."[166] Although Bower earlier indicates that the expulsion occurred in 839, later in his chronicle he added in the margin the date 870 (*anno scilicet domini^d viii^c iii^{xx} x^o*), as the date in which Kenneth "successfully formed one kingdom out of two." This date, the editors point out, is inconsistent with the rest of the narrative and with the historical record.[167] The date may be relevant, however, to the *Scottis Originale*: Bower might have found it in some written source, and if in a manuscript other than Bower's source it had been written *anno scilicet domini^d vii^c iii^{xx} x^o*, with a 'vii^c' mistakenly written for 'viii^c', the year would have been 770, an error not too improbable in light of the three chronicles cited in the preceding paragraph that dated the united Scots kingdom at 750. If the author of the Latin version of the *Scottis Originale* assumed the date of the expulsion of the Picts was 770 and indicated that it took place seven hundred years ago, the year of composition would be ca. 1470. This corresponds with the date the chronicle suggests in its account of the founding of the Scottish nation: Fergus united the Scots more than eighteen hundred years ago in 330 BC, and this too suggests ca. 1470 as the date of composition. This could suggest that it was written at about the time Edward was attempting to weaken the Franco-Scottish alliance in 1471.

---

[165] See Skene, ed., *Chronicles of the Picts*, pp. lv–lvi, lxv, lxvii, 176, 290, 303.

[166] John and Winifred MacQueen, eds, *Scotichronicon* by Bower, gen. ed. Watt, vol. 1, (1993), p. xiii.

[167] Ibid., vol. 2, ed. John and Winifred MacQueen (1989), IV 3, 9 (pp. 272–73, 294–95, 451); vol. 9. ed. Watt (1998), p. 110.

In summary, the Latin source of the *Scottish Originale* and its three Scots versions cannot be confidently dated more accurately than to the last third of the fifteenth-century or the first third of the sixteenth. Aside from ambiguous references to the Franco-Scottish alliance, the extant versions of the translation offer evidence of when the Latin source was written: 1) Fergus united the Scots in 330 BC and Scotland has been independent for over eighteen hundred years; 2) Kenneth mac Alpin expelled the Picts seven hundred years ago. The first reference suggests a date of ca. 1470 or a little later. The second corresponds to the first if the author thought (or wished to think) that the united kingdom that mac Alpin ruled was older than it actually was and dated from the eighth century rather than the ninth. In light of varying dates for mac Alpin's victory, the author possibly thought the date was 770. If so, that reference too points to ca. 1470 as the date of the Latin source, although admittedly it could have been written as late as the 1490s as Chesnutt suggests. The possible allusion to Obrecht's mass in OD and OR, if in the original Latin, would indeed indicate a date in the late fifteenth or early sixteenth century, but that allusion could have been added to the Scots exemplar of OD and OR.

The author

The authors of *Vraie Cronicque*, the original Latin version of the *Scottis Originale*, the Scots translation, and its extant revisions are unknown. However, Dauvit Broun, in correspondence with the editors, suggested that a work written by a Gaelic speaker may be the basis for the introductory legendary part of both the *Vraie Cronicque* and the *Scottis Originale*. Broun points out that Gaelic is referred to as "oure langage" (OD 7, OR 9, OA 8) and "the form 'Gayelglas' (with 'y' rather than 'th') would reflect contemporary Gaelic pronunciation." He believes that a form like "Gathelos" would have been used by non-Gaelic speakers who would have known of him from Fordun or Bower and points out that OD and OA sometimes spell the name with "th." Moreover, he writes, the

> analysis of Portugal, 'Portingale,' as containing the name Gayel reinforces the impression that the author was familiar with thinking of Gathelos as Gàidheal, 'Gayel [Galiel in *VC*].'

The *Vraie Cronicque* and the *Scottis Originale* also both refer to Ireland as *la grant Escoce* (VC 56) and *Scotia Maior* (OD 70, OR 69, OA 57) and to Scotland as *la petite Escoce* (VC 63) and *Scotia Minor* (OR 70, OA 58) or *Less Scotland* (OD 72). Broun suggests:

A Gaelic speaker might also explain the readiness to pick up on the naming of Ireland as *Scotia maior* and Scotland as *Scotia minor* in the Irish Remonstrance of 1318 (which survives only in Bower's *Scotichronicon*): it seems to me that the openness to perpetuating the close tie with Ireland would come naturally to a Gaelic speaker, and less so to someone who was not.

This suggests at least two possibilities: 1) that an author who spoke Gaelic would have written the *Vraie Cronicque* and used the name Galiel, and that the author of the Latin source of the *Scottis Originale* would have based his legendary account on the *Vraie Cronicque*, would also have known Gaelic and thus used the form Gayel Glas; or more probably 2) that the legendary part of the *Vraie Cronicque* is based upon a Latin chronicle written by a Gaelic speaker and that this Latin chronicle was also the source for the legendary part of the presumed Latin source of the *Scottis Originale*.

The *Scottis Originale* and the *Vraie Cronicque*

The relationship between the *Scottis Originale* and the *Vraie Cronicque* is complex, and the best we can do is suggest possibilities as to which was based on the other. The two are similar only in their presentation of the early legendary history (to approximately OD 112, OR 108, OA 99) and in their use of one Latin quotation within that legendary history. The *Vraie Cronicque* has nothing in it about King Arthur,[168] and the two chronicles' presentations of later Scottish history are independent of one another. Since scholars thought for many years that the Scots version of the *Scottis Originale* from OD was written about 1460 and since the *Vraie Cronicque* carries its history down to 1464, they assumed that the French chronicle was derived from it. The surviving Scots versions, however, can be dated from the late fifteenth or early sixteenth centuries rather than from 1460 and are unlikely to be sources for *Vraie Cronicque*. As mentioned above, the non-legendary parts of the presumed Latin source appear to have been written ca. 1470 or later, and the legendary part of the Latin source of the *Scottis Originale* could be based on the *Vraie Cronicque*. Alternatively, both the legendary part of the *Vraie Cronicque* and the legendary part of the Latin source of the *Scottis Originale* could be based upon a common Latin source written before 1464.

Admittedly it is difficult to determine whether the *Vraie Cronicque* drew upon the Latin source of the *Scottis Originale* or whether the Latin source of

---

[168] The source for the *Vraie Cronicque* may not have included the Arthurian material, but even if it did, an author writing for the French may not have found it relevant or believable. The French, unlike the English and Scots, generally considered Arthur a fictional character rather than a historical figure.

the *Scottis Originale* drew upon the *Vraie Cronicque* for its legendary material since passages are often similar in each version. Thus in the French, Galiel's father sends his Greek son to Egypt "avecquez grant nombre de pueple"; and in the Scots, his father sends him to Egypt with "a grete power of men"; in the French, the "Ethyopiens furent desconfiz" and in the Scots, Gayelglas "discomfit the Ethiopis." Judging from such passages, either could be translated from the other. Moreover, both include information not found in the other, and arguments could be made on either side that one could be the source of the other. Even some of the Scots versions' digressions give little clue as to which was the earlier. For example, the *Vraie Cronicque* points out that the Scots' Greco-Egyptian origins are earlier than the Britons' Trojan origin; the Scots version says essentially the same thing but then devotes considerable space to denouncing the Trojans as cowards and traitors, something that would never have appeared in a chronicle designed to win favor for the Scots in France since the French too claimed Trojan descent. One could argue (if the Latin source of the Scots versions were the original) that the author of the *Vraie Cronicque* chose to ignore the denunciation of the Trojans; or (if the French were the original) that the *Vraie Cronicque*'s reference to the Trojan origin of the Britons inspired the Scottish author to add a vituperative harangue against the Trojans.

In the *Vraie Cronicque* Galiel and Scota leave Egypt because of a war the Egyptians are conducting against the children of Israel. Although this could suggest cowardice on the part of the Scots' ancestors, it could instead indicate that the author is trying to keep the ancestors of the Scots free of involvement in a dispute that the Egyptians lose, and where God is on the side of the children of Israel. Furthermore, he provides a partial justification for the Egyptians by suggesting the Israelites are the aggressors. In the Scots version, they simply leave because of "cruell plagis," a reason that might seem sensible.

However, one passage could suggest that a Latin source of the legendary part of the *Vraie Cronicque* may be the source of the legendary part of the Latin version of the *Scottis Originale*. Both the *Vraie Cronicque* and the Scots versions contain a Latin line that puns on the similarity between the Latin for "angulus" (angle, corner) and "Angle" (English). In the French version this is presented as

Autres dient qu'elle est appellee Angleterre *ab angulo, quia veritas non querit angulos, juxta illos versus, Anglicus angelus est cui nunquam credere fas est, dum tibi dicit ave tanquam ab hoste cave.* (VC 119–23)

The three Scots versions give an abbreviated form of this:

> thai war callit Anglici or Angli, *ab Angulo*. Now, *Veritas non querit Angulos nec Anglos*. Tharefore may thai neuer be trew þat come *de Angulo*. (OD 209–11; similarly, OR 211–13, OA 203–05)

It seems probable that the shorter quote in the Scots account would have been derived from the longer one either in the *Vraie Cronicque* or in a possible Latin source of the *Vraie Cronicque*. While this could suggest the Scots version of the legendary material was based upon a Latin chronicle derived from the French version, it is also possible that the legendary part of the Scots translation and the legendary part of the *Vraie Cronicque* were both derived from the same Latin chronicle written sometime prior to 1464.

The *Scottis Originale* and John Hardyng's Chronicle

If the Scots version of the entire chronicle (the legendary part similar to the *Vraie Cronicque* and the later parts that are unrelated to the French chronicle) was written in the 1470s, its hatred of England, comparable to that found in the contemporary epic, Harry's *Wallace* (ca. 1476–78), could reflect the mood of many Scots who were angry that James III was trying to arrange an alliance with Edward IV; and if written in the 1490s it would reflect the hostile feelings toward England during much of James IV's reign before his marriage in 1502 to Margaret Tudor. The political climate of the late fifteenth century could have triggered the vehement rhetoric of the *Scottis Originale*.

If the later parts of the Latin source were written any time after 1465, the author could have been responding to the second or Yorkist version of the English chronicle of John Hardyng, which was completed ca. 1465 and which is far more anti-Scottish than Caxton's *Chronicles of England*. Although some scholars believe that Hardyng's major purpose in writing his chronicle was to argue for a unified England, free of civil war,[169] Hardyng also believed that England should conquer and control the Scots. As Alastair J. MacDonald has observed, he "displays a heartfelt hatred of them" and saw them as a

---

[169] See Felicity Riddy, "John Hardyng's Chronicle and the Wars of the Roses," *Arthurian Literature* 12 (1993), 91–108; Sarah L. Peverley, "Dynasty and Division: The Depiction of King and Kingdom in John Hardyng's *Chronicle*," *The Medieval Chronicle* III, ed. Erik Kooper (Amsterdam: Rodopi, 2004), pp. 149–70; Peverley, "Adapting to Readeption in 1470–1471: The Scribe as Editor in a Unique Copy of John Hardyng's *Chronicle of England* (Garrett MS. 142)," *The Princeton University Library Chronicle* 66 (2004), 140–72; Peverley, "Political Consciousness and the Literary Mind in Late Medieval England: Men 'brought up of nought' in Vale, Hardyng, *Mankind*, and Malory," *Studies in Philology* 105 (2008), 11–17.

people "full of treachery and deceit,"[170] and it was possibly anti-Scottish sentiment that led Grafton to publish two editions of the chronicle in 1543, when such sentiment was politically correct in Henry VIII's England.[171] Hardyng denigrated Scotland's claims to independence and antiquity and praised the Britons and the English, both of whom, according to Hardyng, repeatedly forced the Scots to pay homage.   The Yorkist version of his chronicle survives in twelve complete manuscripts and three fragments and was probably, because of its genealogical information, put into broad circulation as part of Edward's propaganda campaign to justify his claim to the throne.[172] Most surviving manuscripts of this version date from the last third of the fifteenth century, 1470–1500.[173]

Some details in the *Scottis Originale* suggest that it was written in part as a reaction against Hardyng.   Hardyng could have suggested the previously mentioned disparaging allusion to "Maister Walter Maple" and his "buke of ane callit Lanslot [of] the Lake" (OD 154–55, OR 148–49, OA 142–43) since he had used as sources for his chronicle the two Arthurian romances of the Vulgate Cycle that are specifically attributed to Walter Map. Hardyng, unlike most Arthurian chroniclers, includes among Arthur's knights Lancelot, and he is the only English chronicler who adds substantial details from the Vulgate *Queste del Saint Graal* and *Mort Artu*. Moreover, in telling of Mordred's final battle against Arthur, the *Scottis Originale* indicates that Mordred "slew this Arthure, and he him, as the Brute sais" (OD 138–39, OR 133–34, OA 127–28). If the *Originale*-chronicler is referring to the Prose *Brut*, this information is incorrect since the *Brut* simply says that "Mordrede was slayn, and al his folc" and "Arthure himself was wondede to þe deth."[174]   The account of Arthur and Mordred's killing one another first appears in the

---

[170] MacDonald, "John Hardyng, Northumbrian Identity and the Scots" in *North-East England in the Later Middle Ages*, ed. Christian D. Liddy and Richard H. Britnell (Woodbridge: Boydell Press, 2005), p. 34.

[171] See Alfred Hiatt, "Stow, Grafton, and Fifteenth-Century Historiography" in *John Stow (1525–1605) and the Making of the English Past*, ed. Ian Gadd and Alexandra Gillespie (London: The British Library, 2004), pp. 46–51. Also see Hiatt's comments on Hardyng's Chronicle and Anglo-Scottish relations in his *The Making of Medieval Forgeries* (London: The British Library, 2004), pp. 112–19.

[172] See A. S. G. Edwards, "The Manuscripts and Texts of the Second Version of John Hardyng's *Chronicle*" in *England in the Fifteenth Century*, ed. Daniel Williams (Woodbridge: Boydell Press, 1987), pp. 75–84.

[173] For manuscripts see Kennedy, *Chronicles and Other Historical Writing*, p. 2836, and for detailed manuscript descriptions, see Sarah L. Peverley, ed., "John Hardyng's Chronicle: A Study of the Two Versions and a Critical Edition of Both for the Period 1327–1464" (unpubl. Ph.D. thesis, Hull, 2004), pp. 47–118.

[174] *The Brut or the Chronicles of England*, ed. Friedrich W. D. Brie, Pt. 1, Early English Text Society, O.S. 131 (1906; reprint 1960), p. 90.

Vulgate *Mort Artu* (1215–30) and is repeated in the English Alliterative *Morte Arthure* (ca. 1377–1400), in the Latin prose *Brut* known as the *Nova Cronica* (ca. 1438) and its English translation, the *New Croniclys* (perhaps ca. 1444), in the Flemish chronicle of Jehan de Waurin (ca. 1455, final version ca. 1471), and in Hardyng's chronicle.[175] Hardyng writes: "Arthure slewe Mordred . . . / But this Mordred gaue Arthure deaths wound."[176] Although the Scottish author could have derived this information from any of the works mentioned above, Hardyng's chronicle is a likely source.

The unprecedented attack on King Arthur as a tyrant and son of a whore could have been a reaction against Hardyng's idealization of Arthur to the extent of claiming that his kingdom was like heaven on earth. The only English writer prior to Hardyng to present such an idealized portrait of Arthur was John Lydgate in his *Fall of Princes*. The anti-Arthurian sentiments expressed here could have been triggered by Hardyng's account and could be a veiled attack on either Edward IV, who reigned from 1462 to 1483, or Henry VII, who reigned from 1485 to 1509. Both kings claimed Welsh descent and admiration for the Arthurian story, and Henry VII even named his first son Arthur and had him baptized at Winchester, where what was supposedly Arthur's Round Table was (and still is) located.[177]

The Chronicle of the Scots (*The Short Chronicle of 1482*)

The *Chronicle of the Scots* follows Wyntoun's *The Original Chronicle of Scotland* and the *Scottis Originale* in BL Royal MS 17.d.xx. The British Library's catalogue of the Royal manuscripts incorrectly identifies it with the *Brevis Cronica* found at the conclusion of Wyntoun's chronicle in the Advocates MS19.2.4 and also erroneously noted that it occurs at the end of Advocates MS 19.2.3 as well as 19.2.4.[178]

Although the chronicle ends in 1482, it may have been written, as David Macpherson and William F. Skene supposed, ca. 1530 since that may have been the date of the version of the *Scottis Originale* that precedes it in the

---

[175] Their killing one another could also be inferred from the *Polychronicon* ("Arthur fauȝt . . . wiþ Mordredus, and slouȝ hym and was i-slaw"), but although the chronicler mentions Higden, as we indicate in the notes, he probably derived information based on Higden from Bower and may not have known the *Polychronicon* first hand. The quotation is from Trevisa's translation in *Polychronicon Ranulphi Higden Monachi Cestrensis*, ed. Joseph Rawson Lumby, Rolls Series 41, vol. 5 (London, 1871), p. 333.

[176] *The Chronicle of Iohn Hardyng*, ed. Henry Ellis (London, 1812), p. 146.

[177] Simon Jervis, "The Round Table as Furniture" in *King Arthur's Round Table: An Archaeological Investigation*, ed. Martin Biddle (Woodbridge: Boydell Press, 2000), p. 54.

[178] George F. Warner and Julius P. Gilson, *Catalogue of Western Manuscripts in the Old Royal and King's Collections*, vol. 2 (London: The Trustees of the British Museum, 1921; reprint, Munich: K. G. Saur, 1997), p. 257.

same manuscript.[179] As mentioned above, while the other two texts of the *Scottis Originale* indicate that the conquest of the Picts occurred 700 years ago, the scribe of this manuscript adds, "þat is to say, þe ȝeir of our Lord, aucht hundir xxx and od ȝeiris" (OR 164–65). Thus the *Chronicle of the Scots* may have been written ca. 1530 as well. Since, however, it ends in 1482, it may, as Norman Macdougall suggests, have been written in the late autumn of that year,[180] and in that case the scribe of the Royal manuscript could have copied it from an earlier exemplar.

The *Chronicle of the Scots* is primarily a series of brief annals covering important events in the world and in Scotland up to 1482. It begins with a list of the six ages of the world, although, unlike the traditional Augustinian list, the sixth here ends with Christ, and the years after Christ presumably constitute a seventh age. The *Scots*-chronicler, following Fordun (who probably drew upon either Jerome or Martinus Polonus) indicates that the world was created 5199 years before the birth of Christ,[181] instead of ca. 4000 BC, the date often derived from the calculations by scholars in the Middle Ages and Renaissance. The chronicler indicates how long each age lasted, with the dating of the six ages being different from that found in many other chronicles.[182]

Other dates are different from those found in other chronicles edited here. While the *Scottis Originale* and the *Brevis Cronica* tell of the legend of Gathelos and Scota and the origins of the Scots in time of "Moses the prophet," this chronicle does not make such extreme claims for the antiquity of Scottish civilization. While Moses lived 2747 Anno Mundi, the Scots had much later origins in 4315 AM, about one hundred years after Romulus and Remus founded Rome in 4218 AM. By pointing out that the Scots had their origins after the founding of Rome, the chronicler indicates that the Scots had more recent origins than the Trojans, something denied in the other chronicles edited here. In 5139 AM Julius Caesar conquered the world, "all bot Scotland" (S 15). The chronicler omits the claims that some chroniclers made about the Scots being converted to Christianity before the Britons. He says that the Emperor Constantine "first relesyt Haly Kirk" in AD 312 (S 21–22), which would have been when the Britons would have been converted, and then says that "haly Palladius prechit þe fayth to Scottis men" in 433. He is also closer

---

[179] Macpherson, ed., *The Orygynale Cronykil of Scotland* (London, 1795), vol. 1, p. xliii; Skene, *Chronicles of the Picts*, p. lxxiii.

[180] Macdougall, *James III*, pp. 275–76, 312.

[181] S 1–2; Fordun, *Chronicle of the Scottish Nation*, I 7 (vol. 1, p. 6).

[182] See the explanatory notes for details about the chronicler's eccentric dating of world history.

to the truth when he says that the relics of Saint Andrew, which some, including Fordun, claimed arrived in Scotland in the fifth century, reached Scotland in 761. Whether there were relics or not, that is close to the earliest records (AD 747) referring to St Andrews.

This is the least biased of the short chronicles in this book. After the brief introductory account of world history and of early events in Scotland and Britain, most of the entries concern Scotland, beginning with the reign of Malcolm III in 1066. The chronicler pays some attention to occurrences in England and on the Continent, as, for example, to the Emperor Frederic's being "put doun" by the Pope in 1244 (S 77–78). Entries become fuller toward the end of the chronicle where the emphasis is on events during the reign of James III and in England concerning the Wars of the Roses, including the conflict between "the haly man" Henry VI and Edward IV (S 197–211). Although this suggests bias toward Henry the Lancastrian rather than Edward the Yorkist, certainly understandable in light of Edward's designs against Scotland, the tone of this chronicle is nevertheless moderate. It does not appear to have been written like the others as political propaganda but as an effort to teach, in abbreviated form, some of the major events of world and Scottish history. Its model could have been monastic annals.

The chronicle's greatest value is its presentation of Scottish history in the fifteenth century. According to Norman Macdougall, it is one of only two surviving chronicles that preserves a contemporary account of events from 1437 to 1482, and that in only its last two folios. However, the accuracy concerning the dating of events in the years 1479, 1480, and 1482, Macdougall observes, is "impressive," and the chronicler gives good accounts of the slaying of James III's younger brother, the Earl of Mar, because he favored "weches and warloiss" (witches and warlocks) who were burnt that year; of the shortcomings of James III and his reliance on poor counselors; and of the famine of 1482 caused in part by the debasement of currency issued by the government (the "black money" mentioned in 229–30) and in part by the war with England. Macdougall believes the chronicler may have been a supporter of James's brother, Alexander, Duke of Albany, who was banished in 1479 for having participated in a rebellion.[183] Thus this chronicle presents an important contemporary record of events of those years.

---

[183] Macdougall, "The Sources: A Reappraisal of the Legend" in *Scottish Society in the Fifteenth Century*, ed. Jennifer M. Brown (London: Edward Arnold, 1977), pp. 11–12, 20–21. The other contemporary source for these events is the *Auchinleck Chronicle*, cited in n. 5 above.

The Ynglis Chronicle

The *Ynglis Chronicle* is found only in the Asloan manuscript. Its tone is established in the introductory lines: "Heir followis ane tractact of a part of þe ynglis cronikle schawand of þar kingis part of þar ewill & cursit governance." Unlike the other chronicles in this volume, which are devoted to Scottish history, this one covers "a part" of Briton/English history. After an introduction condemning the general treachery of the English and presenting some confused chronology about conquests of the Trojans, Saxons, Danes and Romans and an announcement that he will show, on the basis of evidence from the English *Polychronicon*, that English rulers are descended from the devil, the chronicler proceeds chronologically from Harold to the eighteenth year of Henry VI, with its concluding sentence telling of the arrest of Eleanor Cobham (1440). Almost everything said about the English in this chronicle is negative, with the exceptions of four people: Maud, wife of Henry I, the "gud qwene" who "was douchter to þe haly queen of Scotland"; the martyr Thomas Becket; and Simon de Montfort and Henry VI, both described as "gud."

The chronicler overlooks the distinction between the Britons and English and includes in his introduction elements of two legends about the early settlement of Britain. First he addresses the English as if they were descendants of the legendary Britons: "ʒe ar cummyn of Brutus, þat is þe mast faltyf pepill of all þe warld . . . of quhais wikit fals deidis all þe warld reidis and will do vnto þe end þarof" (Y 10–13). He also draws upon (and modifies) a legend circulating in England that the first inhabitants of the island were Queen Albine (Albina) and her thirty sisters who settled there after rejecting the husbands their father had chosen for them. In one version the women were the Greek daughters of Diocletian; in another, the daughters of Diodicias, King of Syria. The island had been uninhabited except for devils who assumed human form and impregnated the sisters. They gave birth to giants, whose descendants Brutus and his Trojans killed when they arrived on the island. The *Ynglis*-chronicler claims to have found this story in that standard universal history, Higden's *Polychronicon* (Y 18–19). However, it does not appear to have been a part of the *Polychronicon*, although admittedly it could have been added to a now lost manuscript. The story originated as an Anglo-Norman verse account, now known as *Des Grantz Geanz*, which was probably written sometime between the mid-thirteenth century and 1333–34, when it began to appear as a prologue to Anglo-Norman Prose *Brut* chronicles.[184] It

---

[184] Georgine E. Brereton, ed., *Des Grantz Geanz: An Anglo-Norman Poem* (Oxford: Basil Blackwell, 1937), pp. xxxii–xxxiii.

was translated into Latin, probably at Glastonbury in the 1330s,[185] and the Latin version would therefore have been contemporary with the composition of the *Polychronicon*.

Since the story of Albine gained currency in England in the 1330s, it could have been written as a response to Scots' claims of an origin that predated Brutus, particularly the claim, made in the *Processus* of 1301, that Scota herself had conquered Scotland. The English claimed that someone still earlier than Scota, in this case, a Greek princess, Albine and her sisters, had moved to the island, and there was thus continuity from Albine to the giants to Brutus.[186] Moreover, as Lesley Johnson writes, Brutus's arrival is a

> corrective to the earlier, transgressive act of female foundation (brought about, in part, by the refusal of the Greek princesses to cede to the authority of their husbands) which had resulted in the formation of a savage and monstrous community, now cleared by Brutus and his men in preparation for the 'civilized' community which they establish. . . . The events of Albion's foundation and demise could be seen as a curious replay of the antagonism between the Trojans and the Greeks at Troy.[187]

This time the Trojans triumphed over the Greeks.

The *Ynglis*-chronicler uses this story, concocted by the English for their own advantage, against them. These women, who came to the island without men, had offspring by mating with devils. The English should thus understand their "cursit lynnage" and realize that besides being descended from the traitors of Troy, they are, in being descended from Albina and her sisters, "lynealy discendit of þe Devill" (Y 18). He also draws upon the Syrian version of the story by describing them as descendants of "Sarazenis" (Y 34) and thus avoids attributing to them Greek descent since the Scots were of Greek/Egyptian descent.

Furthermore, the English are descended from the Saxons, and "fals Saxonis blud war evir ʒit aganis þe Cristin faith" (Y 40–41). The genealogy of English kings continues to be sinister: drawing upon a story from Higden that was quoted verbatim by Bower and alluded to in the *Scottis Originale*,

---

[185] James P. Carley and Julia Crick, "Constructing Albion's Past: An Annotated Edition of *De Origine Gigantum*," *Arthurian Literature* 13 (1995), 41, reprinted in *Glastonbury Abbey and the Arthurian Tradition*, ed. Carley, p. 347.

[186] See Lesley Johnson, "Return to Albion," *Arthurian Literature* 13 (1995), 25–26; Carley and Crick, "Constructing Albion's Past," pp. 60–61, reprinted in *Glastonbury Abbey and the Arthurian Tradition*, ed. Carley, pp. 364–65.

[187] Johnson, "Return," p. 26.

he explains that William Ross, although thought to be the son of William the Conqueror, was really the son of an evil spirit, and thus Henry II is the grandson of the Devil (a lineage similar to the one he has in the *Scottis Originale*). All subsequent English kings descend from Henry and thus from the devil: "of quhom ar cummyn dovne all þe Saxonis of Yngland lynealy, king be king" (Y 136–37).[188] The only English king described as "gud" is the inept and at times insane Henry VI. The chronicler was perhaps thinking of his reputation for sanctity, but more probably of his being one of the few recent English kings who had had no designs on Scotland and who, with his French queen Margaret, had taken refuge in Scotland when fleeing from the Yorkists.

Although the chronicle ends with a reference to the arrest of Eleanor Cobham for witchcraft in the 1440s, it can be dated to after Henry VII became king in 1485 since it refers to the "law blud" (low blood) of the Tudors (Y 337), and the only justification for this would be if a Tudor were on the English throne at the time it was written. There are further indications of a date after 1440: it was written after Henry VI's death (1471) since it says that Henry "was ane gud man and in his tyme levit all possessionis þat Henry þe Tyrand [i.e., Henry V] had gottin in Fraunce" (Y 335–36). One of its sources, moreover, was Hary's *Wallace* (1476–78) since the chronicle mentions Wallace's invasion of England as far as St Albans and his remaining there until the Queen of England persuaded him to return to Scotland, an event that, so far as anyone knows, Hary invented.[189]

The *Ynglis Chronicle* bears some relation to a verse narrative, "The Ring of the Roy Robert,"[190] but because of the uncertainty of its date and authorship, it is difficult to say what that relation is. Both works deny that Scottish kings have paid homage to English kings. Both list the sequence of conquests of the southern part of the island – by the Saxons under "Horsus" and "Ingest" (i.e, Horsa and Hengest; Y 35; "Ring" 81), by the Danes under "William Hauslot, þe Prince of Denmark" or "Henslot, sone of Denmark king" (Y 42–43; "Ring" 95) and by the Normans under the "Bastard of Normondye" (Y 68; "Ring" 105) – while asserting that the Scots have remained forever under their own kings. The *Ynglis*-chronicler reports that when a Dane was

---

[188] The legend of English descent from the devil also occurs in a sonnet in the early sixteenth-century Bannatyne manuscript (*The Bannatyne Manuscript*, ed. W. Tod Ritchie, 4 vols, STS n.s. 22, 23, 26; 3rd s., 5 (1928–34), vol. 3, pp. 85–86) where the English are said to take their "progeny frome pluto prence of hell," quoted by Terrell, "'Lynealy discendit of þe devil.'"

[189] See McDiarmid, ed., *Hary's Wallace*, vol. 1, p. lxxii, vol. 2, pp. 233–34 and in vol. 1, bk. 8, lines 915–1618, esp. 1170 (pp. 205–27).

[190] *Early Scottish Metrical Tales*, ed. David Laing, new edn. (Glasgow, 1889), pp. 229–35.

quartered in an English house, the occupants were held in servitude (Y 45–52); and the "Ring" tells of a Dane being quartered in each house keeping the occupants in "bondage" ("Ring" 102). The prose chronicle claims that England is "haldin of him [the Pope] for a rent ȝerlie of ane thousand merkis" (Y 170–71) while in contrast the metrical account asserts that "of the Paip nothing we hald" ("Ring" 205).

The name "Hauslot, Prince of Denmark" suggests the influence of the story on Haveloc the Dane at some point in the transmission of sources that both the *Ynglis*-chronicler and the author of "The Ring of the Roy Robert" used. "Hauslot" is probably a corruption of "Haveloc," where the minims for the *v* in "Haveloc" could have been misread as *u*, a carelessly written medial *e* as an *s*, and the final *c* as a *t*. Although most chronicles mention only three Danish kings of England – Cnut, Harold Harefoot, and Harthacnut – several (the Anglo-Norman prose *Brut*, Geffrey Gaimar's *L'Estoire des Engles*, one manuscript of the chronicle of Robert Mannyng of Brunne, and at least one of the English prose *Brut*) include Haveloc as a Danish ruler of England.[191] The first name "William" could have become attached to "Hauslot" if at some point in the transmission the name appeared in a list of conquerors of England, as it does in the *Ynglis Chronicle*, and the eye of the scribe copying the list had skipped ahead to William the Conqueror.

Nomina Omnium Regum Scotorum

The *Nomina Omnium Regum Scotorum* is an eleven-folio Latin summary of either the *Scotichronicon* or one of its abridgments, possibly the *Liber Pluscardensis*. It is found in a miscellany of historical texts written in Latin and Scots in the Dalhousie manuscript formerly at Brechin castle, now at the National Archives of Scotland. It covers the history of the Scots from the time of Gathelos and Scota until the murder of James I in 1437, roughly the same period as the *Scotichronicon*, and like the other short chronicles that tell the origin story, does not include the negative characteristics of Gathelos found in Fordun and Bower. According to Chesnutt, it is related to the *Extracta e Variis Cronicis Scocie* in National Library of Scotland Advocates MS 35.6.13, which was written after 1513[192] and which may have drawn upon the same Latin source. The *Nomina Omnium Regum Scotorum* would have been written by the late fifteenth century since it was used in

---

[191] On the Haveloc story in *Brut* chronicles, particularly the Anglo-Norman ones, see Julia Marvin, "Havelok in the Prose *Brut* Tradition," *Studies in Philology* 102 (2005), 280–306.

[192] Chesnutt, "Dalhousie Manuscript," pp. 77–78; *Extracta e Variis Cronicis Scocie from the Ancient Manuscript in the Advocates Library at Edinburgh*, ed. W. B. Turnbull, Abbotsford Club (Edinburgh, 1842).

annotating a Scotsman's copy of Werner Rolewinck's *Fasciculus Temporum* published ca. 1491.[193]

The purpose for which the *Nomina* was written is suggested by its title. A major function of historical writing in Scotland in the Middle Ages and Early Modern Period was to show the legitimacy of the Scots' claims to independence, and this could be demonstrated by the unbroken lines of kings from ancient times to the present. In England and France such legitimacy was shown by genealogical chronicles of the English kings, which were often elaborate genealogical diagrams richly illuminated and often produced on rolls rather than in codices.[194] In Scotland one finds from early times king-lists (originally continuations of Irish king-lists) that were recited at coronations as well as short Latin chronicles that are little more than lists of kings.[195] Similarly, the previously mentioned Anglo-Norman chronicle inserted into Gray's *Scalacronica* was translated from a Latin chronicle of this type since it is, for the most part, a list of the names of kings, their legitimate descent from their predecessors, and the number of years of each reign. Although the Anglo-Norman chronicle makes a distinction between the rule of the Scots and that of the Picts, it nonetheless points out that Scots and Picts ruled Scotland for 1976 years up to the time of John Balliol.[196] Genealogies of this type were immensely important to the Scots when confronted with threats from England, a land that, the Scots were pleased to point out, had had a number of broken lines in its descent from the various people who had conquered it.

A problem with long chronicles like those of Fordun, Bower, and Boece is that the genealogies tended to be lost in the amorphous subject matter that often covered English and continental history as well as Scottish. Evidence of this problem is indicated by the first (1526/1527) edition of Hector Boece's *Scotorum historia*, which is prefaced by two lists of all of the Scottish kings, one of which includes brief accounts of their reigns. Thus a reader would encounter this genealogy before beginning to read Boece's longer account.

The *Nomina* would have been written for much the same purpose: it is a type of regnal list with most paragraphs devoted to a king and a brief summary of the principal events in his reign. Lacking, like its source, much information

---

[193] Chesnutt, "Dalhousie Manuscript," pp. 78–79.

[194] See n. 80 above.

[195] See Marjorie O. Anderson, *Kings and Kingship in Early Scotland*, rev. edn. (Edinburgh: Scottish Academic Press, 1980); Broun, *Irish Identity*. A number of the brief items in Skene's *Chronicles of the Picts* are of this type. Some king-lists are also edited in Anderson, *Kings and Kingship* and Broun, *Irish Identity*.

[196] Gray, *Scalacronica*, ed. and trans. King, pp. 18–31.

between the reigns of Fergus, son of Feredach (fourth century BC) and Fergus, son of Erc (late fourth century AD), its function as a genealogy begins with the second Fergus and continues until the murder of James I in the fifteenth century. Many of the early accounts of kings, except for that of Gathelos, give just essential details: the date of succession, the king's relation to his predecessor, and the length of his reign, with perhaps generalized references to victories over enemies, notable wicked or virtuous deeds, the influence of God on their actions, and the ways they died. The chronicle offers considerably more detailed accounts of the ninth-century reign of Kenneth mac Alpin, who, the chronicler says, managed to destroy both the Picts and their language at the same time and was thus the first to "rule in Albany," and of the eleventh-century reign of the tyrant Macbeth with details about his struggles against Macduff and Malcolm III (here called Canmore). Its most fully developed sections, however, begin with the attempts of Edward I ("the tyrant") to gain hegemony over Scotland through making John Balliol king, and the struggles of Wallace and Bruce against the English. Although not mentioning the long animosity between the latter two Scots heroes, the chronicler hardly idealizes Bruce: he writes that when Edward invaded Scotland in 1303, "only William Wallace resisted with his followers. At that time, Robert Bruce, the legitimate successor to the throne, was idling on the lands he had in England, as if asleep." A little later, however, Bruce "was touched and awakened by the divine spirit" and a change having been "brought about by the right hand of the most high," he took an "insupportable burden on his own shoulders" for the sake of his country's "liberty and laws."

Although overlooking the hostilities between Wallace and Bruce, this chronicler, like Fordun and Bower, generally does not hesitate to tell of the Scots' treachery against one another. He tells, for example, of Duff, son of Malcolm, "killed by traitorous men of Moray," of the men who "treacherously incited the Countess of Angus" to kill Malcolm, son of Duff, of Constantine III the Bald, who "evilly seized the kingdom," and of Macbeth, who "treacherously" killed Duncan. He points out that James I "having built castles, palaces, and many other religious houses, with the inhabitants living in the greatest peace, . . . was treacherously slain by his own men." Unlike the *Scottis Originale*, this chronicle does not ignore shortcomings of the Scots.

The Brevis Cronica (*The Scottis Cornikle*)

The *Brevis Cronica* (or *Scottis Cornikle*) survives in two sixteenth-century manuscripts: one is National Library of Scotland, Advocates MS 19.2.4, as the concluding part of a manuscript of Andrew of Wyntoun's *The Original Chronicle of Scotland*; the other is the Asloan manuscript. The title *Brevis*

Cronica appears in the Advocates version; in Asloan the chronicle is entitled the *Scottis Cornikle*. The *Brevis* version is included in David Laing's 1879 edition of Andrew of Wyntoun's *Original Chronicle*; the other in W. A. Craigie's 1923 edition of the Asloan manuscript.[197] As mentioned earlier, the British Library's catalogue of the Royal manuscripts incorrectly identifies this chronicle with the *Chronicle of the Scots* (*Short Chronicle of 1482*) discussed above,[198] and this error was repeated in R. L. Mackie's biography of James IV.[199] Moreover, Laing appears to have thought that the *St Andrews Chronicle*, discussed below, was still another copy of the *Brevis Cronica*.

Although W. A. Craigie suggested in his introduction to his edition of the Asloan manuscript that this chronicle was compiled from John of Fordun's *Chronica Gentis Scotorum* "or some similar source" and has "no independent value,"[200] its source is a Latin chronicle closely related to the *Nomina Omnium Regum Scotorum* discussed above.[201] The Scots title in Asloan, not found in the extant Latin version, is "Heir begynnis ane tractat drawin owt of þe Scottis cornikle begynnand in þe thrid age of þe warld." The "Scottis cornikle" is a good translation of Bower's title *Scotichronicon* and suggests that the translator recognized that his source was an abridgment of Bower's work. The Latin title of the Advocates version, *Brevis Cronica,* appears in neither Asloan's copy nor in the *Nomina* and could have been the title of the Latin redaction of the *Nomina* on which the Scots chronicles are based, since this was a fairly common title for short Latin chronicles.[202]

The relationship of the two Scots versions to the surviving Latin *Nomina* is difficult to determine. It is uncertain whether the Asloan and Advocates versions were based on the same Scots exemplar or whether they represent independent translations from Latin. At times the Scots phrasing is identical, thus suggesting that they were copies of the same Scots translation, but at others the phrasing is different, and it is not clear why that would be if they were copied from the same Scots exemplar. In one text (BAd 9–10), for example, one reads Gathelos "was trublyt sair with Spaynʒeartis" and in the other (BAs 12), Gathelos "faucht with þe Spanʒardis." On the other hand, the translations from the Latin are at times identical. It is possible for translators, working independently of one another, to come up with about the same Scots

---

[197] See the editions in the list of primary works cited in the bibliography.

[198] Warner and Gilson, *Western MSS in the Old Royal and King's Collections,* vol. 2, p. 257.

[199] R. L. Mackie, *James IV of Scotland: A Brief Survey of His Life and Times* (Edinburgh: Oliver and Boyd, 1958), p. 13 n. 2.

[200] Craigie, ed., *Asloan*, p. viii.

[201] Chesnutt, "Dalhousie Manuscript," p. 77. Also see Mapstone, "First Readers," p. 38.

[202] Fifty chronicles in the *Encyclopedia of the Medieval Chronicle* have similar titles.

phrasing at times, that two people translating "tempore igitur quo filii Israel in deserto fuerunt" could independently arrive at "Efter þe tyme þat þe childer of Isarell war in þe desert" (BAd 5) and "Eftir, about þe tyme þat þe childer of Israell war in þe desert" (BAs 8–9) since there are not many ways to translate a clause like this. However, the number of nearly identical translations is fairly large. Both the Asloan and the Advocates versions of the *Brevis Cronica*, moreover, include some details, such as both indicating that Gathelos was traveling "with his wyf & peple" (BAd 5–6, BAs 9) and a reference to the battle of Robert Bruce at Beland (or Biland), found in Bower, but not found in the Latin version in the Dalhousie manuscript. The material from Bower could have been added to the Scots versions or, as seems more likely, they could have been based upon a somewhat different version of the Latin chronicle in the Dalhousie manuscript. Furthermore, the Latin text from which the two surviving translations derive either lacked a number of passages that are in the *Nomina* or the translator chose to omit a fair amount of material in order to produce a more concise account. The possibility of their being produced through oral dictation, as Chesnutt suggests for the *Scottis Originale*, can be ruled out since the Advocates version was produced much later than the Asloan (see below), although it could be derived from a manuscript that was orally dictated at the same time as Asloan's exemplar.

The following stemma presents one possibility:

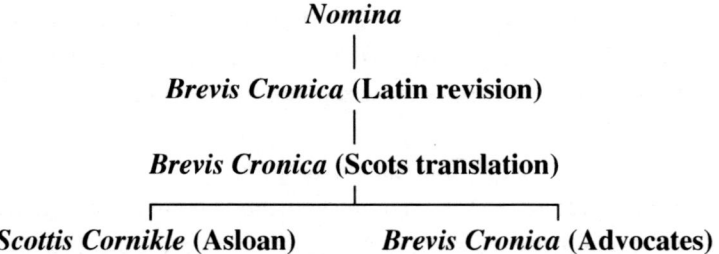

Nomina

|

Brevis Cronica (**Latin revision**)

|

Brevis Cronica (**Scots translation**)

Scottis Cornikle (**Asloan**)   *Brevis Cronica* (**Advocates**)

We acknowledge, on the other hand, other possibilities: the Latin *Brevis* might have been derived from a source shared with the *Nomina* instead of being derived directly from the *Nomina*; the probable revision of the Latin text and the translation might have occurred in a single step; or that the Asloan and Advocates versions might have been based upon separate translations.

The content

The content of the *Brevis Cronica* closely parallels that of the *Nomina*, beginning with the origin myth of Gathelos and Scota and working its way king by king at least to the death of James I, though with even sparer language and detail and with a sharper sense of Scottish nationalism. Text that is found in the Latin version but is missing in the two Scots versions include all verse passages; some accounts of events occurring outside Scotland, like the career of John the Scot at the court of Charles the Bald and his death in England; many short passages of what the *Brevis*-chronicler must have considered excessively circumstantial detail, like the list of body parts not included among St Andrew's relics; some reports damaging to the Scots' reputation, like the flight of Gathelos and Scota from the Egyptian plagues or the homage paid to the King of England for Cumbria; some reports reflecting credit on the English, like the martyrdom of King Edmund; most reflections on the meaning of events, like the discussion of God's help in driving out the Picts and Britons; and several highly rhetorical passages, like the encomium on Wallace's victory at Stainmore. Its few additions are almost entirely matters that concern Scottish history without being integral to the biography of a particular king: the prophecy that Scots will rule wherever the Stone of Scone is; the coming of St Columba to Scotland; Augustine's supposed foundation of the Black Canons (an order that becomes important in Scotland). There are, moreover, many short additions made separately to the surviving versions, and the tone of the *Brevis*-chronicler is at times somewhat more jingoistic than that of the *Nomina*-chronicler. Like Bower, he pronounces against the claim of John Balliol, but he goes further than Bower and the *Nomina* in portraying Edward as a monster "þe fals tratour and foersworne tyrane and aratyk," (BAd 441–42), "ane tyrane" who "oppressit and murtheryt þe pepill without caus or titill" (BAd 450), a "fals tratour" (BAs 358). In his emphasis upon falsity and treachery the *Brevis*-chronicler was perhaps influenced by other texts.[203]

The Asloan version

Of the two Scots versions, Asloan represents the older text, and since Asloan made few changes to the works he copied, aside from some errors in transcription and a few additions such as the reference to James V in the *Scottis Originale*, his version, for the most part, probably closely represents the original translation, and he probably found the title *Scottis Cornikle* in his

---

[203] The *Gesta Annalia* (ch. 94), in a phrase repeated by Bower (XI 25) and, with some modification, in *Liber Pluscardensis* (VIII 23), characterizes Edward mainly as a deceiver, calling him *ille antiquus doli artifex* ("that old master of guile"), and Bower (XI 9) describes this most hated of English kings as one who defeated the Scots primarily by deception: *O ficta dolositas, incantatrix alauda, simulatrix fucata, adulatrix venenosa* ("False, cunning enchantress lark, counterfeit pretender, venomous flatterer"). The passage in the *Gesta Annalia* is translated in Fordun, *Chronicle of the Scottish Nation*, vol. 2, p. 319. The emphasis on Edward's inhumanity in *Brevis* is similar to that found in the *Declaration of Arbroath*: "His wrongs, killings, violence, pillage, arson, imprisonment of prelates, burning down of monasteries, despoiling and killing of religious, and yet other innumerable outrages, sparing neither age nor sex, religion nor order, no one could fully describe or fully understand unless experience had taught him" (Duncan, *Declaration of Arbroath*, p. 35).

exemplar. However, someone, either Asloan or the scribe of his exemplar, added three brief paragraphs to the conclusion of his version of the *Brevis Cronica* to bring it up to date: although the Dalhousie *Nomina* ends, like Bower's *Scotichronicon* and the *Liber Pluscardensis*, with the death of James I, Asloan's concludes with paragraphs concerned with James II, James III, and James IV and brings the chronicle up to James IV's capture of Norham on 28 or 29 August 1513. This conclusion has been used to help date the Asloan manuscript. Since it ends with James IV's victory at Norham, but does not refer to the Scots defeat at Flodden on 9 September of that year and the death of James IV in that battle, Catherine Van Buuren concludes that it could have been written before 9 September:

> As the narrative ends in mid-page the possible loss of a continuation cannot be attributed to a later loss of leaves of the Asloan MS, such as we find elsewhere in the book. It is therefore possible that Asloan or his model ended there, and this would put the date for this item in or not much later than 1513.[204]

Although the chronicle does not begin until the recto side of fol. 124 of the Asloan manuscript, the manuscript was written in fascicles, and its various parts may have been written in an order different from that in which they appear in the manuscript. Thus this chronicle could have been one of the earliest items that Asloan copied. This is somewhat earlier than the date of 1515–1525 that scholars have usually assigned to the Asloan manuscript. Asloan, of course, may have been copying a work that had been completed before September 1513.[205]

The Advocates version

The other surviving version of the *Brevis Cronica*, the Advocates version, includes most of the material found in Asloan except that it breaks off at the end of Robert II's reign in 1390. Norman Macdougall's description of the Advocates version as a summary of Boece's *Scotorum Historia* is partially correct.[206] It is strikingly different from Asloan because its author has supplemented the material it shares with Asloan with material derived from

[204] Van Buuren, ed., *The Buke of the Sevyne Sagis* (Leiden: Leiden University Press, 1982), p. 41.

[205] In a later article, Van Buuren suggests that Asloan began to copy his manuscript ca. 1515 rather than 1513. See Van Buuren, "John Asloan and His Manuscript," p. 50. I. C. Cunningham believes that *Brevis, Scottis Originale, Ynglis*, and the *Auchinleck Chronicle* in the Asloan manuscript could have been written as early as 1513, although "the commonly accepted date of 1515–25 cannot be far from the truth" ("The Asloan Manuscript," p. 133).

[206] Macdougall, *James III: A Political Study* (Edinburgh: John Donald, 1982), p. 312.

John Bellenden's translation of Hector Boece's *Scotorum Historia*. The Advocates version alerts the reader to its use of some material derived from Bellenden by several references toward the end of the chronicle to book and chapter divisions, such as "In þe xii buke, capitulo xvi, xvii" or "in þe xiii buke I, ii, iii." As Mapstone points out in a brief, excellent discussion of the two versions of the chronicle, Boece's Latin text, while divided into books, did not have chapters,[207] and the references to chapters indicate that the author was referring to Bellenden's translation. However, the material taken from Bellenden is largely paraphrased and, as Mapstone indicates, it is difficult to determine whether it refers to the early version Bellenden produced between 1531 and 1533 or to the revision he published sometime between 1536 and 1540.[208] The fact that neither Bellenden nor Boece is mentioned by name but that simply book and chapter references are given suggests that the work was well known and did not need further identification. This further suggests that the author was referring to the printed edition which would have been accessible to many more people than the other manuscript revisions. This version of the *Brevis Cronica* can therefore probably be dated after 1536, and at least the final part of the Advocates manuscript in which it appears was written somewhat later than the date of "early sixteenth century" ascribed to it in the summary catalogue of the Advocates manuscripts and by Wyntoun's editor, F. J. Amours.[209]

The chronicler consulted Bellenden throughout, even deriving from it such minor details as the fact that a dog stolen from the Scots by the Picts was white and that Eugenius III supported Mordred against King Arthur (BAd 56–57, 87–89), but the references to books and chapters in Bellenden occur only in the latter half of the chronicle, from the tenth-century reign of Constantine, son of Ethus (Áed) through kings like Malcolm, David, and Robert Bruce, suggesting that the author thought that his readers would be most interested in the more recent events of Scottish history and that he wanted to direct them to a fuller account, written in Scots, if they wanted to read more about them.

As Mapstone observes, Mair and Boece were replacing Fordun and Bower as the authorities on Scottish history, and the references to Bellenden's version

---

[207] Mapstone, "First Readers," p. 38.

[208] Mapstone, "First Readers," pp. 38, 50 n. 55. The sample quotations that Mapstone checked are similar in both versions of Bellenden. The exact date for the printed edition of Bellenden's version is not known; it was published sometime between 1536 and 1540, and scholars often give the date as "ca. 1540."

[209] National Library of Scotland, *Summary Catalogue of the Advocates Manuscripts* (Edinburgh: H. M. Stationery Office, 1971), p. 108; Amours, ed., *The Original Chronicle of Andrew of Wyntoun*, Scottish Text Society 63, 1 (1914), p. lxiv ("not earlier than the beginning of the sixteenth century").

of Boece makes this apparent.[210] However, it is striking that the author of the *Brevis Cronica* does not refer the reader to the accounts of the kings that reigned between the two Ferguses, most of whose stories appeared for the first time in Boece. This could suggest that the chronicler was skeptical of that part of Bellenden's translation and that he considered Bower, or a work derived from Bower, still the principal authority for those years.

Wyntoun's *The Original Chronicle of Scotland*, which is 426 folios in length, immediately precedes the *Brevis Cronica* in its Advocates manuscript. The compiler must have wanted to append a condensation of Scottish history for those who did not have the time to read Wyntoun and one that drew upon more recent authorities – Bower and Bellenden's version of Boece – than those to which Wyntoun, whose chronicle ends in 1408, had access.

The St Andrews Chronicle[211]

The *St Andrews Chronicle,* published here for the first time, is a damaged 281-line fragment of a Scots summary of part of the early books of Hector Boece's *Scotorum Historia.* Its unique copy is found at the end of a folio manuscript of the first half of the sixteenth century in the St Andrews University Library (DA775.A6 W9), following Wyntoun's *The Original Chronicle of Scotland.* The St Andrews manuscript has been dated 1500–25 but, unless this is a later addition to the manuscript (doubtful since the hands appear to be identical), it must be somewhat later since Boece's *Historia* was published in 1526 or 1527.

When the book was rebound in the nineteenth century one leaf was reversed, so that the last page of the *Original Chronicle* (fol. 449^v) follows the first page of the *St Andrews Chronicle* (fol. 449^r), and the *St Andrews Chronicle* continues from folio 450^r to folio 452^r where much of it on the last folio is illegible. It is different from the Bellenden and Mar Lodge prose versions of Boece discussed above in that it is a summary of early parts of Boece rather than a translation of the book.

The summary consists of abbreviated accounts of the reigns of kings after the first King Fergus until it breaks off with Eugenius (Eochaid Hebdre), son of Congaill (Comgal), and great-grandson of Fergus, son of Erc. Most of the kings between the two Ferguses had been unnamed until the publication of Boece's chronicle, so whoever added the *St Andrews Chronicle* to the Wyntoun manuscript might have been motivated to supplement the *Original Chronicle* with information that would have been unknown to Wyntoun and to other chroniclers prior to Boece (except possibly to "Veremundus," from

---

[210] Mapstone, "Early Readers," pp. 38–39.

[211] The discussion of the *St Andrews Chronicle* is based upon work by Embree, particularly upon a paper that he read at the international conference on the medieval chronicle at Belfast in 2008, with some minor modifications by Kennedy.

whom Boece says he got his information.) Although the chronicler drew upon Boece's chronicle itself for some of the information, the format of his work was possibly suggested by the *Scotorum Regum Catalogus*, a list of Scottish kings with brief summaries of their reigns, which is found at the beginning of the 1526/1527 edition of Boece's *Historia*.

David Laing, in his description of the manuscript in 1879 for his edition of Wyntoun, had vaguely and incorrectly identified it as the *Brevis Cronica*.[212] It is not mentioned in the descriptions of the St Andrews manuscript by W. A. Craigie, and F. J. Amours.[213] So far as is known, it has gone unnoticed since Laing's brief reference to it until Dan Embree identified it in the course of preparing this edition.

That the *St Andrews Chronicle* is not derived from either of the other translations is proven by the large number of instances in which it agrees with either against the other, or more often, disagrees with both. The *St Andrews*-chronicler has made so radical a reduction of his original that it amounts to an abstract or a set of notes. And it is perhaps as a set of notes that the *St Andrews Chronicle* is best read – as a selection of what struck one reader of Boece as worthy of remembrance.

The *St Andrews Chronicle* begins in the middle of Boece's first book, with the Scots landing in Argyll, and Fergus, son of Feradach, establishing himself as the first proper King of the Scots. Since the chronicle begins at the top of the first folio following Wyntoun's chronicle, we do not know if the author included earlier legendary material (the Scots wandering from Egypt to Spain and Ireland) found in Boece. It begins in the middle of the first book, and the first page could have been lost before it was copied in the surviving manuscript. As noted below, another folio has been lost. On the other hand, Dauvit Broun has noted that declining interest in the Irish origins of the Scots is characteristic of late-medieval Scottish historiography, symptomatic of a

---

[212] Laing refers to the *St Andrews Chronicle* in a single sentence of his description of the St Andrews manuscript of Wyntoun's chronicle (*Orygynale Cronykil of Scotland*, 3 vols [Edinburgh, 1872–79], vol. 3, p. xxii): "The last six leaves are occupied with part of the prose Chronicle, beginning with Fergus the first king, and ending with Corane or Gorane Congal." On its face, the phrase "the prose Chronicle" might be thought to mean the *Scottis Originale*, which he had referred to three pages earlier as "The Prose Chronicle at the end [of the Royal manuscript of Wyntoun]." But his index entry for the *Brevis Cronica*, citing page xxii, suggests that he probably meant something like "the prose chronicle that I edit at the end of this volume" – that is, the *Brevis Cronica*; this is how Michael Chesnutt understood the phrase in 1985 ("Dalhousie Manuscript," p. 77). Either way, Laing has misidentified the text. That he did not examine the text closely is suggested by his error in identifying Corane as the last king of the fragment (Corane is followed by Eugenius) and by his failure to recognize it as based on one of the most important monuments of Scottish historiography, Boece's *Scottorum Historia*.

[213] Craigie, "The St Andrews Manuscript of Wyntoun's Chronicle," *Anglia* 20 (1898), 363–80; Amours, ed., *Original Chronicle*, vol. 1, p. lxv.

redefined sense of national identity.[214] Once the author has the Scots ashore in Scotland, he plods dutifully through Boece's roster of legendary or purely imaginary kings, ticking off the years and the most notable events of their reigns at a ratio of about one Scots word to Boece's twenty-five Latin ones.

The first fragment of the chronicle, taken from Books I and II of the *Historia*, runs from the reign of Fergus, son of Feradach, to that of his great grandson, Rether. Following the loss of a folio, the second fragment, taken from the beginning of Book III to the beginning of Book VI, runs from the reign of Ederus to that of Nathalocus. After another missing folio, the third fragment, taken from Books VIII and IX, runs from the reign of Downgard (Domangart) in the early sixth century to the reign of Eugenius (Eochaid Hebdre). There, on fol. 452^r, the chronicle breaks off.

The chronicler may have intended to condense into inconsequence Boece's treatment of the Picts as the traditional hostile in-laws of the Scots. In the *Historia*, the expedition of Fergus to Scotland is taken to drive out the Picts, but he persuades them to join him in attacking the Britons at the last minute. In this version, he comes to attack the Britons "with the help of the Picts," apparently never having contemplated the Picts as enemies. In the rest of the chronicle the Picts are never mentioned except as allies of the Scots. Still, since key passages in Boece – those in which the Picts incur the lasting enmity of the Scots by stealing a white hound and in which, centuries later, Kenneth mac Alpin exterminates them – would fall in the missing sections of the work, we cannot know how, or whether, the chronicler would have dealt with them.

J. B. Black identified as one of the "leading ideas in his [Boece's] presentation of Scottish history" the anachronistic assertion that "throughout this ancient past there ran a tradition that the kings of Scotland were accountable to their people."[215] The author of the *St Andrews Chronicle* instinctively grasped and endorsed this idea. In effecting his reduction of the *Historia*, he was careful to preserve Boece's good-king / bad-king presentation of Scottish history and his belief in consultation with the nobles as the key to proper royal conduct. Many of the entries in his list of reigns consist of little more than evaluations of personal or civic conduct:

> Dornadilla, Mayni sone, ane peciabyll man, renewit þe trewis with þe Brytonis & þe Peichtis. He was ane gret huntar. He maide lawis to þe huntaris & kepit þe lawis weill þat King Ferguss maid, swa þat he sufferit nathing to be jugit or pvnyst bot it þat was red on þe buk of law. (StA 20–23)

---

[214] See Broun, *Irish Identity*, esp. pp. 195–200.

[215] Black, "*Scotorum Historiae*," p. 35.

Nothacus, Dornadillis brother, ane subtell man & falss, rang in tyrandry, brak þe law, reft þe pepill, spul eit & banyst & slew mony nobillis. & in þe secund ȝeir of his ryng, in congregatione of þe nobillis, he was slane be þe Lord of Galloway, and Retherus was crownyt. (StA 25–28)

Moreover, emphasis on law – making, breaking, preserving, and reforming – is maintained throughout the chronicle, with considerable space devoted to words such as "law," "right," "just," "punish," "reprove," "imprison," or "judge" or to vocabulary of personal conduct such as "compassionate," "devout," "peaceable," "sneaky," "false," "vicious," "avarice," "lechery," "well-manered," "wantonness," "defouling," "righteous," "wrongful," "evil," "sloth," "vices," "meek," "pitying," "patience," "covetousness," "wicked," and "witchcraft." The author also emphasizes the vocabulary of civic virtue: "peace," "govern," "consent," "tyranny," "liberty," "despoiled," "robbed," "banished," "wasted," "suppressed [wrongful laws]," and "cared for [the souls of his subjects]."

The *St Andrews*-chronicler understands as well the appeal of Boece's occasional passages dealing with lurid sex, so these get something like full coverage. The rape of daughters, usually in pairs – of the Queen of Britain's daughters by Roman soldiers, of the Lord of Argyll's daughters by King Athirco, of his own daughters and aunts by King Lugthacus – gets ink. So does the setting aside of a queen in favor of another woman. Not so the founding of the Pictish capital of Camelon or the death of Severus the Emperor or even the violence of the tearing apart of a king's assassin by wild horses. In the biography of Erenus, a king possibly invented by Boece, nearly the whole of the space is given over to the king's concubines and the predatory sexual privileges of the lords – also apparently products of Boece's imagination. And later attempts to reform these practices (under Kings Mettellanus and Galdus) are reported, despite being only partly successful because of the "wantonness" and "lechery" of the nobles. Also meriting space is King Mogallus's habit of seizing any married woman who caught his eye. In contrast, when Boece describes with equal detail the hunting laws decreed by Dornadilla, the chronicler finds them lacking in interest. He sums them up in a sentence: "He maide lawis to þe huntaris." And whenever Boece leads his characters into one of his favorite themes – the law of succession of the Scottish throne – he skips ahead to more interesting matter.

The chronicler is also uninterested in the unheard-of marvels with which Boece punctuates his narrative. In the *Historia*, dire events are often presaged by dire signs – bloody seas, falling statues, circling birds – but the translator has no space – or no patience – for them. Merlin, with his prophecy that Wortigern would be conquered by Ambrois and Vter, is not mentioned. Also rejected is an account of a boy who is nightly bedeviled by a vision of a beautiful woman embracing him – a tale that seems much more natural than supernatural, despite the dumbfounded response of the bishop who is consulted. The only vestige of the marvelous in the translation is a single witch, who foretells the murder of King Nathalocus by the servant the king has sent to question her.

The episode of the witch is illustrative of perhaps the most important characteristic of the mind of the chronicler. He is less interested than any of the other chroniclers published here (except perhaps the author of the *Chronicle of the Scots*) in *how* or *why* things happen; he is content to report what. In the *Historia*, the exchange between the servant and the witch is reported as direct discourse; she giving at first a general answer and then, when the servant presses her, the specific identification of the servant as the destined murderer. The servant accuses her of deception and flattery and departs in righteous and almost amused indignation to report this foolish answer to the king. But on the way, he has time to think through the consequences: What if the king believes the prophecy? What if he sends another messenger and gets the same answer? So, of course, the result of this internal dialogue is that the servant decides that his only option is to kill the king, which he does, in a highly circumstantial account, by stabbing the king through the heart while he is seated on the privy, down which the servant then throws his body. In the *St Andrews* version, there is no discourse, no internal dialogue, and in fact no account of the murder: "He wes slane be ane man of Murray for causs he send him [to take co]nsaill at ane wiche, þe quhilk wich said þat he suld sla þe king" (StA 230–32). Thus the deed is so pared of its detail as to all but rob it of its irony. We have, as usual, the what, but only a hint of the why, and nothing at all of the how.

The mechanism of motivation and development of ideas in the *Historia* is, as Nicola Royan has pointed out, the speech – typically paired, between opponents in the council chamber or kings or generals before a battle.[216] Thus when Fergus has landed in Argyll, he addresses a council of the Scots he has come to save, whom he addresses as his children, asking whether they want him to be king or to continue to be ruled by local chiefs. After due consideration, they opt for the protection of this strongman, and Fergus is chosen king. The *St Andrews*-chronicler cuts to the choice: "Fergus . . .

---

[216] Nicola Royan, "The Uses of Speech in Hector Boece's *Scotorum historia*" in *A Palace in the Wild: Essays on Vernacular Culture and Humanism in Late-Medieval and Renaissance Scotland*, ed. L. A. J. R. Houwen, A. A. MacDonald, S. L. Mapstone, Mediaevalia Groningana, n.s. 1 (Leuven: Peters, 2000), pp. 75–93.

chosyne King of Scotland." Or again, when that perpetual Scottish problem, the succession of a minor, threatens the unity of the Scots, Boece puts speeches in the mouths of the Lord of Galloway, who champions the child Rether as the rightful direct descendant, and the Lord of Lorne, who accuses his rival of the murder of the former king and points out the dangers of a child as king. It is clear that both are speaking deceitfully and are really only looking to take the throne for themselves. None of this is of concern to the *St Andrews*-chronicler. He reports merely that there was a great battle fought between these two lords, in which battle nearly everyone died, and then Rether – somehow, it's not important – became king.

In the whole of the surviving adaptation, there is no instance of direct discourse and but a single instance of indirect discourse. When Caritacus (Caractacus) the Briton hero Boece has made into a Scottish king, is asked by a Roman legate why he fights against the Romans without cause, the *St Andrews*-chronicler summarizes his reply in a single sentence: "He said he weryit justlie on þaim for þai dystroyit kingis & reft landis þai had no rycht to" (StA 91–93). The sentence has little relation to the longer and more abstract speech placed in Caritacus's mouth by Boece. Of Caritacus's more famous speech, delivered to Claudius in Rome, reported by Tacitus, and repeated more or less faithfully by Boece, there is no hint in the St Andrews version.

This chronicle was probably intended to give those who could not read Latin a concise Scots account of the kings who, prior to Boece's chronicle, had been unknown, unless the information had circulated in the lost chronicle of Veremundus. It offers some insight into popular taste. It is a result of a process of distillation similar to that which produced the *Brevis Cronica*, a chronicle that, like *St Andrews*, is a short reign-by-reign summary. They both suggest in their sixteenth-century readers, who were presumably not literate in Latin and had other things to do with their time than to read long historical works, something like that skepticism about marvels and impatience with windy rhetoric that has characterized the response of many of Boece's modern readers.

Manuscripts of *La Vraie Cronicque d'Escoce* (Daly)[217]

Paris, BNF, n.a.fr. 20962 [A]

1. "Pour ce que plusieurs,"[218] fols 4^r–53^r.
2. "La Vraie Cronicque d'Escoce," fols 54^v–65^v.

Fifteenth-century (1464–77). 2nd fol. "lesdis Anglois pretendent." 69 vellum fols, 285 × 200mm. 1 quire of 3 fols (1st), 3 quires of 12 fols (2nd, 3rd, 5th), 1 quire of 11 fols (4th), 1 quire of 10 fols (6th), 1 quire of 9 fols (7th).[219] Blank fols 1^r–2^v, 21^v, 54^r, 66^r–69^v. Ruling in pale red ink in a grid, 185 × 125mm., 36 lines per page. Batarde in dark brown ink, with pen cadeaux in red, one in the shape of a face in rubric on fol. 54^v, and simpler cadeaux in black on ascenders on fols 37^v, 45^v and 65^r, 36 lines per page, rubrics in blue, red-mauve (and, once, in gold) lettering. Major textual divisions are marked by 6- or 5-line decorative initials, accompanied by C shaped borders of flowers and acanthus leaves in blue and gold, strawberries and gold ivy leaves; other divisions (paragraphs) are marked by simple two-line initials in blue or gold. A miniature, showing two advocates debating before the kings of France and England, prefaces the first text (fol. 4^r).[220] Stamped brown leather binding. The manuscript belonged to Jacques d'Armagnac, Duke of Nemours (executed 1477), whose arms are painted into the architectural framework of the miniature, and whose signature has been erased from fol. 66^v. A contemporary description of the manuscript added to fol. 69^v is characteristic of his books.[221]

---

[217] I have taken the opportunity to make minor amendments to the description given in Daly, "*Vraie Cronicque*," pp. 130–133. I have not included Paris BNF fr. 7144, fols 77–92, believed by Craig Taylor to be a seventeenth-century copy of the *Vraie Cronicque* (*Pour ce que plusieurs*, p. 289), as this manuscript contains a totally different text, "Li Estrais dou Procés d'Escoce" (fols 75–76), summarizing some documents relating to the Great Cause, and a copy of the treaty of alliance between Charles VIII and James III in 1483. See *Debating the Hundred Years War*, ed. Taylor, 289. Livia Visser-Fuchs, "The Manuscript of the *Enseignement de Vraie Noblesse* Made for Richard Neville, Earl of Warwick in 1464: an Example of Anglo-Burgundian Literary Contact" in *Medieval Manuscripts in Transition: Tradition and Creative Recycling*, ed. G. H. M. Claassens and W. Verbeke (Louvain: Louvain University Press, 2006), pp. 337–62, listed Bibliothèque Nationale MS français 5058 among manuscripts of the *Vraie*, but has since confirmed in a personal communication that *Vraie* is not present in that manuscript.

[218] Designated H by Taylor, *op. cit.*, pp. 277–78, who also gives a description of this manuscript.

[219] A modern fol. (3 bis) has been inserted between fols 3 and 4, and another between fols 66 and 67, which consists of a letter dated 26 Feb. 1896.

[220] Reproduced in Taylor, *op. cit.*, p. 279, fig. 2; it can be located to the Loire valley and was probably the work of the artist Jean Roland III, ibid., p. 278.

[221] "En ce livre a soixante deux feulles et une histoire." A contemporary description inserted on a half-folio (currently fol. 70) relates not to this manuscript, but to another manuscript belonging to Jacques d'Armagnac.

Brussels, Bibliothèque royale, 9469–70 [B]

1. "Pour ce que plusieurs,"[222] fols 1[r]–63[r].
2. "La Vraie Cronicque d'Escoce," fols 64[r]–78[r].

Fifteenth century (1464–67). 2nd fol. "conforme en raison naturelle." 80 vellum fols 310 × 220mm, 10 quires of 8 fols, ruled in a grid, 28 lines per page. Batarde, with some decorative pen cadeaux. Additional rubrics introduce the second and third parts of "Pour ce que plusieurs," and in the "Vraie Cronicque," the Quitclaim of Canterbury. 3-line initials introduce each text, major divisions in the first text are marked by 4-line initials, while 2-line intials mark minor divisions. The first text (fol. 1[r]) is prefaced by a miniature of two advocates debating, while courtiers look on, from the workshop of Guillaume Vrelant (active 1454–81), from Bruges, Flanders.[223] The manuscript belonged to Philip the Good, Duke of Burgundy; it is identified in the ducal inventory compiled after his death in 1467, and was still in the ducal library in 1487.[224] Binding with the arms of Louis XV, King of France.[225]

Geneva, Bibl. pub. et universitaire fr. 166 [G][226]

93 vellum folios, 315 × 215mm., comprising two distinctive parts, first the "Enseignement de la Vraie Noblesse," then the "Vraie Cronicque," to which two short texts (3 and 4 below) were added at a later date.

1. "Enseignement de la Vraie Noblesse," fols 2[r]–81[r]. Completed on 4 September 1464, belonged to Richard Neville, Earl of Warwick (1428–71).
2. "La Vraie Cronicque d'Escoce," fols 83[r]–90[v]. Late 15th century (1483–84? Before John Ireland's death, April/August 1495).

2nd fol., "qui est entre Yrlande," a single quire, ruled in a grid of 190 mm. × 130 mm., 29–37 lines per page. Neat cursive script in brown ink, decorative capitals in brown ink introduce each paragraph. On fol. 82[r], a 13-line space for an initial has been filled by a much later, crude drawing of the royal arms of Scotland, in yellow and red wash. According to a note in a late fifteenth/early sixteenth hand (fol. 90[v]), the book was "fet" (made) by John Ireland, and the manuscript was given by him to Béraud Stuart; the same hand added marginal annotations, or rubrics, to the text (fols 85[v], 87[r]–88[v], 89[v]).

---

[222] Designated K by Taylor, *op. cit.*, pp. 280–282.

[223] Reproduced in Taylor, *op. cit.*, fig. 3, for the artist, see ibid., p. 282 and n. 27.

[224] J. Barrois, *Bibliothèque protypographique* (Paris, 1830), no. 1438, 208, no. 1929, 275; Georges Doutrepont, *La littérature française à la cour des ducs de Bourgogne* (Paris: Champion, 1909), p. xxxiii.

[225] Taylor, *op. cit.*, p. 282.

[226] Only summary descriptions are given of texts other than the *Vraie Cronicque*.

3. "Le droit que le roy Charles pretend au royaulme de Naples," fol. 91^r. Dating to the reign of Charles VIII (1483–98), written on the last leaf of the quire in brown ink in a cursive script, possibly belonged to Bérault Stuart.

4. Legend of St Helena, fols 91^v–93^r. Latin, late 15th–early 16th century, added on the verso of the last folio of the quire and on two added folios, in dark brown ink, in a neat upright script. Of unknown provenance.

Paris, BNF, n.a. fr. 6214 [P]

1. "Pour ce que plusieurs,"[227] fols 1^r–49^v.
2. "La Vraie Cronicque d'Escoce," fols 50^r–62^r.

Fifteenth century (after 1464). The first folio is missing; fol. 1 would have been the original 2nd fol. "-r entrer esdictes matieres" (current second fol. is 'plus amplement'). 62 vellum fols, 300 × 225mm., 1 quire of 7 fols (1st, lacks original 1st fol.), 5 quires of 8 fols (2–6), 1 quire of 10 fols (7th), 1 quire of 5 fols (8th); fol. 65^v blank. Ruling in red-lilac ink in a grid 190 × 136mm. approx. 31–32 lines per page, batarde in dark brown ink; rubrics in red in same style as text. Rare pen cadeaux, washed in yellow; capitals also washed in yellow. Major textual divisions are marked by 5- or 4-line initials in gold and colours, with a very simple decoration of pen rinceaux, leaves and flowers in gold and colours, extending into the inner border; lesser divisions (paragraphs) are marked by 2-line initials, all in gold with alternating blue and mauve infills with geometric patterns in white. On fol. 1, blue or gold 1-line initials with red or black pen decoration respectively; very rare paragraph signs in blue decorated with red ink. Blue calf binding with gold geometric patterns. Provenance unknown; a forged coat of arms (apparently that of the Gilliers family), on fol. 62^r.

Manuscripts of the Latin and Scots chronicles (Embree and Kennedy)
Edinburgh, National Archives of Scotland, GD 45/31/1 - II
The Dalhousie manuscript (formerly Brechin Castle, Panmure manuscript)[228] is a paper folio (270 × 185mm) book of 35 fols, written ca. 1500. It contains:

1. *Ystoria Norwegie*, fols 1^r–12^r.
2. Genealogy of the Orkney Earls, fols 12^v–17^v.
3. List of the Kings of Norway, fol. 18^r–18^v.

---

[227] F in Taylor, *op. cit.*, pp. 276–77, who also gives a description of this manuscript.

[228] The manuscript was once known as the Panmure manuscript until the owner's family name was changed to Dalhousie in 1860. See Chesnutt, "Dalhousie Manucript," p. 64 n. 36; Chesnutt in *Historia Norwegie*, ed. Inger Ekrem and Lars Boje Mortensen, trans. Peter Fisher (Copenhagen: Museum Tusculanum Press, University of Copenhagen, 2003), p. 29 n. 48. A thorough discussion of the manuscript is in Chesnutt's article, and he wrote a briefer description of it for *Historia Norwegie*, ed. Ekren and Mortensen, pp. 28–31.

4. The *Cronycle of Scotland in a Part* (the *Scottis Originale*), fols 18^v–23^r.

5. *Cronica Antiqua Diuersarum Cronicarum Origo*, fols 23^r–23^v.

6. Conclusion of a 1373 Caithness charter, fol. 24^r.

7. *De Johanne Ballialo etc.*, fol. 24^r.

8. *Nomina Omnium Regum Scotorum*, fols 24^r–35^v.

The manuscript is bound behind a printed copy of Werner Rolewinck's *Fasciculus Temporum*. According to Michael Chesnutt, it is probable that "the printed book and the manuscript both circulated for a considerable time in an unbound state."[229] The two texts were bound together ca. 1700 or later, and the book was in the possession of the Earl of Dalhousie at Brechin Castle until deposited in the NAS in 1998.[230]

All eight articles appear to be copied by a single scribe, who wrote in what Chesnutt describes as a "pre-Secretary hand" popular in Scotland in the late fifteenth century.[231] Both the *Scottis Originale* and the *Nomina Omnium Regum Scotorum* are copied in single columns with 30–36 lines per page. The *Originale* is headed *The Cronycle of Scotland In a Part*, and it begins with a tall initial. Otherwise, the text is unadorned and undivided. The *Nomina* is headed by a brief description of the period covered by the chronicle (from before the Incarnation until the reign of James II), followed by an elaborate initial beginning the chronicle proper. It is divided into short sections by reign, each beginning with a raised initial.

Edinburgh, National Library of Scotland, MS 16500

The Asloan manuscript (formerly NLS Acc. 4233) is a paper folio (230 × 170mm) book of 304 folios. It was written during the reign of James V, probably sometime between 1513 and ca. 1533, the approximate date of the death of its major scribe, the Edinburgh notary John Asloan. The manuscript, which was rebound in 1812, was in the hands of the Boswell family from the late seventeenth or early eighteenth century until 1966, when it was purchased by the NLS.

Asloan's book has been described in detail by both I. C. Cunningham and Catherine van Buuren.[232] The manuscript begins with a table of contents in

---

[229] Chesnutt, "Dalhousie Manuscript," p. 58.

[230] Chesnutt, *Historia Norwegie*, ed. Ekrem and Mortensen, p. 28.

[231] Chesnutt, "Dalhousie Manuscript," pp. 88–89; Chesnutt, *Historia Norwegie*, ed. Ekrem and Mortensen, p. 30.

[232] A brief description and complete text is in W. A. Craigie, ed., *The Asloan Manuscript*, v–x. Detailed descriptions are by Cunningham, "The Asloan Manuscript," and Van Buuren, "John Asloan and His Manuscript," 15–51 and in the introduction to Van Buuren's edition, *Buke of the Sevyne Sagis*, 5–20. Van Buuren had written about Asloan's life earlier and

Asloan's hand, indicating that the two volumes of his book originally contained sixty items that included moral, religious, political, geographical and historical works in prose and verse as well as a large body of poetry that includes some of the best known poems of Robert Henryson and William Dunbar. Thirty-four of the items have been lost, and twenty-six survive.[233] All, except for the ninth item (*The Spectacle of Lufe*) and one leaf of the third (*The Buke of the Chess*), were copied by Asloan, and all of the items are written in Scots except for a poem of Lydgate's (no. 49, erroneously attributed to Chaucer) and the third item, the geographical *Cart of the World*, taken from Trevisa's translation of Higden's *Polychronicon*.

The historical works appear in the first volume as items 5–8, 10. The latter is based primarily upon biblical and classical history.

5. The *Scottis Originale* (the *Cronycle of Scotland in a Part*), fols 93^r–98^v.

6. The *Ynglis Chronicle*, fols 99^r–107^v.

7. *Ane Schort Memoriale for Addicioun* (*The Auchinleck Chronicle*), fols 109^r–123^v.

8. The *Scottis Cornikle* (the *Brevis Cronica*), fols 124^r–136^v.

10. *The Sex Werkdayis and Agis*, fols 151^r–166^v.

It is not certain when, or in what order, Asloan copied the items. As Cunningham points out, the manuscript was originally a series of fascicles that were copied at various times and later put together as a book. Although Asloan was still living in December 1532, Van Buuren speculates that most of the items were completed much earlier.

The three texts from this manuscript edited here are written in a cursive secretary bookhand in single columns with 25–31 lines per page. Each has a rubric supplying or implying a title. Each begins with a decorated capital three lines deep and uses large capitals to begin sections and paragraphs. The *Brevis Cronica* is divided into 81 short chapters by centered chapter numbers, and the text of each chapter begins with a raised capital.

London, British Library, MS Royal 17.D.xx

The Royal manuscript is a vellum and paper folio (280 × 205mm) book of 312 folios, originally written perhaps in the last quarter of the fifteenth century, with the two chronicles edited here added in the sixteenth century. It contains:

1. Andrew of Wyntoun's *Original Chronicle*, fols 1^r–298^v.

---

indicated that he had been active in Edinburgh from 1497 until 3 March 1529/30 ("John Asloan, an Edinburgh Scribe," *English Studies* 47 [1966], 365–72). In her article on the manuscript, however, she points out that he was witness to a deed dated 11 December 1532.

[233] Van Buuren lists these in "John Asloan and His Manuscript," pp. 18–20.

2. The *Scottis Originale* (the *Cronycle of Scotland in a Part*), fols 299ʳ–304ʳ.

3. The *Chronicle of the Scots* (the *Short Chronicle of 1482*), fols 304ʳ–308ʳ.

4. *The Letter of Prester John*, fols 310ʳ–311ᵛ.

Originally copied for George Barclay of Achrody in the fifteenth century, it passed through various hands until, according to Amours, it was acquired by the Royal Library in 1661. However, according to the British Library's catalogue of the Royal manuscripts, it does not appear in the old catalogue of Royal manuscripts published in 1666 nor in Edward Bernard's *Catalogi Manuscriptorum Angliae et Hiberniae* (Oxford, 1697).[234]

The two texts from this manuscript edited here are copied in a small cursive secretary hand in single columns with 32–36 lines per page. The *Scottis Originale* is headed by a rubric in red ink. The body of the text begins with a silvered initial four lines deep; the first three words are in red ink. It has no divisions. Latin quotations are written as verse, silvered over red ink. The *Chronicle of the Scots* has no rubric and begins with a smaller (2-line) initial, as if it were a part of (or an appendix to) the *Scottis Originale* – which is how it is printed by Skene.[235] It has subdivisions denoted by slightly enlarged capitals and by a single rubric distinguishing the events before the Incarnation from those after it. The margins of both texts contain pointing fingers, of uncertain date, and corrections and notes in later hands.

Edinburgh, National Library of Scotland, Adv. MS 19.2.4

The Advocates manuscript is a paper folio (270 × 190mm) book of 446 folios. According to the Advocates summary catalogue, it was written in the early sixteenth century, but, as noted above, at least the *Brevis Cronica* was probably written after the publication of Bellenden's translation of Boece ca. 1536–40. It contains:

1. Andrew of Wyntoun's *Original Chronicle*, fols 1ʳ–434ᵛ.

2. The *Brevis Cronica* (the *Scottis Cornikle*), fols 435ʳ–446ʳ.

The manuscript was in the possession of Sir Robert Sibbald at his death in 1722, when it was given to the Advocates Library, now in the National Library of Scotland.

The *Brevis Cronica* is copied in a cursive secretary hand in single columns with 25–35 lines per page. It is divided into short sections by reign, each

---

[234] Amours, *Original Chronicle*, vol. 1, p. lxii. Warner and Gilson, *Catalogue of Western MSS in the Old Royal and King's Collections*, vol. 2, p. 257.

[235] Skene, *Chronicles of the Picts*, pp. 378–390. Skene edited these as one work and entitled it "Chronicle of the Scots."

beginning with a few introductory words in a larger, bolder set hand serving as a heading. All pages except the first have headers, *Brevis* on the versos and *Cronica* on the rectos.

St Andrews University, MS DA 775.A6 W9

The St Andrews manuscript is a paper folio (230 × 170mm) book of 453 folios, written in the first half of the sixteenth century. It contains:

1. Andrew of Wyntoun's *Original Chronicle*, fols 1ʳ–448ʳ, 449ᵛ.
2. The *St Andrews Chronicle*, fols 449ʳ, 450ʳ–452ʳ.

The manuscript has been in the possession of the St Andrews University Library since the middle of the nineteenth century.

The *St Andrews Chronicle* is copied in single columns in the same cursive secretary hand as Wyntoun's *The Original Chronicle*. It is divided into paragraphs beginning with the names of kings, but is otherwise without headings, initials, or decoration of any kind. Folio 449 was reversed when the manuscript was rebound, so that the last page of Wyntoun (fol. 449ᵛ) follows the first page of the *St Andrews Chronicle* (fol. 449ʳ). One folio appears to be missing between fol. 449ᵛ and fol. 450ʳ, and at least one more between fol. 451ᵛ and fol. 452ʳ. The margins have been cropped, and other tears on corners and edges have resulted in the loss of some text; fol. 451ʳ, in particular, is badly damaged. Folio 451ᵛ has other content (pen trials and repeated phrases), so it is clear that the chronicle was not continued.

EDITORIAL METHODS

We have emended what seem to us to be obvious errors and have bracketed emendations and recorded them in the textual notes.

We have modernized capitalization, punctuation, and word division. We have divided the text into sentences and paragraphs according to their apparent divisions of sense. We have indicated folio breaks by insets in the right margin, marking the exact points of the breaks with carets.

We have silently expanded abbreviations, contractions, and suspensions, as far as possible in accordance with the scribe's spelling in unabbreviated practice. We have been conservative in our approach to these expansions, treating some terminal flourishes as otiose; other editors might have added final *E*s in such cases.

We have printed *I*s as vowels and *J*s as consonants; otherwise the spelling is scribal.

We have provided glossaries for the Scots texts and facing translations for the Latin and French texts.

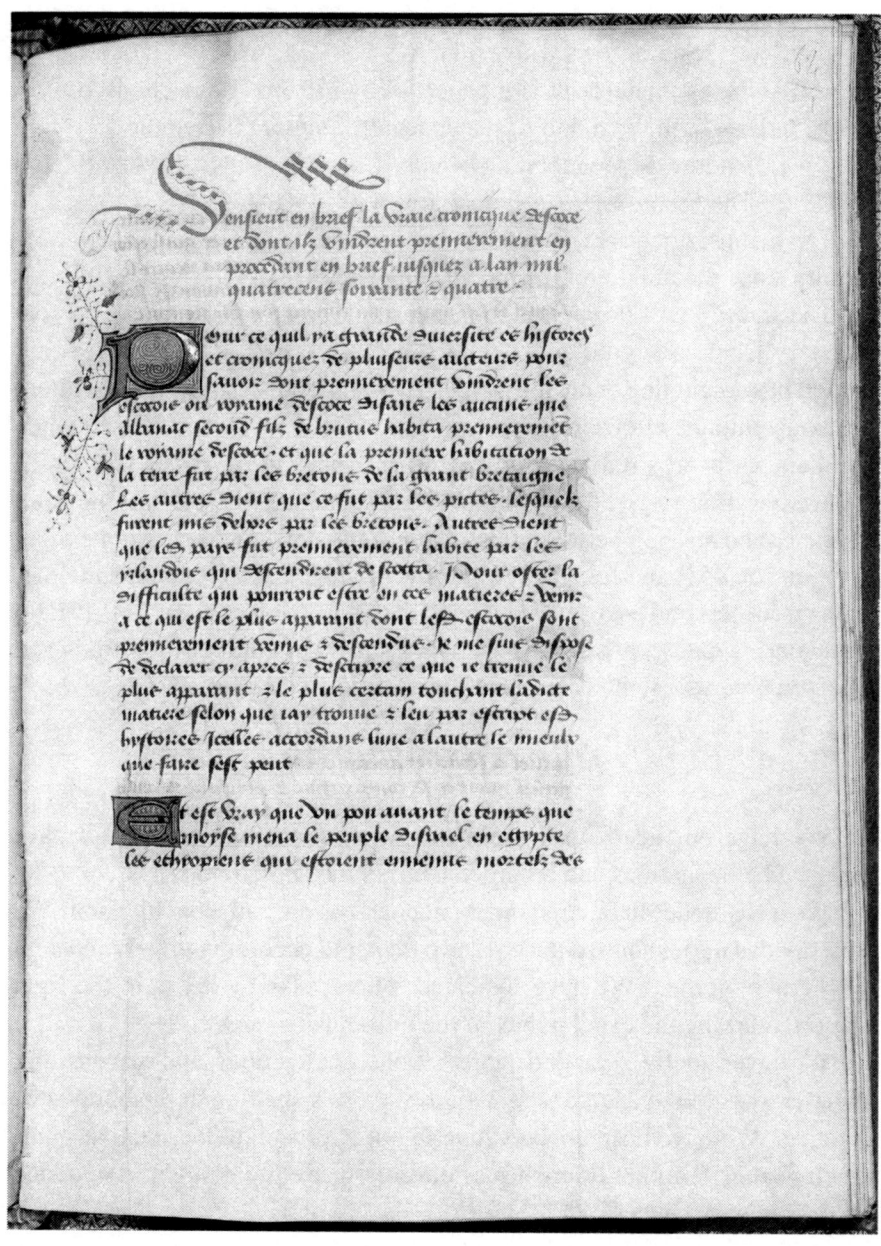

Folio 64r of Bibliothèque royale de Belgique MS 9469–70. © Bibliothèque royale de Belgique.

LA VRAIE CRONICQUE D'ESCOCE

from Brussels, Bibliothèque royale MS 9469-70

S'ensieut en brief la Vraie Cronicque d'Escoce et dont ilz vindrent   **f.64r**
premierement en procedant en brief jusquez a l'an mil quatre cens
soixante et quatre.

Pour ce qu'il y a grande diversité es histores et cronicquez de pluiseurs
5   aucteurs pour savoir dont premierement vindrent les Escoçois ou royame
d'Escoce – disans les aucuns que Albanac, second filz de Brutus, habita
premierement le royame d'Escoce, et que la premiere habitation de la terre fut
par les Bretons de la Grant Bretaigne; les autres dient que ce fut par les Pictes,
lesquelz furent mis dehors par les Bretons; autres dient que ledit pays fut
10   premierement habité par les Yrlandois qui descendirent de Scotta – pour oster
la difficulté qui pourroit estre en ces matieres et venir a ce qui est le plus
apparant dont lesdiz Escoçois sont premierement venus et descendus, je me suis
disposé de declarer cy aprés et descripre ce que je treuve le plus apparant et le
plus certain touchant ladicte matiere, selon [ce] que j'ay trouvé et leu par escript
15   esdites hystoires, icelles accordans l'une a l'autre le mieulx que faire [c]est peut.

There follows in summary the true chronicle of Scotland and where they
first came from, proceeding in brief up to the year one thousand four hundred
and sixty four.

As histories and chronicles by various authors give such different accounts
of how the Scots first came to the kingdom of Scotland – some saying that
Albanac, second son of Brutus, was the first to live in the Kingdom of Scotland,
and that the Britons of Great Britain were the first inhabitants of the country,
others saying that it was the Picts, who were expelled by the Britons, others
saying that the Irish, who descended from Scota, were the first who lived in that
country – to avoid any problem arising from this situation, and to find the most
likely origins and descent of the Scots, I have set out here to explain and
describe what I have found to be most likely and certain about the matter,
according to what I have found and read in the histories, reconciling them as far
as possible.

Et est vray que un pou avant le temps que Moÿse mena le peuple d'Israel en Egypte les Ethyopiens, qui estoient ennemis mortelz des Egyptiens, vindrent oudit pays de Egypte en intention de le conquerir   **f.64v** et invader. Et pour ce qu'ilz estoient fort puissans, le roy d'Egypte

20   envoia devers le roy d'Athenes, son allyé, affin qu'il lui envoyast secours. Lequel le fist ainsi, et lui envoya son filz, nommé Galiel, avecquez grant nombre de pueple. Et se gouverna ledit Galiel si bien et si vaillamment en ladite guerre que par sa vaillance et bonne conduitte, lesdiz Ethyopiens furent desconfiz et chassiez hors d'Egypte.

25   Pour lequel service et aucunement recompenser ledit Galiel, ledit roy d'Egypte lui donna sa fille et heritiere nommee Scotta; et demoura long temps ledit Galiel, avec grande partie du pueple de Grece et ladite Scotta, sa femme, avec lui oudit pays d'Egypte.

Si avint que quant les enfans d'Israel furent entrez ou pays d'Egypte,

30   grande guerre se meut oudit pays entre eulx et les Egyptiens, et firent beaucop de maulx lesdiz enfans d'Israel oudit pays d'Egypte. A l'occasion desquellez choses, lesdiz Galiel et Scotta, et avecquez eulx les Grecs que ledit Galiel avoit en sa compaignie, et pluiseurs de ceulx du pays d'Egypte guerpirent et delaissierent ledit pays et vindrent par mer avec grande

35   quantité de biens, or et joyaulx jusquez au pays d'Auffrique environ   **f.65r** la cité de Cartage, et la demourerent par aucun temps.

Aprés lesquelles choses, lesdiz Galiel et Scotta et ceulx de leur compaignie se partirent dudit pays d'Auffrique, et vindrent passer le destroit de Gybalthar, et prindrent terre en Espaigne, et arriverent premierement en

40   Portugal, lequel pays ilz inhabiterent. Et pour ce que ladite terre de Portugal fut la premiere terre ou lesdiz de Galiel et Scotta si prindrent port oudit pays d'Espaigne, ledit Galiel, aprés son nom, appella ledit pays Portugal, qui est autant a dire comme le port Galiel. Et se estendy ledit Galiel es pays de Byskaye et de Navarre; lesquelz pays il peupla de ses gens, et habita

45   volentiers sur une riviere qui est par dela, nommee Yber; a cause de laquelle riviere de Yber, pour ce que sa femme eut la ung filz, il fist appeller ledit filz Yber, aprés le nom de ladite riviere de Yber; et pour ce que sa femme avoit nom Scotta, il mist nom audit filz Yber-Scotta.

Lequel Yber-Scotta, quant il fut grant et que son pere Galiel fut fort viel,

50   du voloir de sondit pere et par son congié et licence, il assembla grant pueple et navire de ceulx qui estoient venus d'Egypte et de Grece et de leurs enfans, et passa en la derreniere isle occeanne, qui de present on appelle Irlande, laquelle, pour lors, n'estoit habitee fors de gayans, lesquelz   **f.65v** il desconfist, tua et chassa hors du pays. Et habita lui et ses gens

55   oudit pays, et le nomma aprés le nom de sa mere et son seurnom "Scosse".

And in truth, shortly before Moses led the people of Israel into Egypt, the Ethiopians, who were mortal enemies of the Egyptians, entered the land of Egypt intending to conquer and invade it. And as they were very powerful, the King of Egypt sent for help from the King of Athens, his ally. And the latter did so, sending his son called Galiel, with a great number of people. And this Galiel behaved so well and valiantly in that war that, thanks to his valor and good leadership, the Ethiopians were defeated and chased out of Egypt.

The King of Egypt gave Galiel his daughter and heiress, named Scota, as a partial reward for his help; and Galiel remained in the land of Egypt a long time, with his wife Scota and many of the Greek people.

It so happened that when the children of Israel entered the land of Egypt, a great war broke out in that country between them and the Egyptians, and the children of Israel did great harm in the land of Egypt. On this account, Galiel and Scota, together with the Greeks who accompanied Galiel and some from the land of Egypt, abandoned and left that land, and, taking many possessions and jewels, came by sea as far as the land of Africa, around the city of Carthage, and stayed there for some time.

After these events, Galiel and Scota and their companions left the land of Africa, and crossed the straits of Gibraltar, and made landfall in Spain, arriving first in Portugal, and lived in that country. And as Portugal was the first place in the country of Spain where Galiel and Scota landed, Galiel called that country Portugal, which means the port of Galiel, after himself. And Galiel extended his power through the land of Biscay and Navarre, where he settled his people, and lived there on a river called the Yber. As his wife had a son, he called that son Yber, after the name of the river Yber; and as his wife was called Scota, he called his son Yber-Scota.

When Yber-Scota grew up and his father Galiel was very old, at his father's wish and with his leave and permission, he assembled a large number of people and ships from those who had come from Egypt and Greece, and their children, and passed over to the last island in the ocean, which is now called Ireland, which at that time was inhabited only by giants, whom he defeated, killed and expelled from the land. And he and his people lived there, and he called it Scotia after his mother and his own surname.

Et par long temps ledit pays a esté nommé [la] grant Escoce, comme on soloit appeller Angleterre la Grant Bretaigne. Mais les Latins ont pris le propre nom dudit Yber et ont appellé le pays, en latin, Ybernia, et en vulgar est appellé Ybernie ou Irlande.

60 Si avint aprés que le pays fut fort pueplé, et que aucun nombre des gens dudit pays de la grant Escoce passerent le bras de mer qui est entre Irlande et le nort d'Escoce qui est a present, et vindrent habiter ladite terre, laquelle ilz nommerent la petite Escoce. Mais non pourtant ilz n'eurent en ce temps la aucun roy, ains se reputoient trestous subgetz du roy de la grant Escoce.

65 Et les emmena un nommé Rottay, lequel ediffia le chasteau de Rosay, qu'il nomma aprés son nom Rottay, et de present par corruptele est appellé Rosay.

Et certain temps aprés vint oudit pays de la grant Escoce un grant prince d'Egypte nommé Agenor, avec xxx navires tous plains d'hommes sans aucunes femmes, et desiroit habiter oudit pays de la Grant Escoce; mais pour

70 ce que icellui pays estoit fort habité, ilz conseillierent audit Agenor qu'il venist en la Petite Escoce, lequel pays n'estoit pas tant habité ˆ **f.66r** de gens, et que la il trouveroit mieulx son fait pour habiter oudit pays.

Et pour ce qu'il se complaignoit que lui et ses gens n'avoient aucunes femmes, lesdiz de la Grant Escoce lui octroierent de lui baillier et a ses gens,

75 pucelles et vesves assez pour les fournir de ce qu'ilz demandoient.

En ensuivant lequel conseil, ledit Agenor et ses gens vindrent habiter en la Petite Escoce et envoierent en la Grant Escoce pour avoir des femmes et des pucelles, lesquellez leur furent envoyees a grant plenté, et peuplerent fort ledit pays. Et aprés qu'ilz se virent si grant peuple, ilz se voulurent faire

80 seigneurs et maistres dudit pays, et chassier dehors ceux qui premierement l'avoient habité. Laquelle chose venue a la cognoissance du roy de la Grande Escoce, il envoia son filz, nommé Fergows Fferadrach, avec grant nombre de gens d'armes oudit pays de la Petite Escoce, lequel mist en sugession ledit Agenor et toutes ses gens, et prist la couronne dudit pays. Et fut le premier

85 qui s'appella roy de la Petite Escoce. Parquoy appert clerement que la premiere generation des Escoçois n'est point venue de Brutus ne des Bretons, mais est venue des Grecs et des Egyptiens long temps paravant que Brutus venist habiter l'isle d'Albion, que aprés on nomma la Grande Bretaigne.

And for a long while that country was called Great Scotland, just as England is called Great Britain, but the Latins gave the country the name Ybernia, after Yber, and in the vernacular it is called Ybernie or Ireland.

Afterwards, when the country was densely populated, it came about that a number of people from the country of Great Scotland crossed the channel between Ireland and the north of Scotland, as it is at present, and came to live in that country, which they called Little Scotland. But as at that time they had no king, they all considered themselves subjects of the King of Great Scotland. And they were led by a certain Rottay, who built the castle of Rottay, to which he gave his own name Rottay, and at present the name has been corrupted to Rothesay.

Some time afterwards, a great Egyptian prince called Agenor came to the land of Great Scotland, with 30 ships full of men but without any women, and he wanted to live in the country of Great Scotland; but as that country was densely populated, they advised Agenor to come to Little Scotland, as there were fewer people in that country, and as he would find what he needed to make a living more easily in that land. And as he lamented that he and his people had no women, the people of Great Scotland gave him and his people enough maidens and widows for their needs.

Following this counsel, Agenor and his people came to live in Little Scotland and sent off to Great Scotland for women and maidens, who were sent to them in great number and they populated that country. And when they saw they were such a great people, they wanted to be lords and masters of that country, and chase out the original inhabitants. When the King of Great Scotland learned of this, he sent his son, called Fergus Feradrach, with a great number of soldiers, to the land of Little Scotland; he subjugated Agenor and all his people, and took the crown of that land. And he was the first to call himself King of Little Scotland. Thus it is clear that the first generation of Scots were not descendants of Brutus and the British at all, but came from the Greeks and Egyptians long before Brutus came to live in the island of Albion, which was later called Great Britain.

    ‚Touteffoiz pour accorder les differences dessusdites, c'est   **f.66v**

90 assavoir que aucuns dient que les Bretons habiterent premierement
ledit pays d'Escoce, les autres dient que ce furent ceulx de la lignie de Yber
Scota, il est vray que ou royame d'Escoce a deux divers pays. L'un s'appelle
Escoce sauvage, ouquel pays aincoires les gens d'icellui parlent autel
langaige comme les Irlandois. Et est bien a croire que anciennement ilz sont

95 venus d'une mesme generation, tant a cause du langaige comme des
conditions et de la maniere de vivre. Et s'estend ledit pays d'Escoce sauvage
par toutes les montaigne[s] devers le nort et par les Islez aussi du nort, et
jusquez a la mer qui s'appelle Scot Zee, c'est a dire la mer d'Escoce.

    L'autre partie du pays s'appelle l'Escoce anglesse, pour ce qu'ilz parlent

100 autel langaige comme en Angleterre, et aussi ou temps que les Bretons
regnoient en Angleterre, [que] on appelloit lors la Grant Bretaigne, ilz
parloient breton oudit pays. Et a la verité, ladite Escoce anglesche fut
anciennement le partage du second filz de Brutus, nommé Albanac, lequel
fut parti pour sa portion de l'isle de la Grant Bretaigne en la terre qui dure

105 depuis la duchie d'Albanie jusquez a la riviere de Hvvmbre, et ouquel pays
ilz parloient breton comme a Londres, en Galles et en tout le remanant du
pays.

    Et quant les Saxons occupperent l'isle de la Grant ‚Bretaigne et en   **f.67r**
dechasserent les Bretons, ouquel pays ilz semerent leur langaige qui

110 aincoires dure,   semblablement ilz occupperent tout le royame d'Albanye,
et y semerent leur langaige qui aincoires y dure, lequel s'appelle l'Escot
anglois.

    Et s'appellent les Anglois, Anglois, ainsi que dient aucuns a cause d'une
contree nommee Angolus, qui est en Saxoingne, dont premiers vindrent les

115 Saxons. Les autres dient qu'ilz vindrent de Angist, qui fut le premier prince
de Saxoigne, qui amena les Saxons en Bretaigne, et en memoire duquel
lesdiz Saxons, aprés qu'ilz eurent conquesté le royame, ilz le nommerent
Angle ou Anglisten, et depuis Angistland, qui est autant a dire comme la
terre de Angist; et aprés par corruption a esté appellee Ingheland. Autres

120 dient qu'elle est appellee Angleterre *ab angulo, quia veritas non querit
angulos, juxta illos versus :*

        Anglicus angelus est cui nunquam credere fas est,
        dum tibi dicit ave tanquam ab hoste cave.

However, to find some agreement between these different accounts, that is, that some say the first inhabitants in the land of Scotland were the British, while according to others it was the line of Yber-Scota; it is a fact that there are two different regions in the kingdom of Scotland. One is called Wild Scotland, where the people speak the same language as the Irish. And it is credible that in ancient times they descended from the same people, both on account of their language and their way of life. And that land, Wild Scotland, stretches right through the mountains to the north and the northern isles, as far as the sea called the Scots Sea, that is, the Sea of Scotland.

The other part of the country is called English Scotland, because they speak the same language as in England, and furthermore, when the Britons ruled in England, which was then called Great Britain, they spoke British in that country. And for certain, English Scotland was formerly the inheritance of Brutus's second son, Albanac, and was his share of the island of Great Britain, stretching from the duchy of Albany to the river Humber, and in that country they spoke British as in London, in Wales and in all the rest of the country.

And when the Saxons occupied the island of Great Britain and expelled the British, and spread their language, which still survives there, they also occupied the whole kingdom of Albany and spread their language, which still survives there, and which is known as Scots English.

And according to some, the English are called English after a region called Angolus, which is in Saxony, where the Saxons originated. Others say that they came from Hengist, who was the first prince of Saxony, who led the Saxons to Britain, and in memory of whom the Saxons, after they had conquered the kingdom, called it Angle or Anglisten, and later Angistland, which means the same as the land of Hengist. And afterwards it was corrupted into the name "England". Others say that it was named England, from *angulus*, because "truth seeks no corners"; according to the verses:

> Who can possibly believe an Englishman is an angel,
> When he greets you, beware as of an enemy.

Et pour rentrer en ladicte matiere comment la terre d'Escoce fut habitee,
125   il est vray que ceulx d'Irlande, qui furent les premiers Escoçois, habiterent
ladicte terre devers le nort, et y demourerent l'espace de cent soixante et cinq
ans, avant que les Pictez y vensissent demourer; lesquelz Pictez chassierent
partie desdiz Escoçois et aussi partie des Bretons hors d'une partie du
nort et de l'Escoce anglesche, lesquelz pays estoient adont habitez   f.67v
130   partie des Bretons qui estoient venus avec Albanac, et partie des
premiers Escoçois descendus de Scotta. Et demourerent lesdiz Pictez oudit
royame d'Escoce l'espace de mil soixante et ung an et jusques au temps de
[Kyneth], filz de Alpin, lequel estoit roy de l'Escoce sauvage, et chassa tous
les Pictes hors du royame d'Escoce tant sauvage que anglesche, et demoura
135   le royame tout Escoçois, supposé qu'il y eust divers langaiges, c'est assavoir,
que les uns parlaissent escot anglois, c'est a dire autel langaige qu'ilz parlent
en Angleterre, qui estoient Saxons, et les autres parloient l'escot sauvage, qui
est pareil au langaige d'Irlande.

Et pour ce que longue chose seroit reciter tous les roys qui ont esté en
140   Escoce, tant du temps des premiers Escoçois qui habiterent la terre, comme
du temps des Pictez et depuis, je me suis enhardy de seulement reciter les
noms des roys qui ont esté depuis le roy Macolin, fils de Dumkelm; lequel
Macolin espousa Saincte Margarite d'Escoce, a cause de laquelle les roys
d'Escoce pretendent jusquez au jour dhuy avoir droit en la couronne d'
145   Angleterre et icelle leur devoir appartenir.
Et pour entendre ceste matiere, il est vray que le bon roy d'Angleterre
Egar – filz de Emond et nepveu du grant [Adelstan], lesquelz estoient   f.68r
filz du premier Edouart, avant la Conqueste roy d'Angleterre – eut
deux femmes, dont de la premiere issy Sainct Edouart le Martir, roy
150   d'Angleterre, que sa marastre fist tuer, et morut sans hoir issant de sa char;
et de la seconde issy Eldreth, qui regna oudit royame d'Angleterre aprés ledit
Sainct Edouart, et eut beaucop a souffrir en sa vie pour le pechié de sa mere,
et fut grant piece exillié hors du royame et a la fin morut piteusement.
Ledit Eldreth fut deux foiz marié, dont du premier mariage issy Emond
155   Irenside qui regna en Angleterre avec le roy Knoudt le Danois. Et de l'autre
mariage, c'est assavoir de la fille de Richart le second, duc de Normandie,
tante du duc Guillame le Conquereur, issy Sainct Edouart le Confesseur, roy
d'Angleterre, et son frere Alvaret.
Aprés la mort dudit Elreth, ledit Emond Irenside recueilla la succession
160   de son pere et se fist couronner, mais Knout le Danois lui fist si grant guerre,
et avoit si grant faveur et si grant povoir ou royame, qu'il convint par
appointement que ledit royame fust parti en deux, et que chascun desdiz deux
personnages eussent nom et tiltre de roy, et se firent freres adoptis ensemble.

And to come back to the way the land of Scotland was inhabited, it is true that people from Ireland, who were the first Scots, lived in the north of that land, and dwelled there for 165 years, before the Picts came to live there; and the Picts drove out some of the Scots and also some of the British from part of the north, and from English Scotland, a land which was then inhabited partly by the British who came with Albanac, and partly by the first Scots, descendants of Scota. And those Picts lived in the kingdom of Scotland for one thousand and sixty one years, up to the time of Kenneth, son of Alpin, who was king of Wild Scotland, and drove all the Picts out of the kingdom, from Wild Scotland as well as English Scotland, and the kingdom remained entirely Scottish, even though there were different languages, that is, some spoke Scots English, the same language spoken in England by the Saxons, and others spoke Wild Scots, the same language as in Ireland.

And as it would be a lengthy business to list all the kings of Scotland from the time of the first Scots who lived there, and the time of the Picts, and afterwards, I have risked listing only the names of kings since King Malcolm, son of Duncan, who married St Margaret of Scotland, from whom the kings of Scotland claim a right to the crown of England, and that it should belong to them, up to the present day.

And so this matter can be understood, it is true that the worthy King of England Edgar – who was the son of Edmund and nephew of Athelstan the Great, who were sons of the first Edward, King of England before the Conquest – had two wives. St Edward, the martyr King of England, whom his stepmother had put to death, and who died without heirs of his body, was born from the first wife. And from the second came Ethelred, who reigned in the kingdom of England after St Edward, and suffered a great deal in his life because of his mother's sin, and who was for a long time exiled from the kingdom, and in the end died pitifully.

Ethelred was married twice. Edmund Ironside, who reigned in England with King Cnut the Dane, was born from the first marriage. And St Edward the Confessor, King of England, and his brother Alfred, were the result of the other marriage, that is, from the daughter of Richard II, Duke of Normandy, aunt of Duke William the Conqueror.

After Ethelred's death, Edmund Ironside succeeded his father and had himself crowned, but Cnut the Dane waged war against him so fiercely and had such support and such great power in the kingdom, that it was settled that the kingdom should be divided in two, and that each of these two individuals should have the name and title of king, and they became adoptive brothers.

Ne demoura guaires aprés que le conte Eldrich de Wincestre tua **f.68v**
165 ledit Emond Irenside, cuidant complaire audit roy Knoudt. Aprés la
mort duquel Emond, ledit Knoudt chassa hors du royame tous les parens dudit
Emond, et envoia ses deux filz, c'est assavoir Emond et Edouart, devers le roy
de Swave et fut ledit Emond marié a la fille du roy de Hongarie, et ne vesqui
gaires et morut sans enfans. Et au regart dudit Edouart, il fut marié a la niepce
170 de l'Empereur, dont issy Egar Elinger et Saincte Margarite d'Escoce. Lequel
Egar Elinger n'eut aucun enfant legitisme yssant de sa char dont il soit
memoire, par quoy appert clerement que toute la succession dudit Emond
Irenside, roy d'Angleterre, appartenoit de plain droit a Saincte Margarite, suer
dudit Egar Elinger et femme du roy Macolin d'Escoce, desquelz Macolin et
175 Saincte Margarite tous les roys d'Escoce jusquez aujour dhuy sont descendus
en droite ligne de par pere ou de par mere. Et par ce moyen semble que selon
raison, le royame et la couronne d'Angleterre competent et appartiennent et
doivent competter et appartenir au roy d'Escoce.

Vray est que aprés la mort dudit Knoudt et de Herold, son aisné filz, et de
180 Artheknoudt, son second filz, lesquelz regnerent en Angleterre
successivement l'un aprés l'autre, Sainct Edouart le Confesseur, frere **f.69r**
dudit Emond Irenside, prist la couronne d'Angleterre, et morut roy dudit
royame, sans aucuns enfans yssans de lui, ne aussy de Alvarech, son frere, qui
paravant sa mort long temps avoit esté tué par la conspiration du conte
185 Gowinnen.

Aprés laquelle mort dudit Sainct Edouart, Heroldt, filz dudit Gowinnen,
occuppa le royame d'Angleterre, contre lequel vint en bataille le duc Guillame
lequel le desconfist et tua et tous ses freres, et se fist roy, et prist la couronne
d'Angleterre. Et combien que ledit Egar Elinger fist tout son devoir aprés la
190 mort dudit Heroldt de recouvrer le royame de Angleterre comme a lui
appartenant, toutesfoiz pour la puissance et sagesse dudit roy Guillame il n'y
peut parvenir, et aprés pluiseurs grans tribulations qu'il eut en sa vie, il morut
sans aucune sieute de son corps, ainsi que dit est dessus.

Ledit roy Guillame eut quatre filz, c'est assavoir Robert Courteheuse, duc
195 de Normandie, Guillame le Rous, roy d'Angleterre, Joffroy, conte de Bretaigne
de par sa femme, et Henry Beauclerc qui depuis fut roy, lequel espousa
l'aisnee fille dudit roy Macolin et de la Saincte Margarite d'Escoce, nommee
Mathilde, par le moyen duquel mariage et de certains apointemens qui furent
fais entre lesdiz roys Henry Beauclerc et les enfans dudit Macolin, et
200 de certaines terres comme la conté de Hontiton, la conté de Nort **f.69v**
Hombelland et la conté de Combelland, le pays de Tindal et autres
contrees qui furent bailliés par le roy d'Angleterre aux enfans d'icellui Macolin
a les tenir a foy et hommage dudit roy d'Angleterre, ledit roy Henry Beauclerc
demoura paisible roy d'Angleterre, et rentra la couronne en la premiere souche.

Very shortly afterwards, Earl Eadric of Winchester killed Edmund Ironside, hoping to please King Cnut. After Edmund's death, Cnut expelled all Edmund's relatives from the kingdom, and sent his two sons, that is, Edmund and Edward, to the King of Swabia and Edmund married the King of Hungary's daughter, and lived for only a short time afterwards, and died childless. And as for Edward, he married the emperor's niece, and produced Edgar Atheling and St Margaret of Scotland. Edgar Atheling had no known legitimate heir of his body, so it is clear that the whole inheritance of Edmund Ironside, King of England, belonged in all justice to St Margaret, sister of Edgar Atheling, and wife of King Malcolm of Scotland: all the kings of Scotland to this day have descended in direct paternal and maternal line from Malcolm and St Margaret. And by this means it appears that the kingdom and crown of England rightfully belong, and should rightfully belong, to the King of Scotland.

It is a fact that after the death of Cnut and of Harold, his eldest son, and of Harthacnut, his second son, who reigned successively as kings, one after the other, St Edward the Confessor, Edmund Ironside's brother, took the English crown and died as king of that kingdom, and neither he nor his brother Alfred, who had been killed long before Edward's death because of Earl Godwine's plot, left any children.

After St Edward's death, Harold, son of Godwine, seized the kingdom of England; Duke William went into battle against him, and defeated him and killed him and all his brothers, and made himself king, and took the crown of England. And even though after Harold's death, Edgar Atheling did his utmost to recover the kingdom of England as his possession, nevertheless he could not succeed, because of the power and wisdom of King William, and after suffering various great troubles during his lifetime, he died without any issue from his body, as stated above.

King William had four sons, that is Robert Curthose, Duke of Normandy, William Rufus, King of England, Geoffrey, Count of Brittany by his wife, and Henry Beauclerc who was king afterwards, and who married Matilda, the eldest daughter of King Malcolm and St Margaret of Scotland. King Henry Beauclerc remained uncontested King of England, and the crown returned to the original line, as a consequence of that marriage, and on account of certain agreements that were made between the kings, Henry Beauclerc and the children of Malcolm, and on account of certain grants of lands made by the King of England to Malcolm's children, such as the earldom of Huntingdon, the earldom of Northumberland, the earldom of Cumberland, the land of Tynedale, and other regions, to be held in faith and homage from the king of England.

205   Et veulent dire les Anglois que par les moyens dessusdiz, le roy d'Escoce ne puet plus riens demander ne calengier ou royame ne a la couronne de Angleterre.

      Ledit Macolin, lequel commença a regner l'an mil lvi, eut de madame Saincte Margarite d'Escoce six filz, c'est assavoir Edouart, Emond, Elreth,
210   Egar, Alexandre, et David, Mathilde, femme du roy Henry Beauclerc et Marie, femme du conte de Bouloingne.

      Ledit Macolin, lequel commença a regner et ne se tenoit content, ne povoit contenter qu'il n'avoit le royame d'Angleterre, fist guerre en Angleterre et une foiz en revenant dudit royame d'Angleterre avec grans
215   prisez qu'il avoit faittez, fut tué et ses trois premiers filz avecquez luy environ la riviere de Tynne. Et recueilla la succession du royame d'Escoce Egar, son quart filz, lequel morut sans hoir de sa char; et succeda a la couronne Alexandre son frere, v^e filz dudit Macolin, qui morut   **f.70r** semblablement sans enfans, par quoy le royame et toute la succession
220   vint a David qui estoit le derrenier filz dudit Macolin.

      Cellui David eut ung filz nommé Henry qui fut conte de Hontiton, lequel eut trois filz, c'est assavoir Macolin, Guillame et David, et morut ledit Henry avant son pere David, par quoy Macolin, filz dudit Henry, recueilla le royame d'Escoce et la succession du roy David aprés le trespas d'icellui David.

225   Ledit Macolin, filz du conte Henry, fut nourry en la maison du roy Henry Beauclerc et avecquez Henry le second, filz de l'emperris Maheut, lequel il aima merveilleusement, et a ceste occasion aussy pour ce qu'il n'avoit nulz enfans, il donna audit roy Henry le second Northombelland, Combelland, Tindal, et toutes les terres des bordures d'Angleterre et d'Escosse, depuis la
230   riviere de Tynne jusquez a la riviere de Twyth, et depuis la riviere de Reircorsse et Scamor jusques en Sowlway, et si lui fist hommage du royame d'Escoce, dont les Escoçois furent tres malcontens. Et a ceste occasion ilz firent roy d'Escoce Guillame, second frere dudit roy Macolin, lequel fist grans guerres en Escoce et en Angleterre. Et a la parfin, il fut pris et
235   mené en Angleterre, et aprés delivré moyennant qu'il ratiffia tous les   **f.70v** appointemens qui avoient esté fais par le roy Macolin, son frere, avec le roy Henry, tant au regart de l'ommage du royame d'Escoce – et qu'il seroit tenu de venir au parlement du roy d'Angleterre trois foiz l'an, c'est assavoir a la xve d'aprés Noël, a la xve d'aprés Pasques et a la Sainct Michiel – comme
240   des terres d'Angleterre que ledit Macolin avoit transporteez audit roy Henry, et aussi qu'il payeroit tout l'or qui pourroit estre trouvé en tout le royame d'Escoce, et avecquez ce renderoit les terres et chasteaux de Barwyc, Roscheburg, Edymburg et Stremlin. Et si rendy a David, son frere, conte de Hontiton, lequel tenoit la part dudit Macolin et dudit roy Henry, la conté de
245   Galloy, les villes de Dondy, Emerberuby, Langforçon et pluiseurs autres.

And the English want to claim that the King of Scotland cannot ask for or claim anything in the kingdom or from the crown of England on this account.

Malcolm, who began to rule in the year 1056, had six sons from his wife my lady St Margaret of Scotland, that is Edward, Edmund, Ethelred, Edgar, Alexander, and David; (and daughters) Matilda, wife of King Henry Beauclerc and Mary, wife of the Count of Boulogne.

Malcolm, who began to rule and was not satisfied, and could not be satisfied, with what he had in the kingdom of England, waged war in England, and once when he was returning from the kingdom of England with the great prizes he had taken, he was killed with his three eldest sons near the river Tyne. And Edgar, his fourth son, inherited the kingdom of Scotland, dying without an heir of his flesh, and Alexander his brother, fifth son of Malcolm, succeeded to the crown and also died without children, so the kingdom and the whole inheritance came to David, who was the last son of Malcolm.

This David had a son called Henry, who was Earl of Huntingdon, who had three sons, that is, Malcolm, William, and David, and Henry died before his father David, so Malcolm, son of Henry, inherited the kingdom of Scotland, and succeeded King David, after David's death.

Malcolm, Earl Henry's son, was raised in the household of King Henry Beauclerc together with Henry II, son of the empress Matilda, whom he loved to an extraordinary degree, and for this reason, and because he had no children, he gave King Henry II Northumberland, Cumberland, Tynedale and all the lands on the borders of England and Scotland, from the river Tyne to the river Tweed, and from the river Rere Cross and Stainmore to Solway, and paid homage to him for the kingdom of Scotland, which made the Scots very discontented. And for this reason they made William – second brother of King Malcolm – King of Scotland; he waged war fiercely in Scotland and in England. And finally, he was captured and taken to England, and was later freed, provided he ratified all the agreements which had been made by King Malcolm, his brother, with King Henry, both regarding homage for the kingdom of Scotland – and that he would have to come to the Parliament of the King of England three times a year, that is, the fortnight after Christmas, the fortnight after Easter, and at Michaelmas – and homage for the lands in England that Malcolm had transferred to the said King Henry, and also that he would pay all the gold that could be found in the kingdom of Scotland, and, would also give up the lands and castles of Berwick, Roxburgh, Edinburgh, and Stirling. And furthermore he gave David, his brother, Earl of Huntingdon, who had taken the part of Malcolm and King Henry, the earldom of Galloway, the towns of Dundee, Inverbervie, Longforgan, and several others.

Ledit Macolin morut sans hoir et lui succeda ledit roy Guillame, lequel
eut ung filz nommé Alexandre. Et aussy ledit David, son tiers frere, eut trois
filles, c'est assavoir, Margarite qui fut femme Alain de Galloy, Ysabel qui
fut femme de Robert de Brus le premier, et Ade qui fut femme de Henry de
250   Hastinghez.

Icellui roy Guillame fut un vaillant prince et fist par un temps grans
guerres contre les Anglois, et aprés se paciffia avecquez eulx, et fut grant
amy du roy Richart Cuer de Lyon, lequel lui rendy de sa france
volenté les chasteaux de ˆBavvyc, de Rosseburg, de Edymburg et de   **f.71r**
255   Stremlin. Et dient les Escoçois que ledit roy Richart lui quitta
l'ommage d'Escoce, moiennant xi^m mars qu'il en bailla, et aussi comme il
appert par une[s] lettres dudit roy Richart, lesquelles sont fort obscures
touchant ladite matiere, comme par le contenu d'icelles puet plus adplain
apparoir, dont le contenu s'ensieut.

260   Copia littere regi Willermo Scocie, per regem Ricardum primum Anglie
super quittacione hommagii regni Scocie concesse:

*Ricardus Dei gratia, rex Anglie, dominus Hybernie, dux Normannie et
Acquittanie, comes Andegavie et Pictavie, universis archiepiscopis,
episcopis, abbatibus, prioribus, comitibus, baronibus, justiciariis,*
265   *vicecomitibus et omnibus aliis ministris suis ac fidelibus tocius regny sui
Anglie, salutem.*

*Sciatis nos consanguineo nostro Willermo Dei gratia regi Scottorum
reddidisse castra sua de Beruyk, Rosburg, Edymburg et Strevveling, cum
pertinentiis, tanquam jure hereditario ei pertinencia, ab eo et heredibus dicti*
270   *regni imperpetuum possidenda. Preterea ei quittamus omnes consuetudines
et [p]actiones quas bone memorie pater noster Henricus rex per novas
eschattas et captionem dicti Willermy extorsit ita ut ipse faciat nobis integre
et plenarie quod rex Scottorum Macolinus frater eius antecessoribus
nostris fecit pro terris suis in Anglia et de jure facere [et nos facimus*   **f.71v**
275   *ei et successoribus suis quicquid antecessores nostri de jure facere]
debuerunt scilicet in conductu veniendo ad curiam et in redeundo a curia et
in morando in curia et in procurationibus et in omnibus libertatibus,
dignitatibus et honoribus eidem de jure debitis ex antiquitate secundum quod
recognoscetur ex quatuor proceribus regni nostri ab ipso Willermo rege*
280   *electis postquam Willermus bastardus conquestor dicti regni Anglie
predecessor noster et heredes sui Angliam obtinueru[n]t. Si autem fines
regni Scocie vel marchias aliquis nostrorum hominum postquam Willermus
rex Scocie a patre nostro captus fuit usurpaverit aut injuste tenuerit absque
judicio, volumus ut integre restituantur et ad pristinum statum reducantur,*
285   *hiis quibus erant ante eius captionem.*

Malcolm died without heirs, and was succeeded by King William, who had a son called Alexander. Furthermore, David, his third brother, had three daughters, that is, Margaret, who was the wife of Alan of Galloway, Isabel, who was the wife of Robert the Bruce the first, and Ada, who was wife of Henry Hastings.

This King William was a courageous prince, and for a time waged war fiercely against the English, and afterwards made peace with them, and was a great friend of King Richard the Lionheart, who gave him of his own free will the castles of Berwick, Roxburgh, Edinburgh, and Stirling. And the Scots say that King Richard freed him from homage for Scotland, in exchange for 11,000 marks which he handed over, and also as it appears by King Richard's letter, which is most unclear about this affair, as can be seen from its content, which follows.

Copy of the letter granted by Richard I, King of England, to King William of Scotland, regarding the grant of the quitclaim of homage for the kingdom of Scotland:

Richard by the grace of God King of England, Lord of Ireland, Duke of Normandy and Aquitaine, Count of Anjou and Poitou, gives his greeting to all the archbishops, bishops, abbots, priors, earls, barons, justices, sheriffs, and all his other servants and faithful subjects in his whole kingdom of England.

Be advised that we have restored to our kinsman William, by the grace of God King of the Scots, his castles of Berwick, Roxburgh, Edinburgh and Stirling with appurtenances belonging to him by hereditary right, to be held in perpetuity by him and the heirs to the said kingdom forever. Moreover we discharge him of all customary payments and contracts which our father of good memory, Henry the king, extorted through new escheats and the capture of the said William, with the proviso that he shall pay us entirely and fully what his brother Malcolm King of the Scots paid to our predecessors for his lands in England which was owed by law, and we shall do to him and his successors whatsoever our predecessors owed by law, that is, coming to court, returning from court and staying at court, and in the matter of living expenses, and in all liberties, privileges and honors lawfully owed to the same from ancient times, from the time when our predecessor, William the Bastard, the conqueror of the said kingdom of England, and his heirs obtained England, according to the findings of four chief men of our kingdom chosen by the same King William. But if any of our men without legal judgment has usurped or unjustly retained [territory] on the frontiers or marches of the kingdom of Scotland after William King of Scotland was captured by our father, we wish that these be wholly restored and returned to the original state in which they were before his capture.

Preterea de terris suis quas habet in Anglia dominiis vel [feudis] scilicet in comitatu de Hunigenton et in omnibus aliis locis in ea libertate et plenitudine possideat et heredes sui in perpetuum, sicut Macolinus rex Scocie frater eius possidebat et [de] jure hereditario possidere debuerat: nisi

290 *predictus Macolinus aliquid de dictis terris aliquem feodaverit, ita tamen quod si postea infeodata fuit ipsorum feodorum servicia ad eum et heredes suos pertineat: et que si pater noster predicto Macolino aliquid donaverit ratum habemus et pro nobis et heredibus nostris in perpetuum confirmamus atque ad firmum volumus habere, reddimus et eidem ligeancias hominum*

295 *suorum, et omnes cartas quas dictus pater noster de eo habuit, per captionem suam, et si alique alie forte per oblivionem retente et invente fuerint*

ea penitus viribus carere precipimus. **f.72r**

Iste vero Willermus homo noster ligius deveria fecit pro omnibus terris suis in Anglia de quibus antecessores sui homines ligii antecessoribus

300 *nostris fecerunt et nobis fidelitatem juravit. Teste me ipso anno regni nostri primo.*

Aprés lesquelles choses morut ledit roy Guillame l'an mil ii^c xiiii, delaissié ung filz nommé Alexandre, qui fut ung vaillant chevalier et fist de grans guerres au roy de Norweghe, et eut pluiseurs batailles contre lui, et en

305 la fin le desconfist et tua en une bataille qui fut en la conté de Ffise. Pendant laquelle guerre, le roy d'Angleterre, Henry le tiers, filz du roy Jehan, entra en Escoce et y fist de maulz beaucop, disant qu'il ne tendroit point l'appointement qui avoit esté fait par ledit roy Richart avec ledit roy Guillame. Pour laquelle cause ledit roy Alexandre retourna hastivement de

310 devers le nort et se trouverent en champ pour combatre ensemble sur les bordures d'Angleterre et d'Escoce, et fut appointié pour eviter effusion de sang humain crestien qu'ilz combateroient corps a corps; et furent armez et montez a cheval, et leurs lances mises en arrest. Et ainsi qu'ilz vindrent a frapper l'un contre l'autre, ilz jetterent leurs lances a terre, et se

315 entracollerent et baisierent, et fut la paix faitte. Et de la s'en alerent tous deux a Yorc, et firent autel appointement ensemble comme il y avoit eu entre le roy Guillame et le roy Richart, et receut ledit roy Alexandre **f.72v** l'ordre de chevalerie dudit roy Henry. Et firent le mariage de Alexandre, aisné filz dudit roy Alexandre et de Margarite, fille dudit roy

320 Henry, avecquez les grandes aliances ensemble. Et aprés ces choses et pluiseurs autres faittes par ledit roy Alexandre, il morut en l'an de son regne xxxv, qui fut l'an mil ii^c xlix; et fut enterré a Melros.

Moreover, he and all his heirs in perpetuity shall have full and free possession of lands that he holds in demesne or fee, namely in the earldom of Huntingdon and in all other places, just as his brother Malcolm, King of Scotland possessed them and was entitled to possess them by hereditary right, unless the said King Malcolm has enfeoffed any one with any part of the said lands, with this proviso, that if anything from the said lands has been granted in fief, the services due from these fiefs should belong to him and his heirs; and that if our father gave anything to the said Malcolm, we ratify and confirm it on our own behalf and that of our heirs, and it is our wish that it be valid; we restore to him the allegiances of his own men and all the charters which our said father had from him by reason of his capture, and if by chance any others have been retained because they have been overlooked, or any are found in the future, we decree these to be completely invalid.

William himself, our liege man, has done due service for all his lands in England as his predecessors, liegemen of our predecessors, have done, and has sworn an oath of loyalty to us. Witnessed by myself in the first year of our reign.

After these events King William died in the year 1214, leaving a son called Alexander, who was a valiant knight and waged war fiercely against the King of Norway, and had several battles with him, and in the end defeated and killed him at a battle in the county of Fife. During this war, the King of England, Henry III, son of King John, entered Scotland and committed many evils there, saying that he would not keep the agreement which had been made by King Richard with King William. For that reason King Alexander returned quickly from the north, and they met on the field to fight together on the frontiers of England and Scotland and, to avoid shedding Christian blood, it was agreed that they should fight hand to hand, and they were armed and mounted on their horses with their lances in their rests. And just as they were about to strike one another, they threw their lances to the ground and embraced and kissed each other, and made peace. And they went off to York together, and made an agreement like the one between King William and King Richard, and King Alexander was knighted by King Henry. And a marriage was arranged between Alexander, eldest son of King Alexander and Margaret, King Henry's daughter, together with major alliances. And after these and several other deeds had been done by King Alexander, he died in the 35th year of his reign, which was the year 1249, and he was buried at Melrose.

Auquel Alexandre succeda Alexandre, son filz, dont cy dessus est faicte mention, lequel regna xxxvi ans, et morut l'an mil ii^c iiii^{xx} et v; et delaissa de
325   lui et de la royne Margarite, fille du roy Henry le tiers d'Angleterre, deux filz et une fille, c'est assavoir Alexandre et David, et la fille fut appellee Margarite, qui fut mariee au roy de Norwegue, laquelle eut une fille qui morut en bas eage, et n'en issy aucune lignie. Et au regart de David, second filz dudit roy Alexandre le second, il se rompy le col a Rosseburg, a cause duquel accident
330   le roy Alexandre le tiers, son frere, cheut en langueur et morut de desplaisir sans aucuns enfans. Et icy failly toute la lignie et generation dudit roy Guillame, dont a ceste occasion vint la dissention ou royame d'Escoce, pour les trois fillez de David, conte de Hontiton, frere dudit roy Guillame, pour savoir auquel des enfans yssus d'icelles le royame devoit appartenir.
335   [Nota que on dit que iceluy Alixandre, filz de Guillaume, traversa par force tout le royaulme d'Angleterre, pour venir a Douvre parler d'alliances avecques messire Loys de France, filz du roy Philippe le Conqereur; et dient aucunes cronicques qu'ilz firent lesdites aliances, et que ce furent les premieres. Mais si les firent ensemble ou non je ne le trouve point au vray.
340   Item, on dit que le roy Macolin, qui espousa Saincte Marguerite d'Escosse, traversa semblablement tout le royaulme d'Angleterre jusques a Douvre par force, et entra en la mer jusques a la celle de son cheval, disant que s'il y eust eu gré, il fust passé en France pour venir veoir le roy de France, lequel l'amoit fort, et en s'en retournant, fut tué, et ses troys filz,
345   comme dessus est declairé.]

Et pour entendre ceste matiere, il est vray, comme dessus est   **f.73r** declairié, que ledit David, conte de Hontiton, eut trois filles, dont l'aisnee fut nommee Margarite, femme de Alain de Galloy, de laquelle issy une fille nommee Devorguelle, qui fut femme de Jehan de Bailleul, pere de
350   Jehan de Bailleul, lequel fut pere de Edouart de Bailleul. Il yssi aussi de ladite Devorguelle une fille, qui [fut] femme de messire Jehan de Commin, lesquelz deux, c'est assavoir Jehan de Bailleul, filz de Devorguelle et le Commin, a cause de sa femme, pretendoient un mesmez droit en la couronne d'Escoce.
355   La seconde fille fut nommee Ysabel, femme de Robert de Brus le premier, dont descendy Robert de Brus le second, qui querela le royame et fut roy aprés, disant qu'il estoit plus prochain d'un degré que lesdiz de Bailleul et Commin. Et fut pere du grant Robert de Brus qui eut tant de bataillez a l'encontre des Anglois.
360   La tierce fut Adde, qui fut femme de Henry de Hastinghez, dont descendy Henry de Hastinghes, leur filz, lequel aussi pretendoit de son costé la couronne, disant qu'il estoit aussi prochain dudit roy Alexandre le tiers comme estoit Robert de Brus, et plus prochain ung degré que lesdiz Bailleul et Commin.

This Alexander was succeeded by his son Alexander, who has been mentioned earlier, who reigned for 36 years, and died in the year 1285; and he left two sons and a daughter by Queen Margaret, daughter of Henry III of England, that is, Alexander and David, and the daughter, who was married to the King of Norway, was called Margaret; and she had a daughter who died young and had no issue. And as for David, second son of the said King Alexander II, he broke his neck at Roxburgh; because of this accident, King Alexander III, his brother, fell sick and died of sorrow, childless. And that was the end of the whole lineage and descent of King William, and for this reason disagreement arose in the kingdom of Scotland concerning which of the three daughters of David, Earl of Huntingdon, should inherit the kingdom.

[Note that it is said that this Alexander, William's son, crossed the whole kingdom of England by force, in order to reach Dover, to negotiate alliances with my lord Louis of France, son of King Philip the Conqueror, and some chronicles say that they concluded these alliances, and that these were the first ones. But I can't find out for sure whether or not they did so.

Item, they say that King Malcolm, who married St Margaret of Scotland, also crossed the whole kingdom of England by force as far as Dover, and rode into the sea up to his horse's saddle, saying that if he had wanted, he would have gone to France to see the King of France, for whom he had great affection, and as he was returning, he and his three sons were killed, as set out above].

And so this matter may be understood, it is true, as stated above, that David, Earl of Huntingdon, had three daughters, of whom the eldest was called Margaret, wife of Alan of Galloway, from whom descended a daughter called Devorgilla, who was the wife of John Balliol, father to Edward Balliol. The same Devorgilla had a daughter, who was the wife of John Comyn; these two, that is John Balliol, son of Devorgilla, and Comyn, through his wife, both claimed the same right to the crown of Scotland.

The second daughter was called Isabel, wife of Robert the Bruce the First, from whom descended Robert the Bruce the Second, who claimed the kingdom and was afterwards king, saying that he was a degree nearer than Balliol and Comyn. And he was the father of the great Robert the Bruce who had so many battles against the English.

The third was Ada, who was the wife of Henry Hastings, from whom came Henry Hastings, their son, who for his part also claimed the crown, saying that he was as close to King Alexander III as Robert the Bruce, and one degree nearer than the said Balliol and Comyn.

    Sur lesquelles differences et pour appaisier lesdiz questions et debas,   **f.73v**
365   toutes les parties se soubzmirent au dit et ordonnance du roy
d'Angleterre, Edouart le premier de ce nom, autrement dit aux Longues
Gambez. Et dient les Anglois que les Escoçois f[i]rent ladicte submission du
consentement des trois estas d'Escoce, recognoissans que le royame d'Escoce
estoit tenus du royame d'Angleterre [et avoient recours a luy] comme a leur
370   souverain, auquel appartenoit jugier desdites questions et differences. Mais les
Escoçois dient tout [le] contraire, et que la submission ne fut faitte si non
comme a leur plus prochain voisin, et aussi que toutes les parties estoient ses
parens.

    Quoy que ce fust, ladite submission fut faitte par les Escoçois du
375   consentement du parlement d'Escoce et acceptee par ledit Edouart, pardevant
lequel toutes lesdites parties si comparurent a Yorc en ung parlement que
ledit Edouart tint audit lieu pour ladite matiere. Et furent la ordonnez par
ledit Edouart xxiiii personnes notables, xii du royame d'Angleterre et xii du
royame d'Escoce, pour venir oudit royame d'Escoce eulx informer des
380   usages et coustumez dudit pays, affin d'en rapporter la verité audit roy
Edouart a certain autre jour qui fut lors ordonné estre tenus audit lieu d'Yorc,
pour ladicte matiere.

    Et fut deslors dit et declairié par ledit roy Edouart que toutes les   **f.74r**
parties querelans droit en la couronne d'Escoce seroient regecteez et
385   mises hors du procés, excepté lesdiz Bailleul et Brus, lequel Bailleul se disoit
estre descendus de la fille aisnee; et ledit Brus disoit supposé que ainsi fust,
si ne devoit il point venir a la succession, pour ce que ledit Brus estoit plus
prochain un degré dudit roy Alexandre le tiers que ledit de Bailleul n'estoit.

    Au jour limité aux parties par ledit roy Edouart en ladite cité d'Yorc,
390   lesdites parties y comparurent . Aussi fist ledit roy Edouart comme juge, et
les commissaires anglois et escoçois ordonnez et depputez pour le debat des
parties et leur relation oyé, tant au regart du droit des parties comme de
l'obeissance faitte audit Edouart par ceulx d'Escoce – lesquelz avoient mis
tout le royame et toutes les notablez places d'icelles en la main dudit Edouart
395   – icellui Edouart donna sa sentence au prouffit d'icellui Jehan de Bailleul,
lequel il declaira, juga, ordonna, establi et institua roy d'Escoce. Et lui fist
faire par ses subgez d'Escoce toute obeissance, lui bailla la possession de
toutes les places, l'investitude du royame, duquel ledit de Bailleul lui fist
hommage et serement de [feaulté]. Et a ce se consentirent tous les prelas,
400   contez, barons et seigneurs dudit pays qui estoient en la compaignie
desdites parties audit lieu de Yorc, dont tout le pueple d'Escoce fut   **f.74v**
desplaisant et mal se contenta, et dirent que la sentence n'avoit esté
donnee au proufit dudit de Bailleul sinon pour ce qu'il avoit promis de se
faire homme du roy d'Angleterre.

Because of these disagreements, and to settle these questions and disputes, all the parties submitted to the judgment and command of the King of England, Edward I of that name, also known as Longshanks. And the English state that the Scots made that submission with the consent of the Three Estates of Scotland, acknowledging that the kingdom of Scotland was held from the kingdom of England, to which they could appeal as their sovereign, to which belonged the right to judge these issues and disagreements. But the Scots claim the reverse, and that the submission was made only to their nearest neighbor, because all the parties were related to him.

Be that as it may, this submission was made by the Scots with the consent of the Parliament of Scotland and accepted by Edward, before whom all the claimants appeared at York, in a Parliament that Edward held there to deal with that affair. And there 24 notables, 12 from the kingdom of England and 12 from Scotland, were commanded by Edward to go to the kingdom of Scotland and find out about the usages and customs of that country, so that they could inform King Edward, on another day that he appointed to be held in the place of York, about the same matter.

And then King Edward stated and declared that all parties claiming a right to the crown of Scotland were rejected and excluded from the case, except Balliol and Bruce, Balliol claiming to be the descendant of the eldest daughter, and Bruce said that even were this the case, he should not succeed, because Bruce was one degree nearer to King Alexander III than Balliol.

On the day ordained for the parties by King Edward, the said parties appeared in the same city of York. Edward also acted as judge, and once the report of the English and Scottish commissioners ordained and chosen for the dispute between the parties had been heard, regarding both the right of the parties and the obedience paid to the said Edward by the Scots – who had placed the whole kingdom and all the important places in Edward's hands – the same Edward gave his judgment in favor of John Balliol, whom he declared, judged, ordained, established and instituted as King of Scotland. And he ordered his Scottish subjects to give him complete obedience; he granted him possession of all those places, and invested him with the kingdom, for which Balliol paid him homage and gave him the oath of fealty. And all the prelates, earls, barons and lords of that country who accompanied the parties to York consented to this; on this account all the people of Scotland were displeased and discontented, and said that the judgment was only given in favor of Balliol because he had promised to become the man of the King of England.

405 Et a ceste cause un escuier dudit pays d'Escoce nommé Willame Wallez leva grant pueple ou royame d'Escoce, et fist guerre contre ledit de Bailleul et contre les Anglois par longue espace de temps, et gardoit la pluspart du temps les montaignez, et eut pluiseurs bataillez contre les Anglois et ledit Bailleul, dont il gaigna les aucunes, et les autres il perdy, et a la fin il fut pris

410 par les Anglois et par eulx [fut] fait morir piteusement.

Depuis ce temps la, ledit de Bailleul pour aucuns desplaisirs qui lui furent fais par les Anglois se tira par devers le roy de France, dont le roy d'Angleterre fut mal content. Et a ceste occasion, il reprist en grace ledit Robert de Brus, et le fist roy d'Escoce, lequel lui fist hommage dudit royame

415 d'Escoce, comme avoit fait ledit de Bailleul. Et aprés quant il fut ou royame d'Escoce et qu'il eut la possession dudit royame, il ne volut pas garder sa promesse audit roy Edouart, dont a ceste cause se meut grant guerre entre ledit roy Edouart et lui. Et renvoya icellui roy Edouart requerir icellui Jehan de Bailleul, et de rechief l'ordonna et constitua roy d'Escoce, pour

420 dechassier ledit Robert de Brus. Et ne demoura guaires aprés que f.75r ledit roy Edouart d'Angleterre morut, delaissié son filz heritier, Edouart le second, dit de Canervain. Et pareillement morut ledit Jehan de Bailluel, delaissié son filz heritier, Edouart de Bailleul. Et aussi morut ledit Robert de Brus, delaissié Robert de Brus le tiers, son filz heritier.

425 Voyant ledit Edouart de Canervain que ledit Robert de Brus ne lui vouloit obeïr, et que ledit Edouart de Bailleul lui voloit bien faire hommage dudit royame d'Escoce, il le receut audit hommage, et lui bailla grant nombre de gens et de navires pour venir descendre en Escoce. Et descendy ledit Edouart de Canervain a Quincorne, et gaigna la bataille contre ledit Robert de Brus,

430 et fut couronné ledit Edouart de Bailleul roy d'Escoce a Sainct Janscon. Et y eut grant guerre en ce temps la ou royame d'Escoce, et perdy le roy Robert de Brus pluiseurs bataillez contre les Anglois et ledit Edouart de Bailleul, et aussi en gaigna pluiseurs. Et a la parfin, a l'ayde des François, avecquez lesquelz ledit Robert de Brus se allya – dont aincoires aucuns des noms des

435 nobles hommes françois qui vindrent audit secours ont leur posterité en Escoce, comme ceulx de Mombray, d'Estouteville, de Bouloingne, de Sexton, de Neufville, Colleville et pluiseurs autres – il recouvra le royame et chassa ledit Edouart de Bailleul et les Anglois hors d'icellui, et en fut roy paisible.

And for this reason a squire of that country of Scotland, called William Wallace, raised many people in the kingdom of Scotland and made war against Balliol and against the English for a long period of time, and for most of the time, he guarded the mountains, and had several battles against the English and Balliol, some of which he won, and some he lost, and finally he was captured by the English and was cruelly put to death by them.

Afterwards, offended by several acts committed by the English, Balliol turned to the King of France, which displeased the King of England. And for that reason, he took Robert the Bruce back into favor, and made him King of Scotland, as he had previously made Balliol, and [Bruce] paid him homage for the kingdom of Scotland, as Balliol had done. And once he was in the kingdom of Scotland and in possession of that kingdom, he did not want to keep his promise to King Edward, and for that reason a major war broke out between King Edward and him. And King Edward sent away for John Balliol, and ordained and established him as King of Scotland again, to expel Robert Bruce. Then not long afterwards King Edward of England died, leaving as his heir his son, Edward II, "of Caernarfon", as he was known. And John Balliol died as well, leaving Edward Balliol as his son and heir. And Robert the Bruce also died, leaving Robert the Bruce III, his son, as his heir.

Edward of Caernarfon, seeing that Robert the Bruce would not obey him, and that Edward Balliol was really willing to pay homage for the kingdom of Scotland, received homage from him, and gave him a large quantity of men and ships to invade Scotland. And Edward of Caernarfon landed at Kinghorn, and won the battle against Robert the Bruce, and Edward Balliol was crowned King of Scotland at St Johnstown. And at that time a fierce war took place in the kingdom of Scotland, and King Robert the Bruce lost several battles against the English and Edward Balliol, and also won others. And finally with the aid of the French, with whom Robert the Bruce had allied himself, he regained the kingdom, and chased Edward Balliol and the English out of there, and was king in peace. Some French noblemen who came to help him still have descendants in Scotland, for example, Mowbray, Stuteville, Boulogne, Seton, Neville, Colville and several others.

440   Depuis ces choses, ledit Robert de Brus fist paix et appointement   **f.75v**
final avecquez le roy Edouart d'Angleterre le tiers, dit de Windezore,
filz dudit roy Edouart de Canervain, le premier an du regne dudit roy Edouart
le tiers; par laquelle paix fut accordé entr'eulx que ledit roy Edouart
renonceroit a tous les drois qu'il pretendoit en Escoce, et fut fait le mariage

445   de David, filz heritier dudit roy Robert et de Jehanne, suer dudit roy Edouart
le tiers. Et dient les Escoçois que ledit roy Robert donna xxi^m marc[s] audit
roy Edouart pour ladite renonciation. Les Anglois dient que ledit Edouart
estoit jone enfant quant il fist la renonciation, et que la royne Ysabel, sa
mere, et messire Rogier de Mortemer la lui firent faire par argent qu'ilz en

450   receurent sans le consentement du parlement d'Angleterre.

     Et a ceste cause, aprés la mort dudit Robert de Brus, et que ledit Edouart
fut en plus grant eage, il esleva le second Edouart de Bailleul, filz du premier
Edouart de Bailleul, et le constitua roy d'Escoce, et lui bailla grant nombre
de gens et de navires pour venir de rechief en Escoce. Et fut ledit Edouart de

455   Bailleul couronné roy d'Escoce, et chassa le roy David, son filz, [hors du
royame], lequel se retray en France, lui et son frere, devers le roy Phelippe
de Vallois qui pour lors regnoit, et demourerent long temps lesdiz deux freres
ou chasteau de Gaillart en Vecsin.

     Pendant lequel temps fut ouvert traittié de paix entre le roy   **f.76r**

460   Phelippe de Vallois et ledit roy Edouart de Windesore, present les
cardinaulx de court de Romme, qui pour lors estoient a Paris, c'est assavoir,
l'an mil iii^{c}xlii, et demourerent d'accort les ambassadeurs d'Angleterre et les
commissaires du roy de France, en la presence desdiz cardinaulx, de tous les
debas qui estoient entre lesdiz deux roys de France et d'Angleterre, tant a

465   cause de la couronne de France, que de toutes les particularitez du royame,
leurs lettres accordeez, le soupper prest en la grant sale du palais a Paris, les
officiers d'armes, leurs tuniclez vestuez, et ne restoit plus que a crier et
publier par lesdiz officiers d'armes la paix final entre lesdiz deux roys et
royamez de France et d'Angleterre.

470   Quant adont vindrent les ambassadeurs dudit roy David, qui supplierent
au roy de France qu'il voulsist comprendre ledit roy David en sa dicte paix
comme son allié, par vertu des alliances qui avoient esté faittes entre le roy
Robert de Brus et les predecesseurs dudit roy de France, et que par ce moyen
il peust recouvrer son royame d'Escoce, comme ledit roy d'Angleterre

475   devoit recouvrer la duchié de Guyenne par le moyen de ladite paix final.

After these events, Robert the Bruce made peace and a final agreement with King Edward III of England, "of Windsor", as he was known, son of Edward of Caernarfon, in the first year of Edward III's reign. By this peace it was agreed between them that King Edward would renounce all the rights that he claimed in Scotland, and a marriage was arranged between David, son and heir of King Robert, and Joan, sister of King Edward III. And the Scots claim that King Robert gave 21,000 marks to King Edward for this renunciation. The English state that Edward was a young child when he made the renunciation, and that Queen Isabel, his mother, and Lord Roger Mortimer made him do it on account of the money they received for it, without the consent of the Parliament of England.

And for this reason, after the death of Robert the Bruce, when Edward was older, he raised the second Edward Balliol, son of the first Edward Balliol, and created him King of Scotland, and gave him many men and ships to invade Scotland again. And Edward Balliol was crowned King of Scotland, and expelled King David, his son, from the kingdom; the latter withdrew to France with his brother, to King Philip of Valois then reigning, and the two brothers stayed for a long time in Château-Gaillard, in the Vexin.

During this time, peace negotiations began between King Philip of Valois and King Edward of Windsor, in the presence of the cardinals of the court of Rome, who were then at Paris, that is, in the year 1342, and the ambassadors of England and the commissioners of the King of France, in the presence of the cardinals, had agreed on all the points at issue between the two Kings of France and England, concerning both the crown of France and all the specific parts of the kingdom; letters had been agreed and the supper was ready in the great hall of the palace at Paris, the heralds were dressed in their tunics and it only remained for the officers-at-arms to announce and publish the final peace between the two kings and kingdoms of France and England.

At that moment, King David's ambassadors arrived, and begged the King of France to include King David in the peace treaty as his ally, according to the alliances which had been made between King Robert the Bruce and the predecessors of the King of France, so that by this means he could regain his kingdom of Scotland, just as the King of England ought to regain his duchy of Guyenne through the final peace.

Lesquelles choses par l'ordonnance dudit roy de France furent bien adplain remonstrees ₐausdiz ambassadeurs d'Angleterre, en les priant de par lui qu'ilz voulsissent les choses dessusdites accorder et consentir. Lesquellez choses lesdiz ambassadeurs d'Angleterre dirent que

480 pour riens ilz ne le feroient, pour deux causes: l'une qu'ilz n'avoient point de povoir de par le roy d'Angleterre en ceste partie; l'autre que ledit roy d'Angleterre, leur maistre, portoit et soustenoit la part dudit Edouart de Bailleul, et qu'ilz sçavoient bien qu'il ne s'en deppartiroit point.

Oyez lesquelles choses par ledit roy de France Phelippe de Vallois, il dit

485 aussi qu'il ne se deppartiroit point de l'alliance du roy David, et choisy plustost endurer la charge et le peril de la guerre sur luy et sur son royame, que de rompre la promesse et l'alliance qu'il avoit au roy d'Escoce et aux Escoçois, dont a ceste cause la guerre commença entre lesdiz deux roys de France et d'Angleterre; de laquelle ensieuvit grant effusion de sang; et perdy

490 le roy de France deux grossez batailles, [c'est assavoir] le roy Phelippe la bataille de Crecy l'an xlvi, et le roy Jehan la bataille de Poitiers, l'an lvi; a cause desquellez bataillez et des autres maulz que les Anglois firent ou royame de France, ledit royame fut en dangier d'estre de tous points perdu.

Le roy David, depuis ces choses, retourna en Escoce, et a l'ayde

495 du conte de Douglas, il reçouvra grant partie de son royame, et puis   f.77r
morut, delaissié un autre filz, qui avoit nom David, lequel fut allyé de France comme son pere; et fut fort persecuté par les Anglois, comme avoit esté son pere, et a l'occasion de laquelle chose, le roy Charles vi[e] envoia l'admiral de Vienne avecquez grande quantité de François en Escoce au

500 secours dudit roy David, a l'ayde desquelz ledit roy David chassa ses ennemis hors du royame, et demoura paisible en icellui, et s'en retourna ledit admiral de Vienne en France.

Ledit David le second n'eut aucuns enfans maslez, et eut une fille qui fut mariee a Robert Stuwart, autrement dit seneschal, duquel mariage issy deux

505 enfans maslez et pluiseurs filles.

Aprés la mort dudit roy David d'Escoce, fut couronné ledit Robert ou royame d'Escoce, et avoit pluiseurs freres, comme le duc d'Albanye, le conte d'Attel et autres.

Si avint que ledit Robert devint maladif, et se meut grande question entre

510 lui et son filz David, qui estoit duc de Rouzay. A l'occasion duquel debat, pluiseurs sinistrez rappors furent faiz audit roy Robert de son dit aisné filz le duc de Rousay, et tellement que a la promotion desdiz duc d'Albanie et conte d'Attel comme l'en dist, ledit roy Robert ₐbailla commission   f.77v
audit duc d'Albanie pour prendre ledit duc de Rozay, son filz, et le lui

515 amener. Mais ledit duc d'Albanie trespassa sa commission, car il prist le duc de Rozay et le mist prisonnier en un chastel, et la le fist piteusement morir.

These matters were set out very clearly to the English ambassadors, on the orders of the King of France, and on his behalf the English ambassadors were requested to agree and consent to them. The English ambassadors said that on no account could they do it for two reasons: first, they had no authority to do so on the King of England's behalf, secondly, the King of England, their master, supported and maintained the cause of Edward Balliol, and they knew very well that he would not abandon it.

Hearing these things, the King of France, Philip of Valois, also said that he would not abandon his alliance with King David, and chose rather to endure the burden and risks of war for himself and his kingdom, than break his promise to, and alliance with, the King of Scotland and the Scots. And for this reason war broke out between the two Kings of France and England, from which great bloodshed followed; and the King of France lost two great battles, that is to say, King Philip lost the battle of Crecy in the year 1346, and King John, the battle of Poitiers, in the year 1356. As a result of these battles and other evils that the English committed in the kingdom of France, that kingdom was in danger of being completely destroyed.

King David returned to Scotland after these events, and with the help of the Earl of Douglas, he recovered a large part of his kingdom, then died, leaving another son, called David, who was an ally of France like his father; and he was greatly harmed by the English, as his father had been, and for this reason King Charles VI sent the Admiral of Vienne and a large number of Frenchmen to Scotland, to assist King David, with whose help King David expelled his enemies from the kingdom, and stayed peaceably there, and the admiral of Vienne returned to France.

David II had no male children, and he had a daughter who married Robert Stewart, also known as the Steward, from whose marriage two male children and several daughters were born.

After the death of King David of Scotland, the same Robert was crowned in the kingdom of Scotland and had several brothers, such as the Duke of Albany, the Earl of Atholl, and others.

It happened that Robert became ill, and a major dispute arose between him and his son David, who was Duke of Rothesay. As a result of this controversy, several worrying reports were made to King Robert about his eldest son, the Duke of Rothesay, so that, with the encouragement of the Duke of Albany and Earl of Atholl, as it is said, King Robert ordered the Duke of Albany to seize the Duke of Rothesay, his son, and bring him to him. But the Duke of Albany exceeded his instructions, for he took the Duke of Rothesay and imprisoned him in a castle, and there had him cruelly put to death.

Voyant lesquellez choses, ledit roy Robert, lequel estoit perçus d'une jambe et ne se povoit mouvoir du lit, et doubtoit que ses freres en feissent autant a son second filz, Jammez, il ordonna deux navires pour mener sondit
520 filz Jammez en France devers le roy Charles le vi^e, affin qu'il lui pleust le lui garder jusquez a ce qu'il fust en eage pour deffendre son dit pere et le royame.

Et avint que les Anglois eurent cognoissance de ladicte alee, et mirent du navire sur la mer, lequel rencontra ledit Jammez et le prist et mena a Londres
525 devers le roy Henry le quart, ou il demoura prisonnier xxi ans, et ce pendant morut sondit pere, le roy Robert, et eurent le gouvernement du royame sesdiz oncles d'Albanie et d'Attel, avecques leurs adherens.

Aprés la mort dudit roy Henry le [v^e], ledit Jammez fut delivré d'Angleterre, et espousa la niepce du cardinal d'Angleterre, fille du conte
530 de Sombreset, et lui venu ou royame d'Escoce et qu'il fut couronné
et eut prise la possession dudit royame, il fist copper la teste audit   f.78r
duc d'Albanie, son oncle, au prince Stuwart, son filz et au conte de
Lenoz, qui avoit espousé la fille dudit d'Albanie, et demoura paisible en son royame xiiii ans, et maria sa fille aisnee a l'aisné filz du roy de France,
535 Charles le viie, icellui aisné filz pour lors daulphin de Viennois. Et aprés fut tué a saint [Janstan] l'an mil iiii^c xxxvi, au pourchas dudit conte d'Attel, frere dudit [duc] d'Albanie, lequel conte d'Attel fut aprés pris et fait morir tres cruelement par l'ordonnance de la royne et des trois estas du royame d'Escoce.

540 Ledit Jammez delaissa un seul filz nommé Jammes comme le pere, lequel fut un vaillant chevalier et homme de grant corage, et morut environ l'eage de xxviii ans, au siege qu'il tenoit devant Rosseburg, la ou un canon rompy, dont l'un des esclas le vint frapper et le tua; nonobstant laquelle mort pour ce qu'il avoit destraint la place si fort en sa vie, ladite place lui
545 fut rendue aprés sa mort.

Et delaissa deux filz, l'un nommé Jammez qui a present est roy et l'autre . . . qui est prince d'Escoce, duc d'Albanie et conte de la Marche. Et demourerent lesdiz enfans et le royame ou gouvernement de la royne leur mere jusquez a sa mort, qui fut l'an mil cccc lxiii, environ la
550 Toussains.

Fin des Cronicquez d'Escoce.

Seeing these things, King Robert, who was injured in one leg, and could not leave his bed, and feared that his brothers would do the same to his second son James, ordered two ships to take his son James to France, to King Charles VI, so that he would look after him until he was old enough to protect his father and the kingdom.

And it so happened that the English found out about that voyage, and sent out a ship, which met James and seized him, and brought him to London, to King Henry IV, where he stayed a prisoner for 21 years, and in the meantime his father, King Robert, died, and his uncles Albany and Atholl and their faction ruled the kingdom.

After the death of Henry V, James was freed from England and married the niece of the cardinal of England, the daughter of the Earl of Somerset, and once he had returned to the kingdom of Scotland, had been crowned and had taken possession of the kingdom, he had the heads cut off the Duke of Albany, his uncle, the Prince Stewart, his son, and the Earl of Lennox, who had married Albany's daughter, and ruled his kingdom peacefully for 14 years, and married his eldest daughter to the eldest son of the King of France, Charles VII; at that time this eldest son was dauphin of Viennois. And afterwards he was killed at St Johnstown in 1436, at the urging of the Earl of Atholl, brother of the Duke of Albany. The Earl of Atholl was afterwards taken and put to death very cruelly on the order of the queen and the Three Estates of Scotland.

This James left an only son called James like his father; he was a worthy knight and a man with a fine disposition, and he died aged about 28 years, while laying siege to Roxburgh, where a cannon exploded, and one of the fragments hit him and killed him; in spite of his death, because he had besieged the place so strongly in his lifetime, it surrendered to him after his death.

And he left two sons, one named James, who is the current king, and the other . . . who is Prince of Scotland, Duke of Albany and Earl of March. And both children and the kingdom remained under the control of the queen their mother, until her death which was in the year 1463, around All Saints.

End of the Chronicles of Scotland.

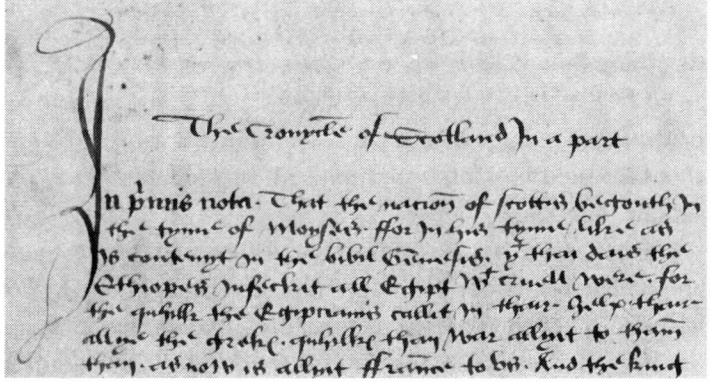

Folio 18v of NAS MS Dalhousie GD 45/31/1–II. Image published with the permission of the Keeper of the Records of Scotland.

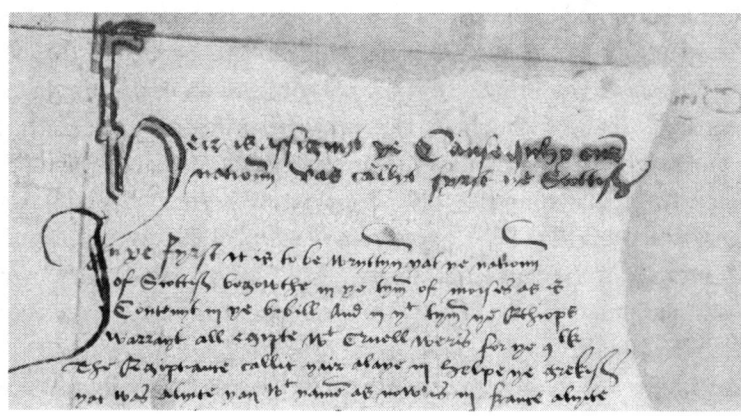

Folio 299r of BL MS Royal 17.D.xx. © The British Library Board.

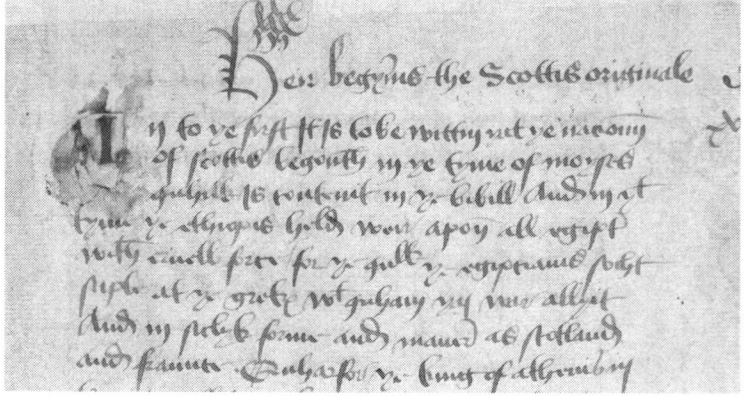

Folio 93r of NLS MS 16500. Image published with the permission of the Trustees of the National Library of Scotland.

110

THE SCOTTIS ORIGINALE
(THE CRONYCLE OF SCOTLAND IN A PART)

from National Archives of Scotland MS Dalhousie GD 45/31/1-II

In primis, nota that the nacioun of Scottis begouth in the tyme of   f.18v
Moyses. For in his tyme, like as is contenyt in the Bibil, Genesis, þat
[in] thai dais the Ethiopes infeckit all Egipt with cruell were, for the quhilk
the Egipcianis callit in thair help thair allye, the Grekis, quhilkis than war
5   allyit to thame than, as now is allyit Fraunce to vs.

---

from British Library MS Royal 17.D.xx

Heir is assignyt þe cause quhy our natioun vas callyt fyrst þe   f.299r
Scottis.
    In þe fyrst, it is to be wryttyn þat þe natioun of Scottis begowthe in þe tym
of Moises, as is contenyt in þe Bibill. And in þat tym, þe Ethiops warrayt all
5   Egipte with cruell weris, for þe quhilk the Egiptiance callit þair alaye in
helpe, þe Grekis, þat was alyite þan with þame, as now is in France alyite
with [w]s Scottis.

---

from National Library of Scotland MS 16500 (Asloan)

Heir begynnis the Scottis Originale.   f.93r
    Into þe first, it is to be wittin þat þe nacioun of Scottis begouth in
þe tyme of Moyses, quhilk is contenit in þe Bibill. And in þat tyme, þe
Ethiopis held weir apon all Egipt with cruell force, for þe quhilk þe
5   Egipcianis socht suple at þe Grekis with quham þai war allyit, and in siclyk
forme and maner as Scotland and Fraunce.

111

And the King of Athenes, in Grece, callit Neolus, send his sone Gayel
Glas, efter quham oure langage Scottis is callit Gayelgaggit, with a grete
power of men in Egipt, and discomfit the Ethiopis, dauntit & abandownit the
Ethiopis ay to the tyme þat Moyses rais. For the quhilk victory, the King of
10   Egipt gave his anerly douchter and aire to the said Gayel, callit Scota, in
mariage. Off the quhilk Scota, we efterwart war all callit Scottis, as
the custume ˏwas that tyme to call naciouns efter wommen, & nocht   **f.19r**
efter men – as Asya, Affrica, and Europa, the thre principale partis of
the warlde. *Juxta illud*:

15   *A muliere Scota vocatur Scocia tota,*
                       Nomen habet, uetito Gathelos ducis audaucto.

Þairfoir þe King of Athenes in Grece, callit Neolius, [send] his sone
Gayelglas, eftir quhome our langage callit is Gayelige, with ane gret power of
10   men into Egipt, and discumfyt þe Ethiops, and abandonyt þame ay to þe tyme
þat Moises rase. For þe quhilk victory, þe King of Egipte gaif his aunly dochtir
and heir, callit Scota, to þis Gayelglas in mariage. Of þe quhilk Scota, we eftir
was callit Scottis, as þe custome was þan to call natioun eftir women, and nocht
eftir man – as is Asya, Affrica, and Europa, þe thre pryncipale partis of þe
15   warld. *Versus*:

                   A Scota nata Pharaonis Regis Egipti,
                   Vt veteres credunt, Scotia nomen habet;
                   A muliere Scota vocitatur Scotia tota,
                   Nomen habet, vetito Gathelas ducis adaucto.

Quharfor þe King of Athenis into Grece, callit Neolus, send his son with
gret power, callit Gathelos, eftir quhom our langag is callit Galeig, with gret
power of men in Egipt, and discomfit þe Ethiopis, and habandonit þam vnto
10   þe tyme þat Moyses rais. For þe quhilk victory, the King of Egipt gaf his
allanerly dochter & air, callit Scota, in mariage to þe said Gathelos. Be
proper name of þe quhilk Scota, we war callit Scottis, as vse and custome was
þat tyme to nacionis to tak dominacioun and name eftir þe proper name of
women, and nocht of men – as Asya, Affrik, & Europe, the thre principale
15   partis of þe warld.

                   A Scota nata Pharaonis regis Egipti,
                   Vt veteres tradunt, Scocia nomen habet.

Sa þat the opynioun of thame may nocht stand þat trowis þat we come of
Brutus, quhilk come of the traytouris of Troye, as is wele kend, lyke as is
contenyt in the story of Troye, Gwydo de Columpna. Bot we ar cummyn of
20   the worthieft nacioun þat euer was in erde, that is the Grekis, of the mannis
syde, Gathelos, off the Egipcianis of the wommannis syde, Scota, quhilkis
war before the destructioun of Troye iii^c ȝere. And efter that, was Brute
borne nere a hunder ȝere. Sa the nacioun of Scottis begouth before the
Britones nere iiii^c ȝere. Sa mycht we neuer cum of thame sen we war sa lang
25   before thame. And þat the Grekis war the worthiest, it apperis, for thai haue
bene twis conquerouris of the warlde – be Ercules and Alexander. And
Troyanis neuer, bot at thair defens and vencust at the last.

---

20   And sa þe opynyoun of þame may nocht stand þat trowis we come [fra]
Brutus, quhilk come of þe traytouris of Troye, as is weill kennyt, and is
contenyt in þe storye of Troye, maid be ane clerk callit Gwido de Columpna.
Bot we ar cummyn of þe maist werschipfull natioun þat euir was in
erd, þat is þe ‿Grekis on þe mannis side, Gayelglas, and of þe   f.299v
25   Egiptians on þe womannis side, Scota, quhilk was before þe
distructioun of Troye thre hundir ȝeir. And sa þe natioun of Scottis was sa
lang befor þame. And þe Grekes was þe maist wirscipfull natioun þat euir
was, for þai haif bene twise conquir[oris] of þe warld – be Ercules and
Alexander. And þe Troiance neuir, bot at þair defence, and vincust at þe last.

Sa þat þe opiniones of þam ar nocht trew þat sayis or trowis þat we come
of Brute, quhilk come of tratouris of Troye, as is wele kend and contenit in
20   þe story of Troye, maid and compylit be þe clerk callit Gwydo de Columna.
For sekerly we ar cummyn of þe mast famous & mast worschipfull
nacioun þat evir was in erd, quhilk is‿of Grece of þe mannis syd, callit   f.93v
Gathele, and of þe Egipcianis of þe woman syd, callit Scota, quhilkis
war befor þe distructioun of Troy mair þan thre hundreth ȝeris. And sa lang
25   þe nacioun of Scottis was befor ony tresoun ras in Troye. And at þe Grekis
war þe mast worschipfull nacioun, for twys þai conquest all þe warld – anys
be þe worthy man callit Herculis and anys be þe famous conquestour
Alexander, þe quhilkis war baith borne Grekis. And þe Troianis did neuir,
bot quhen þai war segit, baid at þar defence, & war vincust and vttrely
30   distroyit.

In cas þat of thaim sensyne ar cummyn diuers worthy men, and ȝit come
thai of thame þat bare the foule surname – þat is to say, Antenor, Eneas, and
30   Helenus, quhilkis all thre procurit the tresoun of Troy, with Polidamas.
In losing of the Grekis, sais Varro, that famous clerk:

> *Grecia cum suis prouinciis est regnorum*
> *domina, milicie nutrix, prophecie mater, omnium scienciarum*
> *inuentrix et magistra, cuius gens bellicosissima*
35   > *dono sapiencie et sciencie predita, sermone des[er]tissima,*
> *legibus subdita, pia, circa extraneos pacifica,*
> *circa incolas et domesticos quieta, contra*
> *hostium iniurias nimium intollerabilis et infesta,*
> *cuius ydeoma omnium clarius et sonancius, & hec.*

---

30   And suppoise of þame sensyne ar cummyn worthy men, ȝite þan þai ar
cummyn of þam þat bair þe foule surname – þat is to say, of Anthenor and
Eneas & Helye, quhilk thre procuryt þe treson of Troye with Pelymades in þe
losyng of þe Grekis.
And sa wraite þe famous clerc:

35   > *Grecia cum suis provinciis, regnorum est*
> *domina, militie nutrix, prophesie omnium scientiarum*
> *invictrix, ac magistra, cuius gens bellicosissima*
> *dono sapientie et scientie predita, sermone decertissima,*
> *legibus subdita, pia, circa extraneos pacifica,*
40   > *circa incolas et domesticos quieta, contra*
> *hostium iniurias nimium intollerabilis et infesta,*
> *cuius ydoneum omnium clarius et sonantius est.*

And suppos of þaim ar cummyn mony noble & worthy men, ȝit þai ar
32   succedit of þam þat bure & beris þe foull surname of þe tresoun of Troye.
And sa wrait þis famous clerk Grecia.

40   This foresaid Gayell & Scota war maryit togeder in the tyme þat the
barnis of Israel passit the Rede Sea. And efter the decess of Pharo, thai
gouernyt the land of Egipt. And for thai saw sik cruell plagis cum of Egipt,
thai decretit to pas with thair folkis þat he brocht out of Grece &
mony of Egipt ˌto seke void landis and vnenhabyte. For he wald   **f.19v**
45 nocht pas in his awin contree agayne, as the maner was that tyme.

      And in siklyke maner left Ethiope Egipt, and come in Grece, for the
plagis þat fell on it.

      And gif ony wald oppone to vs þat we ar cummyn of Egipt of the ta syde
quhilk oppressit the barnis of Israel, that argewis nocht vs the wers tharfore.
50 For rycht sa war Criste the wer þat come of Jowis, quhilk is nocht suthe.
Juxta illud:

      Sicut spina rosam sic genuit Judea Mariam.

      This forsaid Scota and Gayel war maryite togyddir in þe tyme þat þe
bairnes of Israell passyt in þe Reide See, and þe dede of King Pharao þat
45 gouernyt þe land of Egipte. And, for þai saw þe cruele plage þat come ouer
Egipt, þai decretit to pas with þair folk þat þai brocht of Grece, and monye of
Egipte, for to seik woid landis, and to inhabyte þame. For he wald nocht pase
in his cuntre agane, as þe maner was þat tyme.

      And gyf ony wald saye tyll vs þat we ar cummyn of Egipt of þe ta syde
50 quhilk oppressyt þe bairnes of Israell, argue us nocht with þe werst. For rycht
sa come Christ of þe Jowes. *Versus*:

      ˌ*Sicut spina rosam genuit Judea Mariam.*   **f.300r**

      This forsaid Scota & Gathelos war spousit togiddir quhen at þe barnis of
35 Israell past in þe Reid Se. And eftir þe deces of King Pharo, þai gouernit þe
land of Egipt. And for þai saw & wnderstud þe felloun plagis þat come on
Egipt, þai tuke purpos and decretit to pas with þe folk þat þai had of Grece &
Egipt for to seike voide landis and inhabit þam. For he wald nocht pas in his
awne cuntre agane, as þe maner was þat tyme.
40   And gif ony wald say þat we ar cummyn of þe ta syd of þaim of Egipt þat
oppressit þe barnis of Israell, luf ws nocht þe wer þarfor. For þai war ay lele
amangis þaimself. For Jhesu Crist was borne of Jowis.

And als full worthy men mony ar cummyn of the traytouris of Troye.

And als suppos þat thai persewit the barnis of Israel, ʒit thai ressauit Crist
55   in Egipt and nurist him nere vii ʒeris, quhen the generacioun of the samyn
barnis persewit him to the dede and at the last hangit him.

This Gayell and Scota with thair folk past out of Egipt with grete richess
and mony schippis. And be the maist force, thai war lordis and gentillmen
þat past with thame. And first thai arrivit in Affrik and remaynit thare xl ʒere
60   in grete were and vexacioun. Becaus þat thai decretit to inhabyte void landis,
lyke as thai war counseilit be thair pagane goddis, tharefore thai turnyt thyne
and past the Strater of Jupiter, and at the last come in Spanʒe and arryvit in
Portyngale, quhilk ʒit has the name of Gayell, oure forefader, and is callit
Portyng Gayell.

And alsua full worthye men ar cummyn of þe traytouris of Troye.

And suppoise þat þai persuyte þe bairnis of Israell, þai resauyte Christ
55   into Egipt and nurest him ner sevin ʒer, quhen þe generatioun of þe samyn
bairnis persuyt him to þe ded, and at þe last þai crucifyte him.

This Gayele and Scota with þair folk passyt out of Egipt with gret riches
and mony schippis. And be þe maist part, þai war lordis and gentillmen þat
passyt with þame. And first þai arifyt in Aufrice and remanyt þarin fourty ʒeiris
60   in gret weir and wexatioun. And because þai drecretyt to inhabyt woid landis,
as þai [war] consalyt be þair pagan goddis, and son eftir þat, þai ternyt þin and
passyt þe [R]ase of Jubiter, and at þe last þai come into Spaynʒee and aryfyt in
Portingale, þe quhilk has ʒit þe name of Gayele, our foirfadir.

Suppos þai persauit þe barnis of Israell, þai resauit Crist in Egipt
and nurist him ner vii ʒer, quhill þe generacioun of þe samyn ͺbarnis   f.94r
45   persewit Crist to þe deid and crucifyed him.

This Gathelos and Scota passit with þar folk out of Egipt and mony gret
gentillis with þaim with gret riches and mony michti schippis. And þe mast
part war lordis and gentillis þat passit with þaim. And first þai aryvit in
Affrica and remanit þar xl ʒeris with mekle weir & wexacioun. And becaus
50   þai desyrit and had concludit to seike voide landis and inhabit as þai war
counsalit be þar pagane goddis, tharfor þai rasit þar folkis with þar schippis
and past þe Rais of Jubiter, and at þe last þai come in Spanʒe and aryvit in
Portingale, quhilk has name of Gathele, our forfader.

65 And efter, thai come in Navarn and Wisbayn and resydit on the ryuer of
Hyber, quhare Gayell gat on Scota Hyber-Scot. Quham Gayell, quhen he
come to age, send this Hiber his sone till it þat now is callit Ireland. And he
fand it vakand, savand a certane of gyandis, quhilkis he destroyit, and
inhabyte the land, and callit it efter his moder, Scota, Scocia. Quhilk ʒit in
70 all croniclis and storyes is callit Scocia Maior, vnto the tyme þat sum
part of vs come out of it, in oure Scotland, ˌþat now is, and inhabyte **f.20r**
it and was callit Less Scotland. And than was it þat was callit Scocia
Major begouthe to be callit Ybernia efter this foresaid Yber-Scot.
 Sa þat oure nacioun and oure name was foundit, and oure land inhabyte
75 lang tyme before þat Troy was destroyit and lang or Brute was borne, thouch
thai maid na nacioun quhill lang efter þat Brut come in oure ile, þat he efter
callit Britane, quhilk was neuer callit Britane, bot to the Scottis See, and
nocht be north it.

 And eftir þat, þai come into Itavern of Biscaye and duelt apon þe ryver of
65 Ibir, quhar he gat on Scota Iber-Scot. And quhen Iber come to eild, Gayele
send him in þat cuntre þat nowe is callit Irland, and fand it vakande, bot of a
certane of gewictis, þe quhilk he distroyt, and inhabyt þat land, and callit it
eftir his modir, Scota, Scotia. Þe quhilk is in ald cronyclis and storyes is callit
Scotia Maior to þe tyme þat sum part of ws come out of it in our Scotland, þat
70 now is inhybyt, and it was callyt Scotia Minor. And þan Scotia Maior
begowth to be callyt Ibernia eftir þis said Iber-Scot.
 And þan our name was foundyt and our land inhabyt lang tyme on to
Troye was distroyt, and or Brutus was borne. And syne lang eftir þat,
come Brutus in our ˌile, and callit it Britan, þe quhilk was neuir callit **f.300v**
75 Bertan, bot to þe Scottis See, and nocht be northe.

 And eftir þat, þai come in Nawarne & Beskay and duelt apon þe rever of
55 Olor, and syne in þat cuntre þat now is callit Irland, and fande it voide and
fand in it a certane of giandis quhilkis he distroyit and inhabit þe land callit
eftir Scota, Scocia Maior, vnto þe tyme þat part of ws come out of it in our
Scotland, þat now is inhabit and was callit Scocia Minor. And þan Scocia
Maior begouth to be callit Ybernia of þis said Iber-Scot.
60 Sa our nacioun and our name was foundit and our land inhabit lang tyme
or Troye was distroyit and or Brutus was borne. And sa lang tyme eftir come
Brute in our land and callit it Brettane, bot to þe Scottis Sey.

For be north it duelt neuer Brytoun, na it was neuer subject to na
80   Britouns, na to Romanis, na ȝit to nane othir nacioun. *Juxta illud*:

> *Scocia Romanis vi, metu vernula uanis*
> *Non fuit ex euo, nec subit imperio.*

Sen the first þat come out of Mare Scotland in the Less þat now is ouris,
be the grace of God, was ane callit Rothay, efter quham is callit sensyne the
85   Ile and the Castell of Rosay, and But is callit of Sanct Brandano.

And we war neuir subgectis to þe Britons, no to Ramanis, no to nane oþir
natioun fra Scottis See northe.

> *Scotia Romanis vi, metu subdita vanis*
> *Non fuit ex [ev]o, nec paret imperio.*

80   Alsua þe first þat come of Mar Scotland in þe Lesse þat now is ouris, be
þe grace of God, was callyt Rathus Rothia, eftir quhom is callit þe Ile and þe
Castell of Rothissaye, quhilk now is callit Bute eftir Saynte Brandan.

And northehalf þe Scottis Se duelt neuir Brettone, nor was subject to
Bretonnis, nor to Romanis, nor to nane vþir nacioun fra þe Scottis Se north.
65   Item: Þe first þat come out of Mair Scotland in þe Les Scotland
þat now ̣is ouris, be þe grace of God, was ane callit Ethios Rothay,   **f.94v**
eftir quhom is callit þe Ile & þe Castell of Rothissaye, the quhilk is
now callit Bute eftir Sanct Brandane.

118

Syne come thare ane othir callit Symon Brek and inhabyte in oure
Scotland or Brute come in the north partis and the ilis. Syne come Brut and
inhabyte in the south partis, and sa remaynit lang tyme, vnto the tyme of the
Pechtis, þat thai come, quhilkis war chassit out of thair land callit Scithia be
90   a prince of Egipt callit Agenor, and thai come in xxx schippis, but wommen,
and come to Scottis in Ireland, and askit at thame land to duell on. And thai
denyit thame, bot thai counsailit thame to pas to oure ile þat was nocht sa
inhabyte as thair was, & thai suld help thame, gif ony wald gaynstand, and sa
thai did. And becaus thai had na wommen, thai gave thame wedowis and
95   maidins to mak generacioun. Sa the lave of the Pechtis come all of the
wommen of Scottis blude.

And syne þair come ane oþir callit Symon Brieke and inhabyt our Scotland
or Bruk come in þe north partis and in þe ile. Syne come Bructe and inhabyt
85   þe south partis, and sa remanyt lang tym, tyll þe tyme þat þe Pechtis come, for
þai [war] chasyt out of þair awin landis callit Sithia be ane prynce of Egipt callit
Agenor, and þai in thretye schippis, but wemen, & come in Scottis Irland, and
askit at þame land to duell apon. And þai denyit þame, bot þai consalyt þame
to pas in our ile, þe Lesse Scotland, þat was nocht sa weill inhabytyt as þair, and
90   þai suld help þame gyf ony wald aganestand þam, and sa þai dide. And
because þai [war] all men, and had na wemen, þai gaif þame wedois and
madynnis to mak generatioun. And þe lufe of þe Pechtis come be lufe of þe
wemen of Scottis blude.

Of þat ilk, syne come ane noþir callit Symon Surke and inhabit our
70   Scotland or Brute come in þe north partis, and sa remanit lang tymes quhill
þe tyme þat þe Pictis come, quhilk was chasit out of þar awn land callit Sythia
be a prince of Egipt callit Ogenere, and þai come in a navyne thretty schippis
full of men, but women, and aryvit in Scotland Maior, and askit at þe Scottis
land to duell apon. And þai denyit and wald gif þaim nane nor lat þaim mak
75   in þat cuntre ony residence, bot counsalit þaim to cum in Les Scotland, quhilk
was nocht sa inhabit as was Mair Scotland now callit Irland. And þai suld
help þaim gif ony wald ganestand þaim to entre. And becaus þai war desolate
of women, thai deliuerit to þaim ane certane of wedowis and madinnis to mak
generacioun with and multiplie þe cuntre. And sa þe Pictis gat ennteres and
80   fauouris in þis cuntre throw þe women þat þai brocht with þaim out of
Scotland Maior, quhilkis war of blude till ourself.

And lang tyme efter þat thai come in oure Scotland, thai multiplyit
gretely, & begouth to contempne oure Scottis þat duelt thare before,   **f.20v**
and thame þat come oure to thame. And this was tald to the prince of
100   Grete Scotland, and thai war gretly movit thareat. And than the kingis sone,
callit Fergus Feradach, tuke a grete powere of Scottis, and come in oure
Scotland, and tuke the croune of it, and brocht in the armes of Scotland. & he
was the first King of Lytill Scotland. *Juxta illud*:

> *Albion in terris rex primus germine Scot[u]s*
> 105   *Illorum turmis rubri tulit arma leonis*
> *Fergusius fuluo Farchard rugientis in aruo.*
> *Christum tercentis terdenis prefuit annis.*

And lang tyme eftir, þai come in our Scotland and multiplyt greitlye, and
95   begowth to contempin our Scottis þat duelt þair befor. And þis was [tald] to
prince of Gret Scotland, and he was greitlye amufyt þairat. And þan þe
kingis sone, callit Ferguse Farchar, tuk ane gret power of men, and come   **f.301r**
in our Scotland, and tuke þe crovn of it, and brocht in þe armis of
Scotland, þe quhilk is a reide rampand leon in ane scheild of gold. *Versus*:

> 100   *Albioun in terris rex primus germine Scotus*
> *Ipsorum turmis rubri tulit arma leonis*
> *Fergusius fuluo Farchar rug[i]entis in aruo.*
> *Christum tercentis terdenis prefuit annis.*

Syne þai multipliit gretlie and vsurpit apon ws Scottis men and did ws gret
scaith and thocht to put ws out of þe land. Quhilk was tald to þe prince of Gret
Scotland, and he was gretlie amovit þarat. And þan þe kingis son, callit to
85   name Fergus Ferherd, gadderit gret power of Scottis men, and come in
Les Scotland, and tuke þe crovne of it, and was our first king, and   **f.95r**
brocht þe armes of Scotland, the quhilk remanys ȝit ane red rampand
lyoun in a scheld of gold. *Versus*:

> *Albion in terris rex primus germine Scotus*
> 90   *Illorum turmas rubri tulit arma leonis*
> *Fergusius fuluo Ferherd rugientis in aruo.*
> *Liliger llle leo rosidus nunc pingitur auro.*
> *Christum tercentis terdenis prefuit annis.*

120

And sensyne failȝeit neuer kingis in oure Scotland, to this day, of his blude rycht lyne doune to oure souerane lord þat now is, quhilk God kepe and *110* pres[er]ue. Na fra Gayell, oure first king, to the said Fergus, quhilk amountis to nere vi skore of kingis, na neuer strangeare regnyt on vs na had dominacioun.

Sett Arthure that tyrant maid vs were agayne his faith and alye. For before him iiii or v kingis, efter that the Romanis subjectit the Britones, made *115* alye with vs for to help thame agayne the Romanes, quhilk we did, and oft had the victory agayne thame and quhilis had the were. Bot we occupiit the Romanes sa þat we gert thame big twa wallis fra the Est See to the West See to kepe vs fra the Britones þat thai subjectit.

And sensyne failȝit neuir king in our Scotland, to þis day, of richt lyne *105* doune to our souirane lord þat now is king, þe quhilk God kepe. Na ȝit fra Gayele, our fyrst king, to þe said Ferguse, þe quhilk nowmir cummis neir to sax scoir of kingis, na neuir strangeare rignyt on ws na ȝit had dominatioun.

Suppose þat Arthur þe tyran maid wer one ws agane his fayth and alia, *110* for befor him four or fyfe kingis, eftir þat þe Romans subjeckit þe Britons, maid alia with ws to helpe þame agane þe Romans, þe quhilk we dide, and eftir had þe wictory agane þame, and quhil had þe wer, and sa we occupyt þe Romans at we gert þam byg twa wallis fra þe Est See to þe West See to kepe ws fra þe Britons þat þai subjeckit.

And sensyne neuir falȝeit king of þat blud fra þe rigne and þe crovne of *95* Scotland, nor nevir war depryvit, bot has remanit be richt lyne discendand ay dovne fra þe said Fergus till our souerane lord James þe Fyft þat now is, quhom Almychti God conserf. Nor fra Gathele our first progenitor till þe said Fergus, the quhilk novmer of kingis cummis to vi^{xx}, nor neuir stranger rang on ws nor had dominacioun of ws.

100 Suppos Arthur þat tyrand maid weir on ws aganis his faith and promys, and eftir þat þe Romanis dantit þe Brettonnis, þai allyit þaim with ws till helpe þaim agane þe Romanis. The quhilk we held & kepit and wor apon þe Romanis and occupiit þaim sa þat we gart þaim big twa wallis fra þe Est Se to þe West Se to kepe ws fra þe Brettanis þat þai dantit and wan on fors.

And we brak thame ay doune, and slew thair Emperour Seuerus at 3ork,
120 and gaynstude in all Julius Cesar, Claudius, and Waspasiane, quhilk wald
have subjectit vs as thai did the Britones. And for to tell all the process of
this, it war to lang.

Bot this Arthur, nocht agaynstanding þat we & the Pechtis helpit the
Britones to pes, & put out the Romanes, than brak he his allye on vs, and
125 maid were on vs a quhile, and tuke the realme of Britane fra the
rychtwis airis – that was to say, Mordrede and Gawane, quhilkis war   f.21r
Loth of Louthyanis sonys, gottyn on ane of Arthuris sisteris of full
bed, the quhilk was maryit with the said Loth or Arthure was gottyn.

---

115 And we brak þame ay doune, and slew þair Empriour Severus at 3ork, &
aganstude in all thingis Julius Cesar, and Claudius, & Waspasius, Empriouris
of Rome, quhilk wald haf subjeckit ws as þai dide þe Britons. And for to tell
all þe process of þis, it war to lang.

Bot þis Arthur, nocht gaynstandand þat we and þe Pechtis helpyt
120 þe Britons to put out þe Romans, he brak his alya on ws, and maid   f.301v
wer on ws a quhile, & tuke þe rewm of Brytan in debbete resone fra
richtwis heir – þat is to say, Moldreid and Gawan, þat war Loth of Lowdianis
sonnys, gottyn on þe kingis dochtir & heir of Brytan, þe quhilk was Arthuris
sistir, and maryit with þe said Loth or Arthur was gottyn.

---

105 And we straik þaim ay dovne, and slewe þar empriour callit Seuerus at
3ork, and ganestude in all thing Julius Cesar, Claudius, and Vaspasius,
Empriouris of Rome, quhilkis wald haf dantit ws as þai did Brettonnis. Bot
to tell all þe proces of þis, it war to lang.

Bot þis Arthour, nocht ganstanding quhilkis we & þe Pictis helpit   f.95v
110 him and þe Brittonnis to put out þe Romanis quhen þe Romanis had
dantit þaim & wtterly destroyed, had nocht bene our suple, falslie he brak his
allia till ws, and maid weir on ws a quhile, and tuke to him fra þe richtuis air
the crovne of Brettane – that is to say, fra Mordred and Gawane, quhilkis war
Schir Loth of Lothianis sonnis, gottin apon þe kingis dochter and air of
115 Brettan, quhilk was Arthuris sister & mariit with þe said Loth or Arthour was
borne.

And becaus þat the aire of Britane was maryit with a Scottis man,
130 quhen the kynryk vakit, & Arthure was xv ʒeris ald, thay maid him king,
be the devilry of Merlyn. The quhilk Arthur was gottyn on ane othir
mannis wyf be the Duk of Cornwell, Vter. And sa was Arthur, spurius &
a huris sone, sauf reverence, maid a king, and Mordrede, the sone of Loth
of Louthiane, þat was rychtwys aire, for he was Scottis, & was putt by
135 [agayne] his rycht.

The quhilk Mordrede, quhen Arthure was out in his tyrandiis, be all the
statis of Britones and Scottis, was had to London and crownyt for King of
Britones, and in his rychtwis querele, he slew this Arthure, and he him, as
the Brute sais.

---

125 And becaus at þe heir of Brytan was maryit with ane Scottis man quhen
þe kinrik wakit, and Arthur was xv ʒer ald, þe Brytannis maid him king, be
þe devilrie of Merlynge. & þis Arthur was gottyn on ane oþir mannis wiffe,
þe Duc of Carnele. And sa was Arthur spurius, þat is bastard, and ane huris
sone, saife revirence, and maid king, but nocht of law, and Moldreid þe
130 sone of Loth of Lowdian þat was richtwis heir, he was put by.

The said Moldreid, quhen þat Arthur was out of þe cuntre in his
tyraneale, þe estaitis of Brytan & Scottis had him to London & crownyt him
King of Brytan, and syne in his richtwis quierlye slew þis Arthur, and he
him, as þe Brute sais.

And becaus þe air of Brettane was mariit with a Scottis man, and þe
kinrik was fallyn throu werray richt in a Scottis mannis handis, and
Brettane voide of air male, and þis Arthour was xv ʒeris ald, þe Brettonnis
120 maid him king throw þe devilry of Merlyne. This Arthour was gottin apon
ane noþir mannis wyf, þe Duke of Cornwellis spous, and was neuir able to
ane crovne, for he was þe son of adultry. And þir fals Brettonnis be þis
caus bure by Mordred, þar richtuis air & werray wndowtable king.

The quhilk Mordred, quhen Arthour was out of þe cuntre in his
125 tyrandry, he gadderit all þe estatis and Scottis men to Londoun & schew
þaim his richt, and þar awysitly þe Brettonnis chesit him king and crovnit
him incontinent. And in his richtuis querell & defence, he slewe þis
Arthour and Arthur him, as Brute says.

140　　　And the King of Scotland, þat than was callit Sorane, send his ost of Scottis
men with Mordrede agaynis Arthur – a way becaus of Mordredis rycht, and ane
othir way becaus Arthure maid were on him and brak his allye.

For fra the Romanes subject the Britones and nocht vs, euer the Britones
war contrary to vs and wald haue put vs out of this ile or ellis subjectit vs as
145　　thai war. Bot with the help of God, we and the Pechtis agaynstud thame sa
and the Romanis, þat the Romanes war fayne for to leve thame, quhen thai
and thai had maid were on vs iii^c ʒere. Sa þat the Britones war oure naturale
inymyis vnto the tyme þat thai maid allye with vs, quhilk this Arthur brak.
Bot efter his dede it was euer ʒit wele kepit, and trew frendschip to this day.

135　　　And þe King of Scotland, þat þan was callyt Goran, send his ost of Scottis
men with Moldreid agane Arthur – a way because of Moldredis richt, and ane
oþir way because þat Arthur maid were on him, and brak his alia.

For fra þe Romans subjeckit þe Brytons and nocht ws, þe Brytannis was
contrar and wald haif put ws out of þis alia or subject ws as þai war. Bot be
140　　þe help of God, we and þe Pechtis gaynstude þame, sa þat þe Romans
　was fayne to lefe þam, quhen þai & þai maid wer on ws thre hundir　**f.302r**
ʒeir. Sa þat þe Britannis war our naturall enemys to þe tyme þai maid
alia with ws, þe quhilk þis Arthur brak. Bot eftir his dede, it was euir weill
kepit, and ay trew frendschip betuyx ws and þe Brytannis to þis day.

And Gorane, þat tyme King of Scotland, send his ost of Scottis men with
130　　Mordred aganis Arthour – allway becaus of Mordredis richt, and ane
noþir way becaus ˌArthur falsly, agane his allya and band maid betuix　**f.96r**
ws and him, maid weir on ws.

For fra we had maide him in pece of his enemys, he with þe Brettanis rais
apon ws and wald haue put ws out of our cuntre with þe suple þat he had of
135　　Romanis. Bot throu helpe of God, we and þe Pictis resistit þaim all in sic a
wys þat þai war fayne to ces. And quhen þai had maide weir on ws thre
hundreth ʒer, þai saw þai couth nocht wyn at ws. Thai war fayne till ally
þaim with ws. The quhilk allia was lang tyme weile conseruit & kepit vnto
þe tyme þis Arthur brak it. And sensyne to þis hour quhatsumeuer band we
140　　had of þaim, it was neuir wele kepit.

150   And sekirly thare is mekle thing said of this Arthur quhilk is nocht
suthe, & bot fenȝeit, as thai say þat he slew Frelle, King of Fraunce, and als
Lucius, the Procuratour of Rome. For in his dayes thare was nane
sik, ᷓas all storyes of Fraunce beris witnes. And sik mony othir   **f.21v**
[l]esynes ar maid of him, as Maister Walter Maple fenȝeit in his
155   buke of ane callit Lanslot [of] the Lake.

    And in this cruell were þat we and the Pechtis maid in oure defens agayne
the Romaynes and Britones, quhen þat the Romaynes had left thame, than
Wortiger, þat falsly vsurpit the croune of Britones, quhen he mycht nocht
gaynstand vs, he callit in his supplee the fals Saxones, quhilkis bakkit vs
160   mekle, and before Arthure. The quhilk Saxones has remaynit euer still in this
ile sensyne, and in the tyme of Arthur & agayn his will.

---

145   And þar is mekill thing said of þis Arthur, þe quhilk is nocht suth, bot
fenȝit thing. Þai say þat he slew Stallo, þe King of France, and Sir Lucius,
Procuratour of Rome. And in his dais þar was nane sic. And mony oþir
lesyngis ar maid of him, as Maistir Walter Napillis fenȝit in his buke of him,
callyt Lancilot de Lac, bot all þe storyis of France beris witnes in þe contrare.
150   And in þis cruell wer þat we and þe Pechtis maid in our defence agane þe
Romans & Brytannis, quhen þe Romans and þe Brytannis had maid Vorage
King of Brytannis, þat falsly vsurpyt þe crovn of Brytannis, quhen þai mycht
nocht gaynstand ws, þan callit he in help þe fals Saxions, þe quhilk wexit our
land mekill befor Arthuris dais, and euir sensyne has remanyt in þe land, and
155   als in þe tyme of Arthur agane his will.

    And suppos fenȝeouris sayis þis Arthour did gret cruelte in diuers landis
and maid gret conquest, as Master Walter Mapill fenȝeit of him in his
wryting, of þe quhilk þe story beris witnes in þe contrar.

    And [in] þis cruell wer, we and þe Pictis maide sa forsy defence aganis
145   baith Romanis and Brettonnis quhen þis Arthour had falsly vsurpit þe crovne
of Brettane þat þai mycht nocht ganestand ws. Than callit he in helpe of þe
fals Saxonis, quhilk Saxonis wexit our land mekle with Arthour. And in þe
suple of him nochtwithstanding, we put þaim furth scharply. And syne þai
remanit still in Brettane in contrar Arthur and all þat he couth do.

Tharfore it is nocht lyke þat he conquest xxx realmys, þat in his awin proper realme mycht nocht putt out the Saxonis, quhilkis euer maid him were. And quhen thir Saxones war rutit in the land, and bundyn to the Britones and suorne fully, thai brak thair faith and rais agayne thame, and at the last put thame out of the land, the process of the quhilk war lang for to tell.

165

And efter this thare fell a discord betuix vs and the Pechtis, and efter lang were, we putt thame vtterly out of the land for euer be oure king, Kenneth Makalpyne, the quhilk was done vii^c ʒere syne. Sa remaynit the Saxones in the south, & we in the north ay vnto the tyme þat the Danys subject the Saxones, & regnyt on thame wele xxx ʒere.

170

Þarfore it is nocht lyk þat he conquest xxx kingis þat in his awin mycht nocht put out þe Saxons, þe quhilk euir maid him wer. And quhen þe Saxons war rutyt in þe land, and bundyn to þe Brytannis, & sworne falsly, þai brak þar fayth, and rase agane þame, and at þe last put þame out of þe land, of þe quhilk þe proces war lang to wryte; þarfor I man be schort. And þai may be callyt *serpens in gremio, mus in pera, ignis in sinu.*

160

And eftir þis þar fell ane discord betuyx ws and þe Pechtis, and we warrayt on þame lang tyme, and put þame out vtralye of þe land of Scotland, be our king, Kenauthe Makalpyn, þe quhilk was done sewyn hundir ʒeir syne, þat is to say, þe ʒeir of our Lord, aucht hundir xxx and od ˌʒeiris. And sa   f.302v remanyt þe Saxons in þe south, and we in þe north, to þe tyme þat þe Danys subjeckit þe Saxons and rygnyt on þame xx ʒeir.

165

150

And sa it semys nocht to be suth þat he suld conques in ˌhis tyme   f.96v xxx kinrikis that mycht nocht put owt of his awne land þe Saxonis quhilkis lete him neuir sit a daye in pece, quhill þe Saxonis war falslie sworne to þe Bretonnis and bundyn to þam, for þai brak þar faith and rais agane þam and at þe last put þaim out of þe land, of þe quhilk þe proces war lang to wryte. Tharfor I will intromet no forther þarwith. Bot þai may be wele callit *serpens in gremio.*

155

And eftir þat, þar fell ane discord betuix ws and þe Pictis, quharthrou þar rais ane gret weir and lestit lang tyme, quhill at þe last we put þam out of our land of Scotland be our king, Kenneth McCalpyne, the quhilk was done sevyne hundreth ʒeris syne. And sa remanit þe Saxonis in þe south part & we in þe north vnto þe tyme þat þe Danys dantit þe Saxonis and regnit on þaim thretty ʒeir.

160

And syne come William Bastard, and put out the Danys and mony of the
Saxones, and haldis the land as ȝit, the quhilk of grund-rycht suld be the
Kingis of Scotland, be the rycht of Sanct Margaret, the quhilk was Edmound
Irnesydis sonis douchter, the quhilk Edmund was vndoutit King of Ingland.
For suthe it is, a bastard may nocht succede, the veray airis lyfand.

And sa the Pechtis put out be the Scottis, and the Britones be the
Saxones, and syne ͵the Saxones be the Danys, and the Danys be the   f.22r
Bastard. Sa remaynis the ile now occupyit with the Scottis anerly in
Scotland, and with the Normandis & Inglis in Ingland, to this day.

And syne come Wilȝam, Bastard of Normondy, þe Duke of Normondis
bastard sone, and put out þe Danys and mony of þe Saxons, and held þe land
ȝit, þe quhilk of grond-rycht suld be þe Kingis of Scottis be þe rycht of
Edmond Irnsidis sonnys dochtir, Sanct Mergreit, þat was maryit with þe King
of Scottis, callyt Macolm Chanmar, fra þe quhilk þar is discendit lyne be
lyne, till our king þat now is. And [þis] Edmond Irnsidis was wnweddit King
of Ingland. And it is suth þat a bastard may nocht succeid till heritage, þe
heir beand on lyfe.

Alsa þe Pechtis war put out be þe Scottis, and þe Brytannis be þe Saxons,
and syne þe Saxons and þe Danys be þe Bastard of Normondis, and sa
remanys þe ile alanerly occupyt nowe be þe Scottis men in Scotland, and with
Normans and Inglismen in Ingland, to þis day.

And syne [come] Willam Bastard, þe Duke of Normondys bastard son,
and put þe Danis & mony of þe Saxonis out of Brettane, and haldis þat land
as ȝit, quhilk of ground-rycht suld be þe King of Scotlandis throw þe titill and
richt of Edmond Irnsydis sonnis dochter, the quilk was mariit with a King of
Scotland callit Malcome Canmor, callit to name Sanct Margaret, fra þe quhilk
is discendit lyne be lyne our souerane lord þat now is. And þis Edmond
Irnsyd was richtuis King of Yngland. Item: it is suth and just law þat
a bastard may ͵nocht succeid, þe werray air beand on lyf.   f.97r
And þus war þe Pictis werely put out be ws Scottis, and þe
Brettonnis [be] þe Saxonis, and þe Saxonis be þe Danys, and þe Danis be þe
Bastard of Normondye. And sa remanis þe ile allanerlie occupiit with ws
Scottis in Scotland, and Normandis in Yngland, to þis day.

And suppos þat Scotland was lang vexit with were be diuers naciouns –
that is to say, Romanos, Britones, Saxones, Danys, Norwais, Gothis, Pechtis,
and Inglis. Neuertheles thai war put out euer be Scottis be cruell bataillis and
be na morn slepis. *Juxta illud*:

185
Poſt Britones, Noricos, Dacos, Anglos, quoque Pictos,
Necnon Romanos bellica sudore repulsos,
Nobiliter Scoti jus tenuere suum.

180
Suppose þat Scotland was lang tyme wexit with wer of diuers natioun –
þat is to say, Romans, Brytannis, Saxons, Danys, Norweis, Pechtis, Gotis, and
Inglismen. Neuirþeles þai war put out euir be Scottis, be cruele force of
batell, and be na morne slepis.

Post Brytones, Moricos, Adacos, Pictos, & Anglosque,
185
Necnon Romanos belli sudore repulsos,
Nobiliter Scoti jus tenuere suum.

And suppos Scotland was langtyme wexit with weir of diuers nacionis –
175
that is to say, Romanis, Brettonnis, Saxonis, Danys, Pictis, and Normannis.
Neuirþeles we Scottis men put þaim ay out throu cruell force and batell and
with na morne slepis.

Sa þat we may say this *in veritate*: þat there is na land nor ȝit nacioun þat
is nor was fra the begynnyng of the warld þat standis in fredome sa lang tyme
190 – that is to say auchtene hunder ȝere and mare vnconquest or subject till ony
strange nacioun or king, as we do, bot euer vnder oure awin king, of oure
awin blude, rycht lyne descendand fra oure first King Fergus before said, till
him þat now regnis, quham God sauff.

And gif thir fals Inglis wald say þat sumtyme oure kingis obeyit to the
195 Inglis kingis and maid fewtee, suthe it is, bot nocht for Scotland, bot for the
landis þat thai held of him in Ingland, lyke as the Inglis king held and suld
hald of the King of Fraunce his landis þat he has and had in France.

Sa þat we may say þis day in veryte þat þar is na land, no na natioun sa fre
fra þe begynnyng of þe warld, na has standyn sa lang tyme in fredome as has
þe Scottis – for þai hafe beyne xviii hundir ȝeiris and mar vnconquest, and
190 neuir was subjeckit to na natioun or king to þis day, bot euir vndir our
awin king of our awin blude be rycht lyne discendand fra our first king, f.303r
Ferguse befor said, to him þat now rygnys, quhome God keip.

And gyf þir fals Inglismen wald say þat sumtyme our king aliyt to þar
Inglis king, and maid fewtee to þame, gyf þat be suth, it was nocht for þe
195 Kinryk of Scotland, þe quhilk þe worthye King of Scottis brukit of rychtwise
tytill mony ȝeir before þat Inglismen or Brytannis come in þis ile, bot for þe
landis þat þai held of him in Ingland, rycht as þe Inglis king held & suld hald
of þe King of France þe land þat he has & had in France.

Sa þat we may say þis day be werray suthfastnes: þar was neuir land
nor is no land nor nacioun so fre bygane of all þe warld, nor has standing
180 so lang tyme in fredome as we Scottis in Scotland – for we haue bene xviii
hundret ȝeir inconquest, nor neuir was dantit be no nacioun of strange
cuntre or king to þis daye, bot evir wnder our kingis of richt lyne
discendand fra Gathele & Scota, first inhabitaris of þis land, and fra Fergus
forsaid till our souerane lord þat ryngis now present, quhom God kepe and
185 conserf.

And gif þe fa[l]s Ynglismen will say þat our king was sumtyme allyit to
þe King of Yngland and maid fewte to him, gif þat was suth, it was nocht for
þe Kinrik of Scotland. The quhilk þe worthy Kingis of Scottis brukit on
richtuis titill mony ȝeris befor or Inglis or Brettonis come in þat ile,
190 bot for þe landis ˏthai held of him in Yngland, richt as þe Ynglis king f.97v
held and suld hald of þe King of Fraunce.

129

And gif ony wald say þat Fraunce has standyn langar vnconquest, it is
wele wittyn þat Gallia, þat now is Fraunce, war lang tyme tributaris to
200 Romaynes, and thare was diuers kingis of thame. And syne come the
Franchis and optenyt Gallia. Bot within this a m ʒere, the story hereof war
lang to rehers, and of all othir naciouns, thair subjectioun, the
conquest, the changeing ‸of kingis, as the cronyclis can schaw in   f.22v
thameself.
205 And of this xviii^c ʒere þat we haue regnyt in this land, we war neuer iii^c
ʒeris in verray pes, bot ay pressit and persewit with thir naciouns foresaid,
and ʒit langest with thir Normandis, now calland thame Inglis.

Alsa, gyf ony of þame wald say þat France has standyn lang tym
200 vnconquest, it is weill wrytyn be ald croniclis þat Gallica, þat now is callyt
France, was lang tyme tributaris to Romans, and war kingis of it, and sensyne
come doune þe Franche king, and optenyt France. Bot within þir thousand
ʒeris, þe storye hereof war lang to rehers, & of oþir natiounis, subjectionis,
and conquestis, & changis of kingis, þe quhilk I couth schaw and I had tym
205 and oportunyte.
Alsa, ʒe sall wit þat of þis thousand and viii hundir ʒeris þat we Scottis
has rignyt in þis land, we war neuir thre hundir ʒer in pese, bot ay presyt with
þe nationis befor said, & langast with þir Romans, now calland þame
Inglismen.

Item: Gif ony of þaim wald say þat Fraunce stud lang tyme vnconquest,
it is wele wittin be ald cornikillis that Galloy, þat now is callit Fraunce, was
lang tyme trybuteris to þe Romanis, and war king of it. And syne come a
195 Romane dovne and optenit Fraunce and was king of it. Bot within þis
thousand ʒer, þe story herof war lang to tell and of all vþir nacionis, þar
subjectionis, conquest, & changi[s].
Item: ʒe sall wit of þis thousand and viii hundreth ʒeir that we Scottis has
regnit in þis land of Scotland. Of þe quhilk tyme we war neuir thre hundreth
200 ʒeir in pece, bot ay wexit with vþir nacionis, as is forsaid, and langast be þe
Romanis, now callit Ynglismen.

130

And thair land callit Anglia fra a contree of Almane in Saxone callit Anglalus, of the quhilk sumtyme thai war callit Anglici or Angli, *ab Angulo*.

210 Now, *Veritas non querit Angulos nec Anglos*. Tharfore may thai neuer be trew þat come *de Angulo*.

And now the Normannis has tane thair name and thair falshede togiddir. And na wonder is, for thair king is cummyn doune rycht lyne fra the Devill, lyke as thair awin cronycle of Ingland, callit *Policronicon*, beris witnes. For

215 Henricus the Secund þat slew Sanct Thomas of Canterbery, þat was the empericis sone, the quhilk emperice was weddit to the Erle of Dagan, and he gat on hir this Henry the Tyrane, the quhilk erle was bot the secund fra the Devill.

---

210 And þis forsaid land callyt Anglia is said fra a cuntre in Almanȝe callyt Angulus, of þe quhilk sumtyme þai war callyt Anglici or Anguli, fra Angulo. *Sed veritas non quærit Angulos juxta veritatem Evangelii.* Þairfor þai may neuir be trew þat þat come fra Anglulo.

And now þe Romans has tane þair name and þar falshed togyddir. And

215 it is na wondir for þar king is cummyn doune lyne be lyne fra þe Devill, as ald cronyclis of Ingland beris witnes, callyt *Policronicon*.   **f.303v**
It beris witnes of Henry þe Secund, þat slew Sanct Thomas of Cantirbery, þat was þe emprice sone, þe quhilk emprice was weddit with þe Erle of Angean, and he gat on hir þis Henry þe Tyrand, þe quhilk erle was þe

220 secund fra þe Devill, as ald croniclis beris witnes.

And þar land is callit Anglia be ane cuntre in Almane callit Anglius, of þe quhilk þai ar callit Anglici o[r] Angli, *ab Anglo*. *Vnde auctoritas juxta dictum euangelium: Weritas non querit Anglos*. Tharfor þai may neuir be

205 trew þat come *ab Anglo*.

And now þe Romanis has tane þar name & falsnes togidder. And euery man wnderstud genologi of Ynglismen, þar suld few wounder of þam. Suppos þai be werray fals, and þar caus quhy: þar king is cummyn dovne lyne be lyne fra þe Devill, as þar awne cronikle callit *Policornica*

210 proportis and beris witnes of Henry þe Secund that slew Sanct   **f.98r**
Thomas of Canterbery, þat was þe emprys son, the quhilk emprice was weddit with þe Erll of Angeos, and he gat apon hir þis Henry þe Tyrand, the quhilk was secund fra þe Devill carnate, as þar awne ald writ beris witnes.

And all the kingis sensyne ar cummyn of him. The process and the maner
220   hereof I leve for lenth of tyme.

And in the samyn cronycle of Ingland, he sais þat this samyn Henricus,
quhen he was ȝong & nurist in the King of Franchis court, Sanct Bernard
prophecied of him, sayand, "*A Dyabo existi, et ad Dyabolum ibis.*"

And suppos thai mak lesyngis oft tymes of vs, in thair collaciouns, ȝit at
225   the leste, it þat thair awin cronycle beris witnes, we may say semys suthe.
And nocht anerly this, bot mony othir hundreth diuers thingis, quhilkis war
to lang to wryte in a pistil.

And all þe Kingis of Ingland sensyne ar cummyn of þat progenye. And
þe maner heirof is our lang to tell.

And in þe sammyn croniclis of Ingland, it is said þat þis Henry, quhen he
was ȝingir and nurysyt with þe King of France, Sanct Barnard maid prophesie
225   of him and said, "*A Diabolo existi et ad Diabolum ibis.*"

And suppose þat þai dispysit ws oftyme in þar colatiounis, ȝit at þe last,
as þar awin croniclis beris witnes, we may say suth of þame, bot nocht
alanerly þis, bot ane oþir hundir thingis, þe quhilk I couth schaw, bot it war
lang to wryt as now.

---

215   And all þe Kingis of Yngland sensyne ar discendit and cummyn dovne of
þe samyn tyrand.

And þe samyn cornikle of Yngland says that quhen þis said Henry tyrrand
was ane barne in tendirnes in his credill with þe King of Fraunce, Sanct
Bernard come & saw him and spak of him þis prophecye, sayand þus, "*A
220   Diabulo existi et ad Diabolum ibis.*"

And it þat þar awne writtis proportis of þam, how suld we contrar nocht
allanerlie of þis, bot a hundreth mar thingis of þe quhilkis ȝe sall heir
eftirwart of þar wikitnes? & to wryt all, it is to lang to wryt of now.

This is the nature of Inglismen: quhare euer thai mak straytest oblissing of faith and pes, thai dissaue thame erest, for sekerly thay kepe

230 neuer faith langar than thai may se ane opyn tyme of avantage to   **f.23r**
chape, and coueris thame with thair dedis with sophistry, and excusit
with fenȝeit falshede and fals colouris. And this did thai euer til vs all tymes
bygane, bot that suld thai nocht haue done and thai had bene trew.

For we gave thame first faith Cristyndome & doctrine of the Kirk, for we

235 war cristnyt before thame nere iiii^c ȝeris. *Juxta illud*:

> *Christi transactis tribus annis atque ducentis,*
> *Scocia catholicam cepit inire fidem.*

---

230 And trestis hardily þat þis is þe maner of þame: þat quhar euir þai mak
straitast oblysing of fayth & pese þai dissaife erast. For sikkirly þai kepe
neuir suth langir þan þai may see ane opyn tyme, and awantage and coulouris
all þar deidis with solphestry, & exquesyt fals fenȝit coulouris. And þis þai
did euir all tyme till ws, þe quhilk þai suld not haif done and þai had beyne

235 trewe.

For we gaif þame first Christyndome, & fayth & doctryne of Haly Kirk,
for we war chrystynyt befor þame, four hundir ȝeir and mair. *Versus*:

> *Christi transactis tribus annis atque ducentis*
> *Scotia catholicam cepit inire fidem.*

And sekerly this is þe maner of Ynglismen: that quhar þai mak stratest

225 obligacioun & band of pece, thar þai dissaif sonest, as þai haue done all tymes
bygane till ws. Thai kepit neuir langar trewis than þai mycht se apperance of
ony awantage, quhilk war nocht þar commoun and þai war trewe, as þai war
nevir, and had conscience, as þai haf nane.

For þai tuke at ws first faith and Crisendome and doctrine of Haly

230 Kirk, for we war cristinnit befor þaim four hundreth ȝeir and mair.   **f.98v**
Juxta illud metrice dictum:

> *Christi transactis tribus annis atque ducentis*
> *Scocia catholicam cepit inire fidem.*

And for all this thai kepe till vs the kyndenes þat thai schaw.

And in reuengeance of thair falsnes, a King of Scotland callit Gregore
240 subjectit thame to the water of Themes, mare than xxx ȝere, as thair awin
croniclare sais, William Malburrens:

> *Magna pars Danis, sed pars et maxima Scotis,*
> *Et pars Alfredo Regi sed parva remansit.*

> *Et hec de hec epistula explicit.*

---

240 And for all þis þai kepyt till ws þe kyndnes þat ȝe knowe.

& in þe revengeance of þar falshed, þe King of Scottis Gregour subjeckit
þame to þe watir of Temys mair þan xxx ȝeiris, þe quhilk þar awin
croniclis sais, callyt Wilȝam Mamrenence, sayand þis: **f.304r**

> *Magna pars Danys datur, sed maxima Scotis,*
> 245 *Et pars Affrido Regi sic parva remansit.*

Sic as þir I fynd in þar awin bukis, þe quhilk is þe mair autentice agane
þame. Amen.

And for all þis þai kepit till ws kyndnes as men wait in rememberance of
235 þar awne sorow and wengeance.

Ane King of Scotland callit Gregour dantit þam to þe watter of Themes
and held þam at our jurisdictioun mair than xxx ȝer, quhilk þar awne writ
beris witnes and proportis þe samyn.

Heir endis þis small tractact of þe Scottis Originale.

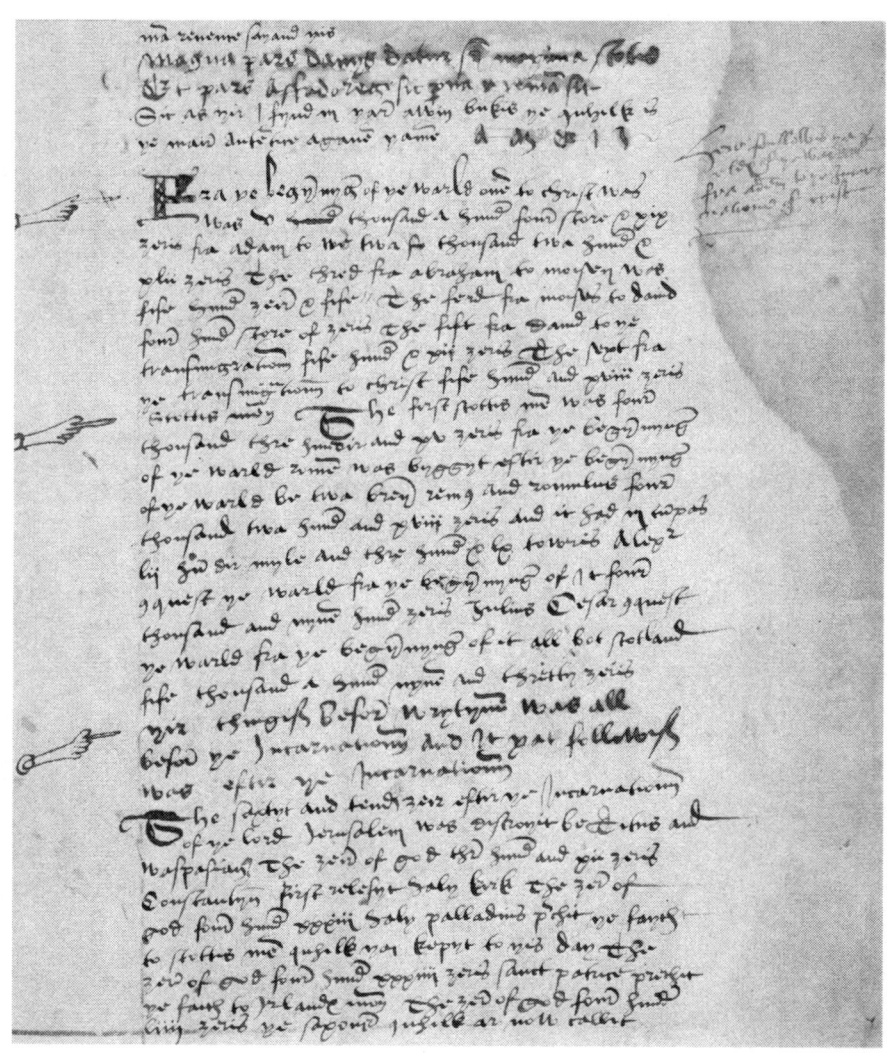

Folio 304r of BL MS Royal 17.D.xx. © The British Library Board.

136

THE CHRONICLE OF THE SCOTS

(THE SHORT CHRONICLE OF 1482)

from British Library MS Royal 17.D.xx

˻Fra þe begynnyng of þe warld one to Christ was v thousand, a   **f.304r**
hundir, four score, & xix ȝeris.

Fra Adam to Noe, twa thousand, twa hundir, & xlii ȝeris.

The thred, fra Abraham to Moisen, was fife hundir ȝeir & fife.

5   The ferd, fra Moises to Dauid, four hundir, score of ȝeris.

The fift, fra Dauid to þe Transmigratioun, fife hundir & xii ȝeris.

The sext, fra þe Transmigratioun to Christ, fife hundir and xviii ȝeris.

Scottis men: The first Scottis men was four thousand, thre hundir, and
xv ȝeris fra þe begynnyng of þe warld.

10   Rome was byggyt eftir þe begynnyng of þe warld be twa breþir, Remus
and Romulus, four thousand, twa hundir, and xviii ȝeris, and it had in
cumpas lii hundir myle and thre hundir & lx towris.

Alexander conquest þe warld fra þe begynnyng of it four thousand and
nyne hundir ȝeris.

15   Julius Cesar conquest þe warld fra þe begynnyng of it, all bot Scotland,
fife thousand, a hundir, nyne and thretty ȝeris.

Þir thingis befor wrytyne was all befor þe Incarnatioun, and it þat
followis was eftir þe Incarnatioun.

The saxtyt and tend ȝeir eftir þe Incarnatioun of þe Lord, Jerusalem was
20   distroyit be Titus and Waspasianus.

The ȝeir of God thre hundir and xii ȝeris, Constantyn first relesyt Haly
Kirk.

The ȝer of God four hundir xxxiii, haly Palladius prechit þe fayth to
Scottis men, quhilk þai kepyt to þis day.

137

25   The ʒer of God four hundir xxxiiii ʒeris, Sanct Patrice prechit þe faith
to Irlandis men.

    The ʒer of God four hundir liiii ʒeris, þe Saxons, quhilk ar
now callit Inglismen, with þar dukis Horse & Hengest, com in   **f.304v**
Brytan, quhar þan rignyt Vortigern king. And in þat tyme was
30   Merlyn.

    The ʒer of God fife hundir and xv ʒeris, Sanct Augustyne was send in
Ingland to preche þe fayth to þame.

    The ʒeir of God sevyn hundir lxi, þe relikis of Sanct Androw þe
Apostle com in Scotland.

35   The ʒer of God sevyn hundir & four score, gret Charlis wan Spanʒe,
France, & Galice fra þe Saraʒens.

    The ʒer of God a thousand lxvi ʒeris, Macolm, þe sone of Duncan, tuke
þe rewm of Scotland in heritage, and rignyt xxxvi ʒeris.

    The ʒer of Christ a thousand lxvi, Mergret þe Quvene was spowsyt with
40   Macolm, and gat on hir vi sonnys: Edward, Edgar, Edmund, Ætheldred,
Alexander, and Dauid; and twa dochtiris: Mald, Quvene of Ingland, and
Marie, Cowntasie of Balane.

    The ʒeir of God a thousand a hundir and viii ʒeris, Edgar, son to þe said
Macolm, in heritage tuke þe kinrik of Scotland and rignyt ix ʒeris.

45   The ʒeir of God a thousand a hundir and vii ʒeris, Alexander, broþir to
þe said Edgar, tuke þe kinrik be successioun and rignyt xvii ʒeris, and he in
þe sewynt ʒer of his rigne foundyt Scone, þe abbay.

    The ʒeir of God a thousand a hundir & vi ʒeris, twa monys was sene in
þe lift.

50   The ʒeir of God ane thousand a hundir and xxiiii ʒeris, þis Alexander,
þe sone of Macolm, discesyt, and þat sammyn ʒer Dauid, his broþir, tuke
þe kinrik.

    The ʒer of God a thousand a hundir xxxvi ʒeris, þis Dauid, king,
foundyt þe abbay of Melrose.

55   The ʒer of God a thousand ane hundir xlii ʒeris, þis King Dauid
foundyt þe abbay of Nowbatile, and in þe nixt ʒer folowand, he foundyt þe
abbay of Jedward.

    The ʒeir of God a thowsand a hundir & l ʒeris, he foundyt þe   **f.305r**
abbay of Homcolens and Kynlose.

60   The ʒeir of God ane thousand ane hundir liii, King Dauid discesyt at
Carlele, and to him succedyt Macolm, þe sone of Henry, Erle of
Huntyngtoun, son to þe forsaid king, King Dauy.

Quhilk in þe ȝer of God a thousand a hundir lxi foundyt þe gret kirk of Sanct Androis in þe tyme of Arnald, bischope of þe sammyn, quhilk alsa þe
65 ȝer of God a thousand a hundir liiii foundyt þe abbay of Cowpir, and in þe nixt ȝer folowand discesyt; and he rignyt xii ȝeris, and to him succedyt Wilȝam, his broþir.

The ȝeir of God a thousand a hundir lxx, Sanct Thomas of Cantirbery was mirtyrit.

70 The ȝer of God a thousand ii hundir, Ingland & Walice war intirdytyt for þar trespas vi ȝeris, and ay sensyne þai ar tributaris to þe Pope for þar relesching.

The ȝeir of God a thousand ii hundir & xvii ȝeris, King Wilȝame discesyt, and he rignyt lii ȝeris.

75 The ȝer of God a thousand ii hundir & xli deyt King Alexander þe Secund, þat rignyt xxxii ȝeris.

The ȝer of God a thousand ii hundir & xliiii ȝeris, Frederic þe Empriour be Innocence þe Pape was put doun.

The ȝeir of God a thousand ii hundir & lxxx, King Alexander, þe sone
80 of Alexander þe Secund, descesyt at Kingorne.

The ȝeir of God a thousand ii hundir and x[c]ii ȝeir, Jhone of Balyole was maid king at Scone.

The ȝer of God a thousand ii hundir x[c]vi ȝeris, þe Inglismen was put out of Scotland, and þe batell of Dunbar was strykyn, and þat sammyn ȝer
85 was strikyn þe batell at þe bryg of Stirlyng.

The ȝer of God a thousand ii hundir & x[c]vii ȝeris, þe batell of
þe Fawkirk was strykyn ͺat þe fest of Sanct Mare Magdalene.   **f.305v**

The ȝer of God a thousand iii hundir & twa ȝer, strikyn was þe batell of Rosslyn.

90 The ȝeir of God a thousand iii hundir and ii ȝer, Wilȝame Wallace was slane, & King Robert þe Broice slew þe Cummyn.

The ȝer of God a thousand iii hundir and vi ȝeris, Robert Broice was maid king at Scone þe vii callend of Aprile, and þe sammyn ȝer was strikin þe batell of Methwyn and þe discumfyt of Dalrye in þe partis of Argyle.

95 The ȝer of God ane thowsand iii hundir and xiiii ȝeris, was strykyn þe batell of Bannokburn, in þe fest of Sanct Jhone þe Baptiste, quhar our ald enemys gat a gret fall.

The ȝer of God a thousand iii hundir and xviii ȝeris, þe greit kirk of Sanct Androis was hallowyt.

100 The ȝer of God a thousand iii hundir & xx ȝeris, haldyn was þe Blak Parliament at Perth.

The ʒer of God a thousand iii hundir & xxix ʒeris, King Robert þe Broice discesyt þe vii day of June.

The ʒer of God a thousand iii hundir & xxx ʒeris, King Dauy was
105 crownyt in þe vii ʒer of his eld, þe xxiii day of Nouember.

And þe nixt ʒer folowand was strykyn þe batell of Duplyn and þe batell of Anand.

The ʒer of God a thousand iii hundir & xxxiii ʒeris, was strykyn þe batell of Holdoun Hill.

110 The ʒer of God a thousand iii hundir xliii ʒeris, was strikyn þe batell of Duram at þe fest of Sanct Luce.

The ʒer of God a thousand iii hundir and l ʒeris, was þe First Mortalite.

The ʒer of God a thousand iii hundyr and lv ʒeris, was þe Brynt Candilmes.

115 The ʒer of God a thousand iii hundir lxvi ʒeris, was þe
coronatioun of King Robert Stewart, þe xvii day of Marche.   **f.306r**

The ʒer of God a thousand iii hundir & lxii ʒer, was þe Secund Mortalite.

The ʒer of God a thousand iii hundir & lxx ʒeris, King Dauid þe Broice
120 discesit.

The ʒer of God a thousand iii hundir and lxxviii ʒeris, was þe gret devysioun in Haly Kirk begunyyn.

The ʒer of God a thousand iii hundir & lxxx ʒeris, was þe Thrid Mortalyte.

125 The ʒeir of God a thousand iii hundir and lxxxv ʒeris, was þe cummyng of Franche men in Scotland.

The ʒeir of God a thousand iii hundir and lxxxviii ʒeris, was strykin þe batell of Otirburn.

The ʒer of God ane thousand iii hundir four scor and ix ʒeris, was þe
130 disces of King Robert Stewart.

The ʒeir of God a thousand iii hundir lxxx & xviii ʒeris, was þe batell of Sanct Jonstoun, xxx for xxx.

The ʒer of God ane thousand iiii hundir ʒer, discesyt Bischop Walter Traile of Sanct Androis.

135 And þe nixt ʒer folowand, was þe batell strykin of Nesbyt Muir.

And þat sammyn ʒeir, was þe Ferd Mortalyte.

The ʒer of God a thousand four hundir and twa ʒer, was þe batell of Homyldone.

And the nixt ʒer folowand, was þe batell of Schreisbery and Coklaw.

140 The ʒer of God a thousand iiii hundir and fife ʒeris, was þe descese of King Robert þe Thrid.

The ȝeir of God a thousand iiii hundir and vi ȝeris, was þe brinyng of Stirwlyng.

The ȝeir of God a thousand iiii hundir and xiii ȝeris, begane þe
145 vniuersyte in Sanct Androis.

The batell of Hairlaw began and was strykyn in þe ȝer of God a
thousand iiii hundir and xi ȝeris.   f.306v

The ȝeir of God a thousand four hundir & xix ȝer, was þe
passage of þe Erle of Buchan and Wigton in France.

150   And þat sammyn ȝer, was þe dry sommyr.

And þe nixt ȝer folowand, was þe Fyft Mortalyte, þe quhilk was callit
the Qwhew.

The ȝer of God a thousand iiii hundir and xxi ȝeris, was þe batell of
Bolgee.

155   The ȝer of God a thousand four hundir and xxiii ȝeris, was þe
coronatioun of James þe First and of his spouse at Scone.

The ȝer of God ane thousand iiii^c & xxxiii ȝeris and in þe moneth of
Julii, was the blak hour generall.

The ȝeir of God i^m iiii^c & xxxvi ȝeris, was the first sege of Roxburgh be
160 King James þe First, and in the nixt Fasteryngis Ewyn, he was slayne in
Sanct Jonstoun be the Erle of Atholle sone and air, and Robert Grayme,
tratouris, and þar complices.

The ȝer of God i^m iiii^c & xxxvi ȝeris, was þe coronatioun of King James
þe Secund with rede scheik, callit James with þe fyr in þe face, he beand
165 bot sax ȝer ald and ane half, in þe abbay of Halyrudhouse, quhar now his
banys lyis.

The ȝer of God a m iiii^c xxxix ȝeris, was þe deir summyr, for þe boll of
meill was for xxiiii s., and þe boll of malt for ii merkis, and þe boll of
quheit for xxx s., and mony deit for hungyr.

170   The ȝeir of God a m iiii^c & xl ȝeris, was hedyt Erle Wilȝem of
Dowglace and Dauid, his broþir, and Malcome Flemyn, Lord of
Cummernald, James þe Secund beand justice.

The ȝeir of God a m iiii^c fyfty and ane ȝeir, began the vniuersite in
Glasgw, purchest be Bishoip Wilȝem Turnbull. And þat ilk ȝeir
175 was þe first pardon of Glasgow of ful remissioun as in þe ȝeir of   f.307r
grace, and lestyt four monethtis, purchest be þe sammyn Bischoip
William Turnbull. The ȝer of God a m iiii^c fyfty & four ȝeris, deit þat
Bischoip Wilȝem Turnbull, to quhome succedit Bischoip Androw
Durriisder.

180　　　The ȝer of God a m iiii^c & lx and thrid day of August, deit King James þe Secund at Roxburgh be þe brekyn of on [of] his awyn gunnis at straik him to deid at þe secund sege of Roxburgh.　And he was erddit in Halyrudhous.

　　　The ȝer of God a m iiii^c and saxty on þe Sanct Laurence day nixt
185　folowand þe deces of James þe Secund, was King James þe Thride, his sone, crownyt in Kelso, he beand aucht ȝeris of eld and ane half.

　　　The ȝer of God a m iiii^c lxiii ȝeris Jhone of Dowglace was slayne in Edynburgh, and Erle James, his broþir, was chasyt in Ingland.

　　　Anno domini m° cccc° lxix°, James þe Thrid of Scotland, þe xiii day of
190　Julii, was maryit in Halyrudhous in gret dignite with Mergret – with þe kingis douchtir of Norway, Dasie, & Swasie, and Demmerk.

　　　And þat sammyn ȝeir was banysyt þe Lord Bowde, & Schir Alexander, lord & knycht, was hedyt in Edynburgh.

　　　Anno domini m° cccc° lxiii° Alexander, Duke of Albany, was tane on
195　þe se be þe Inglismen & honorabilly deliuerit for þe instance of his broþir, King James, be King Edward in Ingland.

　　　Anno domini m° cccc° lxx°, King Edward of Ingland was banysyt be þe Erle of Warwik and passyt in Flanderis & was resawit be þe Duk of Burgunȝe, for þe dukis wyf was his sister.　And King Hary, at was befor
200　banysyt in Scotland be Edwardis fadir, was þan restoryt to þe crown of Ingland.

　　　Anno domini m° cccc° lxxi°, þe said Edward come agane in　f.307v Ingland with gret power of þe Duke of Burgunȝhe and straik ane batell with þe Erle of Werwyk besyd Lundoun and slew þe erle and all his
205　complices, wincust and depriuyt King Hary, & tuke þe croune, and eftirwart slew Hary, þe quhilk was callit ane sanct and mony miraclis kythit in Ingland.

　　　That ilk ȝer, was sene ane mervalouse stern in þe firmament.　And in þat ilk ȝer drownyt þe Bischoipis of Sanct Androise barge, and sum juge
210　þat þe stern seyne aperit for caus of þe drownyn of þat schip, and oþir sum for cause of þe depriwyn & mertyryng of the haly man, King Hary.

　　　Anno domini m° cccc° lxxix°, King James þe Thred banysyt Alexander, his broþir, Duke of A[l]bany, and passyt in France and was maryit þar. And eftir þat, he come in Ingland and maid his residence with King Edward
215　of Ingland.　And þan þe King of Scotland gart sege Dunbar, þe dukis castell, and þe Lord of Bunterdaill was capitane, and he and his stall away be þe se.　& sa þe king gat þe castell.

And þat ȝer was mony weches & warlois brint on Crag Gayt. And
Jhone, þe Erle of Mar, þe kingis broþir was slayne, becaus þai said he
220   faworyt þe weches & warlois.

Anno domini m° cccc° lxxx°, þair raise ane gret wer betuix Ingland &
Scotland. And þat ȝer, þe Erle of Anguys with gret power of Scottis
passyt in Ingland and brynt Balmburgh and lay thre nychtis & thre dais in
Ingland.

225   And þat ȝer, was gret tempestis of weddir for ane gret storme
began at New ȝeir Day and lestyt quhill þe xxvi day of Marche. Þe   **f.308r**
morn eftir Our Lady Day in Lenterin þe storme brak.

And nixt Beltyn Day eftir was ewill Beltyn Day.

Anno domini m° cccc° lxxxii, þar was ane gret hungyr and deid in
230   Scotland, for þe boll of meill was for four pundis, for þar was Blak Cunȝhe
in þe realme strikkin. And ordinyt be King James þe Thred half pennys
and thre-penny pennys innumerabill of coppir. And þai ȝeid twa ȝer and
mair. And als was gret wer betuix Scotland and Ingland, and gret
distructioun throw þe weris was of corne & cattell. And þai twa thyngis
235   causyt baitht hungar and derth, and mony pur folk deit of hungar.

And þat sammyn ȝer in þe monetht of Julii, þe King of Scotland
purposyt till haif passyt in Ingland with þe power of Scotland and passyt on
gaitwart to Lawdyr, and þar þe lordis of Scotland held þar consaell in þe
kirk of Laudir and cryit downe þe blak siluir. And þai slew ane part of þe
240   kingis housald, and oþir part þai banysyt, and þai tuke þe king himself, and
þai put him in þe castell of Edynburgh in firm kepyng, for he wrocht mair
þe consaell of his housald at war bot sympill na he did of þame þat war
lorddis. And he was haldyn in the castell of Edinburgh fra þe Magdalyne
Day quhyll Michaelmes.

245   And þan þe wictall grew better chaip, for þe boll þat was for four
pundis was þan for xxii s. of quhyt siluir.

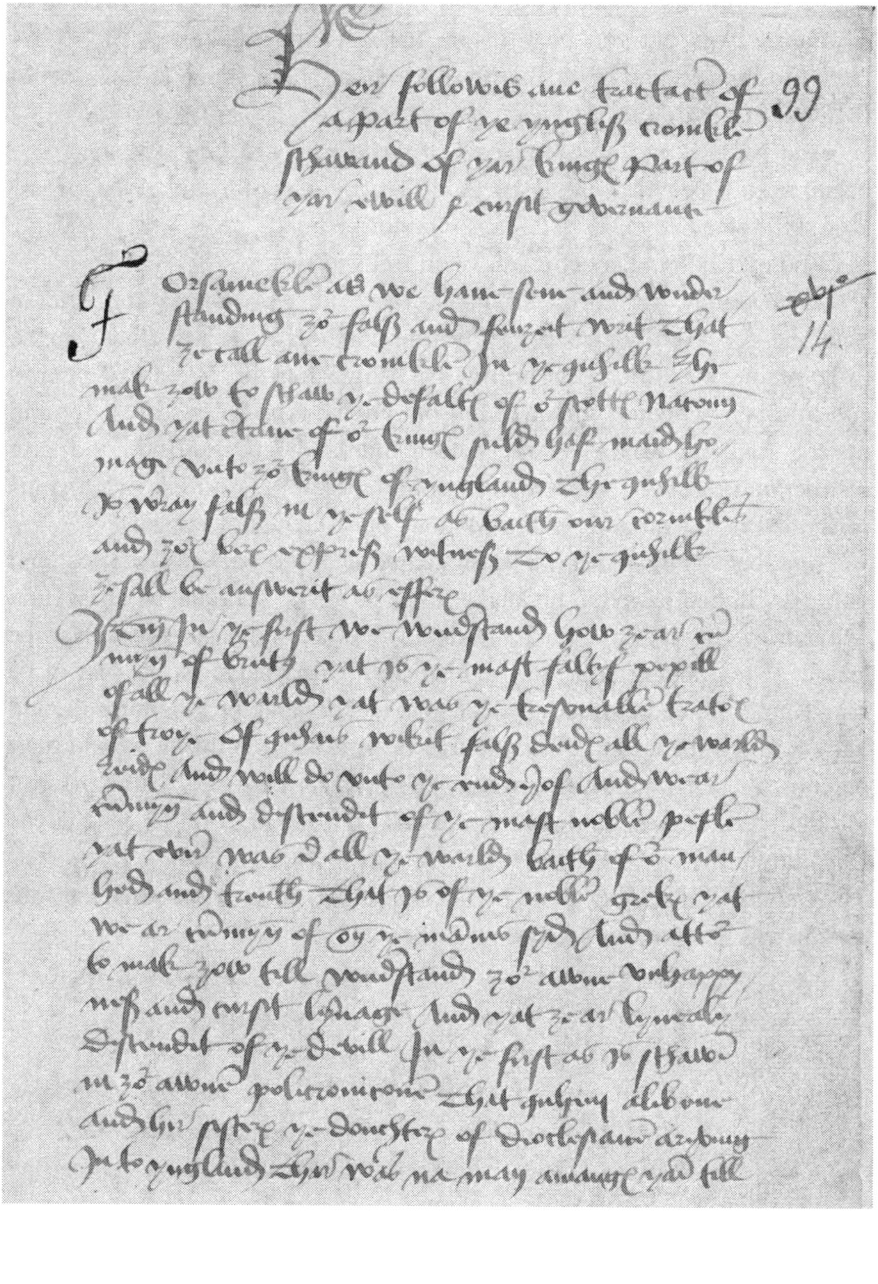

Folio 99r of NLS MS 16500. Image published with the permission of the Trustees of the National Library of Scotland.

THE YNGLIS CHRONICLE

from National Library of Scotland MS 16500 (Asloan)

Heir followis ane tractact of a part of þe Ynglis cronikle   **f.99r**
schawand of þar kingis part of þar ewill & cursit governance.

    Forsamekle as we haue sene and wnderstanding ȝour fals and fenȝeit
writ that ȝe call ane cronikle, in þe quhilk ȝhe mak ȝow to schaw þe
defaltis of our Scottis nacioun and þat certane of our kingis suld haf maid
homage vnto ȝour kingis of Yngland, the quhilk is werray fals in þe self, as
baith our corniklis and ȝouris beris expres witnes to þe quhilk, ȝe sall be
answerit as efferis.

    Item: In þe first, we wnderstand how ȝe ar cummyn of Brutus, þat is
þe mast faltyf pepill of all þe warld, þat was þe tresonable tratouris of
Troye, of quhais wikit fals deidis all þe warld reidis and will do vnto þe
end þarof.

    And we ar cummyn and discendit of þe mast noble peple þat evir was
in all þe warld, baith of our manhed and treuth – that is, of þe noble Grekis
þat we ar cummyn of on þe mannis syd.

    And attour to mak ȝow till wnderstand ȝour awne vnhappynes and
cursit lynnage and þat ȝe ar lynealy discendit of þe Devill, in þe first, as is
schawin in ȝour awne *Policronicone* that quhen Alibene and hir sisteris, þe
douchteris of Dioclesiane, aryving into Yngland, thar was na man
amangis þaim till haue conuersacioun with bot at þe devillis tuke   **f.99v**
liklynes of men and had carnale dele with þam. And sa was ȝour
forbearis þat first inhabit Yngland engenerit & gottin be þe Devill, & þis
ȝour awne corniklis beris plane in þe self, þat ȝe may nocht ganesay.

    Allswa quhar ȝe say that our kingis suld haf haldin of þe kingis of
Yngland, the contrar of þat is werraye treuth, for sen þe first tyme þat þe
Scottis inhabit þis ile, we haf ay liffit wnder a god and ane king and ay
kepit ane armes and sa did ȝe neuir.

145

And as for to schaw þat ȝe liffit nocht ay wnder a god, ȝe haf twys errit sen ȝe come to þe faith, for þe quhilk caus ȝour prestis war changit in þar
30   devyne seruice fra þe Vse of Rome vnto a strater seruice that is callit Salisbery Vse.

And so to schaw þat ȝe haf nocht liffit vnder a kyng, ȝe haue first bene of þe Sarazenis and secundlie of þe Brutis. The quhilk Brutus slew baith his fader and moder and come of þe fals tratouris of Troye.
35   The thrid tyme, of þe paganis of Horsus and of Ingest that come first in Northumbirland & conquest ȝow halely. Sexaburga, þe Qwene of Germany, left behynd hir þe said Horsus and Ingest to be masteris and governouris our ȝow. Eftir þe quhilk Ingest, ȝour realm is callit   f.100r Yngland. The quhilk fals Saxonis blud war evir ȝit aganis þe Cristin
40   faith and as ȝit remanis still amangis ȝow.

Eftir þe Saxonis, [come] þe Danys William Hauslot, þe Prince of Denmark, and conquest ȝow halely and rang on ȝou and held ȝow in sic thrildome that in euirilk hous of Yngland thar was put ane Dene to be master.

Now gentill masteris, I sall schaw ȝow how ȝe lerit ȝour curtasy þat ȝe
45   pryde ȝow samekle in, the quhilk we call deir bocht. For als lang as a Dene was in ony houss of Yngland, þe gud man of þe hous held ay his bonat of, sa lang as þe Dene was in with him. And ay quhen þe Dene spak till him, he knelit at ilka word. And siclyke quhen ony Ynglisman met ane Dene on þe gait, he knelit down on his kne quhidder þe gait was fair or foule quhill
50   þe Dene was gane by him, quharthrow ȝe lerit & was brocht in vse of all ȝour fair flattering langage & subtell deidis and contenewis þarin.

Efter þat, þe Romanis conquest ȝow certane ȝeris.

In þe ȝer of God viiiᶜ & xv, Gregory, the noble King of Scottis, conquest & wan all Yngland till þe watter of Themes and þe mast part of
55   Irland and Walis. The quhilk he held vnder his obeysance to þe end of his lyf. Bot to rehers all his noble deidis, to me it war our   f.100v lang.

And as forsamekle as all Ynglismen ar so presumptuos in þar argumentis and collationis of þar cornikillis and sa proude in þar genology
60   and antecessouris quhen þai commoun with ony vþir nacionis quhilkis ar cummyn of a mair noble hous and of ane worthiar genology þan þai ar – for þat caus and for to stanche & slaike þar pryde, I sall, with þe helpe of God, schaw how þai ar lynealy cummyn dovne fra þe Devill, lyke as ȝour awne principale story and cornikle callit *Pollicronicon* declaris in þe self.
65   It is nocht till haf bene writtin in ȝour croniklis and in autentik bukis les þan it haf bene werite & trewe in þe self.

And heir will I begyn at þe Bastard of Normondye to declair þe story
befor said, eftir þe deid of Sanct Eduard, þe gud haly King of Yngland,
quhilk þamself martyrit falsly.

70 Than regnit Herold, þe sone of þe Erll Godwyne, quhilk falsly brak his
mariage with þe douchter of William, Duke of Normondy. Quharfor
quhen þe said Herold was drevyn in Normondy aganis his will, he fenȝeit
and said he come for mariage. And þan þe Duke of Normondy gaif him
his douchter & gret ritches. And alson as he come hame in

75 Yngland, he cuttit baith hir palpis of and put out hir eyne and send   f.101r
hir sa hame till hir fader on a meyr and hir face till þe meris tale.
Than þe duke, seand þis, callit his twa sonnis þat war of full bed and bad
þam take ane army and pas in Yngland and weir on Herold þat was king
but ony rycht. And þai twa refusit it.

80 And þan he callit William, his bastard sone, quhilk grantit to gang and
come in Yngland with ane gret ost and power, and slewe þar King Herold,
and was crovnit king himself, and liffit lang with rialte þar with his qwene,
on quham he gat mony fair childer. That is to say, Robert Curthose;
William þe Ros; Richert, þat deit in his childhed; Henry Beauclerk; and

85 Mald; with vþir four childer, þat deit in þar ȝouthhed. And at his end day,
he maid Robert Curthos [Duke of Normondye and gaf all Yngland to]
Willam þe Ros, þe secund begottin son, and to Henry Beauclerk all his
tressour, and þan deit, þe xxii ȝer of his regne.

And eftir him regnit þis William Ros, quhilk was engenerit and gottin be
90 ane ewill spreit apon his moder and was callit incobus, quhilk wele apperit be
his deidis, for he was all his days contrar till God and Haly Kirk and
nevir did thingis all his dayis þat soned vnto God, for quhar euir he   f.101v
come, he distroyit Haly Kirk.

Ancelm, Archebischop of Canterbery, becaus he reprevit his wikkit
95 deidis, he exild him of Yngland.

And þis samyn king gart mak þe New Forest. And for to mak þe said
forest, he distroyit & wastit xxvi townis and þar kirkis and lxxx houss of
religioun, and all for þe making of þe said forest. And he was sa wikit of
his dedis that þe thingis þat war plesand to God displesit him. For sa he
100 endit in þis said forest sodandlye amangis his peple be a schot of ane
arrow, and na man wist how, in þe xiii ȝer of his wikitnes.

And þan eftir him was maid king Henry Beaudclerk, his broþir, becaus
he had na childer gottin of his body. And quhen þis Henry Beauclerk was
crovnit, þe ferd ȝer of his regne he spousit Mald, þe gud qwene þat put

105 dovn þe reke penny of Yngland, þat was douchter to þe haly quene of
Scotland, Sanct Margaret. And þis King Henry gat on his wyf Mald iii
sonnis & dochteris, that is to say, William, Richert, and Mald, that was
weddit to þe Empriour of Almanȝe.

And in þe xviii ȝer of his regne, þar rais ane gret debait betuix
110 him and Lowis, King of Fraunce. In þe quhilk weir, he had gret   **f.102r**
helping of þe Erll of Blais, þat spousit Mald, his sister. And quhen
he had endit his weir in Fraunce, he retorned agane in Yngland and left his
twa sonnis to follow him. The quhilkis war drownit in þar hame-cummyng
with gret company of nobillis with þam.

115 And eftir þat, new worde come to þe king þat Henry þe Empriour,
quhilk spousit Mald, his douchter, was deid, and schew till hir fader till
fetche hir out of Normondye. And sa he did, and brocht hir haim into
Yngland, and eftir þat, mariit hir with Galfryde, Erll of Angeos, quhilk
gat on hir a son. The quhilk was callit Henry þe Secund, þe son of þe
120 emprice.

And quhen þis was done, þis forsaid King Henry Beauclerk tuke a gret
seiknes and deit, þe xxxv ȝer of his regne.

And quhen he was deid, Stevyne, quhilk was son till þe Erll of
Ballonȝe and Mald, his sister, was chosin king & come in Yngland throu
125 þe helpe of his fader, þe erll, and counsall of mony gret baronnis of
Yngland, that falsly brak þe aith þat þai had maid befor to Mald þe empris.

In þe ferde ȝer of þe said King Stevynnis regne, Malde þe empris come
furth of Angeos in till Yngland to persew hir richtis, þe quhilk sche did
with gret trawell and pane and oft tymes fled and was chasit diuers tymes
130 throu all Yngland.

And in þe meyntyme þat þis weir was in Yngland betuix þe said   **f.102v**
King Stewyne and þe Emprys Mald, the Erll Galfryd of Angeos
gaif our all Normondy to Henry, his son. The said Erll Galfryd of Angeos
was incobus and gottin betuix a devill & his moder in mannis liknes. And
135 he was fader to þe said Henry, þe empryce sone, of quhom ar cummyn
dovne all þe Saxonis of Yngland lynealy, king be king. And within schort
tyme eftir, þe Erll Galfryd deit. And þan was Henry, his son, Duke of
Normondy and Erll of Angeos.

In þis samyn ȝer, þe King of Fraunce partit with his qwene becaus þai
140 war of blude. And scho was richtuis air of Gasconȝe. And þareftir scho
was spousit with Henry, þe empris sone.

And þan þe said Henry come with ane gret power in Yngland to persew
his richt and maid gret weir throw all Yngland, quhill at þe last it was

accordit betuix þaim þat King Stephyne and Henry, þe emprice sone, suld haf
145 ilk man his part of Yngland. And quha þat first deit, the toþir suld be his air.

And in þis Kyng Stevinnis coronacioun, at þe mes, the pax was forȝet
and nocht gevin. And in all his tyme, he had nevir pece. And sa deit þis
King Stevyne first.

And þan þis Henry was crovnit king of all Yngland. And he   f.103r
150 had with his wyf thre sonnis. That is to saye, Henry, his first
begottin son, & Richert, Erll of Oxinfurd, and Jhon, his ȝoungest son.

And þis Henry, þe emprice sone, was sa contrarius till God and Cristin
faith that he and his sone Henry slewe þe haly martir Sanct Thomas of
Canterbery, amang mony vþiris of þar cursit and wikit deidis aganis God &
155 þe Cristin faith, as þai haue euirmar persewit vnto þis day.

Bot first deit his son Henry, and þan he deit þe xxxvi ȝer of his regne.

And eftir him regnit Richert, his secund son, quhilk was slane at þe
castell of Galȝone be ane of his awne pepill þe ix ȝer of his regne. For his
peple war till him fals, as all Yngland was euir subtell & fals baith to þar
160 awne nacioun and to all vþiris.

And becaus þis King Richert had na childer, his ȝoungast broþir, Jhon,
was maid king eftir him. The quhilk King Jhon was sa contrarious till God
and Haly Kirk that he distroyit neir all þe kirkis of Yngland, and reft fra
þaim þar possessionis and gudis, and distroyit all þe ordour of Sistens
165 within Yngland, baith monkis & nunnis.

For þe quhilk caus, he and all Yngland was interdytit mony ȝeris and ay
quhill it was accordit betuix þe pape & King Jhon þat he resignit
wp þe crovne of Yngland to Pandulf, þe papis legat. And syne on   f.103v
þe papis behalf he tuke it agane of him evirmar to be haldin of him
170 for a rent ȝerelie of ane thousand merkis Ynglis to be payit ȝerelie in name
of tribut þarfor.

And sa may nocht Ingland be callit a fre realme within þe self as vþir
realmes is, bot a realme þat is haldin for tribut, payand þe said sovme
ȝerlie. The quhilk gif þai fale to do, þar infeftment to be of nane avale.
175 The quhilk is to be wnderstanding nocht kepit and sa haf þai tynt þar
infeftment.

And sa he liffit mony ȝeris þareftir. Bot he and his fals pepill war neuir
at accorde. For God for his wikitnes send sic vengeans on him that he had
neuir rest nor pece in all his tyme.

180   This King Jhon had mony fair childer – that is to say, Henry, his air þat
       was king eftir him; Richert, þat was Erll of Cornwell; Eleȝebet, þat was
       Empryce of Rome, and Elene, with mony vþiris þat þar nameȝ ar nocht
       heir.
          And in his tyme, Alexander þe Secund, our king, past throu
185   Yngland with ane gret army till Dover agane King Jhonis will and   **f.104r**
       baid þar xv days and spak with King Lowis of Fraunce and raid in þe
       watter of Dower quhill his hors fletit with him, and syne slang his swerd in
       þe se, and said þar was neuir Scottis man raid ferrar in Yngland þan he did.
       And in his hame-cummyng, King Jhon brak all þe briggis and passagis, and
190   ȝit he come hame in Scotland hale & feir and all his army. And in his hame-
       cummyng, King Jhon was poysonit þe xviii ȝer of his regne. And þan þe said
       King Alexander spulȝeit þe castellis and brocht in Scotland all þe tressour &
       jowellis þat war in þe saidis castellis.

          Item: Nixt eftir þis King Jhon, his son Henry the Thrid was crovnit.
195   And in þis Henryis tyme, Lowis, þe Dalphyne of Fraunce, conquest
       mekle of Yngland and was þarin mony a day.
          And þis samyn Henry and his peple war euir at discord for quhy þai war
       sa fals till him & he to þam þat þar mycht neuir ane of þaim trow ane noþir.
          Than Symond of Montfurde, Erll of Lacister, represit þis kingis vycis,
200   the quhilk causit þe king to haf sic invy at him that he, throu þe helpe of
       Gilbert of Clair, Erll of Glocister, slewe þis gud man, þe Erll of Lacister.
          This Henry þe Thrid had five childer – that is to say, Eduard, Margaret,
       Edmond, Beatrice, and Katryne. And syne he deit þe lv ȝer of his regne.

          And þan was crovnit Eduard, his sone, with þe lang schankis, into
205   quhais tyme þe noble weriour William Wallace was, quhilk followit him
       into Yngland vnto Sanct Albanis and remanit þar fra All Halowe Evyne till
       þe morne eftir Candilmes Day. And þan throu trety of þe Qwene of
       Yngland, þat was a Franche woman, and throw þe fulfilling of his   **f.104v**
       desyris, torned agane in Scotland and brynt and distroyit all
210   Northumbirland to þe New Castell and come hame without batell.
          And þan deit þis Eduard Langschankis at Burgh on þe Sand þe xxxv ȝer
       of his regne. And was dissauit throw a mawment þat spak till him in a
       ryng, sayand þat he suld nocht de till he come to þe Burgh of Jerusalem.
       Bot he was sa begylit. And ȝit ay on syndry, Ynglismen ar dissauit,
215   trowand in þar mawmentis and vse þaim amangis þaim ȝit dayly.

And eftir þis Eduard with þe lang schankis, was crowned his sone
Eduard of Carnauerane, quhilk was þe maist infortunat king þat euir was in
Yngland. And rais sa ewill of governance that he rewlit him all be laddis
and be men of na avale and of law birth, as be Peres of Dammastioun,
220 quhilk was baith hangit & drawin for his fals counsall, and syne eftir be
Schir Hew Spensar þe fader and be Schir Hew Spensar his sone, quhilkis
war baith fals tratouris, as has bene mony ma of þat nacioun, and at þar
endingis war baith hangit and drawin.

This samyn King Eduard was sa contrarious & sa fulfillit with falset
225 and wikitnes that he exilit baith his qwene and his eldest sone out of þe
realme of Yngland into Fraunce to hir fader.

And in þis samyn tyme þe pape send a cardinale into Yngland   f.105r
for to correk þe faltis of Haly Kirk and of errasy quhilk rang evir
still and ȝit dois in þat realm. And he was baith strikin and spulȝeit, and all
230 his gudis reft fra him, the quhilk was ane cursit deid. And all þe land and
peple war cursit *de facto*.

This samyn Eduard tynt þe battell of Bannokburn, loving to God, [in]
quhilk was ane ȝeris provisioun togiddir, and syne was schamefully chast
eftir þe batell fra Striuling to Dunbar and þar stall away in a bait and fled in
235 Yngland.

And he martyrit in his tyme þe haly man Thomas of Lacister, quhilk
lyis at Pomfret and is a sanct of ȝour awne making, as ȝe haf mony ma.
And quhen ilkane of ȝou stikkis & gorris vþir, þan ȝe call þai[m] sanctis of
ȝour making. Bot we Scottis men lufis na sanctis of ȝour making.
240 And for his wikit deidis, he was put downe.

And þan þe hale counsall of Yngland gart crovn his sone Eduard of
Wyndesor, quhilk was callit Eduard þe Thrid.

And þan þis Eduard of Carnauerane was put in preson be his son and his
wyf in þe Castell of Kilemouth, euir to remane till þe end of his lyf.
245 And his kepar was Schir Henry, Sanct Thomas broþir of Lacister,   f.105v
becaus þat he suld remember þe deid of þe haly man, his broþir. Bot
eftirwart he was changit vnto þe Castell of Barklay to be in þe keping of
Schir Jhon Barklay and Schir Jhon Mautyuaris.

And þareftir rang his son Eduard of Wyndissor furth in his cruelnes
250 and ay in tribulacioun and contrarynes. Bot quha hard euir in ony realme
of sic a king of governans of cursitnes and falset as was þis Eduard of
Carnauerane and sa fals and tressonable peple as was his liegis to him?
For þe fader mycht nocht trast þe sone, nor ȝit þe son þe fader nor þe
moder, nor nane of þat nacioun may trast ane noþir, nor ȝit vþir pepill
255 trast þaim.

And quhen Eduard of Carnauerane had bene twa ȝer in presoun, he was be þe counsall of his sone Eduard of Wyndissor and his wyf þe qwene changit of his warde vnto þe Castell of Croif, the quhilk was þe place of þe warld þat he werst lufit.

260 And þar throw command of his son þe new king & of his wyf þe Qwene Eliȝebeth and counsall of þe fals pepill of Yngland, he was murdrest schamefully in þis maner: thai put ane horne in his foundement and þarthrou put ane hate speit wp throw þe horne amang his bowallis and sa slew him. And þis was a gret schame to þe sone to   f.106r 265 sla þe fader on þis maner.

This Eduard of Wyndesor maid fewte to þe King of Fraunce as lord and master.

And þareftir in þe li ȝer of his regne, deit Eduard, his son, þat was Prince of Walis.

270 In þis samyn ȝer was a gret murthour of lordis in Yngland.

And in the lii ȝere of his regne, he deit.

And eftirwart was Richert of Burdeous, Prince Eduardis son, crownit & regnit mony ȝeris eftir in Yngland.

And in þe ferd ȝer of his regne, ras þe commonis of Kent and mony 275 vþir cuntreis and chesit þaim a chiftane callit Jak Stro and ane noþir callit Wat Thrildere, and throw þe commonis and þar chiftanis spulȝeit, reft, & slew our all Yngland a lang tyme for þe gret misgouernans of þis King Richert and his fals counsall.

And in þe fyft ȝer, þe erd quoke and schuke so horribilly in Yngland 280 that all þe pepill was efferit of þar lyvis and said it was for wengeans of þar wariit king and his counsall, as was sene on þaim eftirwart.

In þe xi ȝer of his regne, rais aganis him fyve of þe gretest lordis of all Yngland, that is to saye, Schir Thomas Wodstok, þe kingis eme and Duke of Glocister; þe Erll of Riddisdale; Richert, Erll of   f.106v 285 Werwik; Schir Henry Bollynbroke, Erll of Darby; the fyft, Schir Thomas Mowbray, Erll of Nottynghame. And þir fyve tratouris set ane parliament at Londoun and þar put to ded mony lordis of þe kingis counsall with vþir diuers gret tressonnis aganis þe crovne, the quhilk was neuir red siclyk of na nacioun except þe fals nacioun of Yngland.

290 In þe xvi ȝer, þar come lordis of Scotland into Yngland to do armes. That is to say, þe Erll of Mar challangit þe Erll Marschell of Yngland; Schir William Dalȝell challangit Schir Peris Cortnay, knycht of Yngland; a sqwyer callit Cokburne challangit Schir Nycoll Hanbreke, and did þar armes at Smeithfeld, and retorned agane with honour & victorye.

295   This King Richert distroyit mony abbais & religious placis into Scotland, þat is to say, Jedburgh, Kelso, Melros, Dryburgh, and Newbotill.

        This King Richert murdrest mony of his lordis in Yngland and was exild into Scotland, þe quhilk deit a beggar and out of his mynd and was
300   erdit in þe blak freris of Striuling.

        And þan þis Hary of Longcastell tuke þe crovn in plane parliament be hale consent of þe fals pepill of Yngland but ony titill of richt.

        And þis Hary of Longcastell slew þe quhyte heremyte ˏof   **f.107r**
Yngland and maid a sanct of him, becaus he schew him a visioun
305 þat was schawin to him be þe Haly Trinite. That is to say, þat þe said heremyt saw a place for þe king in Hell and he resignit nocht our þe crovne fra him.

        And þan þe king sperit at him quha suld regne eftir him & he resignit nocht þe crovne.

310   He said, "Eftir þe sall regne ane haly man, and eftir him þe devill, and eftir him þe swerd, and eftir it nane."

        Item: In þe first ӡer of his regne, he murdrest þe Erll of Surry, þe Duke of Exister, þe Erll of Salisbery, þe Erll of Glocister. And in þe samyn ӡer þareftir, Schir Jhon Holland, Duke of Exister, was tane and
315 hedit with mony vþiris þat I knaw nocht þar names.

        Item: Þar rais ane Welche sqwyer aganis him callit Ewyne of Glendour.

        And in þe thrid & ferd ӡer of his regne, he had ane gret batell callit Schrewisbery betuix him & þe Perses of Northumbirland. Thar was slane
320 in þe kingis cot armour þe Erll of Stanfurde & Schir Walter Blunt be a Scottis lord callit Schir Archebald Douglas.

        In þe sext ӡer, þe Erll of Mar passit in Yngland on a conduct and challangit Schir Edmond, Erll of Kent, of certane deidis of armes, þe quhilkis war eschewit manfully, & retorned with honour.

325   ˏItem: Into þe viii ӡer of his regne, he slewe þe Erll of   **f.107v**
Northumbirland & þe Lord Barde.

        In þe xiii ӡer, he deit. And his lyf was evir into tressonable murthour.

        And þan was crovnit his sone Henry þe Fyft, callit Henry þe Tyrand, quhilk spousit Katryne, douchter to þe King of Fraunce.

330   And in þe nynt ȝer of his regne, for þe misgouernance of him anentis God and Haly Kirk and þe haly man, Sanct Fiacrie, his belly raif and all his bowallis come out. And þus he endit his lyf awfully & offerit ane mort to Mahovne.

335   Eftir him regnit his sone Henry þe Sext, quhilk was ane gud man and in his tyme levit all possessionis þat Henry þe Tyrand had gottin in Fraunce.

Item: A sqwyer of Walis of law blud weddit Qwene Katryne and gat apon hir thre sonnis and a douchter. And ane of þaim was Erll of Richemont; þe toþir, Erll of Panbrek; the thrid, ane monk in Westmister.

340   Item: In þe xviii ȝere of King Henryis regne þe Sext, Dame   **f.108r** Elenor of Cobane was arrestit ⌃ . . . .

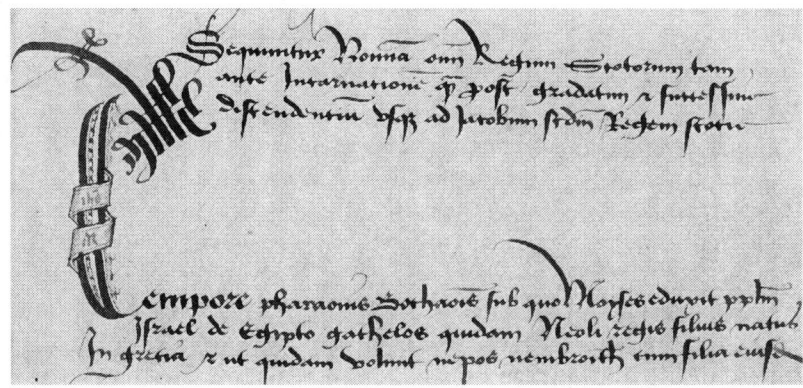

Folio 24r of NAS MS Dalhousie GD 45/31/1–II. Image published with the permission of the Keeper of the Records of Scotland.

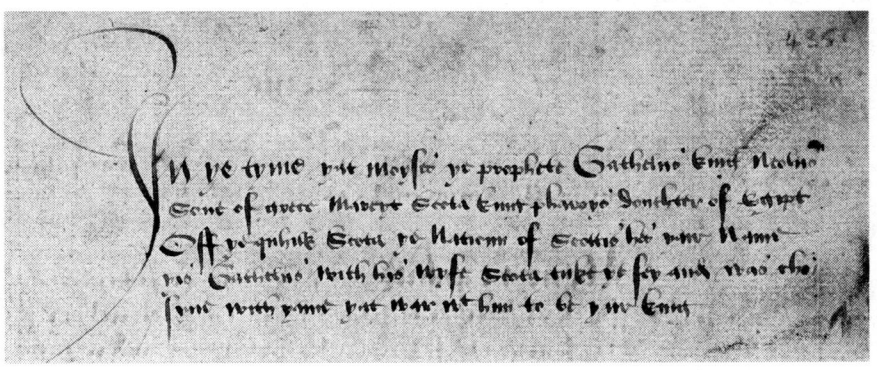

Folio 435r of NLS MS 19.2.4. Image published with the permission of the Trustees of the National Library of Scotland.

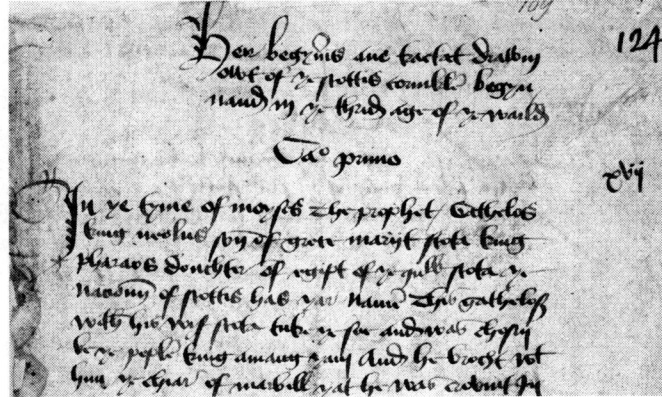

Folio 124r of NLS MS 16500. Image published with the permission of the Trustees of the National Library of Scotland.

NOMINA OMNIUM REGUM SCOTORUM

from National Archives of Scotland MS Dalhousie GD 45/31/1-II

˞Sequuntur nomina omnium Regum Scotorum tam ante incarna-   **f.24r**
cionem quam post, gradatim & successiue distendentium vsque ad
Jacobum secundum Regem Scocie.

Tempore Pharaonis Bochaonis sub quo Moyses eduxit populum Israel de
5   Egipto, Gathelos quidam Neoli Regis filius, natus in Grecia & ut
quidam volunt nepos Nembroith, cum filia eiusdem ˞Pharaonis Scota   **f.24v**
nomine a quo gens Scotorum nuncupatur, ab Egipto exiens propter
cladem Egiptiis illatam cum vniuersis sibi adherere volentibus Egiptiis &
Grecis mari se contulit, electus a Grecie & Egipti nobilibus qui secum erant
10   in regem.

THE BREVIS CRONICA
(THE SCOTTIS CORNIKLE)

from National Library of Scotland MS 19.2.4 (Advocates)

˞In þe tyme þat Moyses þe prophete, Gathelus, King Neolus sone   **f.435r**
of Grece, mareyt Scota, King Pharoys douchter of Egipt, off þe quhilk
Scota, þe natioun of Scottis hes þair name. Þis Gathelus with his wyfe Scota,
4   tuke þe sey, and was chosyne, with þame þat war with him, to be þair king.

156

NOMINA OMNIUM REGUM SCOTORUM

Translation

Here follow the names of all the Kings of the Scots, both before the Incarnation and after, extending by degrees and in succession to James II, King of Scotland.

In the time of Bochaon the Pharaoh, under whom Moses led the people of Israel out of Egypt, one Gathelos, the son of King Neolus, born in Greece and, as some will, grandson of Nimrod, left Egypt with the daughter of that same pharaoh, named Scota, after whom the people of the Scots are called; he left Egypt because of the disaster that fell upon the Egyptians, and, with all the Egyptians and Greeks who wanted to follow him, he took to the sea, and he was chosen king by the Greek and Egyptian nobles who were with him.

THE BREVIS CRONICA
(THE SCOTTIS CORNIKLE)

from National Library of Scotland MS 16500 (Asloan)

Heir begynnis ane tractat drawin owt of þe Scottis cornikle f.124r begynnand in þe thrid age of þe warld.

Capitulo primo: In þe tyme of Moyses the prophet, Gathelos, King Neolus son of Grece, mariit Scota, King Pharaos douchter of Egipt, of þe quhilk Scota, þe nacioun of Scottis has þar name. This Gathelos, with his wyf, Scota, tuke þe see, and was chosin be þe peple king amang þam. And he brocht with him þe chiar of marbill þat he was crovnit in.

157

Tempore igitur quo filii Israeli in deserto fuerunt, Gathelos multis iactatus pro[c]ellis tandem per Ansaga flumen Affricam intrans Numidie quieuit, qua tempore pauco relicta Hispaniam adiit, et super Hiberum flumen ciuitatem condens, & arcem ciuitatem Brigantium nominauit, vbi gens Scotorum
15   multiplicata est valde.

Circa tempus quo Salmon Ruth in vxorem accepit, Gathelos misit filium suum Hiberum, cum Hiemet fratre suo, ad considerandum insulam Ybernie, qui eam armata manu vi simul et ami[c]i[t]ia cepit, tum ad Hispaniam est reuersus & mortuo patre suo successit eidem.

20   Circa tempus Abden judicis in Israel, Micelius, Rex Scotorum in Hispania, misit Hermonium, Partholonium, et Hibertum filios suos recto ad Hiberniam qua obtenta pacifice, Hermonius reuersus est ad patrem in Hispania. Partholonius vero et Hibertus in insula Hibernie cum gentibus suis permanserunt.

25   Circa tempus Ezechie Regis quo tempore Roma condita est, Symon Brek missus est a patre suo Milone, alias Fonduf, Rege Scotorum in Hispania, ad Hiberniam et eadem sibi subiciens regnauit in ea multis annis. Hic portari secum fecit cathedram marmoriam quasi sedem regalem et eam in loco cui nomen Themor locauit.

---

5   Efter þe tyme þat þe childer of Issarell war in þe desert, þis Gathelus, with his wife and pepill, war trublit with tempest of sey, and at þe last, be þe flude or wattir callit Angase, enttrit in Affrik, and fra þine ane litill quhile he come to Spanʒe, and vpoun þe reveir callit Hebete he biggit ane citie and callit þe samyn Brigance, quhair þe Scottis multiplyit, and war trublyt sair with
10   Spaynʒeartis.

About þis tyme Gathelus send his sone Hyber, with his broder Emete, to considder þe Ile of Irland, and be favour and force he tuke it, and syne come agane to Bragance, quhair his fader was deid, and he succedit King of Scottis to him.

15   Sone eftir þis tyme, Mitelus, king of þe saidis Scottis, being in Spainʒe, send furth his sonnis Hermonye, Ptholomye, and Hibert secundly to Ireland, and tuke it. Hermonye [come] agane to Spainʒe, and Ptholomy and Hebert abaid in Irland and keipit it.

Lang eftir þis tyme, Symon Breik, king of þe saidis Scottis, was send be
20   his fader, callit Mylone, out of Spainʒe, with þe chyar of merbill þat was þe kingis sait, in Irland, and subdewit it, and regnit mony ʒeiris, and put þe chyar in ane place callit þe Themore, and þis was quhen Manasses   **f.435v** regnit in Jowrye.

158

Then, when the children of Israel were in the wilderness, Gathelos, tossed by many storms, at last entered Africa by the Ansaga River and came to rest in Numidia. Leaving there after a little time, he went to Spain and built a city on the river Hiber and named that fortress city Brigantium, where the Scots multiplied greatly.

At about the time when Salmon took Ruth as a wife, Gathelos sent his son Hiber, with his brother Hiemet, on a reconnaissance of the island of Ireland; he took it both by force of arms and by diplomacy, and then he returned to Spain. And when his father died, Hiber succeeded him.

At about the time that Abdon was a judge in Israel, Micelius, the king of the Scots in Spain, sent his sons Hermonius, Partholonius, and Hibertus directly to Hibernia. Once it was peacefully occupied, Hermonius returned to his father in Spain, while Partholonius and Hibertus remained in the island of Hibernia with their people.

At about the time of Hezekiah, the king in whose time Rome was founded, Symon Brek was sent to Hibernia by his father, Milo, elsewhere called Fonduf, the king of the Scots in Spain. And he subdued it and reigned there for many years. He had a marble chair like a royal throne carried to there and put it in a place called Themor.

Capitulo secundo: Eftir, about þe tyme þat þe childer of Israell war in þe desert, this Gathelos, with his wyf & peple, was trublit in þe se, and at þe last,
10   þai enterit in Affrike be þe watter callit Angase, and fra thyne þai salit to Spanʒe, and apon þe rever callit Hibet thai biggit þe cite of Brigans, quhar þe Scottis multipliit fair and faucht with þe Spanʒardis.

Capitulo iii⁰: Sone eftir þis, Mitelius, king of þe said Scottis, send his sonnis Hermony, Protholony, and Hibert fra Brigans to Irland and þai tuke it.
15   Hermony come agane to Brigans. Protholony & Hibert abaid still and kepit Irland.

Capitulo iiii⁰: Item. Gathelos send his sone Hiber, with his broþir Hiemet, to consider þe Ile of Irland, and with fauour and with force þai tuke and come agane to Brigans. And þar fader was deid, and Hiber   **f.124v**
20   succedit king to þam.

Capitulo v⁰: Lang eftir this tyme, Symon Breke was send be his fader, king of þe said Scottis, fra Brigans, quhais name was Mylone, to Irland with þe chyar of marbill, and he subdewit Irland, and regnit lang, and put þe chiar in a place callit Themor, in þe tyme þat Manasses regnit in Jowry.

30   Circa tempora Salatiel ducis Judee, quidam populi Picti vocati ortum habentes de Sithia inferiori venerunt ad Hiberniam querentes locum ad manendum qui directa per Scotos Hiberniam inhabitantes ad Albionis insule aquilonarem partem que nunc Scocia dicitur applicuerunt. & eandem inhabitantes acceperunt filias Scotorum in uxores cum nullas haberent, ea
35 [c]um lege vt vbi res veniret in dubium magis de feminea regum prosapia quam de masculina regem sibi eligerent.

        Anno ante incarnacionem Domini ccc xxx^{mo}, Fergusius filius   **f.25r**
Ferchard ex Hibernia venit in partes aquilonares Albiones insule que
nunc dicitur Scocia portans secum cathedram marmoriam quam prius de
40 Hispania ad Hiberniam deportari fecit Symon Brek. & in eadem est primus rex coronatus idem Fergusius apud Scotos in partibus Albionis que nunc Scocia dicitur, prout metrice quid dixit:

> *Albion in terris rex primus germine Scotus*
> *Ipsorum turmis rubri tulit arma leonis,*
45 > *Fergusius fuluo Farchard rugientis in aruo*
> *Christum tercentis terdenis prefuit annis.*

        Circa annum ante incarnacionem Domini c v, Rether, qui Sancto Beda Reuda vocatus est, aliquam partem terre Britonum Regno Scocie jure belli addidit eaque ex nomine suo Retherdale appellans que nunc dicitur
50 Redisdale.

        About þe quhilk [tyme], ane peple callit þe Pichtis come furth of Sythia to
25 Irland, quhair þai hade gevin þaim þe south part of Scotland, callit Albioun, and þe Scottis gaif þame wyffis, of þair childer and douchteris, vndir þis conditioun: þat þe king suld be sonar chosin of wommanis kyne þan of þe mannis kyne.

        Sone eftir, come ane nobill ȝo[un]g man out of Irland to Scotland, callit
30 Fergus Fercharde, and brocht with him þe kingis seyt or chyar of merbill fra Irland, þe quhilk chyar Symon [Breik] brocht out of Spainȝe to Ireland, and Gathelus, þe first king, brocht it out of Egipt, and was crownit þairin. And as prophecyis sayis, quhair euir it be þe Scottis sall regnne. Þis Fergus chesyt þe reid lyoune to his armys, thre hundreth and xiii befoir þe byrth of Cryst.
35   Efter þis tyme, Richert, King of Scottis, with strenth force, conqueist furst of Inglismennis hands þe daill callit Riddisdaill, and callit it eftir him Rycthesdaill, and now is callit Rechisdaill.

At about the time of Shealtiel, the governor of Judea, a certain people called Picts, whose origin was in lower Scythia, came to Hibernia asking for a place to settle. Directed by the Scots who lived in Hibernia, they sailed to the northern part of the island of Albion that now is called Scotland. And those inhabiting it received daughters of the Scots as wives because they did not have any, with this legal provision, that whenever the matter might come in doubt, they would choose their king from the female line rather than the male.

In the 330th year before the Incarnation of the Lord, Fergus, the son of Ferchard, came from Hibernia into the northern parts of the island of Albion, which now are called Scotland, carrying with him the marble throne that Simon Brek had earlier ordered to be carried from Spain to Hibernia. And Fergus was the first to be crowned King of the Scots on this throne in the parts of Albion that are now called Scotland, just as this says in verse:

> The first king of Scottish descent in the lands of Albion
> Carried among his Scottish troops the arms of a red lion,
> Roaring on a yellow field; Fergus Ferchard
> Preceded Christ by 330 years.

About the 105th year before the Incarnation of the Lord, Rether, whom St Bede called Reuda, added by right of war some part of the land of the Britons to the Kingdom of Scotland, naming it Retherdale after himself; now it is called Redisdale.

---

25   *Capitulo vi⁰*: Lang eftir þat tyme, a peple callit þe Pictis come furth of Sithia to Scotland, quhar þai gaf þam þe south part of Scotland, callit Albany, and þe Scottis gaf þaim wyfis, of þar childer & douchteris, vnder þis condicioun: þat þe king suld rather be chosyn of womannis kyn, na of þe mannis.

30   *Capitulo vii⁰*: Sone eftir, come a noble ȝoung man out of Irland to Scotland, callit Fergus Ferherd, and brocht with him þe kingis sete or chiar of marbill out of Irland, þat Symon Brek brocht out of Spanȝe & Gathelos out of Egipt. And quhar euir it be, þe Scottis suld regne be prophecy. This Fergus chesit þe red rampand lioun till his armes, thre hundreth ȝer and threttene

35 befor þe birth of Crist.

    Capitulo viii⁰: Eftir þis, Rether, King of Scottis, conquerit out of Ynglismennis handis a dale and callit it Retherisdale, and eftir him ȝit   **f.125r** it is callit Retherisdale.

161

Anno ante incarnacionem Domini xlix°, Julius Cesar post deuictam Galliam et Britaniam tributariam factam misit legatos suos ad reges Scotorum et Pictorum suadens vt se sponte sua Romanis subicerent alioquin contra eos pugnaret. Qui reges vnanimi voto contradixerunt ei, sicut metrice dicitur:

55   Scocia Romanis vi, metu subdita vanis
          Non fuit ex euo, nec paret imperio.

Et sic infecto negocio, ad Gallias rediit.

Circa annum Domini l[ ] exortum est grauissimum bellum Britannorum contra Scotos et Pictos et durauit annis c liiii usque ad annum Domini c
60 lxxxxiiii, scilicet qui fuit annus xvᵘˢ Severi imperatoris, quo tempore dicte gentes Britanni et Scoti mutua cede et incendio se interemebant nec sexui parcentes nec etati.

Circa annum Domini cc iii, Seuerus imperator venit ad Britanniam propter Britannos tutandos contra Scotorum impetus. Quem Fulgencius, Dux
65 Britannorum, sustinere non audens qui et rebellare contra Romanos instituit ad Scociam fugit et ibi cum regibus Scotorum et Pictorum   f.25v perpetue pacis et vtriusque gentis eterne comitatis fedus iniit, filiis suis duobus obsidibus inter[im] datis. Qui vallum inter Scociam et Britanniam fecit.

The ȝeir before þe Incarnatioun of oure Lord, Julius Cesare, eftir þat he hade ourcuming with force France and Ireland, send to þe Kingis of Scottis and
40 Pychtis to submyt þame wilfully to him – þe quhilk þai withstude and denyit with haill assent and war neuir subdewit, bot euir fre.   f.436r

In þe xii ȝeir of Claudius þe Empriour, þair begane ane greit battaill betuix þe Inglismen þat [ar] callit Brittonnis and Scottis and Pichtis, þe quhilk battaill continewit to þe tyme of Severus þe Empriour, in þe quhilk
45 tyme, baith birnyng and slaying of men and wemen with childrene lestit ane hundreth fiftie and foure ȝeiris.

In þe fyftyne ȝeir of Severus, Fulgentius, Duke of Brittonnis, quhilk wald nocht thoill þe malice of Severus, þat biggit ane wall betuix Scottis and Brittonnis, fled to þe Scottis and maid perpetuall peace and legacy with þame,
50 and left his tua sonnis in hostage for mair souerte. The quhilk Fulgentius, with help of Scottis, ourcome þe said Severus in battaill.

In the 49th year before the Incarnation of the Lord, Julius Caesar, after conquering Gaul and making Britain a tributary, sent his envoys to the kings of the Scots and the Picts, urging them to submit voluntarily to the Romans, or else he would fight them. Those kings defied him with a unanimous will, just as it is said in verse:

Scotland was never, through force or fear, conquered
By the vainglorious Romans, nor does she obey their command.

And so, abandoning the negotiations, he returned to Gaul.

About the year of the Lord 50, there arose a very grave war of the Britons against the Scots and the Picts, and it lasted 154 years until the year of the Lord 194, that is to say, the year that was the 15th of Emperor Severus, at which time the aforesaid peoples of the Britons and the Scots destroyed one another with mutual slaughter and burning, sparing no one because of either sex or age.

Around the year of the Lord 203, Emperor Severus came to Britain to protect the Britons against the attacks of the Scots. Fulgentius, the leader of the Britons, not daring to withstand him, but determined to rebel against the Romans, fled to Scotland, and there with the kings of the Scots and the Picts he made a compact of perpetual peace and eternal alliance with both peoples, his two sons being given as hostages in the meantime. Severus built a wall between Scotland and Britain.

Capitulo ix^o: The ȝer befor þe Incarnacioun of our Lord xlix, Julius Cesar,
40 eftir þat he had ourcummyn Fraunce & Yngland, he send to þe king of Scottis and Pictis and bad þam submit fully to him – the quhilk þai denyit with hale assent and was nevir subdewit.

Capitulo x^o: In þe xii ȝeir of Claudius þe Empriour, thar began a gret batell betuix þe Ynglismen, callit þe Brittonnis, þe Scottis, and Pictis, that
45 continewit till þe tyme of Seuerius þe Empriour, in þe quhilk tyme birnyng, slayng of men, women, & childer lestit a hundreth fyfty & four ȝeris.

Capitulo xi^o: In þe xv ȝer of Seuerius, Fulgencius, þe Duke of Britonnis, þe quhilk wald nocht suffer þe malice of Seuerius, biggit a wall betuix Scottis and Britonnis, and fled to þe Scottis, and maid continewale pece & lege with
50 þam, and left his twa sonnis in ostage for þe mar securite. The quhilk Fulgencius, with þe helpe of Scottis, ourcome þe said Seuerius and Romanis victoriusly in batall.

Anno Domini cc iii°, tempore Victoris primi pape et Seueri imperatoris,
70 Scoti catholicam fidem suscipiunt quam hactenus inuiolabiliter obseruarunt,
vnde metrice dicitur:

> Christi transactis tribus annis atque ducentis,
> Scocia catholicam cepit habere fidem,
> Roma Victore primo papa residente.
75   > Principe Seuero martir et occubuit.

Circa annum Domini cc lxxx iii Scotorum gentes et Pictorum qui venandi
gracia in suarum regionum confinibus conuenerunt, propter molosum quem
Scoti asserebant quendam Pictorum furto abstulisse in se inuicem insurgentes
mutua cede se trucidabant. Et tam leni occasione prime discensionis materia
80 inter easdem gentes ortum habuit. Et qui ante per quingentos annos vna
degentes vnaque tuebantur potencia tam faciliter ad inimicicias prouocantur,
nec aliquando postea sunt reconciliati.

Circa annum Domini ccc xxx iiii, translata sunt ossa beati Andree
apostoli de Patras ciuitate usque ad Constantynopolim preter tres digitos
85 manus dextre et os brachii inter humerum et cubitum dextrum, vnum dentem
et patellam genu eiusdem apostoli que angelo reuelante et imperante seruauit
beatus Regulus episcopus. Qui jussu angelico ductuque, eadem ossa per
multa maris discrimina plurimaque pericula in Scociam deportauit vbi a Rege
Pictorum Gurgust honorifice suscipiuntur et fundata est in honorem Dei et
90 Sancti Andree apostoli ciuitas Kylremont que nunc dicitur ciuitas
Sanctiandree et est sedes metropolitana tocius Scocie.

In þe ȝere of oure Lord tua hundreth and thre, Victore being Paip of Rome,
and þe said Severus empriour, Scotland tuke þe faith of Cryst, and as ȝitt hes
kepit it vndefoulit. And þe said Victor deyt martyr.
55 Ane litill before þe tyme of Dioclesiane þe Emprioure, the pepill of Scottis
and Pichtis huntit in þe marchis of þair regionis and cuntreis, and for ane quhyt
hund stollin away be þe Pychtis þai fell at wariance and war neuir uele aggreit
to þe last distructioun of þe Pychtis, þe quhilk peple keipit gude peax fyve
hundreth ȝeiris togidder befoir þis tyme.
60 In þe tyme of Constantyne þe Empriour, þe baynnis of Sanct Andro **f.436v**
war brocht to Sanct Reuill in Scotland. Þai war ressauit with þe King
of Pychtis, Gurgust, one þe kirk month, now callit Sanct Androis [biggit] be
King Hungus, King of Pychtis þat tyme. Þe quhilk tyme Sanct Austyne, þe
doctour of Yponeus in Affrik, began þe ordour of Blak Channonis.

164

In the year of the Lord 203, in the time of Pope Victor I and Emperor Severus, the Scots received the Catholic faith, which they have observed inviolably to this day, just as is said in verse:

> 203 years after Christ,
> Scotland began to have the Catholic faith,
> When Victor I presided as pope in Rome.
> He died a martyr, when Severus was emperor.

About the year of the Lord 283, the Scots and Picts, who came together to hunt on the border between their territories, rose up against each other because of a hound that the Scots claimed certain Picts had stolen stealthily, and they butchered one another in mutual slaughter. And the cause of the first dispute between these peoples had its origin in so slight a reason. And they who had passed 500 years together before this and had been protected by their united power were so easily roused to hostilities and after that were never reconciled.

About the year of the Lord 334, the bones of the blessed apostle Andrew were translated from Patras to Constantinople, except three fingers of the right hand, the arm bone between the shoulder and the right elbow, one tooth, and a kneecap, which, by the revelation and command of an angel, the blessed Bishop Regulus had saved. Regulus, commanded and guided by the angel, carried the bones away over vast expanses of sea, through many dangers, to Scotland, where they were reverently received by Gurgust, King of the Picts, and in honor of God he founded Kylremont, city of the apostle St Andrew, which is now called St Andrews and is the metropolitan see of all Scotland.

Capitulo xii⁰: In þe ȝeir of our Lord ii^c & thre, Victor beand Pape of Rome, and þe said Seuerius Empriour, Scotland tuke þe faith of Crist and as
55 ȝit has kepit it vndefoulit. The quhilk pape deit martir.

Capitulo xiii⁰: A litill befor þe tyme of Dioclesiane þe Empriour, f.125v
the peple of Scottis and Pictis baith togiddir huntit in þe marchis of
þar regionis, and for þe steling of a hund or ratche þai fell in discord &
fechtting, the quhilk lestit to þe last distructioun of þe Pictis, the quhilk peple
60 had kepit gud pece togiddir five hundreth ȝer befor.

Capitulo xiiii⁰: In þe tyme of Constance þe Empriour, the banis of Sanct Androwe was brocht be Sanct Rewle in Scotland quhar þai war resauit honorabilly with þe King of Pictis, callit Gurgast, and þe kirk of Kilremont was biggit be Hungar, King of Pictis, that is now Sanct Androis. About þe quhilk tyme Sanct
65 Austyne, þe doctor bischop of Yponen, began þe ordour of Blak Channonis.

Circa annum Domini [ccc lxxxxiii], scilicit anno secundo Archadii et Honorii, secundus Fergusius, filius Erth (qui fuit frater Eugenii regis Scotorum in bello prostrati), regnum Scotorum quod a Pictis et **f.26r**

95 Britonibus per xiiii annos dolose occupatum fuit viriliter dimicando recuperauit, hostes in eodem degentes longius fugando. Et sic in Regno Scotorum sibi jure hereditario debito regnauit xxvi annis.

Anno Domini cccc xix, Eugenius secundus, filius predicti Fergusii, successit patri in regnum et regnauit xxxiiii annis. Habuit quoque multas

100 victorias contra Britones et Romanos in Britannia, bis destruendo Grymys Dyke.

Circa annum Domini cccc lii, defuncto Eugenio, successit Dongardus, frater eius, in regnum Scotorum et regnauit quinque annis, mirabiliter regnum defendens.

105 Anno Domini cccc lvii defuncto Dongardo, successit frater eius Constancius, et regnauit annis xxii, et longo morbo consumptus, decessit ab hac luce.

---

65 In þe ʒeir of oure Lord God foure hundreth and thre, Fergus – þe sone of Erthe, þat was þe sone of Ethaid and broþir to Eugeny, King of Scottis, þat was slane in þe feild with Pichtis and Brittonnis – this Fergus recouerit and gat agane þe realme of Scotland out of þe Brittonnis and Pychtis handis, þe quhilk þai hade wranguusly occupyit þe space of foure skoir and thre ʒeiris.

70 Þis draiff away all his inymeis with force and plane baittaill and regnit eftir xvi ʒeiris.

The ʒeir of God iiii^c and xix, Eugeny, þe secund of þat name, þe sone of þe said Fergus, regnit eftir his fader xxxiii ʒeiris. Þis hade greit battaillis and victory apone þe Brittonis, quhill at þe last, one þe south syde of Humbyr, he

75 was slane in ane feild, quhilk feild he wann.

Efter þe quhilk Eugeny, Dongard, his broþir, was crownyt þe ʒeir of God iiii^c lii ʒeiris, and regnit bot thre ʒeiris, and gouernyt þe realme rycht nobilly fra inymeis.

Efter þe quhilk Dongard, Constant, his broþir, was crownit, and regnit

80 xxii ʒeiris.

About the year of the Lord [393], that is to say in the second year of Archadius and Honorius, Fergus II, son of Erth (who was the brother of Eugenius, King of the Scots, killed in battle), by fighting valiantly and driving away the enemies who had long lived there, recovered the kingdom of the Scots, which had been treacherously occupied by the Picts and Britons for 14 years. And thus he reigned in the kingdom of the Scots for 26 years as was due to him by hereditary right.

In the year of the Lord 419, Eugenius II, son of the aforesaid Fergus, succeeded his father in the kingdom and reigned for 34 years. He also had many victories over the Britons and Romans in Britain, twice destroying Grim's Dyke.

Around the year of the Lord 452, when Eugenius had died, his brother Dongard succeeded to the kingdom of the Scots. And he reigned for five years, defending the kingdom wonderfully.

In the year of the Lord 457, when Dongard had died, his brother Constance succeeded him, and he reigned for 22 years, and then, consumed by a lingering disease, he departed from this light.

Capitulo xvᵒ: In þe ȝer of God iiiiᶜ & thre, Fergus, þe son of Erth – þat was þe son of Ethad and broþir till Eugeny, King of Scottis, and slane in þe feld with þe Pictis – the quhilk Fergus recoverit & gat agane þe realm of Scotland out of þe Pictis and Britones handis, the quhilk þai had wranguislie occupiit þe space of iiiiˣˣ ȝeris & thre, and draf away his enemys in plane batell and regnit xvi ȝer eftir þat.

Capitulo xviᵒ: ˛The ȝer of God iiiiᶜ & xix, Eugenius þe Secund of **f.126r** þat name, þe said Fergus son, regnit eftir his fader xxxiii ȝeris and had gret victory and batell apon þe Britonnis, and at þe last, on þe south syde of Humber, he was slane in þe feld fechting.

Capitulo xviiᵒ: Eftir þe quhilk Eugeny, Dongard, his broþir, was crovned þe ȝer of God iiiiᶜ & lii, and regnit thre ȝeris, and defendit þe realm nobilly.

Capitulo xviiiᵒ: Eftir þe quhilk Dongard, Constance his broþir was crovnit þe ȝer of God iiiiᶜ lvii & regnit xxii ȝeris and deit of gret seiknes.

Anno Domini cccc lxxix, Congallus, nepos Constantini ex fratre
Dongardo, regnum suscepit et regnauit xxii annis. Huius tempore incepit
110   bellum inter Scotos et Pictos quod finem non habuit usque ad ultimam
vtriusque sexus Pictorum internecionem.

Anno Domini quingentesimo primo, mortuo Congallo, frater eius
Conranus successit in regnum et regnauit triginta quatuor annis.

Anno Domini quingentesimo [tricesimo] quinto, Eugenius tercius filius
115   Congalli qui Eothodius, occiso Conrano suo patruo, regnum suscepit
Scotorum et regnauit annis xxiii.

Anno Domini v^c lviii, mortuo Eugenio, successit frater eius Conuallus in
regnum et regnauit decem annis.

Anno Domini v^c lxviii, mortuo Conuallo, frater eius Kynnatil siue   **f.26v**
120   Connyd in regno succedens, post annum et tres menses decessit ex hac
vita.

Eftir quhame Congall, þe sone ofe þe said Dongard, was crownit,   **f.437r**
in quhais tyme þe battellis begane betuix Pychtis and Scottis, and
endit neuir to þe last distructioun of þe Pychtis, baith of man, woman, and
barne.

85   The ʒeir of God v^c and ane, Conrane, þe broþir of Congall, regnit xxxiii
ʒeiris. He hade greit weris aganis þe Saxonis be sindry chances of fortoun.
He was beryit in Ycolmekill, and supportit King Arthure, King of Brittonnis,
aganis þe Saxonis.

Efter Conrane, Eugenius, þe thride of þat nayme, regnit, quhilk was sone
90   to Congallus. He supportit Modred, King of Pichtis, aganis þe Brittonis in
þe samyn battaill quhen King Arthure was slane with all þe nobilite of
Brettane. He was crownit þe ʒeir of God v^c xxxv and regnit xxiii. In þat ilk
battaill, Modreid was slane.

The ʒeir of God v^c xlviii, Conwall succedit to his broþir Eugenius, ane
95   devoit and religious prince in all his werkis. He gouernit þe realme in greit
felicite, and deceissit þe tent ʒeir of his regine. In his tyme, Sanct Colme
come in Scotland and biggit mony abbayis.

The ʒeir of God v^c lxviii, Kynnatill, or Comyd, broþir to Convallus, regnit
100   and deceissit within ane ʒeir and thre monethis, in þe presence of Sanct
Colu[m]be, and was entyrit in Ycolmekille, amang þe remanent sepulturis of
kingis.

In the year of the Lord 479, Congall, the nephew of Constantine (the son of his brother Dongard), received the kingdom, and he reigned for 22 years. In his time, a war began between the Scots and the Picts, which had no end until the final destruction of the Picts of both sexes.

In the year of the Lord 501, when Congall had died, his brother Conrane succeeded to the kingdom, and he reigned for 34 years.

In the year of the Lord [535], Eugenius III, the son of Congall, succeeded to the kingdom of the Scots as Eothodius when his uncle Conrane was killed, and he reigned for 23 years.

In the year of the Lord 558, when Eugenius had died, his brother Convall succeeded to the kingdom, and he reigned for ten years.

In the year of the Lord 568, when Convall had died, his brother Kynnatil (or Connyd) succeeded to the kingdom. And he departed from this life after a year and three months.

---

80   *Capitulo xix⁰*: The ȝer of God iiii͡c lxxix, Congall, þe son of þe said Dongard, was crovnit and regnit xxii ȝer. In quhais tyme began þe batell betuix þe Pictis and Scottis, and endit neuir till þe last distruction of þe Pictis, baith man, woman, & childer.

     Capitulo xx⁰: The ȝer of God v͡c and ane, Conran, þe broþir of Congall,
85 regnit xxxiiii ȝer peceably.

     Capitulo xxi⁰: Eftir Conran, Constantyne regnit and was callit Erthody & Heb alsa. And was crovnit þe ȝer of God v͡c xxxv, and he regnit xxiii ȝer. In quhais tyme, Arthur of Yngland was slane ˄and Mordred in þe   **f.126v** batell of Britonnis.

90   *Capitulo xxii⁰*: The ȝer of God v͡c lxviii, Connall succedit to Constantyne and regnit x ȝer. In his tyme, Sanct Colme come in Scotland and biggit mony abbais.

     Capitulo xxiii⁰: The ȝer of God v͡c lxxviii, Kynnatill, or Comyd, regnit eftir his broþir Connall and deit within a ȝer and thre monethis.

Circa annum Domini v^c lxx Sanctus Columba tercio monente eum angelo Aiadanum filium Conrani manum capiti imponens ac benedicens regem ordinauit. Et inter benedicionis uerba de filiis nepotibus et pronepotibus
125 multa prophetauit et regnauit annis xxxv. In cuius tempore claruerunt Sanctus Columba, Sanctus Seruanus, Sanctus Kentigernus, Sanctus Connallus, et Sanctus Baldredus qui defunctus seculo apud Le Bass mirabiliter ad terram delatus est, scilicet diuino remigio; cuius ossa apud Aldhame, Tynnynghame, et Prestoun tres ecclesias miraculo diuino
130 requiescere dicuntur.

Circa hec tempora vates quidam Britonum Merlinus nomine mirabili penitencia et fine ex hac luce migrauit.

Mortuo Aiadano, Kenethus Ker, filius Conualli, coronam regni suscipiens post vnum annum vel, secundum alios, post tres menses,
135 defunctus est.

Vnde anno Domini vi^c vi Eugenius Bynd, quartus eo nomine, successit patri suo Aiadano et regnauit xvi annis. Electus & ipse inter fratres a Sancto Columba sicut pater eius Aiadanus qui in hostes et rebelles ferox fuit et crudelis, legiis et ciuibus mitis valde & misericors. Eius tempore floruit
140 Sanctus Gillenus Scotus apud Atrabatum & Sanctus Columbanus in Galliis.

The ʒeir of God v^c lxx, Sanct Colme was monist be ane angell to bliss þe sone of Conrane befoir said, quhais nayme was Aidane; and quhen Sanct Colme laid his hand one þe said Aidanis heid, he blissit him, and
105 crownit him, and prophecit mekill of him, his kinrik, and freindis. And ⏜f.437v
þis Aidaine regnit xxxv ʒeiris. In his tyme, was Sanct Mungew, Sanct Connall, and Sanct Baldreid, quhilk lyis at Aldhame, Tynnynghame, and Prestoune.

Efter Aidane, Kenneth Ker, sone to Convallus, succeidit to þe croune, and
110 deceissit in þe catar, þe fourth moneth eftir hi[s] coronatioun, and was bureyt in Ycolmekill.

About þis tyme, Merlyng, þe propheit of Brettane, deceissit with greit pennance.

The ʒeir of God vi^c and vj, Eugeny Bynd, vþirwayis Corthedy, succedit
115 to his fader Aidane, and regnit xvi ʒeir. He was chosin and blissit be Sanct Colme, and was to his inymeis als ferce as ane lyoune, and to his rebellis, and was to his trew liegis als meik as ane lamb. In his tyme, Sanct Mungew was one lyfe and schew miraclis in Scotland, and Sanct Colme in France.

About the year of the Lord 570, St Columba, after an angel had admonished him three times, ordained Áedán, the son of Conrane, king, placing his hand on his head and blessing him. And in his benediction, he foretold many future things about his sons, grandsons, and great-grandsons. And Áedán reigned 35 years. In his time, St Columba, St Servanus, St Kentigern, St Connall, and St Baldred were famous. When St Baldred had died to the world at Le Bass, he was carried to land miraculously, that is, by a divine boat; his bones are said to rest by a divine miracle at three churches – Aldhame, Tynnynghame, and Prestoun.

About these times, a certain prophet of the Britons, Merlin by name, went from this light with an extraordinary repentance and ending.

When Áedán died, Kenneth Kerr, the son of Convall, received the crown of the kingdom, and he died after one year or, according to others, after three months.

Then, in the year of the Lord 606, Eugenius Bynd, the fourth of that name, succeeded his father Áedán, and he reigned for 16 years. He was himself chosen from among his brothers by St Columba just as his father Áedán had been; he was fierce and cruel to enemies and rebels, very mild and merciful to his liege men and citizens. In his time, St Gillen the Scot flourished at Arras and St Columban in Gaul.

---

95   *Capitulo xxiiiiᵒ*: The ȝer of God vᶜ lxxix, Sanct Colme was monist be þe angell to blis Aiadane, þe son of Conrane, and quhen he laid his hand on his hed and gaf him his blissing, he ordanit him king and prophecit mekle of him & his frendis. And þis Aiaden regnit nobilly xxxv ȝer. In his tyme, was Sanct Mongow, Sanct Conwall, & Sanct Baldreid on lyf and schawit mony

100   mirakillis. The banis of Sanct Baldred lyis at Aldhame, Tynnyngham, and Prestoun.

    Capitulo xxvᵒ: About þis tyme, þe prophet Merlyne of Brettane deit with gret pennance.

    Eftir þis Aiaden, Kenneth Ker, þe son of Connall, tuk þe crovne and deit

105   eftir a ȝer & thre monethis.

    Capitulo xxviᵒ: The ȝer of God viᶜ & vi, Eugeny Bynd, vþirways ͺcallit Cothody, succedit to his fader Aiaden & regnit xvi ȝer. And þis **f.127r** was chosyn be Sanct Colme. He was a fers lyon to his enemys & to rebellis, and to his liegis a meke lamb. In till his tyme, Sanct Gillen schawit

110   miraklis in Scotland & Sanct Colme in Fraunce.

Defuncto Eugenius Bynd, successit ei filius eius maior natu Ferchardus anno Domini vi^c xxii & regnauit decem annis in pace.

Anno Domini vi^c xxxii, Donaldus Brek, mortuo fratre suo Ferchardo, successit in regnum Scotorum & regnauit annis xiiii; scilicet, ipse
145 benedictionem accipiens cum regno per Sancti Columbe mannum inposicionem.

Circa hec tempora, Rex Oswaldus Nordanhumbrorum cum **f.27r**
fratribus expulsus de Anglia et receptus apud Regem Scotorum et in
eodem permanent regno per xvii annos. Sacri baptismatis vnda renatus est.
150 Et in fide Christi sufficienter instructus. Et mortuis inimicis, adiutus Scotorum nobilibus in Regno Nordanhumbrorum iterum susceptus, misit ad Scociam vbi in Christo renatus fuit ut sibi & genti Anglorum mitteretur antistes ad instruendos in Christi fide populos terre sue quibus preerat. Et missus est Sanctus Aiadanus ordinatus confestim episcopus Lyndysfernensi;
155 qui cum ignoraret linguam Anglicanam, ipse Rex Oswaldus in sermonibus et fidei Christiane instructionibus necessariis fuit interpres qui nouerat optime linguam Scoticanam quam in Scocia didicit.

Ferquharde succeidit to his fader, Eugeny þe Fourt, ane vicious tyrane,
120 and for his demeritis was condampnit to perpetuall presoun, quhair he slew himself for disperatioun, þe xiii ȝeir of his rignne, fra þe Incarnatioun vi^c
xxxii ȝeiris.

Donald Breik, þe fourt of þat name, sone to Eugenyus, succeidit to Ferquharde, his broþir. He supportit King Oswald aganis Saxonis. He perist
125 in Loch Tay, þe xv ȝeir of his regnne, fra þe Incarnatioun vi^c xlvi ȝeiris, and ressauit þe benedictioun of Sanct Colme.

About þis tyme, Sanct Oswald, king of þe north part of Ingland, was banist with his broder to Scotland, and duelt heir xvii ȝeir, and was cristynnit heir. And quhen his inymeis war deid, and he restoryt to his croune,
130 he [send] to Scotland for ane bischop to cum and cristyn his land. **f.438r**
And Sanct Aidane was send to him, and crystynnit þe cuntre, and was
maid Bischop of Durhame. And þis Aidane preichit in his awin speiche, and King Oswald, þat knew baith þe spechis, was þe interpretour to þe pepill.

When Eugenius Bynd died in the year of the Lord 622, his elder son Ferchard succeeded him and reigned for ten years in peace.

In the year of the Lord 632, after his brother Ferchard died, Donald Brek succeeded to the Kingdom of the Scots, and he reigned for 14 years. Of course, he received both a blessing along with the kingdom by the laying on of St Columba's hands.

Around these times, King Oswald of Northumberland was expelled from England with his brothers and was taken in by the King of the Scots; and they remained in that kingdom for 17 years. He was reborn in the water of holy baptism, and he was sufficiently instructed in the faith of Christ. And when his enemies were dead, with the help of Scottish nobles he was received once more in Northumberland, and he sent to Scotland where he had been reborn in Christ requesting that a bishop be sent to him and to the English people to instruct in the faith of Christ the people of his land over whom he ruled. And St Áedán was immediately ordained Bishop of Lindisfarne and sent. Since he was ignorant of the English language, King Oswald himself, who knew the Scottish language, which he had learned very well in Scotland, was the interpreter of the sermons and the necessary instructions for the Christian faith.

Capitulo xxvii°: Ferchard succedit to his fader, Eugeny Bynd, the ʒer of God vi^c xxii & regnit x ʒer in pece.

Capitulo xxviii°: Donald succedit to Ferchard, his broþir, the ʒer of God vi^c xxxii & regnit xiiii ʒer and resauit þe benedictioun of Sanct Colme.

115   *Capitulo xxix°*: About þis tyme, Sanct Oswald, king of þe north part of Yngland, was bannist with his broþir into Scotland, and duelt heir xvii ʒer, and was cristinnit heir. And quhen his enemys war deid, and he restorit to his crovne, he send to Scotland to Aiadene þe bischop and bad him cum & cristin his cuntre. And he maid him Bischop of Durehame. This Aiadane prechit in

120   his tung to þe pepill, and Sanct Oswald interpret it to þam, þat knewe baith þe tungis. And sa was þe north of Yngland cristinnit be Aiadan and Oswald.

Anno Domini vi^c xlvi°, mortuo Donaldo Brek, nepos eius Ferchardus Fod filius Ferchardi ad regni regimen promotus coronatur regnauitque annis xviii
160 in pace.

Anno Domini vi^c lxiiii, defuncto Ferchardo Fode, successit in regnum Scotorum Maldwinus Donaldi Brek regis filius et regnauit xx annis.

Anno Domini vi^c lxxxiiii, defuncto Rege Maldwino, nepos eius Eugenius quintus filius Dongardi fratris Maldwini regnare cepit in Scocia et regnauit
165 annis tribus.

Anno Domini vi^c lxxxvii, Eugenius sextus, filius Fercherdi Fode Regis, in regnum Scotorum successit, et regnauit x annis. Omni tempore suo cum Anglis pacem habuit, cum Pictis bellum. Eius temporibus virtutibus pollens et miraculis Sanctus Adamnanus Scotus floruit. Eius eciam tempore per
170 totam Scociam et Britanniam, sanguinea pluuia per septem dies desuper effluxit et versa sunt in sanguinem omne lac pariter et butirum.

Ferquharde Foid, nepote to Downald þe Fourt, callit Breke, regnit eftir his
135 fader, ane bludy monstour, regnand with insaciabill awarice aboue his subdittis, contempnare of all religioun and peax, and last become penitent of his injuste, and deceissit þe xviii ʒeir of his regnne, fra þe Incarnatioun vi^c lxiiii ʒeiris.

Makdowyne, sone to Downald þe Fourt, callit Breke, succeidit to his
140 fader, and biggit þe Abbay of Ycolmekill, becaus it was ruynus to þe ground, and was slane be tressoun of his awin wyfe for suspicioun of adulteris, fra þe Incarnatioun vi^c lxxxiiii ʒeiris.

Eftir Makdowyne, Eugeny, þe fyift of þat nayme, nepote to King Maldwyne, regnit foure ʒeiris. He vincust in sett battaill Egfreid, King of
145 Inglismen and Saxonis, fra þe Incarnatioun vi^c lxxxviii ʒeiris. Þis Eugeny was sone to Downald.

The ʒeir of God vi^c lxxxvii, Eugeny þe Saxt regnit x ʒeir, þe sone of Ferquharde Foid. In his tyme, he hade gude peace with Ingland and weir with the Pychtis. Sanct Adampnane schew þan miraclis in Scotland and Brittane,
150 [as] it war blude vii dayis, þat all mylk and buttir turnit in blude.

In the year of the Lord 646, when Donald Brek had died, his nephew Ferchard Fod, the son of Ferchard, was promoted to the rule of the kingdom and crowned, and he reigned for 18 years in peace.

In the year of the Lord 664, after Ferchard Fod died, Maldwin, the son of King Donald Brek, succeeded to the kingdom of the Scots, and he reigned for 20 years.

In the year of the Lord 684, when King Maldwin died, his nephew Eugenius V, the son of Dongard, the brother of Maldwin, began to reign in Scotland, and he reigned for three years.

In the year of the Lord 687, Eugenius VI, the son of King Ferchard Fod, succeeded to the Kingdom of the Scots, and he reigned for ten years. In all his time, he had peace with the English and war with the Picts. In his times, St Adomnán the Scot flourished, strong in virtues and miracles. And also in his time, throughout all Scotland and Britain, a bloody rain poured down for seven days, and likewise all the milk and butter were turned into blood.

Capitulo xxx°: The ʒer of God vi^c xlvi, Ferchard Fode, þe newow of Donald, regnit xviii ʒer in pece. This Ferchard ˌwas Ferchardis sone **f.127v** aboue writtin.

125   *Capitulo xxxi°*: The ʒer of God vi^c lxiiii, Maldwyn, Donaldis son, succedit to Ferchard Fode & regnit xx ʒer.

Capitulo xxxii°: Eftir Maldwyne, Eugeny, his broþir, was crovnit þe ʒer of God vi^c lxxxiiii & regnit bot iii ʒer.

Capitulo xxxiii°: The ʒer of God vi^c lxxxvii, Eugeny þe V, þe son of 130   Ferchert Fode, regnit x ʒer. In his tyme, he had gud pece with Yngland and weir with þe Pictis. Sanct Adampnane schawit mirakillis in Scotland. In þis kingis tyme, þar fell dew lyk blud vii days, that all milk, watter, & buttir torned into blud.

Anno Domini vi^c lxxxxvii, defuncto Eugenio sexto, successit in   **f.27v**
regnum Scotorum Ambrikilleth, filius Fyndan, filii Eugenii quinti, et
vno anno regnauit.

175   Cui defuncto, successit eidem Eugenius septimus frater eius, et regnauit
xvii annis. Vir per omnia prudens et modestus et sagaci ingenio, proprium
optimis regendo legibus et ecclesiasticis documentis adornans, tranquillam
feliciter vitam terminauit.

Anno Domini vii^c xv, defuncto Eugenio septimo, successit ei in regnum
180   Scotorum Murdacus nepos eius ex Ambrikilleth [& regnauit xv annis]. Eius
anno ultimo vise sunt in Scocia due comete quarum vna precedebat mane
solem orientem et altera sequebatur vespere occidentem.

Anno Domini vii^c xxx, defuncto Murdaco, successit in regnum Scotorum
Ethfyn, filius Eugenii septimi, et regnauit xxxi annis. Vir regie sullimitatis
185   honore dignus. Pacem habuit usque ad ultimos dies quando cum Pictis cepit
habere bellum.

Post mortem Ethfyn, Eugenius octauus, filius Murdaci alias Nectanius,
adeptus est regnum Scotorum anno Domini vii^c lxi et regnauit duobus annis.

Cui successit Fergusius tercius, filius Ethfyn, anno Domini vii^c lxiii et
190   regnauit tribus annis.

The 3eir of God vi^c lxxxxviii, Amberkelethe, sone to Eugeny þe   **f.438v**
Fyft, ane vicious monstoure, gevin to immoderate lust and avarice,
was slane be ane schot of ane arow quhen he was passand with ane greit army
aganis þe Pychtis, þe secund 3eir of his regine.

155   Eugenius, þe vii of þat nayme, broder to Amberkeleth, ane nobill prince,
regnit xvii 3eir. He was þe first prince þat causit wail3eand deidis of nobill men
to be put in memory. He deceissit at Abernethy, and was buryit in Ycolmekill.

The 3eir of God vii^c xv, Mordak, sone to Amberkeleth, regnit eftir Eugeny
xv 3eir, ane [virtuus] prince, gevand all his justice and peax. In his last dayis
160   war tua cometis seyne, ane in þe mornyng and ane vþir at nycht.

The 3eir of God vii^c and xxx^{ti}, Ethfyne, þe sone of Eugeny þe Sevint,
succeidit to Murdak, and regnit nobilly in tranquillite and justice xxxi 3eir
rychtwyse, and in his last dayis begane to gife battaill to Pychtis.

Efter þe deid of Ethfyne, Eugeny, þe sone of Mordak, vþirwayis callit
165   Tamus, regnit. In þe begyning of his empyre, he appeirit gude, and sone eftir
fell in all maner of vice and crewelte, and was wnhappely slane be his
famyliaris, þe thrid 3eir of his regnne.

Fergus, þe thrid of þat nayme, regnit eftir his fader Ethfyne, and was slane
be industry of his wyfe for suspitioun of adultery, þe thride 3eir of his regnne.

In the year of the Lord 697, when Eugenius VI had died, Ambrikilleth, the son of Fyndan, the son of Eugenius V, succeeded to the kingdom of the Scots, and he reigned for one year.

When he had died, Eugenius VII, his brother, succeeded him and reigned for 17 years. A man in all things prudent, and modest, and of wise character, he improved his own kingdom by ruling with the best laws and ecclesiastical guidance, and he ended his tranquil life happily.

In the year of the Lord 715, when Eugenius VII had died, his nephew Murdac, son of Ambrikilleth, succeeded him to the kingdom of the Scots and reigned for 15 years. In his last year, two comets were seen, one of which preceded the rising sun in the morning, and the other followed the setting sun in the evening.

In the year of the Lord 730, when Murdach died, Ethfyn, the son of Eugenius VII, succeeded to the kingdom and reigned for 31 years. A man worthy of the supreme honor of kingship, he had peace until his last days, when he began to wage war with the Picts.

After the death of Ethfyn, Eugenius VIII (or Nectan), the son of Murdach, obtained the kingdom of the Scots in the year of the Lord 761 and reigned for two years.

Fergus III, the son of Ethfyn, succeeded him in the year of the Lord 763, and he reigned for three years.

Capitulo xxxiiii⁰: The ȝer of God vi^c lxxxxvii, Ambrikellech, þe son of
135   Fyndaw, þe sone of Eugeny þe IIII, succedit to Eugeny þe Fift, and he regnit a ȝer.

     To quhom succedit Eugeny þe VI, a wys man, and rewlit wele & peceablye þe realme xvii ȝer.

     Capitulo xxxv⁰: The ȝer of God vii^c & xv, Murdow, þe son of
140   Ambrikellech, regnit eftir Eugeny þe Sixt xv ȝer. In his tyme, þar was twa cometis sene in þe lift, ane at morne & þe toþir at ewyn.

     Capitulo xxxvi⁰: The ȝer of God vii^c & xxx, Ethfin, þe son of Eugeny þe VI, succedit to Murdow, and regnit nobilly xxxi ȝeir, a   f.128r noble man and ane wys, and in his last dayis began to gif batall to þe
145   Pictis.

     Capitulo xxxvii⁰: Eftir þe deid of Ethsin, Eugeny þe VII, þe sone of Murdow, vþirways callit Tamus, was crownit þe ȝer of God vii^c lxi and regnit bot a ȝer.

     To quhom Fergus þe son of Ethsin succedit & regnit iii ȝer.

Anno Domini vii^c lxvi, defuncto Fergusio, successit ei in regno Selwachius filius Eugenii octaui, et regnauit annis xxi. Et mortuus est in pace.

Anno Domini vii^c lxxxvii, Selwachio defuncto, successit ei in regno Athaius, filius Regis Ethfyn, et regnauit annis xxxii. Huius Athaii diebus
195 amicicia confederacionis inter reges, populos, & regna Francie et Scocie que nostros usque adhuc dies perseuerat, laudes Deo, per magnum Karolum Regem et hunc Athaium inicium habuit.

Huius itaque Athaii Regis frater fuit magnus ille bellator Gilmerius   **f.28r**
qui multis annis in magni Regis Karoli obsequio et excercitu contra
200 christiane fidei hostes strenue militauit, quique multorum in diuers partibus Almanie fundator extitit monasteriorum. Sed et Rome apud Sanctum Paulum insigne hospitale construxit.

Huius eciam diebus fundata est vniuersitas Parisiense per duos Scotos, videlicet Johannem & Clementem.
205 Anno Domini viii^c xix°, defuncto Athayo, Regni Scotorum regimen accepit Coguallus et regnauit quinque annis et mortuus est.

Cui successit in regnum Duncanus alias Dongallus, filius Selwachii Regis, et regnauit annis septem. Cepitque bellum habere cum Pictis durissimum, regnum Pictorum hereditario jure suum esse asserens.

---

170   Soluathius, sone to Eugenius þe VIII, succeidit to Fergus. He   **f.439r**
gouernit his realme in greit felicite and justice, and deceissit þe xx^{ty} ȝeir
of his regnne, fra þe Incarnatioun vii^c lxxxvii ȝeiris.

Quhen Soluathius was deid, Achayus, þe sone of Ethfyne, was crownit þe ȝeir of God vii^c lxxxvii and regnit in greit felicite xxxii ȝeir. In his tyme,
175 begane the band betuix Scotland and France quhilk lastit as ȝitt, thank be till Almychtty God.

Gilmore, þe nobill vereour, was þis Achayus broder, þe quhilk nobill man was in greit weris with Charlis, þe King of France, aganis þe Turkys, and biggit mony abbayis in Almane, and feft þame, þat na man suld duell þair bot Scottis
180 men. This nobill man biggit alsua ane hospitall at Sanct Paullis in Rome.

In þis Achayus tyme, was þe nobill vniuersyte of Parys foundit be tua Scottis men þat war callit Clement and Johnne.

Quhen þis Achayus was deid, Conwallus tuke þe croun, þe ȝeir of God viii^c xix, and regnit v ȝeir.
185 To quhame succeidit Duncane, vþirwayis callit Dongall, þe sone of Soluathius, and regnit vii ȝeir, and began strang battaill with þe Pychtis, and clamyt þe realme of Pichtis to be his be ressoun of þe first conuentioun. He peryst in þe wattir of Spaye.

In the year of the Lord 766, when Fergus had died, Selwach, the son of Eugenius VIII, succeeded him to the kingdom and reigned for 21 years. And he died in peace.

In the year of the Lord 787, when Selwach had died, Athaius, the son of King Ethfyn, succeeded him to the kingdom, and he reigned for 32 years. In the days of this Athaius, the league of friendship between the kings, peoples, and kingdoms of France and Scotland, which has lasted right up to our days, thanks be to God, had its beginning through King Charlemagne and this Athaius.

And so the brother of this King Athaius was that great warrior Gilmer, who for many years in the service and army of King Charlemagne fought vigorously against the enemies of the Christian faith and who was the founder of many monasteries in various parts of Germany. And he built a remarkable hospital at St Paul's in Rome.

Also, in his days, the University of Paris was founded by two Scots, namely John and Clement.

In the year of the Lord 819, when Athayus had died, Cogvall received the rule of the kingdom of the Scots, and he reigned for five years and died.

Duncan (or Dongal), son of King Selwach, succeeded him to the kingdom, and he reigned for seven years. And he began to wage a very hard war against the Picts, claiming the kingdom of the Picts was his by hereditary right.

---

150   *Capitulo xxxviii°*: The ȝer of God vii^c lxvi, Seluache, þe son of Eugeny þe VII, succedit to Fergus & regnit xxi ȝer, ane gud man.

     Capitulo xxxix: Achaius, þe son of Ethsin, was crovnit the ȝer of God vii^c lxxxvii and regnit xxxii ȝer. In his tyme, began þe band betuix Fraunce & Scotland, the gret Charllis beyng King of Fraunce, the quhilk band lestis ȝit,
155   thankit be God.

     Gilmor, þe noble weriour, was þis Achaius broþir, the quhilk nobill man was in greit weris with Charllis aganis þe Turkis, and biggit mony abbais in Almany, and feft þaim to Scottis men for evir. He biggit ane noble hospitale at Sanct Paulis in Rome.

160   In þis Achaius tyme was þe noble vniuersite of Paris foundit be twa Scottis men þat was callit Jhon and Clement.

     Capitulo xl°: Quhen þis Achaius was deid, Cognald tuke þe crown   **f.128v** the ȝeir of God viii^c and xix and regnit v ȝeir and deit.

     To quhom succedit Duncane, vþirwys callit Dongall, þe sone of Selwache,
165   and regnit vii ȝer. He began strang batell agane þe Pictis, and clamit þe realme of Pictis.

210   Anno Domini viii^c xxxi^o, mortuo Dongallo, Alpinus filius Athaii Regis, statim coronatus est, et regnauit tribus annis, et occisus est in bello a Rege Pictorum postquam in bello captus & deditus fuit.

    Filius autem Alpini, Kennedus successit in Regno Scotorum patri suo Alpino anno Domini viii^c xxxiiii, & regnauit iiii annis super Scotos solos, et *215*   superatis Pictis regnauit monarcha xvi annis. Et regnare cepit anno regnacionis Scotorum in Albion, que nunc Scocia dicitur, m^o c^o lxix exitus autem eorum de Egipto sub principe Gathelos, filio Regis Neoli, et uxore sua Scota ii^m iii^c xlix de quo sic scribitur metrice:

        Primus in Albania fertur regnasse Kenedus,
220   Filius Alpini, prelia multa gerens.
        Expulsis Pictis, regnauerat octo bis annis;
        Atque Forteuioth mortuus ille fuit.

    Quhen Dongall was deid, Alpyne, þe sone of Achayus, was crownit, þe *190*   ʒeir of God viii^c xxxi, and regnit thre ʒeir, and slew Feredeth, King of Pichtis, in plane battell. Eftir þat, Brudus and Kenneth, Kingis of Pichtis, war bayth slane, and Brudus þe Feirs chosin king, and faucht with [Alpyne], quhair he was slayne, and þe Scottis discumfyst, and his heid was   **f.439v** strykin of, and put one ane staik, in greit dispyte of Scottis.

195   The sone of Alpyne, callit Kenneth, succeidit to his fader, Alpyne, þe ʒeir of God viii^c xxxiiii, and regnit iiii ʒeir aboue þe Scottis, and ourcome þe Pichtis in plane battell vii tymes one ane day, and he regnit aboue baith xvi ʒeir. And he began to regnne, eftir þe regnne of Scottis, into Albany, þat is now Scotland, ane thousand ane hundreth xix, and eftir þe departing of *200*   Gathelus and Scota of Egipt, ii^m xlix ʒeiris.

    This Kenneth deyt at Forthirnothe.

Memorandum

    The Scottis regnit before þe Pychtis ii^c lxv ʒeiris and thre monethis, and þe Pichtis regnit in þe south part of Scotland, þat is Albany, fra þair first cuming *205*   or þai war distroyit, i^m lxi ʒeiris. Þai war distroyit ʒeir of God viii^c xxxviii.

In the year of the Lord 831, Dongal having died, Alpin, the son of King Athaius, was immediately crowned. He reigned for three years and was killed in battle by the King of the Picts after being captured in battle and surrendering.

Moreover, Kenneth, the son of Alpin, succeeded his father Alpin in the rule of the Scots in the year of the Lord 834. And he reigned for four years over the Scots alone, and then having conquered the Picts, he reigned as their monarch for 16 years. And he began to reign in the 1169th year of the rule of the Scots in Albion, which is now called Scotland, but in the 2349th year after their departure from Egypt under Prince Gathelos, son of King Neolus, and his wife Scota, as is written thus in verse:

> Kenneth is said to have been the first to rule in Albany,
> Son of Alpin, waging many battles.
> Having expelled the Picts, he reigned twice eight years;
> And he died at Forteviot.

Capitulo xli°: Quhen Dongall was deid, Alpine, þe sone of Athaius, was crowned, þe ȝer of God viii[c] xxxi, and regnit iii ȝer, and was slane in batell fechting nobilly aganis þe Pictis.

170   *Capitulo xlii°*: The son of Alpyne, callit Kenneth, succedit to his fader Alpine, the ȝer of God viii[c] xxxiiii & regnit iiii ȝer apon þe Scottis, and ourcome þe Pictis in batell and regnit on baith xvi ȝer. He began to regne, eftir þe regne of Scottis, in Albany, þat is now Scotland, i[m] i[c] lxix ȝeris, and eftir þe parting furth of Gathelos & Scota out of Egipt, ii[m] ccc xlix ȝeris.

175   The Scottis regnit befor þe cummyn of þe Pictis cc lxv ȝeris and thre monethis. And þe Pictis regnit in þe south part of Scotland, callit Albany, fra þar cummyng or þai war distroyit i[m] lxi ȝeris.

Erat is fortis vir prudens perspicacis ingenii atque bellorum executor audacissimus. Hic quatuor ex causis duxit Pictos e terra tollendos. Primo quia
225 patrem suum post dedicionem crudeliter occiderunt. Secundo propter furtum vnius molosi quem nec restituere nec pro eo satisfacere voluerunt sicut dictum est. Tercio quia dixit se probaturum regnum esse suum jure hereditario propter conuencionem factam cum Pictis in dacione vxorum. Sed est quarta causa potissima fuit, quia cum eo tempore in tota Albion insula essent f.28v
230 quatuor gentes, scilicet Scoti et Picti in ea parte que nunc Scocia dicitur, Saxones et Britanni in ea parte que nunc Anglia dicitur, essentque tres earum gentes Christiane religionis cultrices, scilicet Scoti, Picti, et Britanni, et vna sola infidelis, scilicet gens Saxonum pagana qui nunc Angli dicuntur. Isti Picti rupto federe quod habebant cum Scotis Christianis junxerunt se federe
235 Saxionibus paganis ad internecionem Scotorum et Britonum. Et quid[em] Deo permittente Britones eiecti sunt de regno suo, paucis exceptis, in Wallia permanentibus sub dicione Regis Anglie. Scoti vero Deo eis magis propicio auxiliatore Pictorum Regno simul et Scotorum pociuntur pacifice usque in hodiernum diem omni viuente interfecto in Regno Pictorum quod secum non
240 adduxerunt Scoti.

Hic Rex Kenedus xii° regni sui anno sexties vno die bellum commisit contra Pictos et Saxones et septies victor effectus est. Vnde notandum quod Pictorum reges in Albion regnauerunt lxiii per mille ducentos vii annos. Et iste Kenedus vltimum eorum Regem Drustonem commisso grauissimo
245 prelio apud Sconam simulque totam gentem et linguam destruxit.

This Kenneth distroyit þe Pychtis, man, woman, and child, and þair last king at Scone, Dronestane, for foure causs. The first caus was þat þai slew his fader, Alpyne, and put his heyd for dispyt one ane staik. The secund caus, for steling of ane quhyte hoynd, as said is before. The thrid caus, for he
210 clamyt to be king of þe first conventioun. The fourt caus, for þai maid paix with þe Saxonis of Ingland þat war paganis and vncrystynnyt, and sua þai alsua and þe Britonnis, and sua of þir foure nationis war nane vncrystynit bot þe Saxonis.

This Kenneth eikit þe boundis of Scotland to Northumbirland and kest
215 doun Camelon. He maid mony plesand lawis and actis for weill of his subdittis.

In þis tyme, þe Dunbarris tuke þair begyning.

This was a strong, prudent man, of acute intelligence, and a very daring fighter of battles. He caused the Picts to be removed from the land for four reasons. First, because they cruelly killed his father after he had surrendered. Second, because of the theft of a hound which they refused to return or give satisfaction for, as has been said. Third, because he said the kingdom would be proven to be his by hereditary right according to the pact made with the Picts when they were given wives. But it is the fourth cause that was the strongest, that since at that time in all the island of Albion there were four peoples – that is, the Scots and the Picts in that part that is now called Scotland; Saxons and Britons in that part that is now called England. Three of them were people who fostered the Christian faith – namely the Scots, Picts, and Britons – and only one infidel people – namely the pagan Saxon people who are now called English. Those Picts had broken the treaty they had with the Christian Scots and joined themselves by treaty with the pagan Saxons for the destruction of the Scots and Britons. And indeed, by the permission of God, the Britons were cast out of their kingdom, except for a few who persist in Wales under the authority of the King of England. The Scots, God being a very propitious help to them, rule peacefully over the kingdom of the Picts together with that of the Scots right up to the present day, with every living thing in the kingdom of the Picts killed that the Scots did not take with them.

In the 12th year of his reign, this King Kenneth engaged in battle with the Picts and Saxons six times in one day, and seven times he was the victor. It is noteworthy that 63 kings of the Picts reigned in Albion for 1207 years. And this Kenneth fought Drust, the last of their kings, in a very great battle fought at Scone and destroyed all the people and their language at the same time.

And þis Kenneth distroyed þe Pictis and þar last king, Drustone, at Scone. Sevyne tymes on a day he facht & was euir victor. He distroyit man, woman, & child for four causs. Ane was for þai slew his fader. The secund for þe steling of þe hunde or rathe þat is spokin of befor. The thrid for he clamed to be king be ressoun of þe first conuencioun. The ferd for þai **f.129r** maid pece with þe Saxonis of Yngland þat war paganis and brak trewis with him þat was cristinnit. Thar was four nacionis in þis ile, that was to say Scottis, Pictis, & Britones, and þai war cristinnit, and þe ferd vncristinnit, þat was þe Saxonis.

This Kenneth deit at Forthernocht.

Anno Domini viii^c liiii, defuncto Kenedo magno et solempniter celebratis eius obsequiis, successit eidem in Regno Scotorum Donaldus, frater eius et Alpini filius, et regnauit quatuor annis.

Cui successit Constantinus primus, filius Kenedi magni, et regnauit xvi 250 annis, occisus tandem a Danis commisso grauissimo prelio, quo eciam tempore Sanctus Edmundus Rex Anglie ab eadem pagana gente Danorum occiditur et martir Deo effectus est.

Anno Domini viii^c lxxiiii, Constantino defuncto, successit ei in regnum Ethus Alipes, filius magni Kenedy, frater Constantini, et vno anno regnauit. 255 Hic propter maximam quam habuit pedum velocitatem dictus est Alipes quasi habens pedes alatos.

Quo defuncto, successit eidem in regnum ˏScotorum Gregorius   f.29r filius Dongalli Regis, qui apud Sconam coronatus est, anno Domini viii^c lxxv, et regnauit xvii. Hic primo anno regni sui libertatem concessit ecclesie 260 Scoticane et ecclesiasticis personis confirmatam a Johanne Papa octauo Constantinopli in quinto eius synodo. Iste sibi subiugauit totam Yberniam et pro maiori parte Angliam, quam partim vi, partim clemencia subegit.

ˏEfter þe deid of greit Kenneth, Donald, his broder and sone of   f.440r Alpyne, regnit þe ʒeir of God viii^c liiii and regnit iiii ʒeir. He was ane 220 tyrane, gevin to immoderate avarice and lust, and for þe samyn, he tynt all þe landis of Scotland beʒonde Clyde. At þe last, þe nobillis conspyrit aganis him and kest him in presoun, quhair he slew himself for disperatioun.

Efter þe deid of þis Donald, Constantyne, þe sone of Kenneth, regnit xvi ʒeiris, and at þe last he was slane with þe Danis, quhilk war paganis, in ane 225 greit battell callit þe Blak Cow, be Hungar, eftir þat he hade discumfit Hubla and his collegis, and was bureyt in Ycolmekill.

Efter þe deid of þis Constantyne, Ethus, his broder, was maid King of Scottis þe ʒeir of God viii^c lxxiiii, and he regnit bot ane ʒeir, for he was ane man of dull ingyne and abill to nathing les þan the adminstratioun of his 230 realme. He was depryvit of authorite, and put in presoun, quhair he deyt þe secund ʒeir of his regnne, and was bereyt in Ycolmekille.

Efter quhais deithe, Gregoir þe Greit, sone of Congall þat pereist in Tay, regnit þe ʒeir of God viii^c lxxv. This Gregore grantit fredome to Haly Kirk and personnis þairof, and it was confermit be Johnne, viii paip of þat name, in his 235 first synody haldin at Constantinopill. This Gregore subjectit to him all Ireland, and eykit Northumbirland, Cumbyir, and Westmurland to þe Empyre of Scottis, and maid mony nobill lawis, and deceissit þe xviii ʒeir of his regnne, and was bureyt in Ycolmekill, fra oure redemptioun viii^c lxxxxiii ʒeiris.

184

In the year of the Lord 854, when the great Kenneth was dead and his obsequies had been solemnly celebrated, Donald, his brother and a son of Alpin, succeeded him to the kingdom of the Scots, and he reigned for four years.

Constantine I, son of the great Kenneth, succeeded him, and he reigned for 16 years. He was eventually killed in a very great battle waged by the Danes, and at that time, too, St Edmund, King of England, was killed by that same pagan race of Danes and became God's martyr.

In the year of the Lord 874, when Constantine was dead, Ethus the Wing-Footed, son of the great Kenneth and brother of Constantine, succeeded him to the kingdom, and he reigned for one year. Because of his very great speed of foot, this man was called "Wing-Footed" as if he had winged feet.

When he was dead, Gregory, son of King Donald, succeeded him to the kingdom of the Scots; he was crowned at Scone in the year of the Lord 875, and he reigned for 17 years. In the first year of his reign, he granted freedom to the Scottish Church and to clerics, which was confirmed by Pope John VIII at his Fifth Council in Constantinople. He made all of Ireland subject to him and subdued the greater part of England, partly by force and partly by clemency.

Capitulo xliii⁰: Eftir þe deid of þis gret Kenneth, Donald, his broþir and son of Alpine, regnit þe ȝer of God viiiᶜ liiii and regnit four ȝer.

190   To quhom succedit Constantyne, þe son of Kenneth, & he regnit xvi ȝer, and at þe last was slane with þe Danis and paganis, in a gret batell callit þe Blak Cove.

Capitulo xliiii⁰: Ethus Alipes succedit to Constantyne, þe son of Kenneth, his broþir, the ȝer of God viiiᶜ lxxiiii, and he regnit bot a ȝer.

195   *Capitulo xlv⁰:* Eftir quhais deid, Gregory, þe son of Dongall, was crownit the ȝer of God viiiᶜ lxxv and regnit xvii ȝer. This Gregory was þe gretest þat euir was in Scotland, as Arthour in Yngland and Charllis in Fraunce. He subject to his obedience all Irland and Yngland to Themes nere hand and Walis, part with force and part with fauouris. He grantit first fredome

200   to Haly Kirk, and it was confermit be Jhon, þe viii pape of þat name, **f.129v** in his first synode, haldin at Constantinople. This was a noble and a victorius king.

Huius Gregorii tempore floruit Johannes Scotus qui, rogatu Karoli Calui, *Ierarchiam* Dionisii Arriopagite de Greco uerbum e uerbo transtulit in
265 Latinum; sed postea in Anglia apud monasterium Malmisberiense stilis puerorum quos docendos susceperat confossus martir effectus est.

Defuncto Gregorio, successit in Regno Scotorum Donaldus filius Constantini anno Domini viii^c lxxxxii, et regnauit annis xi, et defunctus est apud Fores.

270 Constantinus secundus, filius Hethi Alipedis, Donald[o] mortuo, succedens anno Domini ix^c iii in regem coronatus apud Sconam, regnauit xl annis. Qui xvi regni sui anno dedit Eugenio, filio Donaldi successori sibi sperato; qui tamen ante ipsum Constantinum defunctus est, totam Cumbrie regionem quoadusque regni diadema post eius mortem fuerit obtent[um]. Ac
275 ut eo coronato suus heres proximus ad idem succederet, et quod sic semper de vno herede in alium fieret, instituit.

Huius tempore commissum est grauissimum bellum de Bronyngis felde. Hic diuina gracia inspirante xl^{mo} anno regni sui sponte regno dimisso, religionem intrat apud Sanctum Andree, Kelledeorum abbas effectus, et annis
280 quinque superuixit.

Efter þe deithe of Gregore, Donald þe VI, sone to King f.440v
240 Constantyne þe Secund, was maid King of Scottis. He deceissit þe xi ʒeir of his regnne at Fores, and was bureyt in Ycolmekill. He maid sindry lawis.

In his tyme, þe realme of Normannis and þe Duchery of Flanderis tuke þair begyning.

245 Constantyne þe Thrid, sone to King Ethus, succeidit to Donald þe ʒeir of God ix^c and iii, and regnit xl^{ty} ʒeir. He gaif all Cumbirland to his apperand air, Eugeny, þe sone of þe said Donald, vndir þis conditioun, þat euir þe prince or air of Scotland suld haif it quhill þai war crownit king.

In his tyme, was þe greit battell of Brounyngfeild streikkin, quhair
250 Eugeny, Donaldis sone, was slane. And becaus his army was discumfist, he exonerat him of all princely dignite, and tuke þe habyt of ane channoun regulare, and enterit in religioun, quhair he leiff vi ʒeiris eftir, and deceissit in þe Abbay of Sanct Androis, bot he was bureyt in Ycolmekill. In þe xi buke, capitulo x°.

In the time of this Gregory, John the Scot flourished, who, at the request of Charles the Bald, translated the *Hierarchy* of Dionysius the Areopagite word for word from Greek into Latin. But afterwards, in England at the monastery of Malmesbury, he was made a martyr, stabbed by the styluses of the boys whom he had undertaken to teach.

When Gregory was dead, Donald, son of Constantine, succeeded to the kingdom of the Scots in the year of the Lord 892, and he reigned for 11 years, and he died at Forres.

Constantine II, son of Ethus the Wing-Footed, succeeded when Donald died in the year of the Lord 903; he was crowned king at Scone and reigned 40 years. In the 16th year of his reign, he gave all of the region of Cumbria to Eugenius, son of Donald, his intended successor (who nevertheless died before Constantine himself), until he obtained the crown of the kingdom after Constantine's death. And when Eugenius was crowned, his nearest heir would succeed to Cumbria, and thus Constantine established that it would always pass from one heir to another.

In his time, the very great battle of Brunanburh was fought. Inspired by divine grace, he freely renounced his rule in the 40th year of his reign, and entered the religious life at St Andrews, became abbot of the Culdees, and survived five years more.

Capitulo xlvi⁰: Efter þe deid of Gregory, Donald, þe son of Constantyne, was crownit in þe ȝeir of God viiiᶜ xcii and regnit xi ȝeir and deit at Fores and
205   was erdit in Comekill.

Capitulo xlvii⁰: Constantyne þe Thrid succedit to Donald þe ȝer of God ixᶜ & thre, and regnit xl ȝer. He was Ethus Alipes son. He gaf all Cummerland till his apperand air Eugeny, þe son of þe said Donald, vnder þis condicioun: þat euir þe prince or air of Scotland suld haue it till he war
210   crovnit king, and þan it suld fall to þe air quha euir war nixt prince.

In þis mannis tyme, was þe gret batell of Brownyngisfeld strikin, quhar Eugeny, Donaldis son, was slane. The xl ȝeir of Constantynis regne, he left þe warld and enterit in religioun and levit v ȝeris eftir.

Anno Domini ix^c xliii, Constantinus diuine miseracionis gracia inspirante, sede regia se euacuans, Malcolmo primo filio Donaldi locum regnandi dedit, qui coronatus regnauit annis ix, cui Eadmundus Rex Anglie totam Cumbriam pro amicicia seruanda contra Danos tradidit inperpetuum sub fide jurata
285 possedendam. Decretumque est inter reges et Regni Scocie et Anglie quod temporibus futuris pro bono pacis Scocie et Anglie ut heres   f.29v Regis Scotorum pro tempore existens homagium Regi Anglie prestaret pro regione Cumbrie quam perpetuo possederent.

Malcolmo defuncto, successit Indulfus, filius Constantini filii Hethi
290 Alipedis, et regnare cepit anno Domini ix^c lii, et regnauit ix annis; habuitque bellum maximum contra Danos, contra quos viriliter se defendendo spiculo transfixus capud diem clausit extremum.

Indulfo sic defuncto, successit in Regno Scotorum Duffus, filius Malcolmi, anno Domini ix^c lxi, et regnauit quatuor annis et sex mensibus, qui
295 fuit vir columbine simplicitatis, pacem diligens, sed rebellum predonum et latronum seuerus vltor terribilis et cruentus. Hic tum fuit occisus proditorie & Morauiensibus, et corpus eius absconditum. Sed sol radios non emisit super terram quousque repertum est corpus eius, et in sepulcris patrum collocatum. Vnde de eo metrice dignum:

---

255 Efter þe deid of Constantyne, Malcome þe First, sone to King Donald þe VI, was maid King of Scottis. He was confiderate with Inglismen, and gouernit his realme in greit felicite and peax. Bot at þe last, he was slane be tressoun of Murray men becaus he was ourer scharp pwnissar of justice, and bureyt in Ycolmekill þe xv ʒeir of his rignne, fra oure redemptioun ix^c lix ʒeiris.

260 Efter þe deithe [of] Malcome, Indulphe, sone to Constantyne þe Thrid, was crownit King of Scottis. He defendit his realme nobilly fra inuasioun of Danis. Bot at þe last, he was slane crewellie fechtand to þe deith be Danis in Bouchquhane, þe ix ʒeir of his regnne, þe ʒeir of God ix^c xviii ʒeiris.

Efter Indulphe, Duffus, þe sone of Malcome þe First, was crownit,   f.441r
265 ane just prince, richt deuote, meik, and religious. He was slane in þe nycht be tressoun of Donald, capitane of Fores, and his body was heyd besyde Killois be þe murderaris, vnknawin sax monethis. All þe said tyme nouþir sone, mone, nor sterne war seyne in Scotland, bot þe lyft ourcouerit ay with perpetuall dirknes, quhill his body was tane wp and buryit in Ycolmekill, þe
270 v [ʒeir] of his regine, fra oure redemptioun ix^c lxxii ʒeiris.

He was trublet als be incantatioun of wychis, quhilk roistit him in walx, and hade greit infirmite þairthrow. And becaus he pwnist certane conspiratouris þat war freindis to Donald, he was slane, as said is.

In the year of the Lord 943, Constantine, inspired by the grace of divine compassion, vacated his royal throne and gave it to Malcolm, son of Donald, to reign in his place. He was crowned and reigned for 9 years. To protect their alliance against the Danes, Edmund, King of England handed over all Cumbria to him to be held in perpetuity under a sworn oath. And it was decided between the kings and the kingdoms of Scotland and England that in future times, for the good of the peace of Scotland and England, the heir of the King of the Scots at the time should perform homage to the King of England for the region of Cumbria, which they would possess in perpetuity.

When Malcolm was dead, Indulf, son of Constantine, son of Ethus the Wing-Footed, succeeded him. And he began to reign in the year of the Lord 952, and he reigned for 9 years. And he fought a very great battle against the Danes, and while he was defending himself courageously against them, he ended the last day of his life pierced by an arrow in his head.

When Indulf had thus died, Duff, son of Malcolm, succeeded to the kingdom of the Scots in the year of the Lord 961, and he reigned four years and six months. He was a man of dove-like simplicity, loving peace, but to rebels, robbers, and thieves a severe, frightful, and bloody avenger. Then he was treacherously killed by men of Moray, and his body was concealed. But the sun did not send out its rays upon the earth until his body was discovered and placed in the graves of his ancestors. The following verse was written as a result:

Capitulo xlviii°: Eftir þis Constantyne enterit in religioun, Malcome, þe son
215 of þe said Donald, was crowned in þe ȝer of God ix^c xliii and regnit ix ȝer. And
he was slane be tressoun of Murray men and erdit in Comekill.

ˌ*Capitulo xlix°*: Efter þe deid of Malcome, Indulphe, þe son of   **f.130r**
Constantyne þe Secund, was crownit þe ȝer of God ix^c lii, & regnit ix
ȝer and defendit þe realme nobilly fra þe Danis. And at þe last was slane be
220 þe Danis and erdit in Comekill.

Capitulo l°: Duffus, þe son of Malcome was crownit the ȝer of God ix^c lxi
and he regnit iiii ȝeir and a half. This was ane innocent and ane gud man and
was slane be tresoun of Murray men, and his body was hid, bot þe son schane
nocht on þe erd till he was takin wp & erdit in Comekill.

300   Quatuor et semis Rex Duff regnauit arestis,
      Malcolmo natus, regia jura tenens.
      Hunc interfecit gens perfida Morauiensis,
      Cuius erat gladiis cesus in urbe Fores.
      Sol abdit radios, ipso sub ponte latente,
305   Quo fuit absconsus, qu[o]que repertus erat.

Anno Domini ix^c lxv, Culenus, filius Indulfi Regis, mortuo Duffo, in regem susceptus, et regnauit iiii annis et sex mensibus; ad regni vero regimen per omnia vir inutilis nichil enim regale aut memoria dignum in diebus eius gestum est, nisi quod propter flagicia sua plurima ab insidiantibus occisus est.

310   Anno Domini ix^c lxx°, mortuo Culeno, Kenedus secundus, Malcolmi filius, frater Regis Duffi, regnare cepit et regnauit annis xxiiii et mensibus nouem. Omnibus diebus suis pacem habuit, statimque regno adepto Malcolmum, filium Duffi, suum successorem Regem Cumbrie ordinauit. In diebus   f.30r
eius statutum est, ut regi ex hac vita discedenti superstes sanguine
315   proximus succedere deberet licet infans vnius diei: cum dicatur etas regis in fide subditorum consistere, quamquam usque ad illa tempora semper propinquior de sanguine regis qui ad virilem etatem peruenerat regnauerit, nichil tamen contra statutum suum futuris temporibus hec consuetudo valeret. Vnde ex hoc grauiter indignati multi Comitissam de Angus ut regem perderet proditorie instigant;
320   sicque mulieris prodicione arteque nephanda interemptus est.

Culyne, sone to King Indulphe, was crownit eftir þe deith of Duffus, ane
275   terribill and odious tyrrane, full of infamyt werkis, deflorand virginis and matronys with mony vþir vicious werkis. Neuirþeles, at þe last, he was slane be ane gentillman callit Callard, for defloratioun of his dochter, eftir þat he hade gouernit Scotland v ʒeiris to þe greit displesour of þe pepill, and was buryit in Ycolmekill, fra oure redemptioun ix^c lxxvii ʒeiris.
280   In his tyme, war syndry mervellis seyne in Albioun.
Kenneth þe Thrid, sone to King Malcome, was crownit eftir þe deith of Culyne. He gat ane glorious victour of þe Danis at Loncart, and causit þe nobillis till bring sindry lymmaris to his justice. He slew þe Prince of Scotland, þat his sone mycht succeid to þe croun. He abrogat þe auld lawis concernyng þe
285   electioun of kingis and statute þat þe nerrest blude suld succeid to þe croun, þocht he war ane child of ane ʒeir auld. Quhairfore he was invyit and haitit with mony, and at þe last was slane tresonabilly be Fenella, Countes of Angus,   f.441v
be ingyne maid be ane crocebow, quhilk was ane subtell woman, þe xv
ʒeir of his regnne, and was buryit in Ycolmekill, fra oure redemptioun i^m ʒeiris.

King Duff reigned for four and a half summers,
Son of Malcolm, upholding royal rights.
Treacherous people of Moray killed him,
By whose swords he was cut down in the city of Forres.
The sun put away its rays while he lay hidden under a bridge;
Where he was concealed, he was also discovered.

In the year of the Lord 965, Culen, son of King Indulf, was raised to king after the death of Duff, and he reigned four years and six months. In truth, he was a worthless man for the business of ruling in every way; for nothing royal or memorable was done in his days, except that because of his many shameful acts, he was killed by men lying in wait.

In the year of the Lord 970, on the death of Culen, Kenneth II, son of Malcolm and brother of King Duff, began to reign, and he reigned for 24 years and nine months. He had peace all his days, and as soon as he had attained the kingdom, he appointed Malcolm, son of Duff, his successor as King of Cumbria. In his days, it was decreed that when the king departs from this life, the survivor nearest in blood ought to succeed, even if it is an infant of one day, because it may be said that the age of the king depends upon the loyalty of his subjects, although up to that time, the nearest to the blood of the king who had arrived at adulthood always reigned; but this custom had no power against his law in future times. Because of this, many gravely outraged men treacherously incited the Countess of Angus to destroy the king. And thus he was killed by the treachery and unspeakable cunning of this woman.

---

225   *Capitulo li⁰*: The ȝeir of God ix꜀ lxv, Culene, þe son of Indulphe, regnit efter Duff iiii ȝer and sex monethis, and was wnhappy and curst and at þe last slayne for his cursitnes.

    Capitulo lii⁰: The ȝer of God ix꜀ lxx, Kenneth þe Secund, son of Malcome, was crovnit & regnit xxiiii ȝer. This Kenneth statut & ordanit þat

230 þe nixt of þe blud, suppos he war a child of a ȝer ald, suld succeid to þe crowne. Quharfor he was inwyit and haitit with mony, and at þe last, be þe Countas of Angus he was tratorisly slane & erdit in Comekill.

Post Kenethi Regis mortem, Constantinus tercius caluus, filius Culeni, regnum inuasit, despecta publica constitucione predicta anno Domini ix^c xciiii. In diebus eius facta est incolarum diuisio, plebium strages, turbacio magnatum miseranda cedesque multorum, et effusio sanguinis innocentum.

325 Et sic male arreptum tenuit regnum per annum cum dimedio, et occisus est commisso prelio in Laudania.

Anno Domini ix^c xcvi mortuo Constantino caluo, regnum Scotorum inuasit Grym, filius Kyneduf, eo jure quo predecessor suus. Et multiplicata sunt mala in Regno Scocie regnante eo, et regnauit octo annis quibus

330 regnicolarum dampna increuerunt valide. Tandem occisus est commisso bello cum Malcolmo legittimo regni herede et filio Kenedi Regis.

Victoria potitus Malcolmus non sibi statim regis nomen assumpsit, sed conuocatis regni principibus coronam regni ab eis sibi dari, si jura permitterent, alias non, peciit humiliter. At illi regie successionis legem

335 diebus patris sui statutam per omnia ratam habentes ipsum regem legittimum pronunciant et coronant: et sic regnare cepit anno Domini millesimo quarto, et sic regnauit feliciter annis xxx^{ta}. Hic apud Scotos rex victoriosissimus fuisse perhibetur, quia nusquam ab inimicis victus est.

---

290 In his tyme, þe Hayis tuke þair begyning.

Eftir þe deith of Kenneth, Constantyne, þe ferd of þat name, sone to King Culyne, tuke þe croune, and was slane þe thride ȝeir of his regnne at þe mouth of Awmount, in Louthiane, in ane greit battaill, and Kenneth, his aduersare, baith. In his tyme, was greit murthour and slauchter of innocentis,

295 and mony greit nobillis slayne. He was bureyt in Ycolmekill, fra oure redemptioun i^m iii ȝeiris. In þe xi buke, capitulo xio.

In his tyme, was mervellis seyne in Albioun.

Gryme, nepote to King Duffe, tuke þe croune injustlie. In þe begyning of his regnne, he was ane nobill and vertuus prince, and eftir þat, he become ane

300 maist corruptit tyrane, and was slane be Malcome, þe sone of Kenneth, þe ix ȝeir of his regnne, and was bureyt in Ycolmekill, fra oure redemptioun i^m ix ȝeiris.

Malcome, þe secund of þat name, sone to Kenneth þe Thride, was crownit with consent of his nobillis, keping þe statutis his fader Kenneth maid. He

305 devydit all þe landis of Scotland in baronyis, and gaif þame frelie amang his nobillis, and he gat fra þame þair wairdis and releiffis of all frehaldaris airis, to sustene him, and þair mariages. He was wictorius vpoun Ingland, Irland, Waillis, and all vþiris landis.

After the death of King Kenneth, Constantine III the Bald, son of Culen, usurped the kingdom, disregarding the aforesaid public settlement, in the year of the Lord 994. In his days, there was made a division of the inhabitants, a destruction of the common people, a deplorable disorder of the magnates, a slaughter of many, and bloodshed of the innocent. And having thus evilly seized the kingdom, he held it for a year and a half and was killed in a battle fought in Lothian.

In the year of the Lord 996, when Constantine the Bald was dead, Grym, son of Kyneduf, usurped the kingdom of the Scots by the same right as his predecessor. And evils were multiplied in the kingdom of Scotland while he reigned. And he reigned for eight years, during which the injuries of his subjects increased mightily. At last he was killed in a battle fought with Malcolm, the legitimate heir to the kingdom and son of King Kenneth.

Once he had attained victory, Malcolm did not immediately assume the name of king, but he assembled the princes of the kingdom and petitioned them humbly that they grant him the crown of the kingdom if the laws permitted, and not otherwise. But they, maintaining in all respects the law of royal succession established in the days of his father, pronounced him the legitimate king and crowned him. And so he began to reign in the year of the Lord 1004, and so he reigned successfully for 30 years. Among the Scots he was considered to have been the most victorious king, because he was nowhere vanquished by his enemies.

Capitulo liii°: Efter þe deid of þis Kenneth, Constantyne, Culenis   f.130v
oye, invadit þe crovne and tuke it þe ȝer of God ix^c xciiii and held þe
235   crovne a ȝeir and a half and was slane in þe feld for his cursitnes at þe watter
of Almond in Louthian. In his tyme was gret truble & slauchter of innocentis,
and gret noblis murdrist & slane.

Capitulo liiii°: In þe ȝer of God ix^c xciiii, Gryme, þe son of Duff, with þe
wrang titill of his predecessour, inwadit þe crovne and tuke it. And mekle ill
240   was done in þe realme. And he regnit viii ȝeris, bot at þe last he was slane be
Malcome, the son of Kenneth, þe richtuis air of þe land.

Capitulo lv°: Quhen þis Malcome had þe wictory, he tuke nocht þe crovne
on him till it was grantit him be þe lordis of þe land. And þe noblis of þe land
crovnit him, obseruand and kepand þe statut þat his fader maide, the ȝer of
245   God i^m & iiii ȝeris. And he regnit xxx ȝeris, and was callit mast victorius, for
he was neuir ourcummyn.

Anno regni sui septimo, gracia Dei inspirante, de prediis sibi a Deo
340   collatis ‸nouam sedem episcopalem constituit apud Murtilach et nunc   **f.30v**
dicitur Abirdonensis.   Hic eciam rex mire fuit liberalitatis siue
prodigalitatis quia cum omnes terras regias et redditus inter nobiles regni ac
suos milites distribuisset, nichil sibi retinendo, peciit ab eis sibi prouidere
vnde sue maiestatis regie honestas decusque poterit sustentari, et ut inbecillis
345   plebs contribucionis graui onere non deprimeretur.   At tunc tam a nobilibus
quam plebe constitutum est, vt cunctorum nobilium libere tenencium
cuiuscumque status sint heredes cum terris et dominiis in custodia regis
essent usque vicesimum annum vna cum maritagiis cuiuscumque libere
tenentis.   Hic xxx anno regni sui letaliter a proditoribus vulneratus, quos
350   tamen ipse prius vicerat, ex hac luce migrauit.

Sepulto Malcolmo victoriossimo rege cum patribus, Duncanus nepos eius
ex filia Beatrice et patre Abthano de Dow, regis dyadema suscipiens, regnare
cepit anno Domini m° xxxiiii, et sex annis regnauit, occisus tandem a
Machabeda proditorie.

Bot at þe last, he become be lang aige maist crewell and
310   awaricious tyrane, and ‸was þairfore hurt be conspiratioun of his   **f.442r**
familiaris vndir nycht at Glammys, quhilk war all slane þairfore, and
he deyt of his woundis þe xxxi ȝeir of his regine and was bureyt in
Ycolmekill, fra oure redemptioun i^m xl^ty ȝeiris. He maid ane vþir bischoprik
in Scotland at Murthlak, now callit Abirdene.
315   In his tyme, þe Keithis tuke þair begyning.
Quhen Malcome was deid, Duncane, his nevo of þe douchter of Beatrix,
and his fader was callit Abthane of Dowe, was crownit King of Scottis. He
wincust þe Danis with sindry victoryis, and was slane tresonabilly be
Makbethe, þe saxt ȝeir of his regine, and buryit in Ycolmkill, fra þe
320   Incarnatioun i^m xlvi ȝeiris.
In his tyme, þe Stewartis tuke þair begyning.

In the seventh year of his reign, inspired through the grace of God, he established from the estates conferred on him by God a new episcopal see at Mortlach, now called Aberdeen. This king was also marvelously liberal or prodigal, because when he had distributed all the royal properties and revenues among the nobles of the kingdom and his knights, keeping nothing for himself, he asked them to provide him with something from which he might be able to sustain his majesty and royal honor and distinction and so that the lesser people would not be weighed down by a heavy burden of payment. Then it was granted by both the nobles and commons that the heirs of all the nobles and freeholders of whatever rank, together with their lands and houses, should be in the custody of the king up to their 20th year, together with marriages of each freeholder. In the 30th year of his reign, he was fatally wounded by traitors whom he had earlier overcome, and he migrated from this light.

When the most victorious Malcolm was buried with his ancestors, his grandson Duncan, by his daughter Beatrice and the Abthane of Dull, took the royal diadem and began to reign in the year of the Lord 1034. He reigned for six years, treacherously killed at last by Macbeth.

He maid ane noþir beschoprik in Scotland at Mirtillache, now callit Aberdene. This king regnit apon Scotland, Irland, half Yngland, & Walis. He gaf all þe land of Scotland till his men in fee & heretage and held
250   nathing to himself bot þe hill of Scone till hald his parliament on. f.131r
And þar þe frehaldaris grantit him ward releif & mariage of þar childer. And at þe last at Glammis, he was hurt be tratouris, the qu[hi]lkis he ourcome and slew, bot he deit of his woundis.

    Capitulo lvi°: Quhen Malcome was deid, Duncan, his newo of his
255   douchter Beatrix, and his fader was callit Abthan of Dowe, was crownit the ȝeir of God i^m xxxiiii ȝeris, and he regnit vi ȝeris, and was slane with a tratour callit Makbeth.

355 Qui Machabeda expulsis legittimis heredibus regni, videlicet Malcolmo
Canmor et Duncano Ban, filiis dicti Duncani Regis, in Regno Scotorum se
violenter intrudens, regnare cepit anno Domini m° xl°. Malcolmus filius regis
et legittimus heres regni apud Edwardum Regem Anglie gratanter receptus
est. Donaldus frater eius in insulis se seruauit. Hic Machabeda multos nobiles
360 in diebus suis, veritus ne legittimi aliquando heredes ad regnum redirent,
exulare coegit; et inter ceteros Makduff Thanum siue Comitem de Fyf,
confiscatis eorum prediis bonisque omnibus circa annum regni sui xv.

Circa annum Domini m° liiii Thanus siue Comes de Fyf Makduf adiuit
Malcolmum legittimum heredem Regni Scocie in Anglia suadens ei redditum
365 ad regnum multis racionibus; quod cum Malcolmo placeret, dissim[u]lans
tamen ait, "Priuata," inquit, "vita michi apcius conuenire videtur quam regia
dignitas cum sim vir nullius continencie sed lubricus totus et
luxuriosus." At Makduf inquit, "Puellarum copiam Scocia nutrit;   f.31r
habebis quot volueris." "Aliud grauius me vrget," inquit Malcolmus.
370 "Ardentis auaricie igne succensus cum aliter non liceat rapina furtove
quodlibet optinere michi licere videtur." At Makduf, "Regno," inquit,
"potitus, auri, gemmarum, ceterorumque jocalium omnium opulenciam
habens, plura desines concupiscere." At tercio, Malcolmus, "Dolosus,"
inquit, "sum nulli fidem seruans."

Makbeth, nepote to King Malcome þe Thride, vsurpit þe croun, and put
away þe richtuis airis out of þe land. Þat was Malcome Canmore and Donald
Wann, þe sonnis of þe said Duncane, in Ingland, quhilk war keipit with Sanct
325 Edwart, King of Ingland. This Makbeth did mony plesand actis in þe
begyning of his regnne vnder cullour of justice, bot at last he schew his
crewelte and peruerst mynd, set to scheding of blude mair þan ony zeile of
justice. He exilit Makduff, Thane of Fyife, and confiscat and tuke all his land
and gudis.

When this Macbeth had expelled the legitimate heirs of the kingdom –
that is to say Malcolm Canmore and Donald Ban, the sons of the said King
Duncan – he violently usurped the kingdom of the Scots, and he began to
reign in the year of the Lord 1040. Malcolm, the king's son and the
legitimate heir to the kingdom, was gladly received by Edward, King of
England. His brother Donald kept himself unharmed in the isles. In his time,
this Macbeth, fearing the legitimate heirs might some day return to the
kingdom, forced many nobles into exile; and among them Macduff, Thane or
Count of Fife. He confiscated their properties and all their goods, around the
15th year of his reign.

Around the year of the Lord 1054, the Thane or Count of Fife, Macduff,
went to Malcolm, the legitimate heir of the throne of Scotland, in England,
and urged him for many reasons to return to the kingdom. Although this
pleased Malcolm, nevertheless he dissembled and said, "The private life
seems to suit me better than royal dignity, since I am a man of no self-
restraint, but entirely lecherous and wanton." But Macduff said, "Scotland
nourishes an abundance of girls; you will have as many as you want." "But
something more serious drives me," Malcolm said. "Inflamed by the fire of
ardent avarice, even though it may not otherwise be permitted, it seems to me
permissible to obtain anything I please by theft or plundering." Macduff
said, "Having gained control of the kingdom, you will have a wealth of gold,
gems, and every other trinket, and you will cease to lust after more." But
Malcolm spoke for the third time, "I am deceitful, keeping faith with no one."

Capitulo lvii⁰: This Makbeth put away þe richtuis airis owt of þe land, þat
was Malcome Canmor and Donald Wan, þe sonnis of þe said Duncane, and
violentlie intrusit himself into þe crovne. He began to ryng the ʒer of God iᵐ
& xl ʒeris, and he regnit xvi ʒeris. Malcome Canmor was kepit with Sanct
Eduard, King of Yngland. And Donald Wan abaid in þe out ylis. This
Makbeth exilit mony, dredand þe richtuis aris. In þe xv ʒer of his regne he
exilit Makduf, þe Thane of Fyffe, and confiskit and tuke all his gudis, as he
did of mony vþir nobillis.

375   Quo audito, Makduf velud spiculo confossus profunde suspirans ait, "Ve nobis miseris Scotis quibus vnum de tribus malis est eligendum, aut amissis omnibus temporalibus exilium perpetuum subire, aut tyranno execrabiliter deseruire, aut tibi qui propria confessione indignum te regis nomine profiteris. Sed nec tu," inquit, "nec tirannus ille [me] dominabitur: exilium

380   eligo." Et erumpentibus lacrimis, pugnis collisis, versus boream quo Scocia sita erat respiciens, alto gemitu cordis lamentando ait, "Valeas O Scocia natale solum pro perpetuo." Tunc Malcolmus recedentem Makduff blande reuocat dicens, "Verebar ne tu sicut alii prius in meam perniciem reditum persuaderes. Nunc quia intelligo te dolositatem detestari, ecce vado tecum

385   erisque michi secundus in regno, sed nec lubricum nec auarum aut dolosum recognosces. Sed tu precedere, nuncia amicis meum aduentum instare; ego confestim sequar."

    Precessit Makduf, et Malcolmus assumptis Anglicis qui secum ire vellent venit ad Scociam, vbi Makduf cum plurimis amicorum turmis prestolabantur

390   congratulabantur eius aduentui: statimque excercitus tyranni Makabede minui cepit, et Malcolmi crescere; quem Malcolmus ultra montes insecutus usque Lumfannan et ibi commisso prelio, eum interfecit anno Domini m° lvi° quinto die Decembris.

    Sed non multo post, Lulath, Machabede consobrinus, volens succedere

395   in regno, in sede regali positus est apud Sconam, qui post quatuor menses occisus est, apud Esse prouincie Strabolgy, anno Domini m° lvii tercio die mensis Aprilis ebdomada pasche feria quinta.

---

330   Throu quhilk he past in Ingland, and causit Malcome Canmore, with vþir Inglismen, cum in þair support, and chaisit Makbeth at Dunsynnane, quhair he was slane be Makduffe, þe xvi ʒeir of his regine, and bureyt in Ycolmkill, þe ʒeir of God iᵐ lxi ʒeir. In þe xiii buke, capitulo quarto.

When Macduff heard this, as if pierced by an arrow, he sighed deeply and said, "Woe to us wretched Scots, who must choose one of three evils: to submit to perpetual exile, losing all our worldly goods; or to serve a detestable tyrant; or to serve you who profess yourself by your own confession unworthy of the name of king. But neither you," he said, "nor that tyrant will dominate me: I choose exile." And bursting into tears, banging his fists together, looking to the north where Scotland was, lamenting with a deep groan from the heart, he said, "Farewell, Scotland, land of my birth, forever!" Then Malcolm mildly called Macduff back, saying, "I was afraid that you were persuading me, like others before, to return for my destruction. Now, because I know that you detest deceit, see! I will go with you, and you will be second to me in the kingdom, but you will see no lust or avarice or deceit. But you go ahead and announce to friends that my arrival is imminent; I will follow immediately."

Macduff went ahead, and Malcolm, taking those English who wanted to go with him, entered Scotland, where Macduff waited for him with many troops of friends, and they congratulated one another on his arrival. And immediately the army of the tyrant Macbeth began to shrink and that of Malcolm to grow. Malcolm pursued him over the mountains to Lumfanan and, joining battle there, he killed him in the year of the Lord 1056, on the fifth day of December.

But not long afterwards, Lulach, Macbeth's cousin, desiring to succeed to the kingdom, was placed on the throne at Scone. He was killed after four months at Esse, in the province of Strabolgy, in the year of the Lord 1057, the third day of April, the Thursday before Easter.

Capitulo lviii⁰: Abowt þis tyme, be þe helpe of þis Makduf and part of Ynglismen, Malcome Canmor come hame and chasit Makbeth our þe Month to Lunfannane, and þar a batell was strikin, and Makbeth was f.131v slane, the ȝeir of God iᵐ lvi þe v day of December.

270 Bot Lulach, his cosing, was iiii ȝeris intrusit in þe kingis set, and at Esse in þe province of Strabolgye, he was slane.

Et eodem mense Aprili die Sancti Marci anno eodem coronatus est Rex
Malcolmus et triginta sex annis regnauit. Vltimo anno regni sui
400   fundauit nouam ecclesiam Dunelmensem, & ecclesiam Sancte   f.31v
Trinitatis de Dunfermlyn, et multis refecit donariis. Nupsit autem
sanctissime ac religiosissime mulieri beate videlicet Margarete, filie Regis
Edwardi, Regis Anglie, genuitque ex ea sex filios, quorum tres ante patrem
defuncti, alii tres successiue regnauerunt. Ipse Malcolmus in obsidendo
405   Castrum de Awnwik occisus est xiii die Nouembris; et gloriosa illa ac omni
tempore recolenda Regina Margareta, quarto die sequenti, perceptis in
ecclesia sacramentis ecclesiasticis, animam sanctam celo reddidit etc.

Anno Domini m° xciii defuncto Malcolmo inclitissimo Scotorum Rege,
in regno se intrusit Donaldus Bane, frater dicti Malcolmi, et regnauit sex
410   mensibus; sed expulsus est de regno per Duncanum, filium notum ipsius
Malcolmi, qui et ipse regnauit anno et sex mensibus, et sic occisus est insidiis
dicti Donaldi Bane, quem ipse prius expulerat de regno; et rursus regnauit
Donaldus tribus annis: sicque hii duo male regnauerunt quinque annis.

Efter þe deith of Makbeth, Malcome þe Thride, callit Canmore, was
335   crownit King of Scottis one Sanct Markis Day. He mareyt Margret, douchter
to King Edwart of Ingland, one quhame he gat mony haly chider. The last
ȝeir of his regnne he foundit þe New Kirk of Durhame and þe Kirk of
the Trinite in Dunfermlyng. He was slane at þe sege of Anwyk, in   f.442v
Northumbirland, by ane knycht of Ingland callit Peircy, þe xiii day of
340   Nouember, and was buryit in Dunfermling, fra oure redemptioun i^m lxxxxv
ȝeiris, and haly Sanct Margret deyt foure dayis eftir, and kyithit mony
miraclis. In þe xii buke, capitulo ix, x, xi, xii.

Donald þe VII, broþir to Malcome Cammore, callit Wann, was crownit
eftir his deith aganis þe law, and chasit awaye þe sonnis of his broder, King
345   Malcome, out of þe realme, bot at last he was doung out of Scotland, and
chasit in Ireland [be] Schir Duncane Canmore, bastarde sone to King
Malcome, þe secund ȝeir of his regnne. In þe xii buke, capitulo xiii°.

Duncane þe Secund, bastarde sone to Malcome Cammore, was þan
crownit, and he was slane be slycht of Donald before reheirsit. Thir tua
350   kingis, Downald and Duncane, gouernit þe realme of Scotland, inuading vþir
with continuall injuris v ȝeiris, to þe greit truble of þe pepill, in quhais tyme
þe Ilis war takin fra þe Scottis be Danis and Norwayis. In xii buke, capitulo
xiii.

And in that same month of April, on St Mark's day of the same year, King Malcolm was crowned. And he reigned 36 years. In the last year of his reign, he founded the new church at Durham and the church of the Holy Trinity at Dunfermline and restored it with many gifts. He married a very holy and very religious woman, namely the blessed Margaret, daughter of Edward, King of England, and he fathered six sons with her, of whom three died before their father, and the other three reigned in succession. This Malcolm was killed in the siege of Alnwick castle, the 13th day of November, and that glorious Queen Margaret, who is honored in all ages, four days later received the ecclesiastical sacraments in church and gave back her holy spirit to heaven, etc.

In the year of the Lord 1093, when Malcolm, the most illustrious King of the Scots, died, Donald Ban, brother of the said Malcolm, usurped the kingship, and he reigned for six months; but he was expelled from the kingdom by Duncan, the notorious son of Malcolm himself, and he himself reigned a year and six months, and so he was killed by the treacheries of the said Donald Ban, whom he had earlier expelled from the kingdom. And Donald reigned again for three years. And thus the two reigned wickedly for five years.

Capitulo lix⁰: Than Malcome Canmor was crovnit on Sanct Markis Daye, the ȝer of God iᵐ lvii, and he regnit xxxvi ȝer. The last ȝer of his regne he biggit and foundit þe New Kirk of Durhame and þe Trinite Kirk of Dun-
275 fermling. This Malcom mariit þe blissit Margaret, douchter to þe King of Yngland. And þe xxxvi ȝer of his regne, he was slane at þe sege of Alnwyk, the xiii day of Nouember, and þis haly Sanct Margaret deit four dayis eftir, and schawit mony myraklis, and baith was erdit togiddir at Dunfermling.

Capitulo lx⁰: The ȝer of God iᵐ xciii, quhen þe noble King Malcome was
280 deid, Donald Wan, his broþir, tuke þe crowne and expulsit and put away his childer. And he regnit vi monethis and was put away be Duncan, a bastard son of King Malcommis.

This Duncane regnit a ȝer & sex monethis and was slane be tressoun of þe said Donald. And sa þis Donald regnit agane thre ȝer. Thir twa regnit
285 wranguisly fyve ȝeris without richt.

Cum isto Donaldo congressus est Edgarus, filius Malcolmi predicti
415 senior, et legittimus heres Regni Scocie, et regnauit ix annis et tribus
mensibus; qui fundauit prioratum de Coldynghame, et sic viam vniuerse
carnis ingressus est apud Edynburgh.

Anno Domini m° c vii mortuo sine liberis Edgaro, successit Alexander
frater eius, et regnauit xvii annis: vir per omnia Deo deuotus, clericis et
420 religiosis mitis & clemens, sed subditis aliis satis terribilis, circa pauperes
liberalis. Ecclesiam de Dunfermlyn, a patre et matre fundatam, donariis et
possessionibus ampliauit. Tria monasteria nigrorum canonicorum fundauit
de nouo, scilicet monasterium de Scona et de Sanctiandree in qua prius erant
Kelledei, et monasterium de Emonia Sancti Columbe abbatis; restituitque
425 canonicis Sanctiandree Cursum Apri prius tempore Kelledeorum ablatum.
Iste igitur Alexander Rex etate et sensibus integer quo nemo deuocior
in ecclesiasticos in extraneos munificencior, in malefactores seuerior,   f.32r
in bonos omnes mansuecior, anno Domini m° cxxiiii viii kalendae
Maii debitum vniuerse carnis persoluens, spiritum celo reddidit, sepultus
430 apud Dunfermlyn prope patrem.

This Donald was slane be Edgar, sone to Malcome Canmore and Sanct
355 Margret.   Efter þe deith of Donald, Edgar, sone to Malcome Cammore, tuke
þe croune, and gouernit þe realme in greit felicite, and deceissit but ony
successioun of his body, and was buryit in Dunfermling, fra oure saluatioun
i^m i^c ix ʒeiris. In þis tyme, þe Haly Land was recouerit fra Saraʒenis, and þe
speir þat peirsit oure Lordis hart was found. Alsua, Mauld, eldest douchter
360 to King Malcome, was mareit one þe King of Ingland, and þe ʒoungast
douchter one þe Erle of Bullouny. This Edgar foundit þe Abbay of
Coldinghame in þe honoure of Sanct Cuthbert.

Alexander þe First, callit þe Feirs, þe fyift sone to Malcome   f.443r
Cammore, was crownit eftir Edgar. He was oft inuadit be
365 conspiratioun of his inymeis, bot he dantit þame be singular manheid and
wisdome. He was gude to Haly Kirk, and terribill yneucht to his subdittis.
He gaif greit possessionis to Dunfermling, þat his fader foundit, and ordanit
thre places of Blak Channonis, þat was Scone, Sanct Androis, and Colmes
Kirk of Ymonye. He deceissit þe xvii ʒeir of his regnne but ony successioun
370 of his body and was bureyt in Dunfermling, fra oure redemptioun i^m i^c xxvi
ʒeiris. In þe xii buke, capitulo xv.

Edgar, the elder son of the aforesaid Malcolm and the legitimate heir to the kingdom of Scotland, fought with this Donald, and he reigned for nine years and three months. He founded the priory of Coldyngham, and he went the way of all flesh at Edinburgh.

In the year of the Lord 1107, when Edgar died without children, his brother Alexander succeeded. And he reigned for 17 years, a man in every respect devoted to God, mild and merciful to clerics and monks, generous to the poor, but to other subjects terrifying enough. He enriched the church of Dunfermline, founded by his father and mother, with gifts and possessions. He founded anew three monasteries of black canons, namely the monastery of Scone, and the monastery of St Andrews in which earlier there were Culdees, and the monastery of St Columba at Inchcolm; and he restored the Boar's Raik to the canons of St Andrews, taken from them earlier in the time of the Culdees. In the year of the Lord 1124, the 8th kalends of May, this King Alexander, who was unimpaired in age and wits and than whom no one was more devoted to the clergy, or more generous to strangers, or more severe to criminals, or kinder to all good people, at last paid the debt of all flesh; he restored his spirit to heaven and was buried at Dunfermline near his father.

Capitulo lxi⁰: This Donald was slane be Edgar, Malcommis son and richtuis air. And þis Edgar regnit ix ȝer and thre monethis. He **f.132r** foundit þe monastery of Coldinghame in þe honour of Sanct Cuthbert. And he deit at Edinburgh.

290   *Capitulo lxii⁰*: This Edgar deit without childer, and þan Alexander, his broþir, was crovnit the ȝer of God xiᶜ & vii and regnit xvii ȝeris. This Alexander was gud to Haly Kirk and clergy and terrible yneucht till his subjectis. He gaf gret possessionis to Dunfermling, that his fader foundit, & ordanit and biggit thre placis of Blak Chennonis: in Sanct Androwes, Scone,

295   & þe abbay of Sanct Colmes Ynche, and first callit it Ymonye.

Anno Domini m° c xxiiii Alexandro sine liberis translato, successit ei Dauid frater eius junior natu, et regnauit annis xxix mensibus duobus et tribus diebus. De istis tribus regibus et fratribus mira leguntur sanctitatis preconio collaudari. Nam preter victus parcitatem, elemosinarum copiam, et
435 oracionem assiduitatem, ita domesticum regibus vicium euicerunt ut nunquam feminam in eorum thalamos nisi legittimas vxores fuisse, nec eorum quemquam pelicatu aliquo pudiciciam contristasse legatur.

Iste Dauid habuit in matrimonio Matildam filiam & heredem Waldesi Comitis de Huntyngtoun, filii et heredis Swardi Comitis de Northumbria,
440 habuitque bellum cum Stephano Rege Anglie; sed tandem concordatum est quod Henricus filius et heres apparens huius Dauid homagium faceret Regi Anglie pro Comitatu de Huntyngtoun et Comitatum Northumbrie libere possederet. Iste Henricus mortuus est ante patrem relinquens tres filios superstites, scilicet Malcolmum, Wilelmum, et Dauid.

445 Iste Dauid Rex inuenit in toto Regno Scotorum nisi quatuor episcopatus, et reliquit nouem. Monasteria multa fundauit diuersorum ordinum, videlicet de Calco, de Melross, de Jedwod, de Newbotill, Holmcultrom, Dundranan, monasterium Sancte Crucis prope Edynburgh, Cambuskeneth, Ryeuall, Kynlos, et juxta Berwyk monialium, et aliud juxta Carlioli, et canonicos
450 Premonstratenses de Dryburgh Noui Castelli, et ibi monasterium monialium et aliud nigrorum monacorum.

Dauid, þe first of þat name, vi sone vnto King Malcome, succeidit eftir Alexander þe Feirs. He mareit þe heretour of Northumbirland, and faucht sindry battellis aganis Inglismen in persute þairof. Thir thre, Edgar, Alexander,
375 and Dauid, war thre gude and nobill men, and vsit neuir wemen bot þair awin wyffis, and spendit þair gudis in founding and bigging of kirkis, and in almous deidis.

This Dauid straik ane feild with Stephin, King of Ingland. And it was accordit þat Henry, sone and air to King Dauid of Scotland, suld mak homage
380 to þe King of Ingland for þe Erldome of Huntingtoun, and þe Erldome of Northumbirland he suld bruke fre. This Henry deit before his fader, and left thre sonnis behind him, þat is to say, Malcome, Williame, and Dauid.

This King Dauid fand in all Scotland bot foure bischoprikis, and he left nyne. He foundit and biggit þir abbayis of diuers ordouris: Kelso, Melros,
385 Jedburgh, Newbotill, Holncultrane, Drundanane, Halyrudehous, Cambuskynneth, Revallis, Kinlos, and þe nunnis besyde Berwik.

In the year of the Lord 1124, when Alexander died without children, his younger brother David succeeded him, and he reigned 29 years, two months, and three days. Marvels concerning these three kings and brothers are collected to be greatly praised and for the proclaiming of their sanctity. For besides the austerity of their way of life, the abundance of their alms-giving, the constancy of their prayers, they so conquered the private vice of kings that no woman except their lawful wives was ever in their beds, nor may it be read of them that they darkened their chastity by keeping mistresses.

David married Matilda, the daughter and heir of Waltheof, Count of Huntingdon, who was the son and heir of Siward, Count of Northumbria. He had a battle with Stephen, King of England; but eventually they agreed that Henry, David's son and heir apparent, would do homage to the King of England for the county of Huntingdon, and he would possess the county of Northumbria freely. Henry died before his father, leaving three surviving sons, namely Malcolm, William, and David.

King David found in all the kingdom of the Scots only four bishoprics, and he left nine. He founded many monasteries of diverse orders, namely Kelso, Melrose, Jedburgh, Newbattle, Holm Cultram, Dundrennan, the monastery of Holyrood near Edinburgh, Cambuskenneth, Rievaulx, Kinloss, a convent near Berwick, another near Carlisle, one of Premonstratensian canons at Dryburgh of Newcastle, and a house of nuns there and another of black monks.

Capitulo lxiii°: The ȝeir of God xi hundreth & xxiiii, David succedit to Alexander, his broþir, þat deit without childer, and regnit xxix ȝer, ii monethis, and thre dayis. Thir thre breþir war noble men & gud and vsit neuir women bot þar awne wyfis. Thai spendit þar gudis on kirkis founding,
300   and in bigging of abbais, and in almos to þe pure. This Dauid mariit þe douchter & air of Walden, Erll of Huntingtoun. And þis Walden was air to Northumbirland be his fader, Seward, þe erll.

This Dauid strake a feld with Stephin, King of Yngland. And it was accordit þat Henry, son & air to King Dauid of Scotland, suld mak homage
305   to þe King of Yngland for þe Erldom of Huntingtoun, and þe Erldom of Northumbirland he suld brouke fre. This Henry deit befor his **f.132v** fader, and left thre sonnis behynd him – that is to say, Malcome, William, and Dauid.

This King Dauid fand in all Scotland bot iiii bischoprikis, and he left nyne.
310   He biggit and foundit þir monasteriis of diuers ordouris, *videlicet* Kelso, Melros, Jedburgh, Newbotill, Holyncultran, Dundranan, Halyrudhous besyd Edinburgh, Cambuskynnell, Ryvallis, Kynlos, and þe nunnis besyd Berweke.

Completisque in regno xxix annis, commendauit Malcolmum nepotem suum legiis suis regni successorem esse debere et alterum nepotem Wilelmum Comitem Northumbrie. Ipse vero grandeuus et infirmitate graui depressus
455 apud Carliel feliciter moriens, corpus terre spiritum celo reddidit angelis sociandum; sepelitur in Dunfermlyne apud patrem et fratrem etc.

Anno Domini m° c liii Malcolmus filius Henrici filii Dauid Regis   f.32v defuncti, defuncto & patre suo Henrico, successit in regnum Scotorum. Iste Malcolmus cum regnare cepit decimum tercium annum gerens, at posteaque
460 pubescens exoratus a suis nubere renuit, quia vouens Deo castitatem in pura virginitatis pudicicia permanebat, vni viro se virginem castum exhibere Christo professus est, sicque completis in regno xii annis septem mensibus et tribus diebus hominem exuens angelis sociandus; regnum non amisit sed mutauit.

Anno Domini m° c lxv Malcolmo virgine defuncto, successit Willelmus
465 frater eius, qui propter vite & morum probitatem dictus est amicus Dei, leo justicie, et decus morum apud Scotos. Et anno Domini m° clxxviii fundauit monasterium de Abbirbrothok et mater eius Ada fundauit monasterium monialium de Hadyngtoune. Captus est autem x anno regni sui prodicione Anglorum, et xx anno liberatus, recepit denuo a Rege Anglie Comitatum de
470 Huntyngtoun et Northumbrie, Westmurlandiam, et Cummerlandiam et ciuitatem Ca[r]lioli que prius ab eo extors[a]; ac pro eius redempcione Castrum Puellarum scilicet et omnia alia quecumque ablata erant omnia sunt restituta.

And quhen he hade regnit xix ʒeiris, he left his croune to Malcome, Northumbirland to Williame, and Huntingtoun to Dauid. He deceissit a sanct, at Carleill, and was bureyt in Dunfermling, fra our redemptioun iᵐ iᶜ liii
390 ʒeiris. In þe xii buke, capitulo xvj, xvii.

Efter þis Dauid, Malcome, his ooi, was crownit, callit þe Madyne.   f.443v He gouernit his realme in greit felicite, and deceissit þe xii ʒeir, vi monethis, and iii dayis of his regnne, and wald neuir haif wyfe, bot deyt ane virgyne. He was bureit in Dunfermling, fra oure redemptioun iᵐ iᶜ lx ʒeiris.
395 In þe xiii buke i, ii, iii.

Eftir þe deithe of Malcome þe Madyne, his broder Williame was crownit. He was þe Lyoun of Richtiusnis, þe Freind of God, and Fairnes of Maneris. The ʒeir of God iᵐ iᶜ lxxvii he foundit and biggit þe abbay of Abirbrothok, and Ada, his mod[er], þe nunry of Hadingtoune, and Dauid, his broþir,
400 Lundoris. This nobill King Williame, þe tent ʒeir of his regnne, was tratourysly tane with Inglismen at Anwyk and was deliuerit, with huge miney, þe twenty ʒeir of his regnne. He ressauit agane of þe King of Ingland þe Erldomis of Huntingtoun, Northumbirland, Westmurland, and Cumbyrland, þe quhilk he hade tane with force fra him.

Having completed 29 years of his reign, he commended his grandson Malcolm to the liegemen of his kingdom as his successor, and his other grandson, William, as Count of Northumbria. Being of great age and oppressed by a serious illness, he died happily at Carlisle, and he gave back his body to the earth and his spirit to heaven, to associate with angels; he was buried at Dunfermline near his father and brother, etc.

In the year of the Lord 1153, Malcolm, son of Henry, son of the dead King David, his father Henry also being dead, succeeded to the throne of the Scots. This Malcolm was 13 years old when he began to reign, but even when urged by his men, he refused to marry after reaching puberty, and because he promised his chastity to God, he remained in the pure modesty of virginity – he had promised to offer himself as a pure virgin to one man, Christ. And thus after completing 12 years, seven months, and three days on the throne, he laid aside humanity for the company of angels; he did not lose his kingdom, but exchanged it.

In the year of the Lord 1165, when Malcolm the Maiden was dead, his brother William succeeded, who because of his life and upright conduct was called among the Scots the friend of God, the lion of justice, and the glory of morals. And in the year of the Lord 1178, he founded the monastery of Arbroath, and Ada, his mother, founded the nunnery of Haddington. But he was captured in the 10th year of his reign by the treachery of the English, and in the 20th year freed. He received back from the King of England the county of Huntingdon and Northumbria, Westmoreland, and Cumberland and the city of Carlisle that had earlier been taken from him; and the land for his ransom, namely Maiden Castle, and all the other things whatsoever that had been taken away were restored.

And quhen he had regnit xxix ȝer, he left his crowne to Malcome, Northumbirland to William, and Huntingtoun to Dauid, and deit at Carlele,
315   a sanct, and was erdit in Dunfermlyng.

Capitulo lxiiii°: Eftir þis Dauid, Malcome, his oy, was crovnit, the ȝer of God i^m i^c liii, a child of xiii ȝer, and regnit xii ȝer & vi monethis & thre dayis. He deit a vergin and wald neuir haue wyf.

Capitulo lxv°: Eftir Malcome þe Madyn, his broþir William was crownit, the
320   ȝeir of God i^m i^c lxv and regnit xlix ȝeris. He was callit þe Lyoun of Richttuisnes, þe Frende of God, and Fairnes of Maneris. The ȝer of God i^m i^c lxxviii, he foundit and biggit þe abbay of Arbroth, and Ada, his moder, þe nunry of Hadingtoun, and Dauid, his broþir, Lundoris. This noble King William, þe x ȝer of his regne, was tratourisly takin with Ynglismen apon þe   f.133r
325   marchis, and he was deliuerit, þe xx^ti ȝer of his regne, and resauit agane of þe King of Yngland the Erldomeȝ of Huntingtoun, Northumbirland, Westmurlande, and Cummerland, þe quhilkis had takin with force fra him.

Huius illustrissimi Regis Willelmi famam audiens Papa Lucius et
deuocionem erga sedem apostolicam per abbates de Calco et Melros
475 ambaciatores regis, et in redditu nuncios apostolicos rosam auream preciosam
miro artificio laboratam uirga aurea siue ceptro regali erectam orthodoxo sibi
et Catholico ecclesie filio Regi Willelmo cum paterna benedictione remisit.
Hic xlix° anno regni sui rebus cessit humanis apud Streuelyn defunctus, et
apud monasterium de Abbirbrothoc quod ipse prius fundauerat sepultus est.

480 Anno Domini m° cc xiiii mortuo magnifico Rege Willelmo cum magna
leticia trium statuum regni, coronatus est Alexander secundus dicti Regis
Willelmi filius optime indolis adolescens xvi annorum. Iste tercio anno regni
sui inuito Rege Anglie Johanne, venit per Angliam usque Dovir, et ibidem
moram trahens per quindenam cum Lodouico Rege Francie de arduis
485 negociis Scocie Francie & Anglie tractauit cum eodem. Interim   **f.33r**
Johanne Rege Anglie destruente pontes vada et passagia fluminis de
Tarent ne Rex Scotorum liberum ad propria haberet regressum. Sed disponente
Deo idem Rex Anglie veneno periit per suos ante congressum et excercitus eius
fugatus est. Rex autem Scocie tulit omnes gasas et armamenta bellica Regis
490 Anglie, et cum gloria magna diuiciis quam plurimis potitus reversus est in
regnum Scocie. Et fundauit cum matre monasteria de Balmurynoch, de
Plusqwarty, et de Bewlyn, et Ardcathan. Pacem justiciam et veritatem semper
dilexit, et anno regni sui xxxv componendo pacem cum Ergadiensibus graui
infirmitate correptus defunctus est in Christo et sepultus apud Melros.

---

405 The Paip Lucius send him ane mervalus rois of gold and anamalit, and set
with precious stanis, and rasit one a sceptour of gold, for his vertew and
gudnes. He deceissit at Striuiling, þe xlix ȝeir of his regnne, and was bureyt
in Abirbrothok, þat he foundit, fra oure redemptioun i^m ii^c xiiii ȝeiris. In þe
xiii buke iiii, v, vj, vii, viii, ix, x.

410 Efter þis King Williame, Alexander þe Secund, his sone, was crownit, ane
nobill child of xvi ȝeir of aige. The quhilk Alexander, þe thrid ȝeir of his
regnne, ȝeid throu Ingland aganis King Johnnis will to Dowyr with his army,
and renewit þe band with France, and tareyt þair xv dayis, and spak with
Lowis, þe King of France. And King Johnne brak all briggis be þe gait
415 to stop his way, þat he suld nocht cum hayme. Bot as God wald, King   **f.444r**
Johnne was poissonit with his awin folkis, and King Alexander chaisit
his men and wan þe feild, and spulȝeit þe cuntre before him, and come hayme
with greit riches, artailȝery, joy, and mirth. This Alexander and his moder
biggit and foundit þe abbayis Balmurenoch, Plusqurty, Bowlyne, and
420 Archatane. He luffit peace, justice, and treuth. He deceissit þe xxxv ȝeir of
his regnne, and was bureyt in Melrois, fra oure redemptioun i^m ii^c xlix ȝeiris.
In þe xiii buke, capitulo xi, xii, xiii, xiiii.

Pope Lucius, hearing from the abbots of Calco and Melrose, the king's ambassadors, the fame of this illustrious King William and his devotion to the apostolic see, sent in return papal nuncios, and a precious gold rose wrought with marvelous craft set on a gold stem or royal scepter, with his paternal blessing to King William as an orthodox and catholic son to himself and the Church. In the 49th year of his reign, he withdrew from human affairs and died at Stirling and was buried at the monastery of Arbroath, which he had himself founded earlier.

In the year of the Lord 1214, when the magnificent King William was dead, Alexander II, son of the said King William, a 16-year-old youth of the best nature, was crowned with great joy from the three estates of the kingdom. In the third year of his reign, against the will of King John of England, Alexander went through England to Dover and delayed there for two weeks with King Louis of France and conducted difficult negotiations with him concerning Scotland, France, and England. Meanwhile King John of England was destroying the bridges, fords, and ferries of the River Trent so that the King of Scotland would not have a free passage back to his own land. But God disposed otherwise, and the King of England perished by poison administered by his men, before an engagement, and his army was put to flight. The King of Scotland, on the other hand, carried off all the treasures and armaments of the King of England, and after acquiring, with great glory, as much wealth as possible, he returned to Scotland. And he founded with his mother the monasteries of Balmerino, Pluscarden, Beauly, and Ardchattan. He always loved peace, justice, and truth. And in the 35th year of his reign, while arranging a peace with the men of Argyll, he was seized by a grave illness. He died in Christ and was buried at Melrose.

The Pape Lucius send him ane merwalous ros of gold, annamalit & set with precious stanis and rasit on a sceptur of gold, for his werteu and gudnes.

330 And he deit at Stirling and was erdit in Arbroth.

Capitulo lxvi°: Eftir þis King William, Alexander þe Secund, his son, was crownit, the ȝer of God i^m ii^c & xiiii ȝeris, ane noble ȝoung man of xvi ȝeris ald. And þe thrid ȝer of his regne, he ȝeid throu Yngland aganis King Jhonis will to Dower and tariit þar xv dayis and spak with Lowis, þe King of

335 Fraunce. And þis King Jhon gart brak all þe briggis be þe gait, þat he suld nocht cum hame. Bot as God wald, King Jhon was poysonit with his pepill, and King Alexander had þe victorie of his fowis and brynt & distroyit þe cuntre befor him, and come hame with gret artalȝe, joye, riches, and tryvmphe. This Alexander & his moder biggit and foundit þe monasteriis of

340 Balmerinoche, Plusqwarti, Bowlyne, and Archatane. He lufit pece, justice, & treuth. And þe xxxv ȝer of his regne, he deit & was erdit at Melros.

495   Anno Domini m° cc xlix defuncto Alexandro secundo Rege Scotorum successit Alexander tercius filius eius puer octo annorum. Hic maximam victoriam habuit de Norwegensibus occisis in vno [prelio] xx millibus et confractis centum lxª nauibus: regnauit annis xxxvii. Omnibus diebus suis floruit Christi ecclesia, sacerdotes venerabantur, justicia et virtus regnabant,
500   sed subito apud Kyngorn defunctus est; de corpore suo nullum relinquens successorem preter vnicam filiam filie sue Margarete Regine Norwegie Margaretam nomine, que cum esset desponsata Edwardo apparenti heredi Regis Anglie ante contractum matrimonium carne soluta est.

    Tuncque orta est discensio non minima inter proceres regni de jure
505   successionis regie. Nam Johannes de Baliolo seipsum dicebat ad regnum proximum heredem, quia de Dornagilla maiore natu filia Dauid Comitis de Huntyngtoun et fratris Wilelmi Regis. E contra Robertus Bruce dicebat se ad regnum preferendum, quia quamuis de Ysobella secunda filia dicti processit, primus tamen masculus fuit et vno gradu propinquior, nam nepos ex filia dicti
510   Dauid fuit et dictus Johannes pronepos eiusdem.

    Efter þis Alexander, his sone, Alexander þe Thride, was crownit, a[ne chy]lde of viii ȝeir of age. He hade greit victoryis of Norwayis, an[d s]lew
425   tuenty thousand of þame one ane day, and brynt and destroyit iᶜ and iii skoir of schippis. In his tyme, all gudnes regnit. He deceissit at Kingorne þe xxvii ȝeir of his regnne, and was bureyt in Dunfermling, fra our saluatioun iᵐ iiᶜ lxxxvi ȝeiris. This Alexander hade na airis of his body bot his douchteris douchter, Margret þe Quene of Norwayis dochter, þat deyt sone eftir him, but
430   ony successioun.

    And þan rais greit stryfe for þe croun of Scotland betuix Johnne Baliole and Robert Bruce. And þan war chosin vi keiparis of Scotland, quhill þe mater and richt war decidit. Johnne Baliole clamyt þe croune, Dervergillis sone, þe eldest douchter douchter to Dauid Huntingtoun. And Robert Bruce
435   clamyt þe croune, becaus he was first borne, all gife he come of þe ȝoungest sister, and ane degre nerrar to þe croun. And þan þe law of Scotland gaif it to him. In þe xiii buke, capitulo xvj, xvii, xviii, xix, xx.

In the year of the Lord 1249, when Alexander II, King of the Scots, was dead, his son Alexander III, a child of eight years, succeeded. He had a great victory over the Norwegians; 20,000 of them were killed in one battle and 160 ships destroyed. He reigned 37 years. The Church of Christ flourished all his days; priests were respected; justice and virtue reigned; but he died suddenly at Kinghorn, leaving no successor of his body except the only daughter of his daughter Margaret, Queen of Norway, also called Margaret, who, although she was betrothed to Edward, the heir apparent to the King of England, was released from the bonds of flesh before the marriage was contracted.

And then a not insignificant dissension arose among the nobles of the kingdom about the law of royal succession. For John Balliol declared that he was the nearest heir to the kingdom because he was descended from Dornagilla, the elder daughter of David, Count of Huntingdon and brother of King William. On the other hand, Robert Bruce said that he should be promoted to kingship, because although he was descended from Isabella, the second daughter of the aforesaid, he was the first male and one step closer, for he was the grandson of the said David through his daughter, and the said John was a great grandson of the same.

Capitulo lxvii°: Eftir þis Alexander þe Secund, Alexander þe Thrid was crownit, his son, the ȝer of God i^m ii^c xlix, a child of viii   **f.133v** ȝeris ald. This had gret victorie of Norowayis. He slew xx^m of þaim

345 on a day, and brynt and distroyit a hundreth and thre scor of schippis. He regnit xxxvii ȝer. In his tyme, all gudnes regnit with him. He deit at Kingorne be a fall of a hors and left na air of his body bot his dochter dochter, Margaret þe Qwene of Noroways douchter, þat deit sone eftir him.

And þan rais gret stryf for þe crovne of Scotland betuix Jhon Baliole &
350 Robert Brus. And þan þar was chosin vi keparis of Scotland, quhill þe mater war decidit. Jhon Baliole clamit þe crovne becaus he was þe eldest douchter douchter [son] of Erl Dauid of Huntington. And Robert þe Bruse clamit it becaus he was first borne: howbeit he come of þe ȝoungast sister, he was a degre nerrer þe crovne. The law of Scotland gaf it him to be air richtuis.

Anno Domini m° cc lxxxvi Alexandro tercio Rege Scotorum defuncto, per sex annos et ix menses regnum a custodibus regebatur sex numero, qui interim electi erant ad custodiendum pacem et justiciam in regno donec determinaretur questio de successione regis. Sicque factum est f.33v
515 per sex annos et nonem menses.

Tandem anno Domini m° cc xcii ultimo die Nouembris, Johannes de Baliolo erectus est in regem et coronatus, procurante Rege Anglie Edwardo tiranno, qui apud Scotos vocatus est Langschankis, non quia ad regnum pociora jura habuit, sed quia cecatus ambicione regni homagium facere
520 promisit dicto Edwardo, contra regni libertatem et consuetudinem predecessorum suorum, in ded[e]cu[m] magnum regalis status in perpetuum inuitisque omnibus regni proceribus: quem Rex Anglie quarto anno sequenti depriuauit honore regio, completis in regno tribus annis cum dimedio.

The ʒeir of God iᵐ iiᶜ lxxxvi ʒeiris, quhen Alexander þe Thride was deid, þe realme was sax ʒeir and ix monethis vnder keiparis.
440 And þe ʒeir of God iᵐ iiᶜ xciii, þe last day of Nouember, Johnne Baliole maid king th[row] þe help of þe fals tratour and foresworne tyrane a[nd] aratyk, Edwart Langschankis, King of England. Thi[s] fals tyrane hade ane commissioun fra þe paip to juge in þe mater, and he wist f.444v weill þat Robert Bruce was richtuis air, bot because he wald nocht
445 hald of him and put þe realme vnder subjectioun of Inglismen, he maid Johnne Baliole, his aduersare, þat hade na richt, vnder þat condicioun to be his man and hald of him, contrare þe fredome of þe realme of Scotland, þat euir ʒitt was fre, and agane justice. Þe nobillis withstude, quhairfore Edwart put him doun, quhen he hade regnit thre ʒeiris and ane half, and fa[l]sly lyke
450 ane tyrane, oppressit and murtheryt þe pepill without caus or titill, becaus þai hade na king to defend þame. Bot ane nobill [ʒoung] man, callit Williame Wallace, inspyrit be [God, tuke] part with þe poure pepill, and defendit þe realme, [to þe] greit displesour and confusioun to þe Inglismen, quhill þe cuming of þe Bruce.

In the year of the Lord 1286, after the death of Alexander III, King of Scotland, the kingdom was ruled for six years and nine months by guardians, six in number, who were chosen to maintain peace and justice in the kingdom until the question of the succession of the king was determined. And this took six years and nine months.

Then finally, in the year of the Lord 1292, the last day of November, John Balliol was raised to the throne and crowned, at the instigation of the King of England, Edward the tyrant, who is called Longshanks by the Scots, not because Balliol had the greater right to the throne, but because, blinded by ambition, he promised to do homage for the kingdom to the said Edward, against the liberty of the kingdom and the custom of his predecessors, to the great detriment of the royal estate in perpetuity and against the will of all the nobles of the kingdom. The King of England, in the fourth year following, deprived him of the royal honor, after he had completed three and a half years on the throne.

---

355   *Capitulo lxviii*: The ʒer of God iᵐ cc lxxxvi, quhen Alexander þe Thrid was deid, the realme was sex ʒeris and ix monethis vndir þe keparis.

And þe ʒer of God iᵐ iiᶜ xcii, þe last day of Nouember, Jhon Baliole was maid King of Scotland be help of þe fals tratour Eduard Langschankis, King of Yngland. This Eduard had a commissioun be þe pap to be juge in þat
360   mater, and he wald gif it till nane bot till him þat wald hald it of him. The quhilk Robert þe Brus wald nocht do. And Jhon Baliole grantit þarto, contrar þe fredome of þe crovn, ̣that na noble of þe land wist. Bot **f.134r** eftirward, þe said Eduard put him downe becaus he wald nocht cum and do him seruice, quhen he had regnit thre ʒeris and a half, and murdrest
365   him falsly – the pepill of Scotland þan havand na king to defend þam. Bot William Wallace defendit þe realm, till þe cummyn of þe Brus.

525 Anno Domini m cc lxxxxvi Edwardus Rex Anglie misit excercitum magnum ad obsedendum villam be Berwik, et xxviii naues onustas armatis, et resistentibus Scotis, omnes naues combuste sunt et maior pars hominum interfecta.

Sed anno sequenti venit idem rex cum maiore excercitu & in persona propria, & facta obsidione, cum per longa tempora villam vi capere non 530 possit, finxit se uelle recedere, remouit tentoria, et regirans cum excercitu montem de Halidoun fixit signa bellica Regis Scotorum et nobilium eius, quibus erectis iterum venit ad villam. Videntes autem in villa erant vexillum et signa bellica gentis sue putantesque excercitum Scotorum, quia per aliam viam aduenerant, aperiunt portas, intrant Anglici, statim cognita fraude 535 resistere volentes non valuerunt; sic dolose capitur villa, vbi jussit tirannus omnes vtriusque sexus et etates torculari, vbi occisi sunt vii^m quingenti. Facta sunt hec quarto kalendae Aprilis, scilicet feria sexta in parascheue Domini.

Eodem anno Willelmus de Kyngorn vicarius generalis episcopi Sanctiandree in remotis agentis eiecit omnes Anglicos de Regno Scocie. 540 Cuius eiectionis executor fuit inclitus ille Willelmus Wallace. Contra quem misit Rex Anglie Hugonem Crassynghame thesaurarium suum cum magno excercitu, sed apud pontem de Stryuelyng occisus est idem thesaurarius a predicto Willelmo. Iterum idem Rex Anglie venit furens ob sedem suorum et Scotorum sanguinem si[t]iens.

---

455 The ȝeir of God [i^m] ii^c lxxxxvj, King Edwart send ane greit armye t[o bese]ge Berwik, and alsua send xxviii schippis, with ar[myt m]en and wittellis, bot þe nobill Scottis defendit [þe toune, a]nd brint þe schippis, and slew þe men þat come [þairin].

And þe nixt ȝeir eftir come Edwart þe tyrane [hims]elf, with ane greitar 460 power, and becaus he couth nocht [take] þe toune, he maid him as he wald depart, and gang away with his oist lyk ane tratour theif a litill out of sicht, and come agane ane vþir way, as it hade bene fra Scotland, and brocht with him baneris of þe armes of Scotland, and þe men of þe toune wenyt it had bene þair awin folkis, and leit him in, and sua he tuke þe toune with tresoun lyk ane 465 tratour. And þis fals inhumane tyrane gart sla man, woman, and child, and sua war martyrit vii^c and l pepill one þe Gude Fryday, þe iiii kalend of Aprile.

This ȝeir Williame Kingorne, Vicar Generall of Sanct Androis, put furth all Inglismen beneficit in his diocy, and þe executour þairof was William Wallace in his first begyning. Agane þe quhilk Williame, þe King of f.445r 470 Ingland send his thesaurar, Hew of Cassinghame, bot at þe brig of Striuiling he was slane and his men chasit and taking be Williame Wallace.

In the year of the Lord 1296, King Edward of England sent a great army and 28 ships laden with armed men to besiege the town of Berwick, and when the Scots resisted, all the ships were burned, and the greater part of the men were killed.

But in the year following, the king came again with a greater army and in person, and when the siege was made, since after a long time he was unable to take the town by force, he feigned that he wanted to retreat, struck his tents, and retired with his army to Halidon Hill where he affixed the battle flags of the King of the Scots and his nobles, and with them held high he came again to the town. Those in the town, seeing the standard and battle flags of their people and considering them the army of the Scots, because they came from another direction, opened the gates; the English entered; but although the trick was immediately recognized, and they wanted to resist, they were not strong enough. Thus the town was captured by trickery; and the tyrant ordered everyone of both sexes and all ages to be tortured, and 7500 were killed there. These things were done on the fourth kalends of April, that is, on Good Friday.

In the same year, William Kinghorn, the Vicar General of the Bishop of St Andrews who was serving abroad, threw out all the English from the kingdom of Scotland. The man who carried out this eviction was the renowned William Wallace, against whom the King of England sent Hugh de Cressingham, his treasurer, with a great army, but that treasurer was killed at Stirling Bridge by the aforesaid William. Then the same King of England came again, raging because of the slaughter of his men and thirsting for the blood of Scots.

Capitulo lxix⁰: The ȝer of God iᵐ iiᶜ lxxxvi, King Eduard send a gret army to sege Berwike, and als he send xxviii schippis, with armed men, & wittalis, and vþir stuf, bot þe noble Scottis defendit þam, and brynt þe
370 schippis, and slew þe mast part of Ynglismen.

And þe nixt ȝer eftir, come Eduard þe tyrand himself, with a gretar power, and becaus he couth nocht get þe towne, he fenȝeit himself to depart hamwart, and come agane ane noþir gait, as he had cummyn fra Scotland with baneris of Scotland. And sa þe men of þe towne, trastand þai had bene
375 Scottis men, leit him in. And þar þat fals tyrand martyrit & put to deid viiᵐ & l folkis of men, women, and childer on Gud Fryday, þe ferd day of Aprile.

This ȝer William of Kyngorne, Vicar Generale of Sanct Androwes, put furth all Ynglismen beneficit within his diocy, and þe executor þarof was William Wallace in his first begynnyng. Aganis þe quhilk William
380 Wallas, þe thesaurer, Schir Hew of Crassinghame of Ingland come, **f.134v** bot William Wallas slew him at þe brig of Sterling and all his peple.

545 Cui obuius venit Willelmus Wallace in Anglia apud Stanemure,   **f.34r**
vbi ordinatis aciebus Scotorum et Anglicorum hinc & inde cum jam
putarentur congressioni proximi. Rex Anglie videns Scotos paratos pugnare
pro animabus et ordinate procedere, regirans excercitum suum terga dans
Scotis ignominiose retrocessit. Mira Dei virtus et gracia Scotis ibidem
550 illuxit, vbi tantus rex tanto apparatu et excercitu cum satrapis suis suffultus
contra tam paucos quos pene nullos reputabat, nullo extracto gladio terga
dedit. Scotis autem visum est Anglos non insequentes fore, sed contentos
esse debere de victoria sibi a Deo collata, et sic gracias agentes Deo reuersi
sunt prospere in Scociam, predam omnem in via secum auferentes.

555 Anno Domini m° ccc iii Rex Anglie cum maxima potencia terre sue, cum
Principe Wallie, Vasconie, Normannie, et Ybernie, tam per mare quam per
terram Scociam intrat, et vniuersum regnum acephalum inuadit, vbi omnes
nobiles, communitates, et plebe[o]s ad suam coegit obedienciam,
resistentibus occisis et eorum bonis confiscatis, solo Willilmo Wallas
560 resistente cum sibi adherentibus.

Tunc Roberto de Bruce legittimo regni successore in terris quas in Anglia
habebat moram trahente et quasi dormiente. Sed paulo post spiritu diuino
ipsum tangente et euigelare faciente, facta est mutacio dextre excelsi et
adiuuantibus eum amicis, velud alter Mathathyas, cum esset proximus heres
565 regni pro cuius libertate et legibus onera importabilia propriis humeris
imposuit, insurgendo contra Regem potentissimum Anglie, ducem
Normannie Equitanie et Andegauie dominum Ybernie et Wallie, et supra hec
inuasorem et quasi triennalem occupatorem Regni Scocie, exceptis amicis et
propinquis suis qui reliquis numero comparari non poterant.

And eftir, þis Williame Wallace gadderit ane gretar power, and met with
King Edwart þe tyrane at Stanemuire, bot he fled for dredour of Wallace, and
durst [nocht] abyde in þe feild.
475 The ȝeir of God i^m iii^c and iii ȝeiris, þe King of Ingland enteryt into
Scotland with ane greit [mu]ltitude baith be sey and l[an]d, and slew all his
resistaris, and [tuke] þair gudis, and causit [all þe la]nd, except Williame
Wallace, ob[ey] to him.
That tyme [Robert, bea]nd King of Scotland, was in Ingland, and leiffit
480 [þair, bot] God causit him to ryse sone eftir in defence of his a[win] re[al]me.

216

William Wallace came to meet him at Stainmore in England, where the battle formations of Scots and English were drawn up on either side, since they were already thought to be very close to joining battle. The King of England, seeing the Scots prepared to fight for their lives and to advance in order, whirled his army around, showing their backs to the Scots, and ignominiously retreated. The marvelous strength and grace of God shone on the Scots in that place, where such a king with such equipment and such an army and supported by his lords against so few, whom he considered so insignificant, turned his back without drawing a sword. But it seemed to the Scots that they should not pursue the English, but should be content with the victory bestowed on them by God, and so, giving thanks to God, they returned successfully to Scotland, taking all the spoils on the way with them.

In the year of the Lord 1303, the King of England with a very great army from his land, and with the prince of Wales, Gascony, Normandy, and Ireland, entered Scotland both by sea and by land and invaded the whole country, which was without a leader. There he forced all the nobles, communities and common people into obedience, killing resisters and confiscating their goods, while only William Wallace and his followers resisted.

At that time, Robert Bruce, the legitimate successor to the throne, was idling on the lands he had in England, as if asleep. But a little later, he was touched and awakened by the divine spirit, and a change was brought about by the right hand of the Most High and the assistance of his friends, like another Mattathias, and since he was the next heir to the kingdom, he took insupportable burdens on his own shoulders, for the sake of its liberty and laws, by rising against the most powerful King of England, Duke of Normandy, Aquitaine, and Anjou, Lord of Ireland and Wales, and – over and beyond this – the invader and occupier of the kingdom of Scotland for almost three years, with only his friends and associates, who could not be compared with the rest in number.

And eftirwart, William Wallace gadderit a gret power and ʒeid to Stanemure in Yngland, quhar þe King of Yngland fled and durst nocht abyde feld.

385   *Capitulo lxxᵒ*: The ʒer of God iᵐ iiiᶜ & thre, the King of Yngland enterit apon Scotland with a gret multitud be se & land, and slew all his resistaris, and tuke þar gudis, and causit all þe land obey to him, excepand William Wallas.

Robert þe Bruse, þe richttuis air, abaid in Yngland and levit on his landis
390   þar, bot God causit him awalk and rys agane sa gret a king.

570   Vnde anno Domini m° ccc vi, coronatus est idem Robertus Bruce apud
Sconam vi kalendae Aprilis. Cuius infortunia, fugas, pericula, dampna, tedia,
famem, sitim, vigelias, jeiunia, nudidates, frigora, insidias, exilia propinquorum
ut regine et germanorum fratrum capciones et incarceraciones occisionesque
quibus in principio guerre sue victus fugatusque vbique succubuit, nullam puto

575 ad narrandum sufficere linguam. Nam biennio toto diuersis locis contra
ͺdiuersos Regis Anglie locum tenentes dimicans superatus est. Sed mira   f.34v
Dei clemencia postmodum illuxit Scotorum Regi, et sicut in duobus eius
primis annis in omni euentu bellico infortunatissimus fuerit, ita postea in
omnibus bellis suis nullus ei fortunacior potuit inueniri. Nam primis diebus in

580 conflictibus contra Anglicos xiii vicibus legitur succubuisse devictus.
    Sed postmodum victoriosos triumphos de Anglis legitur habuisse lvii vnde
de multis eis victoriis vnum libet ad memoriam reducere, scilicet quomodo vicerit
ad Bannocburn prope Streuelyng, vbi ex consensu vtriusque Regis Scotorum et
Anglie dies belli prefixus est, anno sequenti in festo Sancti Johannis Baptiste,

585 scilicet anno Domini m° ccc xiiii. Quo die comparuit Rex Anglie cum trecentis
millibus pugnatorum exceptis peditibus, et Rex Scotorum cum xxx millibus vbi
Deo propicio cessit victoria Scotis. Rex autem Anglie fugatus de prelio usque
Dunbar castrum fortissimum per millia circiter xl et de Dunbar in parua nauicula
cum octo tantum comitibus manus Scotorum persequentium se euasit.

590   Rex autem Robertus confortatus usque ad finem vite permansit victoriosus,
regnauit [annis] xxiiii et defunctus. Sepultus est apud Dunfermlyn vii idus Junii.

    The ʒeir [of G]od iᵐ iiiᶜ and xiiii, [þe day was] sett of battell [betuix] King
Robert and þe King of Ingl[and] one Midsymme[r day þat] was to cum, ane ʒeir
eftir, and þe King of Inglan[d come] with thre hundreth thousand fechtand men
of diuers n[acionis], and þe King of Scotland was bot threttie thousand men, and

485 þat day, as God wald, þe victory feld to þe Scottis, and þ[e Ki]ng of Ingland was
chasit be James of Douglas to Dunbar, and eschaipit with viii erlis of his awin
natioun. This battell was strikkin at Bann[ok]burne in Scotland.
    And King Robert deceissit and was [bureyt] in Dunfermling, as said is, fra
oure redemptioun iᵐ [iiiᶜ and] xxix ʒeiris.

490   The ʒeir of God iᵐ iiiᶜ and xvi ʒeiris, Robert Bruce was crownit at Scone, þe
vi kalende. of Aprile. Bot þe first tua ʒeiris he loist, and tynt þe feild, and was
chasit abak, and his freindis tane and trublit, and he hade þe sorrow þat cannocht
be exprymit. He tint xiii battellis þir tua ʒeiris aganis Inglismen, bot
ͺeftirwartis he ourcome þame lvii tymes, at diuerse battellis & juperdeis.   f.445v

495 He was callit þairfore þe recoverar of his realme.
    He deceissit þe xxiiii ʒeir of his regnne, and was bureyt in Dunfermling. In
þe xiii buke, capitulo viii° to þe end.

As a result, in the year of the Lord 1306, that same Robert Bruce was crowned at Scone on the 6th kalends of April. I think no tongue is adequate to tell his misfortune, flights, dangers, harms, weariness, hunger, thirst, sleepless watches, fasts, nakedness, cold, treacheries, exiles of relatives like the queen and his own brothers, and the captures and imprisonments and killings by which he was defeated and put to flight and everywhere brought low at the beginning of his campaign. For in two whole years, struggling against various lieutenants of the King of England, he was defeated in various places. But the marvelous mercy of God afterwards shone upon the King of the Scots, and just as in his first two years he was very unfortunate in every military encounter, so afterwards in all his battles none more fortunate than he could be found. For in the first days of his conflicts against the English, he is reported to have been defeated 13 times.

But soon he is reported to have had 57 victorious triumphs over the English, and I am pleased to recall to memory one of these many victories – namely, how he won at Bannockburn, near Stirling. There, by agreement of both the King of Scotland and the King of England, the day of battle was set for the Feast of St John the Baptist the following year – that is, the year of the Lord 1314. On that day, the King of England appeared with 300,000 soldiers, not counting infantry, and the King of Scotland with 30,000 soldiers, but God being propitious, victory fell to the Scots. Moreover, the King of England fled from the battle to the very strong castle at Dunbar, about 40 miles, and from Dunbar, with only eight earls, he escaped in a small boat from the hands of the Scots following him.

But King Robert, greatly strengthened, remained victorious to the end of his life. He reigned 24 years and died; he was buried at Dunfermline the 7th ides of June.

Capitulo lxxi⁰: The ȝer of God iᵐ ccc & vi ȝeris, Robert Brus was crovnit king at Scone, þe vi kalends of Aprile. Bot þe first twa ȝeris he lost & tynt þe feldis, and was chasit & drevyne abak, & his frendis tane & trublit. And he had þe sorow þat can nocht be tald. He tynt xiii batellis aganis þe Ynglismen þai twa ȝeris. Bot eftirwart, he ourcome þaim lvii tymes and distroyit þaim.

Capitulo lxxii⁰: The ȝer of God iᵐ iiiᶜ xiiii, the day was set of batell betuix King Robert þe Brus & þe King of Yngland on Mydsomer Day a ȝer eftir, and þe King of Yngland come with thre hundreth thousand men, and þe King of Scotland with xxxᵐ men. And þat day God gaf þe victorye to þe Scottis, and þe King of Yngland was chasit fra Sterling to Dunbar. And þar þat tratour gat away in a bait & viii erllis and left all his men slane.

Eftir þat, King Robert wan þe feld at Beland and mony vþir placis and regnit victoriusly xxiiii ȝer, & syne deit, & was erdit in Dunfermling, þe vii ides of June, the ȝer of God iᵐ iiiᶜ xxix ȝeris.

395

400

f.135r

219

Anno Domini m° ccc xxix defuncto Roberto de Bruce Rege Scotorum inclitissimo, fuit idem regnum in custodia Thome Ranulfi Comitis Morauie et nepotis ex sorore dicti Roberti Regis usque ad coronacionem Dauid filii dicti
595 [Regis] Roberti. Qui Dauid vnctus et coronatus est in regem anno Domini m° ccc xxxi, viii kalendae Decembris ab Episcopo Sanctiandree juuenis octo annorum. Et anno sequenti venit Edwardus de Balliolo in Scociam, et viii kalendae Octobris coronam regni more suo suscepit propter quod Rex Dauid apud Regem Francie per octo annos & ultra perendinauit. Sed post regressus
600 ad Scociam cum leticia et honore maximis receptus est, expulso prius eodem Edwardo. Sed iterum idem Rex Dauid captus est ab Anglis in bello prope Durhame et per annos xi in Anglia detentus, tandem tamen liberatus est datis prius pro redempcione sua centum millibus mercarum sterlyngorum.

Restitutus in regno Rex Dauid, regnum optimis legibus innouauit,
605 rebelles secundum justiciam castigando satis austere. Tandem Dei gracia inspirante animo concepit toto annisu ad domandam paganorum feritatem ̣terram sanctam esse petendam, vnde cum spectabili   f.35r potencia militari Jerusalem visitare decreuit. Decretumque perfecisset, si non voluntate diuina morte fuisset preuentus. Mortuus est igitur
610 inclitissimus Rex Dauid secundus Rex Scotorum apud Castrum de Edynburgh anno Domini m° ccc lxx in [festo] cathedra Sancti Petri regni sui anno xxxix° etatis sue anno xlvii et sepultus est in Monasterio Sancte Crucis de Edinburgh.

Eftir þe deithe of [þe] maist vi[ctorio]us King Robert þe B[ruce, ...] k[ei]ping [. . . . . .] Thomas Randell [. . . . .] held greit justice
500 [. . . . .] vnto þe corona[tioun . . . .] þe quhilk was [. . . . .] þe vii kalende of [De]cember [. . . . .]nge. And þe nixt [ʒe]re eftir [. . . . . Joh]n Baliolis sone in Scot[l]and and inva[dit . . . .] quhilk caus Dauid [. . . . .] was þair aucht ʒeires [. . . . .] and put furth þis Edwart [. . . . .] for
505 euirmair. And þe ʒeir of God iᵐ iiiᶜ xx [. . . . .]nge þe auchtenit ʒeir he come agane out of [Ingland.] [Þis] Dauid, eftir mony victoryis þat he h[ad . . . .] and was tane at þe battaill of Durhame [. . . . . ʒ]eir in Ingland and þan was lattin hayme [. . . . . . ra]nsoun payit ane hundreth thousand pund[is sterlyn]g.

Eftir his hame-cuming, he began and [gouernyt þe r]ealme richt weill and
510 nobille, and purposi[t to have] gane to þe Haly Land to fecht aganis þe Turkis, bot he deyt in þe meyntyme at þe castell of Edinburgh, þe xxxix ʒeir of his regnne, and was buryit in [þe] Halyrudehous, befoir þe hie altare, fra oure r[edempti]oun iᵐ iiiᶜ lxx ʒeir. In þe xv buke, capitulo i° to þe end þairof.

In the year of the Lord 1329, when the most renowned Robert Bruce, King of Scotland, was dead, the kingdom was in the care of Thomas Ranulf, Earl of Moray and nephew of the said King Robert through his sister, until the coronation of David, the son of the said King Robert. David, an 8-year-old boy, was anointed and crowned as king in the year of the Lord 1331, the 8th kalends of December, by the Bishop of St Andrews. And the following year Edward Balliol came into Scotland, and on the 8th kalends of October, he seized the crown of the kingdom, in his own right, because King David remained with the King of France for eight years and more. But after his return to Scotland, Edward having been expelled earlier, King David was received with the very great joy and honor. But once again, the same King David was captured by the English in a battle near Durham and was held in England for 11 years, but he was finally released after 100,000 marks sterling had earlier been paid for his ransom.

Returned to his kingdom, King David reformed the kingdom with the best laws, punishing rebels with appropriate severity in accordance with justice. At last, inspired by the grace of God, he had the idea of attacking the Holy Land with all his might to subdue the fierceness of the pagans, and so he decided to go to Jerusalem with a remarkable military force. And he would have carried out this decision had he not, by divine will, been prevented by death. The most renowned King David II died therefore at Edinburgh Castle on the [Feast of the] Chair of St Peter in the year of the Lord 1370, in the 39th year of his reign and the 47th year of his age, and he was buried in Holyrood Abbey in Edinburgh.

---

405   *Capitulo lxxiii°*: Efter þe deid of þe mast victorious King Robert þe Brus, the realme was ii ȝeris in keping of Erll Thomas Randall, King Robertis sister son till þe coronacioun of Dauid Brus, King Robertis son. The quhilk was crovnit þe ȝer of God i[m] iii[c] xxxi, a child of viii ȝeris ald. And þe nixt ȝer eftir, come Eduard Baliole, Jhon Baliolis son, in Scotland and invadit þe

410 crovne, for þe quhilk caus Dauid Brus was with þe King of Fraunce viii ȝer. And eftir þat, he come hame & expulsit & put awaye þe said Eduard & his for euirmar. This Dauid, eftir mony victoriis þat he had in Yngland, he was takin at þe batall of Durhame and haldin xi ȝer in Yngland, and þan lattin hame for i[c] thousand pundis striuling.

415   And eftirwart, he rewlit þe realm richt wele and purpost till haue gane to þe Haly Land, bot he deit at Edinburgh, þe ȝer of his regne xxix, & was erdit in Halyrudhous.

Post mortem Regis Dauid secundi coronatus est Robertus secundus,
615 senescallus Scocie nepos dicti Dauid ex sorore secundum patrie leges in festo
annunciacionis beate Virginis. Iste primam confederacionem cum Rege
Francorum factam renouauit ampliauitque, quam eciam auctoritate apostolica
fecit confirmari. Eius tempore plurima existant preclare gesta contra
Anglicos precipue magna victoria de Ottirburn.

620 Et anno Domini m° ccc lxxxix grandeuus admodum effectus quia filius
eius primogenitus Johannes claudus effectus erat, filium suum secundo
genitum Robertum ducem Albanie et Comitem de Fyf, Regni Scocie
custodem effecit, vocans eum gubernatorem. Itaque propter crebras victorias
contra Anglos pacem ipsis Anglis desiderantibus concedens, regnum in
625 magna tranquillitate relinquens presentis vite finem sortitus est apud
Dundonald, sepultus in Scona xiii kalendae Maii anno Domini m° ccc xc°· Et
sic regnauit xix annis & xxiii diebus.

Mortuo et sepulto Roberto secundo Rege, et regno sub tutela Roberti ducis
Albanie et gubernatoris anno Domini m° ccc xc. Johannes primogenitus
630 eiusdem Roberti secundi regio more vnctus et coronatus est et de consensu
trium statuum vocatus est Robertus tercius, cuius primogenitus Dauid Dux de
Rothisay adultus de magna insolencia accusatus est apud regem patrem suum;
qui misit litteras fratri suo gubernatori ut eum custodie manciparet pro
castigacione. Qui captus ab auunculo suo et positus in castro de Falkland in
635 breue tempore spiritum exalauit.

Efter þe deith of Dauid, Robert Stewart, his susteris sone, was crownit,
515 and gouernit his realme weill, in greit tranquillite. He renewit þe
confideratioun betuix France and Scotland, and hade greit victoryis vpoune
Inglismen at þe field callit Ottirburne. Þe Erle of Northumbirland was tane
with þe Scottis.

This king ＾. . . .   **f.446r**

After the death of King David II, Robert II, the Steward of Scotland and nephew of the said David by his sister, was crowned according to the laws of the country on the Feast of the Annunciation of the Blessed Virgin. He renewed and expanded the first treaty made with the King of France, which he also had confirmed by apostolic authority. In his time very many deeds against the English stand out clearly, chiefly the great victory at Otterburn.

And in the year 1389, when he had become quite old and because his first-born son, John, had become lame, he made his second-born son, Robert, Duke of Albany and Earl of Fife, the guardian of Scotland, calling him the governor. And thus because of numerous victories against the English, he granted the peace that the English themselves desired, and leaving the kingdom in great tranquillity, he reached the end of the present life at Dundonald and was buried at Scone on the 13th kalends of May in the year of the Lord 1390. And thus he reigned 19 years and 23 days.

When King Robert II was dead and buried, and the kingdom was under the guidance of Robert, Duke of Albany and governor, in the year of the Lord 1390, John, the first-born of that same Robert II, was anointed and crowned in accordance with royal custom, and by consent of the three estates he was called Robert III. His first-born, David, Duke of Rothesay, an adult, was accused in the presence of his father the king, of great arrogance, and he sent letters to his brother the governor that he was placing him in confinement as a punishment. He was captured by his uncle and placed in Falkland Castle; in a short time he gave up the ghost.

Capitulo lxxiiii⁰: ˏEfter þe deid of þis Dauid, his sister son, Robert   f.135v
Stewart, was crowned, the ȝer of God iᵐ iiiᶜ lxx. This renewit þe band
420   of Fraunce and had gret victoris apon Ynglismen as at þe batell of Ottirburn,
quhar þe Erll of Northumbirland was tane presoner with þe Scottis.

This king, becaus his eldest son haltit, he maid his nixt sone, þe Duke of
Albany, Robert, kepar of þe land. This at þe last grantit pece till Ynglismen
at þar desyr & left þe land in gret pece. And þe xix ȝer of his regne, he deit
425   at Dundonald and was erdit in Scone.

Capitulo lxxv⁰: Eftir þe deid of þe mast gracious King Robert Stewart, his
eldest son, Robert, was crovnit the ȝer of God iᵐ iiiᶜ lxxxx, bot þe realm was
wnder his broþiris handis as conseruatour. This king had twa sonnis: Dauid,
þat was Duke of Rothissay, and James þe First. This Dauid was complenȝeit
430   to his fader þat he was to wantoun, for þe quhilk his fader wrait lettreȝ to his
broþir þe conseruatour to chasty him, bot he put him in presoun in Falkland
and hungerit him to deid.

Cuius morte audita rex pater contristatus valde timensque vnico filio superstiti Jacobo, disposuit eum Regi Francorum mittendum; qui juvenis xiiii annorum in mari captus est ab Anglis treugarum tempore, ubi per xviii annos custoditus est. Ut autem nunciatum est regi patri suo vnicam filium ab

640 inimicis captum continuo defecit spiritus eius, vigorque corporis emarcuit, et pre ˏnimia tristicia cibum non sumpsit donec Creatori f.35v spiritum reddidit, anno Domini m° cccc iiii, & sic regnauit annis xvi.

Anno Domini m cccc iiii, Robertus dux Albanie, Roberto tercio Rege defuncto et vnico filio suo Jacobo in Anglia captione, gubernator Scocie a

645 tribus statibus rursus eligitur, et regnum in optima pace conseruans, obiit anno Domini m° cccc xix tercio die Septembris: post cuius mortem filius eius primogenitus Murdacus nomine stetit gubernator Regni Scotorum quasi per iiii annos, usque ad liberacionem Regis Jacobi de Anglia: qui gubernator satis remissus erat in factis suis.

650 Anno Domini m° cccc xxiiii circa dominicam in passione, Jacobus primus legittimus heres Regni Scotorum, liber de captiuitate Anglorum effectus, [rediit] ducens secum Johannam sponsam suam, filiam merchionis de Dorset et Comitis de Summerset, & xxi die Maii ipse rex & regina apud Sconam coronantur cum solempnitate et honore debito.

When his father the king heard of his death, he was very sad and afraid for his only surviving son, James, and he arranged to send him to the King of France. The 13-year-old boy was captured at sea by the English in a time of truce and held under guard for 18 years. But when the king his father was informed that his only son had been captured by the enemy, his spirit immediately declined and the strength of his body dwindled, and because of excessive sadness he did not consume food until he returned his spirit to the Creator, in the year of the Lord 1404. And thus he reigned 16 years.

In the year of the Lord 1404, when King Robert III was dead and his only son James in captivity in England, Robert, Duke of Albany, was again chosen as governor of Scotland by the three estates, and, preserving the kingdom in great peace, he died on the third of September in the year of the Lord 1419. After his death, his first-born son named Murdach continued as governor of the kingdom of Scotland for almost four years, until the release of King James from England. As governor, Murdach was rather negligent in his deeds.

In the year of the Lord 1424, about Palm Sunday, James I, the legitimate heir to the kingdom of the Scots, set free from the captivity of the English, returned, bringing with him Joan his wife, daughter of the Marquis of Dorset and Earl of Somerset, and on the 21st day of May the king and queen were crowned at Scone with due solemnity and honor.

For þe quhilk, þe king dred quhen he had bot a son and thocht to send him to þe King of Fraunce. Bot he was tane at Scarisburgh and kepit in Yngland
435   xix ʒer. For þe quhilk, his fader tuke thocht and deit þe xvi ʒer of his regne and [was] erdit at Paslay.

Capitulo lxxvi°:   Efter his deid, Robert, þe Duke of Albany, gouernit þe realme as conseruatour, chosin be þe thre estatis, xv ʒer.   **f.136r**
Efter quhais deid, Murdow, his eldest son, was conseruatour four ʒeris
440   till þe cummyng hame out of Yngland of James þe First. This Murdow was rakles in his doyngis and left gret faltis vnpvnist.

Capitulo lxxvii°:   The ʒer of God i^m iiii^c xxiiii, about Palme Sonday, James þe First of þat name come owt of Yngland and brocht with him Janot, þe Duke of Somersydis dochter, his spous. And þai war crownit baith þe xxi
445   day of May.

655   Iste fundauit monasterium monachorum Cartusiensium ordinis in Valle Virtutum prope Perth sic nominatum.   Et filiam suam primogenitam matrimonio copulari fecit primogenito Regis Francie. Et tandem edificatis castellis palaciis et multis aliis locis, incolis in optima pace de gentibus, proditiose interfectus est a suis in monasterio fratrum predicatorum de Perth, 660   et sepultus est in ecclesia Cartusiensium quam ipse fundauit. Et omnes eius interfectores capti sunt, post equos tracti, suspensi et demembrati sunt.

He founded the monastery of the order of Carthusian monks in the Vale of Virtues near Perth, and thus it was named. And he joined his first-born daughter in matrimony with the first-born of the King of France. And at last, having built castles, palaces, and many other places, with the inhabitants living in the greatest peace among the peoples, he was treacherously slain by his own men in the monastery of the preaching friars at Perth, and he was buried in the church of the Carthusians, which he himself founded. And all of his murderers were captured, dragged behind horses, hanged, and dismembered.

This king foundit þe charterhous of Sanct Jhonstoun, quhar he lyis now. He mariit his dochter with þe Dalphyne of Fraunce and was a man of gret polisy and wisdome, bot he was tratourisly slane in þe Blak Freris of Sanct Jhonstoun the xiii ʒeir of his regne. And þe tratouris þat slew him war hangit,
450   drawin, and quarterit.

Capitulo lxxviii°: Efter þe deid of James þe First, James þe Secund, his sone, was crownit on Our Lady Day in Lentryne, the ʒer of God [iᵐ] iiiiᶜ xxxvi, a child of vii ʒeris ald, and he regnit xxiiii ʒer. He was slane at Roxburgh with a gwn þat brak in þe schutting, and þe wege stert out & slew
455   him. He was erdit in þe Halyrudhous.

Capitulo lxxix°: The ʒeir of God [iᵐ] iiiiᶜ lx, James þe Thrid, his sone, ˏwas crovned at Kelso. And he regnit xxviii ʒer and was slane   **f.136v** in þe feld of Sterling and erdit in Cambuskynnelle.

Capitulo lxxx°: The ʒer of God iᵐ iiiiᶜ lxxxviii, James þe Ferd was
460   crovned at Scone on Sanct Jhon þe Baptistis Day. And apon þe day of þe decollacioun of Sanct Jhon, he wan Norhame, in þe ʒer of God iᵐ vᶜ and xiii ʒeris with mony diuers strenthis & castellis on þe Ynglis bordour.

Folio 449r of University of St Andrews MS DA775.A6W9. Image courtesy of University of St Andrews Library.

THE ST ANDREWS CHRONICLE

from St Andrews University Library MS DA775.A6W9

Fergus þe fyrst King of Scotland, þe King of Irlandis sone, **f.449r**
send in Scotland be his fader, broucht with him þe chyr of marbyll
stane, chosyne King of Scotland, ane famous battell straik aganis þe
Brytonis, with help of þe Peichtis wan þe feild, and slew þe King of
5 Brytonis, callit Coilus, maid peice with þe Peichtis.
    He rang xxv ȝeiris, passand in Irland drownyt at Cragfergus, and beris
þe name throw him.

Feritharis þe Secund, King Fergus brother & tutor to his barnys, rang
xv ȝeiris & gouernyt þe realme rycht weill.
10   Hys brother sone desyrit þe crowne, and he wald haue resygnyt it to
hym, bot þe nobyllis of Scotland wald nocht consent þarto. Apone þe
nycht, he was slane in his bed. Þe verite is nocht schawyne quhydder it
was be awentur or be menys of his brother sone, bot þe fleyng of his
brother sone maid him suspect, for he fled in Bertane & come neuer in
15 Scotland agane.

Maynus, Fergus ȝonngest sone, þe thride king, ane petuous man & just
and deuote efter þe maner of þe gentilis, he techit þe pepill to worschipe
þar goddis. He biggit templis & in gret montanis set gret stanis.
    He resignyte þe crowne to his sone quhen he had regnyt xxix ȝeiris.

20   Dornadilla, Mayni sone, ane peciabyll man, renewit þe trewis with þe
Brytonis & þe Peichtis. He was ane gret huntar. He maide lawis to þe
huntaris & kepit þe lawis weill þat King Fergus maid, swa þat he sufferit
nathing to be jugit or pvnyst bot it þat was red on þe buk of law.
    He regnyt xxviii ȝeiris.

25   Nothacus, Dornadillis brother, ane subtell man & fals, rang in tyrandry,
brak þe law, reft þe pepill, spulȝeit & banyst & slew mony nobillis. & in
þe secund ȝeir of his ryng, in congregatione of þe nobillis, he was slane be
þe Lord of Galloway, and Retherus was crownyt.

Rether, Dornadillis sone, crownit be þe Lord of Galloway, ane gret
30   batell straik suddandly betuix þe Lord of Lor[ne], callit Ferquhard, &
Dowall, þe Lord of Galloway, in þe quhilk batell neir all þe lordis and
nobillis [off Scotland and mony off þe comon pepyll] war slayne, & þe
King of Peichtis.

*   *   *

̖Ederus, Drusti oey, ane nobill man.   He rewlit þe realme in   f.450r
35   gret peis. [In] his tyme, þe Ilysmen inwadit Argyll, bot þe king
come & slew þar captan[e &] hangit mony of þe laif.
    In his tym, ambassatouris come fra þe King of Be[rtane] and askyt help
agane Julius Cesar, & þe King of Scotland send x thow[sand] men to him,
& þe King of Pechtis als mony, & be þe helpe of þaim, þe Bry[tonis] put
40   out Julius Cesar of Brytone.   Bot þe secund ȝeir he come agane [to]
Brytone, & þe King of Scotland offerit þaim helpe, quhilk þe Brytonis
ref[usit], & sa þai war vyncust in battell & maide tributaris to þe
Roman[is].
    And Julius Cesar send to þe King of Scotland & to þe King of
45   [Pechtis] to subdew þaim wilfully to him, quhilk þai refusit baith. And
secundly [he] agane send opprobrius langage & þai als gret wordis to him.
And swa þe empriour, crabbyt, rasyt his ost aganis þaim, bot for c[aus]
France rebellit, he passit thairour.   Inglis cornyklur says he [come] to
Callendair Wod.
50   In þis tym, Murketus, Gilli oey, come owt off Irland [and] hereyt þe
ilys, bot he was hangit with mony off hys men.
    Þis king rang [peissabi]lley xlviii ȝeiris.

Erenus, Ederus sone, crownyt, ane vicious monstur full of aweryce &
lych[ory]. He had ane hundreth concubynes.   He maide ewill lawis: þe
55   fyrst was þat [a] man mycht mary mony wemen at anis; the secund þat þe
commonis w[emen s]uld be comon to þe nobyllis; the thrid þat a vergyne
new maryit suld b[e tane] to þe lardis bed.   Þe quhilk lawis stude to King
Malcome Canmoir ty[m].

Þis king þus vicious was tane be þe nobillis, & þe fyrst nycht efter, ane
60 [ser]wand worryit him in his bed, þe vii ȝeir of hys ryng.

{vii} Mettellanus, Ederus brother sone, crownyt, ane gude man weill
manerit.

In [þis tym], þar wes na battell bot all in peis. Þe lawis þat Erenus maid
he w[ald haue] distroyit, bot þe wantones off þe nobillis wald nocht let.
65 He resauit [amba]ssatouris of Rome rycht sueitly and send to þe
empriour mony to be offer[it at þe] capitoll and gat ferm frendschip off þe
Romanis.

Þe x ȝeir off [hys ryng] wes borne our saluiour Jhesu, fra þe begyning
of Scotland ccc [xxx ȝeiris].
70 Þis Metellanus rang xxxix ȝeiris & deit without barnis.

{viii} Caritacus, Metellanus sister sone, crownit.

He excedit all þe kn[ychtis] in hardyment of battell.

He passit about all Scotland & did just[ice.

Þe King] off Brytonis ambassatouris come to him for help contrar þe
75 Romanis. [Ane] gret battell wes strykyne betuix þe Romanis & þe
Brytoni[s. Þe King] off Brytone wes slayne & mony nobillis with him and
Gne[us Sensius], consolar of Rome & mony nobillis of Rome.

Sone efter þis, þ[e empriour] Claudius & Vespasianus with him come
in Brytone, & let þe Scottis [and þe] Pechtis be, & passit in Orknay, tuk þe
80 cuntre, & had þar tr[ybut].

The King off Brytone, new chosyn, had þe King of Scotla[ndis
sister als] hys wyff, bot he put hyr in presone and tuk ane gret   f.450v
woman of Ro[me vn]lefully in mariage at þe consaile of þe
Romanis. And swa þe nobil[lis off] Brytone tuk gret displesour at þar king,
85 & rais aganis him & þe Roma[ni]s in batell, & chesit þe King of Scotland
to be þar captane, and swa off [Sco]ttis, Peichtis, & Brytonis he gaderyt
ane gret cumpany, & passit in battell aganis [þe] Romanis, in þe quhilk
battell mony wes slane on baith þe sydis, swa þat euery [man] efter þe feild
leit wþer pas þar way.
90 Sone efter þis, þe legait of Rome send to [þ]e King of Scotland &
speryt quhy without caus he mowit weir on þe [Ro]manis. He said he
weryit justlie on þaim for þai dystroyit kingis & reft landis þai had no rycht
to. And swa þe Romanis merwalit þe hardyment off þe Scottis.

[In] þis tym, þe King of Brytonis left þe Romanis & turnyt to þe
95   Brytonis. [T]harfor þe Romanis send to Rome for help, & þe empriour
send to þaim Vespasiane [&] mony with him. And in contrar him in battell
besyd Ȝork, come þe King of Bryto[ne & þ]e King of Scotland & þe King
of Pechtis, in þe quhilk battell neir all þe Bryt[onis, Sco]ttis, & Pechtis war
slane. Þe King of Pechtis wes slane. Þe King of Brytonis [on his k]neis in
100   lynnyng claithtis askyt grace at Vespasiane & gat it. The King [of
Sc]otland & few with him fled in Scotland.

    Efter þat, Vespasiane come to Camelo[n, & t]uk þe towne, & spulȝeit
it, & send ane captane of hys in Carryk, & faucht [agan]is þe King of
Scotland. In þe quhilk battell, thocht þe Romanis wane þ[e feild, m]ony of
105   þaim wes slane & þe King of Scotland sair hurt. The secund d[ay of þ]is
battell, Vespasiane send ane herald to þe king and bad him subdew h[im
to] þe Romanis, & he promesyt hym to be hys frend, bot he refusyt it &
wes red[y to d]ee for þe liberte of Scotland.

    Þane þar come ane messinger to Wespasian[e & he s]chew him þat þe
110   Brytonis rebellit aganis him. & he left Scotland & left ane cap[tane c]allit
Aulus Plautus. The King of Scotland straik ane battell aganis þis cap[t]ane
& tynt mony men, syne fled to Dunstaffage, bot sone efter, þis captane
de[i]t.

    & [th]an ane Romane come & ane callit Ostrio. In contrar him, þe
115   King of Scotla[nd str]aik feild & tynt mony men, & þe king chasyt. And
fynaly his stepmoder, þe [Qweyn] of Galloway, betrasyt þe king & gaif
him in þe Romanis handis.

    And swa [þe] king & his twa brether, his wif, & his dowcthter war all
had presoneris to [Rome]. & quhen he was brocht before þe empriour &
120   all þe senatouris, all merwalit of his [pacie]nce. Neuerþeles þe empriour of
his grace send him in Scotland agane & held [his b]rether in plegis. And
swa efter þat, he remanyt in frendschipe with þe Roman[is, & he] regnyt
xxi ȝeiris.

    [Corbr]edus, Caritatus brother, crownit, ane lang tym kepit faith &
125   frendschip[e with þe R]omanis. He leiffit justlie & kepit justyce scharply.

    In his tym, þe King of [Pechtis] slew þe legait of Rome & mony
Romanis with him, & send ambassatour[is to þe Kin]g of Scotland for
helpe. & þe King of Scotland said þat he wald noht rys [aganis] þe
Romanis without caus maid be þaim.

130   Bot efter, þe Romanis askyt [þe landis] of Galloway. For þe
quhilkis wes strykyn ane batell.   In quhilk, efter slauchter ˌ[on   **f.451v**
baith] þe sydis þat euerilk perte left vþer, & with consent of bai[th]
þe perteis, peis [maid with f]ew tane.

Bot þe Qweyn of Brytonis wes þe King of Scotlandis sister, ca[m] þar
135   to mowe weir on þe Romanis for þe defowling of hyr twa douchteris, [&]
ane gret battell strykyn, in þe quhilk batell þar wes of Romanis lxx
thowsand men slane & of Scottis & Brytonis xxx thowsand.

Bot sone þe empriour send an[e] captane in Brytone callit Paulus
Suetonius, þe quhilk straik ane gret battell, & [tynt] þe maist pert off his
140   horsmen. Neuerþeles he wan þe feild & slew þe Qweyn of Brytone & lxxx
thowsand Brytonis & Scottis men. Þe King of Scotland fled [&] few with
him in Scotland.

Þe remanand of his tym he leiffit in peis. He regn[yt] xviii ʒeiris.

Dordanus, Metellanus oey sone, crownit. In þe begyning of his ring,
145   he simula[t] to be just. Efterwart he wes verray vicious, full of aweryce.

He persewit Corbre[dus] sonnys, þe rychttuus ayris, to þe deid. Bot he
wes deprehendit in þe cryme. Þe th[rid] ʒeir of hys ryng, he was tane &
his heid strekyn off.

Galdus, Corbredus sone, crownit king, ane fortunate man in his letter-
150   day. A[ganis ew]ill kingis þat wes afoir him, he was verray just & wald
fane a put doune þ[e w]rangus lawis þat Erenus maid, bot he prewalyt in
þat þe nobillis su[ld] nocht haif þe commonis wiffis in lychory.

He faucht mony tymes in contrar þe [Ro]manis, fyrst in Kyll, quhar þar
wes slane of Scottis men xii thousand, & þe[r h]urt in hys face & vi
155   thousand Romanis slane.

The secund battell in Calle[endaire] Wod. Þe nomer þat wes slane on
bayth þe sydis is nocht kennit.

In þis tym, þe Ro[manis s]chippis sailand about Scotland, mony
perischit in Pechtland Fyrth, & m[ony] Norway men & Irland men come in
160   help of Scottis men.

The thrid battell ag[anis þ]e Romanis wes betuix Angus & þe Mernys,
quhar þar wes slayne xx t[hou]sand Scottis men & of þar frendis & xii
thousand Romanis. & efter þis, þe Roman[is schi]ppis saylit about all
Scotland & enteryt in Tay & brynt all þe Da[nys] schippis.

165   Þe ferd battell wes in þe Mernys, quhar þe Romanis war [vyncust] &
mony slane.

The fyft battell wes neir Dunkell at Inchtwthill, q[uhar] v thousand Romanis wer slayne & ii thousand Scottis, & þe Romanis [fled].

The sext battell wes in Galloway, quhar þe Romanis war wincust &
170 [fled] to þar pailʒeanis. & swa þai send ambassatouris to þe King of Scotlan[d on] þar kneis gretand, askyt peis at him, puttand þe conditionis of[f it at] his will, & swa he maide peis with þaim, þai leiffand Scotland & Pecht[land].

Þis nobill king regnyt xxx ʒeiris.

175 [L]ugthacus, Galdus sone, crownit, a man of rycht ewill conditionis & [vnlyk] his fader sweir & lychorus, swa þat he sparyt nocht in lychory his ante[s or his] douchteris.

He spulʒeit nobillis of þar gudis & slew mony of þaim, & fy[naly he] wes slane in Dunstaffage, þe thrid ʒeir of his ryng.

180 Mogallus, Galdus douchter sone. In þe begyning of hys ryng, w[ith þe persuasione] of þe King of Pechtis, he mowit battell agan[is þe Romanis] ̦and ourcome þaim in Brytone, & slew mony of þaim, &   **f.451r**
hurt þar gret capt[ane, Lucius] & on þe secund day he slew mony of þe Romanis, þat fled out of þe feild, & [þe] captane of þe Romanis send
185 to þe empriour for help.

& þe Empriour Adriane come per[so]naly in Brytone. & quhen he knew þe maneris of þe Pechtis & Scottis men – þat þai ly out in frost & snaw & weir few claithtis – he wald nocht persew þaim in battell, bot by[g]git ane gret dyk fra Tyne to þe West See, quhilk he gert keip for þe
190 marche bet[uix] þe Romanis & þe Scottis.

Þis Mogallus efterwart fell in sueirnes, aweryce, & lychory, sw[a] þat he wald haif all maryit women comon. He wes þe fyrst þat maid þe law þ[at] þai þat wes condampnyt to deid, þar heretage & gudis suld be eschetit to þe king. Swa for his ewill lyff, he was slane þe xxxvi ʒeir of his ryng.

195 Conarus, Mogallus sone, crownit. He causit his fader to be slayne.

In þe begynin[g] off his ring, he hyd his vicis, bot efter, he wes all viciouss. He vaistit þe substan[ce] of Scotland & askyt ane tax of þe pepyll, þe quhilk þe nobillis displesit gretum[ly], swa þat þe nobillis tuk þe king, & put him in subjectione, & chesit þe Lord off Argyll gouernour.

200 Þe quhilk lord wes rycht just in his begyning, bot in proces of tym he [fell] fra justice & wes argonit & correkkit in parliament. & swa he gouernit þe realme v[i] ʒeiris, in þe quhilk ʒeiris þe king wes kepit in subjectione. And swa þe king d[eit] in subjectione þe xiiii ʒeir of his ryng.

Ethodius, Mogallus sister sone, ane victorious man in battell, in pece
205 just.

Ofty[n] he fleit þe Romanis.

He dantit þe Ilysmen & slew mony of þaim.

He maid la[wis] to huntaris.

In his tym, Lucius, þe King of Bryton, tuk þe Cristyne faith.

210 & fynaly þis nobill king wes slane be ane harppar in his chalmer, for þe
Ilysmen [þat þe] king slew.

He rang xxxiii ȝeiris.

Sathrael, Ethodius brother, ane cruell tyrane baith in þe nobillis & in
þe com[monis.

215 In þe] fourt ȝeir of his ryng, he was slane be his howsald men.

[Do]nald, Ethodius brother, ane meik & petruis prynce.

In his tym, com in Bryt[one þe] Empriour Severus & straik ane gret
battell, in þe quhilk battell wes slayne o[ff Br]ytonis, Scottis, & Pechtis
xxx[ti] thowsand men.

220 Þis wes þe fyrst King of Scotla[nd þat tu]k þe Cristyne faith, & curȝeit
mony, & deit, & herdyt lyk ane Cristyn m[an, þe x]xi ȝeir of his ryng.

[Eth]odius þe Secund, Ethodius sone, ane dull man of ingyne, full of
co[watyc]e of money.

He wes slane in þe congregatione of lordis, þe xvi ȝeir [of h]is ryng.

225 [Athir]co, Ethodius sone, ane wikkyt man, full of lychory.

For þe rewesyn of [þe L]ord of Argyllis twa douchteris, he wes chaist
in plaine feild, & syn sle[w hims]elf þat he suld nocht be tane with his
fayis, þe xii ȝeir of his ring.

[Nath]alocus, Lord of Argyll, intrusyt.

230 He wes cruell & full of tyrane & [turnyt to w]ychcraft. He wes slane be
ane man of Murray for caus he send him [to take co]nsaill at ane wiche, þe
quhilk wich said þat he suld sla þe king.

[He] deit þe xii ȝeir of his ryng.

*   *   *

.[Downgard, Eugenius brother, cro]wnit. Þ[e] Bryt[onis] f.452r

235 [re]belli[t] aganis [þe Scottis and þe Pechtis. Þe King of Sco]ttis
gadderit ane g[ret] cumpany & past ag[anis þe Brytonis, and slew all þe]
plegis, & syne str[aik] ane gret batt[ell, quhar þar wes slayne of þe]
Brytonis xvi thousand & of Scottis & [Pechtis xiv thousand. Downgard
wes buryit in Scot]la[n]d þe fyrst ȝeir of hys ryng.

240   [Constantyne, Dow]ngard bro[ther, wes] vicious, dull, & lychorus. Als
mei[kill al]s Eugenius, hys brother, ekyt he tynt. He relaxit þe trybut of þe
B[ryto]nis & gaif þaim þair strenthtis.

        & fynaly he wes slane be ane Lor[d] off þe Ilys for þe rewesyng of hys
dowchter, worryit in hys bed, þe [xvii] ȝeir of hys ryng.

245   Congaill, Downgard sone, crownit, ane wailȝeand man.

        Þe fyrst b[attell] he straik at þe water of Hwmber, in þe quhilk battell
þe Duk of [Walis] was slane & xx^{ti} thowsand Brytonis with him.

        For þe quhylk þe Bryton[is] feyit þe Saxones to cum in Ingland with
Duk Hengeist. Þe quhylk Saxo[nes], beand paganis, dystroyit þe Crystyne

250 faith in Brytone.

        And twys þa[i faucht] aganis þe Scottis & wan twa feildis on þaim, bot
fynaly þe Brytonis tuk þar king & put him in festnance and chesyt ane oþer
king callyt Wortim[eire]. Þe quhylk Wortimeir gaif to þe Scottis & Pechtis
all Northummerland. And [swa] þe Scottis & Pechtis in battell oppressit þe

255 Saxones and chasyt Hengeist sone to Kentschyr.

        Bot þis King Wortimeir was sone posonyt & deit, & [swa] Goldyne
Ambrois, þe ayr of Brytone, crownyt. He gaif [to þ]e Sc[ottis &] Pechtis
all þe forsaid landis, & be help of Scottis & P[echtis, þis Goldyne]
Ambrois chasyt all þe Saxones owt of Ingland, [& ran] Duk Hengeist

260 throwcht with ane speir.

        Þis ki[ng, efter he rang xx] ȝeiris, he deyt in hys bed.

        Corane or Gorane, Congaill brother, confeder[at with þe Pechtis, come
to Northum]merland. He faucht aganis þe Saxones & tyn[t mony men] . . .
& mony slane. Bot efter þat, he wes with King Art[hur confederat and

265 chasyt] þe Saxones out of Ingland, saiffand þe labo[rious] . . . .

        [Þe] king beand agit, justyce sesyt in Scot[la]nd, [q]uha[rfor . . .
nobillis of] Murray slew þe king in Loch [a . . . .]

        Eugeni[us, Con]gaill sone, . . . fau[cht] . . . .

EXPLANATORY NOTES

In the following notes, we have striven to provide such information as will illuminate or clarify the edited texts. In particular, we have summarized the historical events recorded in the chronicles, indicating whether the chroniclers have reported those events accurately and, to the extent possible, where they have obtained their information.

We have glossed short passages that have seemed to us difficult to understand by simply consulting the glossary.

When the whole passage cited seems to derive from an identifiable source (most commonly Fordun, Bower, or Boece), we have given that source in brackets following the line numbers – for example, "VC 16–55 [Fordun I 8–17, Bower I 9–18]". Other sources are mentioned in the text of the notes.

Citations of ancient and medieval works are given, wherever possible, by book and chapter, so that any edition or translation may be consulted.

Many of the figures in these chronicles appear under various names – Gaelic, Latin, Scots, and French. As a primary reference, we use the form commonly used by modern historians. But we add, in parenthesis, the forms appearing in the chronicle or (for the *Vraie Cronicque* and the *Nomina*) in its translation.

Some confusion in these chronicles, particularly in the *Nomina Omnium Regum Scotorum* and the *Brevis Cronica*, results from the universal late-medieval belief in a unified and continuous kingdom of the Scots with a known linear succession of kings. We have attempted to mitigate this confusion by identifying kings, historical or legendary, by kingdom and dates of reign, to the extent that they are known. But before the end of the ninth century, it is not always clear, even for historical kings, what to call the kingdom they ruled. Dál Riata, the kingdom claimed by much later royal genealogies, though existing at least from the sixth century, probably did not gain ascendancy over the petty kingdoms of the Scots until near the end of the seventh century and may have lost its ascendancy by the beginning of the ninth. It had been made up out of *cenéla*, or kinship groups – the principal being the Cenél Comgaill (in Cowal), the Cenél nGabráin (in Kintyre), the Cenél nEchdach (in upper Lorn), and the Cenél Cathboth (in mid Lorn) named respectively for Comgall and Gabrán, grandsons of the possibly historical Fergus, son of Erc, and for Eochaid and Cathdub, later supposed to be distant descendants of Fergus's putative brother, Loarn. Thus some of the kings credited in later king-lists as ruling Dál Riata may have ruled only a portion of it, and we have identified them accordingly. After periods of Pictish hegemony in the late eighth and early ninth centuries, the name "Dál Riata" disappears from the historical record, followed toward the end of the century by "Pictavia". Kenneth, son of Alpín, and his sons are attested in Irish sources as kings of Picts, and we have given them that title here, but it is certain that the kingdom they ruled was Gaelic as well as Pictish. Contemporary sources do not tell us what to call the kingdom of Eochaid and Giric, who succeeded Kenneth's sons, but we have called them kings of Picts as well. Then, beginning with Domnall, Kenneth's grandson, whom at his death in 900 Irish chronicles call *ri Alban* (variously translated as "king of Alba" or "king of Scots" or "king of Scotland"), the record becomes a little clearer, and we have, somewhat arbitrarily, identified all his successors into the sixteenth century as "kings of Scots".

La Vraie Cronicque d'Escoce

VC 1–3: The *Vraie Cronicque* was likely written as a briefing paper for diplomats preparing for the Anglo-French negotiations scheduled for Saint-Omer in 1464. Those negotiations never took place. The last event recorded is the death of Mary of Guelders in December 1463.

VC 4–15: The origin myths summarized here come respectively from: the version of Geoffrey of Monmouth (*Historia Regum Britanniae* II 1), in which Scotland is inherited by Albanac, the third (but here made the second) son of Brutus, Aeneas's great-grandson (according to Geoffrey of Monmouth) or grandson (according to one account in the *Historia Brittonum*); the version of Bede (*Historia Ecclesiastica Gentis Anglorum* I 1), in which Scotland is settled by the Picts (though with permission of the Irish Scots); and the version popularized by Fordun (*Chronica Gentis Scotorum* I 28) and Bower (*Scotichronicon* I 29), in which Scots led by Eochaid Rothay settle Scotland long before the arrival of the Picts. Not surprisingly, it is the last of these that the chronicler emphasizes (VC 60–66). In subsequent passages, the chronicler will reconcile these versions, as he promises, by restricting the descendants of Brutus to the Lowlands (VC 99–107) and by placing the descendants of Scota in the country before the arrival of the Picts (VC 60–88, 124–31).

VC 16–88 [Fordun I 8–17, Bower I 9–18]: This is the myth by which the Scots give themselves a Greek–Egyptian genealogy and an ancient occupation of Scotland, thus trumping the Brutus myth of the English and the historical antiquity of the Picts in Scotland.

VC 16–28 [Fordun I 8–11, Bower I 9–12]: Moses, of course, led the Israelites *out of* Egypt, not *into* it. The Exodus was then considered a historical event; Bower (I 8) dated it to the fifteenth century BC. The non-Biblical war against the Ethiopians, cited by Fordun and Bower from "another chronicle", was probably suggested by Higden (II 13), where it is Moses who becomes the pharaoh's general.

The Greek prince here called Galiel is known as Gathelos to Fordun and Bower and subsequent historians. The murky origins of Gathelos and Scota are thoroughly discussed by John and Winifred MacQueen (Bower, *Scotichronicon*, vol. 1, pp. xiv–xxxii, 111–13), and by Dauvit Broun (*Irish*

Identity, passim). Bower follows Fordun in presenting alternate portraits of the Greek prince, from sources no longer extant, including versions in which he is accused of mental instability, arrogant and violent behavior, and oppression of the Israelites. But the *Vraie*-chronicler adopts a more favorable portrait, choosing the version in which the prince is sent to Egypt (instead of being run out of Greece) and leaves Egypt voluntarily (instead of being expelled by the people) – a portrait also found in the *Scottis Originale*, below. There is also an earlier positive portrait in the fourteenth-century Anglo-Norman chronicle of Scotland embedded in Gray's *Scalacronica* (pp. 18–19): Gathelos (there called Gaidel) is described as the *cheualerous* son of a noble knight of Athens.

VC 29–36 [Fordun I 11–12, Bower I 12–13]: The charge that the Israelites engaged in a war against the Egyptians and did great harm to the country is not in Fordun or Bower. The *Vraie*-chronicler is trying to keep the ancestors of the Scots free of involvement in a dispute that the Egyptians lose, and in which God is on the side of the children of Israel. Furthermore, he provides a partial justification for the Egyptians' actions by suggesting that the Israelites are the aggressors.

He has also added the references to jewels and to Carthage.

VC 37–48 [Fordun I 14, 17, Bower I 15, 18, Gray pp. 18–19]: Fordun and Bower tell the story of the wanderings of Gathelos and Scota from Egypt to Africa to Spain, in each place engaged in continuous fighting with the prior inhabitants. The mention of the Straits of Gibraltar as well as the eponymous reference to Portugal, here considered part of Spain, is apparently original to the *Vraie Cronicque* and the versions of the *Scottis Originale*. Oporto was called *Portus Cale* in Latin. Fordun and Bower derive the name of the river from Hiber (Éber), the name of a son of Gathelos and Scota, here called Yber-Scotta, but the *Vraie*-chronicler has it the other way around. The Scots' settlement in Spain, located by Fordun, Bower, and Gray at Brigantia (modern A Coruña) and here in Navarre and Biscay, would place them on the Atlantic coast; the Ebro, though it rises in northwestern Spain, flows into the Mediterranean.

VC 49–55 [Fordun I 16–17, Bower I 17–18]: The *Vraie*-chronicler follows Fordun and Bower closely except in having Hiber remain in Ireland after conquering it.

VC 56–59: The Romans' name for Ireland, Hibernia, was actually derived, at least partly, from Latin *hibernus* (wintry). The *Vraie*-chronicler is on solider ground with Scotia Major (Ireland) and Scotia Minor (Scotland).

VC 60–66 [Fordun I 28, Bower I 29]: This is an attempt to prove the antiquity of the Scots in Scotland by force of etymology: Rottay is Eochaid Rothay, the legendary and eponymous leader of early Irish immigrants into Scotland, said to have settled around Rothesay – once the name of the island and now of the town. The name is actually of Norse derivation. The castle at Rothesay, a detail added by the *Vraie*-chronicler, is a late-medieval construction. Historians have generally supposed that the Irish migrated from the kingdom of Dál Riata in northeast Ireland to Argyll in perhaps the fifth century – long after the period claimed by Fordun and Bower. But recent scholarship raises doubts about the reality of such a migration, suggesting that Gaelic speakers may have been occupying the Highlands as early as the Iron Age (see Campbell, "Were the Scots Irish?"). If correct, this theory would make Fordun's claims of the antiquity of the Gaels in Scotland accidentally closer to the truth.

VC 67–75 [Fordun I 29–30, Bower I 30–31]: It is striking that the *Vraie*-chronicler identifies these immigrants only as the followers of an Egyptian prince, and not, as in Bede (I 1), Fordun, and Bower, as the Scythian refugees who become known as the Picts. It may be that he wishes to strengthen their connection to the Scots, since as Egyptians they would be distant cousins. (It is worth noting that in the *Declaration of Arbroath* of 1320, a similar connection is implied, this time by claiming Scythian ancestry for the Scots, ignoring the Egyptians altogether.) Agenor is not otherwise identified in Fordun or Bower; compare the *Scottis Originale* (OD 86–91, OR 83–88, OA 69–74) where Agenor pursues, rather than leads, the Picts. The number of ships is a characteristically particular addition by the *Vraie*-chronicler.

The legend of the Picts' arrival in Ireland looking for a place to settle is taken from Bede (I 1), whose chronicle was completed in 731. Alfred Smyth (*Warlords*, pp. 60–61) thinks the legend was "already old in Bede's day" and considers it "an origin tale foisted on the Picts by the Irish" who already had designs on Pictish territory; but James Fraser (*Caledonia*, pp. 238–41) considers it "virtually certain that the legend was composed ca. 700" and that it was employed by the Picts themselves "to rationalise a single Gaelo-Pictish community of descent, in which the Picts enjoyed precedence but Gaels were not denied honour." In any case, it served the needs of late medieval Scottish historiography as a device by which the Scots established their primacy in Scotland and by which they simultaneously claimed kinship with, and authority over, the Picts.

The Picts, known as "Cruithin" to the Irish and "Pritani" to the southern Britons, were occupying the northeastern parts of Britain when the Romans arrived. They were apparently called Picts (or "painted people") by the Romans, beginning at least in the third century, because of their tattooed or painted bodies. Their language may have been some form of northern Brythonic Celtic with possibly some non-Celtic features, but that and their ethnic identity remain controversial (see Smyth, *Warlords*, pp. 41–52; Forsyth, *Language in Pictland, passim*; Price, "Pictish", pp. 129–30; and Fraser, *Caledonia*, pp. 44–54).

VC 76–88 [Fordun I 34, II 12, Bower I 36, II 12]: Fergus, son of Feredach (Fergows Fferadrach) was a legendary descendant of legendary Irish kings, traditionally the first king of the Scots to rule in Scotland. In fact, no such kingdom existed at the date given by Bower, 330 BC. As is clear from the last sentence of this paragraph, the point of this section is to antedate the foundation myth for Britain based on Brutus, with a foundation myth for Scotland based on characters who trace their ancestry back before the fall of Troy to the

Exodus. Bower (I 8) dates the time of Moses about 250 years before the time of Priam, the last king of Troy. The *Vraie*-chronicler raises the status of Fergus by making him the son of the Irish king, while Fordun and Bower merely say he was a "nobleman . . . descended from the line of ancient kings." The *Vraie*-chronicler also departs from his sources by having Agenor still ruling over the Picts.

VC 89–112 [Fordun II 6–9, Bower II 6–9]: The Scottish Highlands, lying north of the Firth of Forth (Scottish Sea) and corresponding roughly to the boundaries of early medieval Scotia, was an area of Gaelic settlement (though with Pictish and Scandinavian elements). The characterization of its inhabitants as "Wild Scots" derives from Fordun, who calls them "savage and untamed". Froissart (*Chroniques*, vol. II, p. 270) describes Aberdeen as *l'entree de la sauvage Ecosse* ("the entrance to wild Scotland"). The Highlands' Gaelic speech distinguished it from the increasingly Scots-speaking Lowlands. By the time this chronicle was written, the boundaries of Gaelic speech had retreated north and west.

The *Vraie*-chronicler acknowledges the Lowlands as an extension of Britain, ruled by the legendary Albanac and his followers, rather than by the descendants of Scota and Gathelos. During the English–Scottish conflict of the late thirteenth and early fourteenth centuries, Edward I's envoys justified his claim to the whole of Scotland by asserting that Albanac had been granted the whole of Scotland as his portion, but at Bamburgh in 1321, Scottish envoys conceded only that the south of Scotland was settled by descendants of Brutus (see Daly, "Vraie Cronicque", p. 111, n. 14). Fordun and Bower, quoting Geoffrey of Monmouth, allege that the Humber, the Trent Estuary, and the "Scottish Sea" formed the limits of *Scocia*, and that the Britons never set foot further north. The *Scottis Originale* (OD 77–78, OR 74–75, OA 61–62) asserts only that from the Firth of Forth northwards Scotland was never called Britain. In fact, all of Scotland, except possibly the Highlands, had probably once been populated by British (that is Brythonic Celtic) tribes, as well as by the Picts, who may have been Brythonic Celts. By the mid-fifteenth century, it had been settled by Anglo-Saxon, Scandinavian, Norman, as well as French and English immigrants. In culture and language, it was substantially English.

The Anglo-Saxon migration to the east coast of the island of Britain occurred almost simultaneously with the traditionally posited migration of the Irish to the west coast, in the fifth century, though the spread of English culture and language north of the Forth took several more centuries. *Alba* – originally the Gaelic (Irish) name for the island of Britain – became the name of the tenth-century Gaelic-Pictish kingdom of the descendants of Kenneth, son of Alpín. The name apparently provided Geoffrey of Monmouth with his mythical and eponymous hero Albanactus and with the name *Albany* for the entire northern part of the island.

VC 92: *royame d'Escoce*: Apart from passing references to the kingdom supposedly ruled by Albanac (VC 6) and to Fergus as a king (VC 84), this is the first occasion on which the *Vraie*-chronicler uses the term *royaume* (kingdom) rather than *pays* (which in French could also mean a locality, such as a duchy or county).

VC 113–23: Here are three etymologies for the Angles, none found in Fordun or Bower. The first is essentially accurate: the Angles are thought to have come from Angeln in the Danish peninsula. The second is the false derivation of "England" from "Hengist", apparently taken from the Anglo-Norman prose *Brut* (138–39) or the English prose *Brut* (59); it is also found in Y 38–39 below and in the prefatory material of Hector Boece's *Scotorum Historiae* (f. 21). The third is playfully but awkwardly contrived of puns on "Angles", "angles", and "angels". The proverbial phrase "truth seeks no corners" is perhaps inspired by Paul's assertion, in Acts 26:25–26, that his preaching of "truth and soberness" *neque enim in angulo quidquam horum gestum est* ("was not done in a corner"): the play on words, of course, works only in Latin and French.

VC 122–23: The version of these verses given here is also cited in "Pource que plusieurs", a polemical treatise which, like the *Vraie Cronicque*, was composed in preparation for negotiations which were scheduled to take place between the English and French at Hesdin in 1463–64. This treatise accompanies the *Vraie Cronicque* in all its manuscripts except *G*. For possible origins of the verses, see Taylor, *Hundred Years War*, p. 73. They were quoted by Bower, with slight variants (*quem nemo credere potest* replaces *cui nunquam credere fas est*), in passages vituperating the English, once in his account of Æthelred's reign (IV 39) and again in his account of King Edward I's reign (XIII 25). See also Walther, *Initia Carminum*, 1033, p. 53.

VC 124–38: In a hurry to address his major theme of the contradictory claims of the Scots and the English, the *Vraie*-chronicler hastens to eliminate the Picts as important participants in Scottish history. He glances back at the account he has already given of their origins (VC 67–88) and then quickly jumps ahead to summarize their supposed destruction in the middle of the ninth century by Kenneth (Kyneth), son of Alpín, supposed king of Dál Riata. In fact, what little is known about Kenneth or the events of his reign contradicts this account: the Picts were neither destroyed nor expelled; both Picts and Scots were probably much weakened by the depredations of Vikings; Kenneth may have been a Pict himself; and a unified Scottish kingdom still lay in the future. But Kenneth as the conquering and unifying king has obvious utility to the version of history being promoted here, a history apparently conceived and promoted by his descendants.

The Pictish language did disappear, however, in favor of Gaelic – what the chronicler calls Wild Scots. In later centuries, as the Lowlands were alternately under Scottish and English control, Anglo-Norman and then a northern dialect of English, which came to be called Scots, gradually gained currency in the Scottish court and spread north and west. Like Fordun and Bower, the *Vraie*-chronicler equates a geographical with a linguistic zone: the reality was more complex (see McDonald, 'Gàidhealtachd", pp. 71–73).

The 165 years given as the duration of the Scots' settlement in Scotland before the arrival of the Picts is probably an error for 265 years, which is very close to one of the time-spans (265 years and 3 months) given by Bower (I 37). The 1061 years for the duration of the Pictish kingdom is one of three figures given by Bower (IV 10), following King-list D. Counting backward from the traditional date for Kenneth's conquest of the Picts, about 842, one might conclude that the initial Scottish settlement was about 384 BC, or using Bower's figure, about 484 BC. (A well-read fifteenth-century reader might thus have reason to think that Brutus, born a few generations after the fall of Troy in the thirteenth century BC, might have beaten the Scots to Britain after all.)

VC 139–45: Here the *Vraie*-chronicler skips forward four centuries to begin a long, essentially accurate account (VC 145–206) of the succession of the English crown, in which the claims of the descendants of Malcolm III, King of Scots from ca.1058 to 1093, and his queen, Margaret, are advanced. The account is loosely based on Fordun (VI 6–15) and Bower (VI 1, 14–23). Duncan I, King of Scots from 1034 to 1040, was Malcolm's father.

VC 146–53: The *Vraie*-chronicler quickly traces the English royal succession from Alfred's son Edward the Elder, who reigned 899–924, to Edward's sons Athelstan, who reigned 924–39, and Edmund the Elder, who reigned 939–46, then skipping Edward's youngest son, Eadred, and Edmund's first son, Edwy, to Edmund's second son, Edgar, who reigned 957–75, and to Edgar's sons, Edward the Martyr, who reigned 975–78, and Æthelred II, who reigned 978–1016. Edgar apparently had three wives rather than two: the first and third were Æthelflaed and Ælfthryth, and their sons were naturally rivals for the crown when Edgar died. Ælfthryth was thought to have been involved in the murder of Edward in 978 – the *pechié* to which the chronicler alludes here and for which Ælfthryth was remembered throughout the later Middle Ages. Æthelred was troubled throughout his reign by the raids of the Danes, who forced him into exile for a few months in 1014. He died in 1016; the surviving versions of the *Anglo-Saxon Chronicle* are silent on the cause of his death.

VC 154–63: Æthelred's first wife was Ælgifu, by whom he had many children, including Edmund Ironside – so called for his attempts to repel Danish attacks. He reigned for less than a year in 1016, for the last month in a power-sharing arrangement whereby the Danish invader, Cnut, ruled England north of the Thames. Æthelred's second wife was Emma (also named Ælgifu), daughter of Richard the Fearless, the first (not the second) Duke of Normandy. With Æthelred, she had sons Edward the Confessor (later canonized), who reigned 1042–66, and Alfred Atheling, who was killed in 1036. Emma's brother Richard (the second Duke of Normandy) was William the Conqueror's grandfather, and thus she was William's great aunt.

VC 164–78: Eadric Streona, a Mercian aldorman (not Earl of Winchester), who had switched sides at least twice in the struggles of Æthelred and Edmund Ironside against Cnut, was rumored to have plotted the death of Edmund. But the cause of Edmund's death is not certainly known. Edmund's sons Edmund and

Edward Ætheling, still children, were exiled first to Sweden, then to Hungary, despite the orders of Cnut, now ruler of all England, to have them killed. Edmund died without issue, but Edward married Agatha, a noblewoman who is variously reported by medieval authorities, including Bower (VI 1), as the daughter of the Emperor or of the King of Hungary (and niece of the emperor). Edward and Agatha had three children, including Edgar Ætheling and Margaret. At Edward the Confessor's death, Edgar was the last male descendant of Alfred the Great. (Edgar may have later had a son, Gerald Longstride, but the *Vraie*-chronicler may not have known this.) In 1067, Edgar fled with his sister Margaret to Scotland. There she married Malcolm III in 1069; she died in 1093. Following the death of Edgar about 1126, her descendants could therefore lay a theoretical claim to the English throne. The right of the kings of Scotland to the English throne is asserted by Bower (VI 1), who takes it from Jocelin of Furness's *Life* of Waltheof, Earl of Northumbria. The assertion that all subsequent kings of Scotland were descended from Malcolm and Margaret is almost true – but Malcolm's immediate successor was his brother Donald Bán, and Donald's reign was briefly interrupted by that of Duncan II, Malcolm's son by his first marriage.

VC 179–85: Following the death of Cnut, who reigned 1016–35, and of his sons Harold Harefoot, who reigned 1037–40, and Harthacnut, who reigned 1040–42, the English throne passed back to the Anglo-Saxon line with Edward the Confessor, who reigned 1042–66. Edward died without issue. In 1036, during a struggle for the throne between Harold and Harthacnut, Edward's brother Alfred, himself a potential claimant, had returned to England from Normandy. Upon landing, he was arrested by Godwine, Earl of Wessex, one of Harold's partisans, and blinded; he died shortly thereafter.

VC 186–93: At Edward the Confessor's death in 1066, he was succeeded by Harold, Earl of Wessex. Edgar Ætheling was the legitimate heir, but at about fifteen, he was thought incapable of defending the kingdom in the impending crisis. Harold, together with his brothers Leofwine and Gyrth, was defeated and killed at Hastings by William the Conqueror. Harold's brother Tostig was not killed at Hastings, but a few weeks earlier at Stamford Bridge, fighting *against* Harold. Edgar was proclaimed king after the battle of Hastings, but he relinquished his claim soon after without being crowned. Nevertheless he did not really give up his hope of gaining the throne. In 1068, he participated in a rebellion against the Normans and the following year in an invasion from Scotland. In 1106, he was captured fighting against Henry I. Pardoned, he lived at least until 1125.

VC 194–207: William I, the Conqueror, was King of England from 1066 to 1087. He was followed by two of his sons, William Rufus, who reigned 1087–1100, and Henry I, who reigned 1100–35. The eldest son, Robert, inherited William I's other title as Duke of Normandy. Henry, called Beauclerc because of his scholarly reputation, married Matilda, daughter of Malcolm III and Margaret, thus returning the throne of England to *la premiere souche*, the Anglo-Saxon royal line. There was no son Geoffrey; this reference perhaps results from confusion of Alan IV, Count of Brittany, who married William's daughter, Constance, with Geoffrey, son of Henry II, who became Duke of Brittany by marrying another Constance, the great-great-granddaughter of Alan IV by a second wife.

The *Vraie*-chronicler is in error here in associating Scottish claims to these lands with the claim to the English throne. It was King Stephen, not Henry I, who granted the earldom of Huntingdon to Henry, the son of David I, King of Scots, in 1136. In the late eleventh and early twelfth centuries, the borders between Scotland and England were fluid, and the historical situation is therefore more complex. It is probable that Scottish claims to lands which were to become the English counties of Northumberland and Cumberland (including Tynedale) had their roots in the acquisition by the kings of Scots of the former kingdom of Cumbria / Strathclyde and part of Bernicia / northern Northumbria in the mid-tenth century. After the Norman conquest of England, English and Scottish kings competed for influence in the region. Malcolm III invaded Northumbria five times, and although William Rufus and Henry I settled their subjects in south Cumbria, David I was able to seize and control that area after Henry I's death. During the wars for the English throne between Stephen and Matilda, David I consistently claimed Cumbria and Northumbria. His son Henry of Scotland was recognized as Earl of Northumbria by each rival in turn (1139, 1141), and by Henry, Count of Anjou (the future King Henry II of England), in 1149. After Earl Henry's death in 1152, his younger son William (the future King William I) was acknowledged as earl, an arrangement overturned by his brother Malcolm IV's resignation of these debatable lands to Henry II in 1157 (discussed in VC 225–31). See Barrow, *Kingdom of the Scots*, pp. 130–47; and Duncan, *Scotland*, pp. 219–24.

VC 208–20: Here the *Vraie*-chronicler turns his attention back to the Scottish royal succession and Scottish claims to border counties. Malcolm III reigned from 1057 or 1058 (not 1056) to 1093. He pursued an aggressive policy toward England, raiding Northumbria periodically throughout his reign.

Malcolm had nine sons, but the first three, by Ingebjorg, daughter (or widow) of Thorfinn, Earl of Orkney, are ignored by the *Vraie*-chronicler, as they are by Fordun (V 16) and Bower (V 18). Of his sons by Margaret, only the eldest, Edward, died with Malcolm at the battle of Alnwick (well north of the Tyne) on a raid into Northumbria. Edmund supported his uncle, Donald Bán, when he seized the throne; Edmund later became a monk. Ethelred was the lay Abbot of Dunkeld. Edgar (reigned 1097–1107) and Alexander (reigned 1107–24) died childless. Malcolm's daughters' marriages are correctly reported.

VC 221–24: David I reigned from 1124 to 1153. His only son, Henry of Scotland, Earl of Northumbria, had died in 1152, leaving three sons, Malcolm, William, and David. The eldest succeeded his grandfather as Malcolm IV (reigned 1153–65).

VC 225–32: It was Malcolm's grandfather, David I, not Malcolm himself, who spent part of his youth at the court of Henry I of England. And Henry II of England was not raised at that court either, being only two years old when his grandfather, Henry I, died. Henry II was the son of Geoffrey of Anjou and Matilda, called the Empress as the widow of Holy Roman Emperor Henry V.

In 1157, Malcolm yielded back to Henry II Northumberland and Cumberland – territory that Henry, in 1149 while not yet king, had pledged to David I. The *Gesta Annalia* (II–III) and Bower (VIII 3–4) note the discontent of the Scots at this concession.

VC 230–31: *riviere de Reircorsse.* The *Vraie*-chronicler is in error here in identifying the Rere Cross as a river. The Rere or Rey Cross, on the western edge of Stainmore, had been a boundary marker of the late eighth- and ninth-century kingdom of Cumbria or Strathclyde. In the 1136 agreement between King Stephen of England and David I, after David seized Carlisle, the border between their respective kingdoms was fixed at the Rere Cross. See Barrow, *Kingdom of the Scots*, p. 142.

VC 232: Marginal note in G: *le premier homage fet par roy d'Escose.*

VC 232–43: There was a brief rebellion against Malcolm in 1160, but it did not result in his brother William's being placed on the throne – despite the account in the *Gesta Annalia* IV. The historical events reported here occurred after William succeeded. He was King of Scots from 1165 to 1214. In 1173, he invaded Northumberland in support of Henry the Young King against his father, Henry II. William was captured at Alnwick in 1174 and held for seven months. As the price of his release, he concluded the Treaty of Falaise-Valognes, by which he conceded Huntingdon, Tynedale, and Northumberland and surrendered the four castles listed here plus a fifth, Jedburgh, to Henry. But the treaty did not require the payment of all the gold in Scotland or William's frequent attendance at the English court (the anachronistic reference to the *parlement* of England is probably a translation of *curia regis* in the document).

VC 237: Marginal note in G: *le ii^e homage.*

VC 243–45 [*Gesta Annalia* XXX–XXXI, Bower IX 27]: By his statement that David, Earl of Huntingdon, "had taken the part of Malcolm and King Henry", the *Vraie*-chronicler may be referring to David's service as a hostage to Henry in 1163 (see Stringer, *Earl David*, p. 11). David was still a teenager when his brother Malcolm died, so it is unlikely that any more significant political role is contemplated.

There was no earldom of Galloway in the Middle Ages; there was a lordship of Galloway, but David, Earl of Huntingdon never held it. Probably this is a mistake for the Lordship of Garioch, which was granted to David by Malcolm IV, not by William. In 1180, William confirmed David's lordship of Garioch, Dundee, Longforgan, Newtyle, Pitmiddle, Lindores, and Morton.

VC 246–50: Malcolm was succeeded by his brother William in 1165; William was succeeded in turn by his son Alexander II in 1214. Malcolm and William had a younger brother, David, Earl of Huntingdon (1152–1219). David had many children, including the three daughters mentioned here: Margaret, who married Alan, Lord of Galloway; Isabel, who married Robert de Bruce, Lord of Annandale; and Ada, who married Henry de Hastings. These daughters are of interest to the *Vraie*-chronicler because their descendants were to be rival candidates for the throne after 1290.

VC 251–59 [*Gesta Annalia* XX, Bower VIII 48]: A few months after the death of Henry II in July 1189, William went to Canterbury to conclude an agreement with Henry's son, King Richard I. The resulting document, called the *Treaty* or *Quitclaim of Canterbury*, relieved the kings of Scotland from the burdens imposed by the *Treaty of Falaise-Valognes*. The castles of Roxburgh and Berwick were returned; Edinburgh Castle had been returned three years before. Nothing was said about Jedburgh or Stirling or about a cash payment, which the *Vraie*-chronicler reports 1000 marks higher than the amount mentioned by the *Gesta Annalia* and Bower. But John and Winifred MacQueen (Bower, *Scotichronicon*, vol. 8, p. 564) note that several contemporary chronicles mention a payment of 10,000 marks.

VC 256: Marginal note in G: *se que les Escosois dient touchant la quitance de l'ommage*.

VC 260–301 [*Gesta Annalia* XX, Bower VIII 49]: At least two versions of the *Quitclaim of Canterbury* (1189) are known, an "English" version preserved in a document from the English exchequer, and printed by Stones, *Anglo-Scottish Relations*, pp. 6–8; and a "Scottish" version found in the *Gesta Annalia* appended to Fordun's text in some manuscripts. The Scottish version was adopted by Bower and by the *Liber Pluscardensis*. As Stones points out, that version removed the ambiguity present in the English version. It specifies that William I will pay homage only for his lands in England, and that the agreement binds Richard's successors. In the Scottish version, the *Quitclaim* was a counterweight to Edward I's claims that the *Treaty of Falaise-Valognes* proved the King of Scots to be a vassal of the English king for the kingdom of Scotland. Stones assumed that "spurious" passages had been added by Fordun (in fact, by the anonymous author of the *Gesta*). However, it has recently been suggested by David Corner *et al.* (Bower, *Scotichronicon*, vol. 4, pp. 566–67) that the text used by Bower and his source might have been a draft or a variant version of the *Quitclaim* contemporaneous with the English document, circulating in Scotland. As the *Vraie Cronicque* follows the Scottish version, the chronicler's statement here that the letters are *obscures* concerning homage seems rather disingenuous. There are some variants that suggest either that the *Vraie Cronicque* was using another version very close to the Scottish version or that the chronicler "improved" or interpolated his text.

As Bower gives a text very similar to this version, the English translation given by Bower's editors for the *Quitclaim* has been followed, with some minor changes in style and interpretation, except where the *Vraie Cronicque* varies from Bower's text.

VC 262: *dominus Hybernie*: Not in the Scottish or English versions.

VC 264: *prioribus*: Not in the English version.

VC 265: *aliis ministris suis*: Not in the English version.

VC 265: *regny sui*: Not in the Scottish or English versions.

VC 268–69: *Edymburg et Strevveling, cum pertinentiis*: Not in the Scottish or English versions. (See the note to VC 250–58.)

VC 270: *quittamus*: The Scottish version has *acquietavimus*; the English version has *quietavimus*.

VC 270–71: *consuetudines et*: Not in the English version.

VC 272: *eschattas et*: Not in the English version.

VC 274: *pro . . . Anglia*: Not in the English version.

VC 275: *et successoribus suis*: Not in the English version.

VC 278: *ex antiquitate*: Not in the English version.

VC 279–80: *ex . . . electis*: A variant on the phrase found in the Scottish version, which may indicate a scribal error in the transmission of the text of the *Vraie Cronicque*: *a quatuor proceribus ex nostris et a quatuor proceribus regni Scociae a nobis electis.*

VC 280–81: *postquam . . . obtinuerunt*: Not in the English version.

VC 281: *fines*: Not in the English version.

VC 286: *suis . . . in Anglia*: Not in the English version.

VC 287: *locis*: Not in the English version.

VC 288–89: *Scocie . . . eius*: Not in the English version.

VC 289: *jure hereditario*: Not in the English version.

VC 292: The English version mentions only Willliam; the Scottish version mentions Malcolm and adds *vel predicto Willelmo*.

VC 292–94: With the exception of minor variants, *aliquid . . . habere* follows the Scottish version.

VC 298: In place of *deveria fecit*, the Scottish and English versions have *rex devenit*. The wording of the *Vraie Chronicque* seems to lay emphasis on the duties to be paid by the Scottish king, rather than on his status as a liegeman of the English king.

VC 300–01: *Teste . . . primo* follows the Scottish version. The English version gives another formulation and witness list.

VC 302–22: Alexander II (reigned 1214–49) was the son of William I and the father of Alexander III (reigned 1249–86). The chronicler confuses the two Alexanders and muddles the events of the two reigns.

The battle against the King of Norway is probably the battle of Largs. That battle was little more than a skirmish; it took place in 1263, in the reign of Alexander III, not Alexander II; it was fought on the west coast of Scotland, not in Fife; neither Alexander III nor the Norwegian King, Haakon IV (reigned 1217–63), was present; both sides claimed victory; and Haakon died of natural causes a couple of months later, in the Orkneys.

Henry III, King of England from 1216 to 1272, did not invade Scotland; the invasion mentioned here is probably that of Henry's father, John, in 1216, in which Berwick, Haddington, Jedburgh, and Roxburgh were burned.

The fanciful battlefield peace-making described here never occurred. And the meeting between the Scottish and English kings at York may be a conflation of three such meetings over more than 30 years. Alexander II and Henry III signed treaties in York in 1220 and again in 1237, besides one in Newcastle in 1244. Alexander's aim was to return to "an agreement . . . like the one between King William and King Richard", as the *Vraie*-chronicler puts it – that is, to reaffirm the *Quitclaim of Canterbury*, but he was not successful.

It was Alexander III who was knighted by Henry III, in York in 1251. The next day he was married (at the age of 10) to Margaret, Henry's 11-year-old daughter.

VC 323–34: Alexander III's two sons died before him, David as a child in 1281, and Alexander, Prince of Scotland, childless, in 1284. His only daughter, Margaret, married Eric II, King of Norway, in 1281 and died in 1283, perhaps in childbirth; her daughter, also named Margaret (1283–90) and called the Maid of Norway, became the uncrowned heir to the Scottish throne upon the death of her grandfather, but she died in the Orkneys en route to Scotland from Norway.

The chronicler again confuses his Alexanders: having correctly identified David as the son of Alexander III, he then misidentifies him as the son of Alexander II, explicitly making him the brother of Alexander III.

Alexander III did not die of sorrow, but of a fall from a horse. The accident occurred on 19 March 1286. But by the Old Style calendar in use in Scotland until 1600, the new year did not begin until 25 March, so Alexander's death would have been considered to be in 1285. By *toute la lignie et generation dudit roy Guillame*, the chronicler apparently means just the male line, since the Maid of Norway lived until 1290.

David, Earl of Huntingdon, (1152–1219) was the brother of Kings Malcolm IV and William. Thus when the Maid of Norway died, it was from the heirs of David's daughters that the new monarch would be chosen, as explained in VC 343–61.

VC 335–45: This passage has been added only to MS G.

VC 335–39: In the summer of 1216, in league with rebel English barons, Alexander II led a small force all the way to Dover to meet the Dauphin, the future King Louis VIII, who was asserting a claim to the English throne, and with his English allies, had occupied much of southeastern England. Alexander remained there about two weeks, doing homage to Louis for his English territories in exchange for promises of support, and then returned to Scotland.

VC 336: Marginal note in G: *les premieres aliances de France et Escose. Comme ii rois d'Escose ont traversé Angleterre jusques a Douvre.*

VC 340–45: This wholly false account of a raid by Malcolm III is probably based on the raid of Alexander II, described immediately above. In his version of Alexander's exploit, the *Ynglis*-chronicler (Y 184–88) includes the detail of the king riding his horse into the sea, a detail not mentioned by the *Gesta Annalia* (XXXV) or Bower (IX 29). Malcolm was killed on a much less ambitious raid.

VC 346–54 [*Gesta Annalia* LXXV, Bower XI 14]: The eldest of Earl David's three daughters, Margaret of Huntingdon ca. 1194–ca.1233), married Alan fitz Roland, Lord of Galloway. Her daughter Dervorguil la (ca. 1218–90) married John Balliol. Dervorguilla's son John (ca. 1249–1314) was one the competitors for the Scottish throne. Edward Balliol (1282–1364) was the son of the second John, not of the first. One of Dervorguilla's daughters, Alianora, married John II Comyn, Lord of Badenoch, who also claimed the crown, through his wife, but also through his descent from King Donald Bán.

VC 355–59 [*Gesta Annalia* LXXVI, Bower XI 13]: The second daughter, Isabel of Huntingdon (1199–1251), married Robert Bruce (ca. 1195–ca. 1230), fourth Lord of Annandale. Her son, Robert Bruce (ca. 1215–95), fifth Lord of Annandale, was a competitor for the Scottish throne, but never king. His claim was that he was just two generations from Earl David, whereas John Balliol and Alianora Balliol, wife of John Comyn, were three. His son was Robert Bruce (1253–1304), Earl of Carrick, and his grandson was Robert Bruce (born 1274), King of Scots from 1306 to 1329. The chronicler has strengthened the claim of this last Robert by making him one generation closer to Earl David than he was. The *Gesta Annalia* and Bower provide accurate genealogies.

VC 360–63 [Bower XI 14]: The third daughter of Earl David, Ada of Huntingdon (ca. 1216–ca. 1265), married Henry Hastings. Her son was also named Henry Hastings (ca. 1235–69), and her grandson was John Hastings (1262–1313), first Baron Hastings. John, not Henry, was a competitor for the throne.

VC 364–73: Until a successor could be chosen, the kingdom was governed by "Guardians" – a council of two barons, two earls, and two bishops – appointed by the Scottish Parliament in April 1286. At the invitation of at least some of the Guardians and, separately, of some of the earls of Scotland, Edward I of England (called Longshanks, because of his height) undertook to hear the rival claims. Here the chronicler is refusing to commit himself to either the Scottish or the English interpretation of events, but is merely summarizing the claims made by each side in the later dispute about what Edward's role had been. According to the *Gesta Annalia* (LXX) and Bower (XI 2), Edward was asked by the Scots to act as *judex superior* in the case, but he was not accorded overlordship of Scotland or seen as a judge with a legal title – just as a friendly arbiter and distinguished neighbor. On the question of whether the Great Cause was an adjudication or an arbitration, see Stones and Simpson, *Edward I*, pp. 207–08, and Duncan, *Kingship*, pp. 220–65.

VC 367: Marginal note in G: *De la sumision que firent les pretendans d'Escose au roy d'Engleterre*: "Concerning the submission that the claimants to Scotland made to the king of England."

VC 368: *des trois estas d'Escoce*: The term "three communities", equivalent to "three estates", first appears formally in Scotland in 1357 during negotiations for David II's ransom; prior to that date, the term was "the community of the realm" (see Nicholson, *Scotland*, p. 166).

VC 374–82: Edward asserted his overlordship at Norham (not York) in 1291. The Guardians were vague in their reply, probably hoping that the issue would be settled by the future king. However, the claimants to the throne submitted to Edward I's judgment, and on 13 June 1291 at Berwick, the Guardians and magnates swore fealty to Edward as superior and direct lord of Scotland.

The *Gesta Annalia* (LXXI) gives three versions of the number of auditors (80, 40, and 24), drawn from different sources; Bower (XI 2) gives the last figure only. In fact, it appears that Edward's court of claims appointed 104 auditors on 5 June 1291 – 24 from Edward's council (12 barons and 12 ecclesiastics) and 40 each from Balliol and Bruce. The auditors were not sent en masse into Scotland, but Edward asked the Scottish auditors about the laws and customs of Scotland by which he should judge the case, and when they were unable to agree, he sent envoys abroad for advice. And Edward granted a long recess (until June 1292) to search Scottish repositories for documents that one of the claimants (called "Competitors"), Count Florence V of Holland, asserted would uphold his claim.

VC 383–88: From the beginning of the Great Cause, it was apparent to Edward and to most of the Competitors that the case would come down to Balliol and Bruce. For the legal basis of their respective claims, see Stones and Simpson, eds, *Edward I*, pp. 17, 20, and Barrow, *Bruce*, pp. 52–65.

VC 389–404: Edward declared his judgment in favor of Balliol on 17 November 1292 at Berwick (not York), and Balliol was enthroned on St Andrew's Day, 30 November.

The *Gesta Annalia* (LXXII) and Bower (XI 11) assert that Bruce was excluded because he refused to submit the kingdom of Scotland to Edward, whereas Balliol, on the advice of corrupt counselors, acquiesced to Edward's demands. The historical facts do not support this assertion, which seems to reflect retrospective propaganda by Bruce – an inevitable bias in the chronicler since the Scottish kings of the fourteenth and fifteenth centuries were descended from Bruce's grandson, Robert, who ultimately inherited the Bruce claim.

As in the case of the *Treaty of Falaise-Valognes* (above VC 231–32), the chronicler gives the people of Scotland a major (and unhistorical) role in rejecting English claims to overlordship.

VC 399: Marginal note in G: *iii^e hommage.*

VC 405–10: In July 1295, the Scottish Parliament took control of the government from King John Balliol and gave it to a council of twelve magnates. John was captured and imprisoned by Edward a year later. William Wallace (ca.1272–1305), a knight's son from Elderslie near Paisley and later a knight himself, rose from obscurity to lead the Scottish resistance to the English in the power vacuum that followed the abdication of John Balliol, forced by Edward, in 1296. Wallace was betrayed to the English in August 1305, taken to London, sentenced to death, hanged, drawn, and quartered the same month.

The chronicler gives a very simplistic account of these political events. The Scottish clergy and barons played a major part in the initial resistance to Balliol and the English. It was only after the collapse of a magnate rising in the south-west that there was a revolt of the lower classes led by William Wallace, but he fought in the name of King John Balliol. After his defeat at Falkirk in 1298, Wallace was supplanted by aristocratic leaders and a regency government, which invoked the authority of John and the community of the realm.

VC 411–24: A very confused account. Not "afterwards", but in 1294, well before the execution of Wallace, relations between John and Edward had deteriorated when Edward had attempted to require John's attendance at the English Parliament and to exact military service from the Scots for his war with the French, the Scots' allies.

Negotiations between the French and the Scots opened in May 1295. A council of 12 magnates took control of the kingdom from John in July. An alliance was concluded with Philip IV of France in October, although John only learned of this in January 1296. The Scots ratified the treaty in February.

The *Gesta Annalia* (LXXXVIII, XCIV) and Bower (XI 18) both assert that after falling out with John Balliol, Edward offered the Scottish kingdom to Robert Bruce the Competitor, but retracted his offer after winning the battle of Dunbar in 1296. In fact, the Competitor had died the year before. His son, Robert Bruce, Lord of Annandale (1243–1304), and his grandson, Robert Bruce, Earl of Carrick (1274–1329), paid homage to Edward a month before the battle of Dunbar, thus allying themselves with Edward against John.

After Edward I had captured and deposed John Balliol in 1296, the youngest Bruce hoped to be made king, but Edward ruled Scotland in his own right, demoting its status from a "kingdom" to a "land". Bruce took part in the rising against Edward in 1297. Balliol was released from custody, and under the terms of the Anglo-French truce of 1301, there appeared to be some chance that he might be restored to the throne – perhaps the basis for the chronicler's allegation here. In February 1302, fearing a Balliol restoration, Bruce yielded to Edward. By 1306 a civil war was in progress between factions led by Bruce and by Balliol, who was allied with John Comyn, Lord of Badenoch. After his rash murder of John Comyn on 10 February 1306, Bruce was crowned at Scone on 25 March, thus beginning a prolonged struggle against Edward, and following Edward's death in 1307, against his son, Edward II, called Edward Caernarvon from his birthplace in Wales. Oddly, no mention is made here of the signal victory won by King Robert against Edward II at Bannockburn in 1314.

It is noteworthy that the portrait of Bruce in the *Vraie Cronicque* is not particularly flattering. On the varying impact of Bruce propaganda on Scottish historiography, see James E. Fraser, "Swan".

John Balliol lived until 1314, but never regained the throne of Scotland. His son Edward Balliol later claimed the throne.

The Robert Bruce III mentioned here is a double for Robert I – the confusion probably resulting from the fact that the king was the third Robert Bruce, starting with the Competitor. The king had an illegitimate son named Robert, but his heir was David II (1324–71).

VC 414: Marginal note in G: *iiii^e hommage.*

VC 425–39: In 1332, largely at the instigation of the Disinherited – Scots who had lost their Scottish estates for supporting the English – Edward Balliol did homage for Scotland to Edward III (not Edward II) and with his backing (but without his personal accompaniment) invaded Scotland by sea. After landing at Kinghorn, he won a battle at Dupplin Moor against an army led by Donald of Mar on behalf of the child-king David; that Robert I's illegitimate son, Robert Bruce, was a subordinate commander of the Scottish forces may be the source of the chronicler's confusion. Balliol then had himself crowned at Scone, near St Johnstown, but he was run out of the country after a few months.

The French aid cited here probably refers to the *Treaty of Corbeil* of 1326, which had allied Robert I with Charles IV of France.

We have been unable to trace the source for this information about the nobility. According to Bower (XIII 24) members of the Mowbray family were among the Disinherited, thus supporting Edward Balliol, but according to Thomas Gray's mid-fourteenth-century *Scalacronica*, the settlement of the Norman Mowbrays and Colvilles belongs to a much earlier reign, that of William the Lion. (The relevant section is not included in King's edition and translation of the *Scalacronica*, but is in Stevenson's edition, p. 41.) For lists of Disinherited, see also Nicholson, *Scotland*, p. 125, and Barrow, "Families", pp. 315–36, esp. pp. 331–32. For the origins of the Melvilles, see Ritchie, *Normans*, p. 277. Seton and other Scots also played an important role as mercenary soldiers in the pay of Charles VII (see Ditcham, "Mercenaries", p. 183).

VC 427: Marginal note in G: *v^e homage.*

VC 440–50: Following their coup against Edward II in 1327, his queen, Isabella of France, and her lover, Roger Mortimer, negotiated with Robert I for a settlement of Anglo-Scottish disputes. A treaty ratified by the Scots parliament at Edinburgh in March 1328 and by the English parliament at Northampton the following May provided for the restoration of the borders of the time of Alexander III and the waiving of all claims by the English king to overlordship of Scotland in return for a payment of £20,000 (30,000 marks) by the Scots. Edward III (1312–77) was still under the control of Isabella and Mortimer when he approved the treaty. Later he made no secret of his dissatisfaction with it; Nicholson (*Edward III*, pp. 55–56) cites three roughly contemporary chronicles, Gray's *Scalacronica* (p. 156), Geoffrey le Baker's *Chronicon Angliae* (p. 40), and the English prose *Brut* (p. 218), as witnesses to Edward's position. A document apparently prepared for Edward, *Informatio pro Domino meo Rege in facio Scotie*, put forward the thesis that because the king was underage, the treaty was invalid.

In June 1328, Robert I's 4-year-old son and heir, David, was married to Joan, the 7-year-old sister of Edward III.

VC 448: Marginal note in G: *de la renonsiasion de l'ommage, comme dient les Escosois*: "concerning the renunciation of homage, as the Scots claim."

VC 449: *de Mortemer la lui firent faire par argent qu'ilz*: The phrase was omitted in Anstruther's edition.

VC 451–58: This Edward Balliol is a double for the first, and this invasion is a repetition of the one reported above (VC 425–30). Edward Balliol did mount another invasion, in 1335, which was also ultimately unsuccessful. He maintained his claim to the throne in exile in England until 1356, when he was pensioned off to France by Edward III.

Following Scottish defeats at Dupplin Moor in 1332 and at Halidon Hill in 1333, the young David II was taken to the court of King Philip VI of France, where he remained until 1341. Philip established him at Château-Gaillard. He was accompanied by his 13-year-old wife, but his only brother, apparently a twin, had died in infancy.

VC 459–83: In the spring of 1334 (not 1342), peace negotiations were underway in France between the English and the French in the run-up to what would become the Hundred Years' War. The parties had nearly reached an accord when the arrival of David II in his voluntary exile caused Philip to insist that the Scots be included in the peace. Negotiations were broken off, and war ultimately resulted. This imaginative dramatization may have been inspired by the account in the *Grandes Chroniques de France* (V, p. 357): *Mais il ne demoura mie longuement que la chose ala autrement, car il ne furent mie en leur hostieux que le roy les redemanda et leur dist que s'entencion estoit que le roy David d'Escoce et tous les Escos fussent compris en icelle paix*: "But it was not long before things turned out different, because they [the English ambassadors] were barely back to their lodgings before the king called them back and told them that his intention was that King David of Scotland and all the Scots would be included in that peace treaty."

The chronicler emphasizes how much the Scots owed to their alliance with the French. But he neglects to mention that the alliance had its costs as well. He takes no note of the battle of Neville's Cross in 1346, fought in part to relieve the pressure on the French from Edward's campaign in France. The battle, by which a Scottish invasion of England was halted outside Durham, resulted in the capture of David II; he was not ransomed until 1357.

Putting the kingdom of Scotland on a par with the duchy of Guyenne here might be said to weaken the case for Scottish independence from England. Successive French kings claimed that English kings – as Dukes of Guyenne – should pay liege homage to them, and had exacted duties (justice, military service) similar to those that Edward I had claimed from the Scottish king.

VC 465: *les particularitez*: Literally, "details", but here translated as "specific parts".

VC 484–93: The war mentioned here is the Hundred Years War. The two greatest French defeats of the reign of Edward III were Crécy in 1346, under Philip VI, and Poitiers in 1356, in which Edward's son, the Black Prince, captured King John II.

VC 484: Marginal note in G: *Icy monstra grant foy le roy de France aux Escosois a son dommage*: "Here the king of France demonstrated great faithfulness to the Scots, to his cost."

VC 494–502: By "these events" the chronicler does not mean the battles of Crécy and Poitiers. In June 1341 – thus after the invasions of Edward Balliol – David returned to Scotland from his childhood exile in France.

In June 1334, once Edward Balliol was in power, he had granted a large part of the Lowlands to Edward III in perpetuity. David's return from France had been prepared for in April 1341 by the recapture of the castle and town of Edinburgh by William, later Earl of Douglas. Douglas and his allies went on to clear the English out of the Lowlands. Much later, in the spring of 1363, David faced down a short-lived rebellion of Scottish lords, apparently without French assistance. The chronicler has apparently confused that rebellion with the English invasion of 1385 and attached both to a fictitious son, also named David.

In 1383, Robert II (not David) and the government of Charles VI of France agreed that the French would send troops to Scotland in case of an Anglo-Scottish war. A major French expedition, led by Admiral Jean de Vienne, was sent to Scotland in May 1385. In July, a Franco-Scottish force invaded Northumberland, only to retreat in the face of a large army led by Richard II. The English advanced as far as Edinburgh, which they burned, and then themselves retreated. The Franco-Scottish force then raided Cumberland. The French expedition caused considerable ill-feeling on both the French and the Scottish sides – a situation passed over in silence by the *Vraie*-chronicler.

VC 503–05: The chronicler has apparently forgotten the real David I (above, VC 218–24) and thus considers David II to be David I, and his wholly fictitious son to be David II. But since the chronicler has omitted one David and added another, he is accidentally correct in identifying the king who died in 1371 as David II. That David had neither sons nor daughters. It was *Robert I*'s daughter Marjorie who married a Stewart, and that was Walter – not Robert. Her son Robert Stewart succeeded his father as hereditary High Steward of Scotland, and in 1371, succeeded his uncle David as King. Robert II (reigned 1371–90) had no siblings.

VC 506–08: The king here called *ledit Robert* is not Robert II, who succeeded David, but Robert's son, John, renamed Robert on his succession as king, apparently to avoid acknowledging John Balliol as a prior King John. (His name had probably not seemed a problem at his birth in 1340, since his chance of succession must have appeared remote: David II was young and likely to produce an heir; and John was not made legitimate until 1349.) Robert III (reigned 1390–1406) had four legitimate brothers: Robert, Duke of Albany; Alexander, Earl of Buchan; David, Earl of Strathearn; and Walter, Earl of Atholl.

VC 509–16: Robert III's elder son, David, Duke of Rothesay (1378–1402), was appointed Lieutenant (Guardian) in 1399 for a term of three years, replacing his uncle, Robert, Duke of Albany, who had become his rival for control of the government. Bower (XV 12) claims that after David had shown himself too energetic (and violent) in exercising extra-judicial power, and after he had refused to reform, the king wrote to his brother Albany asking that David be confined until he learned to behave himself. Probably in the fall of 1401, Albany arrested David and confined him at Falkland manor, where, at the end of March 1402, he died. According to Stephen Boardman (*Early Stewart Kings*, p. 238), "even if this [Bower's account] were true, . . . the king had no political control over, nor direct involvement in" the plot that resulted in Rothesay's arrest and subsequent death. Bower coyly attributes the death to dysentery "or (as some would have it) . . . hunger", but Boardman (p. 245) notes that his account is probably influenced by Albany's propaganda, intended to promote "the fiction that the prince had died of natural causes." It is notable that the *Vraie*-chronicler isn't buying it.

VC 517–27: Robert III had been kicked by a horse sometime before December 1388; the accident left him lame for the rest of his life. Moreover, his last years were plagued by sickness – one of the factors that rendered him almost without political significance.

Bower (XV 18) reports that Robert, fearing for the safety of his surviving son, James (1394–1437), secretly shipped him off for France. But Stephen Boardman (*Early Stewart Kings*, pp. 292–97) suggests that the voyage may have been an impromptu decision taken when James was threatened by hostile Scottish forces in East Lothian. James's party did not sail in ships ordered by Robert, but in a merchant vessel from Danzig, encountered by chance. James was captured by the English off Flamborough Head, south of Scarborough, in March 1406, then taken to London and imprisoned. He was released in 1424, after more than 18 (not 21) years of captivity. Robert III had died in 1406, two weeks after his son's capture. During the captivity of James I, his uncle Robert, Duke of Albany, continued as Lieutenant until his death in 1420. He was succeeded as Lieutenant and as Duke of Albany by his son Murdoch.

VC 528–39: Henry V of England died in 1422. James I returned to Scotland in April 1424. While still a prisoner, on 2 February 1424, he had married Joan Beaufort, daughter of John Beaufort, Earl of Somerset, and niece of Cardinal Henry Beaufort.

Murdoch, Duke of Albany, and his followers were suspected of delaying the ransom that released James from captivity and of rapacious administration of the government while in power. By May of the following year, James had arrested and beheaded Murdoch, Murdoch's sons Walter and Alexander, and Murdoch's father-in-law (not son-in-law), Duncan, Earl of Lennox. (The *Vraie*-chronicler apparently calls Alexander "prince" in the generic French sense – not in a mistaken belief that he was the heir apparent.)

In 1436, James's daughter, Margaret of Scotland, aged 11, married the Dauphin of Viennois, the future Louis XI of France, aged 12; she died in 1445.

In February 1437 (1436 Old Style), James was staying at the priory of the Dominicans in St Johnstown (Perth). There his uncle Walter Stewart, Earl of

Atholl, had him assassinated. Walter was the half-brother of Robert, Duke of Albany, who had died long before, in 1420. The conspirators were tortured before they were executed – according to *The Dethe of the Kynge of Scotis* (pp. 46–47), because of *suche diligence in pursuing* and *so sodaine vengeaunce* by the queen.

VC 540–45: James II (1430–60) was killed at the siege of Roxburgh, when an artillery piece burst near him; a wedge, used to secure a loaded chamber in place, flew out and tore into his leg. The castle surrendered after his death.

VC 546–50: James II had four sons: James III (ca.1451–88), who was crowned at the age of 8 or 9; Alexander, Duke of Albany and Earl of March; David (who died in infancy in 1457); and John, Earl of Mar. Until her death in December 1463, Queen Mary maintained custody of her son and exercised some influence over the government.

VC 547: *l'autre . . . qui est prince d'Escoce, duc d'Albanie et conte de la Marche.* The missing name should be Alexander, rather than David (the reading found in *A*) as David had died before his father.

The Scottis Originale

We posit four or more persons possibly involved in the production of these texts: the *Originale*-chronicler, who composed the chronicle in Latin; one or more translators; and the three scribes (one or more of whom might also be translators) who copied out its three surviving versions. The scribe of the Asloan version is, of course, John Asloan.

OA 1: *the Scottis Originale*: This title is also given to the chronicle in the last line of this version. The alternate title, *The Chronycle of Scotland in a Part*, is used as a heading in the Dalhousie manuscript.

OR 1–2: The OR-scribe has apparently added this forecast of the chronicle's theme – though, in fact, the matter of the origin of Scotland's name is very quickly disposed of.

OD 1–14, OR 3–15, OA 2–15: This section, though related to Fordun (I 8) and Bower (I 9), seems to be derived directly from the *Vraie Cronicque* (16–28) or its possible Latin source.

OD 1–5, OR 3–7, OA 2–6: The *Originale*-chronicler implies, falsely, that the Scots' Egyptian origins are "contained in the Bible".

The common English enemy made natural allies of the French and Scots: their *Auld Alliance* began informally in the late twelfth century with the alliance of King William with King Louis VII of France, was formalized in 1295, and was renewed in 1326, 1371, 1391, 1428, 1448, 1484, 1492, and 1512. The analogy to the alliance with France is not in Fordun or Bower. By this gratuitous remark, the *Originale*-chronicler reveals at the outset his tendentious vision of history.

OD 1: *In primis, nota*: "In the first place, note", perhaps a phrase carried over from the Latin source.

OR 3, OA 2: *In to þe first / In þe fyrst*: "In the first place".

OR 6–7: *as now is in France alyite with [w]s Scottis*: "as now France is allied with us Scots." The scribe has written *as* instead of *ws*, an error perhaps caused by an eyeskip to the line above.

OD 6–16, OR 8–19, OA 7–17: Clearly these mythical ancestors have derived their names from the language and the people, rather than the other way around. *Gaelic* seems to be derived from a Celtic word meaning "stranger" (applied by the medieval Welsh to the Irish in the form *Gwyddel*); and similarly *Scot* from an Irish verb meaning "raid". Neolus (or Neolius) is probably Neleus, father of Nestor, and grandfather of Peisistratus, legendary king of Athens. For Gathelos (Gayelglas) and Scota, see the notes to VC 16–28, 29–36, 37–48. OD and OR use the form *Gayelglas*, which, as suggested in the note to VC 21, is closer to the Gaelic forms (*Gàidheal, Gayel*) than is OA's form, *Gathelos*, which is derived from Latin accounts. The *Originale*-chronicler follows the *Vraie Cronicque* or its possible Latin source in adopting a favorable portrait of Gathelos. Marjorie Drexler ("Fluid Prejudice", pp. 68–69) points out that the chronicler has smoothed out his character in an attempt to make the origin myth "unassailable by anyone who might try to use it to malign the Scots." It is significant that all three Scots versions refer to Gaelic as *oure langage* – as opposed to the attitude of some Lowlanders (like the poet Dunbar) that Gaelic is a barbaric tongue.

OD 13–14, OR 14–15, OA 14–15: *Asya, Affrica, and Europa*: The folk etymologies of these names are taken from Higden (*Polychronicon* I 11, 19, 21); Higden takes them from Isidore. Higden and Isidore trace "Asia" and "Europe" back to women, but "Africa" to Afer, a son of Abraham.

OD 14, OR 15: *Iuxta illud / Versus*: "According to this" / "Verse": Formulas for introducing verse.

OD 15–16, OR 18–19: "From the woman called Scota, all Scotland takes is name; It has her name, but adding that of the leader Gathelos was forbidden." Fordun (I 27) and Bower (I 28) have a slightly different version of these lines:

> *Scoti de Scota, de Scotis Scocia tota*
> *Nomen habent, vetito Geythelos (Gaythelos) ducis adaucto.*

A still different version is found in the Coupar Angus manuscript of Bower's *Liber Extravagans*, though not in other manuscripts of that text; they appear in a note to line 58 of Broun and Scott's edition (Bower, *Scotichronicon*, vol. 9, p. 109). In Skene's edition (*Chronicles*, p. 334) of the same work (but called *Chronicon Rhythmicum*), they are lines 57–58:

> *Scoti a Scota; de Scotis Scocia nota:*
> *A muliere Scota vocitatur (vocatur) Scocia tota.*

The sentiment expressed in OD 15, OR 18 was apparently considered telling evidence of the antiquity of the Scottish nation, because the line appears in Baldred Bisset's *Processus* (or Pleading) before the Pope in 1301, arguing the

Scots' case against Edward I's claims of suzerainty over Scotland. Bower quotes the line in his transcript of the *Processus* (XI 62) and also in his transcript of the *Instrucciones*, or preliminary materials from which Bisset's pleading was constructed (XI 49).

OR 16–17, OA 16–17: "From Scota, the daughter of Pharoah, the King of Egypt, as the ancestors believe (say), Scotland has its name." These lines are not in Bower; but in the *Vraie Cronicque* (VC 54–55), Yber-Scotta, the son of Scota, names the country after his mother.

OD 17–39, OR 20–42, OA 18–33: This is the *Originale*-chronicler's own argumentative working out of the implications of the mythical descent of the Scots from the Greeks (in Fordun and Bower) in opposition to the mythical descent of the Britons from the Trojans (in Geoffrey of Monmouth). The chronicler is driving home two points: that the Scots reached the island long before the Britons did; and that the Britons were descended from traitors. According to the twelfth-century *Roman de Troie* by Benoit de Sainte-Maure and the thirteenth-century *Historia Destructionis Troiae* by Guido delle Colonne, the Trojans Aeneas, Antenor, and Pollidamas conspired to betray the city to save themselves. Helenus, son of Priam, the Trojan king, revealed to the Greeks how the city could be taken. Brutus, the eponymous founder of Britain, is a descendant of Aeneas (see the note to VC 4–15). The *Originale*-chronicler is going beyond Bower (II 5), who acknowledges that the Britons got to the island first (*Incoluerunt . . . Britones Albionem insulam prius*) and who does not call attention to Aeneas's treason. There is an alternate version of the Scottish foundation myth, which had been related in Bisset's *Processus* in 1301, in which Scota herself leads her followers all the way to Scotland, thus clearly antedating the arrival of Brutus. But because a later passage (OD 65–73, OR 64–71, OA 54–59) makes it clear that only Scota's son makes it even as far as Ireland, the *Originale*-chronicler cannot have this version in mind. The existence of the version in the *Processus* along with the version in OD indicates, however, that there was a tradition, different from that of Bower, that indicated that the Scots arrived on the island before Brutus and the Trojans.

In his description of Hercules as a conqueror of the world, the author is drawing upon a tradition that is found in Chaucer's *Monk's Tale* where Hercules is described as being, in addition to a slayer of monsters, "the sovereyn conquerour" who visited every realm "at bothe the worldes endes" and was so strong that "no man myghte hym lette [hinder]." He set up pillars instead of boundaries "at bothe the worldes endes" (*Riverside Chaucer*, gen. ed. Benson, lines 2095–118).

OD 26–27, OR 29, OA 28–29: *And Troyanis neuer, bot at thair defens*: OD and OR must mean "And the Trojans never *fought*, except in their own defense". OA is clearer: "And the Trojans never fought, but when they were besieged, they remained on the defensive".

OD 28, OR 30, OA 31: *In cas (And suppos) . . . worthy men*: "Even supposing that since then many worthy men are descended from them".

OD 31, OR 32–33: *In losing of the Grekis*: "In praising the Greeks". In OD, the phrase begins a new sentence, and in OR, it appears to be attached to the preceding sentence. Thus in OD the praise is attributed to Varro, and in OR to the traitors. What the OR-scribe apparently means is that the traitors justify switching sides by praising the superior strength of the Greeks.

OD 32–39, OR 34–42, OA 33: "Greece, with its provinces, is the mistress of realms, the nurse of soldiery, the mother of prophecy, the discoverer and the mistress of all branches knowledge, whose most warlike people, endowed with the gift of wisdom and knowledge, with highly skilled debate, subject to laws, devout, peaceful toward foreigners, peaceable toward inhabitants and natives, unable to accept the threats and incursions of enemies, whose idiom more clearly and resonantly . . . and this . . . (whose fitness in all things is more clear and resonant)." We do not find these verses among the works of either Marcus Terentius Varro (116–27 BC) or Publius Terentius Varro (82–c.35 BC). The OA-scribe seems to have mistaken the first word of the verses, which he omits, for the name of the famous clerk. The OR-scribe seems not to know who wrote the verses, but he knows he is famous. Bower (X 2) gives a slightly different version of these verses without attribution.

OD 40–45, OR 43–48, OA 34–39 [Fordun I 10–11, Bower I 11–12, 14, V 29–36]: Fordun and Bower say that following the drowning of the Pharaoh in the Red Sea, Gathelos and Scota were driven out either by a peasant uprising or by the plagues. Gathelos did not want to return to Greece "because of the crimes he had formerly committed there" (*ob perpetrata prius ibidem scelera*). In explaining that Gathelos was acting *as the maner was that tyme*, the *Originale*-chronicler can again be seen following the *Vraie Cronicque* or its source in retouching history to remove pejorative information about the national founder.

OD 46–47 [Fordun I 13, Bower I 14]: *Ethiope*: Fordun and Bower say that many Egyptians fled to Greece to escape the plagues, but say nothing about Ethiopians – whom he had earlier reported to have been driven out of Egypt by Gathelos. *Ethiope* must be a scribal misreading of *Cecrops*, the mythical Egyptian founder of Athens, who Fordun and Bower say was among the refugees.

OD 48–56, OR 49–56, OA 40–45: The *Originale*-chronicler here pauses in his narrative to discuss the implications of ancestry for the national character. He reverses the argument he advanced above (OD 17–30, OR 20–33, OA 18–32) that even worthy Britons are tainted by their descent from traitors. Now he asserts that the Scots are *not* tainted by *their* descent from oppressors of the Israelites: "For by that reasoning, Christ would be the worse for having been born among the Jews – which is not true." Then, inexplicably, he goes further and defends the Egyptians who stayed behind: "And granted that they (the Egyptian ancestors of the Scots) persecuted the Israelites, yet they (their Egyptian descendants) received Christ into Egypt and nourished him for nearly seven years, while the descendants of the Israelites pursued him to the death and at the last hanged him."

OA 41–42: *For þai war ay lele amangis þaim self*: "For they were always loyal among themselves". That is, unlike the Trojans, mentioned above, and the Jews,

260

who persecuted Jesus, the Egyptians did not have traitors among them, even though they persecuted outsiders like the Jews.

OD 52, OR 52: "Just as the thorn bore the rose, so Judea bore Mary." This is a line from a twelfth-century respond, but it is used as the title of a mass for the Virgin written by Jacob Obrecht, probably about 1497–98. This line thus might date the Dalhousie and Royal versions after 1497 and suggests a common exemplar for them. For a discussion of the dating of the mass, see Barton Hudson, "Obrecht's Tribute"; and Bloxom, "Plainsong and Polyphony".

OD 57–64, OR 57–63, OA 46–53 [Fordun I 10–11, Bower I 12–13]: Fordun and Bower tell the story of the wanderings of Gathelos and Scota from Egypt to Africa to Spain, in each place engaged in continuous fighting with the inhabitants. The eponymous reference to Portugal probably comes from the *Vraie Cronicque* or its source, which reports Gathelos's passage of *le destroit de Gybalther* – possibly what the *Originale*-chronicler means by the Strait of Jupiter. The mention of *grete richess* is probably derived from the *Vraie Cronicque*'s reference to a *grande quantité de biens, or et joyaulx*, which has no basis in Fordun or Bower.

OD 65–73, OR 64–71, OA 54–69 [Fordun I 14–17, Bower I 15–18]: Fordun and Bower link Spain and Ireland by their Latin names, Hiberia and Hibernia, deriving both from the Hiber river (the Ebro), and the river's name from Éber (Hyber-Scot, Yber-Scot, Iber-Scot), the son of Gathelos and Scota. The river does in fact seem to have given its name to Hiberia, but Hibernia, the equivalent of the Irish *Erinn*, is probably derived from Latin *hibernus*, for "wintry". (See the note to N 11–15, BAd 5–10, BAs 8–12.) The *Vraie Cronicque* has a similar account (see the note to VC 37–48). OD's *Wisbayn*, OR's *Itavern*, and OA's *Olor* are doubtless scribal errors.

OD 66, OR 65: *quhare Gayell gat on Scota Hyber-Scot*: A reckless addition to Fordun and Bower. Given the 40-year sojourn in Africa, Scota must be at least in her 50s. The *Vraie Cronicque* agrees with this chronicle that the son was named after the river, against Fordun (I 17) and Bower (I 18) who cite "certain writers" as asserting that the river was named after the son.

OD 67–68, OR 66–67, OA 56: *he fand it vakand, savand a certane of gyandis*: Bower cites contradictory authorities, some of whom say the island was empty and some of whom say it was inhabited by giants – an idea derived ultimately from Geoffrey of Monmouth's account of Brutus's finding his new home uninhabited except for a few giants; the giant killer in that account is not Brutus but Corineus, after whom Cornwall was named. OD and OR similarly resolve the contradiction by the mediation of *savand* or *bot*, while OA has it both ways: *fande it voide and fand in it a certane of giandis*. The *Vraie Cronicque* also reports that Hiber finds Ireland uninhabited except for some giants, which he drives out. In OA, the first mention of Hiber has been omitted, so because the *said Iber-Scot* in OA 59 has never been mentioned before, the pronoun *he* in OA 56 seems to credit Gathelos rather than his son with the destruction of the giants.

OR 67: *gewictis*: The parallel terms *gyandis* and *giandis* make it probable that the word means "giants", though we can find no other record of the word. Hector MacLean ("Ancient Peoples", p. 170) speculated in 1891 that it was "a Gaelic form of the name Pict, . . . which would, at first, have C substituted for P, as in the case of *Criuthin* for *Prydyn* . . . ." And Laurence Waddell (*Phoenician Origins*, p. 122) cited the word in 1924 as evidence that the "primitive aborigines of Ireland" were Picts, "especially as it was usual to spell the analogous Wight [as in the Isle] . . . with an initial G." But it seems doubtful that the scribe thinks this is what the word means, because the chronicle is explicit about the much later arrival of the Picts.

OD 74–78, OR 72–75, OA 60–62: The *Originale*-chronicler is asserting the primacy of the myth of the settlement of Ireland by Hiber over the equally spurious myth of the foundation of Britain by Brutus. But since he has not said anything about the date of the Scots' migration from Ireland to Scotland, his conclusion that *oure land [was] inhabyte lang tyme before þat Troy was destroyit* is unsubstantiated. This argument comes not from Fordun or Bower, but from the *Vraie Cronicque* (VC 85–98) or its source, along with the reference to the Scottish Sea (the Firth of Forth) as the limit of the settlement of the Britons.

OD 79–80, OR 76–77, OA 63–64: The claim of independence of foreign domination is more or less true if one is thinking of the imposition of widespread, permanent, and institutional authority, and ignoring the campaigns of Agricola, Severus, and Constantius into the north of Scotland, the two Roman occupations of the lowlands below the Clyde and the Forth, the Viking settlements along the western seaboard and in the Iles, and the invasions of William I and Edward I.

OD 81–82, OR 78–79 [Bower II 15, 64]: "Scotland was never, through force or fear, conquered by (subject to) the vainglorious Romans, nor does she submit to (obey) their command." The verses are also found in N 55–56, in the fifteenth-century text *Tract on the Scots*, lines 11–12 (Skene, *Chronicles*, pp. 330–31).

OD 83–85, OR 80–82, OA 65–68 [Fordun I 28, Bower I 29]: This is another attempt to prove the antiquity of the Scots in Scotland by force of etymology. The reference to Rothesay closely parallels the *Vraie Cronicque*, but the reference to Bute is not in the French chronicle. Rothesay, once the name of the island and now of the town, actually has a Norse derivation, but it is said by Fordun to be derived from Eochaid Rothay (Rothay, Rathus Rothia, Ethios Rothay), a legendary settler from Ireland. Bute is said by Fordun to be derived from *bothe*, the Gaelic word for "cell", because of a hermitage built there by St Brendan. But this etymology is also false: according to John and Winifred MacQueen (Bower, *Scotichronicon*, vol. 1, p. 147), the island was called Bute long before Brendan (ca.486–575) – who is not known to have visited the island anyway.

OD 86–96, OR 83–93, OA 69–81 [Fordun I 27, 29–30, Bower I 28, 30–31]: According to Fordun and Bower, Simón Brecc (Symon Brek, Symon Brieke, Symon Surke) was the legendary leader of the third wave of migration from Spain to Ireland, not a settler of *oure Scotland*. But John and Winifred MacQueen (Bower, *Scotichronicon*, vol. 1, p. 147) point out the contradiction between Bower's statement that Eochaid Rothay, "great-grandson of . . . Simon Brecc" was "the first leader of the inhabitants of these islands" and his later genealogy (V 60), which says that eight generations *before* Simón, his ancestor Rothechtaid "was the first to colonise the islands of Scotia". Apparently Rothay – originally a twelfth-century mistranscription of Eochaid's sobriquet *Buadaig* ("victorious") – and Rothechtaid have been conflated (see Broun, *Irish Identity*, p. 71). Perhaps this contradiction has confused the *Originale*-chronicler: he puts Simón later than Rothay, while Fordun and Bower put them the other way around. His point, now made for the third time, is that the Scots got to Britain before the Britons did.

The legend of the Picts' arrival in Ireland looking for uninhabited land is taken from Bede (I 1). It serves the needs of late-medieval Scottish historiography as a device by which the Scots established their primacy in Scotland before having actually inhabited it, and by which they claimed simultaneous kinship with, and authority over, the Picts (see the note to VC 67–75). The fanciful story has also provided some modern historians with a rationale for the now disputed Pictish custom of matrilineal succession (for discussions of this issue, see Miller, "Matriliny", pp. 133–61, and Smyth, *Warlords*, pp. 57–61). Bede and later Higden report that the Picts came from Scythia. Fordun and Bower cite an unnamed chronicle that says that the Picts were led, rather than chased by Agenor, a claim repeated by the *Vraie Cronicque*. None of these chroniclers mention the 30 ships, a detail that is shared by the *Vraie Cronicque*.

The *Originale*-chronicler is at some pains to distinguish the two Scotias: Ireland, called *Scotia* by the Romans and in OA called *Scotland Maior* or *Mair Scotland*; and Scotland, in OR and OA called *Lesse* or *Les Scotland*. In OD and OR, *our ile* means Scotland, and *thair* (their island) means Ireland.

OD 88–90: *vnto the tyme of the Pechtis, þat thai come, quhilkis war chassit out of thair land callit Scithia be a prince of Egipt callit Agenor*: "until the time of the Picts, when those who were chased out of their land called Scythia by a Prince of Egypt called Agenor, came".

OD 95, OR 93: *the lave (lufe) of the Pechtis*: "the rest of the Picts", i.e., later generations. The second *lufe* in OR 92 apparently means "love"; possibly an eyeskip accounts for the identical spelling of two distinct words.

OD 97–107, OR 94–103, OA 82–93 [Fordun I 34, II 12, Bower I 36, II 12]: Fergus, son of Feredach (here also Farchar and Ferherd), a legendary descendant of legendary Irish kings, is traditionally the first king to rule over the Scots in Scotland. In fact, no such kingdom existed at this date, 330 BC. The royal arms of Scotland (a red lion on a gold field, surrounded by a double border of fleur-de-lys) were apparently first used by King William I (reigned 1165–1214). The *Vraie Cronicque* makes no reference to the coat of arms.

OD 97, OR 94: *And lang tyme efter þat thai come . . . , thai multiplyit / And lang tyme eftir, þai come . . . and multiplyt*: OD probably repeats the syntax of the original text in making "they came" the core of a dependent clause (the *þat* being relative rather than demonstrative): "And for a long time after they came . . . , they multiplied . . ."; OR, by moving "they came" to the independent clause, introduces an inexplicable delay between the Picts' being given license to occupy Scotland and their actually going there: "And a long time afterwards, they came . . . and multiplied . . . ."

OD 98, OR 95, OA 82: *oure Scottis þat duelt thare before / ws Scottis men*: The legendary descendants of Simón Brecc and his followers.

OD 100–04, OR 96–98, OA 83–86: *Grete Scotland*: "Ireland"; *our Scotland / Lytill Scotland / Les Scotland*: "Scotland".

OD 104–07, OR 100–03, OA 89–93: "The first king of Scottish descent in the lands of Albion, Fergus, son of Farchard carried among his Scottish troops the arms of a red lion roaring on a yellow field. (That reddish lion with its fleur-de-lys is now painted with gold.) He preceded Christ by 330 years." The second sentence does not appear in OD or OR. These lines also appear in N 43–46, in Bower (II 12), in the fifteenth-century *Tract on the Scots*, lines 13–17 (Skene, *Chronicles*, p. 331), and in the *Liber Extravagans*, lines 124–27 of the *Poema Scotica* section. They do not occur in the *Vraie Cronicque*.

OD 104, OR 100, OA 89: *Scotus / Scotis*: OR and OA have *Scotus*, apparently intending to agree the word with *primus rex* – "first Scots king". This is also the reading in the *Nomina* (N 43). But OD has Scotis. That is also the reading in Bower, in the *Tract on the Scots*, and in the *Liber Extravagans*.

OD 108–12, OR 104–08, OA 94–99: The succession of Scottish kings from Gathelos to Fergus, son of Feredach, is entirely legendary, from this first Fergus to the later Fergus, son of Erc, mostly legendary, and from that second Fergus to Cinaed, son of Alpín, only intermittently historical. But within the terms of Scottish legend, the *Originale*-chronicler's claim of uninterrupted Scottish sovereignty is more or less true. Dauvit Broun (*Scottish Independence*, pp. 37–70) explores the importance of a "continuous narrative of a kingship's history" to the identity of the Scots and the authority of their king – which narrative took shape in the course of the thirteenth century and was fully developed by 1320, when it is cited by the baronial authors of the *Declaration of Arbroath* as major evidence of Scottish independence from England: "And as the historians of old time bear witness,[the Scots] have held [Scotland] free of all bondage ever since [their arrival from Spain]. In their kingdom there have reigned one hundred and thirteen kings of their own royal stock, the line unbroken by a single foreigner." The *Originale*-chronicler has taken the point and upped the ante: the six-score kings claimed here are in addition to the 113 (which presumably start with Fergus, son of Feredach), since the 120 reach *to* Fergus *from* Gathelos. Fordun and Bower provide various genealogies from Gathelos to Simón Brecc, but skip over the further descent to Fergus. There is a complete genealogy from Gathelos to Fergus, son of Feredach, in the *Ymagines Historiarum* of Ralph of Diss; we are grateful to Dauvit Broun for letting us see the edition he is working on. That genealogy lists only 58 kings. It seems likely that, ignorant of this genealogy, the *Originale*-chronicler simply used an arbitrary average reign, to arrive at a sufficiently impressive number.

The claim of independence from foreign conquest is repeated in OD 188–93, OR 187–92, OA 178–85. Similar claims are twice made in "The Ring of the Roy Robert" (*Metrical Tales*, p. 230, l. 60; and p. 232, lines126–28):

> We war euir fre within our awin!

and:

> Bot of our Realm, I dar weill say
> Was never none hyn to this day,
> Brocht Scotland in subiectioun!

OA 96: *our souerane lord James þe Fyft þat now is*: James V ruled from 1512 to 1542.

OD 113–66, OR 109–61, OA 100–56: This lengthy section, more than a fifth of the whole chronicle, is a largely legendary account of Scottish-British relations in the period between the conquests of Britain by the Romans in the first century and the Saxons in the fifth and sixth centuries. The section is almost wholly devoted to confronting and discrediting the legend of Arthur, who, because of his status as a British hero, later adopted by the English, was a favorite late-medieval target of the Scots. For discussions of Scottish attitudes toward Arthur, see Fletcher, *Arthurian Material*, pp. 241–29; Alexander, "Scottish Attitudes", pp. 17–34; Göller, "King Arthur", 173–84; Boardman, "Matter of Britain", pp. 47–72; Royan, "Representations of Arthur", pp. 9–20; and Royan, "Faint Praise", pp. 43–54.

OD 113–18, OR 109–14, OA 100–04 [Fordun III 14, 17–18, Bower III 14, 17–18]: Bower reports alliances made with the Britons before the reign of Arthur. The Romans built two walls to protect their northern frontier in Britain: Hadrian's Wall, built between 122 and 130, and running from Solway Firth to the mouth of the Tyne; and the more northerly Antonine Wall, built between 140 and 142, and running from the Firth of Forth to the Firth of Clyde.

OD 112–13: *and sa we occupyt þe Romans at we gert þam byg twa wallis*: "we so troubled the Romans that we forced them to build two walls".

OD 119–22, OR 115–18, OA 105–08: Emperor Severus died at York in 211, but of sickness rather than battle; he had campaigned as far north as Aberdeen without being able to engage the Picts in decisive battle. Julius Caesar had never made any attempt to invade the north. During the reign of Emperor Vespasian (69–79), a successful advance had been made into the lowlands.

OD 123–35, OR 119–30, OA 109–23 [Fordun III 24–25, Bower III 24–25]: Bower accepts the Arthurian material of Geoffrey of Monmouth (VIII 19), who says that Merlin gave King Uther drugs that changed his appearance to look like Duke Gorlois of Cornwall, thus enabling Uther to sleep with Gorlois's wife, Igerne, who conceived Arthur as a result. Fordun and Bower champion the Scots Mordred (Moldreid) and Gawain, legitimate sons of Loth of Lothian, over the illegitimate Arthur. Bower adds a detail not in Fordun: Mordred was the older of the two brothers and was thus by implication a closer heir to the throne than Gawain. Loth was married to Anna, who Geoffrey of Monmouth at one point says was the sister of Arthur and at another point says was the sister of King Aurelius, brother of Uther. Most chroniclers after Geoffrey say Anna was Arthur's sister, but since she was conceived after Uther and Igerne were married, she was legitimate. Fordun and Bower both mention the possibility that she was Aurelius's sister, but conclude that her being Arthur's sister was "nearer the truth". Bisset's *Processus* (Bower XI 62) also stresses Arthur's illegitimacy. Geoffrey and Bower do not call Igerne a whore, as OD and OR do. According to them, she was the unwitting victim of what Bower (III 24) calls "the unheard of art of the prophet Merlin". Nor do they say, as OA does, that Mordred was passed over because he was a Scot, but simply because he was a small child, and the Britons needed a warrior king. In attributing Arthur's selection to *the devilry of Merlyn*, the *Originale*-chronicler is probably thinking of the sword in the stone episode in either Robert de Boron's *Merlin* or its adaptation into the French prose romances of the Vulgate and Post-Vulgate cycles. Merlin drops out of the story before Arthur is born, according to Geoffrey of Monmouth and the English chronicles based on his work.

The *Vraie Cronicque* lacks any reference to Arthur or to any Scottish kings between Fergus, son of Feredach, and Kenneth, son of Alpín. It (or its Latin source) is not used again as a source until the *Scottis Originale* comes to Kenneth (OD 167, OR 162, OA 157).

OA 110–11: *quhen þe Romanis had dantit þaim & wtterly destroyed, had nocht bene our suple*: "when the Romans would have defeated and utterly destroyed them, if it had not been for our help".

OD 132: *the Duk of Cornwell, Vter*: Uther, of course, was not the Duke of Cornwall, but the king who slept with the duke's wife.

OD 136–39, OR 131–34, OA 124–28 [Fordun III 26, Bower III 26, Higden V 6]: Fordun and Bower record the battle between Mordred and Arthur, but not the crowning of Mordred in London while Arthur was out of the kingdom. This detail probably comes from Higden.

OD 140–42, OR 135–37, OA 129–32 [Fordun III 21, 24, Bower III 21, 24] Gabrán (Sorane, Goran) was a historical king (and the eponym of the Cénel nGabráin) in Kintyre from about 538 to about 558. Fordun and Bower report that the battle between Arthur and Mordred took place after Gabrán's reign, during the reign of Eugenius, a king possibly invented by Fordun or one of his sources. They do not claim Scottish participation on either side.

OD 143–49, OR 138–44, OA 133–40: Another of the *Originale*-chronicler's periodic summations. In his view of history, the conquest of Scotland had been a major objective of the Romans, and their failure was a reason for their departure from Britain. In fact, when the Romans pulled their legions out of Britain at the beginning of the fifth century, after an occupation of more than 360 years, they were responding to pressures elsewhere in the empire. But he manages to express an essential truth: when the Britons were under Roman occupation, the northern (mostly Pictish) tribes were restrained by a formidable military power to their south; when the Romans abandoned the island, the resulting British kingdoms were too fragmented to pose a very great threat to the Scottish nation that would emerge over the next several centuries.

There is a purely legendary tradition of alliance between the Scots and the Britons in this period. According to Fordun (III 17–18, 21) and Bower (III 17–18, 21), the Scots came to the aid of Vortigern and Aurelius Ambrosius against the Saxons, and it is implicit in their accounts (III 26, III 26) of the probably fictitious King Eochaid Hebdre (called *Eugenius*), who they say reigned 535–58, that there was such an alliance at the time of Arthur.

OD 150–55, OR 145–49, OA 141–43: Geoffrey of Monmouth (IX 11) claims that Arthur defeated Frollo, the King of France, and later (X 11) that Lucius, the Procurator of Rome, was killed in battle "by an unknown hand." Arthur is the slayer of Lucius in the fourteenth-century *Alliterative Morte Arthure*, which may have been known in Scotland. But the likely source of these references to Lucius and Frollo (Frelle, Stallo) are taken from Higden's criticism of Geoffrey (*Polychronicon* V 6), in which Higden claims, wrongly, that Geoffrey attributed Lucius's death to Arthur ("*dicit Arthurum . . . Lucium . . . extinxisse*"). Walter Map (Maple, Napillis, Mapill) (ca.1140–c.1210) was widely (and falsely) credited during the Middle Ages with the Vulgate Cycle, a series of romances including *Lancelot* – and the tale was widely discredited as fiction. It is, of course, the target of the irony of Chaucer's Nun's Priest (*Canterbury Tales*, VII 3211–12):

> *This storie is also trewe, I undertake,*
> *As is the book of Launcelot de Lake,*
> *That wommen holde in ful greet reverence.*

OD 156–61, OR 150–55, OA 144–49: An extremely confused account of the Anglo-Saxon Invasion. When the Romans pulled out of Britain in the early fifth century, incursions by the Picts led the Britons to hire mercenary Saxons to defend them, but by the middle of the sixth century the Saxons had taken over the country for themselves. Vortigern (Wortiger, Vorage) was, according to Bede, the British king who invited the Saxons in. He had, according to Geoffrey of Monmouth, usurped the crown after murdering the young king, Constans. According to Fordun (III 17) and Bower (III 17), once it became clear to the Britons that the Saxons were their real enemies, they forged a series of alliances with the Scots. Part of the confusion is attributable to the *Originale*-chronicler's tendency to conflate actions widely separate in time. The *cruell were þat we and the Pechtis maid in oure defens agayne the Romaynis and Britones* refers to the centuries of Roman occupation, but the period *quhen he (þai) mycht nocht gaynstand vs* refers to the period following the Roman evacuation, when the Picts became the aggressors. Similarly in OA, Arthur, the legendary opponent of the Saxons, is confused with Vortigern, their host: here it is Arthur who *callit . . . in helpe of þe fals Saxonis*. OD and OR stress that the Scots were fighting the Saxons before Arthur was even born. All three texts gloat that, despite Arthur's victories, the Saxons ultimately prevailed.

OA 147–48: *in þe suple of him nochtwithstanding*: "despite his help".

OD 162–66, OR156–61, OA 150–56: The claim that Arthur conquered 30 kingdoms is made by Geoffrey of Monmouth (X 7). The *Originale*-chronicler here repeats Higden's doubts about these victories (V 6). The ultimate triumph of the Saxons over the Britons is offered as proof of the inflation of Arthur's fame.

OA 155–56, OR 160–61: *serpens in gremio, mus in pera, ignis in sinu*: "Snake in the lap, mouse in the wallet, fire in the garment" – things that badly repay hospitality, according to one of Aesop's fables, Number 59 in the version of Odo of Cheriton (d. 1247).

OD 167–71, OR 162–67, OA 157–61: Kenneth (Kenauthe), son of Alpín (Makalpyne, McCalpyne), is traditionally considered the last king of Dál Riata and the first King of Scots, after conquering and expelling the Picts in 842. But Kenneth may have been a Pict himself, and though he ruled Pictland until his death in 858, probably not by right of conquest. (See the note to VC 124–38.)

OD 169, OA 159–60, OR 164–65: The three versions agree that the expulsion of the Picts occurred "seven hundred years ago". From the traditional date of 842, this would seem to date the chronicle to late in the second quarter of the sixteenth century. But OR's explicit dating of the expulsion to *þe ȝeir of our Lord, aucht hundir xxx and od ȝeiris* would date the chronicle, or perhaps just this version, to the 1530s. See the Introduction, pp. 42–43, for a fuller discussion.

OD 170–171, OR 161–67, OA 160–61: *the tyme þat the Danys subiect the Saxones, & regnyt on thame wele xxx ȝere*: 1016–42, when England was ruled by Danish kings Cnut, Harold Harefoot, and Harthacnut.

OD 172–76, OR 168–75, OA 162–69: The *Originale*-chronicler is defending the claim of Edmund II Ironside (and thus the claims of Edmund's Scottish descendants) to the crown of England, while attacking the claims of William the Bastard and his descendants. Edmund reigned over a part of England for a few months in 1016, in a forced division of the kingdom with Cnut; his son Edward the Exile failed to succeed him. About 1069, his granddaughter Margaret married Malcolm III, King of Scots. Margaret was later canonized.

OR 172, OA 166: Malcolm (Macolm), King of Scots from 1057 or 1058 to 1093, was known to the *Originale*-chronicler and to later ages as Malcolm Canmore (Chanmar) – "Great Head". But Archibald Duncan (*Kingship*, pp. 74–75) has argued that this sobriquet properly belongs to his great-grandson, Malcolm IV.

OA 166: *callit to name Sanct Margaret*: "named St Margaret".

OA 166–67, OR 172–73: *fra þe quhilk is discendit lyne be lyne our souerane lord þat now is*. All Kings of the Scots after 1097 were descended from Malcolm and Margaret, so this remark is no help in dating the chronicle. But see OA 96 and note. The wording is similar to that of VC 142–45.

OR 173: *wnweddit*: an unfortunate blunder for *vndoutit*, seeming to asperse the Scottish royal line rather than the English. Doubtless the mistake was made under the influence of the subject being discussed – the bastardy of William the Conqueror.

OD 177–93, OR 176–92, OA 170–85: This section develops the claim of continuous sovereignty made in OD 108–12, OA 94–99, OR 104–08 and announces the theme of continuous warfare in defense of the kingdom that organizes the chronicle to the end.

OD 177–80, OR 176–79, OA 170–73: This is, of course, a gross simplification of the history of Britain, but it is roughly accurate about the passage of sovereignty from people to people: the Picts and Scots grew into a single Gaelic-speaking kingdom; the Britons who were not driven out to Wales, Cornwall, or Brittany were absorbed by the Saxons; the Danish invaders of the ninth century were absorbed by the Saxons (though in the eleventh century, Danes under Cnut ruled England briefly); the English were then conquered by Normans under William the Bastard. The wording of the first sentence of this paragraph seems to come directly from Bisset's *Processus* (Bower XI 61).

OD 182: *Romanos*: The scribe has, perhaps unconsciously, copied the Latin form.

OD 182, OR 181: *Gothis*: Fordun (IV 17, 37) and Bower (IV 17, 40) include Goths, along with Danes, Norwegians, Vandals, and Frisians, in two lists of pirates that preyed upon the English. But here they are included among the attackers of the Scots.

OD 184, OR 183, OA 177: *be na morn slepis*: "not by sleeping late".

OD 185–87, OR 184–86: "After the Britons, Norwegians, Danes, English, and Picts too, and also the Romans driven back by the sweat of war, the Scots nobly kept their own jurisdiction." OR's *Moricos, Adacos* must be scribal errors, as Moors have never invaded Scotland, even in myth, and *Adacos* does not appear to mean anything. The first of these verses and one combining the other two are found in the fifteenth-century *Tract on the Scots*, lines 6–7 (Skene, *Chronicles*, p. 330).

OD 188–93, OR 187–92, OA 178–85: The claim of *auchtene hunder ȝere and mare . . . fra oure first King Fergus* would date the chronicle to the 1470s or later. This contradicts the dating in OD 169, OA 159–60, OR 164–65. The 1800-year period is repeated in OD 205, OA 198–99, OR 206–07.

OD 190: *vnconquest or subject*: Apparently the scribe considers that the negative prefix of *vnconquest* will apply as well to *subject*. The sense is that the Scots have not been conquered by and have not been subjected to a foreign power.

OA 183: Even by the chronicle's own origin myth, of course, Gathelos and Scota were never occupants of Scotland; however, according to the version in Bisset's *Processus*, as quoted by Bower (XI 62), Scota "sailed to Scotland, carrying with her the royal seat which this king of England [Edward I] took away with him . . . She conquered and overthrew the Picts, and took over that kingdom . . . . These Scots are known to have retained the name and country to the present day."

OD 194–97, OR 193–98, OA 186–91: Beginning with David I (1080–1153), several Scottish kings did homage to English kings for lands they held in England independent of the Kingdom of Scotland. The distinction is a key point in Bisset's *Processus* (Bower XI 59, 63). But Malcolm III, William I, and John Balliol apparently all did homage to English kings for Scotland itself. English kings from William I to Edward III did homage to the Kings of France for territory held in France, but this act was last performed in 1329, and Aquitaine, the last continental territory except Calais held by the English, was lost in 1453.

The *Originale*-chronicler's pointed use of the present tense suggests remarkable ignorance of the results of the Hundred Years' War.

OD 198–204, OR 199–205, OA 192–97: The *Originale*-chronicler has a point: in comparison with Celtic Gaul and other continental territories, conquered successively by Roman and Germanic invaders, Scotland has enjoyed relative independence from foreign control.

OD 200: *and thare was diuers kingis of thame*: "and there were diverse kings of the Romans."

OR 201, OA 195: *and war king / kingis of it*: "and the Romans were kings of it."

OA 194–95: *come a Romane dovne*: Comparison with the other versions shows that this should be a Frank.

OD 201–03, OR 203–04, OA 196–97: *the story hereof . . . changeing of kingis*: "the story of the subjections, conquests, and changes of kings – of Gaul and of all other nations – would be too long to tell".

OD 205–07, OR 206–09, OA 198–201: The *Originale*-chronicler does not provide the basis for his calculation of less than 300 years of peace since Fergus, son of Feredach, founded Scottish rule in Scotland, but it is clear from his account that he considers the Scots to have been more or less continuously harassed by Britons, Picts, Romans, Saxons, Danes, and, for the last three centuries, at least, by the Normans and English. It is a not entirely unjustified summation of Scottish history.

OD 207, OR 208, OA 201: *Normandis / Romanis*: The use of *Romanis* for *Normandis* in OA and OR is curious. Since it is repeated in OA 211, OR 222, it looks deliberate.

OD 208–11, OR 210–13, OA 202–05: A cumbersome pun, taken from the *Vraie Cronicque* (see VC 120–24 and note) or its source, based on the Latin word *angulus* or "angle", from which he asserts the Angles have derived their name: "Whence according to the gospel, 'Truth does not seek angles (or Angles).'" The text referred to may be Acts 26:25–26, which is not, of course, a gospel.

OD 212–18, OR 214–20 , OA 206–14[Bower IX 6]: Bower quotes Higden's claim (VII 21) that Henry's father, Geoffrey Plantagenet, Count of Anjou (Dagan, Angean, Angeos), was descended from a countess who rarely attended church and even then left before the secret of the mass. When her husband attempted to prevent her departure, she flew out the window and was never seen again. Higden implies, but does not say, that she was the daughter of the Devil. Henry's mother was Matilda, granddaughter of William I of England, and by a former marriage, wife of Emperor Henry V.

OA 208: *par caus quhy*: "their reason is that".

OD 215–16, OR 218, OA 211: *þat was the empericis sone*: This clause should modify *Henricus the Secund*, of course, and not *Sanct Thomas of Canterbery*.

OD 217–18, OR 219–20, OA 213: *the quhilk erle was bot the secund fra the Devill*: that is, that Henry's father was the second generation from the Devil – a closer relation than Higden or Bower imply, for they have *Comitissa . . . de cuius sobole [semine / femine] Galfridus Plantagenet processit* "Countess . . . from whose progeny Geoffrey Plantagenet came." But OA's removal of the word *erle* changes the reference to Henry instead of his father.

OD 219, OR 221, OA 215–16: In fact, all the Kings of England since Henry II have descended from Henry and therefore from the Count of Anjou. Again, by substituting *þe samyn tyrand* for *him*, OA changes the reference to Henry, whom he has just called *Henry þe Tyrand*.

OD 221–23, OR 223–25, OA 217–20 [Bower IX 7]: Bower quotes Higden (VII 4) on St Bernard's prophecy: "From the Devil you have come, and to the Devil you will go."

OD 224–27, OR 226–29, OA 221–23: The *collaciouns* and *writtis* are the chronicles of the English, probably especially those, like Hardyng's *Chronicle*, that *mak lesyngis . . . of vs*, that is, those that are written to assert English claims to lordship over Scotland. If even these chronicles reveal the wicked deeds of the English, the *Originale*-chronicler argues, then they may very well be believed. A similar appeal to English chronicles as evidence of Scottish claims is made in "The Ring of the Roy Robert" (*Metrical Tales*, p. 232, lines 109–12):

> And gif ye trow this nocht south be,
> Reid the Registar, and ye may see,
> And the croniclis of braid Bartane,
> Quhairout of our authoris ar tane.

OA 221: *And it þat þar awne writtis proportis of þam, how suld we contrar . . . ?*: "How should we contradict what their own writing claims about them?"

OA 222–23: *a hundreth mar thingis of þe quhilkis ȝe sall heir eftirwart of þar wikitnes*: John Asloan's promise that the reader "shall hear afterwards" of these things goes further than the other two versions, which merely assert that these charges *could* be made if space permitted. It is intriguing to note that the *Ynglis Chronicle*, which immediately follows the *Scottis Originale* in the Asloan manuscript, seems to be the fulfillment of this promise: the latter chronicle is a catalogue of the wickedness of English kings; it develops the *Originale*'s use of what might be called the *ipse dixit* trope, deriving evidence of English wickedness from English chronicles; it repeats the charge that, starting with Henry II, all English kings are descended from the Devil; and it has very similar passages asserting English descent from Trojan traitors in contrast to Scottish descent from Greek heroes, and claiming conquest of England by King Gregory.

OD 228–33, OR 230–35, OA 224–28: The *Originale*-chronicler here states his thesis of the inherent falsity of the English a final time.

OD 233: *bot that suld thai nocht haue done and thai had bene trew*: "but they would not have done that if they had been true."

OA 227: *quhilk war nocht þar commoun and þai war trewe, as þai war nevir, and had conscience, as þai haf nane*: "which would not have been their custom if they were honorable (or true to their word), which they never were, and (if they) had conscience, which they do not."

OR 234–35: *þe quhilk þai suld not haif done and þai had beynne trewe*: "which they would not have done if they had been honorable (or true to their word)."

OD 234–37, OR 236–39, OA 229–32: In the course of the seventh century, the Anglo-Saxons received Christianity from missionaries sent separately from the Irish monastery at Iona and from Rome. The Britons had received Christianity during the fourth century under the Roman occupation. There is no evidence in support of the legend that the Scots were converted during the reign of Pope Victor I (189–98).

OR 236: Marginal note: *Scotland was christinyt before Ingland iiii hundir ʒeiris and mair.*

OA 231: *Juxta illud metrice dictum*: "According to this saying in verse."

OD 236–37, OR 238–39, OA 232–33 [Fordun II 37, Bower II 40]: "203 years had passed since Christ when Scotland began to enter upon the Christian faith." The verses are also in N 71–74 and in the fifteenth-century *Tract on the Scots*, lines 17–18 (Skene, *Chronicles*, p. 331).

OD 238, OR 240, OA 234: *And for all this thai kepe till vs . . . kyndenes*: "And because of all this, they continue to show neighborly feeling toward us" – an obviously ironic statement. A similar charge appears in "The Ring of the Roy Robert" (*Metrical Tales*, p. 231, lines 64–66):

> On till ws all, it is weill kend,
> Anent the barnis of auld Brutus,
> That kyndnes hes bene kepit till ws.

OD 239–43, OR 241–45, OA 236–38 [Fordun IV 17–18, Bower IV 17–18]: Giric (Gregore, Gregour), may have been the son of one Dungal, otherwise unknown. He may have reigned from 878 to 889, possibly as a usurper, but the record of this period is very thin. (It is not even certain what to call the kingdom he may have ruled, since there are no contemporary references to the kingdom of Pictavia after 875 and none to the kingdom of Alba until 900.) This Giric may have reigned jointly with or subsequent to Eochaid, grandson of Kenneth, son of Alpín, through a daughter; Eochaid does not appear in Fordun or Bower. The claim that Giric conquered much or all of England (and perhaps Wales and Ireland into the bargain) is a favorite and utterly baseless pillar of legendary Scottish history – important enough to be included in Bisset's *Processus*. Also false is the claim, not found in Bower, of a 30-year reign. The assertion that Giric's control extended as far as the Thames is derived ultimately from a remark of William of Malmesbury that King Alfred (reigned 871–99), at the low ebb his fortunes, had *vix tribus pagis* ("barely three counties") remaining loyal to him; those counties (Hampshire, Wiltshire, and Somerset) lie south of the Thames. It is true that during this period, the Scots were pushing into northern Northumbria. See the extended note by John and Winifred MacQueen (Bower, *Scotichronicon*, vol. 2, pp. 468–69), and compare Y 53–57 and BAd 243–46, BAs 200–01.

OD 242–43, OR 244–45: "A great part remained for the Danes, but an even greater part for the Scots; and a part for King Alfred, but only a small one (A great part is given to the Danes, but the greatest to the Scots, and so a small part remains for King Alfred)." Bower supplies the verses, but he doesn't get them from William.

OD 244: "And here ends this epistle."

The Chronicle of the Scots

S 1–2: Various datings of the Nativity from the Creation were used in medieval chronicles. The year 5199 was calculated by Jerome in the fourth century and popularized by Martinus Polonus in the thirteenth; it is used by Fordun and Bower.

S 1: Marginal note: *Heir foullowis þe ʒeldis* [ages] *of þe wardill* [world] *fra Adem to þe Incarnatione of Crist.*

S 3–7: [Fordun I 7, Bower I 7]: This is a variant of the division of history into ages devised by Augustine of Hippo in the fifth century and used by Fordun and Bower. Augustine's scheme was divided at Noah, Abraham, David, the Babylonian Captivity, and Jesus, with the sixth age in progress. The *Scots*-chronicler has an extra division at Moses, with the seventh age in progress. He omits the duration of the second age, from Noah to Abraham, but it must span, according to his scheme, 1002 years. Except for the first, his dates for the ages do not agree with Fordun's or Bower's.

S 5: *four hundir score*: Apparently "420", since 400-score would be 8000 years – far exceeding the total he has allowed before the Nativity.

S 8–16: These dates do not follow the usual medieval dating systems. By his scheme, the *first Scottis men* would be in 884 BC – some five centuries after Moses was thought to have crossed the Red Sea, which is traditionally contemporaneous with the marriage of Scota and Gathelos and the founding of the Scots race (see OD 1–5, OR 3–7, OA 2–6) and 554 years before the traditional date (330 BC) for the establishment of the Scottish kingdom of Fergus, son of Feredach, in Argyll. Some of the other dates are similarly eccentric: by the *Scots*-chronicler's dating, the foundation of Rome would be in 981 BC (instead of the traditional date of 753 BC), and Alexander's death would be in 299 BC (Bower's date would be 306 BC, and Jerome's, accurately, would be 324 BC). But he puts Caesar's conquest of the world at 60 BC – not far off the completion of his conquests in Gaul, which led to his invasion of Britain in 55 BC.

S 11–12: The *Scots*-chronicler's grasp of space is even worse than his grasp of time: a city 5200 miles in circumference would be the size of Europe. Martinus Polonus, the source of the claim of 360 towers, says that Rome was 42 miles around.

S 19–20: In AD 67, Emperor Vespasian sent his son Titus to Jerusalem to suppress a Jewish rebellion. Jerusalem was captured and its temple destroyed in 70.

S 21–22: In 313, Constantine and his co-emperor Licinius issued the Edict of Milan, legalizing Christian worship.

S 23–26: Palladius and Patrick were successively missionaries and bishops in Ireland – traditionally at roughly the dates given here. But according to T. Charles-Edwards (*Early Christian Ireland*, pp. 202–40), Palladius and his associates operated in the middle third of the fifth century, and though "Not a single date can be given to any event of Patrick's life", he likely operated in the second half of that century. Seventh-century accounts promoted Patrick's achievements at the expense of those of Palladius – who was said to have abandoned his Irish mission, returned to Britain, and died there. The assertion here that Palladius went directly to Scotland is derived from Fordun (III 8) or Bower (III 8), both of whom quote Prosper's *Chronicon* in reporting that Pope Celestine sent Palladius *"ad Scotos in Christum credentes"* ("to the Irish who believe in Christ") – but apparently misunderstanding *Scotos* as "Scots". The *Scots*-chronicler turns this to good account: by simply citing the dates, he is able to imply that Scotland received the Christian faith before either Ireland or England. More subtly, his distinction between *Scottis men* and *Irlandis menn*, together with his earlier omission of the Irish connection traditionally a part of the Scots' origin myth, is evidence of an emphasis on Scottishness at the expense of Irishness in late-medieval Scottish historiography. Dauvit Broun (*Irish Identity*, p. 198) suggests that the absence of references to Ireland in Baldred Bisset's *Processus* of 1301 and in the *Declaration of Arbroath* of 1320 are attempts to make "defence of Scottish independence unassailable."

S 27–30: The traditional date for the arrival of the Saxons under their leaders Hengist and Horsa is 449. But Lewis Thorpe in his translation of Geoffrey of Monmouth, infers, on the basis of information in Geoffrey, that they arrived 450–55. This date and the reference to Geoffrey's invention, Merlin, a British prophet, suggests that the *Scots*-chronicler was using Geoffrey at this point. Vortigern was a possibly historical king the Saxons encountered.

S 31–32: Augustine of Canterbury (d. 604) was sent to England by Pope Gregory the Great as a missionary in 597.

S 33–34: There is no reliable evidence in support of the legend of the translation of St Andrew's bones, but the legend had the support of Fordun (II 46–48), Bower (II 58–60), and others. A large church had been at St Andrews since 737. In the twelfth century, however, priests at St Andrews claimed that the translation had occurred in the fourth century. Fordun and most of his successors followed the fourth-century date. But this chronicle draws upon an early form of the legend that said that St Andrews was established in the eighth century. Dauvit Broun has pointed out to us the intriguing implication of the date 761: in that year died Unuist (*Hurgust* in Bower), the Pictish king who, in the legend, gives the land on which the church was built to house the saint's bones, and whose own bones, in reality, may have been deposited in the St Andrews sarcophagus.

S 33: Marginal note: *The relikis of Sanct And. come into Scotland.*

S 35–36: Charlemagne campaigned against the Saracens in Spain in 778.

S 37–42: Malcolm (Macolm) III (ca. 1031–93), son of the Duncan killed by Macbeth, was King of Scots from 1057 or 1058 to 1093. His second wife was Margaret (Mergret) of Wessex (ca. 1045–93), by whom he had six sons and two daughters, all correctly identified here. Edward died with Malcolm; Edmund, because of his support for his uncle Donald Bán, was forced to become a monk; Ethelred was the Abbot of Dunkeld; Edgar, Alexander, and David later ruled successively. Maud (Mald) married Henry I, King of England; Mary married Eustace, Count of Boulogne (see the note to N 398–407, BAd 334–42, BAs 272–78). The

Scots-chronicler's omission of all earlier Scottish kings, including even the two
Ferguses and Kenneth, son of Alpín, is further evidence of the chronicler's focus
on politically useful details. Malcolm is the logical starting point for his genealogy, as the ancestor of all subsequent Scottish kings except his brother Donald
Bán.

S 43–44: Edgar (ca.1074–1107), son of Malcolm III and Margaret, was King of
Scots from 1097 to 1107.

S 45–47: Alexander I (ca.1077–1124), son of Malcolm III and Margaret, was King
of Scots from 1107 to 1124. He founded an Augustinian Priory at Scone.

S 48–49: The supposed sighting of two moons is taken from the Laud version of the
Anglo-Saxon Chronicle; the date is given as the Thursday before Easter, 1106.

S 48: Marginal note: *Twa monis seyne in þe lyft.*

S 50–59: David I (ca.1080–1153), son of Malcolm III and Margaret, was King of
Scots from 1124 to 1153. He founded the abbeys of Melrose in 1136, Newbattle
in 1140, Jedburgh by 1147, and Kinloss in 1150–51. Holmcultram Abbey was
founded in 1150 by David and his son Henry.

S 60–67: David's son Henry, Earl of Huntingdon, was already dead when his father
died at Carlisle in 1153, so David was succeeded as King of Scots by Malcolm
IV, his grandson. Malcolm reigned until 1165 and was succeeded by his
brother, William I, the Lion, who reigned until 1214. Malcolm founded
Coupar Angus Abbey ca. 1160–64. Construction of the cathedral at St Andrews was begun ca. 1158–60, under Bishop Arnold.

S 64: Marginal note: *Bishop Arnald.*

S 68–69: In December 1170, Thomas Becket, Archbishop of Canterbury, was
murdered in his cathedral.

S 68: Marginal note: *Sant Thomas of Cantirbery vos* [was] ~~vos~~ *martyrit.*

S 70–72: Pope Innocent III placed England under an interdict in 1207 because of
King John's refusal to install Stephen Langdon, Rome's candidate for Archbishop of Canterbury. In 1213, John accepted Langdon and surrendered England
and Ireland to Innocent and received them back as his vassal, in return for an
annual tribute of 1000 marks. In addition, John was to compensate the Church
for his depredations. The interdict was finally lifted in 1214. (For the terms of
the settlement, see Warren, *King John*, pp. 206–10; McLynn, *Richard and John*,
pp. 380–85.)

S 73–74: William I, the Lion, was King of Scots from 1165 to 1214 (not 1217 – a
mistake possibly caused by misreading *xiiii* as *xuii*).

S 75–76: Alexander II was King of Scots from 1214 to 1249.

S 77–78: Pope Innocent III deposed and excommunicated Emperor Otto IV (not
Frederick) in 1210 for invading Sicily against the Pope's wishes. Pope Gregory
IX excommunicated Emperor Frederick II in 1227 because he did not invade the
Holy Land and again in 1229 because he did.

S 79–80: Alexander III was King of Scots from 1249 to 1286. His death at Kinghorn
precipitated a succession crisis that led ultimately to the Wars of Independence.
(See the note to N 495–503, BAd 423–30, BAs 342–48.)

S 79: Marginal note: *King Alex' þe sone of Alex' þe Secund descesit at Kingorn.*

S 81–82: John Balliol, the temporarily successful claimant to the throne, was crowned King of Scots in November 1292. The *Scots*-chronicler or his source has apparently dropped a *c* out of this and the following two dates.

> For an account of Edward's judgment and its consequences, see the note to N 516–23, BAd 440–54, BAs 357–66.

S 83–91: In 1296, after John Balliol had been forced from power (and after some English clergy had been removed from their Scottish benefices), Edward I invaded Scotland. He won a battle at Dunbar on 27 April. After this disaster, William Wallace and Sir Andrew Moray assumed the leadership of the Scottish resistance. Wallace won a great victory at Stirling Bridge on 11 September 1297, after which he was knighted, but he suffered a defeat at Falkirk on 22 July (the Feast of St Mary Magdalene) 1298. A small Scottish force under the command of Sir Symon Fraser and John Comyn defeated a much larger English force at Rosslyn on 24 February 1303. Wallace was captured and executed in 1305 (not 1302 – again a possible misreading of *u* as *ii*). Robert Bruce, grandson of the Robert Bruce who was an unsuccessful Competitor in 1292, served in Edward's forces from 1302 until February 1306, when he assassinated his rival, John Comyn, and shortly thereafter asserted his claim to the Scottish throne. (For a fuller summary of these events, see the notes to N 516–69, BAd 440–80, BAs 357–90.)

S 83: Marginal note: *The Ingllis men wos put outh of Scotland.*

S 88: Marginal note: *The ded of Wallace.*

S 91–93: Robert Bruce had himself crowned King of Scots at Scone on 25 March 1306 (the VIII, not the VII, kalends of April). He was defeated by Edward I's forces twice that summer, at Methven and at Dalry. See the note to N 570–80, BAd 490–95, BAs 391–95.

S 92: Marginal note: *Robert Bruce maid King.*

S 95–97: On 24 June (the Feast of John the Baptist) 1314, Robert Bruce won a great victory over Edward II at Bannockburn. (See the note to N 581–89, BAd 481–87, BAs 396–401.)

S 95: Marginal note: *Banokburne.*

S 98–99: The cathedral of St Andrews was consecrated in 1318, with Robert I in attendance.

S 100–101: The Black Parliament, a judicial rather than a legislative conclave, met at Scone in August 1320 to try a group of barons who were accused of conspiring to kill Robert Bruce and replace him with Sir William Soulis; in fact the so-called "Soulis Conspiracy" probably had as its object the coronation of Edward Balliol. Four of the barons were hanged; Soulis was imprisoned for life; he died the following spring. (See Penman, "A fell coniuracioun", pp. 25–57.)

S 102–03: Robert Bruce died on 7 June 1329.

S 104–05: David II (1323–71), son of Robert I, was crowned on 24 November 1331, at Scone.

S 104: Marginal note: *King Dauid vas crownit.*

S 106–07: On 11 August 1332, the forces of Edward Balliol, son of the deposed King John, defeated the Bruce forces under Donald, Earl of Mar, at Dupplin Moor. The victory made it possible for Balliol to be crowned at Scone, but in December he was defeated by Randolph, Earl of Moray, at Annan.

S 108–09: On 19 July 1333, Edward III defeated a Scots army led by Sir Archibald Douglas at Halidon Hill, near Berwick.

S 110–11: In 1346 (not 1343), David II invaded England in response to a French request to distract the English from military operations in France. On 17 October, at the battle of Neville's Cross, near Durham, the Scots were defeated, and David was captured. The following day was the Feast of St Luke.

S 112: The bubonic plague struck Scotland in the fall of 1349.

S 113–14: Edward III raided the Lowlands in 1356, systematically burning towns as far as the Forth. Because Edinburgh was burned on 2 February, the feast celebrating the presentation of Jesus in the temple, the raid became known as the Burnt Candlemas.

S 115–16: Robert II was crowned at Scone on 26 March 1371 (not 1366), following the death of his uncle, David II.

S 117–18: The plague known as the Second Mortality occurred in 1361–62.

S 119–20: David II died on 22 February 1371 (1370 Old Style).

S 121–22: When Gregory XI died in 1378, Urban VI was elected in Rome. But within a few months, some of the same cardinals held a second election and chose Clement VII, who set up a rival papacy in Avignon. The resulting Western Schism lasted until 1417. Scotland recognized the Avignon popes; England recognized the Roman popes.

S 123–24: In Scotland, the Third Mortality occurred in 1379–80, but in England the plague so designated was in 1369.

S 125–26: A large force of French troops under the command of Admiral Jean de Vienne was sent to Scotland in 1384 to stiffen Scottish resistance to the English.

S 125: Marginal note: *The cumyng of Franche men.*

S 127–28: On 19 August 1388, a raid into England led by the Earl of Douglas culminated in a battle at Otterburn in which the English were badly beaten. (See the note to N 614–19, BAd 514–18, BAs 418–21.)

S 129–30: Robert II died on 19 April 1390.

S 131–32: In 1396, Robert III, in an attempt to resolve a long-standing feud, presided over the "Battle of the Clans", a staged combat near Perth (St Johnstown) between two rival clans with 30 fighters on each side.

S 133–34: Bishop Walter Trail of St Andrews, royal advisor and diplomat, died in 1401.

S 135: On 22 June 1402 (not 1401), a Scottish force on a raid into Northumberland was defeated at Nesbit Moor.

S 136: In Scotland, the Fourth Mortality, by Bower's count (XV 12), was in 1401–02.

S 137–38: On 14 September 1402, a Scottish force led by the Earl of Douglas, which had raided as far south as Newcastle in retaliation for the defeat at Nesbit Moor, was cut to pieces by a stronger English force at Homildon Hill. More than 80 Scottish knights and barons, including Douglas, were captured.

S 139: Cocklaws Castle in Teviotdale, held by the Scots, was being besieged by Henry Percy in the summer of 1403 when he lifted the siege and headed south to join his uncle, the Earl of Worcester, and his brother-in-law, Edmund Mortimer, in revolt against Henry IV. That revolt culminated in the rebels' defeat at Shrewsbury on 21 July.

S 140–41: Robert III died in April 1406, not 1405.

S 142–43: Much of Stirling, including its Church of the Holy Rude, was destroyed by a catastrophic fire in March 1405 (1406 Old Style).

S 144–45: The University of St Andrews, the oldest in Scotland, was founded in 1413.

S 146–47: The battle of Red Harlaw, a pointless and artless slaughter between Highlanders following Donald MacDonald, Lord of the Isles, and Lowlanders raised by the Earl of Mar and the Provost of Aberdeen, was fought on 24 July 1411 near Harlaw, northwest of Aberdeen.

S 146: Marginal note: *The Battell of Hairlaw*.

S 148–49: In 1419, the Scottish Parliament sent an expedition under the command of John Stewart, Earl of Buchan, and his father-in-law, Archibald Douglas, Earl of Wigtown, to France to aid the Dauphin against Henry V.

S 150: Bower (XV 31) says that in 1419, "there was a very great drought in the summer and yet the harvest was abundant."

S 151–52: An epidemic, known commonly as *le qwhew*, occurred in Scotland and the north of England in 1420–23. Bower (XV 32) says that "This sickness, by which not only magnates, but also numberless men of the people were snuffed out, was called *le qwhew* by the common people." In his note to the passage (Bower, *Scotichronicon*, vol. 8, p. 202), D. E. R. Watt says that the term does not seem to be recorded elsewhere.

S 153–54: In the battle of Baugé (Bolgee), fought in Anjou on 22 March 1421, a French force reinforced by Scots under Buchan and Wigtown defeated an English force. Though of little strategic importance, the battle increased the prestige of the Scots as soldiers.

S 155–56: James I (1394–1437) and his wife, Joan Beaufort, were crowned at Scone on 21 May 1424, not 1423.

S 157–58: A total solar eclipse, which was remembered as the "Black Hour", occurred in Scotland on Wednesday, 17 June (not July) 1433.

S 157: Marginal note: *The blak hour gen'ell*.

S 158: Marginal note: *Blak Setterday 1433*. A much later total solar eclipse, on 1 March 1597 (Old Style), was also popularly known as "Black Saturday".

S 159–62: In 1436, James made an unsuccessful attempt to capture Roxburgh Castle, still in the hands of the English. He broke off his siege, in part because of rumors of a conspiracy to kill him. And in fact, on 21 February 1437, James was assassinated in St Johnstown (Perth) by a group of eight conspirators instigated by Walter Stewart, Earl of Atholl, Robert Stewart (Walter's *grand-*

son and heir), and Sir Robert Graham. Walter's son, David, had died earlier in prison. Walter himself was not present at the assassination.

S 160: Marginal note: *King James þe First þat was slane in Sant Jonstoune.*

S 163–66: James II (1430–60) was crowned in Holyrood Abbey in Edinburgh on 25 March 1437 (not 1436), the Feast of the Annunciation, at the age of 6. Under the Julian (Old Style) calendar, this would have been the first day of the year 1437; this may explain the *Scots*-chronicler's mistake with the date. James had a large red birthmark on the left side of his face.

S 167–69: The *Auchinleck Chronicle* also records a famine in Scotland in 1439: *The sammyn tyme þar was in Scotland a gret derth, for þe boll of quheit was at xl s and þe boll of ete mele xxx s. And werraly the derth was sa gret þat þar deit a passing peple for hunger.* (Quoted from the Asloan MS.)

S 170–72: On 24 November 1440, at what came to be called the "Black Dinner", the 10-year-old king hosted the teenaged William, 6th Earl of Douglas, William's younger brother David, and Sir Malcolm Fleming of Cumbernauld at Edinburgh Castle. After dinner, the guests were arrested and executed on the orders of William Lord Crichton, Sir Alexander Livingston, and the boys' great-uncle, James the Gross, Earl of Avondale, under whose control James was. The murders allowed Avondale to succeed as Earl of Douglas. But the real motive was control of the king, and the young earl may have shown signs of drifting out of Avondale's influence into the party of the queen. It is unlikely that the king was *beand justice* – that is, serving as judge. (See Michael Brown, *Black Douglases*, pp. 255–62.)

S 173–79: In 1450, Bishop William Turnbull (ca.1400–54) obtained the charter for the University of Glasgow from Pope Nicholas V; the university was formally founded the next year. He also obtained a papal pardon for visitors to the cathedral in Glasgow during the jubilee year of 1450. Turnbull was succeeded the following year by Andrew de Durisdeer.

S 180–83: James was killed at the siege of Roxburgh in 1460, when a cannon, fired in celebration of victory, burst near him; a wedge, used to secure a loaded charge, flew out and tore into his leg. He was buried at Holyrood Abbey.

S 180: Marginal note: *The ded of King James þe Secund at Rochburgh.*

S 184–86: James III (1451–88) was crowned at Kelso Abbey on 10 August (the Feast of St Lawrence) 1460, at the age of 9.

S 187–88: Following the murder of William, Earl of Douglas, by James II in 1452 – an event that somehow escapes the notice of the *Scots*-chronicler – relations between the Douglases and the crown had deteriorated into rebellion. The new earl, William's brother James, and a younger brother, John, Lord of Dalvenie, had formed an alliance with the King Edward IV of England. The rebellion of the Black Douglases collapsed when John was captured and beheaded at Edinburgh in 1463, and Edward concluded a 15-year truce with James III the following year. (See Michael Brown, *Black Douglases*, pp. 299–316.)

S 189: Here the style of the dates changes from *The ȝer of God* to *Anno domini* and from *m iiii^c* to *m cccc*, suggesting a new chronicler. The scribe does not change.

S 189–91: On 13 July 1469, James III was married to Margaret, daughter of Christian I, King of Denmark and Norway, and formerly (until 1464) King of Sweden. *Dasie* here is apparently Dacia, a term used for Scandinavia in general or Denmark in particular; either way, the *Scots*-chronicler has achieved unconscious redundance.

S 192–93: Robert, Lord Boyd, accused of abducting the king in July 1466, fled to England in 1469 and became a pensioner of Edward IV; his brother, Sir Alexander Boyd, was also involved in the abduction, but did not escape: he was beheaded in Edinburgh that year.

S 194–96: Alexander Stewart (1454–85), Duke of Albany, the brother of James III, was captured at sea by the English in 1464, but was soon released.

S 197–207: In 1470, Edward IV (1440–83) was forced to flee England when a coup organized by Richard Neville, Earl of Warwick, released the deposed Henry VI from the Tower and placed him back on the throne of England. Edward took refuge with his brother-in-law, Charles the Bold, Duke of Burgundy.

Earlier, following the Yorkist victory at Towton in 1461 (fought under Edward rather than his father, Richard, Duke of York, who had died the previous year), Henry had fled to Scotland where he was offered a haven and military support in return for Berwick. But in 1464, finding themselves abandoned by their French allies, the Scots in turn abandoned Henry. He was captured in 1465 and locked up in the Tower.

Edward returned to England in March 1471, and with the support of Burgundian troops, reoccupied London in April, and reimprisoned Henry. On 12 April, Edward defeated Warwick's forces at Barnet, just north of London. Warwick was killed. Henry died on the night of Edward's return to London, probably by violence and probably on Edward's orders. Within a decade of his death, he was popularly considered a saint in England because of his reputation for other-worldliness, enhanced, perhaps, by his periodic bouts of madness. Once Henry Tudor gained the throne in 1485, he gave this popular sentiment an official boost by sponsoring a written account of his great-uncle's saintly deeds and unsuccessfully petitioning three popes for his canonization. If this royal endorsement was what brought Henry's miracles to the attention of the *Scots*-chronicler, it would mean that the chronicle is at least a few years later than the date of its last entry, 1482. (For a critical examination of the saintliness of Henry VI and an account of Henry VII's efforts to turn it to political account, see Wolfe, *Henry VI*, pp. 3–21, 351–58.)

S 208–11: A large comet appeared in December 1471 and lasted until January. In 1472, the *St Salvator*, a great ship built by James Kennedy, Bishop of St Andrews and one of the regents for James III, wrecked on the coast of Northumberland.

S 212–20: In 1479, James moved against his brothers Alexander, Duke of Albany, and John, Earl of Mar, on charges of treason. John, accused of conspiring with witches, was arrested and soon died, apparently murdered. Alexander, accused of violating the peace with England, was not banished, but escaped to France, having left his supporter John Ellem of Butterdean to hold his castle of Dunbar. When royal forces besieged Dunbar Castle, Butterdean and his men escaped to England by sea. In France, Alexander married Anne de la Tour d'Auvergne, daughter of Bertrand II, Count of Auvergne and of Bouillon. In 1482, he was welcomed at the court of Edward IV, who agreed to support his bid for the Scottish throne in return for a pledge to hold the kingdom as his vassal.

The burning of witches in Edinburgh at this time, though a part of popular lore and the subject of a monument on the Royal Mile, is not well documented. Ranald Nicholson (*Scotland*, p. 485) cites Leslie (*History*, pp. 43–44) as reporting in the following century that the Earl of Mar was taken to Cragmillar, a nearby castle; and that *thair wes also mony and divers witches and sorceraris, alsueill men as wemen, suspect of that cryme convict and burnit for the same at Edinburghe*. This may, however, not be corroboration of the *Chronicle of the Scots*, but use of it as a source.

S 213: *and passyt in France*: That is, Alexander, not James, went to France.

S 221–24: In the summer of 1480, Archibald Douglas, Earl of Angus, raided south and burned Bamburgh. Full scale war broke out and continued until 1483.

S 225–27: In the Julian (Old Style) calendar, New Year's day was 25 March, which was also the Feast of the Annunciation or Lady Day. So this was a two-day storm.

S 228: Beltin or Beltane Day is 1 May, when by a tradition dating from the Druids, bonfires are lit on the tops of hills. The day always carries pagan and therefore "evil" implications, but what was particularly evil about the Beltane of 1480 or 1481 we have not discovered.

S 229–35: Norman Macdougall, James's biographer, notes that the conclusion to the *Chronicle of the Scots*, one of only three contemporary records of the crisis of 1482, "goes some way towards explaining the motives of those involved," (*James III*, 1982 edn., p. 158). According to Macdougall, the facts suggest that about 1480, under pressure to increase revenues to meet an impending English invasion, "James III had recourse to the desperate expedient of minting large quantities of very debased coins and putting them into circulation at a false value" (*ibid.*, p. 160). The coins apparently included some of copper and some of debased silver – called "black coins" or "black silver" (S 239) because they would tarnish. The black silver pennies had a third the value of "white" sterling silver pennies (S 246). But elsewhere, Macdougall ("Reappraisal", p. 21) notes that the *Scots*-chronicler "appears to have no clear idea of what 'black money' was. He calls it 'copper' first, suggesting a drastic debasement, but later describes it as 'black silver' which might well be a reference to billon placks, a mixture of silver and copper which had been authorized by parliament in 1466 and 1473, and which remained in circulation for more than ten years. He may therefore be confusing the war crisis of 1480–82, when the king may have conducted a drastic debasement, with stories of earlier parliamentary debasements . . . which inevitably upset basic prices." The result was economic chaos, and according to the *Scots*-chronicler, starvation. Meal prices for 1482 were in fact the highest recorded in the second half of the century: records of the English Exchequer show meal at 6s. 8d. a bushel in 1481, 20s. in 1482, and 8s. 4d. in 1483 in Galloway.

S 233–34: *And als was gret were betuix Scotland and Ingland, and gret distructioun throw þe weris was of corne & cattell*: "And also there was a great war between Scotland and England, and there was much destruction of grain and livestock because of the wars."

S 234: *þai twa thyngis*: That is, the debased coinage and the war.

S 236–44: In July 1482, a large army, led by the Duke of Gloucester and James's brother Alexander, came north to besiege Berwick Castle. James gathered an army and moved south to relieve Berwick, but not, apparently, to push further. Norman Macdougall ("Reappraisal", p. 21) uses this passage to comment on the *Scots*-chronicler's knowledge of events: "It may . . . be doubted whether he either knew, or was prepared to relate, much of what was happening in Scotland in the summer of 1482. For example, he credits James III with preparing to invade England when in fact, this is the reverse of the truth."

On 22 July (the Feast of Mary Magdalene), while in Lauder on the way to Berwick, a group of Scottish magnates seized James along with a number of his court favorites – low-born men, in the view of the magnates, to whom James listened instead of them. Some, including Thomas Cochrane, whom the magnates blamed for the debased coinage, were summarily hanged from Lauder Bridge, and others, including Sir John Ramsay, were spared. James was confined in Edinburgh Castle. He was released, more or less in the custody of his brother, at least by 25 August, though a polite fiction was maintained that his jailers were besieged and that they did not surrender until 29 September (Michaelmas). For details of these arrangements, see Nicholson, *Scotland*, p. 508.

The charge that James cared more for the council of low-born members of his household than for that of his magnates anticipates one of the charges later used in the parliament of 1488 to justify the rebellion that had led to the king's death.

S 245–46: In 1486 the black silver pennies were called in and the crisis eased. The prices cited here suggest a return to earlier levels – less than a third of what they had been in the debased coinage.

S 246: The chronicle apparently ends. Space for about five lines remains on this folio.

The Ynglis Chronicle

Y 1–2: The *Ynglis*-chronicler frankly confesses his purpose: to extract from English chronicles such material as will reveal the evil nature and misgovernment of English kings. He will identify one chronicle later (Y 18, 64) – Ranulph Higden's *Polychronicon*. But he was also using the English prose *Brut* and Bower's

Scotichronicon, as well as other sources, not always identifiable. The term *a part of þe Ynglis Cronikle* is thus not the chronicler's own title, but his collective designation of his sources.

Y 3–8: The chronicle is a rejoinder to those English chronicles written in support of English claims to sovereignty over Scotland. The *Ynglis*-chronicler may have in mind the *Chronicle* of John Hardyng, written in two versions (completed in 1457 and ca.1465) in part to encourage Henry VI and then Edward IV to invade Scotland. But Edward I and Edward III had also searched the chronicles of their day for evidence that Scotland was a dependency of England. Higden himself had been summoned by Edward III to be interrogated on this subject in 1352. The homage paid by some Scottish kings to English kings is a theme stressed by Edward I in his petition to the pope in 1301.

Y 3–4: *ȝour . . . ȝe . . . ȝhe . . . ȝow*: The direct address to the putative English reader contributes to the particular venom of this chronicle.

Y 9–15: Scottish legend has gone British legend one better by tracing Scottish ancestry back to the Greeks, the winners of the Trojan War. Brutus, legendary descendant of Aeneas, was the eponymous founder of Britain, as reported in the *Historia Brittonum*, sometimes attributed to Nennius, and in Geoffrey of Monmouth. According to the twelfth-century *Roman de Troie* by Benoit de Sainte-Maure and its thirteenth-century Latin translation, *Historia Troiana* by Guido de Columna, the Trojan prince Aeneas was one of those who conspired to betray the city to save themselves. The English usually claimed to be successors to the Trojan *civilization* of the Britons – not descendants of Brutus himself, as the *Ynglis*-chronicler here asserts. The English considered the actual descendants of Brutus to be the Welsh. Since, however, this was written after Edward IV's reign and after Henry Tudor had become king (see the note to Y 336–38), this may be an allusion to the claims of these two kings to Welsh ancestry.

Y 16–23: Some versions of the Anglo-Norman and English prose *Brut* begin with a prologue relating the legend of Albine, daughter of King Diocletian (or Diodicias) of Syria (or Greece), who is banished along with her 30 (or 32 or 33) sisters for the murder of their husbands. They sail to an uninhabited island, which is then named Albion after Albine. There the sisters are impregnated by devils in the guise of men, giving birth to a race of giants. Giants, according to Geoffrey of Monmouth, still inhabited the island when Brutus and his Trojans arrived, although Geoffrey says nothing about the Albine legend. The latter story developed in England, first in Anglo-Norman sometime between the beginning of the thirteenth century and the early 1330s; later in that decade it was translated into Latin (see Brereton, *Des Grantz Geanz*, p. xxxii; and Carley and Crick, "Constructing Albion's Past", p. 60). The story was possibly concocted to counteract the Scots' claim that they were the first inhabitants of the island. The Albine story was prefaced to a number of manuscripts of the Anglo-Norman and English prose *Brut*; it was not, however, usually a part of Higden's *Polychronicon*, as is claimed here, although since its Latin translation was composed at about the time the *Polychronicon* was being written, it could have been included in some Higden manuscripts that no longer survive.

Y 22–23: *þis ʒour awne corniklis beris plane in þe self, þat ʒe may nocht ganesay*: "Your own chronicle itself says this plainly, which you may not deny." This is this chronicler's first full expression of the *ipse dixit* trope, the principal rhetorical underpinning of his chronicle. The trope has already been hinted at in Y 6–7 and in Y 17–18 and is most fully expressed in Y 63–66. The trope is used at the end of the *Scottis Originale* (OD 212–18, OR 214–20, OA 206–14; OD 224–27, OR 226–29, OA 221–23; OD 239–41, OR 241–43, OA 236–38; and OR 246–47), and it may in fact have been borrowed from that chronicle (see the note to OA 222–23).

Y 24–27: The legendary Scottish history handed down by Fordun and Bower claims an unbroken succession of kings and an unchanged royal coat of arms from Fergus, son of Feredach, the first king to rule in Scotland, beginning in 330 BC. See N 36–45, BAd 29–34, BAs 30–35 and note. But the chronicler's claim that the Scots have lived under one god since that time is unusual.

Y 28–31: The Use of Salisbury (or Use of Sarum) is a variation of the Roman rite adopted at Salisbury Cathedral in the thirteenth century and later used throughout England. The second "error" likely refers to the New Use of Sarum which developed in the fourteenth century to modify the original Sarum use. By 1457, the Sarum rite was standard in churches of England, Wales, and Ireland (Cross, *Christian Church*, pp. 1456–57).

Y 32–34: The chronicler's accusation is that the British ancestors of the English were descended from two sources, Albine and Brutus, and thus lack the unified tradition of the Scots. Albine and her sisters (above, Y 16–23) were from Syria, according to some versions of the legend that begin appearing in manuscripts of the Anglo-Norman *Brut* that ends in 1333, and thus were, in the chronicler's view, *Sarazenis* (see Brereton, ed, *Des Grantz Geanz*, p. xxxv; Carley and Crick, "Constructing Albion's Past," p. 353; and Johnson, "Return to Albion," p. 21). According to Geoffrey (I 4), the English prose *Brut* (1), and Higden (II 27), Brutus's mother died giving him birth, and when he was 15 he killed his father while hunting.

Y 35–40: Hengist and Horsa were the traditional leaders of the Saxons who began the Anglo-Saxon invasion in the middle of the fifth century. According to Geoffrey of Monmouth, they arrived in Kent, not Northumberland, although they later devastated York and Lincoln. The supposed derivation of "English" from *Hengist* appears in a number of chronicles but seems to have originated with the Anglo-Norman prose *Brut*. See the note to VC 113–23.

Sexaburga is mentioned in the Cadwallader episode toward the end of the history of the Britons in at least five manuscripts of Geoffrey of Monmouth, three of which date from the twelfth century, but not in his account of Hengist and Horsa (line 279). In the manuscripts of Geoffrey in which Sexaburga is mentioned, she is described as the *nobilissima regina Sexburgis* who "assembled a vast crowd of men and women, landed in Northumbria and filled the empty tracts of land from Scotland to Cornwall" (Geoffrey, *Kings*, pp. 278–79). Her name is also found in the Cadwallader episode of at least two manuscripts of Middle English versions of the prose *Brut*, though not in the Brie edition; Lister Matheson edits the passage in which she appears in *The Prose Brut*, pp. 57–61. She is there identified as a *noble queene* who leads one of the *companyes grete þat come fro Germanye* in an invasion of Northumberland. It is possible that this legendary queen was confused with the historical seventh-century Seaxburh, Queen of Kent and mother of King Ecgberht.

Y 41–51: The Danish ruler of England "William Hauslot, Prince of Denmark," is not mentioned by Fordun or Bower who, like most chroniclers, name just three Danish kings of England: Cnut, and his sons Harthacnut and Harold Harefoot. However several chronicles, particularly the Anglo-Norman *Brut* and the chronicle of Geffrey Gaimar, mention the prince Haveloc the Dane as another Danish ruler of England, and the name *Hauslot* is probably a corruption of *Haueloc*. A short passage in the fifteenth-century "Ring of the Roy Robert" (Laing, *Metrical Tales*, pp. 231–32, lines 95–102) makes similar claims about the conquest of England by *Henslot, sone of Denmark king*. The "Ring" also echoes the claim that a Dane was quartered in every house in England and held the occupants in servitude. There is a fuller discussion of these points in the Introduction, pp. 58–59. For the Haveloc story in English chronicles, see Marvin, "Havelok in the Prose *Brut* Tradition" and Moll, "'Nest pas autentik, mais apocrophum': Haveloks and Their Reception in Medieval England".

Y 52: The Roman occupation of Britain lasted from 43 to 410, decades before the invasion of the Saxons and long before that of the Danes. There is apparently confusion here between Romans and Normans – as in OR 208–09, OA 201.

Y 53–57: Giric (Gregory) was perhaps king from 878 until 889. The claim that he conquered much of England, Wales, and Ireland is false. See the note to OD 239–43, OR 241–45, OA 236–38.

Y 58–66: This paragraph serves as a preface to the king-by-king exposés that follow. The promise to explain how the English kings are descended from the Devil (or at least *a* devil) is fulfilled in Y 131–38.

Y 62–64: *I sall . . . schaw how þai ar lynealy cummyn dovne fra þe Devill, lyke as ȝour awne principale story and cornikle callit Pollicronicon declaris in þe self.* The account of Henry II's descent from an evil spirit is in Higden, who is quoted by Bower (IX 6), and Bower could be the direct source here: according to Higden, Henry's mother was married to Geoffrey of Anjou (Plantagenet) who was descended from an evil spirit. Richard I is reported to have said *hit was no wonder þouȝ þey þat comeþ of suche a kynde greved everich oþer, as þey þat comeþ of þe devel and schulde goo to þe devil* (Trevisa's translation of Higden, VII 21).

Y 65–66: *It is nocht till haf bene writtin . . . less þan it haf bene werite & trewe in þe self:* "It would not have been written . . . unless it had been truth and true in itself."

Y 67–69: William I (ca.1028–87), Bastard and Conqueror, had been Duke of Normandy until he conquered England in 1066. King Edward (ca.1003–66), called
the Confessor and canonized in 1161, died naturally – not martyred by the
English. According to Bower (VI 23), he "ended his life with a happy death on
the eve of Epiphany." The *Ynglis*-chronicler has apparently confused Edward
the Confessor with the earlier Edward the Martyr (962–78), whom Bower
discusses in the same chapter. The Martyr ruled briefly (from 975) before being
assassinated, perhaps on the orders of his stepmother, Ælfthryth. Bower asserts
that the decline of the English kingdom began with this act of treachery –
perhaps the reason that the *Ynglis* chronicler begins his catalogue of the crimes
of English kings with this reference.

Y 70–88: Of the many fanciful explanations of the Norman invasion, this surely
ranks among the most lurid and least factual. Edward the Confessor was succeeded by Harold Godwinson (ca.1022–66), who earlier had in fact been ship-
wrecked (but on the coast of Brittany) while on a mission from Edward to
William, the precise nature of which remains a matter of speculation. Harold
did not propose marriage to William's daughter, since he was already married,
and thus did not commit the outrages charged – which seem to be a ramping up
the charges made by Bower (V 14) that Harold blinded her and cut off her hair
before sending her home. William the Duke and William the Bastard are
actually the same person, although the chronicler thinks they are father and son;
William's father was Duke Robert I, and he had no brothers. From this point,
the chronicler's accuracy improves. Harold was killed in battle, and William
became king. He had nine children: Robert Curthose (ca.1051–1134), William
Rufus (ca.1056–1100), Henry Beauclerc (ca.1070–1135), Richard, and five
daughters, none of whom was named Maud (or Matilda). (It is clear from the
references below (Y 111 and Y123–24) to "Mald, his [Henry's] sister" who
married Stephen, Count of Blois, that the daughter he means is Adela of Normandy.) On his death, Robert became Duke of Normandy, William Rufus
became King of England, and Henry was granted £5000 in silver.

Y 75–76: *and send hir sa hame*: "and sent her home in this condition".

Y 77: *of full bed*: "legitimate".

Y 89–101: William II (ca.1056–1100), called Rufus, second son of William I, had
a reputation for cruelty and greed, the latter quality often directed at the assets
of the Church.

Y 94–95: In 1093, William installed Anselm (1033–1109) as Archbishop of Canterbury, but in 1097 exiled him because of a bitter dispute over the right to invest
bishops.

Y 96–101: This passage repeats, almost exactly, lines from the English prose *Brut*
(Chapter 134). The New Forest, a royal hunting preserve in Hampshire, was
established in 1079 by William I, not by his son. But William II became identified with the oppressive Forest Law, which regulated the forest's use, when he
made mutilation a penalty for its violation. Some residents were driven out.
William II was killed in a suspicious hunting accident there in 1100.

Y 102–22: Henry I (ca.1070–1135), called Beauclerc because of his education, succeeded his childless brother in 1100 and reigned until 1135. He married Edith, daughter of King Malcolm III and Queen Margaret of Scotland. Edith took the Norman name of Matilda (or Maud) and was known as "Good Queen Maud" for her intercessions with Henry (see Huneycutt, *Matilda of Scotland*, pp. 82–89). Bower (V 39) reports that Matilda intervened to abolish "a very wicked custom and servile levy", apparently the parish tax here called *þe reke penny*. What follows in Bower is a variant of the Lady Godiva story, which the *Ynglis*-chronicler modestly omits.

In addition to at least 20 illegitimate children whom he acknowledged, Henry had three children by Matilda: William Adelin, Richard (who died young), and Matilda. But the Richard mentioned here is probably Richard of Lincoln, a bastard who died in 1120.

Henry and his sons campaigned in Normandy against Louis VI in 1118–19, in a war that had developed out of a dispute over Henry's attempts to control Normandy and Maine by having his son William swear homage to Louis; Louis refused to accept this homage. Henry was supported by his nephew Count Stephen of Blois (ca.1092–1154), future King of England; Stephen's wife was Matilda (Maud) of Boulogne. The *Ynglis*-chronicler has confused this Stephen with his father, Stephen-Henry (ca.1045–1102), who was married to Henry's sister Adela; Henry did have a sister named Matilda of Normandy, but she married Alain Fergent of Brittany. After Henry's victory, his son and heir, William, and one of his illegitimate sons, Richard, returning to England in November 1120, were drowned in the famous wreck of the White Ship.

Henry's daughter Matilda, better known as Maud the Empress (1102–67), married Emperor Henry V. After his death in 1125, she was summoned home from Germany (not Normandy); she later married Geoffrey of Anjou, with whom she had a son, the future Henry II.

Henry I died at St Denis after eating a "surfeit of lampreys".

Y 116–17: *and schew till hire fader till fetche hir*: "and indicated to her father that he should fetch her".

Y 123–30: Stephen of Blois (ca.1097–1154), Henry I's nephew, was the son-in-law (not the son) of Eustace III, Count of Boulogne, the nephew of Henry's sister, Matilda (Maud) of Normandy. Stephen claimed the crown upon Henry's death. Both Stephen's father and his father-in-law had died long before. Before his death, Henry had compelled his barons to swear an oath in support of his daughter Matilda's succession to the crown. Matilda invaded England in 1139 and began a civil war which lasted until 1153.

Y 131–38: Henry of Anjou succeeded his father Geoffrey as Duke of Normandy in 1150. Geoffrey died the next year.

The story of Geoffrey (and thus of Henry and thus of all future English kings) descending from a devil in the form of an incubus is hinted at by Higden (VII 21) and retold by Bower (IX 6); it has been alluded to earlier in Y 58–66. In Higden and Bower, the demonic ancestor is "one of the countesses of Anjou from whom Geoffrey Plantagenet was descended", but the relationship is made closer here, just as it is in the *Scottis Originale*. The *Ynglis*-chronicler may mean that it is just a devil who is *in mannis likness*, but since the point of Bower's story is that the countess, who flies out a window never to be seen again, is herself a demon, he may mean that both have taken on human form. The *Ynglis*-chronicler here calls Geoffrey himself the incubus – indicating, perhaps that he does not know what an incubus is. See OD 212–20, OR 214–22, OA 206–16 and notes.

Y 139–41: Eleanor of Aquitaine (ca.1122–1204) was married to Louis VII of France, but her marriage was annulled in 1152 on grounds of consanguinity. She promptly married Henry of Anjou, who became Henry II two years later. She held the territory of Aquitaine independently of both her royal husbands.

Y 142–45: In 1153, Henry of Anjou, son of the Empress, invaded England; within the year he and Stephen concluded an agreement whereby Henry would succeed upon Stephen's death. They did not divide England between themselves. This claim is derived from the English prose *Brut* (140); it is not in Higden.

Y 146–48: Higden (VII 18) reports that it was said that when Stephen received the host at his coronation, it disappeared (*disparuit*).

Y 149–56: Henry II (1133–89) had five sons: William, who died in childhood; Henry, who died in 1183; Richard who succeeded his father; Geoffrey, who died in 1186; and John, who succeeded Richard. Before becoming king, Richard was Count of Poitou and Duke of Aquitaine, but not Earl of Oxford.

In December 1170, a long-running dispute between Henry and Thomas Becket, Archbishop of Canterbury, resulted in Becket's murder. Henry later acknowledged that an intemperate remark of his had provoked the act, but he claimed not to have intended it. His son Henry seems not have been involved.

Y 155: *as þai haue euirmar persewit vnto þis day*: "as they (the English kings) have continued to do until this day."

Y 157–60: Richard I reigned from 1189 to 1199. He died from blood poisoning after being struck by an arrow during his siege of the castle of Châlus-Chabrol in France (but the English prose *Brut* wrongly puts his death at his own Chateau-Gaillard). Still, as Châlus-Chabrol was held by Achard, one of Richard's sub-vassals, the death was technically caused by *ane of his awne pepill*. Richard had one son, Philip, but he was illegitimate.

Y 161–76: John (1167–1216) succeeded his brother Richard in 1199. Pope Innocent III placed England under an interdict in 1207 – not because of John's destruction of churches, but because of his refusal to install Stephen Langdon, Rome's candidate as Archbishop of Canterbury. John retaliated by imposing heavy taxes on the Cistericians. In 1209, Innocent excommunicated John. In 1213 at Dover, John capitulated to the Pope's legate, Pandulf, surrendering England to the Pope and receiving it back as the Pope's vassal, in return for an annual tribute of 1000 marks. Bower records these events (IX 4, 19) and provides a copy of the "Golden Charter" by which John surrendered the kingdom (IX 20).

Y 180–83: John had five legitimate children: Henry III; Richard, Earl of Cornwall; Joan, queen of King Alexander II of Scotland; Isabella of England (the name is a Spanish form of Elizabeth), empress of Frederick II; and Eleanor Plantagenet. He had at least twelve illegitimate children. The chronicler's failure to note Joan's Scottish marriage is remarkable; perhaps he does not wish to acknowledge that the descent of this devil extends to the Scottish royal line.

Y 184–93: In August 1216, Alexander II (King of Scots 1214–49) led an army through England and met the future King Louis VIII of France in Dover; John's forces, however, drove the Scots back into Scotland. The account here of Alexander's campaign and of his triumphant return, "without loss and with great treasure and much glory," appears to be based upon Bower (IX 29), although some details, such as Alexander's slinging his sword into the sea, are not in Bower. John actually died of dysentery, but Bower reports that a monk at Newark, fearing that John was going to destroy his monastery, killed him by offering him "a poisoned silver plate full of plums smeared with poison". (See BAd 421–27, BAs 341–47 and notes; compare Warren, *King John*, pp. 253–55.)

Y 194: Henry III (1207–72) succeeded his father in 1216.

Y 195–96: Louis VIII, while still the Dauphin of France, had invaded England in John's reign (not Henry's) and had occupied much of southeastern England with the support of rebel English barons. With John's death, most of the rebels gave their allegiance to the 9-year-old Henry. Within ten months, Louis withdrew. (See Powicke, *Thirteenth Century*, pp. 8–15; and Bower IX 30.)

Y 197–201: Henry III was faced with a number of rebellions, most notably that of Simon of Montfort (ca.1208–65), Earl of Leicester. Simon was an advisor and brother-in-law of Henry, but he became the leader of a party of barons opposed to the king's financial mismanagement. Henry, aided by Gilbert de Clare, Earl of Gloucester, who had defected from the baronial party, defeated and killed Simon at the battle of Evesham in 1265. Simon was long remembered as a hero who had championed reforms that would limit the power of the king.

Y 202–03: Henry III had five children: Edward I, Margaret of England, Edmund Crouchback, Beatrice, and Katherine.

Y 204–10: Edward I (1239–1307), called Longshanks, succeeded his father in 1272. William Wallace (ca.1272–1305) was the son of a Scottish knight who led the Scots against the English from 1297 until his capture and execution. In the fall of 1297, Wallace invaded the north of England, but did not pass south of New-castle or Carlisle. The fanciful account of his meeting with Margaret, Queen of England and daughter of Philip III of France, is taken from Hary's verse romance/chronicle *Wallace* (1476–78); see M. McDiarmid, ed., *Hary's Wallace* 1.lxxii, 2.233–34 and 8.915–1618, especially 8.1170.

Y 211–15: Edward died at Lanercost Priory at Burgh-on-Sands in 1307, after 35 years on the throne, while on his way to campaign in Scotland. The tale of the idol and its deceitful prophecy is not in any of the *Ynglis*-chronicler's usual sources. It is perhaps a confused echo of the tale of Henry IV's death in the

Jerusalem chamber, reported in Robert Fabyan's Chronicle in 1513 – possibly stimulated by Edward's stated intention of returning to the Holy Land.

Y 216–23: Edward II earned the enmity of his lords by his preference for the company and counsel of men of lower rank. His principal favorite (and probable lover) in the early years of his reign was Piers Gaveston, a Gascon knight whom Edward made Earl of Cornwall in 1307. Gaveston was condemned to be hanged as a traitor in 1312, but was instead run through by a Welsh soldier and beheaded by another (Haines, *King Edward II*, p. 86). Gaveston was then replaced in the king's confidence by Hugh Despenser the elder, Earl of Winchester, and in his affections by Hugh Despenser the younger, his chamberlain. In October 1326, Hugh the elder was condemned to death and drawn by horses through the town, suspended on the gallows, and beheaded. In December, the son was drawn by horses, castrated, disemboweled, and cut into pieces (Haines, pp. 181–82, 185, 450 n.50).

Y 218: *And raiss sa ewill of governance that he rewlit him all be laddis*: "And such evil arose that he governed himself entirely by (took advice only from) boys".

Y 224–26: In 1325, Edward's queen, Isabella, took their elder son, Edward, to the court of her brother, Charles IV of France. She was not exiled, though several chronicles (English prose *Brut*, *Historia Roffensis*, *Wigmore Chronicle*) report rumors to that effect; in fact, she appears to have herself contrived the mission of ostensible mediation on which she went to France, where her English allies awaited her, with the heir to the English throne in her custody.

Y 227–31: The English prose *Brut* (189) reports that in 1317 two cardinals, on a mission to make peace between England and Scotland, were robbed on the moor of Wigglesdon. Higden (VII 42) reports the mission of the cardinals, but not the robbery. No *de jure* papal interdict resulted, but the *Ynglis*-chronicler apparently thinks God would have cursed the country without requiring this formality.

Y 232–35: The battle of Bannockburn, in June 1314, was a great victory by Robert Bruce over Edward II near Stirling Castle. Edward fled south after the battle, leaving Stirling, with its valuable stores, to surrender to Bruce. See N 581–89, BAd 481–87, BAs 396–401 and note.

Y 236–39: Thomas Plantagenet, Earl of Lancaster and Earl of Leicester, leader of the baronial opposition to Edward II, was defeated at Boroughbridge in 1322 and beheaded and buried at Pontefract Castle in Yorkshire. He was popularly considered a martyr to Edward's tyranny. Bower (XIII 4) uses the standard formula: "it is said that very many miracles occurred at his tomb." Unsuccessful attempts were made to have him canonized (Haines, *King Edward II*, p. 188).

Y 240: In 1326, the unpopular Edward II was overthrown in a coup led by his wife, Isabella, and her lover, Roger de Mortimer.

Y 241–65: Edward fled London but was captured in Wales in November 1326 by Henry of Lancaster, brother of the murdered Thomas, and imprisoned first at Kenilworth Castle in Warwickshire and then at Corfe Castle in Dorset. After his forced abdication before parliament in January 1327, he was moved to

Berkeley Castle in Gloucestershire and closely guarded by Sir Thomas (not John) Berkeley and Sir John Maltravers. He was murdered there the following September, apparently on the orders of Isabella and Mortimer, by a red-hot poker inserted through a cow's horn into his anus. Later, in a successful attempt to get Edward's half-brother Edmund of Woodstock, to betray himself, Isabella and Mortimer put the story about that Edward was still alive at Corfe Castle.

Edward of Windsor (1312–77) nominally succeeded his father as Edward III, but as he was just 14 years old, Isabella and Mortimer ruled in his name until 1330. Edward III thus probably played no role in the murder of his father. Contemporary chroniclers Adam Murimuth, Geoffrey le Baker, and Henry Knighton all absolve Edward III of responsibility.

Y 243–44, 257, 260: *and his wyf*: Apparently the *Ynglis*-chronicler means Edward II's wife, Isabella, rather than Edward III's wife, Philippa. Edward III did not marry until four months after his father's death.

Y 266–67: Although the 16-year-old Edward III paid homage to Philip VI at Amiens in 1329 for the Duchy of Gascony, he spent most of his 50-year reign attempting to make good his claim to the French throne.

Y 268–69: Edward III's eldest son, Edward of Woodstock, Prince of Wales, died in 1376, a year before his father.

Y 270: This is perhaps an inaccurate reference to the Good Parliament of 1376. Two of Edward's ministers were impeached, and his mistress was banished from court, but no "murder of lords" occurred.

Y 272–73: The son of Edward of Woodstock, Richard of Bordeaux (1367–1400), born at the Abbey of St Andrew in Bordeaux, succeeded his grandfather in 1377. The chronicler's treatment of Richard's reign is characteristic of his approach to English history generally, in that he does not acknowledge any innocent parties: Richard is guilty of *misgouernans* (Y 277), and those who give him counsel are *fals* (Y 302); yet the lords who move against the counsellors are *tratouris* (Y 286); and Richard is guilty of murder (Y 298) when he takes vengeance upon the lords.

Y 274–78: The Peasants' Revolt was a spontaneous uprising of commoners over an oppressive poll tax in June 1381, beginning in Essex, but spreading quickly to Kent, Hertfordshire, Norfolk, Suffolk, and elsewhere. The Essex men were led by Jack Straw, the Kentish men by Wat Tyler. When the rebels converged on London, they burned Savoy Palace, the residence of John of Gaunt, and executed a few important men, including the Archbishop of Canterbury and Richard II's chancellor. The rebels dispersed within a few days.

Y 279–81: On 21 May 1382, a large earthquake struck southeastern England and northern France. Buildings in London, including St Paul's cathedral and Westminster Abbey, were damaged. As was usual with medieval earthquakes, moralists assigned the cause to God's anger: the English prose *Brut*, for example, cites *þe grete vengaunce and grete drede þat our Lorde God schewed and dede*. But we can find no other chronicler that specifies Richard and his council as the proximate cause of this one.

Y 282–89: In 1387, five of Richard's baronial opponents, known as the Lords Appellant, staged a coup against Richard's advisors. They were Richard's uncle Thomas of Woodstock, Duke of Gloucester; Richard Fitzalan, Earl of Arundel (here called Riddisdale); Thomas (not Richard) Beauchamp, Earl of Warwick; Henry Bolingbroke, Earl of Derby; and Thomas Mowbray, Earl of Nottingham. These lords convened a parliament, known since as the "Merciless", which tried and sentenced to death several of Richard's advisors. It is noteworthy that the chronicler considers all parties guilty.

Y 290–94: This account may refer loosely to a tournament that took place at Smithfield, London's tournament ground, in May 1390. A different account of that tournament is given by the English prose *Brut* (240) and repeated by Caxton in his continuation of Higden (7): according to the *Brut*, the Earl of Moray (not the Earl of Mar) was so badly injured by the Earl Marshal (Thomas Mowbray) that he died on his way back to Scotland; Sir William de Dalzell was so soundly bested by Sir Piers Courtenay that he gave up; and the squire Cockburn was unhorsed five times by Sir Nicholas Hauberk. Bower (XV 6) gives a vivid account of a contest between Dalzell and Courtenay and declares the Scot the victor; but D. E. R. Watt (Bower, *Scotichronicon*, vol. 8, p. 156) suggests that Bower may be referring to another, earlier contest.

Y 295–97: The abbeys of Jedburgh, Kelso, Melrose, Dryburgh, and Newbattle, all lying along the invasion route between England and Edinburgh, were routinely sacked by the English – including by Richard on a punitive expedition into Scotland in 1385. The English prose *Brut* (239) and Caxton (3) record the invasion, but not the destruction of abbeys. Bower (XIV 47) mentions the burning of the monasteries at Dryburgh, Melrose, and Newbattle and the church of St Giles in Edinburgh, but not of Kelso or Jedburgh.

Y 298–300: In 1397, Richard took sudden revenge on the leading Lords Appellant, arresting Gloucester, Arundel, and Warwick; the first was murdered while in custody, the second was executed, and the third was imprisoned.

In 1399, Richard was captured by his cousin Henry Bolingbroke and forced to abdicate; he was murdered in prison early in 1400. But rumors that he was alive persisted, and the Scottish court apparently maintained one imposter, Thomas of Trumpington, at Stirling Castle until his death in 1419. Bower (XV 9) has a more detailed account of Richard's exile, concluding with his burial by friars in Stirling, but does not say that he was a beggar or went insane. For an account of the rumors that Richard was still alive, and in Scotland, see Walker, "Rumor, Sedition, and Popular Protest", pp. 31–65.

Y 301–02: Henry Bolingbroke, now Duke of Lancaster, claimed the throne as Henry IV, with the assent of Parliament, in September 1399.

Y 303–11: This account of the White Hermit is taken from Bower (XV 9). It may be an elaborated version of the brief account in both the *Annales Henrici Quarti* and the *Eulogium Historiarum* of a hermit who came to Henry with prophecies and threats. The precise content of his speech is not given in the latter two chronicles, but Henry was not pleased by it: all three report that he ordered the hermit decapitated. The fanciful and symbolic prophecy of succession was a recurring propaganda tool in late medieval England.

Y 307–08: *and he resignit nocht our þe crovne fra him*: "if he did not give up the crown".

Y 312–15: In January 1400, a group of English magnates conspired to assassinate Henry and restore the imprisoned Richard. The plotters included Thomas Holland, Duke of Surrey; his uncle, John Holland, Duke of Exeter and half-brother of Richard II; and John Montagu, Earl of Salisbury. When the coup failed, the conspirators fled. Though Henry executed many other conspirators and their followers, these three were captured and summarily executed by townspeople, Surrey and Salisbury in Cirencester and Exeter near Pleshy, in Essex. Thomas of Woodstock (1355–97), Duke of Gloucester, was not one of the conspirators, being dead before Henry became king. He had in fact been murdered, but on Richard's orders, not Henry's. The Duke of Gloucester in 1400 was Henry's younger son, Humphrey, aged 9.

Y 316–17: Owen Glendower (ca.1359–c.1416), a Welsh prince, led a rebellion against Henry that began in 1400 and lasted for years. Glendower was never captured.

Y 318–21: In 1403, the powerful Percy family (Henry, Earl of Northumberland, and his son Hotspur), allied with the Scot Archibald, Earl of Douglas, rebelled against Henry IV. In July, Hotspur and Douglas were defeated at the battle of Shrewsbury. Douglas was reputed to have killed three knights dressed as Henry, including Sir Walter Blount and Edmund, Earl of Stafford. Douglas was captured, but allowed to live; he was later ransomed.

Y 322–24: Alexander Stewart, Earl of Mar, participated in a tournament in London in 1406 (see *ODNB*). As in the case of the 1393 tournament (above, Y 290–94) the English prose *Brut* has a contradictory account: it says the Earl of Mar was defeated by Edmund Holland, Earl of Kent.

Y 322: *on a conduct*: "with a safe-conduct pass".

Y 325–26: Henry Percy, Earl of Northumberland, submitted to Henry IV following the defeat of his son at Shrewsbury, but in 1405 he rebelled again. In February 1408, Percy and his ally, Thomas, fifth Baron Bardolf, were killed in a battle at Branham Moor by Sir Thomas Rokeby, the sheriff of Yorkshire. However, according to Bower (XV 19), "The king secretly arranged a rendezvous with Rokeby, who trapped the said Percy at Wetherby Moor, where in 1406 he was killed along with the said Lord Bardolf."

Y 327: Henry had suffered from some serious disease since at least 1405; he died in 1413.

Y 328–33: Henry V (1387–1422) became king in 1413. He was married to Catherine of Valois, daughter of King Charles VI of France. St Fiacre was a seventh-century Irish hermit who settled at Brie in France. According to Alain Bouchart's *Grandes Croniques de Bretagne*, Henry took up Fiacre's relics with the intention of returning them to Ireland, but restored them when he fell sick. Henry died of some intestinal disorder, accompanied by diarrhea. After his death his entrails were cut out of his body and buried at the church of Saint-Maur-des-Fossés at Vincennes (Seward, *Henry V*, 212), and this may have led to the rumor that his *belly raif*.

Y 332–33: *offerit ane mort to Mahovne*: "went to Hell." *Mahoune* (Mohammed), although frequently used in medieval English and Scots to refer to a pagan god, was also used as a synonym for the Devil. For a Scots example, see William Dunbar's "The Dance of the Sevin Deidly Synnis," *Poems*, pp. 50–53.

Y 334–35: Henry VI succeeded his father, Henry V, although he was not yet nine months old. He was king from 1422 to 1461 and again for a few months during 1470–71. He was known for his piety, political ineptitude, and periodic madness. He would have been, from the Scottish point of view, a *gud* English king because he had no designs on Scotland and for a time took refuge there. By 1453, the territorial and political gains won by Henry V in France had been lost on the battlefield – not voluntarily abandoned or relinquished, as the chronicler's verb *levit* seems to suggest.

Y 336–38: Sometime between 1429 and 1436, Catherine of Valois, mother of Henry VI, secretly married Owen Tudor, her Welsh clerk of the Wardrobe. Owen was not of "law blud," but of distinguished Welsh ancestry, supposedly descended from the last British king Cadwallader (Bevan, *Henry VII*, 2) and by implication from the family of King Arthur. His union with Catherine produced three sons and three daughters: the eldest son, Edmund Tudor, was made Earl of Richmond; the second son, Jasper, was made Earl of Pembroke; and the third son, Owen, became a monk at Westminster. Edmund married Margaret Beaufort, great-great-granddaughter of Edward III by way of the legitimized liaison of John of Gaunt with Katherine Swynford. In 1485, Edmund's son, Henry Tudor, became Henry VII.

This entry, obviously intended to call attention to the *law blud* of the Tudors, must have been written after Henry became king, because it would otherwise have no place in this catalogue of royal corruption, and thus it provides a *terminus a quo* for the chronicle.

Y 339–40: Eleanor Cobham was the second wife of Humphrey, Duke of Gloucester, uncle of King Henry VI. In 1441, she was accused of plotting against the king with sorcerers; arrested and tried for witchcraft, she was banished to the Isle of Man for life. She died in 1452, five years after Humphrey had himself died.

Nomina Omnium Regum Scotorum and The Brevis Cronica

In the following notes, we posit five persons involved in the production of these chronicles: the *Nomina*-chronicler, who composed the Latin text; the *Brevis*-editor, who reduced the Latin text (perhaps a somewhat different version) to about two thirds its original length; the *Brevis*-translator who rendered it into Scots, producing a text that has survived in two independent and variant versions, one copied by the anonymous BAd-scribe and another copied by the BAs-scribe, John Asloan. (It is possible, of course, that the editor and the translator were the same person, just as it is possible that there may have been other editors, translators, or scribes involved in the descent of these texts.)

We have taken the title of the Latin chronicle from its heading in the Dalhousie manuscript, *Sequuntur nomina omnium Regum Scotorum*, following Laing, who used the whole heading as a title for his edition of part of the chronicle for the *Bannatyne Miscellany*. And we have followed some, but not all, scholars in entitling the Scots chronicle the *Brevis Cronica*. But since that title (or *Breve Chronicon* or *Brevis Historia*) is given to more than fifty short Latin chronicles (but to no other vernacular ones, as far as we know), it is possible that *Brevis Cronica*, rather than *Nomina* was the title the translator found in his Latin version and gave it to his translation – a title the BAd-scribe copied, while Asloan said only that his text was a *tractat* (treatise) that had been *drawin* ("translated" or "extracted") from *Þe Scottis Cornikle*. Since the latter title is a good translation of *Scotichronicon*, it probably indicates that Asloan realized that his text was an abridgement of Bower's work. All we know for sure is that BAd is headed *Brevis Cronica* and BAs is said to *be derived from* (rather than to *be*) *Þe Scottis Cornikle*.

Since the principal source for these chronicles is Walter Bower's *Scotichronicon*, we have given a reference to the appropriate book and chapter of Bower's chronicle at the head of the note to each section. Although the chroniclers do not seem to have consulted John Fordun's *Chronica*, much of what is in Bower is derived from Fordun, so we have also given references to his *Chronica* or to the *Gesta Annalia*, formerly attributed to him. We have given references to Bellenden's translation of Boece's *Historia* where Bellenden is a source for the BAd version, but not to the *Historia* itself, since the BAd-scribe makes explicit reference to Bellenden's book and chapter numbers.

N 1–3, BAs 1–2: The reign of James II of Scotland (1437–60) provides a *terminus a quo* for the composition of the Latin chronicle, as it does for Bower's *Scotichronicon*. The last event the *Nomina* mentions is the execution of the murderers of James I in March 1437, an event not mentioned in Bower. BAs, which carries its account into the reign of James IV, also tells of their execution. BAd breaks off in 1388, during the reign of Robert II.

BAs 2: *þe thrid age of þe warld*: According to a traditional classification derived ultimately from Augustine, the Third Age extended from Abraham to David. This reference is not in N or BAd, which fact suggests that the *Brevis Cronica* may have been translated from a different version of the *Nomina*, or that someone involved in the transmission of the text to BAs may have supplemented his source by consulting Bower (I 7, 9).

N 4–50, BAd 1–37, BAs 3–38: For legends of the origins of the Scots, see the note to VC 16–88, above.

N 4–10, BAd 1–4, BAs 3–7 [Fordun I 8, Bower I 9]: For the myth of Gathelos (Gathelus), Scota, and Neolus, see the notes to VC 16–88 and OD 6–16, OR 8–19, OA 7–17. The departure of Gathelos and Scota from Egypt is dated by

Bower as 1550 BC. No date is given here, but later references (N 213–18, BAd 195–200, BAs 170–74) place this event in 1511 BC.

N 4: *Bochaonis*: Perhaps a scribal error for *Pharaonis*, the corruption being added after the correct form and then possibly being taken as a name. But Boece (I) gives Bocchoris as the name of the succeeding pharaoh, Scota's brother, ruling at the time Scota and Gathelos leave Egypt. Fordun does not name the pharaoh who is Scota's father, but Bower (I 8) identifies him as Chencres, a form derived from the twelfth-century Irish *Lebor Gabála Érenn* ("Book of the Taking of Ireland"), where the pharaoh's name is Cincris.

N 5–6: *Nembroith*: The Nimrod of Genesis 10. The tentative "ut quidam volunt" echoes Bower (I 9), who attributes this information to "another chronicle" – a source that John and Winifred MacQueen (Bower, *Scotichronicon*, vol. 1, p. 113) suggest resembles the *Lebor Gabála Érenn*. For a fuller discussion of the texts that may lie behind Fordun, see Broun, *Independence*, pp. 216–68.

N 6–7, BAd 2–3, BAs 4–5: *Scota nomine a quo gens Scotorum nuncupatur*: The word "Scot" may actually be derived from the Old Irish word for "wanderer" or "bandit".

BAs 7: *þe chiar of marbill*: The Stone of Destiny (actually of red sandstone) upon which much later Scottish kings were crowned, makes its appearance at a later period in N (28–29) and BAd (20–22), when Simón Brecc takes it from Spain to Ireland. BAs here renders definite a suggestion by Bower (I 28) that the chair might have had Egyptian origins. In Baldred Bisset's *Processus*, it is implied that Scota brings the chair to Scotland from Egypt (see *Scotichronicon*, XI 62).

N 11–15, BAd 5–10, BAs 8–12 [Fordun I 11–12, 14, Bower I 12–13,15]: These geographical references, similar to the forms used by Bower, are identified by John and Winifred MacQueen (Bower, *Scotichronicon*, vol. 1, pp. 119, 121): *Ansaga*, the Oued el-Kebir river in Algeria; *Hiberum*, the Ebro river in Spain; *Brigantium*, A Coruña, a port in northwestern Spain (the coastal district near A Coruña is called Bergantiños). Though the river is nowhere near this corner of Spain, both *Ebro* and *Iberia* were thought to be derived from Éber (Hiber, Hyber), Gathelos's son.

N 16–29, BAd 11–23, BAs 13–24 [Bower I 16–18, 21–22, 27–28]: Recorded here are three successive legendary migrations from Spain to Ireland over nearly a millennium – the first two out of order in BAs. The colonists left behind under Hymec (Emete, Hiemet) are, after his death, unable to maintain control of the original inhabitants of Ireland and appeal to their cousins in Spain for help – a set-back omitted by the *Nomina*-chronicler. Míl Espáine (Micelius, Mitelus, Mitelius), king of the Scots in Spain, sends his three sons – Hibertus (Hibert), Hermonius (Hermonye), and Partholomus (Partholonius, Ptholomye) – to restore order. Much later, a civil war between factions of Scots in Ireland leads to a similar appeal and to the coming of Simón Brecc. Dauvit Broun (*Irish Identity*, pp. 63–68) discusses the probable melding of originally separate migration myths into this narrative.

N 16: Ruth was not the wife of Salmon, but his daughter-in-law. As Ruth is said to be David's great-grandmother, the story might be placed about the end of the twelfth century BC.

N 20: *Abden*: Abdon was a judge of Israel, reported (Judges 12:13–15) to have ruled for eight years – perhaps during the eleventh century BC.

N 25–29, BAd 19–23, BAs 21–24 [Bower I 27–28]: This is the third mythical invasion of Ireland recorded here, dated by Bower to the time of "Manasseh, son of Heze-kiah". N retains only the latter part of this reference, BAd and BAs only the former. Hezekiah and Manasseh were kings of Judah, the latter succeeding his father and reigning 687–42 BC. The traditional date for the founding of Rome is 753 BC. Bower initially identifies Simón Brecc's father as Fonduf, a corruption of En Dub, but subsequently, recording the version given in the legend of St Congall, Fordun calls him simply *quidam Scotorum Hispaniae rex* ("a certain king of the Scots in Spain"), and Bower identifies him as Milo. So the *Nomina*-chroni-cler here hedges his bets. Milo was originally another name for Míl Espáine, above, but here has become another and later king. The *Brevis*-translator has apparently not recognized *Milone* as an ablative. *Themore* is Tara, the seat of the High Kings of Ireland.

BAd 19: *king of þe saidis Scottis*: The phrase has evidently been repeated mistakenly from BAd 15; since Mylone is giving the orders, he must still be king.

N 30–36, BAd 24–28, BAs 25–29 [Bower I 30–31]: See the note to VC 67–75. The granting of maidens and widows, on condition of royal succession in the female line, provided some later historians with a rationale for the now disputed Pictish custom of matrilineal succession.

N 30: Salathiel (Salatiel) is named in Matthew 1:12 and Luke 3:27 as an ancestor of Jesus and in Ezra 3:2 and elsewhere as the father of Zerubbabel, a leader of the Israelites at the time of their return from Babylon and the rebuilding of the temple in Jerusalem – thus in the sixth century BC. According to Haggai 2:21, it is Zerubbabel, not Salathiel, who was governor of Judea.

N 31, BAd 24–25, BAs 26: *ad Hiberniam / to Irland / to Scotland*: BAs's reading perhaps registers understandable confusion about how the Scots, resident in Ireland, could grant access to Scotland, where they had not yet been. BAd, like Bower, is clearer about the supposed wanderings of the Picts.

N 37–46, BAd 29–34, BAs 30–35 [Bower I 36]: Fergus (Fergusius) son of Feredach (Farchard, Fercharde, Ferherd), a legendary descendant of legendary Irish kings, is traditionally the first king of the Scots to rule in Scotland. In fact, no such kingdom is known to have existed at this date. Bower dates the beginning of Fergus's rule as 330 BC; the date of 313 BC in BAd and BAs looks like a mistake in translation.

For the arms of Scotland, see the note to OD 97–107, OR 94–103, OA 82–93.

BAd 32–33, BAs 33 [Bower I 28]: The prophecy that the Scots will rule wherever the marble chair (the Stone of Destiny) is – not found in the Latin text – has been taken by the *Brevis*-translator directly from Bower, who, following Fordun

(I 27), applies the prophecy to the kingdoms of enemies who capture the stone. The implication, made more plainly in Fordun and Bower, is that, because Edward I forcibly removed the stone to Westminster Abbey in 1296, where it was made part of the coronation chair, the Scots would eventually rule over England.

BAd 31: *Symon Breik*: The manuscript has Symon *Rorryk*, apparently a misreading by the scribe, who forgot what he had written 12 lines earlier.

BAs 33: *quhar euir it be*: "wherever it might be".

N 41–42: *in partibus Albionis que nunc Scocia dicitur*: The verb should be plural because the antecedent must be *partibus*, not *Albionis*. Only the northern parts of Albion were called Scotland.

N 43–46, BAd 33–34, BAs 33–35 [Bower II 12]: The verses are also found in OD 104–07, OR 100–03, OA 89–93; for other occurrences, see the note to those passages.

N 47–50, BAd 35–37, BAs 36–38 [Bower II 13]: Bower took the story of Reuda (Rether, Richert) from Fordun (II 13), who found it in Bede (I 1). John and Winifred MacQueen (Bower, *Scotichronicon*, vol. 1, pp. 353–54) explain this false etymology for Redesdale in Northumberland: it does not mean "Rether's portion", but simply "red valley". The importance of the passage to the *Nomina*-chronicler is that it establishes a Scottish claim to this border territory – in his time, part of England. It is probably significant that though according to the legend of St Congall, cited by Fordun and Bower, Rether took the territory of the Britons "with excessive greed", the *Nomina*-chronicler justifies Rether's conquests "by the right of war." Neither Bede nor Bower supplies a date.

N 51–57, BAd 38–41, BAs 39–42 [Bower II 14–15]: Julius Caesar's two invasions of southern Britain were in 55 and 54 BC. They did not involve the Scots or Picts in any way. Both N and BAs follow Bower in dating Caesar's letter to 49 years before the Incarnation; BAd lacks the number. This would be in all likelihood an error resulting from eyeskip, since it would have been known to educated and uneducated alike from the Christmas story (Luke 2:1) that Christ was not born in the days of Julius Caesar.

N 55–56: The verses are also found in OD 81-82, OR 78-79 and in the fifteenth-century *Tract on the Scots*, lines 11–12 (Skene, *Chronicles*, pp. 330–31).

N 58–62, BAd 42–46, BAs 43–46 [Bower II 25]: The BAd and BAs versions of this passage repeat Bower nearly verbatim; the N version provides different, but indefinite dating, since the N-scribe has left a space after the *l*. Claudius was emperor AD 41–54, Severus 193–211. So, following BAd and BAs, from Claudius's twelfth year (53) to the beginning of Severus's reign is 140 years (not 154). But N is no more accurate: 154 years after the year 50 is 204 (not 194) – which is the eleventh (not the fifteenth) year of Severus's reign. The supposed war between the Scots and the Picts is in any event unhistorical.

N 63–68, BAd 47–51, BAs 47–52 [Bower II 38]: The story of Fulgencius (Fulgentius) is unhistorical. As Stephen Boardman ("Matter of Britain", pp. 56–58) has pointed out, the hero is derived ultimately from Geoffrey of Monmouth's creation, Sulgenius (V 2). But Emperor Severus did come to Britain in 208 to put an end to the incursions of the Picts. He did not build a new wall, but simply repaired the wall built by Hadrian between 122 and 128. Though he invaded the north as far as Aberdeen, he was unable to engage the Picts in decisive battle. He died of sickness in York in 211. The claim that Severus was killed in battle (in BAd and BAs, but not in N) is in Fordun and is repeated by Bower alongside an alternate version, attributed to Bede, in which Severus died of sickness. In BAs, the omission of a *þat* before *biggit* and the addition of an *and* before *fled* makes Fulgencius the builder of the wall and nonsense of the history.

N 69–75, BAd 52–54, BAs 53–55 [Bower II 40]: Victor I was Pope 189–98. There is no evidence that he suffered martyrdom. Nor is there evidence that Christianity reached Scotland during Victor's reign.

N 72–75: A date 203 years after Christ would be too late for Victor and Severus. The verses are taken from Bower. They are also found, slightly altered, in the fifteenth-century *Tract on the Scots* (Skene, *Chronicles*, lines 18–21, p. 331); the first three are in the fifteenth-century *Liber Extravagans*, formerly called *Chronicon Rhythmicum*, (Skene, *Chronicles*, lines 115–17, pp. 335–36, n. 3); and the first two are in OD 236–37, OR 238–39, OA 232–33.

N 76–82, BAd 55–59, BAs 56–60 [Bower II 42]: Bower dates this legendary conflict to "the time of Diocletian or a little before". Diocletian ruled 284–305. So there has been a period of more than 600 years of peaceful coexistence since the legendary arrival of Fergus, son of Feredach, in 330 BC.

BAd 56–57: *ane quhyt hund*: The color of the hound is not in Fordun or Bower, but is in Bellenden (VI 5).

N 83–91, BAd 60–64, BAs 61–65 [Bower II 58–60]: Andrew is the patron saint of Scotland. There is no historical evidence in support of the legend of the translation of Andrew's bones. Regulus, a non-historical figure, is known only through this legend. Gurgust (Gurgast) is a misrendering of the Pictish king Bower calls Hurgust and credits with granting the land at Kylrymont to St Regulus. Bower's King Hungus (Hungar), omitted by the *Nomina*-chronicler, but included by the *Brevis*-translator, is a later benefactor of the church. These are probably confused and temporally displaced references to one of two Uurguists, both fathers of Pictish kings named Unuist – Unuist I (reigned 729–61) and Unuist II (reigned 820–34) – both of whom were associated with the foundation or building of St Andrews. (See MacQueen, *Scotichronicon*, vol. 2, pp. 456, 461; and Henderson and Foster, "Introduction", *St Andrews Sarcophagus*, p. 17.) Dauvit Broun ("Birth", p. 18) explains that Hungus / Hurgust has been divided "in an attempt to resolve the [St Andrews foundation] legend's chronological connections: 'Hurgust' was adopted for the mid-fourth-century part to distinguish him from Hungus who was retained in the later part, and was placed in the ninth century."

BAd 60, BAs 61: *Constantyne / Constance*: Fordun and Bower have *Constancius imperator filius Magni Constantini* ("Constantius, the son of Constantine the Great"). Constantius was emperor 337–61.

N 83, BAd 60, BAs 61: As in N 76, BAd 55, BAs 56, N supplies a specific year, while BAd and BAs follow Fordun and Bower in simply dating by reign.

BAd 62: *þe kirk month*: "the church hill", i.e., Kylrymont or St Andrews.

BAd 63–64, BAs 64–65 [Bower II.64]: *Þe quhilk tyme* . . . *Blak Channonis*: An addition, probably by the *Brevis*-translator. By jumping ahead several chapters in Bower, and by his casual use of the phrase *Þe quhilk tyme*, he has made events that are separated by half a century seem contemporary. St Augustine, Bishop of Hippo 395–430, did not found an order of canons, but was credited with writing a rule for canons, who later came to bear his name. From the twelfth century, the term Black Canons was used in England and Scotland to describe canons who lived by this rule.

N 92–97, BAd 65–71, BAs 66–71 [Bower II 57, III 1–2]: Fergus (Fergusius) II, son of Erc (Erth), and grandson of Eochaid Muinremor (Ethaid, Ethad), is a legend-ary or possibly historical leader of the Gaelic-speaking Celts who were in southwestern Scotland, which came to be called Dál Riata, in the fifth century. The traditional date of his death is 501 – a century after the traditional date of the events reported here. John and Winifred MacQueen (Bower, *Scotichroni-con*, vol. 2, pp. 187–88) suggest that Fordun has backdated Fergus and his immediate successors in order to establish a Scottish kingship before the arrival of the Anglo-Saxons. Dauvit Broun (*Irish Identity*, pp. 69–72) offers a plausible explanation of the back-dating as an attempt (by Fordun's source, rather than Fordun) to fix Fergus's death in accordance with late-medieval claims that it occurred 811 years before the death of William the Lion in 1214. From this point to the middle of the ninth century, the supposed kings of the Scots given in the chronicle are derived, through Fordun and Bower, from one or other of the various and conflicting lists of kings of Dál Riata – apparently from a list of the X type. For a more historically accurate list and genealogy, see Marjorie Anderson, *Kingship*, pp. 228–30.

The account of Fergus's supposed return to Scotland is confusing because the *Nomina*-chronicler has omitted, probably out of patriotism, the disastrous (though quite unhistorical) events that led up to it. According to Bower, the Picts had revolted against the Scots, allied themselves with the Britons and the Romans, and driven the Scots out of Scotland. After the king, Eochaid (Eugenius, Eugeny), was killed in battle, his brother Echadius and nephew Erc had fled back to Ireland. (But Eochaid and Echadius, if they had any historical existence at all, may have been one person, since Echadius is identified elsewhere as Eochaid Muinremor, King of Dál Riata in Ireland – the kingdom from which the Scottish Dál Riata supposedly derived. In any case, the *Nomina*-chronicler has omitted Echadius and a generation, making Erc the brother, rather than the nephew, of Eochaid. The inclusion of Echadius by the *Brevis*-editor once again shows that he was either working from a different version of the *Nomina* or consulting Bower directly.) According to Bower, in 403, the Picts, who had subsequently been subdued by the Romans, invited Fergus to return and push out the Romans. The omission in BAd and BAs of any mention of the Romans is perhaps intended to focus the reader's enmity on the Picts.

N 92, BAd 65, BAs 66 [Bower III 1]: Once again, the dating of BAd and BAs is closer to Bower's than N's dating is. Bower (following Fordun) dates Fergus's invasion to 403 – which he accurately terms "the sixth year of the emperors Honorius and Archadius". N leaves a space for the year, but the mathematics of its account (a reign of 26 years ending in 419) implies an invasion no later than 393. N also has a much shorter period of exile for the Scots – 14 years instead of the 43 found in Bower, or the 83 in BAd and BAs.

N 98–101, BAd 72–75, BAs 72–75 [Bower III 5, 10–11,14]: Eugenius (Eugeny) II, son of Fergus, does not appear in the king-lists. John and Winifred MacQueen (Bower, *Scotichronicon*, vol. 2, p. 195) think he is probably an invention of Fordun, inserted to fill a gap in the chronology from 419 to 453, but Dauvit Broun (*Scottish Independence*, pp. 235–68) suspects that the role of restructuring Scottish history is more likely to belong to Richard Vairement, a mid-thirteenth-century Culdee of St Andrews, putative author of a chronicle lying two stages behind Fordun's, and possibly the "Veremundus" whom Boece names as one of his sources. Bower reports Eugenius's attacks upon the Britons and then attacks upon the Saxons in support of the Britons. Eugenius's death in battle, not found in N, is reported in Bower alongside an alternate death from illness. Eugenius's victory in death is added in BAd. For the confusing adoption of "Eugenius" as the Latin equivalent of various Gaelic names, see Broun, "Birth", 18–20.

N 100–01: Grim's Dyke is a name given to iron age or Roman earthworks in various parts of England, but Bower (III 5) explains that he is referring to the Antonine Wall, called Grim's Dyke "by the local inhabitants". By the fifth century, the wall had been long abandoned.

N 102–04, BAd 76–78, BAs 76–77 [Bower III 14]: Domangart (Dongardus, Dongard), son of Fergus, appears in some king-lists as King of Dál Riata (a kingdom that probably did not yet exist) from about 501 to about 506. N follows Fordun and Bower in saying that he reigned for five years, rather than three.

N 105–07, BAd 79–80, BAs 78–79 [Bower III 16–18]: Domangart's brother does not appear in the king-lists. He is another probable invention, inserted to reign from 457 to 479 (see the note to N 98–101, BAd 72–75, BAs 72–75). N's confusion over his name – *Constancius* in N 106, but *Constantinus* in N 108 – is reflected in the Scots chronicles, where he is *Constant* in BAd 79, but *Constance* in BAs 78.

N 108–11, BAd 81–84, BAs 80–83 [Bower III 18]: Comgall (Congallus, Congall), son of Domangart, was a historical king and eponym of the Cénel Comgaill in Kintyre from about 506 to about 538.

N 112–13, BAd 85–88, BAs 84–85 [Bower III 21, 24:] Gabrán (Conranus, *Conrane*), brother of Comgall, was a historical king and eponym of the Cénel nGabráin from about 538 to about 558. Bower, who calls him *Gouranus*, puts his death in 535. He reports that he made alliances with Aurelius and Uther, rather than

with Arthur. On the other hand, the claim in BAs of a peaceful reign is contra-
dicted not only by BAd, but by Fordun and Bower, who say that between treaties
Gabrán fought a war against the Britons. Fordun and Bower say that he was
buried at Iona. The reference in BAd to that island as *Ycolmkill* is anachronistic,
because the name means "cell of Columba", and Columba would not settle there
until decades later.

N 114–16, BAd 89–93, BAs 86–89 [Bower III 24, 26]: Eochaid Hebdre (Eugenius,
Eothodius, Constantyne, Erthody, Heb), putative son of Comgall, does not
appear in the king-lists. He is another probable invention, inserted to reign from
535 to 558 (see the note to N 98–101, BAd 72–75, BAs 72–75). With this
fictitious reign, the chroniclers' chronology has caught up with history. Fordun
and Bower also call him *Eugenius* or *Eochaidius Hebdre*, but apparently not
Constantine; that name may have resulted from Asloan's confusion of Eugenius
with Constantine, King of Cornwall, whom Fordun and Bower mention in the
same chapter. Fordun and Bower say that Eochaid ambushed and killed his
uncle Gabrán. They record the battle between Arthur and Mordred, but do not
support the claim in BAd that Eugenius supported Mordred; that story apparently comes from Bellenden (IX 11).

N 117–18, BAd 94–97, BAs 90–92 [Bower III 26]: Conall (Conuallus, Conwall,
Connall), son of Comgall, was a king of the Cénel Comgaill from about 558 to
about 576. Fordun and Bower fix the start of his reign at 558, as does the
Nomina-chronicler. Asloan agrees with Bellenden (IX 13) by fixing it at 568. The
BAd-scribe, with characteristic independence or carelessness, has 548. Bellenden
is possibly the source of the assertions in BAd of Conall's religious devotion or
felicitous reign; these claims are not in Fordun or Bower.

BAd 96–97, BAs 91–92: Columba (ca.521–97) was an Irish abbot who founded an
abbey on Iona in 565 and subsequently other houses, including Durrow and
perhaps Derry in Ireland, and Hinba and Mag Luinge in Scotland.

N 119–21, BAd 98–101, BAs 93–94 [Bower III 26]: Kynnatil or Connyd (*Kynnatill*
or *Comyd*), does not appear in the king-lists. The assertion in BAd that he died
in the presence of Columba is not in Fordun or Bower, but it is in Bellenden
(IX 14).

N 122–30, BAd 102–08, BAs 95–101 [Bower III 27]: Áedán (Aiadanus, Aidane,
Aiadane), son of Gabrán, was a king of Dál Riata from about 576 to about 609.
The source for Columba's prophecy is the *Vita Sancti Columbae*, written by
Adomnán, a seventh-century abbot of Iona. Dauvit Broun ("Aedán mac
Gabráin", *Oxford Companion*, p. 5) notes that if the story of Áedán's ordination
by Columba is true, it is "among the earliest instances of an overtly Christian
ceremony of royal inauguration in Europe."

N 125–30, BAd 106–08, BAs 98–101 [Bower III 29]: Servanus (better known as
Serf) was, according to the *Oxford Dictionary of Saints* (p. 431), a sixth-century
Scottish bishop, according to A. Macquarrie (*Saints of Scotland*, pp. 145–59),
possibly a Pict of anywhere from the seventh to the ninth centuries, and according to James Fraser (*Caledonia*, pp. 255–56), possibly a son of Clinoch, a

seventh-century Pictish king. It is notable that he is not mentioned by Bower or, apparently, by the *Brevis*-translator. Kentigern, better known as Mungo (Mungew, Mongow), was an Irish monk and friend of Columba who became Bishop of Strathclyde; he died in 612 and was buried at Glasgow. Comgall (Connallus, Connall, Conwall) was a contemporary of Columba and the first abbot of Bangor in Ireland; he died about 601 and was buried at Bangor. Baldred (Baldreid) was an eighth-century hermit at Tyninghame and Le Bass. The *Historia Dunelmensis Ecclesiae* says he died in 756. Thus he cannot have been Kentigern's disciple and successor; that tradition may have arisen because he was said to have memorized the facts of Kentigern's life. Baldred's bones were divided among Scottish churches he had founded, including Aldhame, Tyninghame, and Preston Kirk, but the legend reported by Bellenden (IX 16) and the *Brevis*-translator is that Baldred's corpse multiplied itself into three to satisfy competing claims. Fordun does not mention Baldred – one of several indications that the *Nomina*-chronicler was using Bower rather than Fordun.

N 131–32, BAd 112–13, BAs 102–03 [Bower III 31]: This is an allusion to *Kentigern and Lailoken* (*Vita Merlini Silvestris*), in which Kentigern gives the last rites to a repentant Lailoken, sometimes called Merlin. Bower gives an abbreviated account of the story, which is not in Fordun at all. For a translation of the longer version, see Basil Clarke, ed., *Vita Merlini*, Appendix I.

N 133–35, BAd 109–11, BAs 104–05 [Bower III 38]: Kenneth Ker (Kenethus Ker, Connad Cerr), son of Conall, may have reigned briefly as a king of Dál Riata about 629 – thus after, or simultaneously with, Eochaid Buide (Eugenius Bynd), below. James Fraser (*Caledonia*, p. 156) suggests that Kenneth and Eochaid may have "partitioned Áedán's legacy between them." The *Nomina*-chronicler follows Fordun and Bower in placing Kenneth before Eochaid.

N 136–40, BAd 114–18, BAs 106–10 [Bower III 39–40]: Eochaid Buide (Eugenius Bynd), son of Áedán, was possibly a king of Dál Riata (or, according to the *Annals of Ulster*, a king of the Picts) from about 605 to about 629, and thus before, or simultaneously with, Kenneth Ker. He was the fourth Eugenius in Fordun's and Bower's lists, but the only Bynd. Fordun and Bower provide an alternate name, *Aido*; it is unclear how the *Brevis*-translator came by the name *Corthedy* or *Cothody*, but it may be by a process of scribal corruption similar to that by which an earlier *Eochaid* became *Eothodius* in N 115 and *Erthody* in BAs 86. According to legend, Columba foretold that Eochaid Buide would rule instead of his three older brothers.

N 139–40, BAd 117–18, BAs 109–10: Kilian (Gillenus, Gillen) was a seventh-century Irish missionary in France – not to be confused with another Kilian who was a missionary in Germany. Kilian does not seem to have had any important connection with Scotland, nor do Fordun or Bower claim any such connection – which might account for the substitution in BAd of the already-mentioned Kentigern / Mungo (N 126, BAd 106, BAs 99).

The *Brevis*-translator has perhaps conflated two *Sanct Colme*s into one. The reference in BAd 115–16, BAs 108 was to Columba, but here it should be to

Columbanus (ca.543–615), an Irish monk who was trained at Bangor and later founded monasteries in Gaul.

N 141–42, BAd 119–22, BAs 111–12 [Bower III 41]: Ferchar (Ferchardus, Ferquharde, Ferchard), the son of Kenneth Ker (rather than of Eochaid Buide), was a king of Dál Riata from about 638 to about 650; he may have shared part of his reign with his distant cousin Domnall Brecc (below), whom he outlived by about seven years (see Marjorie Anderson, *Kingship*, pp. 110–11; and Fraser, *Caledonia*, pp. 164–66). Fordun and Bower say that *In cuius nichil actum est tempore* ("in his time, nothing happened") – the probable source of the claim here that he ruled in peace, though what little is known of his reign indicates it was a period of considerable conflict. The claim of suicide in BAd may be taken from Boece and Bellenden (IX 18), who have filled in the gap in historical knowledge by making Ferchar not only a tyrant but a heretic who scoffed at Roman Catholic doctrine on infant baptism and confession of sins and who took his own life.

N 143–46, BAd 123–26, BAs 113–14 [Bower III 41, 45]: Domnall Brecc (Donaldus Brek, Donald Breik), son of Eochaid Buide (and thus a distant cousin rather than brother of Ferchar), was a king of the Cenél nGabráin from about 631 to about 643. Bellenden (IX 19) is the source of BAd's report that Domnall supported Oswald, the Bernician King, against the Saxons. But the reverse might be closer to the truth: James Fraser (*Caledonia*, p. 172) speculates that Oswald might have supported Domnall against his rivals in the last, disastrous years of Domnall's reign. Bower says that Columba prophesied of Domnall that he would die in his bed. But Bellenden (IX 20), who does not report this prophecy, says he drowned while fishing in the Tay. In fact, he was killed at the battle of Strathcarron, fighting against the Britons.

BAd 123: The designation of Domnall Brecc as *Donald Breik, þe fourt of þat name* probably reflects the influence of Boece as translated by Bellenden. Bellenden has previously listed (but not numbered) three King Donalds: Donald, nephew of Mogallus; Donald, son of Athirco; and a usurper, Donald of the Isles – before arriving at Donevald (Domnall Brecc), son of Eugenius. The BAd-scribe has not listed any previous Donalds.

N 147–57, BAd 127–33, BAs 115–21 [Bower III 40–44]: Oswald (ca. 605–42), son of Æthelfrith, King of Bernicia, was forced to flee with his mother and brothers to the court of Eochaid Buide when he was 11 years old. During a long exile in Dál Riata, while Bernicia and Deira were ruled by his father's rival, King Edwin, Oswald was educated and converted at the monastery at Iona. In 633, Edwin having been killed, Oswald returned with troops lent by Domnall Brecc and established his control of all Northumbria. In response to Oswald's request for a bishop, Áedán, a monk from Iona, established himself at Lindisfarne. Oswald may have acted as his interpreter at the beginning of his mission. After Oswald was killed in battle against Penda, the pagan King of Mercia, he was considered a martyr and saint. This story is ultimately derived from Bede (III 1–3). Bower and these chronicles emphasize the Scottish role in the conversion of Northumbria, though during Oswald's exile, Paulinus had begun that work and had made headway in Edwin's court.

N 158–60, BAd 134–38, BAs 122–24 [Bower III 45]: Ferchar Fota (Ferchardus Fod, Ferquharde Foid, Ferchard Fode), was not a son of Ferchar or a close relative of Domnall Brecc, but a distant descendant of Loarn, brother of Fergus, son of Erc. He was a king of the Cenél nEchdach in Lorn and possibly of a united kingdom of Dál Riata for an indefinite period ending about 697. Fordun's chronology, followed by Bower and the *Brevis*-translator, has fallen behind history again as a result of omitting five kings missing or misplaced in the king-list he used. As with the earlier Ferchar (N 141–42, BAd 119–22, BAs 111–12), Ferchar Fota gets a good report from Fordun and Bower and a vicious one from Bellenden (IX 20), from whom the account in BAd is derived. The BAd version contradicts itself by saying that Ferchar Fota succeeded his supposed father, Ferchar, but places him after his supposed uncle, Domnall Brecc.

Ferchar Fota apparently ruled for more than 18 years and not in peace. He was defeated by a British army in 677, and warred more successfully against rival kings in Lorn to become King of Dál Riata at the end of his life (see Fraser, *Caledonia*, pp. 207, 244).

N 161–62, BAd 139–42, BAs 125–26 [Bower III 48]: Máel Duin (Maldwinus, Makdowyne, Maldwyne), son, not of Domnall Brecc, but of Domnall's brother Conall Crandamnae (a king omitted by Fordun), was a king of the Cenél nGabráin from 672 to 688 – before the reign of Ferchar Fota, rather than after. Again, the BAd version contradicts itself by saying that Máel Duin succeeded his supposed father (actually his uncle), Domnall Brecc, although he has just said that Domnall was succeeded by Ferchar Fota. The confusion here, as elsewhere, derives from the scribe's pardonable belief in a single Dalriadan kingdom resembling the Kingdom of the Scots in which he lived. In fact, Máel Duin and Ferchar Fota reigned simultaneously over different parts of the Dalriadan territory.

The rebuilding of the abbey at Iona and Máel Duin's murder by his wife are in Bellenden (IX 21), but not in Fordun or Bower.

N 163–65, BAd 143–46, BAs 127–28 [Bower III 51]: Eochu (Eugenius, Eugeny V) was a king of Dál Riata for a brief period about 697. He was the son of Doman-gart (Dongardus), son of Domnall Brecc; Domangart is a king omitted here, although accurately reported by Bower. He was not the brother of Máel Duin, but his cousin. BAd's Downald is apparently Máel Duin's brother Domnall Dond, whom the scribe has confused with Domangart; if Eochu had been this Domnall's son, he would indeed have been Máel Duin's nephew. It was not Eochu, but Brude (or Bridei), King of the Picts, who defeated Ecgfrith, King of Northumbria at the battle of Dunnichen (or Nechtansmere) in Angus in 685. The misappropriation of the victory is in Bellenden (IX 22); Fordun and Bower do not involve the Scots in the battle.

N 166–71, BAd 147–50, BAs 129–33 [Bower III 51]: Eugenius V / VI apparently did not exist. John and Winifred MacQueen (Bower, *Scotichronicon*, vol. 2,

p. 250) speculate that Bower's Eugenius V is the "possibly spurious Eogan, son of Ferchard Fota." Up to this point, N and BAd have agreed with Bellenden (IX 23) in counting the Eugeniuses from the uncle of Fergus, son of Feredach (N 93–94, BAd 66–67, BAs 67–68). BAs began that way, but altered the count when it called Eochaid Hebdre (Eugenius) Constantine (N 114–16, BAd 89–90, BAs 86–87). Bower does not number any Eugenius until the son of Domangart (N 163–65, BAd 143–44, BAs 127–28), whom he calls Eugenius IV. So from this point, N and BAd agree with Bellenden, and BAs with Bower. Since N was presumably written before Boece's *Historia* or Bellenden's translation of it, the *Nomina*-chronicler must have drawn upon one of the same sources as Boece for his numbering of the Eugenius kings or coincidentally counted the Eugenius kings the same way.

Adomnán (ca.628–704) was an abbot of Iona and the biographer of Columba; he wrote a law, the *Lex Innocentium*, to protect the status of women and children as non-combatants.

The bloody rain and milk are reported in Britain in the F-version of the *Anglo-Saxon Chronicle* for 685 and in Britain and Ireland in the *Annales Cambriae* for 689. Bower (III 51), drawing on Fordun (III 43), extends these phenomena to Scotland and makes them last a week. No specific significance is attached to them in any of these sources.

N 172–74, BAd 151–54, BAs 134–36 [Bower III 52]: Ainbcellach (Ambrikilleth, Amberkelethe, Ambrikellech) son of Ferchar Fota (Fyndan, Fyndaw), was King of the Cenél nEchdach in Lorn for a brief period about 698. He was apparently deposed in that year, but lived to be killed in battle by his brother, Selbach, about 20 years later. BAs follows Fordun and Bower, who identify him as "son of Findan son of Eochaid IV." Bellenden (IX 24) identifies him as the *nepoitt* of Eugenius V, consistent with Fordun and Bower's *nepos* if those terms are taken in their broadest senses (kinsman), since Fordun and Bower's genealogy makes Eugenius IV and Eugenius V second cousins; Ainbcellach is thus a fourth cousin twice removed to Eugenius V. BAd follows Bellenden in linking him to Eugenius V, but cuts out all the middle men, making him his son. In fact, all of this is wrong: he belonged to a completely different branch of the royal family. Fordun and Bower report his death, but say nothing of his character; N agrees with Bellenden in calling him a monster and in accusing him of lust and avarice.

N 175–78, BAd 155–57, BAs 137–38 [Bower III 53]: Eochaid (Eugenius VI / VII), son of Eochu, was King of the Cenél nGabráin from about 721 to 731, when he entered a monastery, his kingdom under military pressure from Selbach, King of the Cenél nEchdach; he died in 733, long after the period assigned by Fordun, Bower, and these chronicles. He was not a brother of Ainbcellach, but a very distant relative. N gives him a virtuous character derived from Bower. The claims in BAd that he founded Scottish historiography and that he died at Abernethy, near Perth, are found in Bellenden (IX 24); Bower says he died in Lorn.

N 179–82, BAd 158–60, BAs 139–41 [Bower III 53]: Muiredach (Murdacus, Mordak, Murdow), son of Ainbcellach, was King of the Cenél nEchdach from 733 to 736.

These comets are reported as occurring in 729 by Bede (V 23), from whom Bower (via Fordun) has his information. No such comets are otherwise known. See the note by John and Winifred MacQueen (Bower, *Scotichronicon*, vol. 2, p. 253); they quote speculation by Robert Newton (*Chronicles*, p. 671) that these were two sightings of the same comet.

BAd 159: *vertuus*: The manuscript has *viciouss*, but the sense of this passage and the testimony of the sources suggest a scribal error, probably an eyeskip from BAd 152. The sense of *gevand all his iustice and peax* is apparently "giving his justice and peace to all".

N 183–86, BAd 161–63, BAs 142–45 [Bower III 54]: Áed Find (Ethfyn), son of Eochaid, son of Eochu, was King of Dál Riata for perhaps 30 years ending in 778. For most of his reign, Dál Riata was dominated by the Picts. The war with the Picts he is said to have had in "his last days" is the only trace of the Pictish conquest to be found in Fordun, Bower, or these chronicles. A battle supposedly fought by Áed Find against the Picts in 768 has been conventionally thought to mark the beginning of Dalriadan resurgence, but James Fraser (*Caledonia*, p. 326) wonders whether he was in fact the Pictish king's "colleague", engaged in a struggle against common rivals.

N 187–88, BAd 164–67, BAs 146–48 [Bower III 55]: There was no Eugenius VII / VIII. Áed Find had a son named Eochaid, but he was not a king. Nor is Muiredach known to have had a son of this name. Fordun and Bower give the alternate name as *Nectanius*. Several eighth-century Nechtans are known, but they are Picts and have no known connection to Áed Find. Apparently the *Brevis*-translator left off the first three letters of *Nectanius* and misread the three minims of the *ni* as an *m* – thus producing *Tamus*. Fordun and Bower say nothing about his reign, but Bellenden (IX 27) provides BAd's story of degeneration and betrayal.

N 189–90, BAd 168–69, BAs 149 [Bower III 55]: Fergus (Fergusius) III, son of Eochaid and therefore brother rather than son of Áed Find, was King of Dál Riata from 778 to 781. He is probably the king known as Vurguist, whose sons Constantin and Onuist were kings of the Picts – a fact these chroniclers would doubtless have found unwelcome had they known it. The story of his murder by his outraged wife is in Fordun, Bower, and Bellenden (IX 28).

N 191–92, BAd 170–72, BAs 150–51 [Bower III 56]: Selbach (Selwachius, Soluathius, Seluache), son of Ferchar Fota, had been King of the Cenél nEchdach (and eventually of Dál Riata) perhaps from 699 to 723 – two-thirds of a century earlier than the position Fordun has given him here. Selbach is the first of four kings (followed by Eochaid Angbaid, Dungal, and Alpín) who, in a king-list no longer extant, were shifted forward together, with the result that this Alpín becomes one with the later Alpín who is the father of Kenneth. Marjorie Anderson (*Kingship*, p. 46) thinks this shift is a scribal error, Dauvit Broun

(*Irish Identity*, pp. 147–53) that it is a deliberate reorganization of the list. Fordun and Bower acknowledge the supposed peace of Selbach's reign, but attribute it to his sloth and negligence. Bellenden (IX 29) gives him a much better reputation, calling him noble and saying that he would have done more if the fates had been favorable. In fact, Selbach was an aggressive and violent king, and his reign was far from peaceful. He overcame rivals, including his brother, within his own Cenél nEchdach, fought land and sea battles against Cenél Cathboth, Cenél nGabráin, and neighboring Britons, and following abdication and four years in a monastery, came out of retirement to resume fighting for his son's kingdom (see Fraser, *Caledonia*, pp. 252, 282–85).

N 193–97, BAd 173–76, BAs 152–55 [Bower III 57]: There was no king named Athaius (Achayus, Achaius). John and Winifred MacQueen (Bower, *Scotichronicon*, vol. 2, p. 258) suggest that the long reign helps make up for the omission of a number of historical kings.

There was no formal treaty between the French and the Scots before the thirteenth century.

N 198–202, BAd 177–80, BAs 156–59 [Bower III 57]: Gilmerius Scotus is the unidentified brother of a nonexistent king. Bower has embellished Fordun's invention (III 48) by attributing to him the foundation of a number of Irish Benedictine monasteries in Germany. As John and Winifred MacQueen point out (Bower, *Scotichronicon*, vol.2, p. 258), these houses were founded long after Charlemagne's time – from the late tenth century to the mid-twelfth. Gilmerius's foundation of a hospital in Rome is also Bower's addition.

N 203–04, BAd 181–82, BAs 160–61 [Bower III 60]: The University of Paris was not founded until the twelfth century. Nor does the account of Clement and John have any basis in fact. As John and Winifred MacQueen have explained (Bower, *Scotichronicon*, vol. 2, pp. 260–61), the story is derived ultimately from the *Gesta Karoli* (I 1) of Notker Balbulus; Notker's account refers to Irish scholars named Dungal and Clemens.

N 205–06, BAd 183–84, BAs 162–63 [Bower III 64]: Conall (Coguallus, Conwallus, Cognald) was really two kings of Dál Riata: Conall, son of Tadg, who had been a Pictish king until deposed in 789 and who became king of Dál Riata from 805 to 807; and Conall, son of Áedán, who appears to have killed his predecessor and reigned from 807 to 811 – markedly earlier than placed by Fordun. According to Alex Woolf (*Pictland to Alba*, p. 59), the killing of one Conall by the other "is the last explicit reference to the secular history of the kingdom [Dál Riata] in any contemporary source."

N 207–09, BAd 185–88, BAs 164–66 [Bower III 64]: Duncan or Dongall may also be a conflation by Fordun or his source of two earlier kings: Donngal, son of Selbach, who was a king of the Cenél nEchdach from 723 to about 734; and Domnall, son of the Pictish king Constantine, who, according to Dauvit Broun ("Pictish Kings", p. 81) may have imposed Domnall as a sub-king on a weakened Dál Riata from 811 to 835. This king's claim to the Pictish kingdom, reported by Fordun and Bower, may thus be an implicit acknowledgment of a

Pictish connection to the Dalriadan throne while reversing its political polarity: the fiction of a Scots king asserting lordship over the Picts may be helping to obscure the fact of Pictish hegemony.

Bower says Dungal died in battle; Bellenden (X 6) says he drowned in the Spey, a loch and river in Perthshire.

BAd 187: The *first conuentioun* was the supposed original agreement between the Scots and Picts for matrilineal succession of the Pictish kingship.

N 210–12, BAd 189–94, BAs 167–69 [Bower IV 2]: Alpín (Alpinus, Alpyne), son of Eochaid, son of Áed Find, may have been a king in Dál Riata, but he is also recorded as a king of the Picts. Though somewhat obscure himself, he is supposed to be the father of the solidly historical Kenneth (see Benjamin T. Hudson, *Kings*, p. 32). Alpín died in 834.

BAd 191–94: Bellenden (X 7) supplies the names of the Pictish kings who fought Alpín. The Pictish king-lists of the X group agree that the last kings before the one defeated by Kenneth, son of Alpín, were Ferech, son of Bacoc; Brude, son of Ferech; Kineth, son of Ferech; and Brude, son of Fokel. Bower says that Alpín was beheaded; Bellenden adds the detail that Alpín's head was put on a stake.

BAd 193: *he was slayne*: That is, Alpín was slain.

N 213–22, BAd 195–201, BAs 170–74: [Fordun IV 3–4, 8–9, Bower IV 3–4, 9–10]: By tradition, Kenneth (Cináed), son of Alpín, (d. 858), has been regarded as the last King of Dál Riata, from about 842, and has been credited with the conquest and destruction of the kingdom of the Picts about two years later, absorbing it into what was then called the kingdom of Alba. In fact, Kenneth himself may have been a Pict (see Woolf, *Pictland to Alba*, pp. 93–98), and a process of unification had been underway for nearly a century (see Benjamin T. Hudson, *Kings*, pp. 34–36), so there was likely no conquest, no expulsion, and no eradication of the Picts, then or later, and the kingdom of Alba does not appear in the historical record until the next century. It is clear that Kenneth was King of the Picts, not so clear that he was King of Dál Riata. Nevertheless, the perceived importance of this non-event to the Scottish version of history is shown by the efforts of these chroniclers and their probably twelfth-century sources to fix it chronologically. But as so often in medieval chronology, what is known definitely is known differently. Fordun, Bower, and N all agree that the destruction of the Picts occurred in 838 or 839, and BAs agrees with Fordun and Bower that this was 2349 years from the departure of Gathelos and Scota from Egypt and 1169 years after the coming of the Scots to Scotland. But BAd has 2049 years and 1119 years for these periods – this time the variants are not provided by Bellenden, as they often are. A span of 1169 years accords almost exactly with N's date of 330 BC for the invasion of Fergus, son of Feredach (N 45–46).

BAd 198–99, BAs 172–73: *he began to regnne, eftir þe regnne of Scottis, into Albany, þat is now Scotland*: "He began, after the period that he had reigned over the Scots alone, to reign over Albany, that is now Scotland."

N 219–22: The verses are taken from Bower, who took them from the thirteenth-century king-list edited by Skene as the *Cronicon Elegiacum* (Skene, *Chronicles*, lines 1–4, p. 177), but also known as the *Verse Chronicle*. Bower may have found the list in the version contained in the *Chronicle of Melrose Abbey*; see the note by John and Winifred MacQueen (Bower, *Scotichronicon*, vol. 2, p. 445).

N 216, 219, BAd 198, 204, BAs 173, 176: *Albion / Albania / Albany*: The term *Albany* comes ultimately from Gaelic *Alba* (Dumville, "Britain and Ireland", pp. 175–83), used by the Irish as the name of the whole island. But from the beginning of the tenth century, contemporary sources used *Alba* to refer to the kingdom that had succeeded the separate kingdoms of the Dál Riata Scots and the Picts. When, from the mid-tenth century, the Scots began to push east through Lothian to the Tweed, and by the early eleventh century they had taken over Cumbria, so that their late-medieval border with England approximated the modern one, the term *Albany* traveled with them. The identification of the Scots' kingdom as *Albany* was given literary and legendary form in the twelfth century by Geoffrey of Monmouth (II 1), in which the third part of the island of Britain is said to have been inherited by Albanactus, Brutus's third son: "Albanactus, the youngest, took the region which is nowadays called Scotland in our language. He called it Albany, after his own name." These late fifteenth-century chroniclers are thinking of Albany as what they consider Scotland, as their placement of *Scotland* and *Albany* in apposition makes clear: *Albany, þat is now Scotland*; *Scotland, þat is Albany*. Thus Kenneth ruled over, according to these chroniclers, what was to become modern Scotland. This supports their claim of the long independence of the nation.

N 222, BAd 201, BAs 187: Kenneth died at Forteviot, the palace of the kings of the Pictish kingdom of Fortriu on the river Earn, southwest of Perth.

BAd 202–05, BAs 175–77: The Scots texts belabor the mathematics of the domination of the Picts further than N. For the duration of Pictish rule, they have 1061 years against the 1207 years of Fordun and Bower. Their 265 years for Scots rule in Ireland before coming to Scotland is one of three alternative spans offered by Bower.

N 223–45, BAd 206–216, BAs 178–86 [Bower IV 3]: These justifications for the supposed eradication of the Picts are taken from Bower. Except for the claim that Alpín was killed after he surrendered, these charges are based on information already provided.

BAd 209: *ane quhyte hoynd, as said is before*: As above (BAd 56–57), BAd follows Bellenden (VI 5) in reporting that the stolen hound was white.

N 227–28, BAd 209–10, BAs 181–82: What BAd and BAs call *þe first conventioun* is the original requirement of matrilineal succession supposedly imposed on the Picts by the Scots. The implication is that Kenneth claimed the Pictish crown through a Pictish mother or perhaps grandmother.

BAd 211–12: *and sua þai alsua and þe Britonnis*: This passage makes no sense, and though comparison with N and BAs makes it easy to see where the BAd-scribe was going, it is difficult to see how his sentence might be emended to get him there. He means, of course, that of the four peoples then living in Britain, only the Saxons were pagan; the Britons, Picts, and Scots were all Christian. Bower says only that the Saxons were pagan.

N 241–45, BAd 205–06, BAs 178–80: The various king-lists of the X group show 56–65 Pictish kings, of which the last is Drust, son of Ferach. Bower lists Drust as sixty-third and gives 1207 years as the span of Pictish rule. If the final battle is assumed to have been in Kenneth's twelfth year, that would be 854. But according to J. L. Roberts (*Lost Kingdoms*, p. 15), there is no contemporary evidence that such a battle even took place.

The claim of multiple victories is perhaps based ultimately on the statement in the *Chronicle of the Kings of Alba* that Kenneth invaded Northumberland six times (see Marjorie Anderson, *Kingship*, p. 250). N's seven victories in six battles may result from the resemblance of *septies* and *sexties* in some hands. BAs follows Bower in reporting seven victories in one day.

However it occurred, the loss of the Pictish language was nearly total. Almost all that remains are kings' names, place names, and a few inscriptions.

BAd 214–15: Kenneth was engaged in warfare on several fronts – against the Britons in Strathclyde, the Vikings around Perth, and the Saxons in Lothian or Northumbria. Camelon was an important Pictish town. It is now part of Falkirk.

BAd 215–16: Kenneth is traditionally credited with promulgating a set of laws called the MacAlpin Code. The laws may in fact be the work of his brother and successor Donald I. In either case, the intention may have been to extend traditional Scots custom to the Picts (see Benjamin T. Hudson, *Kings*, p. 48).

BAd 217, Bellenden (X 10) tells this apocryphal tale of a noble named Bar, the leader of Kenneth's vanguard in one of the battles against the Picts, who was rewarded with a castle (or *dun*). In fact, the name of the castle long antedates the earls of Dunbar, the first of whom was granted the castle in the late eleventh century.

N 246–48, BAd 218–22, BAs 188–89 [Bower IV 15]: Kenneth died in 858. Donald I, son of Alpín, and thus Kenneth's brother or half-brother, was King of the Picts from 858 to 862. Bower gives him a wholly laudatory reputation; Bellenden (X 12–13) tells the lurid tale repeated in BAd.

N 249–52, BAd 223–26, BAs 190–92 [Bower IV 15–16]: Constantine (Constantinus, Constantyne) I (unnumbered in BAd and BAs), son of Kenneth, was King of the Picts from 862 to 876. He was continually occupied with maintaining his hold over the Pictish territory and with repelling Viking raiders. There are various traditions of the place and manner of his death – one of which, provided by Fordun and Bower, is that he was captured and killed by Vikings at the *Nigra Specus* or Black Cave. Bellenden (X 14–15) gives the names of the Viking leaders as Hungar and Hubba and says that Constantine was beheaded. Edmund, King of East Anglia from 865 to 869, was captured and killed by Vikings in Suffolk; subsequently a legend grew that he had died for his faith, and he was revered as a martyr and saint.

N 253–56, BAd 227–31, BAs 193–94 [Bower IV 16]: Áed (Ethus), called *Alipes* or "wing-foot", son of Kenneth, was King of the Picts from 876 to 878. He is the last king to be referred to as "king of the Picts" in the Irish chronicles. One of the traditions of his death, reported by Fordun and Bower, is that he was killed in battle by Giric (below) near Rossie. But contemporary sources say only that he was killed "by his companions" at "Nrurim", which has not been satisfactorily identified (see Benjamin T. Hudson, *Kings*, pp. 54–55; and Woolf, *Pictland to Alba*, pp. 116–17).

BAd 228–30: *he was . . . abill to nathing les þan the adminstratioun of his realme*: "there was nothing he was less capable of than the administration of his realm."

N 257–62, BAd 232–38, BAs 195–202 [Bower IV 17–18, Bellenden X 17–19]: Giric (Gregoir, Gregory), was not a son of Donald, but possibly of a Dungal (Dongall), otherwise unknown. For his reign, see the note to OD 239–43, OR 241–45, OA 236–38. The BAd-scribe conflates this Dungal with the earlier king he had called Dongal, then miswrites his name as Congall, and finally confuses the Spey with the Tay; see the note to N 207–09, BAd 185–88, BAs 164–66.

The claim that Giric granted liberty to the Scottish Church comes from one of the early king-lists. Marjorie Anderson (*Kingship*, p. 198) suggests that he may have ended the proprietary rights that landowners exercised over churches and granted them something like the autonomy of the Irish monastic churches. It is not recorded that such measures were ratified by Pope John VIII, who reigned from 872 to 882 and who approved the decisions of a council held at Constantinople in 879–80, referred to by Fordun as the Fifth Council of Constantinople, and mistakenly in BAd as the First.

Except for the continued pressure of the Scots southward on Strathclyde and Northumberland, the claims of empire for Giric are false. For both his ecclesiastical and his military achievements, see the extended note by John and Winifred MacQueen (Bower, *Scotichronicon*, vol. 2, pp. 468–69).

BAd 238: *fra oure redemptioun*: This formula for dates is used habitually in BAd (but never in BAs) from this point forward. It is Bellenden's usual translation of Boece's *anno saluti* or *anno humanae saluti*. Fordun and Bower typically use *anno domini*. This formula precedes by 14 lines BAd's first citation of Bellenden by book and chapter.

N 263–66 [Bower IV 19]. John Scottus Eriugena (ca. 810–ca. 877) was not from Scotland, but from Ireland – the *Eriu* of his name means "Ireland". At the request of Charles the Bald (West Frankish king from 843 to 877 and emperor from 875 to 877), he translated the *Celestial Hierarchy* of Pseudo-Dionysius from Greek into Latin. Pseudo-Dionysius was possibly a Syrian Christian of the fifth century whose writings were ascribed to Dionysius the Areopagite, a Greek whose conversion by Paul is reported in Acts xvii 34. John may have taught at the abbey at Malmesbury, but the story of his murder by his students is false.

N 267–69, BAd 239–42, BAs 203–05 [Bower IV 20]: Donald II, son of Constantine I, was King of Scots from about 889 to 900; he is the first to be called King of

Alba in the Irish chronicles – Alba designating the Gaelic-speaking kingdom of Scots and Picts that would become the kingdom of Scotland in succeeding centuries. He may have been killed at Dunnottar; according to John and Winifred MacQueen (Bower, *Scotichronicon*, vol. 2, p. 473), the place name was later misunderstood to mean Forres.

BAd 239-40: The designation of the son of Constantine as the sixth Donald is consistent with the BAd-scribe's designation of Domnall Brecc as the fourth Donald – since Donald, son of Alpín, had reigned between them. The designation of the son of Kenneth as the second Constantine is derived from Boece as translated by Bellenden, whose first Constantine appears above (N 105–07, BAd 79–80, BAs 78–79) as Constancius and Constantinus in N and Constant in BAd. The scribe maintains his augmented count, so that Donald Bán is designated Donald VII and Constantine, son of Culen, is designated Constantine IV.

BAd 243–44 [Bower IV 18]: Norwegian Vikings, led by Rollo (ca. 860–ca. 932) raided the coast of France in the last decades of the ninth century. In 911, by the treaty of St Clair-sur-Epte, they were given part of Neustria, which came to be called Normandy. The County of Flanders was founded in 864 by Charles the Bald, who gave it to his son-in-law, Baldwin, as a reward for victories over the Vikings. This addition is taken from Bellenden (X 20).

N 270–76, BAd 245–48, BAs 206–10 [Bower IV 21, Bellenden XI 1]: Constantine (Constantyne) II / III, son of Áed, was King of Scots from 900 to about 943; he died in 952. The agreement between BAd and BAs in calling the son of Áed the third Constantine appears to be a mistake on the part of the latter scribe, Asloan, since he calls the same king Constantine II in BAs 218.

BAd 245: *Constantyne þe Thrid, sone to King Ethus*: The identical words appear in Bellenden's *Chronicles of Scotland* (XI 1). But the modern editors, Edith Batho and Winifred Husbands, have punctuated them differently: *Constantyne, þe thrid sone to King Ethus*. It is worth noting that no elder brothers have been mentioned.

The account of Constantine's setting up a system of succession is taken from Bower, but the supposed first beneficiary of the system, *Eugenius, son of Donald*, is not otherwise known.

N 277–80, BAd 249–54, BAs 211–13: [Bower IV 24–25]: In 937, Constantine, in support of an army of Vikings, attacked the English forces of King Æthelstan at a now unidentified place called Brunanburh, roughly translated by the *Brevis*-translator as Browningfield, somewhere in Northumberland. The English victory is celebrated in the Old English poem, *The Battle of Brunanburh*, included in the *Anglo-Saxon Chronicle*. Bower does not say that a son of his cousin Donald was killed there, but the *Chronicle of the Kings of Alba* says that Constantine's own son was killed. After Constantine's forces were slaughtered, he abdicated in favor of Malcolm, the son of Donald, and retired to the monastic life, probably at St Andrews. N quietly omits mentioning that the Scots were badly beaten, and only BAd gives the defeat as the reason for Constantine's abdication. He may have lived longer than 5 or 6 years; the *Ulster Annals* say he died in 952.

Culdees (from *céli Dé* meaning "companions of God") were zealous but loosely organized religious communities, often attached to collegiate or cathedral churches.

BAd 250–52: The phrase *exonerat . . . of . . . princely dignite* and the detail that Constantine became a regular canon are apparently taken directly from Bellenden (XI 1–2).

BAd 253–54: *In þe xi buke, capitulo x⁰.* Bellenden covers Constantine's reign in XI 1. From this point to the end, BAd frequently supplies references to Bellenden. Except where they are corrected in these notes, the references are accurate.

N 281–88, BAd 255–59, BAs 214–16 [Bower IV 26–27]: Malcolm I, son of Donald II, was King of Scots from about 943 to 954. Malcolm and Edmund the Elder, King of England, entered into an alliance against Cumbria (also called Strathclyde and extending far north of present-day Cumbria), a kingdom of Britons whose flexible boundaries and allegiances are imperfectly understood. After the English had subdued the territory, the Scots occupied it and collected its revenues.

Since the end of the ninth century, the Scots had controlled part of Strathclyde, customarily installing the heir to their throne as sub-king. The concession in N that Malcolm had done homage to Edmund for the territory is perhaps overly generous, since the territory was given to an ally rather than to a vassal. But the chronicler is providing the standard defense against the claims of later English kings of overlordship over Scotland by acknowledging that some areas of northern England – but not Scotland itself – were held from the English king.

Malcolm was apparently killed by Scots, but there are conflicting traditions about whether in Mearns or Moray. John and Winifred MacQueen (Bower, *Scotichronicon*, vol. 2, p. 480) and Benjamin T. Hudson (*Kings*, p. 88) suggest that the Latin forms of the place names may have been confused. According to the *Prophecy of Berchán*, Malcolm was buried at Dunnotar, near the place of his death; Bower says he was buried at Iona.

BAd 258, BAs 216, 223: *Murray men*: The *Brevis*-translator's reference to *Murray men* is anachronistic, doubtless due to confusion in translating *Morauiensibus* – "men of Moray". The Murray family, descended from a Flemish mercenary employed by David I in the twelfth century, was, centuries later, very powerful in Moray and in the North generally. In the fifteenth century, the close association of the Murrays with their cousins the Douglases may have suggested them as rebels against the crown long before their dynasty began.

N 289–92, BAd 260–63, BAs 217–20 [Bower IV 27]: Indulf (Indulfus, Indulphe, Ildulb), son of Constantine II, was King of Scots from 954 to 962. He apparently died in a battle with Vikings in Buchan.

N 293–99, BAd 264–70, BAs 221–24 [Bower IV 28]: Dubh (Duffus, Dub), son of Malcolm I, was King of Scots from 962 to 966. According to some Irish king lists, he was murdered at Forres in Moray by unidentified hands, and his corpse remained hidden under a bridge at Kinloss during a solar eclipse (probably 20 July 966) – an indefinite period in Fordun and Bower, extended absurdly in Bellenden (XI 4) to six months and the blackout made to include the moon and the stars.

N 300–05: The verses are taken from Bower, who took them from the king-list edited by Skene as the *Cronicon Elegiacum* (*Chronicles*, lines 39–44, p. 179), but also known as the *Verse Chronicle*.

BAd 271–73: The tale of Donald, the witches, and the wax image of Dubh is from Bellenden (XI 4) and has no basis in Bower.

N 306–09, BAd 274–79, BAs 225–27 [Bower IV 29]: Culen (Culenus, Culene, Culyne), son of Indulf, was King of Scots from 966 to 971. There are various accounts of his death: in battle against the Britons of Strathclyde, in a burned house, while trying to collect taxes, or, as reported here, by an outraged nobleman.

BAd 280: These *syndry mervellis* are not reported for the reign of Culen by Bower or, surprisingly, by Bellenden. But Fordun (IV 27) reports at the end of his account of Culen a tale he says he forgot to tell earlier (and which Bower has moved back to its proper place in IV 18) – the opening of the earth to swallow an army of Scots who had plundered the church at Lindisfarne. If this is what BAd is referring to, then its placement here is the only evidence of direct use of Fordun in these chronicles. On the other hand, the near-verbatim repetition of this claim for the reign of Constantine III (below, BAd 297), where it does have a source in Bellenden, suggests that the scribe has simply misplaced it.

N and BAs, following Bower, count the Kenneths from the son of Alpín, BAd, following Bellenden (XI 6), from Kenneth Ker. The supposed victory over the Danes at Luncarty in 980 is reported by Bellenden (XI 7), but not by Bower.

Fordun is the earliest existing source of the claim that Kenneth tried to institute direct succession to the Scottish monarchy, but Benjamin T. Hudson (*Kings*, p. 103) warns that this claim "need not be set aside immediately," because the period is characterized by "much innovation in the matter of succession." For Bower, Bellenden, and these chronicles, the method of succession is a theme running through the accounts of several of the following kings. Gordon Donaldson (*Scottish Kings*, p. 12) notes that up to Kenneth's time, "In so far as there can be said to have been a rule of succession in Alba, it was that the eldest, or ablest, male of the royal house, and not the heir of line, should inherit the throne," but with the expansion of the kingdom to include English speakers in the southeast, "Tension arose between native influence on one hand and external, southern influence on the other". These chroniclers, despite the disastrous consequences (in serial minorities) of strictly hereditary succession in later centuries, are defenders of this "modern" idea and of Kenneth's supposed law that embodied it. In subsequent entries, the *Nomina*-chronicler will adopt a vocabulary of illegitimacy for the first time, reporting that Constantine III (N 322) and Grym (N 327–28) each "usurped" (*inuasit*) the kingdom, that Macbeth (N 356–57) and Donald Bán (N 409) each "intruded himself" (*se intrudens / se intrusit*) into the kingship, and that John Balliol (N 518–19) was made king "not because he had the greater right" (*non quia . . . pociora jura habuit*).

A development of the succession theme is the murder of the anachronistically-titled "Prince of Scotland" – the Tanist or designated heir to the throne. This story is in Bellenden (XI 8), but not in Bower; Bellenden names the Prince as Malcolm Duff, Lord of Cumber. Dauvit Broun (*Independence*, p. 259) thinks it likely that the idea comes from Richard Vairement (see the note to N 98–101, BAd 72–75, BAs 72–75).

The story of Kenneth's assassination by means of an arrow-firing statue is found in both Bower and Bellenden (XI 9); the trick was contrived by Fynbhellis, daughter of the mormaer of Angus, whose son Kenneth had executed. Though this tale is clearly fictional, some of the annals indicate that Kenneth was the victim of treason.

N 310: *Kenedus secundus Malcolmi filius*: It is possible that the chronicler meant "Kenneth, the second son of Malcolm", and that would have been an accurate statement, since Kenneth had an older brother, Dubh. But his practice elsewhere suggests that he meant "Kenneth II, son of Malcolm".

BAd 290: The legendary foundation of the Hay family, apparently unknown before Boece and Bellenden (XI 7), was at the legendary battle of Luncarty. Kenneth II was saved from defeat by a farmer named Hay and his two sons, who defended the king with farm implements and were ennobled as a reward.

N 321–26, BAd 291–96, BAs 233–37 [Bower IV 37]: Constantine (Causantín) III, son of Culen, was King of Scots from 995 to 997. Little is known about his short reign except the tradition of continued conflict over succession to the throne and his death at the mouth of the Almond at the hands of one Kenneth – according to Bower and Bellenden (XI 10), a bastard uncle of Malcolm, son of Kenneth II, who also died in the fight, but possibly, as suggested by Benjamin T. Hudson (*Kings*, p.104), the cousin of Malcolm, who survived the fight to become Kenneth III.

BAd 297: These marvels, as listed by Bellenden (XI 10), include rains of stones, fish washed up on the shore, a bloody moon, and failed crops.

N 327–31, BAd 298–302, BAs 238–41 [Bower IV 37, 41]: Grym is apparently a mistake for Kenneth III, son of Dubh, who was King of Scots from 997 to 1005. Benjamin T. Hudson (*Kings*, p. 105) suggests that since *greimm* is Middle Irish for "authority", *grim* may mean "chief". In the king-lists of the X type (F, I, and K) the king's sobriquet has been taken for his name – a mistake perpetuated by Fordun and Bower. The spurious Kyneduf was probably created when the N-scribe garbled *Keneth filius Duff* into *filius Kyneduf* – a blunder not in the source of the *Brevis*-translator. Bower recounts the destruction of the kingdom through civil war between Grim and the direct-succession candidate, Malcolm, son of Kenneth II.

N 332–50, BAd 303–14, BAs 242–53 [Bower IV 43–44, 46, 48]: Malcolm II (ca.954–1034), son of Kenneth II, was King of Scots from 1005 to 1034. He claimed the crown under the law of direct succession established by his father. The events of his reign are treated in different orders by N, BAd, and BAs.

Malcolm was engaged in warfare against invaders for much of his reign, defeating Danes at Mortlach in 1010 and holding Northumbrians at bay at Carham in 1018. On the other hand, he was forced by Cnut to do homage for Cumbria in 1031. He fought no battles in Ireland or Wales. During his reign, Scotland reached its present borders.

There is an uncertain tradition that Malcolm established the see at Mortlach, but also an alternate tradition that this was done by his grandson Malcolm III. In the reign of David I (1124–53), the see was transferred to Aberdeen.

Fordun and Bower criticize Malcolm II for excessive generosity in giving away all his lands except for the Moot Hill at Scone. They note that he kept the revenues from wardships, reliefs, and marriages. John and Winifred MacQueen (Bower, *Scotichronicon*, vol. 2, p. 501) note the similarity of the language of Fordun and Bower on this matter to that of the *Leges Malcolmi Makkenneth*, but point out that that document reflects the language of more than a century later.

Bower says that Malcolm was ambushed at night near Glamis by descendants of the previous kings Constantine and Grim, whom he had killed. Bower labels Malcolm's actions just and his murderers treacherous; the claim that he had grown avaricious in his old age comes from Bellenden (XI 18).

BAd 307: *and pair mariages*: The noun is syntactically parallel to *wairdis and releiffis,* not to *him.*

BAd 315: According to a legend supplied by Bellenden (XI 16), the Keith clan is descended from a young warrior who, in 1010, killed an invading Viking leader named Camus and was rewarded by Malcolm II with estates in East Lothian.

N 351–54, BAd 316–20, BAs 254–57 [Bower IV 43, 49]: Duncan I, grandson of Malcolm I through his mother, Bethoc (Beatrice, Beatrix), was King of Scots from 1034 to 1040; his father was Crinán, Abbot of the secular monastery of Dull (or Dunkeld). Bower follows Fordun in taking pains to explain, mistakenly, that an *abthane* is not an abbot, but a lay lord.

Duncan became king in 1034 – as Archibald Duncan notes (*Making of the Kingdom*, p. 99), "the first instance of succession in the direct line since the mid-ninth century." But Gordon Donaldson points out (*Scottish Kings*, pp. 12–13) that this was "contrary to the old rules" and he was attacked by Macbeth, who, "by native principles" claimed the throne – in "a native, or Celtic, reaction against the new southern ways."

During his reign, Duncan did indeed fight with Vikings, led by Thorfinnr, Jarl of the Orkneys, but it was Thorfinnr who had the sundry victories, conquering much of the north and west of Scotland. Donnchad was killed by his cousin Macbeth (Machabeda, Makbethe), the ruler of Moray, probably in battle in 1040. He was buried at Iona.

BAd 321: [Bellenden XII 5]: Boece traces the history of the Stewarts from the bastard son of Fleance, son of the murdered Banquo, and the daughter of the Prince of Wales. The story of Macbeth in Holinshed's chronicle was based upon the Latin chronicle of Boece and the version of Bellenden published ca.1536–40, and Holinshed was in turn the source for Shakespeare's play. See Mapstone, "Shakespeare and Scottish Kingship", 158–98, and Royan and Broun, "Versions of Scottish Nationhood," 179.

N 355–62, BAd 322–29, BAs 258–65 [Bower IV 51, 54]: Macbeth (Machabeda, Makbethe) was King of Scots from 1040 to 1057. He had been the ruler of Moray before he became king. Macbeth's genealogy is disputed, but Bellenden's account (XII 1) that he was a grandson of Malcolm II is the probable source of BAd's claim that he was the *nepote* of Malcolm III. He gained the throne after Duncan was killed in internal strife, apparently brought on by his inability to contain attacks by the English and the Vikings. Macbeth initially had a reputation as a generous and pious ruler, but he eventually alienated some members of the Scottish aristocracy. Duncan's sons, Malcolm and Donald Bán (or Wan, meaning white), both still children, were taken out of Scotland, the former possibly finding refuge with King Edward of England, the latter perhaps in the Hebrides. Macduff, a descendant of Dubh, was apparently a laird of Fife, but most of what Fordun and later historians tell us of him is unsupported by historical evidence.

N 356, BAd 323, BAs 259: *Canmor*: See the note to OR 172, OA 166.

N 363–87 [Bower V 1–6]: John and Winifred MacQueen (Bower, *Scotichron-icon*, vol. 3, pp. 179–81) speculate that the dialogue between Malcolm and MacDuff was already a literary development of the Macbeth story by the time Fordun recorded it. They characterize it as "a brief Manual of Kingship which has relevance for times later than those of Macbeth."

N 388–93, BAd 330–33, BAs 266–69 [Bower V 7]: In 1054, King Edward of England sent Malcolm's uncle, Siward, Earl of Northumbria, north with an army to put Malcolm on the throne. After bloody fighting, Siward managed to establish Malcolm in Lothian and Cumbria, while Macbeth remained in power north of the Mounth. On 15 August 1057 (not 5 December 1056), Malcolm fought Macbeth at Lumphanan, near Aberdeen, and killed him. BAd confuses Lumphanan with Dunsinane, a hill in Perthshire where Macbeth had survived a defeat in 1054.

N 394–97, BAs 270–71 [Bower V 8]: Upon Macbeth's death, Lulach, called the Fool, his stepson, the son of Gruoch (Shakespeare's Lady Macbeth), was made king by Macbeth's followers at Scone in opposition to Malcolm. He was killed at Essie in Strathbogie in Aberdeenshire in 1058. His rule, such as it was, lasted seven months, not four years as reported in BAs.

BAd 333: *In þe xiii buke, capitulo quarto*: Bellenden covers Macbeth's reign in XII 4–7.

N 398–407, BAd 334–42, BAs 272–78 [Bower V 9, 17–18, 25–26]: Malcolm III, son of Duncan I, was King of Scots from 1058 to 1093. He assumed the crown on St Mark's Day (25 April) 1058. The next year he married Ingebjorg, daughter (or possibly widow) of Thorfinn, Earl of Orkney; with her he had three sons. After she died, about 1069, he married the great-niece (not the daughter) of King Edward of England, the saintly and fecund Margaret (ca.1045–93), by whom he had six more sons and two daughters. Malcolm and Margaret founded a priory at Dunfermline shortly after their marriage. Malcolm laid a cornerstone of the Norman cathedral of Durham in the last year of his life. While invading Northumberland, Malcolm was killed on 13 November 1093 at Alnwick (much later the seat of the Percies) by an English force under Robert de Mowbray, Earl of Northumberland. Margaret died four days later. Malcolm and Margaret were buried in Dunfermline Priory – a significant break with the traditional royal burial at Iona. Margaret was canonized in the thirteenth century. Edward, the eldest son of Malcolm and Margaret, was killed with his father; Malcolm's other sons survived him.

N 408–13, BAd 343–53, BAs 279–85 [Bower V 29–30]: Donald III, called Bán (or Wan), younger brother of Malcolm III, was King of Scots from 1093 to 1094 and again from 1094 to 1097. He seized the throne upon his brother's death, ignoring the claims of Malcolm's surviving sons – four of whom did ultimately wear the crown. Within six months, Duncan, a legitimate son of Malcolm by his first marriage, succeeded in driving his uncle out of Scotland and having himself made king as Duncan II. (Duncan is regarded by Fordun and Bower and their successors as illegitimate, since it was the offspring of Margaret who would continue to rule Scotland.) In another six months, in November 1094, Duncan was killed in battle against his half-brother Edmund. Donald then returned and reigned for another three years. Bower reports that while the Scots were busy fighting one another, Norwegians under King Magnus Barelegs conquered the Orkneys and the Western Isles, but these conquests actually occurred in 1098, during the reign of Edgar.

N 414–17, BAd 354–62, BAs 286–89 [Bower V 34–35]: In 1097, Donald was captured, blinded, and imprisoned by another nephew, Edgar, the third (not the "elder") son of Malcolm III and Margaret and the second oldest of the five who were still alive; Donald died in prison, probably in 1099. Edgar was King of Scots from 1097 to 1107. He died in Edinburgh Castle. Coldingham Priory had been founded in the seventh century, but in 1098 was given by Edgar to the Benedictine monks of St Cuthbert in Durham.

BAd 358–59 [Bellenden XII 14]: The First Crusade (1095–1100) resulted in the capture of Jerusalem. In June 1098 in Antioch, a lance unearthed under the cathedral was declared to be the one that had pierced Jesus's side. The significance of this for the BAd-scribe is apparently that the location of the lance was supposedly revealed by St Andrew in a vision. The scribe uses almost the same phrase as Bellenden: þe spere þat persit Cristis hart.

BAd 359–61: Malcolm's elder daughter, Eadgith, also called Matilda, married King Henry I in 1100. His younger daughter, Mary, married Eustace, Count of Boulogne, in 1102.

N 418–30, BAd 363–71, BAs 290–95 [Bower V 36, 40–41]: Alexander I, fifth son of Malcolm III and Margaret, was King of Scots from 1107 to 1124. He was called "the Fierce" for his suppression of a rebellion in Moray – one of several insurrections he put down. He was a benefactor of the Church, founding an Augustinian Priory at Scone and projecting the construction of a church at Inchcolm (which was actually built later by his brother David). Inchcolm is an island, originally called *Emonia*, in the Firth of Forth; *Inchcolm* means "Island of Columba". The priory at St Andrews was projected by Alexander, but was not founded until 1140, in the reign of David I. Robert, the first prior, "probably wished from the beginning to recruit the *céli Dé* (Culdees) as canons", but failed "despite papal and royal approval" (Duncan, "Foundation", p. 1). (For Culdees, see the note to N 277–80, BAd 249–54, BAs 211–13.) Alexander married late in life and died without issue. He was buried at Dunfermline Priory.

N 424–25: *Cursum Apri*: The area around St Andrews was once called Cursus Apri, apparently indicating the feeding ground of boars. It is now called Boar's Raik.

BAd 365: *dantit pame be singular manheid*: This phrase closely follows Bellenden's wording (XII 15): *dantit thevis with singulair manhede*.

BAs 295: *and first callit it Ymonye*: "and [he] first called it Emonia."

N 431–37, BAd 372–77, BAs 296–302 [Bower V 41–44]: David I, sixth son of Malcolm and Margaret, was King of Scots from 1124 to 1153. This praise of the three royal brothers is ultimately derived from William of Malmesbury (*Gesta Regum Anglorum* V 400), whom Fordun and Bower cite.

N 438–44, BAd 378–82, BAs 303–08: A decade before becoming king, David had married Matilda, daughter of Waltheof, the long-dead Earl of Huntingdon and Northumberland, who was in turn the son of Siward, one of King Cnut's Danish retainers. By this marriage, David himself became the Earl of Huntingdon and thus a vassal of Henry I. When Henry died in 1135, civil war broke out between his daughter Matilda and his nephew Stephen. David supported Matilda, his niece. In August 1138, he fought Stephen in the battle of the Standard in Yorkshire. It was a defeat for the Scots (a defeat these chronicles neglect to mention), but the pressure of Matilda's forces elsewhere convinced Stephen to cut a deal with David. The next year Henry of Scotland, David's only surviving son, did homage to Stephen for Huntingdon and Northumberland – possession of which would remain tenuous and disputed. Henry died a year before his father, in 1152, leaving sons Malcolm and William, who would reign in turn, and David, who became Earl of Huntingdon.

BAd 363–74: The claim that David had to fight *sindry battellis* to defend his claims as Earl of Huntingdon seems to be the BAd-scribe's elaboration on his source. Such a claim is not is Bower, N, or BAs.

N 445–51, BAd 383–86, BAs 309–12 [Bower V 48]: When David became king, there were active dioceses at Moray, Dunkeld, Glasgow, and St Andrews; during his tenure, dioceses were added or revived at Ross, Brechin, Dunblane, Caithness, Aberdeen, and Galloway. Monastic foundations during David's reign include Kelso in 1128, Melrose in 1136, Jedburgh in 1138, Newbattle in 1140, Holm Cultram in 1150, Dundrennan in 1142, Holyrood in 1128, Cambuskenneth in 1140, Kinloss in 1150–51, Berwick (a convent) before 1154, and Dryburgh in 1150. Rievaulx, founded in 1132, was not a Scottish foundation, but David was a patron of it. Tynemouth Priory, of the Benedictines (black monks), had been founded in 1085. There was a Benedictine convent at Newcastle, founded either by 1086 or by 1135; the latter date would be during David's reign. According to John and Winifred MacQueen (Bower, *Scotichronicon*, vol. 3, p. 264) no convent in Carlisle is known. They also note (p. 263) that this praise of David comes originally from the *Eulogium* of Ailred of Rievaulx as transmitted by Fordun (V 38), and that the claim of bishoprics established by David was expanded by Fordun to twelve, then reduced by Bower back to nine.

N 452–56, BAd 387–90, BAs 313–15 [Bower V 44]: Following his son Henry's death in 1152, David compelled the Scottish barons to swear allegiance to his grandsons Malcolm (aged 10) as heir to the throne and William (aged 9) as Earl of Northumbria. The third grandson, David, became Earl of Huntingdon. King David died at his residence at Carlisle in May 1153 and was buried in the Church of the Holy Trinity in Dunfermline Abbey. He had a reputation for piety, but despite the testimony of BAd and BAs, he was not considered a saint.

N 457–63, BAd 391–95, BAs 316–18 [Bower VIII 1–11]: Malcolm IV, grandson of David I, was King of Scots from 24 May 1153 to 9 December 1165 – 12 days longer than he is given credit for here. He was called the Maiden for his failure to marry. He was only 24 when he died. He was buried in the Church of the Holy Trinity in Dunfermline Abbey.

N 464–72, BAd 396–404, BAs 319–27 [Bower VIII 12, 22, 24–25, 39]: William I, called the Lion, brother of Malcolm IV, was King of Scots from 1165 to 1214. G. W. S. Barrow (*Scotland and its Neighbours*, pp. 69–70) notes William's reputation for sanctity despite his "pitiless ferocity" against the English, his excommunication by Pope Alexander III, and his half dozen acknowledged bastards. In 1178, the abbeys of Arbroath and Lindores and the convent of Haddington were founded by, respectively, William, his brother David, and their mother, Ada. In July 1174, William was captured by the English near Alnwick, owing more to his own foolhardiness than to English craft. He was held as a prisoner until February 1175 – an imprisonment of 7 months rather than 10 years – and then exchanged for his brother David and 21 lords as hostages (the *huge miney* of BAd 394) and English control of five Scottish castles. The losses to King Henry II were restored to the Scots by his son, Richard, when he became king in 1189. By the Quitclaim of Canterbury, the *status quo ante* was largely reaffirmed: William regained his sovereignty over Scotland; he continued to hold lands as Richard's liegeman in Huntingdon and Northumberland, though he was no longer recognized as earl of the latter.

N 473–79, BAd 405–409, BAs 328–30 [Bower VIII 79]: In 1182, upon the settlement of a dispute with the papacy that had led to the imposition of an interdict, Pope Lucius III sent a golden rose to William as a sign of restored favor. Bower says that Osbert, Abbot of Kelso, and Arnold, Abbot of Melrose, were among the ambassadors who carried word of the king's "zeal for God" and "efforts to [guard] the laws of his kingdom." William died at Stirling Castle and was buried at Arbroath.

N 480–94, BAd 410–22, BAs 331–41 [Bower IX 1, 29, 47, 63]: Alexander II, son of William I, was King of Scots from 1214 to 1249. In the summer of 1216, in league with rebel English barons, Alexander took a small force all the way to Dover to meet the Dauphin, the future King Louis VIII, who was asserting a claim to the English throne, and with his English allies, had occupied much of southeastern England. Alexander remained there about two weeks, doing homage to Louis for his English territories in exchange for promises of support, and then returned to Scotland. King John of England was not poisoned by his servants, but died of dysentery while campaigning against English rebels in October 1216; the claim that he was murdered is not in Bower or Bellenden. Alexander founded Pluscarden Abbey in 1230, and his mother, Ermengarde de Beaumont, founded Balmerino Abbey in 1225. Beauly and Ardchattan Priories, both founded in 1230, were not royal foundations. In 1249, Alexander led an expedition against Ewen MacDougal, Lord of Argyll, who was claiming authority over all the Isles under the protection of King Haakon IV of Norway. Alexander died of fever at Kerrera on 8 July. He was buried at Melrose Abbey.

BAs 337: *victorie of his folkis*: "victory over his [John's] followers".

BAd 422: *In þe xiii buke, cap⁰ xi, xii, xiii, xiiii*. Bellenden's coverage of Alexander's reign extends to Chapter 15.

N 495–503, BAd 423–30, BAs 342–48 [Bower X 1, 15–16, 40, XI 1–3, 10]: Alexander III, son of Alexander II, was King of Scots from 1249 to 1286. In 1263, a large Norwegian force led by King Haakon IV attempted to invade Scotland, but was inhibited by weather and the death of the king, though not in battle. An indecisive skirmish was fought at Largs between a small Scottish force led by Alexander Stewart – not by King Alexander – and a landing party of Norwegians. The skirmish resulted in nothing like the 20,000 Norwegian casualties reported here and by Fordun and Bower – or the 24,000 reported by Bellenden.

When Alexander was killed at Kinghorn in 1286 by a fall from his horse, his two sons and his daughter Margaret, Queen of Norway, were already dead. Margaret's daughter, also named Margaret, was not yet three years old; she died in Orkney en route from Norway to Scotland in 1290. Negotiations had been carried on between the guardians of the Scottish throne and Edward I of England for the marriage of Margaret to Edward's even younger son, Edward of Caernarfon.

N 504–10, BAd 431–37, BAs 349–54 [Bower X 1, 15–16, 40, XI 1–3, 10]: Margaret's death left the succession in dispute, and there were initially thirteen claimants. Since many of the claimants descended from the illegitimate offspring of William I, the choice eventually narrowed to John Balliol and Robert Bruce, Lord of Annandale and grandfather of the Robert Bruce who later became king. Both Balliol and Bruce were descendants of David, Earl of Huntingdon, younger brother of Malcolm IV and William I: Balliol, the grandson of David's eldest daughter, Margaret; and Bruce, the son of David's second (not youngest) daughter, Isabel. Dervorguilla (Dervergillis, Dornagilla), David's granddaughter (not daughter), was Balliol's mother. The statement that the law of Scotland favored Bruce's claim is in Bower, but not in Bellenden, though Bellenden shares these chroniclers' preference for that claim – an inevitable preference since the Scottish kings of the fourteenth, fifteenth, and sixteenth centuries were descended from Bruce's grandson, Robert, who ultimately inherited the Bruce claim.

BAd 437: *In þe xiii buke, cap° xvi, xvii, xviii, xix, xx.* Bellenden covers the reigns of Alexander and John Balliol in XIII 16–21 and XIV 1.

N 511–15, BAd 438–39, BAs 355–56: Until a successor could be chosen, the kingdom was governed by Guardians – a council of two barons, two earls, and two bishops – appointed by the Scottish Parliament in April 1286. They served until Edward I's judgment in favor of John Balliol in November 1292 – a period of just over six years and seven months.

N 516–23, BAd 440–54, BAs 357–66 [Bower XI 11, 28]. At the invitation of at least some of the Guardians and separately of some of the earls of Scotland (but not at the invitation of the Pope), Edward I of England, called Longshanks, undertook to adjudicate the rival claims. His ultimate judgment in favor of John Balliol was given on 17 November 1292; Balliol was inaugurated as King of Scots on 30 November, St Andrew's Day. Both candidates (not just Balliol) had been forced to recognize in advance that Edward had some form of lordship over Scotland. According to Norman Reid ("Great Cause", *Oxford Companion*, p. 281), "there is no evidence, despite subsequent popular myth, that there was any contemporary feeling that Balliol's elevation to the kingship was unjust or corrupt."

In July 1295, the Scottish Parliament took control of the government from John Balliol and gave it to a council of twelve magnates – apparently this coup is what the BAd-scribe means by *Þe nobillis withstude.* William Wallace (ca. 1272–1305), a knight's son and later a knight himself, rose from obscurity to lead the Scottish resistance to the English in the power vacuum that followed the abdication of John Balliol in 1296. The assertion that Wallace was *inspyrit be God* apparently comes from Bower's statement (XI 28) that God *omnia eius opera dirigebat* ("directed all his works"). Robert Bruce (1274–1329), grandson of the Robert Bruce who had claimed the throne in 1291 and son of the Robert Bruce who had succeeded to that claim in 1295 and who died in 1304, joined with Wallace in 1297, but went over to Edward in 1302, and then changed sides again and seized the Scottish crown in defiance of Edward in 1306, the year after Wallace's death. The reference to *þe cuming of þe Bruce* glosses over these changes to allow three generations of Robert Bruces to seem to be one and to make Wallace and Bruce appear to be allied heroes of a seamless and continuous Scottish resistance. In fact, it is clear from one of Wallace's charters (cited by Barrow, *Bruce*, p. 91) that he considered himself fighting "in the name of the famous prince the Lord John, by God's grace illustrious King of Scotland."

N 524–37, BAd 455–66, BAs 367–76 [Bower XI 20]: On 30 March 1296 (the Friday after Easter, not Good Friday; and the III, not the IV kalends of April), King Edward attacked Berwick simultaneously by sea and land. He captured the town without resorting to a ruse and without heavy losses, except for a few ships that had landed prematurely and were burned by the Scots. Thousands of the male inhabitants may have been slaughtered after capture. When Edward returned the following year, it was not to recapture the town, but to relieve an English garrison that had been besieged by the Scots. In misdating the attack, these chronicles are following Bower. In underestimating the casualties, Asloan is following Bower; the BAd-scribe has apparently dropped a zero.

N 538–44, BAd 467–71, BAs 377–81 [Bower XI 21, 29–30]: During the absence of the Bishop of St Andrews from the country in 1296, his two vicars-general, William of Kinghorn and Peter de Campagne, removed 26 members of the English clergy from their benefices. Wallace does not seem to have been *þe executour þairof* or indeed to have played any part in this action, although Bower says he was involved in it. But in September 1297, Wallace won a significant victory over an English army at Stirling Bridge; Edward's treasurer, Hugh Cressingham, was killed. In the wake of this victory, Wallace was knighted and proclaimed "Guardian" of the kingdom.

N 545–54, BAd 472–74, BAs 382–84: At Stainmore in Cumbria, the English army withdrew from the battlefield before fighting began. These chronicles omit all reference to Wallace's defeat at Falkirk in 1298.

N 555–60, BAd 475–78, BAs 385–88 [Bower XII 3]: Edward campaigned in Scotland in 1298, 1300, and 1301 as well as in 1303, finally gaining effective control over the country in 1304. The claim that Edward *slew all his resistaris* is not true, but is perhaps based on Bellenden's statement (XIV 6), that Edward *wan sindry castellis of Scotland be force, and slew all þat war foundin in þe samyn*. In fact, Edward hanged some of the garrison of Caerlaverock Castle when it surrendered in 1298. Wallace remained temporarily at large, where these chroniclers are content to leave him, making no mention of his betrayal to Edward by fellow Scots in 1305, his trial at Westminster, or his savage execution. As these matters are clear in their sources, they must have been omitted intentionally.

N 555–56: *cum Principe Wallie, Vasconie, Normannie, et Ybernie*: Edward Caernarfon, the Prince of Wales, accompanied his father on this campaign. Bower (XII 3) has *cum potencia magna nimis Anglie videlicet Wallie et Hibernie Vasconie et Sabawdie cuius comes personaliter secum fuit et eciam princeps Wallie* ("with a very large force drawn from England, Wales, Ireland, Gascony, and Savoy, whose count was also present with him in person, and also the Prince of Wales").

N 561–69, BAd 479–80, BAs 389–90 [Bower XII 4, 8]. Robert Bruce, the future Robert I, did not spend 1302–04 living in England, but in the service of Edward campaigning against Scottish holdouts like Wallace, Simon Fraser, and John Comyn, Lord of Badenoch. When his father died in 1304, Bruce inherited large estates in England and a claim to the throne of Scotland. His assumption of the burden to which, according to the chronicler, God called him, began in February 1306 with his assassination of his chief rival, John Comyn, at the altar of Greyfriars' kirk in Dumfries. None of these chroniclers betrays any knowledge of these unsavory details.

N 564: *Mathathyas*: Mattathias was a second-century BC Jewish priest who led a guerrilla revolt against the Seleucid king, Antiochus IV. He was succeeded by his son Judas Maccabeus. This allusion is apparently based on the *Declaration of Arbroath*, which describes Bruce as *velut alter Machabaeus aut Josue* ("like another Maccabeus or Joshua").

N 566–67: *Regem potentissimum Anglie, ducem Normannie Equitanie et Andegauie dominum Ybernie et Wallie*: Edward I's titles.

N 570–89, BAd 481–87, 490–95, BAs 391–401: The BAd-scribe has reversed the order of events, putting the battle of Bannockburn before Robert's coronation. N and BAs have the correct order and the correct dates.

N 570–80, BAd 490–95, BAs 391–95 [Bower XII 9, 11]: After four years of grudging submission and service to Edward I, and shortly after his rash murder of John Comyn, Robert Bruce had himself crowned King of Scots at Scone on 25 March 1306 (the VIII, not the VI, kalends of April – the misdating is from Bower). The sudden coronation provoked the retaliation of the ailing Edward, even as the murder ignited civil strife with the powerful Comyn clan and its allies. Bruce was immediately put on the defensive, and after being defeated that summer at Methven and Dalry, he was reduced to hiding in the mountains and keeping constantly on the move. In the fall of 1306, Bruce's second wife, Elizabeth de Burgh, was captured and imprisoned; Bruce's sister Mary, captured at the same time, was kept in a cage. Bruce's brothers Thomas, Alexander, and Neil were captured and executed. By the end of 1306, Bruce had been forced out of the country. Early in 1307, however, he was strong enough to return, and by a skillful employment of guerrilla tactics, he gradually reduced English control to a few castles and fortified towns in the south and east.

N 581–89, BAd 481–87, BAs 396–401 [Bower XII 20, 22]: In the summer of 1313, Stirling Castle was still occupied by English forces, though under siege. The commander of the garrison agreed to surrender it to Bruce if he was not relieved by Midsummer Day the following year. Thus challenged, Edward II, the inept son of and successor to Edward I, brought a large army to rescue the castle from a much smaller force under Bruce. Edward foolishly placed his forces where they could not maneuver, hemmed in by the Forth on their flank and by a small creek, called Bannockburn, to their rear. When Bruce attacked, the English were slaughtered on the field or drowned in the creek. Pursued by James, Lord of Douglas, Edward escaped to Dunbar with a force of several hundred, and from there took a boat to Berwick. Some details of Edward's escape are not in Bower, but are in Bellenden (XIV 11) and in John Mair's chronicle.

BAd 493–94, BAs 394–95: *xiii battellis . . . lvii tymes*. This martial bookkeeping is derived from John Barbour's *The Bruce* (VIII, lines 432–33), where the battles of Sir James Douglas, rather than of Robert Bruce, are summarized. The *Brevis*-translator may have misunderstood the passage, in which both Bruce and Douglas are mentioned, or he may have transferred Douglas's military exploits to Bruce on the grounds that Douglas was the king's trusted lieutenant.

N 590–91, BAd 488–89, 496–97, BAs 402–04 [Bower XIII 13]: Robert Bruce retook Berwick in 1318 and defeated Edward at Mytton-on-Swale in 1319. In the fall of 1322, he led a raid into Yorkshire and defeated the English at Byland Moor. He died in June 1329 and was buried at Dunfermline Abbey. The BAd-scribe has so confused his chronology that he has him die twice. Apparently he once had the two obituaries in reverse order, since the earlier contains the phrase *as said is*, meaning "as I said before".

BAd 496–97: *In þe xiii buke, cap. viii° to þe end.* Bellenden covers the reign of Robert Bruce in the final chapters (8–17) of his Book XIV (not XIII).

N 592–603, BAd 498–508, BAs 405–14 [Bower XIII 20–27, 48, XIV 1, 12, 18]: Thomas Randolph, Earl of Moray, was Robert Bruce's nephew, the son of the king's half-sister Isabel. On Robert's death, he became guardian for Robert's son, David, aged 5. David was crowned King of Scots at Scone in 1331. Randolph died shortly thereafter. Within months, Edward Balliol, son of John Balliol, invaded Scotland with tacit English backing. Following Scottish defeats at Dupplin Moor in 1332 and at Halidon Hill in 1333, David was taken for his safety to the French court, where he remained until 1341. Edward Balliol was crowned in 1332, but was able to hold on to power for only a few months. He maintained his claim to the throne in exile in England until 1356, when he was pensioned off to France by Edward III. In 1342, David successfully raided Northumberland. In 1346, in response to a French request to distract the English from military operations in France, David invaded England. At the battle of Neville's Cross, near Durham, the Scots were defeated, and David was captured. He remained a captive until 1357, when he was released for a promised ransom of 100,000 marks.

BAd 498–508: This passage is only partly readable because of damage to the manuscript, but it is obvious that it cannot accommodate Laing's version of the text. Whereas Laing normally takes about 28 lines of print to transcribe one manuscript page, he takes 41 lines to transcribe this one, clearly allowing himself longer emendations than the lacunae permit.

N 604–613, BAd 509–13, BAs 415–17 [Bower XIV 34]: David expressed an interest in undertaking a crusade, but nothing came of the project. In 1371, he died suddenly at Edinburgh Castle and was buried at Holyrood Abbey. The present Palace of Holyrood House was built between 1498 and 1501, at about the time the Scots versions of the chronicles were written, and the Scots writers would surely have known that he would not have been buried there. The reference to Holyrood House in the *Brevis* texts may be an allusion to the guesthouse on the grounds of the abbey where members of the Scottish royalty lived in the early fifteenth century before the palace was built. James II was born there in 1430. But it is not certain that the house was there in the late fourteenth century, and so this may be an anachronism. The BAd-scribe repeats Bellenden very closely, but the mention of the high altar is from Bower.

N 614–19, BAd 514–18, BAs 418–21 [Bower XIV 36, 41, 50]: David II having died in February 1371 without a son, his nephew Robert, son of David's half-sister Marjorie, became King of Scots and reigned until 1390. His coronation was on 26 March – the day after the Feast of the Annunciation. In 1383, Robert II renewed an alliance with the French. In 1388, a raid into England led by the Earl of Douglas, culminated in a battle at Otterburn; Henry Percy (Hotspur), son of the Earl of Northumberland, was captured by the Scots. The *Brevis* texts' confusion of Hotspur with his father the earl, also named Henry, is apparently attributable to Bellenden (XVI 1, 7), who elsewhere distinguishes father from son, but in this passage is not as careful to distinguish them as Bower is.

BAd 519: The *Brevis Cronica* breaks off here in the Advocates manuscript. But Laing's edition includes additional text, which we record here:

> . . . *after a long trane of glorious works, baith in peace and weir, finding himself infirme in his auld age, appointed his secund sone, Robert Earle of Fyfe, governour of þe kingdom in þe zeir ane þousand þree hunder auchty and nyne. Þe ambasodouris of France and Ingland came to begg of þis king a trews for þe Inglismen, which þai kneeld to obtain, and was grantit þame in favour to his confederate þe French king. He recoverit out of þe handis of Inglismen þe haill landis which þai hade possest þemselves off in þe regnne of þe tyrrane of Ingland, and so, haveing settled his kingdome in great peace and tranquilite, leaving naþing in þe hands of Inglismen belonging to Scotland except þe þree casteles of Berwyk, Jedbrugh, and Roxbrught, he deyt of a schort seiknes att his castell of Dundonald, quhence he was brocht and royallie burried at Scone, þe zear of oure redemptioune ane þousand þree hundreth and nyntie, xiii kallends of May þat zeir he dieyt, and þe þride day of Agust he was burieyt. He leiffit sevinty and foure zeir, and did raigne over Scotland nintene zeir and twenty-three dayis.*

Since Laing himself says that "The short Chronicle in prose at the end [of the Advocates manuscript] fills eleven leaves, but is incomplete, ending with the succession of Robert II in 1371" (*Orygynale Chronykil*, III, p. xxiv), this additional material presumably was not in the manuscript. He provides no account of its origin. Given the license Laing has assumed in filling lacunae (see the note to BAd 498–508), this text should be considered skeptically.

N 620–27, BAs 422–25 [Bower XIV 53–54]: In 1384, the Scottish parliament forced the incompetent Robert II to appoint his eldest son, John, Guardian of the realm. But four years later, when John had also proven unable to maintain order, they forced him to set John aside, on the pretext of his having been kicked in the leg by a horse, and to appoint his second son, Robert, Duke of Albany, Guardian in his brother's place. In 1390, Robert II died at Dundonald Castle and was buried at Scone.

N 628–35, BAs 426–32 [Bower XV 1]: When Robert's son John succeeded to the throne, he changed his name, becoming King Robert III. See the note to VC 506–08.

But since the new king was still considered incompetent, his brother, Robert, Duke of Albany, continued as Guardian. Robert III's eldest son, David, Duke of Rothesay (1378–1402), was appointed Lieutenant (Guardian) in 1399 for a term of three years, replacing his uncle, who had become his rival for control of the government. This rivalry led ultimately to David's arrest, confinement, and death in the custody of his uncle – probably without the involvement of his father. See the note to VC 509–16.

N 636–42, BAs 433–36 [Bower XV 18]: This is substantially the account given by Bower. But see the note to VC 517–27. James was 11 years old at the time of his capture at sea off Flamborough Head – a little south of Scarborough. Robert III died two weeks later, in April 1406 – not 1404; he was buried in Paisley Abbey. Oddly, though the chronicler has the year wrong, he has the length of reign right. N follows Bower in correctly stating the length of James's captivity at 18 years (until April 1424); BAs has added a year.

N 643–49, BAs 437–41 [Bower XV 37]: During the captivity of James I, his uncle Robert, Duke of Albany, continued as Lieutenant until his death in 1420. He was succeeded by his son Murdoch, who proved inadequate to the responsibility. The faults left unpunished, mentioned in BAs, included those of his own wild sons.

N 650–54, BAs 442–45 [Bower XVI 27]: James I returned to Scotland in April 1424. While still a prisoner, on 2 February 1424, he had married Joan Beaufort, daughter of John Beaufort, Earl of Somerset, and Margaret de Holand – the latter apparently confused here with her sister-in-law, Margaret de Neville, wife of Thomas Beaufort, Earl of Dorset. James and Joan were crowned at Scone on 21 May.

N 655–61, BAs 446–50: In 1429, James founded a Carthusian monastery (Charterhouse) in Perth, known as the Vale of Virtue. In 1436, James's 11-year-old daughter Margaret married Louis, Dauphin of France, later Louis XI. In February 1437, James was staying at the priory of the Dominicans (Black Friars) in Perth. There he was assassinated by a group of eight conspirators headed by Sir Robert Graham and his own uncle Walter Stewart, Earl of Atholl. The assassins were aided by Sir Robert Stewart, the king's chamberlain. The conspirators were tortured before they were executed. James was buried in the monastery he had founded.

BAs 451–55: James II, son of James I, was King of Scots from 1437 to 1460. He was crowned in Holyrood Abbey in Edinburgh on 25 March 1437 (the Feast of the Annunciation), at the age of 6. He was accidentally killed at the siege of Roxburgh, when a cannon exploded near him. He was buried at Holyrood Abbey.

BAs 456–58: James III, son of James II, was King of Scots from 1460 to 1488. He was crowned at Kelso in 1460, at the age of 9. A coalition of nobles, joined by his son, the future James IV, defeated him at Sauchieburn, near Stirling. He was killed there, apparently in battle. He was buried at nearby Cambuskenneth Abbey.

BAs 459–62: James IV, son of James III, was King of Scots from 1488 to 1513. He was crowned at Scone on 26 June, 1488 – two days after the Feast of John the Baptist. On the night of 28 or 29 August 1513 (the latter day being the commemoration of the beheading of John the Baptist), James captured Norham Castle, on the south side of the Tweed, the border with England. James was killed three weeks later at the disastrous Scottish defeat at Flodden. John Asloan apparently chooses to mention neither the defeat nor the death, but allows his chronicle to end with a Scottish victory; but Van Buuren suggests that Asloan's exemplar (or perhaps just the fascicle of the Asloan manuscript in which this chronicle appears) was written in 1513 after the victory at Norham, but before the defeat at Flodden in September. If the exemplar ended with the victory at Norham, "perhaps Asloan did not care to bring it up to date, or he was not asked to do so" (*Buke of the Sevyne Sages*, p. 41).

The St Andrews Chronicle

The notes to each section of the *St Andrews Chronicle*, each organized around the reign of a supposed Scottish king, include a reference to its source in Hector Boece's *Historia Scotorum* by book number.

StA 1–7 [Boece I]: Fergus, the legendary son of the legendary King Feredach of Ireland, is traditionally the first king of the Scots living in Scotland, according to Fordun (II 12) and Bower (II 12) in the fourth century BC. The *chyr of marbyll stane* means the Stone of Destiny (actually of red sandstone), upon which much later Scottish kings were crowned. Boece (but not Fordun or Bower) reports that Fergus came to Scotland to defend the Scots who were already living there against the Picts, but once the armies of the Scots and Picts were drawn up to fight one another, he concluded an alliance with the Picts, and with their help, defeated the army of the Britons, led by King Coilus. But the *St Andrews*-chronicler has omitted any indication of the enmity of the Picts.

Returning to Ireland, Fergus drowned when his ship was wrecked off the coast of Ulster on a rock subsequently named for him – modern Carrick-fergus in Northern Ireland. Fordun and Bower do not mention any kings between Fergus and Rether (StA 29–33).

StA 6–7: *and beris þe name throw him*: "and it has its name from him."

StA 8–15 [Boece II]: According to Boece, Fergus's brother Feritharis tried to resign his crown in favor of Fergus's son, but his council would not agree. Feritharis was subsequently murdered. The nephew then fled south to the Britons.

StA 16–19 [Boece II]: Maynus, Fergus's younger son, is given a good report by
Boece. He is credited with erecting the ancient stone monuments that have
survived to the chronicler's times.

StA 20–24 [Boece II]: The chronicler has not mentioned any previous truce with
the Britons, but Boece has said that Fergus granted one after defeating them.

StA 20: *Mayni sone*: The chronicler has preserved the Latin genitive of *Maynus*,
as he does later with *Drusti* (StA 34) and *Gilli* (StA 50).

StA 25–28 [Boece II]: The Lord of Galloway who kills Nothacus is identified in
StA 31 as Dowall. Boece calls him Lord of Brigantia, the Romans' name for
the territory, occupied by the British tribe of the Brigantes, lying north of the
Humber and Mersey and south of the Solway Firth. The chronicler routinely
changes all occurrences of *Brigantia* to *Galloway*, thus moving the territory
and its associated history within the borders of modern Scotland.

StA 29–33 [Boece II]: Rether appears in the *Nomina* and the *Brevis Cronica* (N
47–50, BAd 35–37, BAs 36–38) as the eponym for Redesdale, and Fordun (II
13) and Bower (II 13) mention him only in connection with that story. To
them he is the great-great-grandson of Fergus, rather than, as here, his great-
grandson. According to Boece, Rether, still a child, was made king by Dowall,
without regard for the laws of election. Boece identifies Dowall as chief of
the Brigantes, actually a British tribe living south of the Tyne, not in
Galloway. According to Boece, Ferquhard, Lord of Lorne, was the father-in-
law of Nothacus, and the King of the Picts was Gethus, who fought on
Rether's side.

StA 32–33: *& þe King of Peichtis*: As comparison with Boece makes clear, this
is an addition to the list of those slain, not the subject of a new clause.

One folio appears to be missing here. The reigns of eight kings summarized
by Boece (Rutha, Thereus, Iosyne, Fynnanus, Durstus, Ewyne I, Gillus, and Ewyne
II) have passed when the text resumes on fol. 450ʳ. Neither these kings nor those
to follow, down to Eochaid, great-uncle of Fergus, son of Erc, appear in Fordun
or Bower.

StA 34–36 [Boece III]: According to Boece, Ederus was the grandson of King
Drustus (or Durstus). As a child, he was hidden away by his nurse and thus
survived when his father and brothers were killed by the tyrant Gillus in his
drive to become king. Gillus was killed by Ewyne, who succeeded to the
crown and then died. Ederus then became king, and Bredus of the Isles
invaded Argyll from Ireland to avenge the death of his kinsman Gillus. Ederus
defeated him and executed his followers.

StA 37–52 [Boece III]: With the coming of the Romans, there begin to be written
records of British history, among which is Julius Caesar's *Gallic Wars*, the
basis for most of this entry. Caesar's two reconnaissances in force occurred
in 55 and 54 BC. Neither expedition lasted more than a few weeks, but the
second extracted statements of submission and promises of tribute from a few

330

of the tribes of southeastern Britain before Caesar, "because of the sudden rebellions in Gaul" (V 22), returned to the continent. There was, of course, no "King of Britain". The Scots and Picts were not engaged.

By *Callendair Wod*, Boece may have had in mind the Callendar Wood near Falkirk where Wallace was defeated in 1297, but the name is loosely given to the Caledonian Forest, a term that might refer to any part of the vast forest that once covered much of Scotland – in any case, an area that would not see a Roman soldier until the invasion of Agricola, 137 years later. The *Ingliss cornyklur* is Thomas Gray, indeed an English chronicler, though the chronicle he wrote, *Scalacronica*, is in Anglo-Norman. Boece calls it a vulgar (vernacular) chronicle, and the *St Andrews*-chronicler has mistakenly supposed that to mean it is in English. Gray mentions a stone house *de la le boys de kalenter* ("of the Callendar Wood"), which he describes as Caesar's *pauilloun*. Homer Nearing ("Caesar Traditions", p. 225) credits Gray with the earliest connection of the building to Caesar. Fordun (II 4) may be referring to the same building when he describes a small stone structure as a landmark built by Caesar "marking the extreme limit of the Roman possessions to the north-west." He locates it "not far from the mouth of the river Caron", which flows into the Firth of Forth. The structure, later known as Arthur's O'on (oven), survived into the eighteenth century.

StA 50–51: Gillus is one of the kings presumably recorded on the missing folio, above. The harrying expedition of Murkettus, his nephew, is another attempt to avenge Gillus's killing by Ederus.

StA 52: Boece puts the end of Ederus's reign in the 26th year of the reign of Augustus, which would be 18 BC.

StA 53–58 [Boece III]: Erenus is apparently another creature of the imagination of Boece or his source – as are these laws of sexual license. Boece says that only his third law, the legendary *droit du seigneur*, lasted until Malcolm III's time. In fact, there is no credible evidence of the custom in Scotland.

StA 59–60: Erenus was arrested by the nobles for his crimes. During his first night in prison he was murdered by a servant, who thought he would win favor by this crime; but the servant was hanged instead.

StA 61–70 [Boece III]: Metellanus is a possibly historical and perhaps Pictish king, but there is no evidence of diplomatic relations with Rome. Boece, or his source, makes him the nephew of Ederus. The traditional date for the founding of the kingdom of Fergus, son of Feredach, is 330 BC. If Metellanus was in his tenth year at the birth of Jesus and reigned a total of 39 years, then he would have died about AD 29.

StA 71–80 [Boece III]: Caratacus (Caritacus) is a historical, though not a Scottish king. Known to Cassius Dio and Tacitus and surviving as Caradoc in Welsh legend, he was the successor of Cunobelinus (Shakespeare's Cymbeline) as king of the Catuvellauni in southern Britain at the time of the Claudian invasion of AD 43. Boece, or his source, has pressed him into service as the King of Scotland at a time when there was no Scotland, and indeed there were probably few Scots in what would later be Scotland. To fill the gap thus created in the equally nonexistent British kingdom, Boece provides a King of Britain named Guiderius.

In AD 43, Emperor Claudius sent an expedition under Aulus Plautius into Britain to conquer it. Eutropius (VII 13) mentions Gnaeus Sentius, who had been consul under Caligula, as a co-commander of this force. Vespasian, later emperor, commanded one of the four legions in this force. Plautius won a decisive Roman victory over Caratacus at a crossing of the Medway, but Caratacus escaped to the west. Apparently Gnaeus Sentius was not killed. Claudius joined his army in time to watch them take Colchester, then returned to Rome. According to Tacitus, the Romans conquered the Orkneys much later, during the governorship of Agricola (78–84); probably they did little more than land on the islands.

StA 81–89 [Boece III]: The British king mentioned here is Aviragus, a probably legendary king mentioned by Geoffrey of Monmouth, made by Boece the brother-in-law of Caratacus, Boece's supposed King of Scotland. Aviragus supposedly married a Roman woman, Genuissa Claudia, in AD 45. The battle referred to here is probably a dim reflection of the one fought in AD 51, somewhere in Wales, in which the Romans defeated Caratacus for the last time. Caratacus escaped once again.

StA 90–93: According to Tacitus (*Annals* XII 37), something like the exchange reported here did take place, but not with a Roman legate. When Caratacus was captured, taken to Rome, and brought before Claudius, Tacitus has him say to the emperor, "If you want to rule the world, does it follow that everyone else welcomes enslavement?"

StA 94–123: This is a confused retelling of the guerrilla war of Caratacus against the Romans (AD 43–51), summarized above (StA 81–93), but now, perhaps conflated with the campaigns of Agricola (79–84), it is presented as new material.

StA 94–113: These events are almost entirely the imaginings of Boece or his source. Vespasian was a general in the Claudian invasion of AD 43 and remained in Britain until 51, but he never campaigned in Scotland, and he never returned to Britain after that. As emperor (69–79) he sent his governors Petillius Cerialis and Julius Agricola into the north, but Caratacus had been long since captured by then.

In Boece's account, Aviragus, supposed King of Britain, believes the Romans will ultimately be defeated, so he breaks his alliance with them and "turns to the Britons" – that is, joins the Britons who are already fighting the Romans. Vespasian, sent from Rome, defeats Aviragus at York, then pursues the Picts to their capital of Camelon, while a subordinate, Aulus Plautius, moves against Caratacus's supposed capital of Caricton. In the meantime, Caratacus escapes to Dunstaffage, in Argyll. Plautius dies before he can capture Caratacus. (In fact, Aulus Plautius had been the leader of the Claudian invasion and thus Vespasian's superior; he had returned to Rome in 47.)

StA 114–23: This is the mostly true story of Caratacus's betrayal and capture. In AD 51, Plautius's replacement as governor, Publius Ostorius Scapula, defeated Caratacus in Wales. Caratacus escaped, but was turned over to Scapula by Cartimandua, Queen of the Brigantes. She was not his stepmother. He and his family were taken to Rome, where they were well treated by Claudius, though probably never returned to Britain. Caratacus had two brothers, but one, Adminius, had been his enemy since before the invasion, and the other, Togodumnus, had been killed at the battle for the Medway crossing.

StA 124–43 [Boece IV]: Corbredus seems to be the creature of Boece or his source.

StA 126–29: Boece identifies this legate as the official who appears above as Ostrio (StA 114) – Publius Ostorius Scapula. Ostorius died suddenly, but not in battle, sometime in the winter of AD 51–52.

StA 130–33: Boece identifies the Roman general who fought this battle as Caesius Nasica, so it is clear that this section refers to the suppression of two revolts (AD 51–57 and 71–74) of the Brigantes under Venutius, the former husband of Cartimandua. After 51, Venutius and Cartimandua were bitter enemies, he succeeding Caratacus as the leader of the insurgency, she allying her faction with the Romans. When Venutius revolted the second time, the Romans decided that it was no longer viable to entrust their northern flank to a client state, and invaded and subdued the whole territory. Boece makes this the occasion for a territorial dispute between the Roman province and the supposed Kingdom of Scotland. According to Boece, the Romans claimed to have granted Brigantia (here called Galloway) to Caratacus for life, and since he was dead, they demanded it back. The revolts were treated simultaneously by Tacitus, so Boece's collapses them into one.

StA 134–42: Paulus Suetonius is the historical Gaius Suetonius Paulinus, Governor of Britain AD 58–61. In 59, following the rape of her daughters by Roman officials, Boudicca, Queen of the Iceni, led a massive revolt against the Romans, sacking Camulodulum (Colchester), Verulamium (St Albans), and Londinium (London). Suetonius Paulinus, who had been campaigning in Anglesey when the revolt broke out, encountered and defeated Boudicca's vastly superior forces somewhere between there and London. Tacitus, whom Boece cites, estimates 70,000 "Roman and provincial deaths" in the cities sacked, but only 400 in the battle itself, as against nearly 80,000 British deaths in the battle. Boece reports, incorrectly, that there were two battles, with 30,000 British deaths in the first.

StA 144–48 [Boece IV]: Dordanus is apparently another of Boece's creations.

StA 149–74 [Boece IV]: Boece has apparently modeled Galdus after Galgacus (or Calgacus), whom Tacitus credits with leading the Caledonii against the Romans at Mons Graupius. Boece has adapted him to his mythical narrative by making him the nephew of Caratacus, leader of the Catuvellauni, but he is in fact the first historically recorded Pict to appear in Boece's history.

StA 151: *bot he prewalyt in*: "but he prevailed only in". That is, of the three evil laws mentioned above (StA 54–57), Galdus succeeded in rescinding only the second.

StA 153–73: Under Petillius Cerialis, Governor of Britain AD 71–74, the Romans attempted to pacify Brigantia, campaigning as far north as modern Carlisle and Newcastle, then withdrawing. Under Agricola, governor 77–84, they reoccupied Brigantia, and then advanced into Galloway, Strathclyde, and Lothian and up the east coast. Agricola supported his operations with fleets off both coasts of Britain, and during the last year of his campaigning he sent a fleet all the way around the island. Boece's account of these campaigns is fanciful, not least because the British and Picts seem to have been fighting a guerrilla war, avoiding pitched battles, at least until Mons Graupius, somewhere in the Grampian Highlands in 84, which ended in the destruction or flight of the native army. Boece's sixth battle is placed back in Brigantia, perhaps reflecting the eventual Roman abandonment of Scotland after Agricola left Britain in 84. Boece's place-names, if not the sites of battles, were at least areas of Roman occupation: Kyle is near Ayr; Callendar Wood is near Falkirk; Tay Firth leads to Perth; the Mernyss is the Mearns; Inchtuthil, near Dunkeld, was a Roman fort.

Tacitus's *Agricola* has been Boece's main source for the Roman occupation. Now beyond that work, Boece returns to purely imaginary history. Not until Downgard (StA 234–39) does he record another historical king.

StA 175–79 [Boece V]: According to Boece, Lugthacus, son of Galdus, was killed at Dunstaffage when he ordered the arrest of nobles he suspected of plotting rebellion because of his crimes.

StA 179–93 [Boece V]: Mogallus, nephew of Lugthacus, is not historical, but his attack on Roman Britain reflects the reality of the period. The Roman *gret captane* wounded in battle with Mogallus is identified by Boece as Lucius Anthenous; we can find no record of such an officer.

StA 186–90: When Emperor Hadrian came to Britain in 122, he ordered a wall to be built across the country from the mouth of the Tyne to Solway Firth to keep the tribes of the north from raiding south.

StA 191–94: In old age, Mogallus committed Boece's two favorite crimes, assaulting the women and the property of his nobles, and so was pursued and killed.

StA 195–203 [Boece V]: Conarus, son of Mogallus, was arrested by his nobles and confined, the kingdom being entrusted to Argade, Lord of Argyll. When Argade himself began to exhibit the same vices, he was rebuked by his council, whereupon he reformed. Conarus died in prison. Boece dates these events to the reign of Emperor Marcus Aurelius (161–80).

StA 204–12 [Boece V]: Ethodius I, cousin of Conarus, pacified the Isles – in fact, a region with a partly Celtic and partly Scandinavian population, which would not be brought under external authority until late in the Middle Ages.

StA 209: Lucius was a legendary King of Britain. According to an early form of the legend, he wrote to Pope Eleutherus (174–89), asking for missionaries to be sent to Britain.

StA 210: *pis nobill king*: Ethodius, not Lucius.

StA 213–15 [Boece V]: Sathreal, brother of Ethodius I, was strangled in his bed by his servants because of his tyranny.

StA 216–21 [Boece V]: Donald, another brother of Ethodius I, joined with the Picts and the Britons in fighting Emperor Severus on the Tyne and were decisively defeated. In fact, Severus campaigned in the north of Britain, including Scotland, 208–11.

    There is no evidence that the Gaels or Picts received Christianity a century earlier than the Britons.

StA 220–21: *& cur3eit mony & deit & herdyt lyk ane Cristyn man*: "and cared for the souls of many, and died, and was buried like a Christian".

StA 222–24 [Boece V]: Ethodius II was so avaricious that his nobles placed the government in the hands of his council, *pe congregatione of lordis*, who ruled without his control. When his greed grew even greater, the council had him killed.

StA 225–28 [Boece VI]: Athirco raped the daughters of a nobleman named Nathalocus, who then pursued him to the Isles. When Athirco saw that he would be captured, he killed himself.

StA 229–33 [Boece VI]: Nathalocus usurped the crown when Athirco's brother and nephews, fearing they too would be killed, fled to the kingdom of the Picts. Nathalocus sent a trusted nobleman of Moray to a witch in Iona (Colmkill) to find out whether any of his court were treacherous. The witch revealed to the nobleman that he himself would kill Nathalocus. At first shocked by the prophecy, but coming to fear that Nathalocus will hear it from another source, he carries it out. (It is worth observing that this episode receives uncharacteristically dramatic treatment in Boece, who makes us privy to the internal debate of the nobleman once he has talked to the witch, but it is stripped of its irony and psychological realism by the *St Andrews*-chronicler.)

At least one folio has been lost following the entry for Nathalocus. Missing is the summary of Boece from the first third of Book VI to the first quarter of Book VIII, covering ten kings: Fyndocus, Donald, Crathlinthus, Fyncormacus, Romachus, Angusiane, Fethelmacus, Eugenius, Fergus, and another Eugenius. With Fergus, son of Erc, though not with Eugenius, his fictive son, Boece and the *St Andrews*-chronicler regain a tenuous grasp on history, for Fergus may be the historical founder (or at least the leader) of the kingdom of Scots in Argyll at the end of the fifth century. See the notes to N 92–97, BAd 65–71, BAs 66–71 and N 98–101, BAd 72–75, BAs 72–75.

StA 234–39 [Boece VIII]: Domangart (Downgard), son of Fergus II, appears in some king-lists as a king of Dál Riata – the Gaelic settlements in southeastern Scotland that were much later to be known by that name.

StA 240–44 [Boece VIII]: Constantine does not appear in the king-lists. He is apparently an invention by Fordun or his source. Boece, in a section probably summarized on the preceding folio, now missing, claimed that Eugenius, elder brother of Domangart and Constantine, had annexed Northumbria by force. It is this land that Constantine loses.

StA 245–61 [Boece VIII]: Comgall (Congaill), son of Domangart, was the king and eponym of the Cénel Comgaill from about 506 to about 538 – more than two decades later than the reign Fordun (III 18, 21) and Bower (III 18, 21) give him (479–501) and more than a half century after the traditional date of the Anglo-Saxon Invasion. But underlying the fanciful details embellished by Boece from Bede, Geoffrey of Monmouth, and Fordun, the outline of historical events is discernible: the southward depredations of Scots and Picts in the vacuum created by the departure of the Romans, the hiring of Saxon mercenaries by the Britons, and the conquest of Britain by the Saxons.

Boece identifies the Duke of Wales, slain in battle by the Scots and Picts, as Guitellus. The King of the Britons who invites the Saxons in is Vortigern, his son and successor is Vortimere (Wortimeir), his successor is Aurelius Ambrosius (Goldyne Ambroiss), and the leader of the Saxons is Hengist (Hengeist).

StA 262–67 [Boece IX]: Gabrán (Corane or Gorane), brother of Comgall, was the king and eponym of the Cénel nGabráin from about 538 to about 558. According to Boece, he was initially successful in expanding into Pictish territory, but was killed in battle with the Picts. (Fordun and Bower say he was killed in an ambush by his nephew, Eochaid Hebdre; see the note to N 114–16, BAd 89–93, BAs 86–89.) Boece has him joining with the Picts and Britons, the latter under Arthur, against the Saxons. He says the Saxons were forced to return to the continent, except for those who agreed to be baptized. According to Boece, Corane and his chief justice used the rigor of the law to raise revenue through the confiscation of the goods of criminals. When some merchants were executed for slight offenses in Forres, some nobles of Murray, who were related to the merchants, killed the king in his bedchamber in Inverlochy, by Boece's dating, in 535.

StA 268 [Boece IX]: Eugenius is another apparent creature of Fordun (III 24) or his source, there made a nephew of Gabrán named Eochaid Hebdre. Boece says that he fought alongside Mordred, King of the Picts, against Arthur in the battle in which both Mordred and Arthur were killed. See the note to N 114–16, BAd 89–93, BAs 86–89.

TEXTUAL NOTES

LA VRAIE CRONICQUE

VC 1–2: S'ensieut en brief ... et quatre]
om. G; Cy apres s'ensuit la cronique
d'Escoce abregié faisant mencion dont
premiers vindrent les Escoçois. Et pour
cause de briefté delaisse tous les roys
qui ont esté oudit pays. Et commence
au roy Macolin qui espouse Sainte
Marguerite d'Escoce *A;* Ci commence
la Vraie Cronique d'Escoce abregié *P.*

VC 14: ce] *G; om. A B P.*

VC 15: cest] sest *B P.*

VC 34–35: grande quantité de biens, or]
grande quantité de biens, argent *P.*

VC 35: et joyaulx] et autres choses *add. G.*

VC 46: sa femme] Scota *add. A G P.*

VC 56: Et par long temps ledit pays a esté
nommé la grant Escoce] *om. P.*

VC 56: la] *A G;* le *B.*

VC 97: montaignes] montaigne *B.*

VC 101: que] *G; om. A B P.*

VC 118–19: Angistland, qui est autant a
dire comme la terre de] *om. G.*

VC 133: Kyneth] *A G P;* Knout *B.*

VC 147: Adelstan] *G;* Adelean *B;* Adelcan
A P.

VC 179–80: et de Artheknoudt, son second
filz] *om. A P*

VC 212: commença a regner et ne se tenoit
content] *om. G.*

VC 214–15: grans prisez qu'il avoit faittez]
ou royame d'Angleterre pour la guerre
qu'il leur commença a faire en
retournant de faire une course *add. P.*

VC 226: Beauclerc et avecquez] le roy
add. A G P.

VC 230: de Tynne jusquez a la riviere de
Twyth, et depuis la riviere de] *om. G.*

VC 253–54: de sa france volenté] *om. A G
P.*

VC 257: unes] *A P;* une *B G.*

VC 258–301: comme par le contenu ...
regni nostri primo] *om. A.*

VC 260–61: Copia littere regi ... regni
Scocie concesse] *om. G.*

VC 272: pactiones] factiones *G P.*

VC 274–75: et nos facimus ei et
successoribus suis quicquid
antecessores nostri de jure facere] *P;
om. B G.*

VC 281: obtinuerunt] obtinuerut *B.*

VC 286: vel feudis] *G;* ve vel ferdis *B;* ve
vel feodis *P.*

VC 289: de] *om. B G P.*

VC 310–11: les bordures d'Angleterre et
d'Escoce] lesdiz roy Henry et roy
Alexandre *add. A G P.*

VC 312–13: et furent ... a cheval] et
furent montez a cheval et armez *A;* et
furent montez a cheval et bien armés
P.

VC 335–45: Nota que on dit ... dessus
est declairé.] *G, om. A B P.*

VC 351: fut] *A G P; om. B.*

VC 367: firent] *A G P;* furent *B.*

VC 369: et avoient recours a luy] *G;* et
avoit recours au roy d'Angleterre *A P;
om. B.*

VC 371: le] *A G P om. B.*

VC 399: feaulté] *A G;* foyauté *B P.*

VC 399–404: Et a ce se consentirent ...
roy d'Angleterre] dont tout le peuple
d'Escosse fut desplaisant et se mal
contenta et dirent que la sentence ja
n'avoit donnee au proufflit dudit
Baileul si non pource que il avoit
promis de se faire homme du roy
d'Angleterre. Et a ce se consentirent
tous les prelaz, contes, barons, et
seigneurs dudit pays qui estoient en la
compaignye desdites parties audit lieu
de *G.*

VC 401: Yorc] *om. G.*

VC 410: fut] *G; om. A B P.*

VC 422–23: Edouart le second, dit de
Canervain. Et pareillement morut ledit
Jehan de Bailluel, delaissié son filz
heritier] *om. A;* delaissié son filz
heritier, Edouart *om. P.*

VC 446: marcs] *P;* marc *B G;* mars *A.*

VC 452–53: filz du premier Edouart de
Bailleul] *om. G P.*

VC 455–56: son filz, hors du royame] hors
son filz du royame *A B G*; filz dudit
Robert de Brus hors d'Escoce du
royaume *P*.

VC 517: perçus] perchuz *G*; percluz *A*.

VC 518: mouvoir] bouger *A G*.

VC 528: Henry le ve] *A G P*; Henry le
quart *B*.

VC 534–35: l'aisné filz . . . Charles le viie]
l'aisné filz de France le viie *A*; l'aisné
filz du roy de France le viie *G*; l'aisné
filz de France Charles le viie *P*.

VC 536: Janstan] *G;* Jaspin *A B*; Jaspis *P*.

VC 537: duc] *G*; conte *A B P*.

VC 543: tua] toute roidde *add. G*.

VC 547: . . .] *left blank in B G P*; David *A*.
See explanatory note.

VC 550: Toussains] et Noël *add. G*.

VC 551: Fin . . . Escoce] *om. G*; Fin du
cronique d'Escoce abregié *A*; Fin de la
cronique d'Escoce abregié *P*.

THE SCOTTIS ORIGINALE

OD 3: in] *om.*

OR 8: send] *om.*

OR 11: rase] ~~was~~ rase.

OR 20: fra] *om.*

OD 23: Sa] ~~Fra~~; Sa *added above line in
same hand.*

OR 28: conquiroris] conquirit.

OD 35: desertissima] destissima.

OR 39: pacifica] ~~et~~ (*or perhaps* ~~at~~)
pacifica.

OR 49: vs] *added above line in a different
hand.*

OD 74: foundit and] foundit ~~in~~ and.

OR 61: war] *om.*

OR 62: Rase] Vase.

OR 79: evo] uno.

OR 83: ane] ~~ane þe north~~ ane.

OR 86: war] *added above line in modern
hand, in brackets, apparently in pencil.*

OR 91: þai war] *added above line in
modern hand, in brackets, apparently
in pencil.*

OR 95: tald] *om.*

OR 96: he] ~~he~~ he.

OR 102: rugientis] ruguentis.

OD 110: preserue] presue.

OR 121: debbete] debbete *overwritten to*

dedbete; dedbait *added in margin in a
different hand.*

OD 134: &] ~~þat~~ &.

OD 135: agayne] *om.*

OD 154: lesynes] besynes.

OD 155: of] *om.*

OA 144: in] *om.*

OA 162: come] *om.*

OR 173: þis] þar.

OA 171: be] *om.*

OA 184: present] pnt', *perhaps
unconsciously copied from the Latin
source.*

OA 186: fals] fas.

OA 194: Romanis] Romanis and war king
of it. *Apparently an eyeskip from the
following line.*

OA 197: changis] changit.

OA 205: or] of.

OA 221: if] it.

OR 221: of Ingland] *inserted above line,
possibly in same hand.*

OR 232: neuir] *short word crossed out in
red and then scraped before* neuir.

THE CHRONICLE OF THE SCOTS

S 1: was] was was.

S 1: thousand] ~~hundir~~ thousand.

S 3: thousand] ~~s~~ thousand.

S 39: Christ] ~~God~~ Christ.

S 40: hir] *added in margin in another
hand.*

S 46: he in] he ~~be~~ in.

S 55: ȝer] *inserted above line in another
hand.*

S 81: xcii] xii.

S 83: xcvi] xvi.

S 86: xcvii] xvii.

S 142: brinyng] ~~begynnyng~~; brinyng
added above.

S 181: of] *om.*

S 194: m°] ~~a~~ m°.

S 213: Albany] Abbany.

S 216: away] away ~~&~~.

S 237: in] *inserted above line in another
hand.*

S 245: for four] ~~þan~~ for four

S 246: xxii] *corrected from* xxxi.

THE YNGLIS CHRONICLE

Y 42: come] *om.*

Y 87: Duke of Normondye and gaf all Yngland to] *An eyeskip has caused these words to appear earlier, after* Robert Curthose *in Y 83, and then again in their proper place, in Y 86:* That is to say, Robert Curthose Duke of Normondy and gaf all Yngland to William þe Ross Richert þat deit in his childhed Henry Beauclerk and Mald with vþir four childer þat deit in þar ʒouthhed and at his end day he maid Robert Curthoss Duke of Normondye and gaf all Yngland to Willam þe Ross þe secund begottin son.

Y 206: William] ~~Sir~~ William.

Y 216: trowand] trowand trowand.

Y 233: in] *om.*

Y 239: þaim] þai.

Y 241: And for his wikit deidis] *An eyeskip has caused these words to appear earlier, after the first ʒour making in Y 239.*

Y 308: fra] ~~till~~. fra *inserted above line, possibly in the same hand.*

NOMINA OMNIUM REGUM SCOTORUM

N 8: vniuersis] vniuerss.

N 12: procellis] protellis.

N 17: cum] *inserted above line.*

N 18: amicitia] amiticia.

N 35: cum] tum.

N 47: c v] c ~~Sanctus~~ v.

N 58: anno Domini l] *space left after* l.

N 68: interim] intermi.

N 86: imperante] imper-i-ante.

N 92: ccc lxxxxiii] *space left for number.*

N 114: tricesimo] *om.*

N 180: & regnauit xv annis] xv annis & regnauit.

N 183: xxx] ~~xl~~ xxx.

N 204: videlicet] *inserted above line.*

N 209: esse] ~~ces~~ esse.

N 224: e] ~~c~~ e.

N 226: nec] *inserted above line.*

N 228: est] *inserted above line.*

N 235: quidem] quid.

N 250: grauissimo] grauissimo ~~grauissi~~.

N 264: Dionisii] ~~Dios~~ Dionisii.

N 270: Donaldo] Donaldi.

N 274: obtentum] obtentus.

N 305: quoque] quique.

N 308: enim] ~~enim~~, enim *inserted above line.*

N 313: successorem] successorēs.

N 317: etatem] *inserted above line.*

N 334: legem] ~~legis~~ legem.

N 365: dissimulans] dissimilans.

N 379: me] mei.

N 459: decimum tercium] ~~xtercū~~ decimum tercium *inserted in margin.*

N 467: de] *inserted above line.*

N 471: Carlioli] Calioli.

N 471: extorsa] extorss.

N 475: ambaciatores] ~~anb~~ ambaciatores.

N 475: preciosam] *inserted above line.*

N 488: eius] ~~est~~ eius.

N 489: armamenta] armenta, *with* ma *inserted above.*

N 497: prelio] *om.*

N 521: dedecum] dedicus.

N 544: sitiens] siciens.

N 558: plebeos] o *inserted above line.*

N 591: annis] *inserted above line.*

N 595: regis] *inserted above line.*

N 611: festo] *om.*

N 644: captione] capti– *inserted in margin, disappearing into gutter* .

N 652: rediit] *om.*

THE BREVIS CRONICA

BAd 11: with] ~~his~~ with.

BAd 17: come] cone.

BAd 24: tyme] *om.*

BAd 29: ʒoung] ʒomg

BAd 31: Breik] Rorryk.

BAs 33: quhar euir it be] quhar it euir it be.

BAd 43: ar] *om.*

BAd 46: foure] ~~tua~~ foure.

BAd 56: and Pichtis huntit] ~~huntit~~ and Pichtis huntit.

BAd 62: biggit] *om.*

BAd 100: Columbe] Colunbe.

BAd 110: his] hir.

BAd 130: send] *om.*

BAd 150: as] *smudged.*

BAd 159: virtuus] vitiouss.

BAd 192: Alpyne] *om.*

BAd 260: of] *added above line in another hand.*

BAd 270: ȝeir] *om.*

BAd 346: be] Bot.

BAd 368: Colmess] ~~Ch~~ Colmess.

BAd 399: moder] *smudged.*

BAd 423–24: ane chylde] *hole in MS,* ane childe *added in margin in another hand.*

The last two folios of the Advocates MS are badly damaged. Unless otherwise noted, all BAd emendations here are attempts to restore the resulting losses. Where we have not been able to propose emendations we have left gaps, filled with spaced periods, of appropriate length.

BAs 348: son] *om.*

BAd 449: falsly] fasly.

BAd 451: Williame] ~~Wal~~ Williame.

BAd 474: nocht] *om.*

BAs 436: was] *om.*

BAs 452: i^m] *om.*

THE ST ANDREWS CHRONICLE

The manuscript has been severely damaged by cropped and torn margins and, particularly on the last folio, by large pieces that have been torn or worn off. Unless otherwise noted, all emendations here are attempts to restore the resulting losses. Where we have not been able to propose emendations we have left gaps, filled with spaced periods, of appropriate length.

StA 30: Lorne] lord.

StA 32: off Scotland and mony off þe comon pepyll] *These words were apparently omitted and then added on the next (and final) line of the page. Uncorrected, the MS reads:* neir all þe lordis and nobillis war slayne, & off Scotland and mony off þe comon pepyll þe King of Peichtis.

One folio is apparently missing between StA 33 and 34.

Folio 451 has been rebound backwards, so that f.451^v precedes f.451^r.

StA 152: þat] þat þat.

One folio is apparently missing between StA 233 and 234.

BIBLIOGRAPHY

In accordance with the *Chicago Manual of Style*, we include publishers for only those books published in 1900 or later.

Primary

Brevis Cronica (*Scottis Cornikle*):
> Andrew of Wyntoun, *The Orygynale Cronykil of Scotland*, ed. David Laing. 3 vols. London, 1872–79. 3.321–338. (Advocates)
> *The Asloan Manuscript*, ed. W. A. Craigie. Scottish Text Society n.s. 14, 16. Edinburgh: William Blackwood, 1923, 1925. 1.185–96.

Chronicle of the Scots (*Short Chronicle of 1482*):
> *Chronicles of the Picts, Chronicles of the Scots, and Other Early Memorials of Scottish History*, ed. William F. Skene, Edinburgh, 1867. 378–86.
> MacDougall, Norman. *James III: A Political Study*. Edinburgh: John Donald, 1982. 311–313. (extract covering the reign of James III)
> Pinkerton, John. *History of Scotland*. 2 vols. London, 1797. 1.502–504 (extract covering 1400–82)

Nomina Omnium Regum Scotorum:
> *Bannatyne Miscellany*, vol. 3, ed. Laing. 44–60 (abridged from Dalhousie).

Scottis Originale (*Chronicle of Scotland in a Part*):
> *Asloan*, ed. Craigie. 1.245–70.
> *The Bannatyne Miscellany*, vol. 3, ed. David Laing. Bannatyne Publications 19. Edinburgh, 1855; reprint New York: AMS, 1973. 35–43. (Dalhousie)
> *Chronicles of the Picts*, ed. Skene, 386–90. (Royal)

Vraie Cronicque:
> *La Vraie cronicque d'Escoce, Pretensions des Anglois à la couronne de France, Diplôme de Jacques VI, roi de la Grande Bretagne*, ed. Robert Anstruther. Roxburghe Club. London, 1847. 2–29.

Ynglis Chronicle:
> *Ane Tractat of a Part of ye Ynglis Cronikle*, ed. A. Boswell. Frondes Caducae 16. Auchinleck, 1818.
> *Asloan*, ed. Craigie. 1.197–214.

Other Primary Works Cited

Andrew of Wyntoun. *The Original Chronicle*, ed. F. J. Amours. 6 vols. Scottish Text Society 50, 53–54, 56–57, 63. Edinburgh: W. Blackwood, 1903–14.
_____. *The Orygynale Cronykil of Scotland by Andrew of Wyntoun*, ed. David Laing. 3 vols. Historians of Scotland 2, 3, 9. Edinburgh, 1872–79.

_____. *The Orygynale Cronykil of Scotland,* ed. David Macpherson. London, 1795.

Anglo-Scottish Relations 1174–1328: Some Selected Documents, ed. and trans. E. L. G. Stones. London: Nelson, 1965.

Bede, the Venerable. *Historia Ecclesiastica Gentis Anglorum* (Latin & English), ed. Bertram Colgrave and R. A. B. Mynors. Oxford: Clarendon Press, 1969.

Bellenden, John, trans. *The Chronicles of Scotland, Compiled by Hector Boece*, ed. R. W. Chambers, Edith C. Batho, and H. Winifred Husbands. 2 vols. Scottish Text Society, 3rd s., 10, 15. Edinburgh: William Blackwood, 1938–41.

Bisset, Baldred. "Incipit processus Baldredi contra figmenta Regis Anglie." In Bower, *Scotichronicon*, gen. ed. Watt, vol. 6, pp. 168–89.

Boece, Hector. *Scotorvm historiae a prima gentis origine.* Paris, 1526/1527.

Bower, Walter. *A History Book for Scots: Selections from "Scotichronicon,"* ed. and trans. D. E. R. Watt. Edinburgh: Mercat Press, 1998.

_____. *Scotichronicon*, gen. ed. D. E. R. Watt. 9 vols. Aberdeen: Aberdeen University Press, 1987–1998.

The Brut or The Chronicles of England, ed. Friedrich W. D. Brie, EETS o.s. 131, 136 (1906, 1908).

Buchanan, George. *History of Scotland*, trans. James Aikman. 4 vols. Glasgow, 1827.

Chaucer, Geoffrey. *The Riverside Chaucer*, 3rd edn., gen. ed. Larry D. Benson. Boston: Houghton Mifflin, 1987.

Debating the Hundred Years War: "Pour ce que plusieurs (La Loy Salicque)" and "A declaration of the trew and dewe title of Henrie VIII," ed. Craig Taylor. Cambridge: Cambridge University Press, 2006.

The Dethe of the Kynge of Scotis, trans. John Shirley. In *Death and Dissent: Two Fifteenth-Century Chronicles*, ed. Lister M. Matheson. Woodbridge: Boydell Press, 1999.

Dunbar, William. *Poems*, ed. James Kinsley. Oxford: Clarendon Press, 1958.

Edward I and the Throne of Scotland, 1290–1296: An Edition of the Record Sources for the Great Cause, ed. E. L. G. Stones and Grant G. Simpson. 2 vols. Oxford: Oxford University Press, 1978.

Extracta e Variis Cronicis Scocie from the Ancient Manuscript in the Advocates Library at Edinburgh, ed. William B. Turnbull. The Abbotsford Club. Edinburgh, 1862.

Fordun, John of. *Chronica Gentis Scotorum*, ed. William F. Skene, and *John of Fordun's Chronicle of the Scottish Nation*, trans. Felix J. H. Skene. 2 vols. Edinburgh, 1871–72. Trans. rptd. in 2 vols. Lampeter, Wales: Llanerch, 1993.

Froissart, John. *Chronicles of England, France, Spain and the Adjoining Countries*, trans. Thomas Johns. London, 1868.

Geoffrey le Baker. *Chronicon Angliae temporibus Edwardi II et Edwardi III*, ed. J. A. Giles. Caxton Society 7, 1847. Reprint, New York, B. Franklin [1967].

Geoffrey of Monmouth. *The History of the Kings of Britain*, ed. Michael D. Reeve, trans. Neil Wright. Woodbridge, Suffolk: Boydell Press, 2007.

_____. *The History of the Kings of Britain*, trans. Lewis Thorpe. Harmondsworth: Penguin, 1966.

Bibliography

Gesta Annalia. In John of Fordun, *Chronica Gentis Scotorum*, ed. W. F. Skene, 254–383. *Chronicle of the Scottish Nation*, ed. Felix J. H. Skene, 249–374. [The *Gesta Annalia* was formerly attributed to Fordun.]

Gray, Sir Thomas. *Scalacronica 1272–1363*, ed. and trans. Andy King. Surtees Society 209. Woodbridge: Boydell Press, 2005.

_____. *Scalacronica: A Chronicle of England and Scotland from A.D. MLXVI to A.D. MCCCLXII*, ed. Joseph Stevenson. Edinburgh: Maitland Club, 1836.

Hardyng, John. *The Chronicle of Iohn Hardyng*, ed. Henry Ellis. London, 1812.

Hary's Wallace, ed. Matthew P. McDiarmid. 2 vols Scottish Text Society, 4th s., 4, 5 Edinburgh: William Blackwood, 1968–69.

Higden, Ranulf. *Polychronicon Ranulphi Higden Monachi Cestrensis*, ed. Churchill Babington (vols 1–2) and Joseph Rawson Lumby (vols 3–9). 9 vols Rolls Series 41. London, 1865–86.

Historia Brittonum:

    The Historia Brittonum, ed. David N. Dumville. Cambridge: D. S. Brewer, 1985.

    Nennius, *British History and the Welsh Annals*, ed. and trans. John Morris London: Phillimore, 1980.

Historia Norwegie, ed. Inger Ekrem and Lars Boje Mortensen, trans. Peter Fisher. Copenhagen: Museum Tusculanum Press, University of Copenhagen, 2003.

Leslie, John. *History of Scotland*, ed. T. Thomson, Bannatyne Club. Edinburgh, 1830.

_____. *Historie of Scotland*, trans. James Dalrymple, ed. E. G. Cody and William Murison, Scottish Text Society 5, 14, 19, 34. Edinburgh, 1888–95

Liber Pluscardensis, ed. Felix J. H. Skene. Historians of Scotland 7. Edinburgh, 1877; *The Book of Pluscarden*, trans. Felix J. H. Skene. Historians of Scotland 10. Edinburgh, 1880.

Lindesay (Lindsay), Robert, of Pitscottie, *The Historie and Cronicles of Scotland*, ed. Æ. J. G. Mackay, 3 vols, Scottish Text Society 42, 43, 60. Edinburgh: William Blackwood, 1899–1911.

Major (Mair), John. *A History of Greater Britain as well England as Scotland*, trans. Archibald Constable. Edinburgh, 1892.

Mannyng, Robert, of Brunne. *The Chronicle*, ed. Idelle Sullens. Medieval and Renaissance Texts & Studies. Binghamton, NY: Binghamton University, 1996.

The Mar Lodge Translation of the History of Scotland, ed. George Watson. Scottish Text Society, 3rd s., 17. Edinburgh: William Blackwood, 1946. [This is "Vol. 1" and covers the first seven books of the Mar Lodge Translation. Vol. 2 was never published.]

The Oldest Anglo-Norman Prose "Brut" Chronicle, ed. & trans. Julia Marvin. Medieval Chronicles. Woodbridge: Boydell Press, 2006.

Protocol Book of John Foular, 1528–1534, ed. John Durkan, Scottish Record Society, n.s. 10. Edinburgh: Scottish Record Society, 1985.

"The Ring of the Roy Robert." *Early Scottish Metrical Tales*, ed. David Laing. Edinburgh, 1826.

Bibliography

The Sex Werkdays and Agis: An Edition of a Late Medieval Scots Universal History from the Asloan Manuscript, ed. L. A. J. R. Houwen. Groningen: Egbert Forsten, 1990.

Skene, William F., ed. *Chronicles if the Picts, Chronicles of the Scots, and Other Early Memorials of Scottish History.* Edinburgh, 1867.

Stewart, William, trans. *The Buik of the Croniclis of Scotland; or a Metrical Version of the History of Hector Boece*, ed. William B. Turnbull. 3 vols Rolls Series 6. London, 1858.

Dictionaries

Craigie, William A. (William Alexander), et al. eds. *A Dictionary of the Older Scottish Tongue, from the Twelfth Century to the End of the Seventeenth.* 12 vols Chicago, Ill., The University of Chicago press; London, H. Milford, Oxford University Press [1937]–2002. [Vol. 6, pt. 34 and vol. 8 pt. 42 published by Aberdeen University Press].

Grant, William, et al. eds. *The Scottish National Dictionary.* 10 vols Edinburgh: Scottish National Dictionary Association, 1931–75.

The above have been combined as the on-line *Dictionary of the Scots Language* <www.dsl.ac.uk>.

Secondary Works

Alcock, Leslie. *Arthur's Britain: History and Archaeology.* New York: Penguin, 1971.

Alexander, Flora. "Late Medieval Scottish Attitudes to the Figure of King Arthur: A Reassessment." *Anglia* 93 (1975), 17–34.

Anderson, Benedict. *Imagined Communities: Reflections on the Origin and Spread of Nationalism*, rvsd. edn. London: Verso, 1991.

Anderson, Marjorie O. *Kings and Kingship in Early Scotland.* 1973; rvsd. edn. Edinburgh: Scottish Academic Press, 1980.

Bannerman, John. "The Scottish Takeover of Pictland and the Relics of Columba." In *Spes Scotorum: Hope of Scots*, ed. Broun and Clancy. 71–94.

Barrois, Joseph. *Bibliothèque protypographique.* Paris, 1830.

Barrow, G. W. S. *The Anglo-Norman Era in Scottish History.* Oxford: Clarendon Press, 1980.

_____. *The Kingdom of the Scots.* London: Edward Arnold, 1973; 2nd edn., Edinburgh: Edinburgh University Press, 2003.

_____. *Kingship and Unity: Scotland 1000–1306.* 2nd edn. Edinburgh: Edinburgh University Press, 2003.

_____. *Robert Bruce and the Community of the Realm of Scotland.* 4th edn. Edinburgh: Edinburgh University Press, 2005.

_____. *Scotland and its Neighbours in the Middle Ages.* London: Hambledon Press, 1992.

Bernau, Anke. "Myths of Origin and the Struggle over Nationhood in Medieval and Early Modern England." In *Reading the Medieval in Early Modern England*, ed. Gordon McMullan and David Matthews. Cambridge: Cambridge University Press, 2007. 106–18.

Bibliography

Bevan, Bryan. *Henry VII: The First Tudor King*. London: Rubicon, 2000.

Biddle, Martin, ed. *King Arthur's Round Table: An Archaeological Investigation*, Woodbridge: Boydell Press, 2000.

Bjørn, Claus, Alexander Grant and Keith J. Stringer, eds. *Nations, Nationalism and Patriotism in the European Past*. Copenhagen: Academic Press, 1994.

Black, J. B. "Boece's *Scotorum Historiae.*" *University of Aberdeen Quatercentenary of the Death of Hector Boece*. Aberdeen: The University Press, 1937. 30–53.

Bloxam, M. Jennifer. "Plainsong and Polyphony for the Blessed Virgin: Notes on Two Masses by Jacob Obrecht." *The Journal of Musicology* 12 (1994), 51–75.

Boardman, Stephen. *The Early Stewart Kings: Robert II and Robert III, 1371–1406*. East Linton: Tuckwell Press, 1996.

_____. "Late Medieval Scotland and the Matter of Britain." In *Scottish History: The Power of the Past*, ed. Edward J. Cowan and Richard J. Finlay. Edinburgh: Edinburgh University Press, 2002. 47–72.

_____. "Lennox family (*per* ca. 1300–1425)." *Oxford Dictionary of National Biography*, 2004. [subsequently *ODNB*]

Bonner, Elizabeth. "Scotland's 'Auld Alliance.'" *History* 84 (1999), 5–30.

Brereton, Georgine E., ed. *Des Grantz Geanz: An Anglo-Norman Poem*. Oxford: Basil Blackwell, 1937.

Brie, Friedrich. *Die nationale Literatur Schottlands von den Anfängen bis zur Renaissance*. Halle: Niemeyer, 1937.

Broadie, Alexander. "Mair, John." *ODNB*.

Broun, Dauvit. "The Birth of Scottish History." *Scottish Historical Review* 76 (1997), 4–22.

_____. "Dunkeld and the Origin of Scottish Identity." In *Spes Scotorum: Hope of Scots*, ed. Broun and Clancy. 95–110.

_____. *The Irish Identity of the Kingdom of the Scots in the Twelfth and Thirteenth Centuries*. Woodbridge: Boydell Press, 1999.

_____. "A New Look at the *Gesta Annalia* Attributed to John of Fordun." In *Church, Chronicle and Learning in Medieval and Early Renaissance Scotland*, ed. Barbara E. Crawford. Edinburgh: Mercat Press, 1999. 9–30.

_____. "Pictish Kings 761–839: Integration with Dal Riata or Separate Development?" In Foster, ed., *St Andrews Sarcophagus*. 71–83.

_____. *Scottish Independence and the Idea of Britain: From the Picts to Alexander III*. Edinburgh: Edinburgh University Press, 2007.

_____ and Thomas Owen Clancy, eds. *Spes Scotorum: Hope of Scots*. Edinburgh: T & T Clark, 1999.

Brown, Jennifer M., ed. *Scottish Society in the Fifteenth Century*. London: Edward Arnold, 1977.

Brown, Michael. *The Black Douglases: War and Lordship in Late Medieval Scotland 1300–1455*. East Linton: Tuckwell, 1998.

_____. "Stewart Monarchy (1371–1513)." In *Scotland: The Making and Unmaking of the Nation c. 1100–1707*. Vol. 1: *The Scottish Nation: Origins to c. 1500*, ed. Harris and MacDonald. 48–64.

_____. *The Wars of Scotland 1214–1371*. Edinburgh: Edinburgh University Press, 2004.

Bibliography

Bryan, Elizabeth. "Prose Brut, English." *Encyclopedia of the Medieval Chronicle*, gen. ed. Dunphy, vol. 1. 1239–40.

Bukofzer, Manfred F. *Studies in Medieval and Renaissance Music*. New York: Norton, 1950.

Burns, J. H. "Ireland, John (c. 1440–1495)." *ODNB*.

_____. *The True Law of Kingship: Concepts of Monarchy in Early-Modern Scotland*. Oxford: Clarendon Press, 1996.

Calmette, J. and G. Périnelle, *Louis XI et l'Angleterre (1461–1483)*. Paris: A. Picard, 1930.

Cameron, Jamie. *James V: The Personal Rule 1528–1542*. East Linton: Tuckwell, 1998.

Campbell, Ewan, "Were the Scots Irish?" *Antiquity* 75 (2001), 285–92.

Campbell, James. "England, Scotland and the Hundred Years War in the Fourteenth Century." In *Europe in the Late Middle Ages*, ed. J. R. Hale, R. Highfield, B. Smalley. London: Faber & Faber, 1965. 184–216.

Campbell, John G. *The Gaelic Otherworld*. Edinburgh: Birlinn, 2008.

Carley, James P. and Julia Crick. "Constructing Albion's Past: An Annotated Edition of *De Origine Gigantum*." *Arthurian Literature* 13 (1995), 41–114, reprinted in *Glastonbury Abbey and the Arthurian Tradition*, ed. James P. Carley (Cambridge: D. S. Brewer, 2001), 347–407.

Charles-Edwards, T. M. *Early Christian Ireland*. Cambridge: Cambridge University Press, 2000.

Chesnutt, Michael. "The Dalhousie Manuscript of the *Historia Norvegiae*." *Bibliotheca Arnamagnæana* 38 (1985), 54–94.

Clancy, Thomas Owen and Murray Pittock, eds. *The Edinburgh History of Scottish Literature*, Vol. 1, *From Columba to the Union (until 1707)*. Edinburgh: Edinburgh University Press, 2007.

Claassens, G. H. M. and Verbeke, W., eds. *Medieval Manuscripts in Transition: Tradition and Creative Recycling*. Louvain: Louvain University Press, 2006.

Clarke, Basil, ed. and trans. *Life of Merlin / Vita Merlini*. Cardiff: University of Wales Press, 1973.

Cohen, Jeffrey Jerome, ed. *Cultural Diversity in the British Middle Ages: Archipelago, Island, England*. New York: Palgrave Macmillan, 2008.

Contamine, Philippe. "The Contents of a French Diplomatic Bag in the Fifteenth Century: Louis XI, Regalian Rights and Breton Bishoprics." *Nottingham Medieval Studies* 25 (1981), 52–72.

_____. "Entre France et Écosse : Bérault Stuart, seigneur d'Aubigny (vers 1452–1508) : chef de guerre, diplomate, écrivain." In *The Auld Alliance: France and Scotland over 700 Years*, ed. Laidlaw. 59–76.

_____. "Froissart and Scotland." In *Scotland and the Low Countries 1124–1994*, ed. Simpson. 43–58.

_____. "Stuart, Bérault (1452/3–1508)." *ODNB*.

Cowan, Edward J. *"For Freedom Alone": The Declaration of Arbroath, 1320*. East Linton: Tuckwell Press, 2003.

_____. "Myth and Identity in Early Medieval Scotland." *Scottish Historical Review* 63 (1984), 111–35.

Craigie, W. A. "The St. Andrews MS of Wyntoun's Chronicle." *Anglia* 20 (1898), 363–80.

Crawford, Barbara E., ed. *Church, Chronicle and Learning in Medieval and Early Renaissance Scotland*. Edinburgh: Mercat Press, 1999.

Cross, F. L., ed. *Oxford Dictionary of the Christian Church*. London: Oxford University Press, 1966.

Cunningham, I. C. "The Asloan Manuscript." In *The Renaissance in Scotland*, ed. MacDonald, Lynch and Cowan. 107–35.

Daly, Kathleen. "The *Vraie Cronicque dEscoce* and Franco-Scottish Diplomacy: An Historical Work by John Ireland?" *Nottingham Medieval Studies* 35 (1991), 106–33.

De Laborderie, Olivier. "A New Pattern for English History: The First Genealogical Rolls of the Kings of England." In *Broken Lines,* ed. Radulescu and Kennedy. 45–61.

Déprez, E. *Les préliminaires de la Guerre de Cent Ans*. Paris: A. Fontemoing, 1902.

Ditcham, B. "The Employment of Foreign Mercenaries in the French Royal Armies 1417–1470." Unpublished Ph. D. thesis, Edinburgh University, 1979.

Ditchburn, David. "The Place of Guelders in Scottish Foreign Policy, c. 1449–c. 1542." In *Scotland and the Low Countries*, ed. Simpson. 59–75.

Doutrepont, Georges. *La littérature française à la cour des ducs de Bourgogne; Philippe le Hardi – Jean sans Peur – Philippe le Bon – Charles le Téméraire*. Paris, Champion, 1909.

Drexler, Marjorie. "The Extant Abridgements of Walter Bower's *Scotichronicon*." *Scottish Historical Review* 61 (1982), 62–67.

_____. "Fluid Prejudice: Scottish Origin Myths in the Later Middle Ages." In *People, Politics and Community in the Later Middle Ages*, ed. Rosenthal and Richmond. 60–76.

Dumville, David N. "Ireland and Britain in Táin Bó Fráich." *Études Celtiques* 32 (1996), 175–87.

Duncan, Archibald A. M. "The Foundation of St Andrews Priory, 1140." *Scottish Historical Review* 84 (2005), 1–37.

_____. *The Kingship of the Scots 842–1292: Succession and Independence*. Edinburgh: Edinburgh University Press, 2002.

_____. *The Nation of Scots and the Declaration of Arbroath (1320)*. London: The Historical Association, 1970.

_____. *Scotland: The Making of the Kingdom*. Edinburgh: Oliver and Boyd, 1975.

Dunphy, Graeme, gen. ed. *Encyclopedia of the Medieval Chronicle*. 2 vols Leiden: E. J. Brill, 2010.

Easson, Edward. *Gavin Dunbar, Chancellor of Scotland, Archbishop of Glasgow*. Edinburgh: Oliver and Boyd, 1947.

Edwards, A. S. G. "The Manuscripts and Texts of the Second Version of John Hardyng's *Chronicle*." In *England in the Fifteenth Century*, ed. Williams. 75–84.

Falkus, Malcolm and John Gillingham, eds. *Historical Atlas of Britain*. New York: Continuum, 1981.

Farmer, David Hugh. *The Oxford Dictionary of Saints*. 2nd edn. Oxford: Oxford University Press, 1987.

Ferguson, William. *The Identity of the Scottish Nation: An Historic Quest*. Edinburgh: Edinburgh University Press, 1998.

Bibliography

_____. *Scotland's Relations with England: A Survey to 1707*. Edinburgh: John Donald, 1977.

Finlayson, W. H. "The Boyds in Bruges." *Scottish Historical Review* 28 (1949), 195–96.

Fisher, Matthew. "Genealogy Rewritten: Inheriting the Legendary in Insular Historiography." In *Broken Lines*, ed. Radulescu and Kennedy. 123–41.

Fletcher, Robert Huntington. *The Arthurian Material in the Chronicles, Especially Those of Great Britain and France* (1906), 2nd edn., ed. Roger Sherman Loomis. New York: Burt Franklin, 1966.

Forde, Simon, Lesley Johnson, and Alan V. Murray, eds. *Concepts of National Identity in the Middle Ages*. Leeds Texts and Monographs, n.s. 14. Leeds, School of English, University of Leeds, 1995.

Forsyth, Katherine. *Language in Pictland: The Case against Non-Indo-European Pictish*. The A. G. Van Hamel Lecture for 1995. Munster: Nodus Publications, 1997.

Foster, Sally M., ed. *The St Andrews Sarcophagus: A Pictish Masterpiece and Its International Connections*. Dublin: Four Courts Press, 1998.

Fraser, James E. *From Caledonia to Pictland: Edinburgh: Scotland to 795*. Edinburgh: Edinburgh University Press, 2009.

_____. *The Roman Conquest of Scotland: The Battle of Mons Graupius AD 84*. Stroud: Tempus, 2005.

_____. "'A swan from a raven': William Wallace, Brucean Propaganda and *Gesta Annalia II*." *Scottish Historical Review* 81 (2002), 1–22.

Gallacher, Patrick J. and Helen Damico, eds. *Hermeneutics and Medieval Culture*. Albany: State University of New York Press, 1989.

Gaussin, Pierre Roger. *Louis XI; un roi entre deux mondes*. Paris: A. Nizet, 1976.

Girvan, Ritchie, ed. *Ratis Raving and Other Early Scots Poems on Morals*. Scottish Text Society, 3rd s., 11. Edinburgh: W. Blackwood, 1939.

Göller, Karl Heinz. "King Arthur in the Scottish Chronicles," trans. Edward Donald Kennedy. In *King Arthur: A Case Book*, ed. Kennedy. New York: Garland, 1996; reprint New York: Routledge, 2002. 173–84. (Originally published as "König Arthur in den schottischen Chroniken," *Anglia* 80 [1962], 390–404.)

Goldstein, R. James. *The Matter of Scotland: Historical Narrative in Medieval Scotland*. Lincoln: University of Nebraska Press, 1993.

_____. "The Scottish Mission to Boniface VIII in 1301: A Reconsideration of the Context of the *Instructiones* and *Processus*." *Scottish Historical Review* 70 (1991), 1–15.

Grant, Alexander. "Aspects of National Consciousness in Medieval Scotland." In *Nations, Nationalism and Patriotism in the European Past*, ed. Bjørn, Grant and Stringer. 68–95.

_____. *Independence and Nationhood: Scotland 1306–1469*. London: Edward Arnold, 1984.

Green, Judith A. *Henry I: King of England and Duke of Normandy*. Cambridge: Cambridge University Press, 2006.

Guenée, Bernard. *Histoire et culture historique dans l'Occident médiéval*. Paris: Aubier Montaigne, 1980.

_____. *States and Rulers in Later Medieval Europe*, trans. Juliet Vale. Oxford: Blackwell, 1985.

Haines, Roy Martin. *King Edward II: Edward of Caernarfon: His Life, His Reign, and Its Aftermath, 1284–1330*. Montreal: McGill-Queen's University Press, 2003.

Harris, Bob and Alan R. MacDonald, eds. *Scotland: The Making and Unmaking of the Nation c. 1100–1707*. Vol. 1. *The Scottish Nation: Origins to c. 1500*. Dundee: Dundee University Press, 2006.

Hiatt, Alfred. *The Making of Medieval Forgeries: False Documents in Fifteenth-Century England*. London: The British Library, 2004.

_____. "Stow, Grafton, and Fifteenth-Century Historiography." In *John Stow (1525–1605) and the Making of the English Past*, ed. Ian Gadd and Alexandra Gillespie. London: The British Library, 2004. 45–55.

Hirschman, Elizabeth Caldwell and Donald N. Yates. *When Scotland Was Jewish*. Jefferson, NC: McFarland, 2007.

Honeycutt, Lois L. *Matilda of Scotland: A Study in Medieval Queenship*. Woodbridge: Boydell Press, 2003.

Hudson, Barton. "Obrecht's Tribute to Ockeghem." *Tijdschrift van de Vereniging voor Nederlandse Muziekgeschiedenis*, D. 37ste. (1987), 3–13.

Hudson, Benjamin T. *Kings of Celtic Scotland*. Westport, CT: Greenwood Press, 1994.

Jacob, E. F. *The Fifteenth Century 1399–1485*. Oxford History of England. Oxford: Clarendon Press, 1961.

Jervis, Simon. "The Round Table as Furniture." In *King Arthur's Round Table*, ed. Biddle. 31–57.

Johnson, Lesley. "Return to Albion." *Arthurian Literature* 13 (1995), 19–40.

Keeler, Laura. *Geoffrey of Monmouth and the Late Latin Chroniclers, 1300–1500*. Berkeley: University of California Press, 1946.

Kelly, Susan. "The Arthurian Material in the *Scotichronicon* of Walter Bower." *Anglia* 97 (1979), 431–38.

Kendrick, T. D. *British Antiquity*. 1950; reprint London: Methuen, 1970.

Kennedy, Edward Donald. "The Antiquity of Scottish Civilization: King-Lists and Genealogical Chronicles." In *Broken Lines*, ed. Radulescu and Kennedy. 159–74.

_____. "Arthurian Material." *Encyclopedia of the Medieval Chronicle*, gen. ed. Dunphy, vol. 1. 114–18.

_____. *Chronicles and Other Historical Writing. A Manual of the Writings in Middle English*, vol. 8, gen. ed. A. E. Hartung. New Haven, CT: Connecticut Academy of Arts and Sciences, 1989.

_____. "Chronicum Scotorum." *Encyclopedia of the Medieval Chronicle*, gen. ed. Dunphy, vol. 1. 424–25.

_____. "John Hardyng and the Holy Grail." *Arthurian Literature* 8 (1989), 185–206, reprinted in *Glastonbury Abbey and the Arthurian Tradition*, ed. Carley. 249–68.

_____. "The *Chronicle of Scotland in a Part* and the *Chronicle of John Hardyng*." In *The Medieval Book and a Modern Collector: Essays in Honor of Toshiyuki Takamiya*, ed. Takami Matsuda, Richard A. Linenthal, and John Scahill. Cambridge: D. S. Brewer, 2004. 357–70.

Kersken, Norbert. *Geschichtsschreibung im Europa der "nationes": National-geschichtliche Gesamtdarstellungen im Mittelalter*. Cologne: Böhlau, 1995.

Kirby, J. L. *Henry IV of England*. London: Constable, 1970.

Laidlaw, James, ed. *The Auld Alliance: France and Scotland over 700 Years.* Edinburgh: University of Edinburgh Press, 1999.

Laing, David, ed. *Early Scottish Metrical Tales.* New edn. Glasgow: Thomas D. Morrison, 1889.

Legge, M. Dominica. "La Piere d'Escoce." *Scottish Historical Review* 38 (1959), 109–13.

Lewis, C. S. *English Literature in the Sixteenth Century excluding Drama.* Oxford History of English Literature 3. Oxford: Clarendon Press, 1954.

Liddy, Christian D. and Richard H. Britnell, eds. *North-East England in the Later Middle Ages.* Woodbridge: Boydell Press, 2005.

Linehan, P. A. "A Fourteenth-Century History of Anglo-Scottish Relations in a Spanish Manuscript." *Bulletin of the Institute of Historical Research* 48 (1975), 106–22.

Lynch, Michael, ed. *Oxford Companion to Scottish History.* Oxford: Oxford University Press, 2007.

_____. *Scotland: A New History.* London: Century, 1991; reprinted London: Pimlico, 2004.

MacLean, Hector. *The Ancient Peoples of Ireland and Scotland Considered.* London: Harrison and Sons, 1890.

MacDonald, A. A., Michael Lynch and Ian B. Cowan, eds. *The Renaissance in Scotland.* Leiden: E. J. Brill, 1994.

MacDonald, Alastair J. "John Hardyng, Northumbrian Identity and the Scots." In *North-East England in the Later Middle Ages*, ed. Liddy and Britnell. 29–42.

Macdougall, Norman. *An Antidote to the English: The Auld Alliance, 1295–1560.* East Linton: Tuckwell Press, 2001.

_____. *James III: A Political Study.* Edinburgh: John Donald, 1982; rvsd edn. 2009.

_____. *James IV.* Edinburgh: J. Donald, 1989.

_____. "Monypenny, William." *ODNB.*

_____. "The Sources: A Reappraisal of the Legend." In *Scottish Society in the Fifteenth Century*, ed. Brown. 10–32.

Mackay, J. *William Wallace.* Edinburgh: Mainstream, 1995.

Mackie, R. L. *James IV of Scotland: A Brief Survey of His Life and Times.* Edinburgh: Oliver and Boyd, 1958.

MacKinnon, Kenneth. "Scottish Gaelic." In *Languages in Britain and Ireland*, ed. Price. 44–57.

Macpherson, David, ed. *The Orygynale Cronykil of Scotland.* London, 1795.

Macquarrie, Alan. *Saints of Scotland: Essays in Scottish Church History AD 450–1093.* Edinburgh: John Donald, 1997.

MacQueen, John. "National Spirit and Native Culture." In *Who Are the Scots? and The Scottish Nation*, ed. Menzies. 161–76.

Mapstone, Sally. "A Mirror for a Divine Prince: John Ireland and the Four Daughters of God." In *Bryght Lanternis*, ed McClure and Spiller. 308–23.

_____ and Juliette Wood, eds. *The Rose and the Thistle.* East Linton: Tuckwell Press, 1998.

_____. "The *Scotichronicon*'s First Readers." In *Church, Chronicle and Learning*, ed. Crawford. 31–55.

_____. "Shakespeare and Scottish Kingship: A Case History." In *The Rose and the Thistle*, ed. Mapstone and Wood. 158–89.

Bibliography

Marvin, Julia. "Havelok in the Prose *Brut* Tradition." *Studies in Philology* 102 (2005), 280–306.

Mason, R. A. "Kingship, Nobility, and Anglo-Scottish Union: John Mair's *History of Greater Britain* (1521)." *Innes Review* 41 (1990), 182–222.

Matheson, Lister. *The Prose "Brut": The Development of A Middle English Chronicle*. Tempe, AZ: Medieval and Renaissance Texts and Studies, 1998.

Matthews, William. "The Egyptians in Scotland; The Political History of a Myth." *Viator* 1 (1970), 289–306.

McClure, J. Derrick and Michael R. G. Spiller, eds. *Bryght Lanternis*. Aberdeen: Aberdeen University Press, 1989.

McDonald, R.A. "The Western Gàidhealtachd in the Middle Ages." In *Scotland: The Making and Unmaking of the Nation c. 1100–1707. Vol. I. The Scottish Nation*, ed. Harris and Macdonald. 66–89.

McGladdery, Christine. *James II*. Edinburgh: John Donald, 1990.

McLeod, Wilson. *Divided Gaels: Gaelic Cultural Identities in Scotland and Ireland c.1200–c.1650*. Oxford: Oxford University Press, 2004.

McNamee, Colm. *The Wars of the Bruces: Scotland, England, and Ireland 1306–1328*. East Linton: Tuckwell Press, 1997.

McNeill, Peter G. B. and Hector L. MacQueen, eds. *Atlas of Scottish History to 1707*. Edinburgh: Scottish Medievalists and Dept of Geography, University of Edinburgh, 1996.

Menzies, Gordon, ed. *Who Are the Scots? and The Scottish Nation*. 1971, 1972; reprint, Edinburgh: Edinburgh University Press, 2002.

Miller, M. "Matriliny by Treaty: The Pictish Foundation Legend." In *Ireland in Early Mediaeval Europe*, ed. Whitelock, McKitterick, and Dumville. 133–64.

Moll, Richarrd J. "'Nest pas autentik, mais apocrophum': Haveloks and Their Reception in Medieval England", *Studies in Philology* 105 (2008), 165-206.

Morris, John. *The Age of Arthur: A History of the British Isles from 350 to 650*. 1973; reprint, London: Phoenix Press, 1995.

Mossé, Fernand, ed. *Handbook of Middle English*, trans. James A. Walker. Baltimore: Johns Hopkins University Press, 1952.

Newton, Robert R. *Medieval Chronicles and the Rotation of the Earth*. Baltimore: The Johns Hopkins University Press, 1972.

National Library of Scotland. *Summary Catalogue of the Advocates Manuscripts*. Edinburgh: H.M. Stationery Office, 1971.

Nicholson, Ranald. *Edward III and the Scots*. Oxford: Oxford University Press, 1965.

_____. *Scotland: The Later Middle Ages*. Edinburgh: Oliver & Boyd, 1974.

Norbye, Marigold Anne. "Genealogies in Medieval France." In *Broken Lines*, ed. Radulescu and Kennedy. 79–101.

Oram, Richard. *The Canmores: Kings and Queens of the Scots 1040–1290*. Stroud: Tempus, 2002.

_____. *David I: The King Who Made Scotland*. Stroud: Tempus, 2004.

_____, Michael Penman, Chistine McGladdery, and Maureen Meikle, eds. *The Kings and Queens of Scotland*. Stroud: Tempus, 2004.

Pearsall, Derek. "Interpretative Models for the Peasants' Revolt." In *Hermeneutics and Medieval Culture*, ed. Gallacher and Damico. 63–70.

Bibliography

Penman, Michael. "'A fell coniuracioun agayn Robert the douchty king': The Soules Conspiracy of 1318–1320." *Innes Review* 50.1 (1999), 25–57.

Peverley, Sarah L. "Adapting to Readeption in 1470–1471: The Scribe as Editor in a Unique Copy of John Hardyng's *Chronicle of England* (Garrett MS. 142)." *The Princeton University Library Chronicle* 66 (2004), 140–72.

_____. "Dynasty and Division: The Depiction of King and Kingdom in John Hardyng's *Chronicle*." *The Medieval Chronicle* III, ed. Erik Kooper. Amsterdam: Rodopi, 2004. 149–70.

_____, ed. "John Hardyng's Chronicle: A Study of the Two Versions and a Critical Edition of Both for the Period 1327–1464." Unpubl. Ph.D. thesis, Hull, 2004.

_____. "Political Consciousness and the Literary Mind in Late Medieval England: Men 'brought up of nought' in Vale, Hardyng, *Mankind* and Malory." *Studies in Philology* 105 (2008), 1–29.

Powicke, F. M. *The Thirteenth Century 1216–1307.* 2nd edn. Oxford: Clarendon Press, 1962.

Price, Glanville, ed. *Languages in Britain and Ireland.* Oxford: Blackwell, 2000.

_____. "Pictish." In *Languages in Britain and Ireland*, ed. Price. 127–31.

Purdie, Rhiannon and Nicola Royan, eds. *The Scots and Medieval Arthurian Legend.* Cambridge: D. S. Brewer, 2005.

Radulescu, Raluca L. and Edward Donald Kennedy, eds. *Broken Lines: Genealogical Literature in Medieval Britain and France.* Turnhout: Brepols, 2008.

Reid, Norman H. "Alexander III." *ODNB.*

Renoir, Alain and C. David Benson. "John Lydgate." In *A Manual of the Writings in Middle English.* Vol. 6, gen. ed. Albert E. Hartung. New Haven: Connecticut Academy of Arts and Sciences, 1980. Nos. 100–02, pp. 1864–65, 2125–27.

Reynolds, Susan. "Medieval *Origines Gentium* and the Community of the Realm." *History* 68 (1983), 375–90.

Riddy, Felicity. "John Hardyng's Chronicle and the Wars of the Roses." *Arthurian Literature* 12 (1993), 91–108.

Ritchie, R. L. Graeme. *The Normans in Scotland.* Edinburgh: Edinburgh University Press, 1954.

Roberts, John L. *Lost Kingdoms: Celtic Scotland and the Middle Ages.* Edinburgh: Edinburgh University Press, 1997.

Robinson, Christine and Roibeard Ó Maolalaigh, "The Several Tongues of a Single Kingdom: The Languages of Scotland, 1314–1707." In *The Edinburgh History of Scottish Literature*, Vol. 1, ed. Clancy and Pittock. 153–63.

Rosenthal, Joel and Colin Richmond, eds. *People, Politics and Community in the Later Middle Ages.* Gloucester: Alan Sutton, 1987.

Royan, Nicola. "Boece [Boethius], Hector." *ODNB.*

_____. "The Fine Art of Faint Praise in Older Scots Historiography." In *The Scots and Medieval Arthurian Legend*, ed. Purdie and Royan. 43–54.

_____. "'Na les vailyeant than ony uthir princes of Britane': Representations of Arthur in Scotland 1480–1540." *Scottish Studies Review* 3.1 (2002), 9–20.

_____. "The Relationship between the *Scotorum Historia* of Hector Boece and John Bellenden's *Chronicles of Scotland*." In *The Rose and the Thistle*, ed. Mapstone and Wood. 136–57.

_____. "The *Scotorum Historia* of Hector Boece: A Study." Oxford University D. Phil. Thesis, 1996.

_____. "The Uses of Speech in Hector Boece's *Scotorum Historia.*" In *A Palace in the Wild: Essays on Vernacular Culture and Humanism in Late-Medieval and Renaissance Scotland,* ed. Houwen, MacDonald, and Mapstone. 75–93.

_____ with Dauvit Broun, "Versions of Scottish Nationhood, c. 850–1707." In *The Edinburgh History of Scottish Literature*, Vol. 1, ed. Clancy and Pittock, 168–83.

Salway, Peter. *The Oxford Illustrated History of Roman Britain.* Oxford: University Press, 1993.

Seton-Watson, Hugh. *Nations and States.* Boulder, CO: Westview Press, 1977.

Saul, Nigel. *Richard II.* New Haven: Yale University Press, 1997.

Seward, Desmond. *Henry V: The Scourge of God.* 1987; reprint New York: Viking, 1988.

Sheppard, Alice. *Families of the King: Writing Identity in the "Anglo-Saxon Chronicle."* Toronto: University of Toronto Press, 2004.

Simpson, Grant G., ed. *Scotland and the Low Countries 1124–1994.* East Linton: Tuckwell Press, 1996. 43–58.

_____. *Scottish Handwriting 1150–1650: An Introduction to the Reading of Documents.* Edinburgh: Bratton Publishing, 1973.

Smith, G. Gregory, ed. *Specimens of Middle Scots.* Edinburgh: William Blackwood, 1903.

Smyth, A. P. *Warlords and Holy Men: Scotland AD 80–1000.* London: E. Arnold, 1984.

Snyder, Christopher A. *An Age of Tyrants: Britain and the Britons A.D. 400–600.* University Park, PA: Pennsylvania State University Press, 1998.

Spiegel, Gabrielle M. *Romancing the Past: The Rise of Vernacular Prose Historiography in Thirteenth-Century France.* Berkeley: University of California Press, 1993.

Stenton, Frank. *Anglo-Saxon England.* 2nd edn. Oxford: Clarendon Press, 1947.

Stones, E. L. G. "The Appeal to History in Anglo-Scottish Relations between 1291 and 1401: Part I." *Archives* 9, no. 43 (1970), 11–21, 80–83.

Stringer, K. J. *Earl David of Huntingdon, 1152–1219: A Study in Anglo-Scottish History.* Edinburgh: Edinburgh University Press, 1985.

Summerfield, Thea. "Teaching a Young King about History: William Stewart's Metrical *Chronicle* and King James V of Scotland." In *People and Texts: Relationships in Medieval Literature*, ed. Thea Summerfield and Keith Busby. Amsterdam: Rodopi, 2007. 187–98.

Terrell, Katherine H. "'Lynealy discendit of þe devill': Genealogy, Textuality, and Anglophobia in Medieval Scottish Chronicles." *Studies in Philology* 108 (2011), 320–44.

_____. "Subversive Histories: Strategies of Identity in Scottish Historiography." In *Cultural Diversity in the British Middle Ages,* ed. Cohen. 153–72.

Turville-Petre, Thorlac. *England the Nation: Language, Literature and National Identity 1290–1340.* Oxford: Clarendon Press, 1996.

Vale, M. G. A. *The Angevin Legacy and the Hundred Years War 1250–1340.* Oxford: Blackwell, 1990.

Van Buuren, Catherine, ed. *The Buke of the Sevyne Sagis*. Leiden: Leiden University Press, 1982.

_____. "John Asloan, an Edinburgh Scribe." *English Studies* 47 (1966), 365–72.

_____. "John Asloan and His Manuscript: An Edinburgh Notary and Scribe in the Days of James III, IV and V (c. 1470–c. 1530)." In *Stewart Style 1513–1542*, ed. Williams. 15–51.

Visser-Fuchs, Livia. "The Manuscript of the *Enseignement de Vraie Noblesse* Made for Richard Neville, Earl of Warwick in 1464: An Example of Anglo-Burgundian Literary Contact." In *Medieval Manuscripts in Transition*, ed. Claassens and Verbeke. 337–62.

Waddell, Laurence. *The Phoenician Origins of Britons, Scots and Anglo-Saxons*. London: Williams and Norgate, 1924.

Walker, Simon. "Rumor, Sedition, and Popular Protest in the Reign of Henry IV." *Past and Present*, No. 166 (Feb. 2000), 31–65.

Walther, Hans. *Initia carminum ac versuum Medii Aevi posterioris Latinorum. Alphabetisches Verzeichnis der Versanfänge mittellateinischer Dichtungen*. 2nd edn. Göttingen: Vandenhoeck & Ruprecht, 1969.

Warner, George F. and Julius P. Gilson. *British Museum Catalogue of Western Manuscripts in the Old Royal and King's Collections*. Vol. 2. London: The Trustees of the British Museum, 1921; reprint Munich: K. G. Saur, 1997.

Warren, W. L. *King John*. New edn. New Haven: Yale University Press, 1997.

Watt, D. E. R. "A National Treasure? The *Scotichronicon* of Walter Bower." *The Scottish Historical Review* 76 (1997), 44–53.

_____. "Fordun, John." *ODNB*.

Webb, Keith. *The Growth of Nationalism in Scotland*. Glasgow: Molendinar Press, 1977.

White, Hayden. *The Content of the Form: Narrative Discourse and Historical Representation*. Baltimore: the Johns Hopkins University Press, 1987; reprinted 1992.

Whitelock, Dorothy, Rosamond McKitterick, and David Dumville, eds. *Ireland in Early Mediaeval Europe*. Cambridge: Cambridge University Press, 1982.

Williams, Daniel, ed. *England in the Fifteenth Century*. Woodbridge: Boydell Press, 1987.

Williams, Janet Hadley, ed. *Stewart Style 1513–1542: Essays on the Court of James V*. East Linton: Tuckwell Press, 1996.

Williamson, Arthur H. "Scots, Indians and Empire: The Scottish Politics of Civilization 1519–1609." *Past and Present* 150 (Feb. 1996), 46–83.

Wood, Juliette. "Where Does Britain End? The Reception of Geoffrey of Monmouth in Scotland and Wales." In *The Scots and Medieval Arthurian Legend*, ed. Rhiannon Purdie and Nicola Royan. Cambridge: D. S. Brewer, 2005.

Woolf, Alex. *From Pictland to Alba 789–1070*. Edinburgh: Edinburgh University Press, 2007.

Woolliscroft, D. J. and B. Hoffman. *Rome's First Frontier: The Flavian Occupation of Northern Scotland*. Stroud: Tempus, 2006.

Young, Alan. *Robert the Bruce's Rivals: The Comyns, 1212–1314*. East Linton: Tuckwell Press, 1997.

GLOSSARY

Words in Scots that vary substantially in form or meaning from Modern English equivalents are glossed here. The line references are given to the first three instances of each form and meaning in each chronicle unless there are only four, in which case the fourth is given as well. Line numbers in square brackets indicate that the word is partly or wholly an emendation. Cross references are given from variant or inflected forms unless they are within three entries of the main entry. Within an entry, line references are to the preceding form and meaning.

Two letters are not found in Modern English: þ (thorn) and ȝ (yogh). We have followed the practice of the *Dictionary of the Older Scottish Tongue* in listing words beginning with thorn after those beginning with *t*, and those beginning with yogh after those beginning with *y*.

Abbreviations for Scots chronicles, in their order in this edition:

OD	*Scottis Originale* – Dalhousie MS	Y	*Ynglis Chronicle*
OR	*Scottis Originale* – Royal MS	BAd	*Brevis Cronica* – Advocates MS
OA	*Scottis Originale* – Asloan MS	BAs	*Brevis Cronica* – Asloan MS
S	*Chronicle of the Scots*	StA	*St Andrews Chronicle*

Abbreviations for grammatical forms:

adj.	adjective		*poss.*	possessive
adv.	adverb		*ppl.*	participle
conj.	conjunction		*pr.*	present
comp.	comparative		*prep.*	preposition
ger.	gerund		*pron.*	pronoun
imper.	imperative		*refl.*	reflexive
n.	noun		*subj.*	subjunctive
num.	numeral		*super.*	superlative
pa.	past		*v.*	verb
pl.	plural			

a: *adj.* one OD 141, 201, OR 136, S 1, 16, 37, etc., Y 26, 28.

a: *see* **haf**.

abaid: *see* **abyde**.

abak: *adv.* back BAd 492, BAs 393.

abandonyt: *v. pa.* subdued OR 10; **abandownit**: OD 8; **habandonit**: OA 9.

abbay: *n.* abbey S 47, 54, 56, etc., BAd 140, 253, 361, 398, BAs 295, 322; **abbais**: *pl.* Y 295, BAs 92, 157, 300; **abbayis**: BAd 97, 179, 384, 419.

abill: *adj.* able; **abill to**: capable of, deserving of BAd 229; **able to**: eligible for OA 121.

abowt: *prep.* about BAs 266.

abrogat: *v. pa.* abrogated BAd 284.

abthan(e): *n.* lord of the thanes *(see explanatory note)* BAd 317, BAs 255.

abyde: *v.* stay, endure BAd 474, BAs 383; **abaid**: *pa.* BAd 18, BAs 15, 262, 389.

accordit: *v. pa. ppl.* agreed Y 144, 167, BAd 379, BAs 304.

actis: *n. pl.* ordinances BAd 215; deeds BAd 325.

aduersare: *n.* adversary BAd 294, 446.

adultry: *n.* adultery OA 122; **adulteris**: *pl.* BAd 141.

Affrica: *n. pl.* Africa OD 13, OR 14, OA 49; **Affrik(e)**: OD 59, OA 14, BAd 7, 64, BAs 10; **Aufrice**: OR 59.

afoir: *adv.* before StA 150.

agane: *adv.* again OR 48, OA 39, S 202, Y 112, 169, 209, 294, BAd 13, 17, 68, etc., BAs 15, 19, 68, etc., StA 40; **agayne**: OD 45, [135]; **agane**: back BAd 402, BAs 373, StA 46, 121.

aganis: *prep.* against OA 100, 130, 144, Y 39, 72, 154, etc., BAd 86, 88, 90, etc., BAs 157, 169, 333, etc., StA 3, 47, 85, etc.; **agane**: StA 38; **aganis**: compared to StA [150]; **agane**: OR 109, 111, 112, etc., OA 102, 131, 153, Y 185, BAd 448, BAs 166, 390; **agayn(e)**: OD 113, 115, 116, etc.; **agaynis**: OD 141.

aganestand: *v.* withstand, resist OR 90; **agaynstud**: *pa.* OD 145; **aganstude**: OR 116; **nocht agaynstanding**: *conj.* notwithstanding OD 123.

aggreit: *adj.* agreed, in accord BAd 57.

agit: *adj.* aged StA 266.

aige: *n.* age BAd 309, 411.

air(e): *n.* heir OD 10, 129, 134, OA 11, 112, 114, etc., S 161, Y 140, 145, 180, BAd 247, 248, 379, 444, BAs 208, 209, 210, etc.; **ayr**: StA 257; **airis**: *pl.* OD 126, 176, BAd 306, 323, 428, BAs 258; **ayris**: StA 146; **aris**: BAs 263.

aith: *n.* oath Y 126.

alanerly: *adv.* solely, only OR 178, 228; **allanerly**: OA 11; **allanerlie**: OA 172, 222.

alaye: *n.* ally OR 5; **allye**: OD 4.

ald: *adj.* old OD 130, OR 68, 126, 200, etc., OA 119, 193, 213, S 96, 165, BAs 230, 333, 344, etc.; **auld**: BAd 284, 286.

alia: *n.* alliance OR 109, 111, 137, etc.; **alya**: OR 120; **alye**: OD 113, 115; **allia**: OA 112, 138; **allya**: OA 131; **allye**: OD 124, 142, 148.

aliyt: *v. pa.* allied OR 193; **allyit**: *pa.* OA 101; *pa. ppl.* OD 5[1], 5[2], OA 5, 186; **alyite**: OR 6[1], 6[2].

allanerly: *see* **aunly**.

all gife: *conj.* although BAd 435.

allswa: *adv.* also Y 24; **alsua**: OR 53, 80, BAd 180, 212, 359, 456; **alsa**: BAs 87; **als**: OD 53, 54, 151, OR 155, S 233, BAd 271, BAs 368.

allway: *adv.* always OA 130.

allye: *see* **alaye**.

Almane: *n.* Germany OD 208, OA 202, BAd 179; **Almany**: BAs 158; **Almanʒe**: OR 210, Y 108.

almychti: *adj.* almighty OA 97; **almychtty**: BAd 176.

almos: *n. pl.* alms BAs 300; **almous deidis**: acts of charity BAd 376-77.

alson: *adv.* as soon Y 74.

als: *adv.* as BAd 116, 117, Y 45, StA 39, 46, [82], etc.

als: *see* **allswa**.

amang: *prep.* among Y 154, BAd 100, 305, BAs 6; into Y 263; **amangis**: among OA 42, Y 20, 40, 100, 215.

ambassatouris: *n. pl.* ambassadors StA 37, 74, [127], 170.

amountis: *v. pr.* amounts OD 110.

amovit: *v. pa. ppl.* moved, disturbed OA 84; **amufyt**: OR 96.

anamalit: *adj.* enameled BAd 405.

and: *conj.* if OD 233, OR 234, OA 206, 227, Y 306; **&**: Y 308.

ane: *adj., pron.* one OD 84, 127, 155, OA 66, S 50, 55, 60[1], etc., Y 27, 158, 170, etc., BAd 45, 85, 99, etc., BAs 84, 140, 180, StA 54, 114.

ane: *indef. art.* a, an OD 86, 131, 141, 230, OR 9, 22, 83, etc., OA 69, 78, 87, etc., S 165, 186, 203, etc., Y 1, 4, 26, etc., BAd 7, 8, 22, etc., BAs 1, 144, 151, etc., StA 3, 16, 20, etc.

ane othir: *pron., adj.* another OD 86, 131, 141-42; **ane vþir**: BAd 160, 313, 462; **ane oþir**: OR 83, 127, 136-37, 228; **ane noþir**: OA 69, 121, 130-31, Y 198, 254, 275, BAs 247, 373.

anentis: *prep.* in the sight of Y 330.

anerly: *see* **aunly**.

antes: *n. pl.* aunts StA [177].

apon(e): *see* **vpoun(e)**.

apperance: *n.* prospect OA 226.

apperand: *adj.* apparent BAd 246, BAs 208.

apperis: *v. pr.* is apparent OD 25; **apperit**: *pa.* Y 90; **appeirit**: appeared, seemed BAd 165.

ar: *v. pr.* are OD 19, 28, 48, etc., OR 23, 30[1], 30[2], etc., OA 18, 21, 31[1], etc., S 27, 71, Y 9, 13, 15, etc., BAd [43]; **wes**: *pa.* was StA 63, 68, 75, etc.; **vas**: OR 1. **war(e)**: were OD 4, 22, 24, etc., OR 12, 43, 58, etc., OA 5, 12, 24, etc., S 70, 242[1], 242[2], Y 29, 39, 56, etc., BAd 4, 5, 6, etc., BAs 8, 62, 117, etc., StA 32, 42, 98, etc.; **bene**: *pa. ppl.* been OD 26, 233, OR 28, OA 111, 180, Y 32, 65, 66, BAd 462, 463, BAs 374; **beyne**: OR 189, 234; **beyng**: *pr. ppl.* BAs 153; **beand**: OR 175, OA 169, S 164, 172, 186, BAd [479], BAs 53, StA 249, 266.

aratyk: *n.* heretic BAd 442.

argewis: *v. pr.* alleges OD 49; **argue**: *imper.* OR 50.

argonit: *v. pa. ppl.* addressed StA 201.

aris: *see* **air(e)**.

armis: *n. pl.* escutcheon, coat of arms OR 98; **armes**: OD 102, OA 87, Y 27, BAd 463, BAs 34; tournament warfare Y 290, 294, 323.

armyt: *adj.* armed BAd [456].

arow: *n.* arrow BAd 153.

artailȝery: *n.* artillery BAd 418; **artalȝe**: BAs 338.

aryfyt: *v. pa.* arrived OR 62; **arifyt**: OR 59; **aryvit**: OA 48, 52, 73; **arrivit**: OD 59; **arryvit**: OD 62; **aryving**: *pr. ppl.* Y 19.

as: *conj.* as if BAd 460, 462, BAs 373.

askyt: *v. pa.* requested, demanded StA 37, 100, 130, etc.; **askit at**: asked of OD 91, OR 88, OA 73.

assignyt: *v. pa. ppl.* adduced, declared OR 1.

at: *rel. pron.* that, which, who OR 113, 125, OA 25, 34, S 181², 199, 242, Y 20.

attour: *adv.* moreover Y 16.

aucht: *adj.* eight OR 165, S 186, BAd 503.

auchtene: *adj.* eighteen OD 190.

auchtenit: *adj.* eighteenth BAd 505.

Aufrice: *see* **Affrica**.

aunly: *adj.* only OR 11; **anerly**: OD 10; **allanerly**: OA 11.

autentik: *adj.* authentic Y 65; **autentice**: OR 246.

avale: *n.* use, authority Y 174, 219.

awalk: *v.* awake BAs 390.

awantage: *n.* advantage OR 232, OA 227; **avantage**: OD 230.

awarice: *n.* avarice BAd 135; **aweryce**: StA 53, 145, 191.

awaricious: *adj.* avaricious BAd 310.

awentur: *n.* chance StA 13.

awfully: *adv.* dreadfully, inspiring fear Y 332.

awin: *adj.* own OD 45, 162, 191, etc., OR 86, 156, 191, etc., BAd 132, 141, 375, etc.; **awyn**: S 181; **awn(e)**: OA 39, 71, 151, etc., Y 16, 18, 23, etc., BAs 299.

awysitly: *adv.* advisedly, after reflection OA 126.

ay: *adv.* ever, always OD 11, 119, 170, 206, OR 10, 115, 144, 207, OA 41, 95, 105, etc.; **ay quhill**: continually Y 166-67.

ayr, ayris: *see* **air(e)**.

bad: *v. pa.* commanded, requested Y 77, BAs 41, 117, StA 106.

baid: *v. pa.* stayed OA 29, Y 185.

bair: *v.* bear, carry OR 31; **beris**: *pr.* OA 32, StA 6; states Y 23; **beris witnes(s)**: testifies OD 153, 214, 225, OR 149, 216, 217, etc., OA 143, 210, 214, 238, Y 7; **bure**: *pa.* bore, carried OA 32; **bure by**: thrust aside OA 123.

bairnis, bairnes: *see* **barne**.

bait: *n.* boat Y 234, BAs 401.

baith: *adj.* both OA 28, 145, Y 7, 14, 33, etc., BAd 45, 83, 133, etc., BAs 57, 83, 120, etc., StA 45, 88, [132], etc.; **baitht**: S 235; **bayth**: BAd 191, StA 157.

bakkit: *v. pa.* repressed, harmed OD 159.

banis: *n. pl.* bones BAs 61, 100; **banys**: S 166; **baynnis**: BAd 60.

band: *n.* bond, alliance OA 131, 139, 225, BAd 175, 413, BAs 153, 154, 419.

baneris: *n. pl.* banners BAd 463, BAs 374.

banyst: *v. pa.* banished StA 26; **banysyt**: S 212, 240; *pa. ppl.* S 192, 197, 200; **banist**: BAd 128; **bannist**: BAs 116.

barne: *n.* child OA 218, BAd 84; **barnis**: *pl.* OD 41, 49, 54, 56, OA 34, 41, 43, 44, StA 70; **barnys**: StA 8; **bairnis**: OR 54, 56; **bairnes**: OR 44, 50.

baronnis: *n. pl.* barons Y 125; **baronyis**: BAd 305.

batall: *n.* battle BAs 52, 144, 413; **batell**: OR 183, OA 176, S 84, 85, 86, etc., Y 210, 234, 318, BAs 43, 71, 74, etc., StA 30, 31, 85, etc.; **battell**: Y 232, BAd 191, 197, 225, etc., StA 3, 42, 63, etc.; **battaill**: BAd 43, 44, 51, etc.; **batellis**: *pl.* BAs 394; **battellis**: BAd 82, 374, 493, 494; **bataillis**: OD 183; **battaillis**: BAd 73.

bayth: *see* **baith**.

be: *prep.* by OD 26, 58, 61, etc., OR 22, 28, 58, etc., OA 11, 20, 27¹, etc., S 10, 20, 46, etc., Y 22, 89, 90, etc., BAd 6, 12, 19, etc., BAs 6, 10, 21, etc., StA 2, 13¹, 13², etc; from, on account of OA 8, 202.

beand: *see* **ar**.

befoir: *adv., prep.* before BAd 34, 59, 103, 512.

begylit: *v. pa. ppl.* begiled, deceived Y 214.

begyn: *v.* begin Y 67; **begynnis**: *pr.* OA 1, BAs 1; **begouth(e)**: *pa.* OD 1, 23, 73, 98, OA 2, 59; **begowth(e)**: OR 3, 71, 95; **begunyyn**: *pa. ppl.* S 122; **begynnand**: *pr. ppl.* BAs 2.

begyning: *ger.* beginning BAd 166, 217, 244, etc., StA 68, 144, 180, etc.; **begynnyng**: OD 189, OR 188, BAs 379, S 1, 9, 10, etc.

bene: *see* ar.

beneficit: *v. pa. ppl.* beneficed, provided with a benefice BAd 468, BAs 378.

bereyt: *v. pa. ppl.* buried BAd 231; **beryit**: BAd 87; **buryit**: BAd 157, 269, 279, etc., StA [239]; **bureyt**: BAd 110, 226, 238, etc.; **bureit**: BAd 394.

beris: *see* **bair**.

Bertane: *see* **Brettan(e)**.

besege: *v.* besiege BAd [456].

beschoprik: *see* **bischoprik**.

besyd(e): *prep.* near S 204, BAd 266, 386, BAs 311, 312, StA 97.

betrasyt: *v. pa.* betrayed StA 116.

betuix: *prep.* between OD 167, OA 131, 157, S 221, 233, Y 109, 131, 134, etc., BAd 43, 48, 82, etc., BAs 44, 48, 82, etc., StA 30, 75, 161, [190]; **betuyx**: OR 144, 162.

beyne, beyng: *see* ar.

beȝonde: *prep.* beyond BAd 221.

big: *v.* build OD 117, OA 103; **byg**: OR 113; **biggit**: *pa.* BAd 8, 48, 97, etc., BAs 11, 48, 91, etc.; **byggit**: StA [189]; **biggit**: *pa. ppl.* BAd [62]; **byggyt**: S 10.

bigging: *ger.* building BAd 376, BAs 299.

bischop(e): *n.* bishop S 64, 133, BAd 130, 132, BAs 65, 118, 119; **bischoip**: S 176, 178¹, 178²; **bishoip**: S 174; **bischoipis**: *poss.* S 209.

bischoprik: *n.* bishopric BAd 313; **beschoprik**: BAs 247; **bischoprikis**: *pl.* BAd 383, BAs 309.

blis: *v.* bless BAs 96; **bliss**: BAd 102; **blissit**: *pa.* BAd 104, 115.

blissing: *n.* blessing BAs 97.

blissit: *adj.* blessed BAs 272.

blud(e): *n.* blood OD 96, 109, 192, OR 93, 191, OA 81, 94, Y 39, 140, 336, BAd 150¹, 150², 285, 327, BAs 132, 133, 230.

bludy: *adj.* bloody BAd 135.

bocht: *v. pa.* bought Y 45.

boll: *n.* measure of grain S 167, 168¹, 168², etc.

bonat: *n.* cap Y 46.

bordour: *n.* border BAs 462.

bot: *conj.* but OD 19, 92, 116, etc., OR 23, 88, 119, etc., OA 29, 75, 95, etc., Y 56, 156, 173, etc., BAd 41, 253, 257, etc., BAs 223, 240, 253, etc., StA 11, 13, 35, etc.; unless, except StA 23; **bot at**: but that, unless Y 20.

bot: *prep.* except, without OD 27, 77, OR 29, 66, 75, OA 62, 190, 195, S 15, BAd 179, 212, 375, etc., BAs 250, 298, 360; **but**: OD 90, OR 87, OA 73, Y 79, 302, BAd 356, 369, 429; **bot of**: except for OR 66.

bot: *adv.* only OD 151, 217, S 165, 242, BAd 76, 228, 383, 484, BAs 128, 148, 194, etc.

boundis: *n. pl.* boundaries BAd 214.

bowallis: *n. pl.* bowels Y 264, 332.

brek: *v.* destroy BAs 335; **brak**: *v. pa.* Y 189, BAd 414; burst BAs 454; broke, violated OD 124, 142, 148, 165, OR 120, 137, 143, 158, OA 111, 139, 153, S 227, Y 70, 126, BAs 183, StA 26; **brak . . . doune**: defeated OD 119, OR 115.

brekyn: *ger.* breaking, exploding S 181.

Brettone: *n.* Briton OA 63; **Brytoun**: OD 79; **Bretonnis**: *pl.* OA 64, 153; **Brettonis**: OA 189; **Brettonnis**: OA 101, 107, 119, etc.; **Brettanis**: OA 104, 133; **Britones**: OD 24, 114, 118, etc., BAs 185; **Britonnis**: BAd 211, BAs 47, 49, 74, 89; **Brittonnis**: BAd 43, 47, 49, etc., BAs 44; **Brittonis**: BAd 74, 90; **Britouns**: OD 80; **Britanis**: OR 142; **Brytannis**: OR 126, 138, 144, etc.; **Brytons**: OR 138; **Brytonis**: StA 4, 5, 21, etc.; **Britones**: *poss.* BAs 69.

Brettan(e): *n.* Britain OA 62, 113, 115, etc., BAd 92, 112, BAs 102; **Britan(e)**: OD 77¹, 77², 125, 129, OR 74; **Brittane**: BAd 149; **Brytan**: OR 121, 123, 125, etc., S 29; **Bryton(e)**: StA 40, 41, 76, etc.; **Bertan(e)**: OR 75, StA 14, [37].

brig: *n.* bridge BAd 470, BAs 381; **bryg**: S 85; **briggis**: *pl.* Y 189, BAd 414, BAs 335.

brint: *v. pa.* burned BAd 457; **brynt**: S
223, Y 209, BAd 425, BAs 337, 345,
369, StA 164; **brint**: *pa. ppl.* S 218;
brynt: S 113.

brinyng: *ger.* burning S 142; **birnyng**:
BAd 45, BAs 45.

broder: *n.* brother BAd 11, 128, 155, etc.;
broþer: S 171; **broþir**: S 45, 51, 67,
etc., Y 102, 161, 245, 246, BAd 66, 76,
79, etc., BAs 17, 67, 76, etc.; **broþiris**:
poss. BAs 428; **brether**: *pl.* StA 118,
[121]; **breþir**: S 10, BAs 298.

brocht: *v. pa.* brought OD 43, 102, OR 46,
98, OA 80, 87, Y 50, 117, 192, BAd
30, 31, 32, etc., BAs 7, 31, 32, etc.,
StA 119; **broucht**: StA 2.

bruke: *v.* have use or possession of BAd
381; **brouke**: BAs 306; **brukit**: *pa.* OR
195, OA 188.

Brutis: *n. pl.* followers of Brutus Y 33.

bryg: *see* **brig**.

Brytan, Bryton(e): *see* **Brettan(e)**.

buk(e): *n.* book OD 155, OR 148, BAd
254, 296, 333, etc., StA 23; **bukis**: *pl.*
OR 246, Y 65.

bundyn: *v. pa. ppl.* bound by oath OD
164, OR 158, OA 153.

bure: *see* **bair**.

buttir: *n.* butter BAd 150, BAs 132.

bureit, bureyt, buryit: *see* **bereyt**.

bygane: *adv.* past OD 233, OA 226; in
times past OA 179.

callend: *n.* kalends S 93.

callit: *v. pa.* called OD 4, 69, 78, 159, OR
5, 67, 74, 153, OA 62, 146, Y 77, 80,
BAd 8², 36², BAs 37; *pa. ppl.* OD 6, 7,
10, etc., OR 8, 9, 12, etc., OA 7, 8¹, 8²,
etc., S 28, 151, 164, 206, Y 30, 38, 64,
BAd 7, 8¹, 20, etc., BAs 10, 11, 24,
etc., StA 5, 30, 114; **callyt**: OR1, 70,
71, etc.; **calland**: *pr. ppl.* OD 207, OR
208; **callit to name**: called by name
OA 84-85, 166.

cannocht: *v.* cannot BAd 492.

capitane: *n.* captain, castellan S 216, BAd
266; **captane**: StA [36], 86, 103, etc.

capitulo: *n.* chapter (Latin) BAd 254, 296,
333, etc., BAs 3, 8, 13, etc.

carnate: *adj.* incarnate OA 213.

cas: *n.* case OD 28.

castell: *n.* castle OD 85, OR 82, OA 67, S
216, 217, 241, 243, Y 158, 210, 244,
etc., BAd 511; **castellis**: *pl.* Y 192,
193, BAs 462.

catar: *n.* catarrh, rheumatism BAd 110.

cattell: *n.* cattle, property S 234.

causit: *v. pa.* caused Y 200, BAd 156,
282, 330, etc., BAs 387, 390, StA 195;
causyt: S 235.

caus: *n.* cause, reason BAd 208, 209, 210,
etc., BAs 410, Y 29, 62, 166, StA 91,
129; **causs**: *pl.* BAd 207, BAs 180; **for
caus**: because S 210, StA [47], 231.

certane: *n.* unspecified number OD 68,
OA 56, 78; **certane**: OR 67.

certane: *adj.* some not specified Y 5, 52,
323, BAd 270.

ces: *v.* cease OA 136; **sesyt**: *pa.* StA 266.

chaip: *n.* bargain; **better chaip**: cheaper S
245.

chaisit: *v. pa.* chased, pursued BAd 331;
chasit: BAd 344; **chasyt**: StA 255,
259, [265]; **chaisit**: *pa. ppl.* BAd 416;
chasit: OA 71, Y 129, BAd 346, 471,
486, 492, BAs 393; **chasyt**: OR 86, S
188; **chaist**: StA 226; **chassit**: OD 89;
chast: Y 233.

challangit: *v. pa.* challenged Y 291, 292,
293, 323.

changit: *v. pa. ppl.* changed Y 29, 247,
258.

changeing: *ger.* changing, succession OD
203.

changis: *n. pl.* changes, succession OR
204, OA [197].

channoun: *n.* canon BAd 251;
channonis: *pl.* BAd 64, 368, BAs 65;
chennonis: BAs 294.

chalmer: *n.* chamber St 209.

chape: *v.* escape OD 231.

chasit, chassit, chast: *see* **chaisit**.

chasty: *v.* chastise, correct BAs 427.

chasyt: *see* **chaisit**.

chesit: *v. pa.* chose Y 275, BAs 34, StA
85, 199; **chesyt**: BAd 33, StA 252;
chosin: *pa. ppl.* Y 124, BAd 27, 115,
192, 432, BAs 6, 350, 438; **chosyn(e)**:
BAd 4, BAs 28, 107, StA 3, 81.

chiar: *n.* chair BAs 7, 31; **chyar**: BAd 20,
22, 30, 31, BAs 23.

chiftane: *n.* chief, leader Y 275;
chiftanis: Y 276.

childer: *n. pl.* children Y 83, 85, 103, etc.,
BAd 5, 26, BAs 8, 27, 46, etc.; **childir**:
BAs 8, 83; **chider**: BAd 336.

chosin, chosyn(e): *see* **chesit**.

claithtis: *n. pl.* clothes StA 100, 188.

clamed: *v. pa.* claimed BAs 182; **clamit**:
BAs 164, 351, 352; **clamyt**: BAd 187,
210, 433, 435.

collaciouns: *n. pl.* discussions, collections
(of chronicles) OD 224; **collationis**: Y
59; **colatiounis**: OR 226.

collegis: *n. pl.* companions BAd 226.

colouris: *see* **cullour**.

com(e): *see* **cum**.

commonis: *n. pl.* commons, the common
people Y 274, 276, StA [214]; *poss.*
StA 56, 152.

comon: *adj.* ordinary StA [32]; shared StA
56, 192.

commoun: *n.* custom OA 227.

commoun: *v.* communicate, have dealings
with Y 60.

complices: *n. pl.* accomplices S 162, 205.

complenȝeit: *v. pa. ppl.* complained of
BAs 429.

compylit: *v. pa. ppl.* compiled OA 20.

condampnit: *v. pa. ppl.* condemned BAd
120; **condampnyt**: StA 193.

conduct: *n.* safe-conduct pass Y 322.

confederat: *adj.* allied StA [262], [264];
confiderate: BAd 256.

confermit: *v. pa. ppl.* confirmed BAd 234,
BAs 200.

confideratioun: *n.* alliance BAd 516.

confiscat: *v. pa.* confiscated BAd 328;
confiskit: BAs 264.

congregatione: *n.* gathering, assembly StA
27, 224.

conquerit: *v. pa.* conquered BAs 36.

conques: *v.* conquer OA 150; **conquest**:
pa. OD 162, OR 156, OA 26, S 13, 15,
Y 36, 42, 52, etc.

conquestour: *n.* conqueror OA 27.

conquiroris: *n. pl.* conquerors OR [28].

consaell: *n.* council S 238; counsel, advice
S 242; **consaile**: StA 83; **consaill**: StA
[231]; **counsall**: Y 288.

consalyt: *v. pa.* counseled, advised OR 88;
pa. ppl. OR 61; **counseilit**: OD 61;
counsalit: OA 51.

conserf: *v.* preserve, maintain OA 97, 185;
conseruit: *pa. ppl.* OA 138.

conspyrit: *v. pa.* conspired BAd 221.

conseruatour: *n.* conservator, guardian
BAs 428, 431, 438, 439.

contempin: *v.* despise OR 95;
contempne: OD 98.

contempnare: *n.* despiser BAd 136.

contenewis: *v. pr.* continues Y 51;
continewit: *pa.* BAd 44, BAs 45.

contenit: *v. pa. ppl.* contained OA 3, 19;
contenyt: OD 2, 19, OR 4, 22.

continewale: *adj.* continual BAs 49.

contrar(e): *n.* opposite Y 25; **in þe
contrar(e)**: to the contrary OR 149,
OA 143; **in contrar**: in spite of OA
149; in opposition to StA 96, 114,
153.

contrar: *adj.* contrary, hostile OR 139, Y
91.

contrar: *v.* speak against, contradict OA
221.

contrar: *prep.* against StA 74.

contrarius: *adj.* contrary, hostile Y 152;
contrarious: Y 162, 224.

contree: *n.* country OD 45, 208; **cuntre**:
OR 48, 66, 131, 210, OA 39, 55, 75,
etc., BAd 131, 417, BAs 119, 338,
StA 80; **cuntreis**: *pl.* BAd 56; counties
Y 275.

conuencioun: *n.* convention BAs 182;
conuentioun: BAd 187 *(see
explanatory note)*.

cornikillis, corniklis: *see* **cronikle**.

corne: *n.* grain S 234.

cornyklur: *see* **croniclare**.

correk: *v.* correct Y 228; **correkkit**: *pa.*
StA 201.

corruptit: *adj.* corrupted BAd 300.

cosing: *n.* kinsman BAs 270.

cot armour: *n.* coat of arms, surcoat worn
over armor Y 320.

coueris: *v. pr.* covers OD 231.

coulouris: *v. pr.* glosses over OR 233.

coulouris: *see* **cullour**.

counsall: *see* **consaell**.

countas: *n.* countess BAs 232; **countes**:
BAd 287.

couth: *v.* could OR 204, 228, OA 137,
149, BAd 460, BAs 372.

cowatyce: *n.* covetousness StA [223].

crabbyt: *adj.* angered StA 47.

credill: *n.* cradle OA 218.

crewell: *adj.* cruel, fierce, causing
extreme suffering BAd 306; **cruell**:
OD 3, 42, 156, OR 5, 150, OA 4, 144,
176.

crewellie: *adv.* cruelly BAd 262.

crewelte: *n.* cruelty BAd 166, 327; cruelte: fierceness, warlike deeds OA 141.

Cristin: *adj.* Christian Y 39, 152, 155; Cristyn(e): StA 209, 220, 221; Crystyne: StA 249.

cristin: *v.* convert to Christianity BAs 117; cristyn: BAd 130; crystynnit: BAd 131; cristinnit: *pa. ppl.* OA 230, BAs 117, 121, 184, 185; cristynnit: BAd 128; cristnyt: OD 235.

croniclare: *n.* chronicler OD 241; cornyklur: StA 48.

cronikle: *n.* chronicle OA 209, Y 1, 4; cronycle: OD 214, 221, 225; cornikle: OA 217, Y 64, BAs 1; croniklis: *pl.* Y 65; croniclis: OD 70, OR 200, 220, 223, etc.; cronyclis: OD 203, OR 68, 216; cornikillis: OA 193, Y 59; corniklis: Y 7, 23.

croun(e): *n.* crown OD 102, 158, S 205, BAd 109, 129, 183, etc.; crovn(e): OR 98, 152, OA 86, 94, 113, etc., Y 168, 288, 301, etc., BAs 104, 118, 234, etc.

crovn: *v.* crown Y 241; crovnit: *pa.* OA 126, BAs 244; crownit: BAd 105; crovnit: *pa. ppl.* Y 82, 104, 189, etc., BAs 7, 78, 81, etc.; crownit: *pa. ppl.* BAs 147, 195, 204, etc., BAd 32, 79, 81, etc, StA 29, 71, 124, etc.; crownyt: OD 137, OR 132, S 105, 186, BAd 76, StA 28, 53, 61, 257.

cruell: *see* crewell.

cruelte: *see* crewelte.

cryit: *v. pa.* cried; cryit downe: forbade, suppressed S 239.

Crystyne: *see* Cristin.

crystynnit: *see* cristin.

cullour: *n.* color, appearance BAd 321; coulouris: *pl.*; fals fenȝit coulouris: pretended position or attitude OR 233; fals colouris: OD 232.

cum: *v.* come, descend OD 42, OA 75, BAd 130, 331, 415, 482, BAs 118, 336, 363, StA 248; cummis: *pr.* amounts OR 106, OA 98; cum: *pa.* OD 24; com(e): OD 46, 50, 62, etc., OR 45, 51, 62, etc., OA 36, 52, 54, etc., S 28, 34, 202, 214, Y 29, 34, 35, etc., BAd 7, 12, [17], etc., BAs 15, 19, 25, etc., StA 14, 36, 37, etc.; cummyn: *pa. ppl.* OD 19, 28, 48, etc., OR 23, 30, 31, etc., OA 21, 31, 40, etc., Y 9, 13, 15, etc., BAs 373.

cuming: *ger.* coming BAd 204, 454, 509; cummyng: BAs 177, Y 113, 189, 191, BAs 440; cummyng: S 125; cummyn: BAs 175, 366.

cumpas: *n.* circumference S 12.

cuntre, cuntreis: *see* contree.

cunȝhe: *n.* coinage S 230.

cursit: *adj.* cursed Y 2, 17, 154, etc.; curst: BAs 226;

cursitnes: *n.* cursedness, wickedness Y 251, BAs 227, 235.

curtasy: *n.* courtesy Y 44.

curȝeit: *v. pa.* cared for the spiritual welfare StA 220.

cuttit: *v. pa.* cut Y 75.

daill: *n.* dale BAd 36.

dais: *n. pl.* days OD 3, OR 147, 154, S 223; dayes: OD 152; dayis: Y 92, BAd 150, 159, 163, etc., BAs 144, 277, 298, etc.

Danis: *n. pl.* Danes OA 163, 171, BAd 224, 262[1], 262[2], etc., BAs 191, 219, 220; Danys: OD 170, 172, 178, etc., OR 167, 169, 177, etc., OA 161, 171, 175, Y 41; *poss.* StA [164].

dantit: *v. pa.* defeated OA 101, 104, 161, 236, BAd 365, StA 207; dauntit: OD 8; dantit: *pa. ppl.* OA 107, 111, 181.

Dasie: *n.* Denmark? S 191 *see explanatory note.*

debait: *n.* debate, war Y 109; in debbete resone: by right of war? OR 121 *see textual note.*

deceissit: *v. pa.* deceased BAd 96, 99, 110, etc.

deces: *n.* decease OA 35, S 185; decess: OD 41; descese: S 140; disces: S 130.

decidit: *v. pa. ppl.* decided BAd 433, BAs 351.

declair: *v.* relate Y 67; declaris: *pr.* Y 64.

decollacioun: *n.* decollation, decapitation BAs 461.

decretit: *v. pa.* decided OD 43, 60, OR 46, OA 37; drecretyt: OR 60.

ded(e): *n.* death OD 56, 149, OR 44, 56, 143, Y 287; deid: OA 45, S 182, 229, Y 68, 246, BAd 164, 218, 223, etc., BAs 146, 188, 195, etc., StA 146, 193; deith(e): BAd 232, 239, 260, etc.

dee: *v.* die StA [108]; **de**: Y 213; **deit**: *pa.*
S 169, 177, 180, 235, Y 84, 85, 88,
BAd 381, BAs 55, 79, 94, etc., StA 70,
[113], [203]; **deyt**: S 75, BAd 54, 201,
230, etc., StA 261; **was (war) deid**:
had died Y 116, 123, BAd 13, 129,
173, etc.; BAs 19, 117, 162, etc.

defaltis: *n. pl.* faults Y 5.

defendit: *v. pa.* defended BAd 261, 445,
452, BAs 77, 219, 366, 369.

defens: *n.* defense OD 27, 156.

deflorand: *ger.* deflowering BAd 275.

defloratioun: *n.* deflowering BAd 277.

defowling: *ger.* violation StA 135.

deid: *n.* deed Y 230; **deidis**: *pl.* OR 233, Y
11, 51, 56, etc., BAd 156, 370; **dedis**:
OD 231, Y 99.

deid, deith(e): *see* **ded(e)**.

deid: *see* **dee**.

deir: *adj.* dear, expensive S 167.

deir: *adv.* dearly, expensively Y 45.

deit: *see* **dee**.

dele: *n.* dealings; **carnale dele**: sexual
intercourse Y 21.

deliuerit: *v. pa.* gave, handed over OA 78;
pa. ppl. released S 195, BAd 401, BAs
325.

demeritis: *n. pl.* faults BAd 120.

Demmerk: *n.* Denmark S 191.

Dene: *n.* Dane Y 43, 45, 47, etc.

denyit: *v. pa.* refused OD 92, OR 88, OA
74, BAd 41, BAs 41.

deprehendit: *v. pa. ppl.* discovered StA
147.

depriuyt: *v. pa. ppl.* deposed OA 95, S
205; **depryvit**: deprived BAd 230.

depriwyn: *n.* deposition S 211.

derth: *n.* dearth, scarcity S 235.

descendand: *v. pr. ppl.* descending OD
192.

descese: *see* **deces**.

descesyt: *v. pa.* deceased S 80; **discesyt**: S
51, 60, 66, etc.

destroyit: *v. pa.* destroyed OD 68, BAd
425; **distroyit**: OA 56, Y 93, 97, 163,
etc., BAd 206, BAs 179, 337, 345,
395; **distroyed**: BAs 178; **distroyt**: OR
67; **dystroyit**: StA 92, 249; **destroyit**:
pa. ppl. OD 75; **distroyit**: OA 30, 61,
S 20, BAd 205[1], 205[2], BAs 177, StA
64; **distroyt**: OR 73.

desyr: *n.*desire BAs 424; **desyris**: *pl.* Y
209.

desyrit: *v. pa.* desired OA 50, StA 10.

devilrie: *n.* deviltry OR 127; **devilry**: OD
131, OA 120.

deuote: *adj.* devout BAd 265, StA 17;
devoit: BAd 95.

devydit: *v. pa.* divided BAd 305.

devyne: *adj.* divine Y 30.

devysioun: *n.* division, schism S 122.

deyt: *see* **dee**.

dignite: *n.* dignity, honor S 190, BAd
251.

diocy: *n.* diocese BAd 468, BAs 378.

dirknes: *n.* darkness BAd 269.

discendit: *v. pa. ppl.* descended OR 172,
Y 13, 17, OA 167, 215; **discendand**:
pr. ppl. OR 191, OA 95, 183.

disces: *see* **deces**.

discesyt: *see* **descesyt**.

discomfit: *v. pa.* defeated OD 8, OA 9;
discumfyt: OR 10; **discumfit**: *pa. ppl.*
BAd 225; **discumfist**: BAd 250;
discumfyst: BAd 193.

disperatioun: *n.* desperation, despair BAd
121, 222.

displesit: *v. pa.* displeased Y 99, StA 198.

displesour: *n.* displeasure StA 84.

dispysit: *v. pa.* despised OR 226.

dispyt(e): *n.* despite, contempt BAd 194,
208.

dissaue: *v.* deceive OD 229; **dissaif(e)**:
OR 231, OA 225; **dissauit**: *pa. ppl.* Y
212, 214.

distroyed, distroyit, distroyt: *see*
destroyit.

diuers: *adj.* diverse, various OD 28, 181,
OR 180, OA 141, 174, Y 129, 288,
BAd 384, 484, BAs 310, 462.

dochter: *n.* daughter OA 11, 114, 165,
BAd 277, 429, BAs 347[2], 444, 447;
dochtir: OR 11, 123, 171; **douchter**:
BAd 316, 335, 359, etc., BAs 4, 255,
275, etc., Y 71, 74, 105, etc.;
douchtir: S 191; **dowchter**: StA 244;
dowcthter: StA 118; **dochter**: *poss.*
BAs 347[1]; **douchter**: BAs 351, StA
180; **douchteris**: BAd 428; **dochteris**:
pl. Y 107; **dochtiris**: S 41;
douchteris: Y 19, BAd 26, BAs 27,
StA 135, 177, 226.

dois: *v. pr.* does Y 229.
dominacioun: *n.* rule OD 112, OA 13, 99; **dominatioun**: OR 108.
doun(e): *adv.* down OD 109, 119, 213, OR 105, 202, 215, S 78, BAd 215, 449, StA 151; **dovn(e)**: OA 96, 105, 195, etc., Y 63, 105, 136; **downe**: S 239, Y 240; **cryit downe**: forbade, suppressed S 239.
doung: *v. pa. ppl.* forced BAd 345.
dowchter, dowcthter: *see* **dochter**.
doyngis: *n. pl.* doings, deeds BAs 441.
draf: *v. pa.* drove BAs 70; **draiff**: BAd 70; **drevyn(e)**: *pa. ppl.* Y 72, BAs 393.
drawin: *v. pa. ppl.* drawn Y 220, 223, BAs 1, 450.
dred: *v. pa.* dreaded, feared BAs 433; **dredand**: *pr. ppl.* BAs 263.
dredour: *n.* fear BAd 473.
drevyn(e): *see* **draf**.
drownyn: *n.* drowning, sinking S 210.
drownyt: *v. pa.* drowned S 209, StA 6; **drownit**: *pa. ppl.* Y 113.
duchery: *n.* duchy BAd 243.
duell: *v.* dwell OD 91, OR 88, OA 74, BAd 179; **duelt**: *pa.* OD 79, 98, OR 64, 95, OA 54, 63, BAd 128, BAs 116.
dukis: *n. poss.* duke's S 199, 215; **dukis**: *pl.* leaders S 28.
durst: *v. pa.* dared BAd 474, BAs 383.
dyk: *n.* wall StA 189.
dystroyit: *see* **destroyit**.

efferis: *v. pr.* is appropriate Y 8.
efferit: *adj.* afraid Y 280.
efter: *prep.* after OD 7, 12, 13, etc., Y 52, BAd 5, 35, 76, etc., BAs 203, 217, 226, etc., StA 17, 78, 88, etc.; **eftir**: OR 9, 13, 14, etc., OA 13, 54, 57, etc., S 10, 18, 19, etc., Y 38, 41, 68, etc., BAd 15, 19, 36, etc., BAs 13, 21, 25, etc.
efter: *adv.* afterwards OD 65, 76, OA 61, StA 59, 112, 130, 196; **eftir**: OR 12, 94, 112, Y 137, 220, 273, BAd 29, 70, 165, etc., BAs 8, 30, 213, etc.
efter that (þat): *conj.* after OD 114; **eftir þat**: OR 110, OA 101, BAd 38, 225, 277, BAs 40.

efterwart: *adv.* afterwards OD 11, OA 223, StA 145, 191; **eftirwart**: S 206, Y 247, 272, 281, BAs 382, 395, 415; **eftirwartis**: BAd 494; **eftirward**: BAs 363.
eikit: *v. pa.* added to BAd 214; **ekyt**: added StA 241.
eild: *n.* age OR 65; **eld**: S 105, 186.
electioun: *n.* choosing BAd 285.
ellis: *adv.* else OD 144.
eme: *n.* uncle Y 284.
emprice: *n.* empress OR 218², OA 211, Y 120; **emperice**: OD 216; **empris**: Y 126, 127; **emprys**: Y 132; **empryce**: Y 182; **emprice**: *poss.* OR 218¹, Y 144, 152; **empericis**: OD 216; **empris**: Y 141; **emprys**: OA 211; **empryce**: Y 135.
empriour(e): *n.* emperor OR 115, OA 105, Y 108, 115, S 77, BAd 42, 44, 53, etc., BAs 43, 45, 54, etc., StA 47, 66, [78], etc.; **empriouris**: *pl.* OR 116, OA 107.
endingis: *n. pl.* endings, deaths Y 223.
endis: *v. pr.* ends OA 239; **endit**: *pa.* Y 100, 332, BAd 83, BAs 82; *pa. ppl.* Y 112.
enemys: *n. pl.* enemies OR 142, OA 133, S 97, BAs 70, 108, 117; **inymeis**: BAd 70, 77, 114, etc.; **inymyis**: OD 148.
engenerit: *v. pa.* engendered Y 22, 89.
ennteres: *n.* entrance OA 79.
entre: *v.* enter OA 77; **enterit**: *pa.* BAd 252, BAs 10, 213, 214, 385; **enteryt**: BAd 475, StA 164; **enttrit**: BAd 7.
entyrit: *v. pa. ppl.* interred BAd 100.
erast: *adv. super.* soonest OR 231; **erest**: OD 229.
erd(e): *n.* earth OD 20, OR 24, OA 22, Y 279, BAs 224.
erdit: *v. pa. ppl.* buried Y 300, BAs 205, 216, 220, etc.; **erddit**: S 182.
errit: *v. pa.* erred Y 28.
erle: *n.* earl OD 216, 217, OR 219¹, 219², S 61, 149, 161, etc., BAd 361, 517; **erll**: OA 212, Y 70, 111, 118, etc.; **erlis**: *pl.* BAd 486; **erllis**: BAs 401.
errasy: *n.* heresy Y 228.
eschaipit: *v. pa.* escaped BAd 486.

eschetit: *v. pa.* escheated StA 193.

eschewit: *v. pa. ppl.* parried Y 324.

estatis: *n. pl.* estates, ranks of society OA 125, BAs 438; **estaitis**: OR 132.

euerilk: *adj.* each, every StA 132; **euirilk**: Y 43.

euir: *adv.* ever OR 23, 27, 143, etc., Y 159, 197, 217, etc., BAd 33, 41, 247, 448, BAs 33, 179, 197, etc.; **evir**: OA 22, 182, Y 13, 39, 228, 337, BAs 158; **euer**: OD 20, 143, 149, etc.

euirmar: *adv.* evermore Y 155, BAs 412; **euirmair**: BAd 505.

ewill: *n.* evil Y 218.

ewill: *adj.* evil, unfortunate, disastrous S 228, Y 2, 90, StA 54, [150], 175, 194.

ewyn: *n.* eve, evening S 160, BAs 141.

excedit: *v. pa.* exceeded StA 72.

excepand: *prep.* excepting BAs 387.

excusit: *v. pa.* excused OD 231.

exilit: *v. pa.* exiled Y 225, BAd 328, BAs 263, 264; **exild**: Y 95; *pa. ppl.* Y 299.

exonerat: *v. pa.* resigned BAd 251.

exprymit: *v. pa. ppl.* expressed BAd 493.

expulsit: *v. pa.* expelled BAs 280, 411.

exquesyt: *adj.* carefully chosen OR 233.

eyne: *n. pl.* eyes Y 75.

facht: *see* **fecht**.

fader: *n.* father Y 34, 76, 116, etc., BAd 13, 20, 73, etc., BAs 19, 21, 73, etc., StA 2, 176, 195; **fadir**: S 200.

fale: *v.* fail Y 174; **failȝeit**: *pa.* fell vacant OD 108; **failȝit**: OR 104.

fallyn: *v. pa. ppl.* fallen OA 118.

falshed(e): *n.* falsehood OD 212, 232; OR 214, 241; **falset**: Y 224, 251.

falsly: *adv.* falsely OD 158, OR 152, 158, OA 145, BAd [449]; **falslie**: OA 111, 152.

fals: *adj.* false OD 159, 194, 232, OR 153, 193, 233, OA 122, 147, [186], 208, Y 3, 6, 11, etc., BAd 441, 442, 465.

faltis: *n. pl.* faults Y 228, BAs 441.

faltyf: *adj.* faulty Y 10.

familiaris: *n. pl.* servants BAd 311; **famyliaris**: BAd 167.

fand(e): *v. pa.* found OD 68, OR 66, OA 55, 56, BAd 383, BAs 309.

fane: *adv.* eagerly StA 151.

Fasteryngis: *n. poss.* Lent's S 160.

faucht: *see* **fecht**.

faworyt: *v. pa.* favored, supported S 220.

fayis: *n. pl.* foes StA 228.

fayne: *adj.* eager, willing OD 146, OA 136, 137; **fayne**: OR 141.

fayth: *n.* pledged word OR 109, 158, 231; **faith**: OD 113, 165, 229, 230, OA 100, 153, StA 124; **fayth**: Christian faith OR 236, S 23, 32.

fecht: *v.* fight BAd 510; **facht**: *pa.* BAs 179; **faucht**: BAd 192, 373, BAs 12, StA 103, 153, [251], etc.; **fechting**: *pr. ppl.* BAs 75, 169; **fechtand**: BAd 262.

fechtand: *adj.* fighting BAd 483.

fechtting: *ger.* fighting BAs 59.

fee: *n.* inheritable estate BAs 249 *(see explanatory note).*

feft: *v. pa.* enfeoffed, gave as a fief BAd 179, BAs 158.

feild: *n.* battle BAd 67, 75^1, 75^2, etc, StA 4, 88, [104], etc.; **feld**: BAs 68, 75, 235, etc.; **feldis**: *pl.* BAs 393; **feildis**: *pl.* StA 251.

feir: *adj.* strong Y 190.

feirs: *adj.* fierce BAd 192, 363, 373; **ferce**: BAd 116; **fers**: BAs 108.

feld: *v. pa.* fell BAd 485.

feldis: *see* **feild**.

felicite: *n.* felicity, happiness BAd 96, 171, 174, etc.

felloun: *adj.* fierce, destructive OA 36.

fenȝeit: *v. pa.* feigned OD 154, OA 142, Y 72; **fenȝit**: OR 148.

fenȝeit: *adj.* feigned, false OD 151, 232, Y 3; **fenȝit**: OR 146, 233.

fenȝeouris: *n. pl.* feigners, pretenders OA 141.

ferce: *see* **feirs**.

ferd(e): *adj.* fourth S 5, 136, Y 104, 127, 274, 318, BAd 291, BAs 182, 185, 376, 459, StA 165; **fourt**: *adj.* fourth BAd 119, 123, 134, etc., StA 215.

ferm: *adj.* firm StA 66.

ferrar: *adv.* further Y 188.

fers: *see* **feirs**.

fest: *n.* feast S 87, 96, 111.

festnance: *n.* imprisonment StA 252.

fewte: *n.* fealty OA 187, Y 266; **fewtee**: OD 195, OR 194.

feyit: *v. pa.* engaged StA 248.

fife: *adj.* five S 4^1, 4^2, 6, etc.; **fyfe**: OR 110; **fyve**: Y 282, 286, BAd 58, BAs 285.

fift: *adj.* fifth S 6, BAs 135; **fyft**: OA 96, S 151, Y 279, 285, 328, BAd 152, StA 167; **fyift**: BAd 143, 363.
fiftie: *see* **fyfty**.
fleit: *v. pa.* routed, put to flight StA 206.
fletit: *v. pa.* floated Y 187.
fleyng: *ger.* fleeing StA 13.
flude: *n.* river BAd 6.
foirfadir: *n.* forefather, ancestor OR 63; **forefader**: OD 63; **forfader**: OA 53.
folk: *n.* people S 235; followers OD 57, OR 46, 57, OA 37, 46; **folkis**: *pl.* OD 43, OA 51; BAd 416, BAs 337.
followis: *v. pr.* follows S 18; **followit**: *pa.* Y 205; **folowand**: S 56, 66, 106, etc.
forbearis: *n. pl.* forebears Y 22.
forefader, forfader: *see* **foirfadir**.
forsamekle: *conj.* forasmuch Y 3; **as forsamekle as**: since Y 58.
fors: *n.* force; **on fors**: by force OA 104; **maist force**: greatest number OD 58.
forsy: *adj.* strong OA 144.
forther: *adv.* further OA 155.
fortoun: *n.* fortune BAd 86.
forʒet: *v. pa. ppl.* forgotten Y 146.
foule: *adj.* foul, inclement Y 49; degrading OD 29, OR 31; **foull**: OA 32.
foundement: *n.* anus Y 262.
foundit: *v. pa.* founded BAd 337, 361, 367, etc., BAs 274, 288, 293, etc.; **foundyt**: S 47, 54, 56, etc.; **foundit**: *pa. ppl.* OD 74, OA 60, BAd 181, BAs 160.
fourt: *see* **ferd(e)**.
fra: *prep.* from OD 110, 117, 118, etc., OR [20], 77, 105, etc., OA 64, 94, 96, etc., S 1, 3, 4, etc., Y 30, 63, 163, etc., BAd 7, 30, 77, etc., BAs 10, 14, 22, etc., StA 37, 68, 189, 201; because OD 143, OR 138, OA 133.
Franche: *adj.* French OR 202, S 126, Y 208.
Franchis: *n. pl.* Franks OD 201.
Fraunce: *n.* France OD 5, 151, 153, etc., OA 6, 191, 192, etc., Y 110, 112, 139, etc., BAs 40, 110, 153, etc.; **Franchis**: *poss.* OD 222.
fre: *adj.* free, independent OR 187, OA 179, Y 172, BAd 41, 448; without obligation BAd 381, BAs 306.
fredome: *n.* freedom from outside control OD 189, OR 188, OA 180, BAd 233, 447, BAs 199, 362.

frehaldaris: *n. pl.* freeholders BAd 306, BAs 251.
freind: *n.* friend BAd 397; **frend(e)**: BAs 321, StA 107; **freindis**: *pl.* BAd 105, 273; **frendis**: BAs 98, 393, StA 162.
frelie: *adv.* freely, generously BAd 305.
frendschip(e): *n.* friendship OD 149, OR 144, StA 66, 122, [125].
freris: *n. pl.* friars Y 300, BAs 448.
ful: *adj.* complete S 175; **of full bed**: legitimate Y 77.
fulfillit: *v. pa. ppl.* filled Y 208, 224.
full: *adv.* very OD 53.
furst: *adv.* first BAd 35; **fyrst**: StA 153.
furth: *adv.* forth OA 148, Y 128, 249, BAd 16, 24, 467, 504, BAs 25, 174, 378.
fyfe: *see* **fife**.
fyft, fyift: *see* **fift**.
fyfty: *num.* fifty S 173, 177, BAs 46; **fiftie**: BAd 46.
fyftyne: *num.* fifteenth BAd 47.
fynaly: *adv.* finally StA [178].
fyr: *n.* fire S 164.
fyrst: *see* **furst**.
fyrst: *adj.* first OR 3, 106, StA 1, 55, 59, etc.
fyve: *see* **fife**.

gadderit: *v. pa.* gathered OA 85, 125, BAd 472, BAs 382, StA 236; **gaderyt**: StA 86.
gaf, gaif: *see* **gif(e)**.
gait: *see* **gayt**.
gaitwart: *adv.* on the way S 238.
ganesay: *v.* deny Y 23.
ganestand, ganestude: *see* **gaynstand**.
gang: *v.* go Y 80; *pa.* BAd 461; **gane**: *pa. ppl.* Y 50, BAd 510, BAs 415.
gart: *v. pa.* caused, ordered, compelled OA 103, S 215, Y 96, 241, BAd 465, BAs 335; **gert**: OD 117, OR 113, StA 189.
gat: *v. pa.* got, obtained OA 79, S 97, 217, BAd 68, 282, 306, BAs 68, 401, StA 66, 100; begot OD 66, 217, OR 65, 219, OA 212, S 40, Y 83, 106, 119, 336, BAd 336; **gottin**: *pa. ppl.* obtained Y 335; begotten OA 114, 120, Y 22, 89, 103, 134; **gottyn**: OD 127, 128, 131, OR 123, 124, 127.
Gayelgaggit: *n.* Gaelic OD 7; **Gayelige**: OR 9; **Galeig**: OA 8.

gaynstand: *v.* withstand, resist OD 93, 159, OR 153; **ganestand**: OA 77, 146; **gaynstude**: *pa.* OD 120, OR 140; **ganestude**: OA 106; **nocht gaynstandand**: *conj.* notwithstanding OR 119.

gayt: *n.* way, street, road S 218; **gait**: Y 49¹, 49², BAs 373; route BAd 414, BAs 335.

generacioun: *n.* descendants OD 55, OA 44, **generatioun**: OR 55; **mak generacioun**: *v.* beget children OD 95; **mak generatioun**: OR 92.

genology: *n.* lineage Y 59, 61; **genologi**: OA 207.

gentill: *adj.* gentle, aristocratic Y 44.

gentillis: *n. pl.* gentility OA 47, 48; **gentilis**: pagans StA 17.

gentillman: *n.* gentleman BAd 277; **gentillmen**: *pl.* OD 58, OR 58.

gert: *see* **gart**.

gewictis: *n. pl.* giants? OR 67 *(see explanatory note).*

gif(e): *v.* give OA 74, BAd 163; **gaf**: *pa.* OA 10, Y 86, BAs 26, 27, 97, etc.; **gaif**: OR 11, 91, 236, Y 73, 133, BAd 26, 246, 305, etc., StA 116, 242, 253, 257; **gevin**: *pa. ppl.* Y 147, BAd 25, 152, 220; **gevand**: *pr. ppl.* BAd 159.

goddis: *n. pl.* gods OD 61, OR 61, OA 51, StA 18.

gorris: *v. pr.* gores Y 238.

gottin, gottyn: *see* **gat**.

gouernyt: *v. pa.* governed OD 42, OR 45, BAd 77, [502], StA 9; **gouernit**: OA 35, BAd 95, 171, 256, etc., StA 202; **gouernit**: *pa. ppl.* BAd 278.

gouernour: *n.* governor, guardian StA 199; **governouris**: *pl.* Y 38.

governans: *n.* conduct Y 251; **governance**: Y 2, 218.

grantit: *v. pa.* agreed Y 80, BAs 361; granted BAd 233, BAs 199, 251, 423; *pa. ppl.* BAs 243.

greit: *adj.* great S 98, BAd 42, 73, 86, etc.; **gret(e)**: OD 7, 57, 60, etc., OR 9, 57, 60, etc., OA 8¹, 8², 47¹, etc., S 35, 63, 97, etc., Y 74, 81, 109, etc., BAs 43, 74, 79, etc., StA 18¹, 18², 21, etc.; **greitar**: *comp.* BAd 459; **gretar**: BAd 472, BAs 371; **gretest**: Y 282, BAs 196.

greitlye: *adv.* greatly OR 94, 96; **gretely**: OD 98; **gretly**: OD 100; **gretlie**: OA 82, 84.

gretand: *v. pr. ppl.* greeting StA 171.

gretumly: *adv.* greatly StA [198].

ground-rycht: *adj.* heritable right, right of possession OA 164; **grond-rycht**: OR 170; **grund-rycht**: OD 173.

gud(e): *adj.* good Y 46, 68, 104, etc., BAd 58, 148, 165, etc., BAs 60, 130, 151, etc., StA 61.

gudis: *n.* goods Y 164, 230, BAd 329, 376, 477, BAs 264, 299, 387, StA 178, 193.

gudnes: *n.* goodness BAd 407, 426, BAs 329, 346.

gwn: *n.* gun BAs 454; **gunnis**: *pl.* S 181.

gyandis: *n. pl.* giants OD 68; **giandis**: OA 56.

gyf: *conj.* if OR 49, 90, 193, etc.; **gif**: OD 48, 93, 194, 198, OA 40, 77, 186, etc.

habyt: *n.* habit, clerical dress BAd 251.

habandonit: *see* **abandonyt**.

haf: *v.* have OR 117, OA 107, Y 5, 24, 65, etc.; **haif**: OR 139, 234, S 237, BAd 248, 393, StA 152, 192; **a**: StA 151; **haf(e)**: *pr.* OR 189, OA 228, Y 26, 28, 32, etc.; **haif**: OR 28; **hes**: BAd 3, 53; **havand**: *pr. ppl.* BAs 365.

haill: *adj.* whole BAd 41; **hale**: Y 190, 241, 302, BAs 41.

haim: *see* **hame**.

haitit: *v. pa. ppl.* hated BAd 286, BAs 231.

hald: *v.* hold OD 197, OR 197, OA 191, BAd 445, 447, BAs 250, 360; **haldin**: *pa. ppl.* BAd 235, BAs 201, 413.

hale: *see* **haill**.

halely: *adv.* wholly Y 36, 42.

hallowyt: *v. pa. ppl.* consecrated S 99.

haltit: *v. pa.* limped BAs 422.

haly: *adj.* holy OR 236, OA 230, S 21, 23, 122, 211, Y 68, 91, 93, etc., BAd 233, 336, 341, etc., BAs 200, 277, 292, 416.

hame: *n.* home Y 74, 76, 190, 210, BAs 267, 336, 338, etc.; **haim**: Y 117; **hayme**: BAd 415, 417, 508.

hame-cummyng: *n.* home-coming Y 113, 189, 190-91; **hame-cuming**: BAd 509.

hamwart: *adv.* homeward BAs 373.

handis: *n. pl.* hands OA 118, BAd 68, BAs 37, 69, 428, StA 117.

hangit: *v. pa.* hanged OD 56, StA 36; *pa. ppl.* Y 220, 223, BAs 449, StA 51.

hard: *see* **heir**.

hardyment: *n.* deeds of valor StA 72; boldness, hardihood StA 93.

harppar: *n.* harper StA 210.

hart: *n.* heart BAd 359.

hate: *adj.* hot Y 263.

havand: *see* **haf**.

hayme: *see* **hame**.

hed: *n.* head BAs 97; **heid**: BAd 104, 193, StA 148; **heyd**: BAd 208.

hedit: *v. pa. ppl.* beheaded Y 315; **hedyt**: S 170, 193.

heir: *v.* hear OA 222; **hard**: *pa.* Y 250.

heir: *adv.* here Y 67, 183, BAd 128, 129, BAs 116, 117.

heirof: *prep.* hereof OR 222.

helpit: *v. pa.* helped OD 123, OA 109; **helpyt**: OR 119.

herdyt: *v. pa.* buried StA 221.

heretage: *n.* inheritance BAs 249, StA 193; **heritage**: OR 174.

heretour: *n.* heiress BAd 373.

hereyt: *v. pa.* harried StA 50.

hes: *see* **haf**.

heyd: *see* **hyd**.

hie: *adj.* high BAd 512.

him: *see* **hym**.

hir(e): *pron., adj.* her OD 217, OR 219, OA 212, S 40, Y 18, 37, 75[1], etc.; **hyr**: StA 82, 135.

houss: *n. pl.* houses Y 97.

howsald: *adj.* household StA 215; **housald**: S 240, 242.

hund(e): *n.* hound, dog BAd 57, BAs 58, 181; **hoynd**: BAd 209.

hunder: *num.* hundred OD 23, 190; **hundir(e)**: OR 26, 141, 164, etc., S 2, 3, 4, etc.; **hundreth**: OA 24, 137, 159, etc., BAd 34, 46, 52, etc., BAs 34, 46, 60, etc., StA 54; **hundret**: OA 181; **hundyr**: S 113.

hungar: *n.* hunger S 235[1], 235[2]; **hungyr**: S 169, 229.

hungerit: *v. pa.* starved BAs 432.

huntar: *n.* hunter StA 21; **huntaris**: *pl.* StA 22, 208.

huris: *n. poss.* whore's OD 133, OR 128.

hyd: *v. pa.* hid StA 196; **heyd**: *pa. ppl.* BAd 266.

hym: *pron.* him StA 11, 107; **him**: *refl.* himself Y 218, BAd 251, 307, 382, etc., BAs 243, 307.

hys: *pron.* his StA 51, 60, [68], etc.

hyr: *see* **hir(e)**.

ile: *n.* isle OD 76, 85, 92, etc., OR 74, 81, 84, etc., OA 67, 172, 189, Y 26, BAs 18, 184; **ilis**: *pl.* OD 87, BAd 352; **ylis**: BAs 262; **ilys**: StA 51, 243.

ilka: *adj.* each Y 48.

ilkane: *pron.* any Y 238.

ilysmen: *n. pl.* men of the Isles StA 35; **ilysmen**: StA 207, 211.

incobus: *n.* incubus Y 90, 134.

inconquest: *adj.* unconquered OA 181.

incontinent: *adv.* immediately OA 127.

industry: *n.* contrivance BAd 169.

infamyt: *adj.* infamous BAd 275.

infeckit: *v. pa. ppl.* infected OD 3.

infeftment: *n.* enfeoffment Y 174, 176.

infortunat: *adj.* unfortunate Y 217.

Ingland: *see* **Yngland**.

Inglis(s): *see* **Ynglis**.

Inglismen, Inglismenis: *see* **Ynglisman**.

ingyne: *n.* intelligence BAd 229, StA 222; ingenuity, cleverness BAd 288.

inhabitaris: *n. pl.* inhabitants OA 183.

inhabyt(e): *v.* inhabit OD 60, OR 47, 60; *pa.* OD 69, 71, 86, OR 67, 83, 84; *pa. ppl.* OD 74, 93, OR 72; **inhabytyt**: OR 89; **inhybyt**: OR 70.

injuris: *n. pl.* injuries BAd 351.

injuste: *adj.* unjust BAd 137.

injustlie: *adv.* unjustly BAd 298.

innocentis: *n. pl.* innocents BAd 294, BAs 236.

innumerabill: *adj.* innumerable S 232.

insaciabill: *adj.* insatiable BAd 135.

inspyrit: *v. pa. ppl.* inspired BAd 445.

instance: *n.* request, urging S 195.

interdytit: *v. pa. ppl.* interdicted Y 166; **intirdytyt**: S 70.

into: *prep.* in OA 2, 7, Y 204, 295, 325, 327, BAd 198.

intromet: *v.* deal (with), occupy oneself (with) OA 155.

intrusit: *v. pa.* intruded, thrust into office BAs 260; *pa. ppl.* BAs 270; **intrusyt**: StA 229.

inuasioun: *n.* invasion BAd 261.
invy: *n.* hostility Y 200.
invyit: *v. pa. ppl.* envied BAd 286; **inwyit**: BAs 231.
inwadit: *v. pa.* invaded StA 35; **invadit**: usurped BAd [502], BAs 234, 409; **inwadit**: BAs 239; **inuadit**: *pa. ppl.* attacked BAd 364; **inuading**: *pr. ppl.* BAd 350.
inymeis, inymyis: *see* **enemys.**

jowellis: *n. pl.* jewels Y 193.
Jowry(e): *n.* Judea BAd 23; BAs 24.
joye: *n.* joy BAs 338.
juge: *n.* judge BAs 359.
juge: *v.* judge S 209, BAd 443; **jugit**: *pa. ppl.* StA 23.
juperdeis: *n. pl.* hazards, dangers BAd 494.
justlie: *adv.* justly StA 92, 125.
justyce: *n.* justice StA 125, 266.

kalend(e): *n.* kalends BAd 466, 491, 501.
kend: *v. pa. ppl.* known OD 18, OA 19; **kennit**: StA 157; **kennyt**: OR 21.
kepar: *n.* warden Y 245; guardian BAs 423; **keparis**: *pl.* BAs 350, 356; **keiparis**: BAd 432, 439.
kepe: *v.* keep OD 109, 118, 229, 238, OR 105, 114, 231, OA 104, 184; **keip**: OR 192, StA 189; **kepit**: *pa.* OA 102, 226, 234, BAs 15, StA 22, 124, 125; **keipit**: BAd 18, 58; **kepyt**: OR 240, S 24; **kepit**: *pa. ppl.* OD 149, OR 144, OA 138, 140, Y 27, 175, BAd 54, BAs 55, 60, 261, 434, StA 202; **keipit**: BAd 324; **kepand**: *pr. ppl.* BAs 244; **keiping**: BAd [499]; **kepe . . . kyndenes**: continue to practice goodwill OD 238; **kepyt . . . kyndnes**: *pa.* OR 240; **kepit . . . kyndnes**: OA 234.
keping: *ger.* keeping, guarding Y 247; **kepyng**: S 241.
kest: *v. pa.* cast BAd 214, 222.
kingis: *n. poss.* king's OD 100, OR 97, 123, OA 84, 114, S 191, 219, 240, Y 199, 283, 287, 320, BAd 21, 30, BAs 31, 132, 270; *pl.* OD 108, 111, 114, etc., OR 107, 110, 156, etc., OA 98, 182, 188, 215, Y 2, 5, 6, etc., BAd 39, 101, 191, etc., StA 92, 150.

kinrik: *n.* kingdom OR 126, OA 118, 188, S 44, 46, 52, BAd 105; **kinryk**: OR 195; **kinrikis**: *pl.* OA 151; **kynryk**: OD 130.
kirk: *n.* church OD 234, OR 236, OA 230, S 22, 63, 98, etc., Y 91, 93, 163, etc., BAd 62, 233, 336, etc., BAs 63, 200, 274, etc.; **kirkis**: *pl.* Y 97, 163, BAd 376; *poss.* BAs 299.
knaw: *v. pr.* know Y 315.
kne: *n.* knee Y 49; **kneis**: *pl.* StA [99], 171.
knelit: *v. pa.* kneeled Y 48, 49.
knycht: *n.* knight S 193, Y 292, BAd 339; **knychtis**: StA [72].
kyithit: *v. pa.* performed, revealed (miracles) BAd 341; **kythit**: S 206.
kyn(e): *n.* kin BAd 27, 28, BAs 28.
kyndnes: *n.* goodwill, neighborly feeling OR 240, OA 234; **kyndenes**: OD 238.
kynryk: *see* **kinrik.**

laborious: *adj.* devout StA [265].
laddis: *n. pl.* boys Y 218.
laif: *n.* rest, remander StA 36; **lave**: OD 95; **lufe**: OR 92[1].
landis: *n. pl.* lands OD 44, 60, 196, 197, OR 47, 60, 86, 197, OA 38, 50, 141, 190, BAd 221, 305, 308, BAs 389, StA 92, [130], 258.
lang: *adj.* long OD 75[1], 88, 97, etc., OR 72, 85, 94, etc., OA 60, 61, 70, etc., Y 57, 204, 277, BAd 309, StA 124.
lang: *adv.* long OD 24, 75[2], 76, 181, OR 27, 73, 160, OA 25, Y 45, 47, 82, BAd 19, BAs 21, 23, 25; **langar**: *comp.* OD 198, 230, OA 226; **langir**: OR 232; **langest**: *super.* OD 207; **langast**: OR 208, OA 200.
langag(e): *n.* language OD 7, OR 9, OA 8, Y 51, StA 46.
lardis: *see* **lordis.**
lastit: *v. pa.* lasted BAd 175.
lat: *v.* let, permit OA 74; **leit**: *pa.* BAd 464, BAs 375, StA 89; **lete**: OA 152; **lattin**: *pa. ppl.* permitted (to go) BAd 508, BAs 413.
lave: *see* **laif.**
law: *adj.* low Y 219, 336.
lawis: *n. pl.* laws BAd 215, 237, 242, 284, StA 21, 22, 54, etc.
lefe: *see* **leve.**

legacy: *n.* alliance BAd 49.
legat: *n.* papal legate Y 168; **legait:** military commander StA 90, 126.
lege: *n.* covenant, alliance BAs 49.
leiff: *see* **liffit.**
leiffand: *see* **leve.**
leiffit: *see* **liffit.**
leit: *see* **lat.**
lele: *adj.* loyal OA 41.
lenth: *n.* length OD 220.
Lentryne: *n.* Lent BAs 452; **Lenterin:** S 227.
leon: *n.* lion OR 99; **lyon:** BAs 108; **lyoun(e):** OA 88, BAd 34, 116, 397, BAs 320.
lerit: *v. pa.* learned Y 44, 50.
les, less(e): *adj.* minor, lesser OD 72, 83, OR 80, 89, OA 65, 75, 86.
les: *adv.* less BAd 229.
les þan: *conj.* unless Y 65-66.
leste: *adj.* least OD 225.
lestis: *v. pr.* lasts BAs 154; **lestit:** *pa.* BAs 46, 59; **lestyt:** S 176, 226.
lesyngis: *n. pl.* lies OR 148, OD 224; **lesynes:** OD [154].
let: *v.* be hindered StA 64².
lete: *see* **lat.**
letter-day: *n.* latter days, end of life StA 149-50.
lettreჳ: *n. pl.* letters BAs 430.
leve: *v.* leave OD 146, 220; **lefe:** OR 141; **leiffand:** *pr. ppl.* StA 172.
levit: *v. pa.* relinquished Y 335.
liegis: *n. pl.* lieges Y 252, BAd 117.
liffit: *v. pa.* lived Y 28, 82, 177; **levit:** BAs 213, 389; **leiff:** BAd 252; **leiffit:** BAd 479, StA 125, 143; **liffit:** *pa. ppl.* Y 26, 32; **lyfand:** *pr. ppl.* OD 176.
lift: *see* **lyft.**
liknes: *n.* likeness Y 135; **liklynes:** Y 21.
litill: *adj.* little BAd 7, 55, 454, BAs 56.
lordis: *n. poss.* lord's BAd 359; **lardis:** StA 57; **lordis:** *pl.* OD 58, OR 58, OA 48, S 238, Y 270, 282, 287, BAs 243, StA 31, 224.
losing: *ger.* praising OD 31; **losyng:** OR 33.
lufe: *n.* love OR 92².
lufe: *see* **laif.**
lufis: *v. pr.* loves Y 239; **luffit:** *pa.* BAd 420; **lufit:** Y 259, BAs 340; **luf:** *imper.* OA 41.

ly: *v.* lie, sleep StA 187; **lyis:** *pr.* S 166, Y 237, BAd 107, BAs 100, 446.
lychorus: *adj.* lecherous StA 176, 240.
lychory: *n.* lechery StA [54], 152, 176, etc.
lyfand: *see* **liffit.**
lyf(e): *n.* life Y 56, 244, 327, 332; **lyff:** StA 194; **lyvis:** *pl.* Y 280; **on(e) lyf(e):** alive OR 175, BAd 118, OA 169, BAs 99.
lyft: *n.* sky BAd 268; **lift:** S 49, BAs 141.
lyk(e): *prep.* like BAd 449, 461, 464, BAs 132; **lyk(e) as:** OD 18, 61, 196, 214, Y 63.
lyk(e): *adj.* likely OD 162, OR 156.
lymmaris: *n. pl.* criminals BAd 283.
lyne: *n.* descent OD 109, 192, 213, OR 104, 191, OA 95, 182; **lyne be lyne:** generation after generation OR 172-73, 215, OA 167, 209.
lynealy: *adv.* lineally Y 17, 63, 136.
lynnage: *n.* lineage Y 17.
lynnyng: *n.* linen StA 100.
lyon, lyoun(e): *see* **leon.**

ma: *n.* more Y 222, 237.
madyn(e): *n.* maiden, virgin BAd 391, 396, BAs 319; **madinnis:** *pl.* OA 78; **madynnis:** OR 92; **maidins:** OD 95.
mair: *adj.* greater OA 65, 76; **mar(e):** OD 83, OR 80.
mair: *adv. comp.* more OR 237, 242, 246, OA 24, 231, 237, S 233, 241, Y 61, BAd 50, 327; **mar(e):** OD 190, 240, OR 189, OA 222, BAs 50; **maist:** *super.* OD 58, OR 23, 27, 58, Y 217, BAd 300, 309, 498, StA 139; **mast:** OA 21¹, 21², 26, 47, Y 10, 13, 54, BAs 245, 370, 405, 426.
maister: *n.* master OD 154; **maistir:** OR 148; **masteris:** Y 37, 44.
mak: *v.* make OD 95, 224, 228, OR 92, 230, OA 74, 78, 224, Y 4, 16, 96¹, 96², BAd 379, BAs 304; **maid(e):** *pa.* OD 76, 113, 125, etc., OR 109, 111, 120, etc., OA 100, 112, 120, etc., Y 86, 143, 266, BAd 49, 210, 215, etc., BAs 49, 119, 183, etc., StA 5, 14, 21, etc.; *pa. ppl.* OD 133, 147, 154, OR 22, 129, 148, 151, OA 20, 131, 136, Y 5, 102, 126, BAd 132, 227, 240, etc., BAs 358, StA 42, 129, [133].

man: *v.* must OR 160.

maner: *n.* manner OD 46, 219, OR 222, OA 6, Y 262, 265; custom OD 45, OR 48, 230, OA 39, 224, StA 17; **maneris**: *pl.* StA 187; manners, forms of courtesy BAd 396, BAs 321; **all maner of**: all kinds of BAd 166.

manerit: *pa. ppl.* mannered StA 62.

manhed: *n.* courage, strength Y 14; **manheid**: BAd 365.

mannis: *poss.* man's OD 20, 132, OR 24, 127, OA 22, 118, 121, Y 15, 134, BAd 28, BAs 29, 211.

marbill: *n.* marble BAs 7, 23, 32; **marbyll**: StA 2; **merbill**: BAd 20, 30.

marche: *n.* march, border StA 190; **marchis**: *pl.* marches, borderlands BAd 56, BAs 57, 325.

mar(e): *see* **mair**.

mareit, mareyt, mariit: *see* **mary**.

merkis: *n. pl.* marks (currency) S 168, Y 170.

martir: *n.* martyr Y 153, BAs 55.

martyrit: *v. pa.* martyred Y 69, 236, BAs 375; *pa. ppl.* S 69, BAd 466.

mary: *v.* marry StA 55; **mariit**: *pa.* Y 118, BAs 4, 275, 300, 447; **mareit**: BAd 373; **mareyt**: BAd 2, 335; **maryit(e)**: *pa. ppl.* OR 43, 124, 125, 171, OD 40, 128, 129, S 190, 213, StA 57, 192; **mariit**: OA 115, 117, 165; **mareit**: *pa. ppl.* BAd 360.

mast: *see* **mair**.

masteris: *see* **maister**.

mater: *n.* matter BAd 433, 443, BAs 350, 360.

matronys: *n. pl.* married women BAd 276.

mawment: *n.* false god, idol Y 212; **mawmentis**: *pl.* Y 215.

meik: *adj.* meek BAd 117, 265, StA 216; **meke**: BAs 109.

meill: *n.* meal S 168, 230.

mekill: *n.* much BAd 105; **meikill**: StA [241]; **mekle**: Y 196, BAs 97.

mekill: *adv.* much OR 154; **mekle**: OD 160, OA 147.

mekill: *adj.* much, many OR 145; **mekle**: OD 150, OA 49, BAs 239.

mennis: *see* **mannis**.

menys: *n. pl.* means StA 13.

merbill: *see* **marbill**.

meris: *see* **meyr**.

merkis: *see* **markis**.

mertyryng: *ger.* martyring S 211.

mervalouse: *adj.* marvelous S 208; **mervalus**: BAd 405; **merwalous**: BAs 328.

mervellis: *n. pl.* marvels BAd 280, 297.

merwalit: *v. pa.* marveled StA 93, 120.

mes: *n.* mass Y 146.

meyntyme: *n.* meantime Y 131, BAd 511.

meyr: *n.* mare Y 76; **meris**: *poss.* Y 76.

michti: *adj.* mighty OA 47.

midsymmer: *n.* BAd [482].

miney: *n.* money, ransom BAd 401.

miraclis: *n. pl.* miracles S 206, BAd 118, 149, 342; **miraklis**: BAs 110; **mirakillis**: BAs 100, 131; **myraklis**: BAs 278.

mirtyrit: *see* **martyrit**.

misgouernance: *n.* misgovernance Y 330; **misgouernans**: Y 277.

moder: *n.* mother OD 69, Y 34, 90, 134, 254, BAd [399]; **modir**: OR 68.

mone: *n.* moon BAd 268; **monys**: *pl.* S 48.

moneth: *n.* month S 157, BAd 110; **monetht**: S 236; **monethis**: *pl.* BAd 99, 203, 267, etc., BAs 94, 105, 176, etc.; **monethtis**: S 176.

monist: *v. pa. ppl.* admonished BAd 102, BAs 95.

monstour(e): *n.* monster BAd 135, 152; **monstur**: StA 53.

montanis: *n. pl.* mountains StA 18.

month: *n.* mound, hill BAd 62.

mony: *n.* money StA 66.

mony(e): *n.* many OD 44, 53, 172, OR 46, 169, OA 163, S 169, Y 298, BAd 287, BAs 231, 263, StA [32], 36, 39, etc.

mony: *adj.* many OD 58, 153, 226, OR 58, 147, 196, OA 31, 46, 47, 189, S 206, 218, 235, Y 83, 125, 154, etc., BAd 21, 97, 179, etc., BAs 91, 99, 156, etc., StA 26, 55, 76, etc.

monys: *see* **mone**.

mort: *n.* death Y 332.

mortalite: *n.* mortality, plague S 112, 118; **mortalyte**: S 124, 136, 151.

mowe: *v.* make, instigate (war) StA 135; **mowit**: *pa.* StA 91, 181; **movit**: *pa. ppl.* disturbed OD 100.

multiplie: *v.* populate OA 79; **multiplyit**: *pa.* multiplied, increased OD 97, BAd 9; **multiplyt**: OR 94; **multipliit**: OA 82, BAs 12.

murderaris: *n. pl.* murderers BAd 267.

murdrest: *v. pa.* murdered Y 298, 312, BAs 364; **murtheryt**: BAd 450; **murdrest**: *pa. ppl.* Y 262: **murdrist**: BAs 237.

murthour: *n.* murder Y 270, 327, BAd 294.

mycht: *v.* might OD 24, 158, 163, OR 152, 156, OA 146, 151, 226, Y 198, 253, BAd 284, StA 55.

myle: *n. pl.* miles S 12.

mylk: *n.* milk BAd 150.

na: *adj., adv.* no OD 76, 79^2, 94, etc., OR 91, 183, 187^1, etc., OA 177, Y 19, 101, 103, etc., BAd 179, 428, 446, 451, BAs 347, 362, 365, StA 63.

na: *conj.* nor OD 80^2, 111^2, OR 107; than S 242, BAs 28; **na . . . na**: neither . . . nor OD 79^1-80^2, 79^2-80^1, 111, OR 107; **no . . . no**: OR 76.

nacioun: *n.* nation, people OD 20, 23, 74, etc., OA 2, 22, 25, etc., Y 5, 160, 222, BAs 5; **natioun**: OR 1, 3, 13, etc., BAd 3, 487; *pl.* OR 180; **nacionis**: OA 13, 174, 196, 200, Y 60, BAd [484], BAs 184; **naciouns**: OD 12, 181, 202, 206; **natiounis**: OR 203; **nationis**: OR 208.

namme3: *see* **nayme**.

nane: *pron.* none OD 152, OR 147, OA 74, 228, Y 254, 311, BAd 212, BAs 360.

nane: *adj.* no, not any OD 80, OR 76, OA 64, Y 174.

nathing: *n.* nothing BAd 229, BAs 250, StA 23.

nationis, natiounis: *see* **nacioun**.

navyne: *n.* fleet OA 72.

nayme: *n.* name BAd 89, 103, 143, etc.; **name3**: *pl.* Y 182.

neir: *adv.* near, nearly OR 106, Y 163, StA 31, 98, 167; **ner(e)**: OD 23, 24, 55, etc., OR 55, OA 44; **nere hand**: BAs 198.

nepote: *n.* nephew, grandson, kinsman BAd 134, 143, 322; **newow**: BAs 122; **nepote**: son BAd 298; **newo**: grandson BAs 254; **nevo**: BAd 316.

nerrer: *adj. comp.* nearer BAs 354; **nerrar**: BAd 436; **nerrest**: *super.* BAd 285.

neuer: *adv.* never OD 24, 26, 77, etc., StA 14; **neuir**: OR 29, 74, 76, etc., OA 28, 63, 94, etc., Y 27, 177, 179, etc., BAd 41, 57, 83, etc., BAs 82, 246, 298, 318; **nevir**: OA 95, 228, Y 92, 147, BAs 42.

neuerþeles: *adv* nevertheless StA 120, 140; **neuirþeles**: OR 182, OA 176; **neuirþeles**: BAd 276.

nevo, newo, newow: *see* **nepote**.

nixt: *pron.* next BAs 230.

nixt: *adj.* next S 56, 66, 106, etc.

nixt: *adv.* next Y 194, BAd 459, 502, BAs 210.

no . . . no: *see* **na**.

nobilite: *n.* nobility BAd 91.

nobill(e): *adj.* noble BAd 29, 155, 156, etc.

nobillis: *n. pl.* nobles BAd 221, 282, 295, etc., StA 26, 27, 32, etc.; **noblis**: BAs 237, 243; **nobyllis**: StA 11, 56.

nobilly: *adv.* nobly BAd 77, 162, 261, BAs 77, 98, 143, etc.; **nobille**: BAd 510.

nocht: *adv.* not OD 12, 17, 45, etc., OR 13, 20, 47, etc., OA 14, 18, 38, etc., BAd 48, 415, 444, etc., BAs 48, 224, 242, etc.; **noht**: StA 128.

nocht gaynstandand: *conj.* notwithstanding OR 119; **nocht ganstanding**: OA 109.

nochtwithstanding: *conj.* notwithstanding OA 148.

nomer: *n.* number StA 156; **novmer**: OA 98; **nowmir**: OR 106.

northehalf: *adv.* on the north side of OA 63.

noþir: *see* **oþir**.

nouþir: *conj.* neither BAd 267.

nunnis: *n. pl.* nuns Y 165, BAd 386, BAs 312.

nunry: *n.* nunnery BAd 399.

nurist: *v. pa.* nourished OD 55, OA 44; **nurest**: OR 55; **nurist**: *pa. ppl.* OD 222; **nurysyt**: OR 224.

nycht: *n.* night BAd 160, 266, 311, StA 12, 59; **nychtis**: *pl.* S 223.

nyne: *num.* nine S 14, 16, BAd 384, BAs 309.

nynt: *num.* ninth Y 330.

obeyit: *v. pa.* submitted OD 194.

oblissing: *ger.* pledge, commitment OD 228; **oblysing**: OR 231.

occupiit: *pa.* concerned, troubled OD 116, OA 103; **occupyt**: OR 112; **occupiit**: *pa. ppl.* occupied, held OA 172, BAs 69; **occupyt**: OR 178; **occupyit**: OD 179, BAd 70.

oey: *see* **oy(e)**.

of: *adv.* off Y 46, 75, BAd 194.

off: *prep.* of, from OD 11, 21, BAd 2, StA 32¹, 32², 50, etc.

offerit: *v. pa.* Y 332, StA 41, [66].

oftyme: *adv.* often OR 226.

oftyn: *adv.* often StA [206].

oist: *see* **ost**.

on: *num.* one S 181.

one: *prep.* on OR 109, S 1, BAd 62, 73, 102, etc.

ony: *adj.* any OD 48, 93, 190, 198, OR 49, 90, 199, OA 25, 40, 75, etc., Y 46, 48, 60, etc., BAd 327, 356, 369, 430.

ooi: *see* **oy(e)**.

oppone: *v.* object OD 48.

oppressit: *v. pa.* oppressed, victimized OD 49, OA 41, StA 254; **oppressyt**: OR 50.

optenyt: *v.* pa. obtained, possessed OD 201; **optenit**: OR 202; **optenit**: OA.195.

opyn: *adj.* opportune OD 230, OR 232.

opynyoun: *n.* opinion OR 20; **opynioun**: OD 17.

or: *adv.* before OD 75, 87, 128, OR 73, 84, 124, OA 61¹, 61², 70, 115; until BAd 205, BAs 177.

or . . . or: *conjs.* either . . . or OA 189.

ordanit: *v. pa.* founded BAd 367, BAs 294; appointed, invested BAs 97; ordered BAs 229; **ordinyt**: *pa. ppl.* S 231.

ordour: *n.* religious order Y 164, BAd 64, BAs 65; **ordouris**: *pl.* BAd 384, BAs 310.

originale: *n.* origin chronicle OA 1.

ost: *n.* host, army OD 140, OR 135, OA 129, StA 47, Y 81; **oist**: BAd 461.

ostage: *n.* hostage; **in ostage**: as hostages BAs 50.

othir: *pron.* other OD 86; **oþir**: OR 83; **noþir**: OA 69.

othir: *adj.* other OD 80, 131, 142, etc.; **oþir**: OR 76, 127, 137, etc.; **noþir**: OA 121, 131.

ouer: *prep.* over OR 45; **our**: Y 38, 277, BAs 267.

ourcome: *v. pa.* overcame BAd 51, 196, 494, BAs 51, 172, 253, 395, StA 182; **ourcuming**: *pa. ppl.* BAd 39; **ourcummyn**: BAs 40, 246.

ourcouerit: *pa. ppl.* covered over BAd 268.

our(e): *adv.* over OD 99, Y 133, 306; overly, too OR 222, Y 56; **ourer**: BAd 258.

out: *adj.* outer BAs 262.

oy(e): *n.* grandson, nephew BAs 234, 316; **oey**: StA 34, 50; **ooi**: BAd 391; **oey**: *poss.* StA 144.

pailȝeanis: *n. pl.* pavilions, tents StA 170.

paip: *see* **pap(e)**.

paix: *see* **pece**.

palpis: *n. pl.* breasts, nipples Y 75.

pane: *n.* pain Y 129.

pap(e): *n.* pope S 78, Y 167, 227, BAs 53, 55, 200, etc.; **paip**: BAd 52, 234, 405, 436; **papis**: *poss.* Y 168, 169.

pas(e): *v.* pass, go OD 43, 45, 92, OR 46, 47, OA 37, 38, Y 78, StA 89; **passit**: *pa.* OD 41, OA 46, 48, Y 322, StA 48, 73, 79, 87; **passyt**: OR 44, 57, 59, 62, S 198, 213, 223, etc.; **past**: OD 57, 59, 62, OA 35, 52, Y 184, BAd 330, StA 236; **passand**: *pr. ppl.* BAd 153, StA 6.

payit: *n. pa. ppl.* paid Y 170, BAd 508; **payand**: *pr. ppl.* Y 173.

pece: *n.* peace OA 133, 152, 200, 225, Y 147, 179, BAs 49, 60, 112, etc., StA 204; **peice**: StA 5; **peis**: StA 35, 63, 133, etc.; **pes(e)**: OD 124, 206, 229, OR 207, 231; **paix**: BAd 210; **peax**: BAd 58, 136, 159, 257; **pax**: Y 146.

peceably(e): *adv.* peaceably BAs 85, 138; **peissabilley**: StA [52].

Pechtis: *n. pl.* Picts OD 89, 95, 123, etc., OR 85, 92, 119, etc., StA 39, [45], 79, etc.; **Peichtis**: StA 4, 5, 21, etc.; **Pichtis**: BAd 24, 43, 56, etc.; **Pictis**: OA 71, 79, 109, etc., BAs 25, 41, 44, etc.; **Pychtis**: BAd 40, 57, 58, etc.; **Pictis**: *poss.* BAs 69.

Pechtland: *v.* Pictland, Kingdom of the Picts StA 159, [173].

peciabyll: *adj.* peaceable StA 20.

peice: *see* **pece**.

peirsit: *v. pa.* pierced BAd 359.

peis: *see* pece.

peissabilley: *see* peceably(e).

pennys: *n. pl.* pennies S 231, 232.

pepill: *n.* people Y 10, 158, 177, etc., BAd 6, 55, 133, etc., BAs 120, 336, 365, StA 17, 26; pepyll: StA 32, 198; peple: Y 13, 100, 159, etc., BAd 24, 58, BAs 6, 9, 25, etc.

perist: *v. pa.* perished BAd 124; peryst: BAd 188; pereist: BAd 232; perischit: StA 159.

persew: *v.* attack StA 188; sue, claim Y 128, 142; persewit: *pa.* persecuted StA 146, OD 54, 56, OA 45; persauit: OA 43; persuyt(e) OR 54, 56; persewit: *pa. ppl.* OD 206; continued Y 155.

persute: *n.* pursuit (of a claim) BAd 374.

pert: *n.* part StA 139.

perte: *n.* party, side StA 132; perteis: *pl.* StA 133.

peruerst: *adj.* perverse BAd 327.

pes(e): *see* pece.

petruis: *adj.* compassionate? StA 216.

petuous: *adj.* compassionate StA 16.

Pichtis, Pictis: *see* Pechtis.

pistil: *n.* epistle, letter OD 227.

plage: *n.* plague OR 45; plagis: OD 42, 47, OA 36.

plane: *adj.* open BAd 70, 191, 197, BAs 70, Y 301; plaine: StA 227.

plane: *adv.* plainly Y 23.

plegis: *n. pl.* hostages StA 121, 237.

plesand: *adj.* pleasing Y 99, BAd 215, 325.

poissonit: *v. pa. ppl.* poisoned BAd 416; posonyt: StA 256; poysonit: Y 191, BAs 336.

polisy: *n.* policy BAs 448.

Portingale: *n.* Portugal OR 63, OA 53; Portyngale: OD 63; Portyng Gayell: OD 64.

poure: *adj.* poor BAd 452.

power(e): *n.* army OD 8, 101, OR 9, 97, OA 8, 9, 85, S 203, 222, 237, Y 81, 142, BAd 460, 472, BAs 371, 382.

poysonit: *see* poissonit.

preche: *v.* preach S 32; prechit: *pa.* S 23, 25, BAs 119; preichit: BAd 132.

preson(e): *n.* prison Y 243, StA 82; presoun: Y 256, BAd 120, 222, 229, BAs 431.

presoner: *n.* prisoner BAs 421; presoneris: *pl.* StA 119.

presserue: *v.* preserve OD 110.

pressit: *v. pa. ppl.* pressed OD 206; presyt: OR 207.

prewalyt: *v. pa.* prevailed StA 151.

procurit: *v. pa.* procured OD 30; procuryt: OR 32.

promesyt: *v. pa.* promised StA 107.

promys: *n.* promise OA 100.

prophecit: *v. pa.* prophesied BAd 105, BAs 97.

prophecyis: *n. pl.* prophecies BAd 33.

propheit: *n.* prophet BAd 112.

proportis: *v.* purports, claims OA 210, 238.

pundis: *n. pl.* pounds S 230, 246, BAd [508], BAs 414.

pur(e): *n.* poor S 235, BAs 300.

purpos: *n.* purpose OA 37.

purposyt: *v. pa.* intended, resolved S 237; purpost: BAs 415; purposit: BAd [510].

puttand: *v. pr. ppl.* putting StA 171.

pwnissar: *n.* punisher BAd 258.

pwnist: *v. pa.* punished BAd 272; pvnyst: StA 23.

quarterit: *v. pa. ppl.* quartered BAs 450.

quene: *see* qwene.

querele: *n.* quarrel OD 138; querell: OA 127; quierlye: OR 133.

quha: *pron.* who Y 250, 308; quha þat: whoever Y 145; quha euir: BAs 210.

quhais: *pron.* whose Y 11, 205, BAd 82, 103, 232, 351, BAs 22, 81, 88, etc.

quham(e): *pron.* whom OD 7, 66, 84, 193, OA 5, Y 83, BAd 81, 185, 336; quhom(e): OR 9, 81, 192, OA 8, 67, 97, 184, S 178, BAs 137, 149, 164, 190.

quhar(e): *adv.* where OD 66, OR 65, OA 224, S 29, 96, 165, Y 24, BAs 11, 26, 33, etc., StA 153, 162, 165, etc.; quhair: BAd 9, 13, 25, etc.

quhar(e) euir: *adv.* wherever OR 230, Y 92; quhare euer: OD 228; quhair euir: BAd 33.

quharfor: *adv.* for which reason OA 7, Y 71, BAs 231, StA [266]; quhairfore: BAd 286, 448.

quharthrou: *adv.* because of which OA 157; **quharthrow:** Y 50.

quhatsumeuer: *adv.* whatever, no matter what OA 139.

quheit: *n.* wheat S 169.

quhen: *adv.* when OD 55, 66, 130, etc., OR 55, 65, 125, etc., OA 29, 34, 110, etc., Y 18, 47, 48, etc., BAd 22, 91, 103, etc., BAs 96, 117, 162, etc., StA 19, 119, 186.

quhidder: *conj.* whether Y 49; **quhydder:** StA 12.

quhil: *adv.* sometimes OR 112; **quhilis:** OD 116.

quhile: *n.* while OD 125, OR 121, OA 112, BAd 7.

quhill: *prep.* until S 226, Y 49, BAd 446; **quhyll:** S 244.

quhill: *conj.* while OA 44, 152, Y 186; until OD 76, OA 70, 158, Y 143, BAd 74, 248, 269, 432, BAs 350; **ay quhill:** until Y 166-67.

quhilk: *pron., adj.* who, whom, which OD 3, 9, 11, etc., OR 5, 11, 12, etc., OA 3, 4, 10, etc., S 24, 27, 63, etc., Y 4, 6, 7, etc., BAd 2, 24, 31, etc., BAs 5, 41, 45, etc., StA 31, 41, 45, etc.; **quhylk:** StA 248, 249, 253; **quilk:** OA 165; **quhilkis:** OD 4, 21, 30, etc., OA 24, 28, 56, etc., BAs [252],327.

quhilkis: *conj.* that OA 109.

quhom(e): *see* **quham(e).**

quhy: *conj.* why OR 1, OA 208, StA 91; **for quhy:** because Y 197.

quhyll: *see* **quhill.**

quhylk: *see* **quhilk.**

quhyt(e): *adj.* white S 246, Y 303, BAd 56, 209.

quierlye: *see* querele.

qulkis: *see* **quhilk.**

quoke: *v. pa.* quaked Y 279.

qwene: *n.* queen Y 36, 82, 104, etc., BAs 348; **qweyn:** StA [116], 134; **quene:** Y 105, BAd 429; **quvene:** S 40, 42.

qwhew: *n.* suffering S 152 *(see explanatory note).*

raid: *v. pa.* rode Y 186, 188.

raif: *v. pa.* burst Y 331.

rais, raise: *see* **ryse.**

rais: *n.* channel, strait OA 52.

rakless: *adj.* reckless BAs 441.

Ramanis: *see* **Romane.**

rampand: *adj.* rampant OA 87, BAs 34.

rang: *see* **regne.**

ransoun: *n.* ransom BAd [508].

ras(e): *see* **ryse.**

rasyt: *v. pa.* raised StA 47; **rasit:** OA 51; *pa. ppl.* mounted BAd 406, BAs 329.

ratche: *n.* hunting dog BAs 58; **rathe:** BAs 181.

rebellis: *n. pl.* rebels BAd 116, BAs 109.

rebellit: *v. pa.* rebelled StA 48, 110, [235].

recouerit: *v. pa.* recovered BAd 67, 358; **recoverit:** BAs 68.

redy: *adj.* ready StA [108].

reft: *v. pa.* plundered StA 26, 92, Y 163, 276; *pa. ppl.* Y 230.

refusit: *v. pa.* refused Y 79, StA [42], 45; **refusyt:** StA 107.

regionis: *n. pl.* regions BAd 56, BAs 58.

regne: *n.* reign Y 88, 104, 109, etc., BAs 173, 212, 263, etc.; **regnne:** BAd 125, 137, 167, etc.; **regine:** BAd 96, 154, 270, etc. **rigne:** OA 94, S 47; **rignne:** BAd 121, 259; **ring:** StA 144, 196, 228; **ryng:** StA 27, 60, [68], etc.

regne: *v.* reign, rule Y 308, 310, BAs 33, 172; **regnne:** BAd 33, 198; **ryng:** BAs 260; **regnis:** *pr.* OD 193; **rygnys:** OR 192; **regnit:** *pa.* OA 161, Y 70, 89, 157, etc., BAd 21, 23, 71, etc., BAs 23, 24, 70, etc.; **regnyt:** OD 111, 171, StA 24, 122, [143], 174; **rignyt:** OR 107, S 29, 38, 44, etc.; **rygnyt:** OR 167; **rang:** OA 99, Y 42, 228, 249, StA 6, 8, 25, etc.; **regnand:** *pr. ppl.* BAd 135; **regnit:** *pa. ppl.* OA 199, BAd 387, 449, BAs 313, 364; **regnyt:** OD 205, StA 19; **rignyt:** OR 207.

rehers(e): *v.* recount OD 202, OR 203, Y 56; **reheirsit:** *pa. ppl.* BAd 348.

reid(e): *adj.* red OR 44, 99, OA 35, BAd 34.

reidis: *v. pr.* reads Y 11; **red:** *pa. ppl.* Y 289, StA 23.

reke: *n.* rake; **reke penny:** Y 105 *(see explanatory note).*

relaxit: *v. pa.* relinquished? StA 241.

releif: *n.* relief (legal obligation) BAs 251; **releiffis:** *pl.* BAd 306 *(see explanatory note).*

relesching: *ger.* releasing S 72.

relesyt: *v. pa.* released, granted freedom to S 21.

religioun: *n.* religious order Y 98, BAd 252, BAs 213, 214; religion BAd 136.

relikis: *n.* relics S 33.

remane: *v.* remain Y 244; **remanis**: *pr.* Y 40, OA 172; **remanys**: OR 178, OA 87; **remaynis**: OD 179; **remanit**: *pa.* OA 49, 70, 149, 160, Y 206; **remanyt**: OR 59, 85, 166, StA 122; **remaynit**: OD 59, 88, 169; **remanyt**: *pa. ppl.* OR 154; **remanit**: OA 95; **remaynit**: OD 160; **remanent**: *pr. ppl.* BAd 100.

remanand: *n.* remaining part StA 143.

renewit: *v. pa.* renewed BAd 413, 515, BAs 419, StA 20.

rent: *n.* tribute Y 170.

reprevit: *v. pa.* reproved Y 94, 199.

resauit: *v. pa.* received BAs 114, 325, StA 65; **ressauit**: BAd 126, 402; **resauit**: *pa. ppl.* BAs 62; **ressauit**: BAd 61; **resauit**: *pa.* sheltered OA 43; **resauyte**: OR 54; **ressauit**: OD 54; **resawit**: *pa. ppl.* S 198.

resignit: *v. pa.* relinquished Y 308; **resignyte**: StA 19; **resignit wp**: Y 167-68; **resignit . . . our**: Y 306.

ressoun: *n.* reason BAd 187, BAs 182.

restorit: *v. pa. ppl.* restored BAs 117; **restoryt**: S 200, BAd 129.

resydit: *v. pa.* resided OD 65.

retorned: *v. pa.* returned Y 112, 294, 324.

revengeance: *n.* revenge OR 241.

reveir: *n.* river BAd 8; **rever**: OA 54; BAs 11; **ryver**: OR 64; **ryuer**: OD 65.

revirence: *n.* reverence OR 129.

rewesyn: *n.* rape StA 226; **rewesyng**: StA 243.

rewlit: *v. pr.* ruled Y 218, BAs 137, 415, StA 34.

rewm: *n.* realm, kingdom OR 121, S 38.

rialte: *n.* royal pomp 82.

richt: *n.* right, just claim OR 136, OA 118, 126, 130, 165, Y 143, 302, BAd 433, 446, BAs 285; **rycht**: OD 135, 141, 174, OR 170, Y 79, StA 92; **richtis**: *pl.* Y 128.

richt: *adj.* correct OR 104, OA 95, 182; **rycht**: OD 109, 192, 213, OR 191.

richt: *adv.* just, exactly, OR 197, OA 190; **rycht**: OD 50, OR 50; **richt**: very, quite BAd 265, 509, BAs 415; **rycht**: BAd 77; StA 9, 65, 175, 200.

richtiusnis: *n.* virtue BAd 397; **richttuisnes**: BAs 320.

richtuis(s): *adj.* virtuous, just OA 127; **richtwis**: OR 133; **rychtwis**: OD 138; **richtuis(s)**: rightful, legitimate OA 112, 123, 168, 189, Y 140, BAd 323, 444, BAs 241, 258, 263, etc.; **richtwis**: OR 122, 130; **rychttuus**: StA 146; **rychtwis**: OD 126; **rychtwys**: OD 134; **rychtwise**: OR 195.

rigne, rignne: *see* **regne**.

ring: *see* **regne**.

ritches: *n.* riches Y 74; **richess**: OD 57.

roistit: *v. pa.* roasted, heated BAd 271.

Romane: *n.* Roman OA 195; **Romanes**: *pl.* OD 115, 117, 124, etc.; **Romanis**: OD 80, 114, 146, OA 64, 101, 102, etc., Y 52, BAs 51, StA [43], 67, 75, etc.; **Romaynes**: OD 157[1], 157[2], 200; **Ramanis**: OR 76; **Romanos**: OD 182.

ros: *n.* rose BAs 328; **rois**: BAd 405.

rutit: *v. pa. ppl.* rooted OD 164; **rutyt**: OR 157.

ruynus: *adj.* ruinous, delapidated BAd 140.

rycht: *see* **richt**.

rychttuus, rychtwis(e), rychtwis: *see* **richtuis(s)**.

rychtwyse: *adv.* virtuously BAd 163.

ryng: *see* **regne**.

rys(e): *v.* rise BAd 480, BAs 390, StA 128; **ras(e)**: *pa.* OR 11, 159, OA 25, Y 274; **rais(e)**: OD 9, 165, OA 10, 133, 153, 157, S 221, Y 109, 218, 282, 316, BAd 431, BAs 349, StA 85.

ryuer, ryver: *see* **reveir**.

sa: *adv., conj.* so OD 23, 24[1], 24[2], etc., OR 20, 26[1], 26[2], etc., OA 25, 33, 61, etc., S 217, Y 21, 27, 47, etc., BAs 121, 284, 374, 390, StA 42; **swa**: StA 22, 47, 84, etc.; **sua**: BAd 211, 212, 464, 465.

saidis: *adj.* said, previously mentioned Y 193, BAd 15, 19.

saiffand: *prep.* except StA 265; **savand**: OD 68; **saife revirence**: saving your reverence, with all due respect OR 129; **sauf reverence**: OD 133.

sair: *adv.* sorely BAd 9, StA 105.

sais: *v. pr.* says OD 31, 139, 221, 241, OR 134, 243; **sayis**: OA 18, 141, BAd 33; **sayand**: *pr. ppl.* OD 223, OR 243, OA 219, Y 213.

sait: *see* seyt.

salit: *v. pa.* sailed BAs 10; **saylit**: StA 163; **sailand**: *pr. ppl.* StA 158.

sall: *v.* shall OR 206, OA 198, 222, Y 7, 44, 62, 310, BAd 33.

saluatioun: *n.* salvation BAd 357, 427.

saluiour: *n.* savior StA 68.

samekle: *adv.* so much Y 45.

sammyn: *adj.* same OR 223, S 51, 64, 84, etc.; **samyn**: OD 55, 221[1], 221[2], OA 44, 216, 217, 238, Y 96, 139, 197, etc., BAd 9, 91, 220; **samyn**: OR 55.

sanct: *n.* saint S 25, 31, 33, etc., Y 68, 106, 153, etc., BAd 60, 61, 62, etc., BAs 61, 62, 64, etc.; **saynte**: OR 82; **sanctis**: *pl.* Y 238, 239.

Saraȝens: *n. pl.* Saracens, Arabs S 36; **Saraȝenis**: BAd 358; **Sarazenis**: Y 33.

sauf reverence: *see* saiffand.

sauff: *v. subj.* save OD 193.

savand: *see* saiffand.

sax: *num.* six OR 107, S 165, BAd 267, 439.

saxt: *see* sext.

saxty: *num.* sixty S 184.

saxtyt: *num.* sixtieth S 19.

sayand: *see* sais.

saylit: *see* salit.

saynte: *see* sanct.

scaith: *n.* harm OA 83.

sceptour: *n.* scepter BAd 406; **sceptur**: BAs 329.

schame: *n.* shame Y 264.

schamefully: *adv.* shamefully Y 233, 262.

schane: *v. pa.* shone BAs 223.

schankis: *n. pl.* shanks Y 204.

scharp: *adj.* severe BAd 258.

scharply: *adv.* severely OA 148, StA 125.

schaw: *v.* show OD 203, 238, OR 204, 228, Y 4, 28, 32, etc.; **schawit**: *pa.* BAs 99, 109, 131, 278; **schew**: Y 116, 304, BAd 118, 149, 326; **schawyn**: *pa. ppl.* Y 18, 305; **schawand**: *pr. ppl.* Y 2.

sche: *pron.* she Y 128; **scho**: Y 140[1], 140[2].

scheding: *ger.* shedding BAd 327.

scheik: *n.* cheek S 164.

scheild: *n.* shield OR 99; **scheld**: OA 88.

schew: *see* schaw.

schip: *n.* ship S 210; **schippis**: *pl.* OD 58, 90, OR 58, OA 47, 51, 72, StA [158], [163], 164.

schir: *n.* sir OA 114, Y 221[1], 221[2], 245, etc., BAd 346, BAs 380.

scho: *see* sche.

schort: *adj.* brief OR 160, Y 137.

schot: *n.* shot Y 100, BAd 153.

schuke: *v. pa.* shook Y 279.

schutting: *ger.* shooting BAs 454.

scoir: *see* skore.

se: *v.* see OD 230, OA 226; **seyne**: *pa. ppl.* BAd 160, 268, 280, 297; **seyne**: S 210; **sene**: Y 3, 29, 281, BAs 141; **sene**: S 48, 208; **seand**: *pr. ppl.* Y 77.

se, see: *see* sey.

secund: *adj.* second OD 215, 217, OR 217, 220, OA 210, 213, S 76, 80, 117, etc., Y 87, 119, 157, 184, BAd 72, 154, 208, etc., BAs 72, 180, 218, etc., StA 8, 27, 40, etc.

secundlie: *adv.* secondly Y 33; **secundly**: BAd 16, StA 46.

sege: *n.* siege S 159, 182, BAd 338, BAs 276.

sege: v. besiege S 215, BAs 368; **segit**: *pa. ppl.* OA 29.

seiknes: *n.* sickness Y 122, BAs 79.

seke: *v.* seek OD 44; **seik(e)**: OR 47, OA 38, 50; **socht**: *pa.* OA 5.

sekerly: *adv.* certainly OD 229, OA 21, 224; **sekirly**: OD 150; **sikkirly**: OR 231.

self: *n.* self; **þe self**: itself Y 6, 23, 64, etc.

semys: *v. pr.* seems OD 225, OA 150.

sen: *adv.* since OD 24, Y 25, 29.

send: *v. pa.* sent OD 6, 67, 140, OR [8], 66, 135, OA 7, 129, Y 75, 178, 227, BAd 11, 16, 39, etc., BAs 13, 17, 40, etc.; *pa. ppl.* S 31, BAd 19, 131, BAs 21, StA 38, 44, 46, etc.

sene: *see* se.

sensyne: *adv.* afterwards, from that time on OD 28, 84, 108, etc., OA 94, 139, 215; **sensyne**: OR 30, 104, 154, 221, S 71.

sepulturis: *n. pl.* sepulchers BAd 100.

serwand: *n.* servant StA [60].

sesyt: *see* **ces**.

set(e): *see* **seyt**.

sett: *conj.* although OD 113.

sett: *adj.* pitched BAd 144.

sewyn: *num.* seven OR 164; **sevin**: OR 55; **sevyn(e)**: OA 159, S 33, 35, BAs 179.

sewynt: *num.* seventh S 47; **sevint**: BAd 161.

sex: *num.* six BAs 226, 283, 356.

sext: *num.* sixth S 7, Y 322, 334, 339; **sixt**: BAs 140; **saxt**: BAd 147, 319.

sey: *n.* sea OA 62, BAd 4, 6, 476; **se**: OA 63, 64, 103, 104, S 195, 217, Y 187, BAs 386; **see**: OD 77, 117¹, 117², OR 44, 75, 77, etc., BAs 6, StA 189.

seyne: *see* **se**.

seyt: *n.* seat, throne BAd 30; **set(e)**: BAs 31, 270; **sait**: BAd 21.

sicht: *n.* sight BAd 461.

sik: *adj.* such OD 42, 153¹, 153²; **sic**: OR 147, 246, OA 135, Y 42, 178, 200, 251.

sikkirly: *see* **sekirly**.

siklyke: *adj.* suchlike, similar OD 46; **siclyk(e)**: OA 5, Y 289.

siclyke: *adv.* similarly Y 48.

siluir: *n.* silver S 239, 246.

simulat: *v. pa.* pretended StA [145].

sindry: *adj.* sundry, various BAd 86, 241, 283, etc.; **syndry**: BAd 280.

sistir: *n.* sister OR 124; **susteris**: *poss.* BAd 514; **sisteris**: *pl.* OD 127, Y 18.

sixt: *see* **saxt**.

skore: *num.* score OD 111; **skoir**: BAd 69, 425; **scoir**: OR 107.

sla: *v.* slay Y 265, BAd 465, StA 232; **slayne**: *pa. ppl.* S 160, 187, 219, BAd 193, 295, BAs 227, StA 32, 76, 162, etc.; **slane**: S 91, Y 157, 319, BAd 67, 75, 91, etc., BAs 67, 75, 88, etc., StA 12, 27, 88, etc.

slaike: *v.* abate Y 62.

slang: *v. pa.* slung Y 187.

slauchter: *n.* slaughter BAd 294, BAs 236, StA 131.

slayne: *see* **sla**.

slayng: *ger.* slaying BAs 46.

slepis: *n. pl.* sleeps OD 184, OA 177.

slycht: *n.* trickery BAd 349.

snaw: *n.* snow StA 188.

socht: *see* **seke**.

sodandlye: *see* **suddandly**.

solphestry: *n.* sophistry OR 233.

sommyr: *see* **summyr**.

sone: *n.* sun BAd 268.

sone: *n.* son OD 6, 67, 100, etc., OR 8, 97, 130, etc., S 37, 51, 61, etc., Y 70, 80, 135, etc., BAd 1, 11, 65, etc., BAs 17, 123, 135, etc., StA 1, 10, 13, etc.; **sonis**: *poss.* OD 175; **sonnis**: OA 165; **sonnys**: OR 171; **sonys**: *pl.* OD 127; **sonnis**: OA 114, Y 77, 107, 113, etc., BAd 16, 50, 324, etc., BAs 14, 50, 259, etc.; **sonnys**: OR 123, S 40, StA 146.

son(e): *adv.* soon OR 61, BAd 15, 29, 165, etc., BAs 13, 30, 348, StA 78, 90, 112, etc.; **sonar**: *comp.* BAd 27; **sonest**: OA 225.

soned: *v. pa.* were in accord with Y 92.

souerane: *adj.* sovereign OD 109, OA 96, 167, 184; **souirane**: OR 105.

souerte: *n.* surety BAd 50.

sovme: *n.* sum Y 173.

spak: *v. pa.* spoke OA 219, Y 47, 186, 212, BAd 413, BAs 334.

Spanȝe: *n.* Spain OD 62, OA 52, S 35, BAd 8, BAs 11, 32; **Spaynȝee**: OR 62; **Spainȝe**: BAd 15, 17, 20, 31.

sparyt: *v. pa.* spared StA 176.

Spaynȝeartis: *n. pl.* Spaniards BAd 10: **Spanȝardis**: BAs 12.

speiche: *n.* language BAd 132; **spechis**: *pl.* BAd 133.

speir: *n.* spear BAd 359, StA 260.

speit: *n.* spit Y 263.

spendit: *v. pa.* spent BAd 376, BAs 299.

sperit: *v. pa.* asked Y 308; **speryt**: StA 91.

spousit: *v. pa.* married Y 104, 111, 116, 329; *pa. ppl.* OA 34, Y 141; **spowsyt**: S 39.

spreit: *n.* sprite, spirit Y 90.

spulȝeit: *v. pa.* despoiled Y 192, 276, StA 26, 102, 178, BAd 417; *pa. ppl.* Y 229.

sqwyer: *n.* squire Y 293, 316, 336.

staik: *n.* stake BAd 194, 208.

stall: *v. pa.* stole, sneaked S 216, Y 234.

stanche: *v.* extinguish Y 62.

standis: *v. pr.* stands OD 189; **stud(e)**: *pa.* OA 192, StA 57; **standyn**: *pa. ppl.* OD 198, OR 188, 199; **standing**: OA 179.

stane: *n.* stone StA 3; **stanis**: *pl.* BAd 406, BAs 329, StA 18.

statut(e): *v. pa.* decreed as law BAd 285, BAs 230.

statut: *n.* law BAs 245; **statutis**: *pl.* BAd 304.

steling: *v. pr. ppl.* stealing BAd 209, BAs 58, 181; **stollin**: *pa. ppl.* BAd 57.

sterlyng: *adj.* BAd [508].

stern(e): *n.* star S 208, 210, BAd 268.

stert: *v. pa.* sprang BAs 454.

stikkis: *v. pr.* stabs Y 238.

stollin: *see* **steling**.

story(e): *n.* history OD 19, 201, OR 22, 203, OA 20, 143, 196, Y 64, 67; **storyes**: *pl.* OD 70, 153, OR 68; **storyis**: OR 149.

strange: *adj.* foreign OD 191, OA 181.

strangeare: *n.* foreigner OD 111, OR 107.

straik: *v. pa.* struck OA 105, S 181; **strykin**: *pa. ppl.* BAd 194; **strekyn**: StA 148; **strikin**: beheaded Y 229; **strikkin**: stamped (coinage) S 231; **straik**: *pa.* fought S 203, BAd 378, StA 3, 30, 111, etc.; **strake**: BAs 304; **strikin**: BAs 211; **strikkin**: BAd 487; **strikyn**: S 85, 88, 110; **strykin**: S 135; **strykyn(e)**: S 84, 87, 95, etc., StA 75, 131, 136; **streikkin**: BAd 249.

strater: *n.* strait OD 62.

strater: *adj.* more austere Y 30; **straytest**: *super.* OD 228; **stratest**: OA 224; **straitast**: OR 231.

strenth: *adj.* strong BAd 35.

strenthis: *n. pl.* fortresses BAs 462; **strenthtis**: StA 242.

strikin, strikkin, strikyn: *see* **straik**.

stryf(e): *n.* strife BAd 431, BAs 349.

strykin, strykyn(e): *see* **straik**.

stud(e): *see* **standis**.

stuf: *n.* materials, supplies BAs 369.

sua: *see* **sa**.

subdew: *v.* subdue StA 45, 106; **subdewit**: *pa.* BAd 21, BAs 23; *pa. ppl.* BAd 41, BAs 42.

subdittis: *n. pl.* subjects BAd 136, 216, 366; **subgectis**: OR 76.

subjectioun: *n.* subjection, conquest OD 202, BAd 445; **subjectionis**: *pl.* OR 203, OA 197; **subjectione**: confinement StA 199, 203[1], 203[2].

subjeckit: *v. pa.* conquered, subjected OR 110, 114, 138, etc.; **subjectit**: OD 114, 118, 240, BAd 235; **subject**: OD 143, 170, BAs 198; **subjeckit**: *pa. ppl.* OR 117, 190; **subjectit**: OD 121, 144; **subject**: OR 139.

subtell: *adj.* subtle Y 51, 159, BAd 288, StA 25.

succede: *v.* succeed OD 176; **succeid**: OR 174, OA 169; **succedit**: *pa.* S 178, BAd 13, 94, 114, etc., BAs 20, 90, 107, etc.; **succedyt**: S 61, 66; **succeidit**: BAd 109, 119, 123, etc.; **succedit**: *pa. ppl.* descended OA 32.

suddandly: *adv.* suddenly StA 30; **sodandlye**: Y 100.

sueirnes: *n.* sloth StA 191.

sueitly: *adv.* agreeably StA 65.

sufferit: *v. pa.* suffered, permitted StA 22.

suld: *v.* should, would OD 93, 173, 196, etc., OR 90, 170, 197, 234, OA 76, 150, 164, etc., Y 5, 24, 144, etc., BAd 27, 179, 248, etc., BAs 28, 33, 209, etc., StA [56], [152], 193, etc.

sum: *adj., pron.* some OD 70, OR 70, S 209; **oþir sum**: some others S 210.

summyr: *n.* summer S 167; **sommyr**: S 150.

sumtyme: *adv.* at one time, formerly OD 194, 209, OR 193, 211, OA 186.

suorne: *see* **sworne**.

suple: *n.* help OA 5, 111, 134, 148; **supplee**: OD 159.

suppos(e): *conj.* although, even if OD 54, 181, 224, OR 109, 180, 226, OA 31, 43, 100, etc., BAs 230; **suppoise**: OR 30, 54.

surname: *n.* epithet OR 31.

sustene: *v.* sustain BAd 307.

susteris: *see* **sistir**.

suth(e): *n.* truth OD 50, 151, 176, etc., OR 145, 174, 194, etc. OA 150, 168, 187.

suthfastness: *n.* truth, truthfulness OA 178.

swa: *see* **sa**.

Swasie: *n.* Sweden S 191.
sweir: *adj.* lazy StA 176.
swerd: *n.* sword Y 187, 311.
sworne: *v. pa. ppl.* sworn OR 158, OA 152; **suorne:** OD 164.
syd(e): *n.* side OD 21¹, 21², 48, OR 49, OA 22, 23, 40, Y 15, BAd 73, BAs 74; **sydis:** StA 88, 132, 157.
sympill: *adj.* of humble origin S 242.
syn(e): *adv.* since, then, afterwards OD 86, 87, 169, etc., OR 73, 83, 84, etc., OA 55, 69, 82, etc., Y 168, 203, 220, 233, BAd 12, BAs 403, StA 112, 227, 237.
syndry: *pron.* various matters Y 214.
synode: *n.* synod BAs 201; **synody:** BAd 235.

ta: *adj.* one (as opposed to another) OD 48, OR 49, OA 40.
tak: *v.* take OA 13; **tuk(e):** *pa.* OD 101, 102, 125, OR 97, 98, 121, OA 37, 86, 112, 229, S 37, 44, 46, etc., Y 20, 121, 169, 301, BAd 4, 12, 17, etc., BAs 6, 14, 18, etc., StA 79, 82, 84, etc.; **takin:** *pa. ppl.* BAd 352, BAs 224, 324, 327, 412; **taking:** BAd 471; **tane:** OD 212, OR 214, S194, OA 206, Y 314, BAd 269, 401, 404, etc., StA [57], 59, 133, etc.
tald: *v. pa. ppl.* told OD 99, OR [95], OA 83, BAs 394.
tareyt: *v. pa.* tarried, stayed BAd 413; **tariit:** BAs 334.
techit: *v. pa.* taught StA 17.
templis: *n. pl.* temples StA 18.
tend: *num.* tenth S 19; **tent:** BAd 96, 400.
tendirnes: *n.* infancy OA 218.
thai: *adj.* those OD 3.
thai, thame, thameself, thair: *see* þai.
thairour: *adv.* over there StA 48.
thar(e): *see* þair.
tharefore, tharfor(e): *see* þairfore.
thankit: *v. pa. ppl.* thanked BAs 155.
thesaurer: *n.* treasurer BAs 380; **thesaurar:** BAd 470.
thocht: *n.* thought BAs 435.
thocht: *v. pa.* thought OA 83, BAs 433.
thocht: *adv.* though StA 104; **thouch:** OD 75; **þocht:** BAd 285.
thoill: *v.* endure BAd 48.

thred: *adj.* third S 4, 212, 231; **thrid(e):** S 123, 141, 180, etc., Y 35, 194, 202, etc., BAd 89, 167, 168, etc, BAs 2, 181, 206, StA 16, 56, [147], 179.
threttene: *adj.* thirteen BAs 35.
thretty: *adj.* thirty OA 72, 161, S 16; **threttie:** BAd 484; **thretye:** OR 87.
thrildome: *n.* slavery Y 43.
throu: *prep.* through OA 118, 135, 176, Y 124, 130, 184, etc., BAd 330, 412, BAs 333; **throw:** OA 80, 120, 164, S 234, Y 143, 208, 212, etc., BAd [441], StA 7; **throwcht:** StA [260].
thyne: *see* þin(e).
till: *prep.* to OD 67, 190, 192, etc., OR 173, 174, OA 81, 96, 97, etc., S 237, Y 16, 20, 47, etc., BAd 175, 283, BAs 67, 208, 250, etc.; **til:** OD 232; **tyll:** OR 49; **till:** as BAs 34; **tyll:** OR 85; **till:** with regard to OD 238, OR 240, OA 234; until Y 206, 213, 244, BAs 45, 82, 209, etc.; **in till:** into Y 128, BAs 109.
tint: *see* tynt.
titill: *n.* title OA 164, 189, Y 302, BAd 450, BAs 239; **tytill:** OR 196.
to: *adv.* too, excessively OD 122, 227¹, OR 118, OA 108², 223², BAs 430².
togeder: *adv.* together OD 40; **togidder:** BAd 59; **togiddir:** OD 212, OA 34, 206, Y233, BAs 57, 60, 278; **togyddir:** OR 43, 214.
torned: *v. pa.* turned Y 209, BAs 133; **turnit:** BAd 148; **turnyt:** OD 61, StA 94, [230]; **ternyt:** turned OR 61.
toune: *n.* town BAd [457], 460, 463, 464; **townis:** *pl.* Y 97.
towris: *n. pl.* towers S 12.
toþir: *pron.* other Y 145, 338, BAs 141.
tractat: *n.* treatise BAs 1; **tractact:** OA 239, Y 1.
Transmigratioun: *n.* Babylonian Captivity S 6, 7.
trast: *v.* trust Y 253, 254, 255; **trastand:** *pr. ppl.* BAs 374; **trestis:** *imper.* OR 230.
tratourisly: *adv.* traitorously BAs 324, 448; **tratourysly:** BAd 401; **tratorisly:** BAs 232.

tratour: *n.* traitor BAd 441, 465, BAs 256, 358, 401; **tratouris**: *pl.* S 162, Y 10, 34, 222, 286, BAs 252, 449; **traytouris**: OD 18, 53, OR 21, 53.

tratour: *adj.* traitorous, treacherous BAd 461.

trawell: *n.* travail, suffering Y 129.

treson: *n.* treason OR 32; **tresoun**: OD 30, OA 25, 32, BAd 464, BAs 223; **tressoun**: BAd 141, 257, 266, BAs 216, 283; **tressonnis**: *pl.* Y 288.

tresonabilly: *adv.* treasonably, treacherously BAd 287, 318.

tresonable: *adj.* treacherous Y 10; **tressonable**: Y 252, 327.

tressour: *n.* treasure Y 88, 192.

trestis: *see* **trast**.

trety: *n.* entreaty Y 207.

treuth: *n.* truth Y 14, 25, BAd 420, BAs 341.

trew(e): *adj.* true, faithful, true to one's word, honorable OD 149, 211, 233, OR 144, 213, 235, OA 18, 205, 227, Y 66, BAd 117.

trewis: *n.* truce OA 226, BAs 184, StA 20.

tributaris: *see* **trybuteris**.

trow: *v.* believe Y 198; **trowis**: *pr.* OD 17, OR 20, OA 18; **trowand**: *pr. ppl.* Y 215.

Troyanis: *n. pl.* Trojans OD 27; **Troianis**: OA 28; **Troiance**: OR 29.

truble: *n.* trouble BAd 351, BAs 236.

trublit: *v. pa. ppl.* afflicted BAd 6, 492, BAs 9, 393; **trublyt**: BAd 9; **trublet**: BAd 271.

tryvmphe: *n.* pomp BAs 339.

trybut: *n.* tribute StA [80], 241.

trybuteris: *n. pl.* tributaries, payers of tribute OA 194; **tributaris**: OD 199, OR 201, S 71, StA 42.

tua: *see* **twa**.

tuenty: *adj.* twenty BAd 425.

tuk(e): *see* **tak**.

tung: *n.* tongue, language BAs 120; **tungis**: *pl.* BAs 121.

turnyt: *see* **torned**.

twa: *adj.* two OD 117, OR 113, OA 103, S 3^1, 3^2, 10, etc., Y 77, 79, 113. 256, BAs 50, 140, 160, etc., StA 118, 135, 226, 251; **tua**: BAd 50, 52, 160, etc.

twis(e): *adv.* twice OD 26, OR 28; **twys**: OA 26, Y 28, StA 251.

tyll: *see* **till**.

tym(e): *n.* time OD 1, 2, 9, etc., OR 3, 4, 10, etc., OA 3^1, 3^2, 10, etc., S 29, 64, Y 25, 35, 137, etc., BAd 1, 5, 11, etc., BAs 3, 8, 21, etc., StA 35, 37, 50, etc.; **tymes**: *pl.* OD 232, Y 129^1, 129^2, BAd 197, 494, BAs 179, 395, StA 153.

tynt: *v. pa.* lost Y 232, BAd 220, 484, BAs 392, 394, StA 112, 115, [139], etc.; **tint**: BAd 493; **tynt**: *pa. ppl.* Y 175.

tyrand: *n.* tyrant OR 219, OA 100, 213, 216, Y 328, 335; **tyrrand**: OA 217; **tyran(e)**: OD 217, OR 109, BAd 119, 220, 300, etc., BAs 371, 375; **tyrrane**: BAd 275.

tyrandry: *n.* tyranny OA 125, StA 25; **tyrandiis**: *pl.* OD 136.

tyraneale: *n.* tyranny OR 132.

tytill: *see* **titill**.

þai: *pron.* they OR 28, 30, 45, etc., OA 5, 26, 29, etc., S 24, 71, 219, etc., Y 60, 61, 63, etc., BAd 25, 40, 57, etc., BAs 10^1, 10^2, 14, etc., StA 42, 45, 46, etc.; **thai**: OD 25, 29, 41, etc., OA 137, 190, 226, Y 262, BAs 11, 299; **þaim**: *obj.* OA 31, 40, 47, etc., Y 20, 144, 164, etc., BAd 25, BAs 27, 158, 344, etc., StA 39, 41, 45, etc.; **þam(e)**: OR 6, 10, 20, etc., OA 9, 18, 32, etc., S 32, 242, Y 21, 78, 114, 198, BAd 4, 26, 40, etc., BAs 6, 20, 26, etc.; **thame**: OD 5, 17, 24, etc.; **þaimself**: *refl.* OA 42; **þamself**: Y 69; **thameself**: OD 204; **þame**: OR 208; **thameself**: OD 207, 231; **þair**: *poss.* OR 5, 29, 46, etc., BAd 3, 4, 26, etc., StA 242; **þar(e)**: OR 158, 193, 241, etc., OA 29, 46, 51^1, etc., S 28, 71^1, 71^2, etc., Y 2^1, 2^2, 29, etc., BAs 5, 19, 27, etc., StA 18, 36, 80, etc.; **þair**: theirs OR 89; **thair**: OD 93.

þai: *adj.* those BAs 395.

þair: *pron., adv.* there S 221, OR 83, 95, BAd 42, 179, 413, etc.; **þar(e)**: OR 145, 147, 162, etc., OA 49, 126, 157, etc., S 213, 229, 230, 238^1, Y 82, 109, 185, etc., StA 63, 109, 134, etc.; **thar(e)**: OD 59, 86, 98, OA 225, Y 19, 43, 319, BAs 43, 184; **þer(e)**: StA [154].

þairfore: *adv.* therefore, for that reason
BAd 310, 311, 495; þairfoir: OR 8;
þarfor: OA 41, OR 156, 160, 212;
tharfor(e): OD 49, 162, 210, OA 51,
155, 204, StA [95]; tharefore: OD 61.

þairin: *adv.* therein, in that, there BAd 32,
[458]; þarin: OR 59, Y 51, 196.

þairof: *adv.* thereof, of that BAd 234, 374,
468; þarof: Y 12, BAs 378.

þairthrow: *adv.* through that, because of it
BAd 272; þarthrou: Y 263.

þam(e), þamm(e), þamself: *see* þai.

þan: *adv.* then OR 6, 13, 30, etc., OA 58,
84, S 29, 200, 215, etc., Y 73, 80, 88,
etc., BAd 149, 348, 431, etc., BAs 210,
290, 349, etc.; than: OD 4, 5, 72, etc.,
OA 146, Y 70, 77, 199, BAs 272.

þan: *conj.* than OR 232, 242, OA 24, Y
61, 66, BAd 27, 229, 327.

þarat: *adv.* thereat, at that OR 96, OA 84.

þareftir: *adv.* thereafter, after that Y 140,
177, 249, etc.

þarto: *adv.* thereto, to that BAs 361, StA
11.

þarwith: *adv.* therewith, with that OA 155.

þe: *pron.* you Y 310.

þin(e): *adv.* thence OR 61, BAd 7; thyne:
OD 61.

þir: *pron., adj.* these OR 193, 202, 208,
246, OA 122, S 17, Y 286, BAd 212,
384, 493, BAs 310.

þis: *pron., adj.* this OR 12, 71, 95, etc.,
OA 33, 59, 80, etc., S 24, 50, 53, 55, Y
22, 26, 77, etc., BAd 3, 5, 11, etc., BAs
13, 27, 36, etc., StA 50, 52, 59, etc.

þocht: *see* thocht.

þus: *adv.* thus OA 170, 219, Y 332, StA
59.

uele: *see* wele.

vaistit: *see* wastit.

vakand(e): *adj.* vacant OD 68, OR 66.

vakit: *v. pa.* (throne) became vacant OD
130; wakit: OR 126.

vas: *see* ar.

vencust: *see* vincust.

vengeans: *see* wengeance.

veray: *adj.* true, certain, utter OD 176;
verray: OD 206, StA 145, 150;
werray(e): OA 118, 123, 169, etc., Y
6, 25.

vereour: *see* wereour.

vergin: *n.* virgin BAs 318; vergyne: StA
56; virgyne: BAd 394; virginis: BAd
275.

verite: *n.* truth StA 12; veryte: OR 187;
werite: Y 66.

vertew: *n.* virtue BAd 406; werteu: BAs
329.

vertuus: *adj.* virtuous BAd 299; virtuus:
BAd [159].

vexacioun: *n.* vexation OD 60;
wexacioun: OA 49; wexatioun: OR
60.

victorie: *n.* victory BAs 337, 344;
wictory: OR 112, BAs 241; victoriis:
pl. BAs 412; victoris: BAs 420;
victoryis: BAd 318, 424, 506, 516.

victorius: *adj.* victorious: BAs 202, 245;
wictorius: BAd 308.

victoriusly: *adv.* victoriously BAs 52,
403.

victour: *n.* victor BAd 282.

vincust: *v. pa.* vanquished BAd 144;
wincust: S 205, BAd 318; vencust:
pa. ppl. OD 27; vyncust: StA 42,
[165]; vincust: OR 29, OA 29;
wincust: StA 169.

violentlie: *adv.* violently BAs 260.

virginis, virgyne: *see* vergin.

virtuus: *see* vertuus.

visioun: *n.* vision Y 304.

void(e): *adj.* uninhabited OD 44, 60, OA
38, 50, 55; woid: OR 47, 60; voide:
devoid OA 119.

vnconquest: *adj.* unconquered OD 190,
198, OR 189, 200, OA 192.

vncristinnit: *adj.* unconverted to
Christianity BAs 186; vncrystynit:
BAd 212; vncrystynnyt: BAd 211.

vndefoulit: *adj.* undefiled BAd 54, BAs
55.

vndoutit: *adj.* undoubted OD 175.

vnder: *prep.* under OD 191, Y 32, 55,
BAd 326, 439, 445, 446, BAs 27, 208;
vndir: OR 190, BAd 26, 247, 311,
BAs 356; wnder: OA 182, Y 26, 28,
BAs 428.

vnenhabyte: *adj.* uninhabited OD 44.

vnhappynes: *n.* misfortune Y 16.

vniuersite: *n.* university S 173, BAs 160;
vniuersyte: S 145, BAd 181.

vnknawin: *adj.* unknown BAd 267.

vnlefully: *adv.* unlawfully StA [83].

vnlyk: *prep.* unlike StA [176].

vnpvnist: *adj.* unpunished BAs 441.

vnto: *prep.* unto, to Y 6, 30, 92, etc., BAd 372; until OD 70, 88, 148, 170, OA 9, 57, 138, 160, Y 11, 155.

vpoun(e): *prep.* upon BAd 8, 307, 517; **apon(e):** OR 64, 88, OA 4, 54, 74, etc., Y 90, 337, BAs 11, 74, 171, etc., StA 11.

vs: *pron.* us OD 5, 48, 49, etc., OR 49; **ws:** OR [7], 69, 107, etc., OA 41, 57, 82[1], etc.

vse: *n.* use OA 12, Y 50; form of liturgy Y 30, 31.

vse: *v.* use Y 215; **vsit:** *pa.* had sexual relations with BAd 375, BAs 298.

vsurpit: *v. pa.* usurped OD 158, OA 82, BAd 322; **vsurpyt:** OR 152; **vsurpit:** *pa. ppl.* OA 145

vtterly: *adv.* utterly OD 168; **vttrely:** OA 29; **vtralye:** OR 163; **wtterly:** OA 111.

vþer: *pron.* other StA 132; **vþir:** Y 238, BAd 160; **vþiris:** *poss.* BAd 308; *pl.* Y 154, 160, 182, 315; **vþir:** *adj.* OA 64, 196, 200, Y 60, 85, 172, etc., BAd 276, 313.

vþirwayis: *adv.* otherwise BAd 114, 164, 185; **vþirways:** BAs 106, 147; **vþirwys:** BAs 164.

vycis: *n. pl.* vices Y 199; **vicis:** StA 196.

vyncust: *see* **vincust.**

wailȝeand: *adj.* valiant BAd 156, StA 245.

wairdis: *n. pl.* wards BAd 306 *(see explanatory note).*

wait: *see* **wit.**

wakit: *see* **vakit.**

wald: *v.* would OD 44, 48, 93, etc., OR 47, 49, 90, etc., OA 38, 40, 74, etc., BAd 47, 393, 415, etc., BAs 48, 318, 336, etc., StA 10, 11, [64[1]], etc.

Walice: *n.* Wales S 70.

wallis: *n. pl.* walls OD 117, OR 113, OA 103.

walx: *n.* wax BAd 271.

wan(e), wann: *see* **wyn.**

wantones: *n.* wantonness StA 64.

wantoun: *adj.* wanton BAs 430.

war(e): *see* **ar.**

wariance: *n.* disagreement BAd 57.

wariit: *adj.* hated Y 281.

warld(e): *n.* world OD 14, 26, 189, OR 15, 28, 188, OA 15, 26, 179, S 9, 10, 13, 15, Y 10, 11, 14, 259, BAs 2, 213.

warlois: *n. pl.* warlocks S 218, 220.

warrayt: *v. pa.* defeated OR 4, 162.

wastit: *v. pa.* devastated Y 97; **vaistit:** wasted, squandered StA 197.

water: *n.* river OD 240, StA 246; **watter:** OA 236, Y 54, 186, BAs 10, 235; **watir:** OR 242; **wattir** BAd 7, 188.

weches: *see* **wich(e).**

weddir: *n.* weather S 225.

weddit: *v. pa.* wedded Y 336; *pa. ppl.* OD 216, OR 218, OA 212, Y 108.

wedowis: *n. pl.* widows OD 94, OA 78; **wedois:** OR 91.

wege: *n.* wedge BAs 454.

weir: *v.* wage war, fight Y 78; **wor:** *pa.* OA 102; **weryit:** StA 92.

weir: *v. pa.* wore StA 188.

weill: *n.* well-being, prosperity BAd 215.

wele: *adv.* well OD 18, 149, 171, 199, OA 19, 140, 155, 193, Y 90, BAs 137, 415; **weill:** OR 21, 89, 143, 200, BAd 444, 509, 515; **weile:** OA 138; **uele:** BAd 58.

wemen: *see* **wommanis.**

wengeance: *n.* vengeance OA 235; **wengeans:** Y 280; **vengeans:** Y 178.

wenyt: *v. pa.* thought, believed BAd 463.

wer: *adv. comp.* worse OA 41; **werst:** *super.* Y 259.

wer(e): *n.* war OD 3, 60, 113, etc., OR 109, 121, 137, etc., OA 144, S 221, 233; **weir:** OR 60, OA 4, 49, 100, Y 110, 112, 131, 143, BAd 148, BAs 131, StA 91, 135; **weris:** *pl.* OR 5, S 234, BAd 86, 178; BAs 157.

wer(e): *adj. comp.* worse OD 50, 116, OR 112; **wers:** OD 49; **werst:** *super.* OR 50.

werely: *adv.* in a warlike manner OA 170.

weriour: *n.* warrior Y 205, BAs 156; **vereour:** BAd 177.

werite: *see* **verite.**

werkis: *n. pl.* deeds BAd 95, 275, 276.

werray(e): *see* **veray.**

werschipfull: *adj.* honorable OR 23; **worschipfull:** OA 21, 26.

werteu: *see* **vertew.**

wes: *see* **ar.**

wexacioun: *see* **vexacioun.**

wexit: *v. pa.* vexed, troubled OR 153, OA 147; *pa. ppl.* OR 180, OA 174, 200.

wich(e): *n.* witch StA 231, 232; wychis: *pl.* BAd 271; weches: S 218, 220.

wictall: *n.* food S 245; wittalis: *pl.* BAs 369; wittellis: BAd 456.

wictorius: *see* victorious.

wictory: *see* victorie.

wiffe, wiffis: *see* wyf(e).

wincust: *see* vincust.

wit: *v.* know OR 206, OA 198; wait: OA 234; wist: *pa.* Y 101, BAd 443, BAs 362; wittin: OA 2, 193; wittyn: OD 199.

with: *prep.* by OD 179, 180, 206, etc., OR 178, 207, 208, 224, OA 172, 200, BAd 6, 9, 61, etc., BAs 63, 68, 191, etc., StA 227.

wnder: *see* vnder.

wnderstand: *v.* understand Y 9, 16; wnderstud: *pa.* OA 36, 207; wnderstanding: *pa. ppl.* Y 3, 175.

wndowtable: *adj.* undoubtable, undeniable OA 123.

wnhappely: *adv.* unfortunately BAd 166.

wnhappy: *adj.* unfortunate BAs 226.

wnweddit: *adj.* unwedded (but see explanatory note) OR 173.

wod: *n.* wood StA 49, 156.

woid: *see* void(e).

wommanis: *n. poss.* woman's BAd 27; womannis: OR 25, BAs 28; wommannis: OD 21; wommen: OD 12, 90, 94, 96; wemen: OR 87, 91, 93, BAd 45, 375, StA 55, [56].

wor: *see* weir.

worryit: *v. pa.* attacked, strangled StA 60, 244.

worschipfull: *see* werschipfull.

wounder: *v.* wonder OA 207.

wrait(e): *see* wryt(e).

wrang: *adj.* wrong BAs 239.

wrangus: *adj.* unjust StA [151].

wranguusly:*adv.* unjustly, illegally BAd 69; wranguislie: BAs 69; wranguisly: BAs 285.

writ: *n.* writing OA 213, 237, Y 4; writtis: OA 221.

wrocht: *v. pa.* followed the advice of S 241.

wryt(e): *v.* write OD 227, OR 160, 229, OA 155, 223^1, 223^2; wrait(e): *pa.* OR 34, OA 33, BAs 430; wryttyn: *pa. ppl.* OR 3; wrytyn(e): OR 200, S 17; writtin: Y 65, BAs 124.

wrytyng: *ger.* writing OA 143.

ws: *see* vs.

wtterly: *see* vtterly.

wychcraft: *n.* witchcraft StA [230].

wychis: *see* wich(e).

wyf(e): *n.* wife OD 132, OA 121, S 199, Y 106, 150, 244, etc., BAd 3, 141, 169, 393, BAs 6, 9, 318; wyff: StA 82; wiffe: OR 127; wyfis: *pl.* BAs 27, 299; wyffis: BAd 26, 376; wiffis: StA 152.

wyn: *v.* win, conquer, capture OA 137; wan(e): *pa.* OA 104, S 35, Y 54, BAd 417, BAs 402, 461, StA 4, 104, 140, 251; wann: BAd 75.

wys: *adj.* wise BAs 138, 145.

wys: *n.* manner OA 136.

ylis: *see* ile.

yneucht: *adv.* enough BAd 366, BAs 289.

Yngland: *n.* England OA 168, 173, 187, etc., Y 6, 19, 22, etc., BAs 40, 88, 115, etc.; Ingland: OD 175, 180, 196, etc., OR 174, 179, 197, etc., S 32, 41, 70, etc., Y 172, BAd 127, 148, 211, etc., BAs 377, StA 248, 259, 265.

Ynglis: *n., adj.* English OA 190, Y 1, 170; Inglis(s): OD 180, 183, 194, etc., OR 194, 197, OA 189, BAs 458, StA 48.

Ynglisman: *n.* Englishman Y 48; Ynglismen: *pl.* OA 207, 186, 201, 224, BAs 44, 264, 321, etc.; Inglismen: OD 228, OR 182, 193, 196, 209, S 28, 83, 195, BAd 43, 145, 256; Inglismennis: *poss.* BAd 36; Ynglismennis: BAs 37.

ȝe: *pron.* you OR 206, 240, OA 198, 222, Y 4, 7, 9, etc.; ȝhe: Y 4; ȝou: *obj.* you Y 42, 238; ȝow: Y 4, 16, 36, etc.; ȝour: *poss. adj.* Y 16, 18, 21, etc.; ȝouris: *poss. pron.* Y 7.

ȝeid: *v. pa.* went S 232, BAd 412, BAs 333, 382.

ʒeir: *n.* year OR 165, S 19, 21, 33, etc.,
BAd 38, 42, 47, etc., BAs 43, 53, 163,
etc., StA 27, 40, 60, etc.; **ʒer(e)**: S 23,
25, 27, etc., Y 53, 88, 101, etc., BAd
52, BAs 39, 47, 66, etc.; **ʒeiris**: *pl.* OR
59, 165, 189, 242, BAd 21, 46, 59,
etc., StA 6, 9, 19, etc.; **ʒeires**: BAd
503; **ʒeris**: OD 55, 130, 206, 235, OR
203, 206, OA 24, 49, 119, etc., S 2, 3,
5, etc., Y 52, 166, 177, etc., BAs 46,
70, 73, etc.; **ʒeir**: OR 26, 142, 164,
etc., OA 161, 181, 198, etc., S 4, 81^2,
173^2, BAs 143, 163^2, 204^2, etc.; **ʒer(e)**:
OD 22, 23, 24, etc., OR 55, 126, 207,
OA 44, 137, 196, 237, S 137, 148, 233,
BAs 34, 60, 71, etc.

ʒerelie: *adv.* yearly Y 170^1, 170^2, 173.

ʒhe: *see* ʒe.

ʒit(e): *adv.* yet OD 28, 54, 63, etc., OR
30, 63, 105, etc., OA 31, 87, 164, Y
39, 40, 190, etc.; **ʒitt**: BAd 53, 175,
448, BAs 37, 55, 154.

ʒong: *adj.* young OD 222; **ʒingir**: *comp.*
OR 224; **ʒoung**: BAd [29], [444], BAs
30, 332; **ʒonngest**: *super.* StA 16;
ʒoungast: Y 161, BAd 360, BAs 353;
ʒoungest: Y 151, BAd 435.

ʒou, ʒour, ʒouris: *see* ʒe.

ʒouthhed: *n.* youth Y 85.

ʒow: *see* ʒe.

zeile: *n.* zeal BAd 327.

INDEX

Persons, places, and some important events are here indexed by the page numbers of their references in the texts of the chronicles – but not in the facing translations. All persons reported in the chronicles are indexed here, without any attempt to distinguish the historical from the non-historical – that task being reserved for the explanatory notes. Persons are indexed under the most common current forms of their names or titles, followed, in parenthesis, by the alternate forms found in the chronicles themselves.

Index

Lightning Source UK Ltd.
Milton Keynes UK
UKOW052351100113

204697UK00004B/7/P